Educational Psychology

An Integrated Approach to Classroom Decisions

Thomas Fetsco
Northern Arizona University

John McClure
Northern Arizona University

PEARSON

Boston | New York | San Francisco
Mexico City | Montreal | Toronto | London | Madrid | Munich | Paris
Hong Kong | Singapore | Tokyo | Cape Town | Sydney

This book is dedicated to
our wives, Shelley and Peggy,
and our children, Tim and Jessica,
whose patience and support
have made the completion of this book possible.
We would also like to acknowledge
the students we've taught and from whom we have learned.

Senior Editor: Arnis Burvikovs
Senior Development Editor: Mary Kriener
Series Editorial Assistant: Kelly Hopkins
Senior Marketing Manager: Tara Whorf
Composition Buyer: Linda Cox
Manufacturing Buyer: Andrew Turso

Senior Editorial-Production Administrator: Karen Mason
Editorial-Production Service: Denise Botelho
Text Designer: Carol Somberg
Photo Research: PoYee Oster, PhotoQuick Researchers
Electronic Composition: Omegatype Typography, Inc.
Cover Administrator: Kristina Mose-Libon

For related titles and support materials, visit our online catalog at www.ablongman.com.

Between the time Website information is gathered and then published, it is not unusual for some sites to have closed. Also, the transcription of URLs can result in typographical errors. The publisher would appreciate notification where these errors occur so that they may be corrected in subsequent editions.

Library of Congress Cataloging-in-Publication Data
Fetsco, Thomas.
    Educational psychology : an integrated approach to classroom decisions / Thomas Fetsco,
John McClure.
        p. cm.
    Includes bibliographical references and index.
    ISBN 0-321-08088-2 (alk. paper)
    1. Educational psychology. 2. Learning, Psychology of. 3. Effective teaching. I.
McClure, John, 1953- II. Title.

LB1051.F43 2005
370.15—dc22
                                                                    2004055300

Printed in the United States of America

10 9 8 7 6 5 4 3 2 1   VHP   10 09 08 07 06 05 04

Photo credits are located on page 524, which constitutes a continuation of this copyright page.

Brief Contents

Contents

Refer to pages xi–xii for a complete listing of features in each chapter.

PART 2: Principles into Practice   197

C H A P T E R   *7*

Using Effective Instructional Techniques, Strategies, and Technology   197

C H A P T E R 8

Teaching for Transfer and Problem Solving   241

C H A P T E R 9

Utilizing Instructional Design   281

Features-at-a-Glance

(continued)

$\mathcal{P}$reface

Educational Psychology: An Integrated Approach to Classroom Decisions was conceived and designed with the idea that learning is the core focus of educational psychology and that it can be fostered through active engagement with theory and practical applications. To a large extent, the decisions involved in writing this text were analogous to the types of decisions teachers make as they plan courses, curriculum, and lessons. Specifically, we began by establishing our goals and then created an organization, pedagogical plan, and supplements that would support those goals. We had four primary goals or writing themes for this text.

1. To help students develop a meaningful understanding of the role of educational psychology theory in classroom teaching by providing clear connections between theories of learning and motivation and a variety of important classroom decisions.
2. To facilitate a comparison and synthesis of different theoretical approaches while helping the reader integrate theory into practice.
3. To provide instructors with flexibility by having stand-alone coverage of content that may not be covered in all educational psychology courses.
4. To emphasize the many similarities among learners, while also acknowledging the importance of learner differences.

Through the use of a carefully integrated approach, we involve students in the analysis and decision making teachers undergo on a day-to-day basis. The result is a book that we hope is practical and relevant to classroom teaching and one that reflects how many instructors structure their own educational psychology classes.

Organization of This Book

Educational Psychology: An Integrated Approach to Classroom Decisions includes the core content typically addressed in an educational psychology text, but with a unique overall organizational plan. The book is organized into three sections: Learning and Motivation Theories, Classroom Applications of Theory, and Learner Differences and Assessment. While other texts typically provide coverage of a theory and its applications in a single chapter, Thomas Fetsco and John McClure incorporate an integrated learning approach by beginning with a discussion of learning and motivation theories and then distribute further coverage and their applications throughout the first two sections of the text.

The design of this book reflects all four of the authors' goals. First, the theoretical principles developed in the first section of the text provide an organizational structure for the second section on classroom applications. This will help students to think about theories in terms of their explicit connections to a number of important classroom decisions. Such organization is an application of the idea that learners are better able to understand and apply what they've learned if they revisit those ideas over time and in different contexts.

Second, the applications of different theories for a particular set of classroom decisions, such as classroom management, are contained in the same chapter. This encourages the reader to compare and contrast different theories in terms of their applications, to select applications that are consistent with the decisions that need to be made, and to find areas that overlap or possibilities for theoretical synthesis.

Third, the final section of this text contains stand-alone coverage of topics such as exceptionality and assessment of learning. Often, these topics may not be included in an educational psychology course, depending on how teacher education curricula have been designed. Presented as it is, instructors can decide how best to include these topics, allowing them to be incorporated at any point in the course without disturbing the integrated nature of the rest of the text.

Finally, the decision to integrate coverage of learner diversity into every chapter, with expanded coverage in Chapters 11 and 12, is based on the authors' fourth goal. By recognizing that learners differ from each other, the authors also show how they share similar needs and issues. The theories presented in Chapters 2 through 6 help the readers understand those shared needs and issues. For example, motivation theory and research suggest that students need to believe that they can succeed with effort. By placing the theoretical chapters first, these common needs and issues are brought to the forefront. Later in the third section of this text, learner differences are explored more deeply in order to provide a greater understanding of these common issues and needs as they apply to a diverse student population.

Features in This Text

Throughout the book, special features draw the reader's focus to issues of recurring importance to teachers of reading as well as to aid with review and understanding of key concepts in reading instruction.

- A **unique pedagogical plan** integrates theory and practice to provide preservice teachers with opportunities to reflect on common classroom decisions. Each piece of this connected plan is identified by a magnifying glass.
  —Two **Close-ups on the Classroom** vignettes appear at the beginning of each chapter, the first involving the classroom experiences of an elementary school teacher and the second involving the experiences of a secondary teacher. These stories introduce readers to teachers and decisions they are trying to make that are informed by the content of the chapter. Each vi-

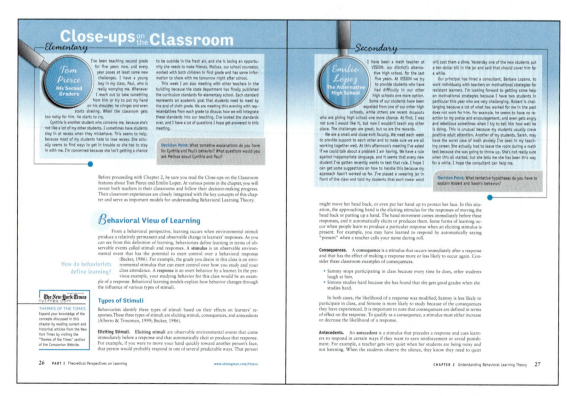

gnette concludes with a "Decision Point" that involves the reader in the early stages of that teacher's decision-making process.

—**Looking in on** features continue the ongoing integrated learning approach by following the progress of both teachers introduced in the opening vignettes. These follow-up features appear throughout the chapter and provide examples of the two teachers integrating concepts and principles from the chapter into their decision-making process. Each Looking in on experience concludes with a question, or "Decision Point," which gives the reader the opportunity to reflect on the applications of chapter concepts and principles that are informing the teachers' practices, as well as the chance to become involved in the teachers' decision-making. The authors extend this discussion by offering their own perspectives on the "Decision Points" on the Companion Website for the book (www.ablongman.com/fetsco).

—**Principles into Practice** and sections at the end of every chapter provide a final analysis of each teacher's decision-making process throughout the chapter, reviewing the use of key concepts and principles, and encouraging readers to consider alternative actions.

• **Focus on Learner Diversity** boxes provide information about how the literature on learner differences can enhance the application of chapter principles and concepts. Each feature concludes with a question to help students understand and apply information on learner diversity. Again, the authors extend this discussion by offering their own perspectives on the Companion Website for the book.

ENRICHING YOUR UNDERSTANDING
The Good Behavior Game

The Good Behavior Game and its variants are examples of an interdependent group-oriented contingency system to help manage the disruptive behavior of elementary school students (Barrish, Saunders, & Wolf, 1969). In the Good Behavior Game, students are divided into teams. Team names are written on the board, and a point is entered under a team name any time a member of that team exhibits one of the target misbehaviors. The team with the fewest points, or any team that meets a preestablished criterion for points, earns a reinforcer. The Good Behavior Game has been shown to be effective in reducing disruptive behaviors during instruction and independent work (Fishbein & Wasik, 1981; Harris & Sherman, 1973; Medland & Stachnik, 1972; Tankersley, 1995).

Two variations of the Good Behavior Game are the Good Behavior Game plus merit (Darveaux, 1984; Wielkiewicz, 1995) and the Good Student Game (Babyak, Luze, & Kamps, 2000; Landrum & Tankersley, 1997). In the Good Behavior Game plus merit, students can also erase points by engaging targeted appropriate behaviors. The Good Student Game differs from the Good Behavior Game in a number of ways, but two key differences are that students self-monitor their behavior during the game, and the game can also be set up as an individual contingency.

• What do you see as the strengths and weaknesses of these approaches? (For your authors' perspective on this question, go to the text website for this chapter.)

www.ablongman.com/fetsco

332 PART II Principles into Practice

• **Enriching Your Understanding** boxes offer information that supplements understanding of important text concepts and principles. As with all the features in the book, Enriching Your Understanding features end with a question to consider, and the authors' perspectives on these questions can be found on the Companion Website.

• The **Study Guide** at the end of every chapter includes a list of key terms, alternative and constructed response test items, decision-making exercises, INTASC activities, and Web resources. These activities are intended to help students create a meaningful understanding of text content and to assess their own learning.

• **Margin notes throughout the text** pose questions that encourage students to reflect on concepts and to check their understanding of the text. These activities are important for building a meaningful understanding of text content, which is an important component of being able to apply that content successfully.

• **Theoretical principles** introduced in Chapters 2 through 6 serve as common organizers for integrating theory and practice for later discussions of applications in Chapters 7 through 10.

• **Alignment to INTASC Standards** at the beginning of each chapter identify the INTASC standards that are the focus of each chapter. The complete list of INTASC Standards is provided on page xvii of the text. Follow-up standards exercises appear in the Study Guide.

• *Educational Psychology: An Integrated Approach to Classroom Decisions* also includes two special Internet connections that encourage readers to go beyond the text to learn as much

The New York Times
nytimes.com

THEMES OF THE TIMES
Expand your knowledge of the concepts discussed in this chapter by reading current and historical articles from the New York Times by visiting the "Themes of the Times" section of the Companion Website.

as possible about educational psychology. The first connection can be seen at the start of each chapter in the form of a **Themes of the Times** icon, which directs you to the Companion Website (www.ablongman.com/fetsco) and specially selected *New York Times* articles. These articles present differing perspectives on contemporary topics pertinent to the field of educational psychology.

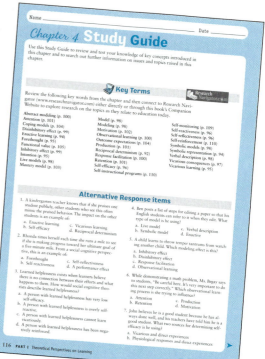

• The second connection appears at the end of each chapter in the **Key Terms** section where the reader is prompted to use **Research Navigator**. This powerful research tool allows readers to investigate key concepts and terms from the book using a collection of resources available to online at www.researchnavigator.com, including EBSCO's ContentSelect Academic Journal Database and the *New York Times*. Purchase of this book allows free access to this exclusive pool of information and data. A personal code and access instructions are included on the inside cover of this book. See page xvii for more information on the contents of Research Navigator.

Key Terms   Research Navigator.com

Review the following key words from the chapter and then connect to Research Navigator (www.researchnavigator.com) either directly or through this book's Companion Website to explore research on the topics as they relate to education today.

Using Research Navigator™

Educational Psychology with Research Navigator™ is designed to integrate the content of the book with the valuable research tool, Research Navigator™, a collection of research databases. Instruction and contemporary publications are available online at www.researchnavigator.com.

In the Key Terms section of the Study Guide in every chapter special Resea prompts cue readers to visit the Research Navigator website to expand on the concepts of the text and to further explore the work being done in the field of educational psychology. To gain access to Research Navigator, go to www.researchnavigator.com and log in using the passcode found on the inside front cover of this text. Research Navigator learning aids include the following components.

EBSCO's ContentSelect Academic Journal Database   EBSCO's Content Select Academic Journal Database contains scholarly, peer-reviewed journals. These published articles provide readers with a specialized knowledge and information about research topics. Academic journal articles adhere to strict scientific guidelines for methodology and theoretical grounding. The information obtained in these individual articles is more scientific than information found in a popular magazine, newspaper article, or on a Web page.

***New York Times* Search by Subject Archive**   Newspapers are considered periodicals because they are issued in regular installments (e.g., daily, weekly, or monthly), and provide contemporary information. Information in periodicals—journals, magazines, and newspapers—may be useful, or even critical, for finding up-to-date material or information to support specific aspects of your topic. Research Navigator™ gives you access to a one-year, "search by subject" archive of articles from one of the world's leading newspapers—the *New York Times.*

"Best of the Web" Link Library   Link Library, the third database included on Research Navigator™, is a collection of Web links, organized by academic subject and key terms. Searching for key terms will provide the reader with a list of five to seven editorially reviewed websites that offer educationally relevant and reliable content. The Web links in Link Library are monitored and updated each week, reducing the chance of finding a "dead" link.

In addition, Research Navigator™ includes extensive online content detailing the steps in the research process including:

- Starting the Research Process
- Finding and Evaluating Sources
- Citing Sources
- Internet Research
- Using your Library
- Starting to Write

For more information on how to use Research Navigator go to **http://www.ablongman.com/aboutrn.**

Text Supplements

Written by the authors to ensure accuracy, quality, and close alignment with the text, supplements for instructors and students reinforce the message of "Principles into Practice" by further emphasizing the complete integration of the project.

For the Instructor

- *Instructor's Manual with Test Items*   The instructor's manual provides a number of elements to support the goals of the text, and to support different learning formats for an educational psychology course. Each chapter contains instructional principles or objectives, principles into practice tables, a teaching outline, focus on learner challenges, Web activities, classroom demonstration activities, observation/interviews for courses that have access to classroom teachers and students, and decision-making activities that provide a structure for discussing the instructor's decision making as it relates to teaching educational psychology.

- *Computerized Test Bank*   The printed test bank is also available electronically through our computerized testing system: TestGen EQ. Instructors can use Test-Gen EQ to create exams in just minutes by selecting from the existing database of questions, editing questions, or writing original questions. The test bank contains a variety of testing items including multiple choice, true/false, short answer, two levels of essay questions (conceptual and reflective), and concept integration items that ask students to apply a combination of concepts and principles to a written teaching scenario.

- *PowerPoint™ Presentation*   This presentation is ideal for lectures or student handouts. (Available for download from Supplement Central at www.suppscentral.ablongman.com.)

- *Allyn & Bacon Transparencies for Educational Psychology IV*   This updated package includes over 150 full-color acetates.

- *My LabSchool*   Discover where the classroom comes to life! From videoclips of teachers and students interacting to sample lesson, portfolio templates, and standards integration, Allyn & Bacon brings your students the tools they'll need to succeed in the classroom—with content easily integrated into your existing courses. Delivered within Course Compass, Allyn & Bacon's course management system, this program gives your students powerful insights into how real classrooms work and a rich array of tools that will support them on their journey from their first class to their first classroom.

- *VideoWorkshop for Educational Psychology*   This is a new way to bring video into your course for maximized learning! This total teaching and learning system includes quality video footage on an easy-to-use CD-ROM plus a Student Learning Guide and an Instructor's Teaching Guide. The result? A program that brings textbook concepts to life with ease and that helps your students understand, analyze, and apply the objectives of the course. VideoWorkshop is available for your students as a value-pack option with this textbook. (Special package ISBN required from your representative.)

For the Student

- *Companion Website* (www.ablongman.com/fetsco)   This robust site is organized by chapter and provides a link to additional study items, special *New York Times* articles, a complete guide to conducting research on the Internet, additional Focus on Diversity and Enriching Your Understanding features as well the authors' analysis and perspectives on those questions addressed in the book, additional INTASC activities, and updates of changes to IDEA and/or NCLB.

- *Preparing for Licensure Guides*   This helps students prepare for special state licensure tests, such as Praxis, with exercises closely tied into the specific case studies from the book. Special guides have been prepared for Praxis and four state-specific certification tests: Texas, Florida, New York, and California.

- *"What Every Teacher Should Know About" Series*   This series of short booklets covers the basic concepts of key topics in education from assessment to classroom management. (Speak with your ABLongman representative for more information.)

Acknowledgments

The authors would like to thank the professionals who took time out from busy schedules to share with us their support and expertise and provided us with the valuable feedback that helped to shape this project. From reviews of the original proposal to ongoing reviews of various drafts of chapters to an intense focus group at AERA, the discussions in this book reflect your valuable input and guidance. We can't thank you enough: Margaret Anderson, SUNY-Cortland; Jennifer Austin, University of Southern Florida; Marcy A. Blackburn, Cameron University; Bruce Burnam, California State University, Los Angeles; Jerrell Cassady, Ball State; Li Cao, State University of West Georgia; Lee Cohen, Montclair State; Alice Corkill, University of Nevada Las Vegas; Gregory Cutler, Bay de Noc Community College; Sandra Deemer, Millersville University; Cindy Dell, Montana State University-Billings; Gypsy M. Denzine, Northern Arizona; Peter Doolittle, Virginia Tech; Jayne Downey, Montana State; Rosemary Fahey, Chapman University; Kathleen Fox, Salisbury State; Christopher M. Hakala, Lycoming College; Laurie Hanich, Millersville University; Stanley Hartzler, Midwestern State University; Jan Heinitz, Concordia University; William Herman, SUNY-Potsdam; Jacqueline Hughes, California State University, Northridge; John Hummel, Valdosta State University; John Isch, Martin Luther College; Jean Kueker, Our Lady of the Lake University; Kerrie Laguna, Lebanon Valley College; Yuliang Liu, Southern Illinois University; Paula Miller, Crichton; Linda Morse, Mississippi State University; Wetonah R. Parker, Meredith College; Jim Persinger, Emporia State University; William Ritchie, Tunxis Community College; Krista Robertson, Rhode Island College; Dan Robinson, University of Texas; William Roweton, Chadron State; Penee Stewart, Weber State University; Rosemary Sutton, Cleveland State University; Yuma Tomes, Virginia Commonwealth University; Raymond Webster, East Carolina University; Jann Weitzel, Lindenwood University; and Michael Verdi, California State University—San Bernardino.

Last but not least, a special thank you to everyone at Allyn & Bacon for their dedication to this project: Senior Acquisitions Editor, Arnis Burvikovs; Senior Development Editor, Mary Kriener; Senior Production Editor, Karen Mason, as well as Denise Botelho. Their advice and patience have been invaluable.

Coverage of Interstate New Teacher Assessment and Support Consortium (INTASC) Standards for Beginning Teacher Licensing and Development

The following is a listing of the INTASC standards on education and a correlation of where those standards are addressed within *Educational Psychology: An Integrated Approach to Classroom Decisions*.

INTASC STANDARD	CHAPTER COVERAGE
1. *Knowledge of Subject Matter:* The teacher understands the central concepts, tools of inquiry, and structures of the subject being taught and can create learning experiences that make these aspects of subject matter meaningful for students.	Chapter 8
2. *Knowledge of Human Development and Learning:* The teacher understands how children learn and develop, and can provide learning opportunities that support their intellectual, social, and personal development.	Chapters 2, 3, 4, 5, 6, 7, 9, 10
3. *Adapting Instruction for Individual Needs:* The teacher understands how students differ in their approaches to learning and creates instructional opportunities that are adapted to diverse learners.	Chapters 2, 3, 5, 6, 7, 8, 9, 10, 11, 12
4. *Multiple Instructional Strategies:* The teacher uses various instructional strategies to encourage students' development of critical thinking, problem solving, and performance skills.	Chapters 3, 5, 6, 7, 8, 9
5. *Classroom Motivation and Management:* The teacher uses an understanding of individual and group motivation and behavior to create a learning environment that encourages positive social interaction, active engagement in learning, and self-motivation.	Chapters 2, 6, 7, 9, 10
6. *Communication Skills:* The teacher uses knowledge of effective verbal, nonverbal, and media communication techniques to foster active inquiry, collaboration, and supportive interaction in the classroom.	Chapter 7
7. *Instructional Planning Skills:* The teacher plans instruction based on knowledge of subject matter, students, the community, and curriculum goals.	Chapters 2, 8, 9, 11, 12
8. *Assessment of Student Learning:* The teacher understands and uses formal and informal assessment strategies to evaluate and ensure the continuous intellectual, social, and physical development of the learner.	Chapters 1, 13
9. *Professional Commitment and Responsibility:* The teacher is a reflective practitioner who continually evaluates the effects of his/her choices and actions on others (students, parents, and other professionals in the learning community) and who actively seeks out opportunities to grow professionally.	Chapters 1, 2, 3, 7, 9, 10, 11, 12, 13
10. *Partnerships:* The teacher fosters relationships with school colleagues, parents, and agencies in the larger community to support students' learning and well-being.	Chapters 11, 12, 13

Introduction to the Study of Educational Psychology

I f you are reading this chapter, you are most likely beginning a course in educational psychology that is part of a teacher-training program. Like most people in your position, you are likely to be asking yourself two questions:

● "Exactly what is educational psychology?"
● "Why do I need to study educational psychology?"

The answers to these questions are related and complex. This chapter begins with brief answers. The remainder of the chapter clarifies and elaborates those answers. However, you should keep in mind that this first chapter is only the beginning of an explanation and that the entire book is, to a certain extent, an attempt to help you answer these questions.

Close-ups on the Classroom

Elementary

I am really enjoying student teaching in the fourth grade with Greg Henson. I'm learning so much that I know will help me when I get my own classroom. One thing I've learned about teaching is that I didn't know as much about it as I thought. We really only barely scratched the surface in my methods classes, and it's a lot harder and more complex than I thought it was going to be.

I've been observing and helping out for three weeks, but now Mr. Henson wants me to plan and teach my own lesson for next week. This will be the first lesson of a unit on fractions and will introduce the basic concept of fractions and their uses. Now that I am going to teach a real lesson to real kids, I have a number of questions. For instance, what is the best learning activity to use? I've noticed that Mr. Henson uses quite a variety of techniques, but I'm not sure how he decides what to use when. I am also worried about the students' motivation and discipline during my lesson. I wonder if the kids will behave as well for me as they do for him. Finally, I am concerned about how to deal with student differences. The students come from a variety of different ethnic backgrounds, and there are several students whose families have recently emigrated from other countries.

When I raised these questions with Mr. Henson, he asked that I try to put together a lesson tonight and then suggested we could talk about it tomorrow before class starts. We both always arrive early, so we should have a good hour to talk before we have to get ready for the first lesson.

Decision Point: What information about the learners in Mr. Henson's class might help Maria answer her questions?

Before proceeding with Chapter 1, be sure you read the Close-ups on the Classroom features about Maria Lucero and Jeffrey Larkin. At various points in the chapter, you will revisit both teachers in their classrooms and follow their decision-making progress. Their classroom experiences are closely integrated with the key concepts of this chapter and serve as important models for understanding Educational Psychology.

What Is Educational Psychology?

What is educational psychology? An exact answer to this question depends on whom you ask. However, for the purposes of this book, educational psychology is defined as that branch of psychology that is concerned with the study of the mental processes and behaviors associated with human learning and instruction. Educational psychologists ask questions about the nature of learners and learning, the characteristics of effective teaching, and how the nature of classrooms affects learning.

Educational psychologists study a wide range of phenomena associated with learning, both in the laboratory and in the classroom. Over the last thirty years, however, educational psychologists' interest in classroom learning has increased dramatically. A review of research reported in recent issues of the *Journal of Educational Psychology* reveals the breadth of questions investigated by educational psychologists. In 1999, the *Journal of Educational Psychology* reported the results of studies investigating the teaching and learning of writing (four studies), mathematics and problem solving (eight studies), and reading (fifteen studies). In addition, some studies investigated questions about the effects of technology on learning, individual student differences affecting school achievement, and the effects of social influences on students.

When educational psychologists ask questions about learning, they apply the methods of science, careful observation, and rational analysis to answer their questions. The answers to their questions are used to formulate and assess theories that teachers use in their decision making.

Teaching is a complex activity, and effective teaching requires a complex set of knowledge and skills. These characteristics have been organized into various sets of standards that are used by many states in the certification of teachers, such as those

Jeffrey Larkin

Student Teaching in Ninth Grade General Science

After three and a half years of study I'm finally starting my student teaching, the last step before I get my certificate. For the next fifteen weeks I'll be working with Mr. William Goodman and his ninth grade general science classes. I've been observing the class for a week and have finally had my first one-on-one meeting with Mr. Goodman. He told me that he wants me to prepare a science unit on magnetism to be taught around the first of November.

As we talked, I told him that my most immediate concern was how to deal with the wide range of student diversity in his classes. Mr. Goodman suggested that we begin with the sequence of objectives for the unit and try to plan lessons that would help the average student reach each object in the sequence. Then we could go lesson by lesson and determine how we might modify each lesson to accommodate the differences of any student or group of students within the class.

Mr. Goodman has also told me that I would have to design an assessment plan for the unit. I told him that I wasn't sure which assessment method would be best. Mr. Goodman said that I should choose an assessment method that made sense with respect to my objectives and the teaching activities within the unit. He suggested that I get started organizing objectives and roughing out some lesson plans, and then we would think about how to assess the students' learning.

Decision Point: What decisions will Jeffery have to make as he prepares his instructional unit? If you were in Jeffery's position, what questions would you have for your supervising teacher?

developed by the Interstate New Teacher Assessment and Support Consortium (INTASC), shown in Table 1.1. A glance at the principles that make up the INTASC standards will give you an idea of how important an understanding of psychology is to teacher effectiveness. Effective teaching results in student learning. Learning is a psychological process, and to influence this process teachers must understand the nature of this process and their students.

This book is intended to help you develop an understanding of learning and learners, in accordance with the INTASC principles. Our approach to this objective is based on three assumptions. The first is that teachers must make decisions in complex multidimensional environments, and that the quality of their decisions influences their effectiveness. The second assumption is that the scientific study of teaching and learning can provide teachers with information that helps them better understand their classrooms and therefore improve the quality of their decision making. The scientific study of teaching and learning leads to formal theories about how people learn and how teachers may assist and guide the learning process. The final assumption is that no single theory of learning or teaching is optimal for every situation that teachers will face in the classroom. Teachers need to know about, and flexibly apply, a variety of theories to make effective classroom decisions. Knowing how research is used to develop and evaluate theories allows teachers to make better decisions about which theory to use when. In summary, we believe that an understanding of scientific theories and how research is used to develop and modify theories can help you apply theories and research to your own classroom.

What are the three assumptions of this text?

Science, Theories, and Educational Practice

Without initiation into the scientific spirit one is not in possession of the best tools which humanity has so far devised for effectively directed reflection. (Dewey, 1916, p. 223)

Science is a method of studying the world. This method includes the collection and analysis of data and the generation of logical explanations for the data that have been gathered so far. These logical explanations are called theories. The effectiveness of

TABLE 1.1   INTASC Standards: What Beginning Teachers Should Know and Be Able to Do

Standard	Description
1 Content Pedagogy	The teacher understands the central concepts, tools of inquiry, and structures of the discipline(s) he or she teaches and can create learning experiences that make these aspects of subject matter meaningful for students.
2 Student Development	The teacher understands how children learn and develop, and can provide learning opportunities that support their intellectual, social, and personal development.
3 Diverse Learners	The teacher understands how students differ in their approaches to learning and creates instructional opportunities that are adapted to diverse learners.
4 Multiple Instructional Strategies	The teacher understands and uses a variety of instructional strategies to encourage students' development of critical thinking, problem solving, and performance skills.
5 Motivation and Management	The teacher uses an understanding of individual and group motivation and behavior to create a learning environment that encourages positive social interaction, active engagement in learning, and self-motivation.
6 Communication and Technology	The teacher uses knowledge of effective verbal, nonverbal, and media communication techniques to foster active inquiry, collaboration, and supportive interaction in the classroom.
7 Planning	The teacher plans instruction based upon knowledge of subject matter, students, the community, and curriculum goals.
8 Assessment	The teacher understands and uses formal and informal assessment strategies to evaluate and ensure the continuous intellectual, social, and physical development of the learner.
9 Reflective Practice and Professional Growth	The teacher is a reflective practitioner who continually evaluates the effects of his/her choices and actions on others (students, parents, and other professionals in the learning community) and who actively seeks out opportunities to grow professionally.
10 School and Community Involvement	The teacher fosters relationships with school colleagues, parents, and agencies in the larger community to support students' learning and well-being.

Source: The Council of Chief State School Officers, Washington, D.C.; available at website http://www.ccsso.org/intasc.html

teachers' decisions depends on their ability to understand their students and classrooms. Developing this understanding is the goal of reflective practice. As the quote by John Dewey suggests, the scientific approach provides teachers with one of the most effective means of achieving this understanding.

How do theories affect our ability to solve problems and make decisions?

In general, a **theory** is a set of beliefs about how the world works, or at least how some part of it works. Such beliefs help explain the world and allow us to make predictions and modify the world to achieve our objectives. For every aspect of our day-to-day lives we have sets of beliefs that we use to understand our situation and guide our response. Therefore, in a sense, anybody who tries to solve a problem begins with a theory.

For many people, such beliefs take the form of informal intuitions developed from their encounters with similar problems. These informal beliefs are sometimes referred to as common sense or **implicit theories** (Clark & Peterson, 1990). Teachers might have implicit theories about how students learn, how they are motivated, or the causes of students' misbehaviors. Research has shown that the implicit theories of teachers do influence their teaching practice (Ignatovich, Cusick, & Ray, 1979; Munby, 1983; Olson, 1981; Smith, 1989; & Torff, 1999).

Scientific theories are a set of formal statements that describe variables and relationships that are important to the understanding of some part of the world. For example, information-processing theory proposes that the rate of learning is limited by learners' ability to pay attention. That scientific theories comprise such a set of formal statements is important because it makes it easier to test the accuracy or precision of the described relationships. By testing these relationships, we develop a more accurate understanding of the world and are able to make more accurate predictions. For instance, a researcher might investigate what kinds of distractions are most likely to influence the rate of learning. In general, experts are more likely to use these types of formal theories when they solve problems within their domains of expertise.

It is important to note that scientists don't think of their theories as *the truth*. Theories are the best explanation they have so far. The development of theories is an evolutionary process. Theories compete to explain what we know, and as new information comes to light, some theories are modified and survive, whereas others are abandoned (Kuhn, 1970). The theories of educational psychologists are subject to these same evolutionary forces, meaning that as we learn more about human nature, the theories of educational psychologists change. Driving this evolutionary process is the scientific method.

Theories help teachers improve their practice by helping them understand how their students are motivated to learn.

Research and the Evolution of Scientific Theories

Scientific inquiry begins and ends with a theory. After developing a theory, the researcher uses the theory to formulate research questions. The questions that a scientist tries to answer are influenced by the scientist's theory. To answer these questions, scientists conduct research. The research is designed to gather information in a way that helps answer the research question. After planning their research, researchers make observations and gather data. The data are then analyzed to answer the original question. Sometimes the result of this research strengthens the theory that generated the question, but often the results of research require that the theory be refined or modified in some way. Frequently, the research process causes researchers to ask new questions and the process begins again. This cyclic process is illustrated in Figure 1.1.

What are the steps involved in a scientific inquiry?

Comparing Theories

Teaching is a complex task and classrooms are complex environments. To study this complexity, researchers tend to focus on limited aspects of the teaching task or classroom environment. Generally, they choose their research topics based on their individual knowledge and interests. As a result, no single theory of teaching and learning exists. An important task for teachers is to compare various theories and select that theory that is most appropriate for a given situation.

Theories may be compared along three dimensions.

- The theory's characteristics, including the scope of the theory as well as the constructs and processes of the theory;
- Epistemic value, or the theory's potential to explain and make predictions about the world; and
- Applicability, or the theory's ability to guide people's decision making in everyday problem situations.

Characteristics of Theories. Because human beings are so complex, psychologists often focus on some restricted aspect of human nature. Their research concentrates on answering questions about a small set of psychological

FIGURE 1.1 The Theory/Research Cycle: The Relationship between Theory and Research

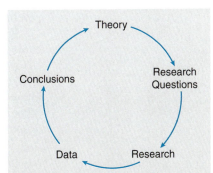

Looking in on

Maria Lucero

1.1

My meeting with Mr. Henson this morning has answered some of my questions, but has given me even more to think about. I think he was a little overwhelmed with my questions, because he suggested that we first plan the lesson and then worry about things like motivation, discipline, and the differences among the learners.

We began our discussion of the lesson by going over the plan I had developed the night before. My idea was to adapt an activity that I had learned in my mathematics methods class for my lesson on fractions. I had always found the activity enjoyable and thought it would be fun for our students as well. Mr. Henson thought the activity was creative, but seemed unsure about its appropriateness for this lesson. He suggested that maybe a better way to start would be to make a list of instructional objectives, in other words, things we wanted the students to learn from the lesson. We did some brainstorming and eventually came up with three objectives for the lesson. Then Mr. Henson asked

me to think about what the students could do that would prove to me that they had learned these three things. With Mr. Henson's help I came up with a set of questions and exercises I thought the kids should be able to do if they understood the concepts I would be presenting. Finally, Mr. Henson asked me what kind of activities would help the kids answer the questions and complete the exercises I had listed.

After our meeting I think I have a better idea about the lesson planning process, but I still have many questions. Mr. Henson has suggested that I work on the lesson and then we will meet again to discuss any other issues I might have.

● **How would you describe Mr. Henson's theory of learners and learning?**

Decision Point: Is it possible to adapt this approach to lesson planning to other subjects?

---

phenomena, and the resulting theory tries to explain these phenomena. This characteristic is referred to as the scope of the theory. The **scope** of a theory refers to the type of phenomena that the theory attempts to explain. Because of this, it is important to consider the focus of different theories when making comparisons. For a teacher, the question becomes, "What classroom situations will this theory help me understand?" Consider the science teacher who wishes his or her student to learn how to use an analytic balance. This teacher needs a theory that describes the process of learning and the factors that affect it. Alternatively, a teacher evaluating a character-education curriculum might need a theory that specifically describes the factors that affect children's empathy and their ability to understand other people's perspectives.

How are psychological constructs and psychological processes different?

All theories describe some aspect of the world, and psychological theories attempt to describe the human mind and human behavior. These theories involve the description of psychological constructs and psychological processes. A **psychological construct** is a hypothetical human characteristic that is used to explain patterns of behavior. Learning style, intelligence, mood, and personality are examples of psychological constructs. **Psychological processes** are actions that create or modify psychological constructs. Learning, motivation, and development are three psychological processes that are of particular interest to educational psychologists and teachers. The description of these processes is an objective in Chapters 2 through 6. Psychological theories differ in terms of the psychological constructs and processes used to explain human performance.

Psychological constructs may vary in terms of their permanence. A **trait** is a psychological construct that represents a relatively permanent and consistent mental characteristic. Personality and intelligence are typically described as traits. For instance, you may have friends who have been very outgoing for as long as you have known them. They enjoy meeting new people, and they like to interact socially with other people. You might explain the person's behavior by saying that she or he is friendly or extroverted. In other words, you seem to believe that there is some underlying psychological trait that explains this consistent pattern of behavior. A mental characteristic that arises from a specific situation and then goes away when the situation changes is called a **state**. Many emotions are examples of states. In psychologically healthy people, fear or anxiety are mental states brought on by some situation. For instance, a student may feel anxious before an important test, but when the test is over, the anxiety subsides. The emotion is tied to the student's situation.

Different theories may use different psychological processes and constructs to explain the same event. These differences produce different ways of understanding a situation. For example, developmental theorists may use the psychological construct of readiness and the process of maturation to explain differences in children's academic performance and behavior across grade levels. From this perspective, if a child is having trouble in school, the problem may be that the child is just not mature enough to achieve at the expected level. The solution would be to provide the students with tasks that are appropriate for their levels of development. On the other hand, learning theories might explain students' performance in terms of the psychological construct of knowledge, which results from the psychological process of learning. Learning theory would explain a child's academic problem as indicating a lack of knowledge and suggest that instruction be designed to make use of what the child already knows to develop the knowledge necessary to achieve in the classroom.

Epistemic Value of a Theory.   Howard (1985) suggests that scientists judge a theory based on its contribution to understanding the world, guided in their judgment by what he has termed epistemic value. **Epistemic value** refers to the power of a theory to contribute to our understanding of a specific situation or the world in general. Epistemic value includes the following:

- Predictive accuracy, or how closely predictions derived from a theory match real world outcomes;
- Internal coherence, or the degree to which the constructs and processes proposed by a theory are logically related;
- External consistency, or how well the theory describes objects and events in the real world;
- Unifying power, or the ability of a theory to identify, incorporate, and explain similarities in data from different fields of research;
- Fertility, or the ability of the theory to inspire and guide research that results in useful information; and
- Simplicity, or the number of constructs or processes comprising the theory. All things being equal, simpler theories are preferred.

What are the six characteristics of a theory that contribute to its epistemic value?

Practical Application.   The practical application of the theory is a final comparison point for theories. Some theories provide attractive descriptions of situations, but are weak in terms of their applicability. Practitioners need theories that provide explanations and suggest a course of action to solve the problems they face. In some cases an older theory may simplify a problem even though the theory is known to be an incomplete, narrow, or inaccurate description of the world. For example, sailors still use a system of celestial navigation based on the assumption that the earth is at the center of the universe and the stars are in fixed positions relative to each other in space. These assumptions are incorrect, but by making these assumptions the calculation of their geographic position is simplified with no noticeable loss of accuracy.

One way to judge the practical application of a theory is to consider the types of principles that can be developed from that theory. By making predictions and testing the accuracy of the predictions, we are able to make judgments about the accuracy of our theories. When repeated test results reveal a consistent relationship between specific situations, actions, and outcomes, the relationship may be stated as a **principle**. For instance, cognitive learning theory proposes that learning depends on the active participation of the learner. This being the case, one prediction that might be made is that learners' intentions affect what they take away from a learning activity.

Maria Lucero

1.2

After looking over my lesson plan, Mr. Henson said that he had only a few suggestions, but that overall it was pretty good. Then we began talking about student motivation and differences.

Mr. Henson said that he thinks about classroom motivation and discipline in terms of behavioral learning theory. He noted that this theory has some practical recommendations for classroom teachers. He said he has found that by reinforcing the learners for doing things correctly and obeying the rules he is able to keep the kids on task most of the time. When I said that I hadn't seen him giving out any candies or gold stars as rewards Mr. Henson laughed and said he uses social reinforcers such as praise. He said candy and gold stars don't work all the time and can be somewhat expensive. Mr. Henson says most of his kids respond very well to praise, if it is sincere and explicitly related to a specific performance. One side effect of this is that the students seem to enjoy the class more

and are more willing to put effort into participating in new classroom activities. Another advantage of behavioral approaches is that they assume that people are people. For example, people generally like it when others who are important to them recognize their accomplishments. A teacher realizes that he has to modify how he shows recognition based on the students' background experiences and expectations, but he knows that it's helpful to find a way to recognize each student's accomplishments.

● **What is the advantage of learning a theory that has many practical applications?**

Decision Point: When you are trying to make a decision, how will you decide which psychological theory will be most useful?

This prediction has been supported by numerous studies. A principle that can be derived from these consistent research findings is: Learning is an active, goal-directed process.

Principles serve an important role in the application of theory. Principles often serve as the foundation for making decisions and formulating a solution to a problem. A good decision maker uses a theory to understand a problem. This understanding allows the decision maker to select the relevant principle. The principle then serves as the basis for a solution to the problem. This is how Ramona Mahoney applies this approach.

➤ I believe that what students learn from a lesson is greatly influenced by the students' intentions. Sometimes students need help in this area. One way to help the students is to begin with some activity designed to encourage them to set appropriate goals for the lesson. For instance, for my science unit on electricity I begin by having students observe the deflection of a compass needle when it is placed near a wire connected to a dry-cell battery. The students are always surprised, and the unexpected behavior of the compass needle arouses their curiosity. They then set out to discover what is causing this effect.

Using Theory and Research to Improve Teaching

As a teacher, you will make hundreds of decisions daily. As you plan for your classes, you must decide what to teach, how to teach, and how to assess your students' learning. As you deliver your lessons, you must decide if students are motivated and learning, or if a change of plan is required. To manage the classroom effectively, you must decide how to respond to the unique problems and behaviors of each student. After you have presented a lesson, you will probably start thinking about how to improve future lessons. Other decisions are associated with the administrative and housekeeping actions required by schools, districts, and other governmental agencies. Teaching is the act of making decisions, acting on those decisions, and evaluating the effects of those decisions.

Teachers make their decisions in complicated environments. Classroom teaching requires the successful completion of many different types of tasks, a concept known as *multidimensionality* (Doyle, 1986). Teachers are managers, instructors, mediators, counselors, and at times medics. They are responsible for teaching a wide-ranging curriculum that includes facts, skills, problem solving, as well as interpersonal skills and attitudes. In addition, they must be able to relate effectively to their students and the adults in their students' lives.

The variety of the decisions that teachers face makes teaching complex and demanding. However, the teacher's task is made even more complex because teachers' decisions are rarely independent of decisions made previously. For example, a teacher deciding what concepts or skills to teach needs to consider the concepts and skills that were previously taught. A teacher deciding how to respond to a student's disruptive behavior may need to consider the student's past responses to similar situations.

The multidimensionality of teaching means that knowledge of a single theory may be insufficient for all the situations faced by teachers. No single theory is likely to be the most useful theory in all situations. Part of the decision-making process for teachers, therefore, is the selection of the theory that is most useful for a given situation. To make an informed selection of a theory, you need some method for comparing theories, and you need to know something about the nature of the educational research behind the theories.

The Contribution of Scientific Study to Teacher Decision Making

A decision is the end product of an often complex thought process. Research has focused on three aspects of teachers' decision making: their thinking processes as they plan for the various aspects of their classes; their thinking while they are interacting with students; and the nature and effects of the teachers' theories and beliefs on their planning and decision making (Clark & Peterson, 1986). It is this last aspect that is most directly affected by scientific research.

On which aspects of decision making does scientific research have the most direct impact? Why?

What people know or believe plays a central role in how they think and act in any given situation (Borko & Putnam, 1996). This applies to teachers and their decision making. Teachers' beliefs about the nature of their students and how they learn, about the purpose of education, and about themselves as teachers all influence their decision making (Calderhead, 1996). Specifically, teachers' knowledge and beliefs influence how they set goals in their classrooms, which student characteristics they identify as critical, and the instructional and management strategies they apply.

The theories that result from the scientific study of teaching and learning can be valuable tools that help teachers organize and clarify their thinking, thus improving the quality of their decisions and teaching practice. Much of what expert teachers know and believe about teaching is grounded in personal experience; and their decisions are often based on the intuitions derived from this experience. However, even experienced teachers may be stumped by unfamiliar circumstances or an unusual problem. In these situations, the results of the scientific study of teaching may be helpful.

For new teachers, understanding the insights derived from the scientific study of teaching can be even more valuable. As a new teacher you may lack the experiences and intuitions of experienced teachers; however, you will be required to make decisions the moment you enter your first classroom. Where will you begin? The theories derived from a scientific study of teaching can provide a valuable starting point for your decision making. Your purpose in studying educational psychology is to develop a theoretical base in preparation for making decisions in your future classroom.

Theories and Decision Making

How do theories affect the decision-making process of teachers? To answer this question, we first need to think about the nature of decision making and what makes a good decision maker. Then, we need to think about how theory might assist the decision-making process.

Decision Making as Problem Solving.   Making a decision is a form of problem solving that usually means choosing a course of action. Psychologists who study human problem solving typically identify a series of steps in the process of solving a problem. These steps include (a) understanding the nature of the problem, (b) developing a plan to solve the problem, (c) implementing the plan, and (d) looking back and evaluating the effectiveness of the planned solution (Polya, 1985).

How are the steps of the problem-solving process similar to a scientific inquiry?

To understand the nature and role each of these steps plays in the problem-solving process, researchers have compared the problem-solving performances of experts and novices. An expert is someone who has demonstrated a great deal of proficiency in solving problems in a particular area, such as classroom teaching, chess, physics, mathematics, and so on. A novice is someone with limited experience within a specific domain. Typically, experts are better able to understand the important characteristics of a problem and formulate effective solutions more efficiently than are novices (Chi, Feltovich, & Glaser, 1981).

What accounts for these observed differences? Experts' ability to understand and solve problems in their domain of expertise seems to be related to their extensive and well-organized knowledge of the problem domain (Glaser, 1984). Experts' knowledge makes them especially sensitive to important relationships among the elements that define the problem situation. Having an effective theory allows them to:

- Identify the important characteristics of the problem situation and ignore unimportant characteristics;
- See the underlying pattern of relationships in the problem situation; and
- Identify principles that can be used to guide the generating of a solution.

To illustrate these points, consider how an expert teacher might use her understanding of behavioral learning theory to respond to a child whose talking is disrupting learning. First, she focuses on the misbehavior as part of a sequence rather than as a single event. By taking this focus, the teacher is able to identify those factors that trigger the misbehavior. Perhaps the student's talking only occurs during certain types of activities or when the student is with a particular student or students. By seeing the student's misbehavior as a sequence, the teacher also focuses on the consequence of the misbehavior. The teacher may try to determine what rewards the student receives for the misbehavior.

By understanding these cause-and-effect relationships, the teacher may try to use principles derived from behavioral learning theory to modify the disruptive behavior. For instance if the student talks when with certain students, the teacher can arrange for these students not to be together. Alternatively, she may arrange her class to make some other behavior more attractive than talking.

Expert teachers' theories about teaching also influence how they perceive a problem and the principles that they apply in the classroom. You probably already have developed some of these theories, and certainly others will develop as you gain experience as a teacher. The intent of this book is to supplement these personal theories with knowledge of some scientific learning and teaching theories. We believe that understanding these scientific theories of instruction and learning is an important step toward becoming an expert decision maker in your classroom.

The next section gives you suggestions for how theory and research can help improve your classroom teaching. One of the major goals of this text is to provide you with a mechanism for evaluating theories that are proposed for classroom use.

Decisions in the Classroom

A lot is required of teachers as decision makers, and your authors believe that the scientific study of teaching can help you make more effective decisions in your multidimensional world. One approach that scientists frequently use when studying a complex process is to break the process into parts and study the parts separately. Once the parts of the process have been adequately described, the scientist may then study the relationships between the parts. The advantage of this approach is that it makes it easier to ask and find the answers to specific questions. To simplify the discussion of the kinds of decisions teachers make, your authors have decided to divide the teaching process and the types of decisions teachers make into three areas, referred to as decision points. The three decision points are:

1. *Planning decisions.* These include decisions that are made before a specific interaction with the learners occur.
2. *Teaching and managing decisions.* These decisions include those made while interacting with the students.
3. *Assessment decisions.* These decisions are made to assess the effectiveness of an interaction with a student.

This division aids our discussion of how the various psychological theories may help your practice as a teacher, but it is important to keep in mind that all types of decisions are interconnected. Decisions that are made while planning a lesson often determine the types of interactions you have with the students. For instance, if you decide to have your students do group work, you are presented with a set of opportunities and challenges that differ from those you would have face if you had decided to do a lecture. Group work may present you with more opportunities to monitor students' understanding one on one than will a lecture. The challenge of keeping the students focused and on task is also likely to be greater if you decide to do group work rather than present a lecture. Relationships also exist between the decisions you make when planning and the decisions you face when assessing the effectiveness of your lesson, and between the decisions you make while teaching and your assessment decisions. While reading the following chapters, keep in mind how the choices you make in one part of your teaching activity influence the decisions you will need to make later on.

A Decision-Making Guide for Selecting Theories

As noted earlier, theories that may help you understand and make a decision in one situation may not be useful in another situation. So the first step in making a good decision is to select a theory that is appropriate to the situation. When making this first decision, you may want to consider and weigh all the dimensions we just discussed. Your goal is to find the theory that gives the best description of and provides the best practical guidance for the situation you are facing.

Teachers and Research

The development of theories is an evolutionary process, that is, theories change as new information becomes available. This means that for teachers to get the most benefit from theories, they must keep up with current developments in the field. In other words, teachers should be aware of and use current research to expand and modify their understanding and application of theory. Although the actual impact of educational research on classroom teaching can be debated, we tend to believe that a conceptual understanding of educational research can be beneficial to teachers in two ways: as consumers of research and as researchers in their own right.

Teachers as Consumers of Research

First, teachers may benefit as consumers of the information produced by others. Teachers have multiple sources of information about learning and teaching in classrooms. They are exposed to interpretations of educational research in their college classes, through on-site training experiences, through informal conversations with colleagues, through professional journals, and through other outlets such as the Internet. It is important that you become critical consumers of the information you gather. A critical interpretation of research helps you understand and appropriately apply the results of research to your own teaching.

Teachers as Researchers

Research is not an activity limited to professional researchers. Teachers conduct research every day in their own classrooms. When they evaluate the effectiveness of new ideas, instructional techniques, or materials, teachers are conducting a form of research. For example, a teacher who is trying different instructional approaches to help a student who is having trouble grasping the course content is conducting research. While not formally stated, the teacher is testing a hypothesis about the nature of learning and the learner. The results of this informal research may help the teacher improve his or her ability to teach the learner and improve professional skills.

A more formal approach to teacher research in classrooms is action research. Action research is defined as teacher-initiated, school-based research (Gay & Airasian, 2000). Consider how an action-research approach might be used in the example given in the preceding paragraph. First, the teacher would use the information the teacher had about the student, the course content, and the teacher's beliefs about learning to make an explicit statement of the problem. The statement might include information about the student and the learning situation that the teacher believed was relevant. The statement would also describe the current state of the student's learning and a description of what a solution would accomplish. Here is an example of a problem statement developed by Jane Forbes for a student in her tenth grade chemistry class:

> William is not doing well on his chemistry examinations. He seems to be bright and motivated, but doesn't volunteer to participate much in either large group discussions or when working within his lab group. I talked to him about his work and he seemed embarrassed. He appeared to understand chemistry concepts at a very basic level, but had difficulty discussing what he knew. He says he finds the textbook and class discussions hard to follow. I talked to some of his other teachers and they have confirmed that his reading skills are poor. The school psychologist has told me that William's performance on tests of reading comprehension are below average, but that he doesn't have a disability. I believe if I can improve his comprehension of the text and class discussions, he will do better on the tests.

Next the teacher would identify specific instructional modifications that might help the student and apply the modifications and collect data through appropriate observational techniques to determine which modifications yielded results that were closest to the desired solution. Here's how Jane Forbes decided to handle William's situation.

> I've talked to William and he has agreed to try a new reading comprehension strategy called concept mapping. I will teach him how to construct concept maps, then for each reading assignment I will require him to create a map from the main concepts of the assignment. At first I will identify the concepts for him, but eventually I want him to find the main ideas for himself. I will also provide him questions for each reading assignment. He will justify his answers with reference to his concept map. He has a study hall during my prep-period

so he will stop by to discuss his map and answers before class starts. In addition to monitoring his performance on quizzes and test, I will keep track of how often he contributes to class and group discussions.

Finally, having determined which techniques were most effective for the student, the teacher would apply the technique more generally to the instruction of that student. This is how Jane Forbes accomplished this last step.

Use other teachers' experiences to improve your teaching and to stay up-to-date in the profession.

▶ It took a while for William to master the concept mapping techniques, but his maps gradually improved. As his maps improved so did his answers to the assigned questions and his ability to explain his answers during our pre-class meetings. I kept a record of William's participation in class discussions and found that as his maps improved he seemed to be participating more in the class discussions and lab groups. His test scores have also improved, but not to the level I would expect. Maybe he needs help in developing some test-taking strategies. The concept mapping approach seems to have worked, and I have suggested he try it with some of his other classes. I have talked to Bob Carson, William's history teacher, and he is enthusiastic about Bill's concept mapping in his class also.

As can be seen, action research is typically more focused on the specific problems and decisions of a teacher or group of teachers. As with all forms of research, action research is a systematic approach to problem solving and decision making in the classroom. Gay and Airasian identify four steps in the action research process: (1) problem/topic identification; (2) data gathering; (3) decision making; and (4) action.

Note the similarity between the steps in action research and the theory/research cycle presented in Figure 1.1 on page 5. Problem identification corresponds to the theory and research portions of Figure 1.1. The problems that teachers identify derive from their own unique situations, but the teacher's perception of a problem and the questions the teacher asks are influenced by the teacher's theories about learners and learning. Data gathering corresponds to the research and data portions of Figure 1.1. In action research, decision making is similar to the conclusion portion of Figure 1.1.

In action research, the decision leads directly to action on the part of the teacher. Action research is based on a specific classroom and directed toward solving a specific problem or answering a specific question within that classroom. For this reason the decision made is more likely to lead to a specific teacher action. The teacher's action leads directly to another question; that is, was the action effective? With this question the whole process begins again.

Some General Insights about Educational Research

Your authors would like to help you in your interpretation and application of educational research by providing some general insights gained from our own reading and interpretation of educational research:

- Different research questions require different data collection procedures.
- An effective understanding of classrooms requires both qualitative and quantitative data.
- There can be multiple competing explanations for the same data.
- The range of differences among individuals, even within the same group, is greater than the range of differences between groups.
- Learning is complex, and classroom learning must be understood in the context of many interacting variables.

Looking in on

Mr. Goodman has been working with me on developing objectives and lessons for my unit on magnetism, and now we are looking to see what accommodations we might need to make for student differences. The first lesson in the unit is a lab activity designed to familiarize the students with the general properties of magnets. Specifically, the students are to learn that different magnets produce magnetic fields of differing strengths, and that these differences can be measured. The students will be working in groups following the instruction in the lab manual and recording their observations in their notebooks.

At first I thought this lesson would be appropriate for students from all different backgrounds, but Mr. Goodman suggested that we look at the lesson more closely. First, he pointed out that because the students came from a wide variety of socioeconomic backgrounds, there might be some students who have played with magnets or observed their properties and other students who have not. Differences in the students' experiences with magnets may help or hinder

Jeffrey Larkin

1.1

their observations and comprehension of the lab results. Mr. Goodman also pointed out that there are several students who speak English as a second language. Differences in students' English proficiency may affect their ability to complete and benefit from the lab activity.

Mr. Goodman suggested that we give careful thought to how we organize the groups so that differences in students' previous experiences would not prove a barrier to successful completion of the lab and may actually improve the overall learning of all of the students in the class.

● **What might be the advantages and disadvantages of Mr. Goodman's approach to dealing with his students' differences?**

Decision Point: In what way is the process of accommodating diversity in the classroom similar to the general processes of problem solving or research?

Varied Data Collection Procedures. When teachers or researchers ask a research question, they must decide what type of data would be most useful in answering the question, and the best way to gather those data. Three commonly used data collection procedures are helpful for different types of questions: direct observation, performance assessment, and self-report.

If researchers or teachers want to know how often, how long, or under what circumstances a behavior occurs, they might use direct observation techniques. Direct observation techniques require an observer to record those behaviors as they occur. If researchers wanted to know how often teachers ask questions during an hour, then it makes sense to use direct observation techniques. The researcher might sit in the back of the room or watch a videotape of the classroom. Each time the teacher asks a question, the researcher might make a mark on a recording sheet. If a teacher wants to know how often a student participates in class, she might move a token from her left pocket to right pocket with every instance of participation. Later, a count of the chips in the right pocket provides an estimate of the amount of participation.

> **List examples of assessment situations for which a teacher might use direct observation.**

If researchers and teachers want to know if students understand and can apply what they have learned, they might employ performance assessments. Performance assessments evaluate students' learning by having them complete a predetermined task. For example, if a science teacher wants to know if students can correctly prepare a microscope slide, then that teacher could evaluate students as they prepare a slide. If researchers want to know if students can apply some problem-solving skills, then they could have those students problem solve and observe the desired skills.

If researchers and teachers want to know how people feel, or what they are thinking, they may want to use self-report techniques. Self-report techniques ask people to report or discuss their perceptions, beliefs, and thought processes. For example, teachers or researchers who want to understand students' math problem solving might ask students to talk aloud about their thinking as they solve problems. If they want to know how students feel about themselves, they might ask them to fill out a self-esteem inventory or survey.

Obviously, the three techniques can be used for other purposes than those included in these examples, and other data collection techniques exist besides these three. The purpose is to show how a data collection procedure should be matched to the type of research questions being asked. As researchers, we want to make sure we collect the data we need for decision making.

Qualitative and Quantitative Data. Our questions determine the types of data collection techniques we use, and the data collection techniques determine the types of data that result from our procedures. There are two general categories of data, qualitative data and quantitative data. Qualitative data are observations of essential characteristics or differences and often take the form of verbal descriptions of a person, group, or situation. Quantitative data are a measure of the quantity or amount of something and are expressed as numbers such as scores or counts.

Collecting qualitative data is more than recording observations; it also involves an interpretive process. Through this interpretive process, the researcher tries to understand the significance of observed events. In his book, *Life in Classrooms*, Philip Jackson (1990) noted that when elementary school students raised their hands to attract the teacher's attention, they often supported the raised right arm by placing their left hand just under the elbow. The significance attached to this observation was that the arm was heavy, and children must often keep their hand up for long periods of time before the teacher responds. These qualitative data were combined with others to help understand classrooms as crowded places with limited resources. Extending this interpretation still further, Jackson concluded that in elementary schools children must learn to wait and be patient.

The process of collecting quantitative data often begins by creating an **operational definition** that describes the characteristic being measured in terms of a score or some other type of numerical observation. For example, in assessing the effectiveness of a specific instructional method, the researchers Jane Stallings and Eileen M. Krasavage (1986) collected quantitative data on (a) the quality of instruction, (b) student engagement during instruction, and (c) student learning. To assess the quality of instruction, trained observers assigned a score to teachers' classroom performances. The students' engagement during instruction was operationally defined by the proportion of time students were observed to be *off-task* (chatting, disrupting, waiting, etc.) during a class period. The researchers addressed students' learning by the change in their performance on standardized achievement tests.

Quantitative and qualitative data each have advantages and disadvantages. Quantitative data can be analyzed using powerful statistical methods to find patterns and make comparisons across many observations. As a result, the conclusions drawn from quantitative data are often more generalizable. The **generalizability** of a conclusion refers to the number of different situations to which the conclusion may be applied. A disadvantage of quantitative data is that sometimes important details are lost.

For example, consider a teacher who is assessing his students' mathematical problem-solving skills. One approach might be to give the students a set of word problems and ask them to solve the problems showing all their work. The quantitative data that may result from this might be a score indicating the proportion of problems correctly solved, or partially correct. However, the information that might be lost

Direct observation is an important way to assess students' progress.

How are qualitative and quantitative data different?

is the types of errors that the students are making. Examining the students' responses qualitatively may reveal patterns that point to students' misconceptions about various parts of the problem-solving process. This kind of information may allow teachers to give specific help to some students or alert them to problems with the way the problem-solving concepts and skills have been taught.

Qualitative data allow the researcher to preserve the fine details of observed situations. This often leads to important and interesting insights about the situation being studied. The trade-off is that qualitative data are often so specific to a particular situation that the researcher can only draw valid conclusions about the particular person or group being studied.

Returning to the previous example, through a qualitative analysis of students' problem-solving performance a teacher may identify a student's misconception. But, do all the students in the class share the same misconception? Because many student differences may affect whether or not a particular student develops a similar misconception, it would be dangerous to assume that all the students have the same problem. The question cannot be answered without completing a qualitative analysis of each student's response to the problem-solving exercise.

Multiple Competing Explanations.   To explain their data, researchers try to make logical connections between the data and other knowledge possessed by the researcher, including theoretical knowledge. Researchers want these explanations to be valid. Validity refers to the quality or the correctness of an explanation or a decision. Researchers try to increase the likelihood that their explanations are valid by considering alternative explanations for their data. By eliminating alternative explanations, researchers can have more confidence in the conclusions they draw from their research.

Once researchers have collected and analyzed data, they are ready to draw some conclusions. Frequently, the researcher's conclusion is an explanation of the results. The idea that the same observation or data can have multiple explanations is an important idea for both teachers and researchers. It helps us avoid jumping to incorrect conclusions.

Consider a hypothetical study of the effectiveness of a new classroom management program in a school. The program is introduced enthusiastically by the principal, who states that this program will work and that discipline referrals to the principal's office will be a measure of its effectiveness. Not surprisingly, referrals to the principal's office do decrease once the program has been instituted. Certainly, the decreased referral rate could be attributed to the program. However, another plausible explanation is that teachers stopped referring discipline problems because they thought it would make them look bad to the principal. What other data do you think could be collected to evaluate which of these two hypotheses is correct?

Teachers also must consider the various plausible explanations for their observations. If their explanations are incorrect, they may select interventions that don't match the problem. For example, one explanation for why a student does not turn in his homework is because the student doesn't care. Obviously, there are other explanations, such as the student doesn't understand the lessons, or his home is so chaotic he can't complete his homework. Can you see how failure to consider alternative explanations in this case might prevent you from making good choices about how to help your student?

Within-Group and Between-Group Differences.   Within-group differences and between-group differences are ideas that are borrowed from statistics. The within-group differences are how much members of the same group differ from each other. Between-group differences are how much members of one group differ, on average, from members of another group. In research as well as in classroom teaching, it's helpful to remember that the within-group differences often equal or exceed between-group differences. This is particularly important for issues of learner diversity. For example, although children with different ethnic backgrounds may differ in important (between-group) ways, there are also important differences within each ethnic group. Assuming all the children from the same ethnic group learn the same way can cause problems for both researchers and teachers. Researchers may miss important subgroups they need to study, and teachers run the risk of stereotyping individual students from a particular group.

Each child has his or her own unique set of abilities and needs.

The Complexity of Learning. Much of the research conducted by educational psychologists and teachers is focused on answering questions about how instruction influences student learning. Trying to answer this question is a complex problem. Many factors affect how and what a person will learn in any given situation. In an effort to make sense of this situation, Jenkins (1979) proposed a model of learning research called the theorist's tetrahedron or simply **the tetrahedral model.** The tetrahedral model is a model of four key instructional variables and how they affect each other. Figure 1.2 provides a drawing of the tetrahedral model modified for use with both research and classroom learning.

Focus on Learner Diversity

Cross-Cultural Research

The influence of culture on many aspects of a person's experience, including experiences in the classroom, is generally recognized. However, consideration of some of the problems and issues of cross-cultural research suggests that teachers should be cautious about making inferences about individual students based on their cultural background.

Leung (1989) points out that one of the difficulties in conducting cross-cultural research is observer bias. Bias in this case refers to the unintentional influence of the observer's own background on the conclusions based on the observations made. This type of bias is especially likely in situations in which the observer has a cultural background different from that of the person observed (Banks, 2001). For instance, a researcher may observe that students with high levels of academic performance ask more questions during class. The researcher may conclude that learners ask questions because they are interested in the subject and are therefore motivated to engage in more behaviors that result in learning. While this interpretation may apply in some cultures it may not apply to students from a culture in which questioning elders is considered impolite. If a learner from such a culture is having academic difficulty, attempting a motivational remedy may be ineffective or even harmful.

Errors may also be made when the general characteristics associated with a particular cultural group are ascribed to an individual from that culture. Researchers may fail to appreciate the amount of variation among the members of a particular cultural group (Padilla & Lindholm, 1995). Members of different cultural groups may vary widely in terms of the socioeconomic class, education level, language proficiency, and acculturation, all of which may affect the experiences that an individual brings to the classroom.

The interaction between people and their culture is complex. Both researcher bias and variation among the members of cultural groups make cross-cultural research complex and researchers' conclusions tentative. In the meantime, teachers should keep an open mind and avoid judging students based on their cultural backgrounds. In other words, teachers should treat all students as individuals with unique abilities and motives.

● **How might the effects of observer bias and variation among members of a culture affect a teacher's decision making? (For your authors' perspective on this question, go to the text website for this chapter.)**

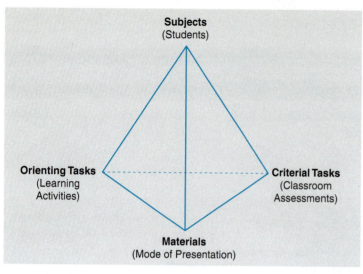

FIGURE 1.2 Adapted Tetrahedral Model

(Adapted from Jenkins, J. J. (1979). Four points to remember: A tetrehedral model of memory experiments. L. S. Cermak & F. I. M. Creik (eds.). *Levels of processing and human memory.* Hillsdale, NJ: Lawrence Erlbaum Associates.)

A tetrahedron is a three-sided pyramid. In the model proposed by Jenkins, each of the four points of the pyramid is an important variable that affects learning. The four variables of the tetrahedral model are orienting tasks, materials, criterial tasks, and subjects. **Orienting tasks** refer to the type of instruction and learning activities being used by the teacher. For example, is the student to memorize a list, summarize the gist of a poem, and so on? **Materials** are the way in which the learning task is presented. Is it presented orally, on a computer, through earphones, and so on? **Criterial tasks** refer to the way in which learning is to be assessed. Will the teacher assess learning by asking learners to recognize learned materials, to recall learned materials, or to complete some more complex performance? **Subjects** refer to the learners. In any learning situation it is important to consider any learner characteristics that might influence the learning process. Some of the important learner characteristics include abilities, interests, knowledge, and purposes.

A second important characteristic of the tetrahedron is that each point of the tetrahedron is connected to each of the other three points. Jenkins was trying to show with his model that a comprehensive understanding of classroom learning requires that we consider how each variable interacts with the other three. For example, the criterial tasks should make sense with the type of learning that is being studied.

Jenkins proposed the tetrahedral model as a way to conceptualize the key variables in learning research. However, the tetrahedral model can be adapted to describe and guide understanding of classroom situations. In your classroom setting the orienting tasks refer to the actions you expect of your students during a lesson. These expected actions might include taking notes, manipulating materials, or discussing a concept. Materials refer to the type of media you use in your lessons, for example, videos, diagrams, or books. It is interesting to note that as the teacher you may be considered part of the media from which your students are expected to learn. Criterial tasks refer to the way you test your students and assign grades. The subjects are your students and their diverse characteristics.

Identify examples of the four variables of the tetrahedral model in a classroom you have recently observed.

Both teachers and researchers can use the tetrahedral model to frame important questions. Both might be interested in how learner characteristics interact with different forms of media. For example, do some students do better with computerized instruction than others? Both might be interested in how learner characteristics interact with criterial tasks or assessment procedures. For example, are there important gender or cultural differences that affect performance on some forms of assessment? The tetrahedral model provides a useful framework for considering how different variables affect learning.

Theory, Research, and Textbook Reading

At the beginning of this chapter, it was noted that knowledge of research and theories allows educators to make better decisions. By knowing about and understanding theory teachers are better able to understand how and why their students learn. This allows them to make better decisions when planning lessons, when delivering a lesson, or when evaluating and improving on the effectiveness of a lesson. Knowledge of research allows teachers to understand the latest techniques and strategies and to incorporate those strategies and techniques into their own classrooms. However, it is not only teachers who can benefit from an understanding of learning;

Looking in on

I have made good progress in developing lesson plans for the unit on magnetism. Today Mr. Goodman and I began discussing how I would assess whether or not the students reached our objectives. I told Mr. Goodman that the one thing I have learned about this process is how all the decisions are related. Choosing an objective affects the kind of learning activities that make sense. He pointed out that the same thing applied to thinking about assessment. Assessment tasks had to make sense given our objectives and given the learning activities we used to help the students reach those objectives.

However, one of my concerns was whether the assessment would be fair to all of the students regardless of their backgrounds. Mr. Goodman suggested that we use the same strategy for developing fair assessments as we used for developing the lessons. First, we would develop an assessment that made sense with regard to our objectives, and then we would consider which student differences might interfere with making a fair assessment of the students' progress. One approach was to consider what knowledge and skills beyond what was taught were required to successfully perform on an assessment. If some students lacked those skills, we might have to modify the assessment procedure or integrate the teaching of those skills into our lessons.

● **How does the approach to designing lessons and assessment activities relate to the tetrahedral model presented in Figure 1.2?**

Decision Point: What does the tetrahedral model suggest about the need for teachers to be flexible in planning and performance?

---

students may also benefit from such understanding. Good learners are, in a sense, their own teachers and make good decisions about what and how to study. By learning about how good readers learn from text you can help your students use their textbooks more effectively. In this section we present some theory and research that will help you as a learner use this text to your best advantage.

Mayer (1984, 1999) suggests that there are three different types of readers and that these types may be classified by how well they are able to learn from the texts they read. After reading a passage from a textbook some learners remember only a small amounts of the information and are unable to apply the information from the reading to new situations. Other learners can remember many of the facts and details of what they have just read, but are nevertheless unable to apply the information to new situations. Finally, some readers remember the main ideas from the reading and apply what they've read to new situations. The difference in these three groups seems to be in the way they mentally process the concepts from the material they are reading.

Starting from a constructivist/information-processing theory Mayer (1984, 1999) suggests that meaningful learning depends on how well learners perform three cognitive activities: (a) selecting important information, (b) organizing the information selected, and (c) integrating the organized information with what they already know. Readers who fail to select important concepts within the text are able to remember very little of what they read. Readers who are able to select the important ideas are able to recall what they read, but if they fail to organize and integrate the new material, they will not be able to apply the material to new situations.

Selecting Important Information

Selection refers to the process of focusing attention. In any situation, what is learned is determined by how attention is directed. Things we attend to are likely to be remembered, and things that do not attract our attention are more likely to be forgotten. Whether or not a reader focuses on some idea or concept depends on the reader's knowledge and the characteristics of the material being read (Cook & Mayer, 1988). If the reader is familiar with a topic he or she is able to select important ideas from what is read. When the information presented is new, then the selections are likely to be less efficient.

Authors can assist readers unfamiliar with the material by providing cues within the text that signal the importance of the concepts presented (Mayer, 1984, 1999). In the current text, we signal the importance of a concept by changing the font, for instance, using either bold or italicized letters, by separating important concepts by bulleting and by questions in the margins that can be answered by attending to specific facts or concepts within the text. As you read this text, attending to these cues will help you select those ideas that are most important. This in turn will prepare you for the next learning process, organization.

Organizing Information

Organization refers to the learner's creation of logical connections among ideas and concepts presented in the text (Mayer, 1984). Research suggests organizing the information presented in a text helps learners form a mental representation or model that increases their ability to recall and apply what they remember (Mayer, 1989). As with selection, organization also depends on the knowledge of the reader. But in addition to knowledge of the content, readers' abilities to organize the information from a passage also depends on whether or not they are able to recognize the underlying structure of the text. If readers are able to recognize these structures, they are better able to organize the new information.

Science texts, such as the one you are reading, have organizational structures that are different from those found in narratives. Cook and Mayer (1988) investigated whether training readers to recognize structure in scientific texts lead to better understanding. They found that even good readers benefited from learning how to recognize some of the common ways in which science books organize information. Some of the structures that appear in our text book include:

- *Generalizations.* This structure is built around a topic sentence that presents a main idea or concepts. Additional information in the passage describes various aspects of the main idea or provides examples. The key to organizing this type of passage is to identify the main idea and then understand how the additional information relates to that idea.
- *Sequence.* This structure describes a series of events or steps of a process. To organize information from this type of structure you first identify the topic, then list the steps in the sequence, and finally describe the change that occurs from one step to the next.
- *Classification.* This type of structure organizes facts, concepts, or events into categories. The structure is often hierarchical in that the passage may describe subcategories within categories. To organize this information you first need to identify the main class or category, then find the subcategories, and note what distinguishes each subcategory from the others at the same level.
- *Compare and Contrast.* These structures identify the similarities and differences between two concepts. To organize this structure, you first must identify the two concepts being compared. Then list their similarities and differences.

Looking for these structures and using them to organize the information being read have been shown to increase readers' ability to recall and apply what they have read (Cook & Mayer, 1988; Mayer, 1999). As you read this text, be on the lookout for these types of structures. Headings, bullets, diagrams, and tables have been included to provide you with clues to help you find these structures and organize what you are reading. Developing coherent organization for the facts and concepts you have learned allows you to take the next step toward meaningful learning, integration.

Integrating Information

Integration refers to actions that learners take to find connections between new facts and concepts and things that are already known (Mayer, 1984, 1993). As with selection and organization, the ability of readers to integrate new information depends on the reader's initial knowledge base. Obviously, readers cannot connect what they've learned with things they don't know, but even when readers have knowledge that could be usefully connected with the information presented in a text, readers may still fail to make the connection. In this case, there are text features that can help readers remember what they already know and make the connections. Examples of some of the text features that serve this function are analogies, examples, cases, and questions that remind readers of previously presented materials. You will find features such as these in this text. Remember, the purpose of these features is to help you integrate the information being presented.

Selection, organization, and integration are all actions that are under the control of the learner. What this means is that the meaningfulness of what you learn depends on choices you make. This text provides some guidance for your choices and additional guidance is likely to come from your instructor. But ultimately, you must make the choice to learn and invest the effort needed to select, organize, and integrate what is presented.

What text features may help you as a reader integrate the important facts, concepts, and ideas within a chapter?

Teachers as Decision Makers

A major theme of this text is that teachers are decision makers. To give you a feel for how theories can guide decision making, you were asked to think about questions and issues as you read about the teachers presented in two cases. In this section we present our perspectives on the cases and then discuss how the learning principles of this chapter may be connected to applications in later chapters.

Maria Lucero's Decision Points

Planning a lesson always requires a consideration of characteristics that can be placed in one of two categories: (a) characteristics that affect the students' ability, and (b) characteristics that affect their motivation to learn. While different theories provide different perspectives on what these characteristics are and how they relate to students' performance in classrooms, there are some that seem to turn up in all theories. One of the characteristics that affects students' ability to learn is the things they've learned through their previous experiences. Previous experiences affect what people are able to do and what they choose to do. Therefore, in Maria's case she might want to know what experiences these kids have had, in and out of school, that might be relevant to her lesson topic.

One of Maria's concerns is that she provide a lesson that will help all her students learn regardless of their backgrounds or individual differences. The strategy recommended by her supervising teacher is to begin the lesson planning process by considering her instructional objectives, planning the lesson, and then making adaptations for student differences as necessary. This strategy can be applied to the planning of any lesson and is the perspective taken in this text. The idea is that not all individual differences are relevant to students accomplishing all instructional objectives. A well-planned lesson is likely to be effective for a majority of students. Once this initial plan is made, the teacher can consider modifications that address those student differences that are logically related to the objectives the students are to reach.

Mr. Henson and Maria are approaching their decision making from the perspective of behavioral learning theory, which is presented in Chapter 2. Different theories let you think about problems and decisions in different ways. One theory may be useful in one situation, whereas another theory may be more useful in a different situation. One of the purposes of courses in educational psychology and this text is to provide you with information about various psychological theories so that you choose the theory that will be most helpful to your own decision making.

Jeffrey Larkin's Decision Points

Jeffrey's situation is similar to Maria's, and once again Jeffrey, will need to think about what experiences his students have had, that will influence their ability to benefit from the learning activities. In addition, Jeffrey must consider how a sequence of lessons fits together. The questions that Jeffrey will ask will depend on his beliefs about learners and learning. Learning theories are formal expressions of such beliefs, and because of the scientific process, are likely to be more precise and consistent in the way they formulate a decision-making situation.

The strategy for accommodating diversity used by Mr. Goodman and Jeffrey is very similar to the one applied by Maria and her supervising teacher. In both cases the goal of instruction is to assist all students to reach the objectives of the lessons. The theory chosen will help the teacher determine what activities students must engage in to reach the objectives, and which student characteristics will affect the ability of students to reach the lesson's objective.

The tetrahedral model is a meta-theoretical perspective of the learning situation. It provides teachers a way to think about instruction in their classrooms. The model suggests that there are a series of interacting variables that teachers must keep in mind as they make decisions in their classrooms. Because of the complexity of these interactions, much of the decision making of teachers is really a parallel process that requires the teacher to consider decisions in light of decisions already made. In addition, teachers must sometimes reconsider decisions made previously in light of later decisions.

Looking Ahead

The theme of this book is that effective teachers are good decision makers. In order to make good decisions in the complex, multidimensional environment of the classroom, teachers must be able to organize their thinking about students, learning, and instruction. Theories provide teachers with a valuable perspective, a frame of reference, from which to analyze and understand classrooms and students.

Once teachers understand a situation, they must make a decision and act on it. This means that teachers must formulate and implement plans. They must then monitor the progress of the plans to determine if they are working, and if any modification of the plans is required. Principles, derived from theories, provide a framework for the formulation of a plan of action.

A goal of educational psychology is to provide teachers with tools to assist in their analysis and understanding of classrooms. Developing theories and identifying principles of learning and instruction accomplish this goal. The purpose of this text is to provide prospective teachers with a foundation of theories and principles that will help them: (a) understand students and classrooms, (b) make decisions and formulate plans, and (c) monitor the effectiveness of their actions.

Name _____ Date _____

Chapter 1 Study Guide

Use this Study Guide to review and test your knowledge of key concepts introduced in this chapter and to search out further information on issues and topics raised in this chapter.

 **Key Terms**

Review the following key words from the chapter and then connect to Research Navigator (www.researchnavigator.com) either directly or through this book's Companion Website to explore research on the topics as they relate to education today.

Action research (p. 12)
Between-group differences (p. 16)
Criterial tasks (p. 18)
Decision points (p. 11)
Direct observation (p. 14)
Educational psychology (p. 2)
Epistemic value (p. 7)
Generalizability (p. 15)
Implicit theory (p. 4)
Integration (p. 20)
Materials (p. 18)

Operational definition (p. 15)
Organization (p. 20)
Orienting tasks (p. 18)
Performance assessments (p. 14)
Principle (p. 7)
Psychological construct (p. 6)
Psychological process (p. 6)
Qualitative data (p. 15)
Quantitative data (p. 15)
Scientific theory (p. 4)
Scope (p. 6)

Selection (p. 19)
Self-report techniques (p. 15)
State (p. 7)
Subjects (p. 18)
Tetrahedral model (p. 17)
Theory (p. 4)
Trait (p. 6)
Validity (p. 16)
Within-group differences (p. 16)

Alternative Response Items

1. What term best describes a set of formal statements describing relationships that explain events in the real world?

   a. Implicit theory
   b. Scientific theory
   c. Principle
   d. Psychological construct

2. Which statement best defines the psychological concept of a trait?

   a. A mental characteristic that arises from a specific situation and changes when the situation changes.
   b. A mental characteristic that remains relatively constant from one situation to another.
   c. A mental process that is associated with a specific situation stops when the situation changes.
   d. A mental process that remains constant from one situation to the next.

3. Which of the following is best thought of as a state?

   a. Intelligence
   b. Personality
   c. Friendship
   d. Emotion

4. Which of the following research topics would be examples of the types of research questions typically addressed by educational psychologists?

   a. How does learners' prior knowledge affect their ability to problem solve?
   b. How does the amount of teacher praise affect learning in a classroom?
   c. How does frequency of reinforcement affect learning of new behaviors?
   d. All of the above

5. Research consistently indicates that practice results in an increase in performance speed and a reduction in the error rate. What term refers to a statement that describes this relationship?

   a. Scientific theory
   b. Implicit theory
   c. Principle
   d. Psychological process

6. What term best describes the actions of a classroom teacher who develops an explicit description of a classroom problem, develops a plan for dealing with the problem, collects data to analyze the effectiveness of the plan, and then uses the results to deal with similar problems in the classroom?

   a. Action research
   b. Scientific research
   c. Explicit research
   d. Principle development

7. What term best describes data in the form of rich complex verbal descriptions?

   a. Quantitative data
   b. Qualitative data
   c. Subjective data
   d. Observational data

8. Mr. Garrison decides not to use a particular learning theory because it only seems suitable for understanding how students learn science. With which characteristic of a theory is he concerned?

   a. Scope
   b. Predictive accuracy
   c. Internal coherence
   d. External consistency

9. When comparing qualitative data with quantitative data, which of the following statements is most correct?

   a. Conclusions made from qualitative data are less likely to be generalizable.
   b. Conclusions made from quantitative data are less likely to be generalizable.
   c. Conclusions made from qualitative data are less likely to be valid.
   d. Conclusions made from quantitative data are less likely to be valid.

10. Which of the following is an example of data collected through self-report?

   a. Test scores from a standardized achievement test.
   b. A school psychologist's notes on a student's demeanor while taking an intelligence test.
   c. The results of career counseling survey that indicates students' likes and dislikes.
   d. Letter grades assigned to student presentations in a speech communications class.

Constructed Response Items

Short Answer/Completion Items

1. Teachers who have developed an intuitive understanding of what works and what doesn't work in their classes may be said to have a(n) _____ theory.

2. What are the steps of action research?

3. What are the five aspects of the epistemic value of a theory?

4. Traits and states are both examples of _____.

Essay Items

1. Describe the relationship between theories and research.

2. Discuss how knowledge of psychological theories might help teachers become better decision makers.

3. Compare and contrast the nature and utility of quantitative and qualitative data.

Practicing Your Decision Making

In this chapter, we've described three decision points in the teaching process. Because teaching and learning are closely related activities, it is possible to apply the same decision points to understanding the decisions that learners must make. Use this idea to analyze your own studying. What decisions must you make when you are planning to study, while you are studying, and when you assess the effectiveness of your study?

INTASC in Action

Use the following activity to think about how research and theory relate to INTASC Standard 9.

Standard 9: Reflective Practice and Professional Growth. Teachers learn a lot through their personal experience in the classroom. However, what are the limitations of relying solely on their personal experience for these types of decisions?

- A school district must decide whether or not to purchase a thinking skills curriculum.

- A school district needs to determine whether or not an educational program has been successful.

How might educational research help with these decisions?

Web Resources

If you would like to read more about scientific theories and their applications, go to the following sites.

American Educational Research Association (AERA)
www.aera.net/index.htm

AERA is the premier educational research organization in the country. Visit their homepage to become familiar with the scope of research conducted in education.

American Psychological Society (APS)
www.psychologicalscience.org/

The is the homepage of the American Psychological Society (APS) and will allow you to become familiar with the psychological issues that may be investigated through empirical research.

Eisenhower National Clearinghouse Online
www.enc.org/topics/

ENC Online is a K–12 math and science teacher center dedicated to disseminating useful information and offering products to improve K–12 mathematics and science teaching and learning. The Educational Topics section of the site will help you locate articles that cover some of today's most important topics for math and science educators and parents.

Understanding Behavioral Learning Theory

By the time you have finished this chapter, you will have learned how to use concepts from behavioral learning theories to interpret and respond to the types of situations discussed in the Close-ups on the Classroom feature. The following behavioral learning theory concepts presented in this chapter have been combined to form a few key learning principles. In later chapters, you will learn how to use these principles to design and deliver instruction and to manage classroom behavior.

- Principle 2.1: Learning is measurable and observable.
- Principle 2.2: Learning complicated behaviors occurs gradually and step by step.
- Principle 2.3: Learning results from the effects of stimuli on responses.

Standards in This Chapter

Although learning the concepts and associated principles presented in this chapter will contribute to your mastery of all of the INTASC standards, the material presented in Chapter 2 is most strongly related to the following standards:

- **Standard 2:** Student Development
- **Standard 3:** Diverse Learners
- **Standard 5:** Motivation and Management
- **Standard 7:** Planning
- **Standard 9:** Reflective Practice and Professional Growth

Close-ups on the Classroom

Elementary

Tom Pierce
His Second Graders

I've been teaching second grade for five years now, and every year poses at least some new challenges. I have a young boy in my class, Paul, who is really worrying me. Whenever I reach out to take something from him or try to put my hand on his shoulder, he cringes and even starts shaking. When the classroom gets too noisy for him, he starts to cry.

Cynthia is another student who concerns me, because she's not like a lot of my other students. I sometimes have students stay in at recess when they misbehave. This seems to help, because most of my students hate to lose recess. She actually seems to find ways to get in trouble so she has to stay in with me. I'm concerned because she isn't getting a chance to be outside in the fresh air, and she is losing an opportunity she needs to make friends. Melissa, our school counselor, worked with both children in first grade and has some information to share with me tomorrow night after school.

This week I am also meeting with other teachers in the building because the state department has finally published the curriculum standards for elementary school. Each standard represents an academic goal that students need to meet by the end of sixth grade. We are meeting this evening with representatives from each grade to discuss how we will integrate these standards into our teaching. I've looked the standards over, and I have a lot of questions I hope get answered in this meeting.

Decision Point: What tentative explanations do you have for Cynthia and Paul's behavior? What questions would you ask Melissa about Cynthia and Paul?

Before proceeding with Chapter 2, be sure you read the Close-ups on the Classroom features about Tom Pierce and Emilio Lopez. At various points in the chapter, you will revisit both teachers in their classrooms and follow their decision-making progress. Their classroom experiences are closely integrated with the key concepts of this chapter and serve as important models for understanding Behavioral Learning Theory.

Behavioral View of Learning

How do behaviorists define learning?

From a behavioral perspective, learning occurs when environmental stimuli produce a relatively permanent and observable change in learners' responses. As you can see from this definition of learning, behaviorists define learning in terms of observable events called stimuli and responses. A **stimulus** is an observable environmental event that has the potential to exert control over a behavioral response (Becker, 1986). For example, the grade you desire in this class is an environmental stimulus that can exert control over how you study and your class attendance. A **response** is an overt behavior by a learner. In the previous example, your studying behavior for this class would be an example of a response. Behavioral learning models explain how behavior changes through the influence of various types of stimuli.

Types of Stimuli

Behaviorists identify three types of stimuli based on their effects on learners' responses. These three types of stimuli are eliciting stimuli, consequences, and antecedents (Alberto & Troutman, 1999; Becker, 1986).

Eliciting Stimuli. Eliciting stimuli are observable environmental events that come immediately before a response and that automatically elicit or produce that response. For example, if you were to move your hand quickly toward another person's face, that person would probably respond in one of several predictable ways. That person

Emilio Lopez
The Alternative High School

I have been a math teacher at VISION, our district's alternative high school, for the last five years. At VISION we try to provide students who have had difficulty in our other high schools one more option. Some of our students have been expelled from one of our other high schools, while others are recent dropouts who are giving high school one more chance. At first, I was not sure I would like it, but now I wouldn't teach any other place. The challenges are great, but so are the rewards.

We are a small and close-knit faculty. We meet each week to provide support to each other and to make sure we are all working together well. At this afternoon's meeting I've asked if we could talk about a problem I am having. We have a rule against inappropriate language, and it seems that every new student I've gotten recently wants to test that rule. I hope I can get some suggestions on how to handle this because my approach hasn't worked so far. I've placed a swearing jar in front of the class and told my students that each swear word

will cost them a dime. Yesterday one of the new students put a ten-dollar bill in the jar and said that should cover him for a while.

Our principal has hired a consultant, Barbara Lozano, to work individually with teachers on motivational strategies for resistant learners. I'm looking forward to getting some help on motivational strategies because I have two students in particular this year who are very challenging. Robert is challenging because a lot of what has worked for me in the past does not work for him. For example, he seems to have no reaction to my praise and encouragement, and even gets angry and rebellious sometimes when I try to tell him how well he is doing. This is unusual because my students usually crave positive adult attention. Another of my students, Sarah, may have the worst case of math anxiety I've seen in my teaching career. She actually had to leave the room during a math test because she was going to throw up. She's not really sure when this all started, but she tells me she has been this way for a while. I hope the consultant can help me.

Decision Point: What tentative hypotheses do you have to explain Robert and Sarah's behavior?

might move her head back, or even put her hand up to protect her face. In this situation, the approaching hand is the eliciting stimulus for the responses of moving the head back or putting up a hand. The hand movement comes immediately before these responses, and it automatically elicits or produces them. Some forms of learning occur when people learn to produce a particular response when an eliciting stimulus is present. For example, you may have learned to respond by automatically saying "present" when a teacher calls your name during roll.

Consequences. A consequence is a stimulus that occurs immediately after a response and that has the effect of making a response more or less likely to occur again. Consider these classroom examples of consequences.

- Sammy stops participating in class because every time he does, other students laugh at him.
- Simone studies hard because she has found that she gets good grades when she studies hard.

In both cases, the likelihood of a response was modified; Sammy is less likely to participate in class, and Simone is more likely to study because of the consequences they have experienced. It is important to note that consequences are defined in terms of effect on the response. To qualify as a consequence, a stimulus must either increase or decrease the likelihood of a response.

Antecedents. An antecedent is a stimulus that precedes a response and cues learners to respond in certain ways if they want to earn reinforcement or avoid punishment. For example, a teacher gets very quiet when her students are being noisy and not listening. When the students observe the silence, they know they need to quiet down and pay attention if they want reinforcement from the teacher or if they want to avoid punishment. The silence is an antecedent that cues the students' behaviors.

Together, antecedents, behaviors (responses), and consequences are often referred to as the ABCs of learning (Kazdin, 1994; Martin, 1981). When you use the ABCs to understand your students' behaviors, you are looking for the antecedents that cue a behavior and the consequences that affect the likelihood of a behavior occurring again. For example, every time you praise a student in front of the class, he responds by acting out, and you have to send him to detention. Because of detention, he is less likely to act out for a while. If you examine the ABCs of this situation, the public praise seems to be an antecedent for the acting out, and the detention is a consequence for acting out. Note that by identifying the ABCs, you provide yourself with some choices. You may try to eliminate the acting out by continuing to send the student to detention (consequence), or you could try to prevent the behavior by modifying the way you provide praise (antecedent).

What do the letters ABC stand for in a behavioral view of learning?

Learning Is Measurable and Observable

Because both stimuli and responses can be observed and measured directly, behaviorists believe that learning can be observed and measured. For example, if students could not multiply two digits together and now they can, that change in behavior can be observed and measured. If a student becomes less likely to interrupt others during class discussion, that change in behavior can be observed and measured. When teaching or managing classroom behavior, therefore, teachers identify the specific behavioral changes they want and the stimuli that will help produce those changes. In addition, teachers collect data on their students' behavior by measuring or observing their students' behavior before, during, and after an intervention. For example, you count how many times a student interrupts other students, and then you intervene and observe whether the number of interruptions changes.

*B*ehavioral Learning Models

Behaviorists explain learning by developing models of how stimuli can produce relatively permanent changes in behavior. Contiguity learning and classical conditioning are two behavioral learning models that focus exclusively on the role of eliciting stimuli in producing learning, while operant conditioning is the behavioral learning model that uses antecedents and consequences to explain learning.

Contiguity Learning

A combination of stimuli which was accompanied by movement will on its reoccurrence tend to be followed by that movement. (Guthrie, 1935, p. 26)

This quotation from the work of Edwin R. Guthrie (1886–1959) describes the contiguity principle, which is the basis for contiguity learning. Contiguity learning occurs when an eliciting stimulus and response become connected because they have occurred together. As a result of this connection, when the eliciting stimulus occurs in the future, the connected response tends to occur. In classrooms, this often is accomplished by having students practice the desired response when the eliciting stimulus occurs. For example, students learn to respond to fire alarms by practicing certain responses during fire drills. They may learn their math facts by producing the correct response to the eliciting stimulus of a flash card or worksheet. Practicing them together connects the problem (stimulus) and answer (response).

How does contiguity learning occur?

Contiguity learning often occurs in classrooms through *drill and practice* activities. Drill and practice activities have been criticized because they tend to emphasize the learning of low-level skills at the expense of meaningful, conceptual understanding. For example, knowing that two times two is four does not mean that a student understands why two times two is four. Although this criticism has merit, it also can be argued that a conceptual understanding of mathematics will not guarantee that math facts have been committed to memory (Harris & Graham, 1996). Although contiguity learning may not be the best choice for all learning objectives, it is a good choice when the goal is simply for students to connect a response to an eliciting stimulus, as is the case for simple factual learning.

Classical Conditioning

Classical conditioning is the second behavioral model that explains how eliciting stimuli can produce learning. Classical conditioning typically involves situations in which two stimuli become associated, and as a result, they both now elicit a similar response (Domjan, Cusato, & Villarreal, 2000; Simpson, 2000). Although Ivan Pavlov (1849–1936) is usually credited with the discovery of the classical conditioning model, he was assisted greatly by colleagues in his laboratory. Also, as sometimes happens with scientific discoveries, similar findings were recorded independently of Pavlov and at about the same time (Windholz, 1993). (See the below Enriching Your Understanding.)

Ivan Pavlov
(1849–1936)

Pavlovian Example.   While studying the salivation response in dogs, Pavlov and his colleagues noted that the dogs in the laboratory starting salivating to environmental stimuli other than food. For example, they would salivate at the appearance of the lab technician who fed them (Pavlov, 1902). Pavlov and his associates began studying this phenomenon systematically by pairing the presentation of food with a second stimulus such as a bell, light, buzzer, metronome, or touching device (Gray, 1979). In this famous work with dogs, Pavlov and his colleagues found that if food

ENRICHING YOUR UNDERSTANDING
E. B. Twitmyer and Classical Conditioning

Ivan Pavlov is traditionally given credit for discovering classical conditioning. There were, however, others who discovered the same phenomenon, but who have not received the same level of credit (Coon, 1982; Dallenbach, 1959; Fernberger, 1943; Windholz, 1993). Edwin B. Twitmyer is one of those psychologists. Twitmyer was a doctoral student at the University of Pennsylvania who was completing a dissertation on variability in the human knee jerk response. In his experimental trials, a bell would be rung to signal the start of a new trial. Shortly after the bell was rung, the patellar reflex was initiated by striking the patella with a hammer. Twitmyer noticed that after a number of trials, some of his subjects started emitting the knee jerk reflex at the sound of the bell, but before the hammer blow. The reflex was being initiated by the sound of the bell. The results of this experiment were originally privately published, but Twitmyer did present the findings at the Christmas meeting of the American Psychological Association in 1904. According to his obituary, Twitmyer was disappointed when his presentation did not elicit a single comment from the audience (Fernberger, 1943). Later, his pioneering work was compiled and published (Twitmyer, 1974), but he never did receive the level of acclaim awarded to Pavlov.

● **Is Twitmyer's work an example of classical conditioning? See if you can translate his experiment into a diagram similar to Figure 2.1. (For your authors' perspective on this question, go to the text website for this chapter.)**

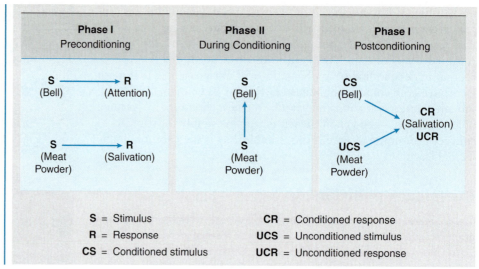

FIGURE 2.1 Pavlov and Classical Conditioning

Phase I	Phase II	Phase I
Preconditioning	During Conditioning	Postconditioning

Phase I — Preconditioning:
S (Bell) → R (Attention)
S (Meat Powder) → R (Salivation)

Phase II — During Conditioning:
S (Bell) ↑ S (Meat Powder)

Phase I — Postconditioning:
CS (Bell) → CR (Salivation) UCR
UCS (Meat Powder) →

S = Stimulus   **CR** = Conditioned response
R = Response   **UCS** = Unconditioned stimulus
CS = Conditioned stimulus   **UCR** = Unconditioned response

was presented with one of these other stimuli, the two stimuli became associated, and they then both elicited salivation. Pavlov's basic experimental work is summarized in Figure 2.1.

As can be seen from Figure 2.1, Pavlov's classical conditioning experiment occurred in three phases. In the preconditioning phase, two separate and preexisting stimulus-response connections were present in the dogs. First, it was noted that the presence of meat powder in the dog's mouth would elicit the response of salivating. As this stimulus-response connection was unlearned and reflexive, Pavlov called the meat powder an **unconditioned stimulus,** and the salivation response to the meat powder an **unconditioned response.** The second stimulus, in this case, a bell, elicited an orienting or attention response such as looking in the direction of the sound.

In the Pavlovian experiment, why is salivating to meat powder an example of an unconditioned response?

During the conditioning phase, Pavlov established a connection between the meat powder and the bell by presenting them together over a number of trials. The goal was to connect the two stimuli by having them occur together (a form of contiguity).

During the postconditioning phase, the dogs had learned to connect the bell to the meat powder, which now elicited the response of salivation. Pavlov called the bell a **conditioned stimulus,** and the salivation response to the bell a **conditioned response.**

Why is salivating to the bell a conditioned response?

Classroom Implications of Classical Conditioning.   The Pavlovian experiments are of tremendous historical importance, but they may not be particularly informative about the role of classical conditioning in classrooms. You probably will not be interested in getting your children to salivate to a bell or in creating new eliciting stimuli for reflexes such as eye blinking or knee jerking. However, classical conditioning is important to teachers because it provides a useful explanation for how students acquire important emotional responses and attitudes (Tauber, 1990).

In the case of emotional responses, students can learn to associate an initially neutral school stimulus with stimuli that already elicit strong emotions. Eventually, they respond to those school stimuli with the same emotions. Consider the following examples of classical conditioning in schools.

- John feels nervous if he does poorly in front of others. In the past he has done poorly on a number of math assignments and tests. Now when any math teacher says take out a piece of paper for a test, his palms sweat and he starts to feel ill.
- Sally feels happy and contented when adults praise and support her. Her teachers are warm and supporting, so she feels happy when she talks or thinks about school.

- Sarah was in two plays in elementary school, and in both cases she forgot her lines on stage. This made her feel anxious and embarrassed. Now a request that she participate in a play makes her feel anxious.
- When Mr. Joseph was in high school he got into a lot of trouble and did poorly. Eventually, he felt so uncomfortable in school that he quit coming. Today as a parent coming back for a parent conference, just the sight of the school building makes him feel uncomfortable.

Classical conditioning can also explain how we implicitly learn certain attitudes (Houwer, Thomas, & Baeyens, 2001; Olson & Fazio, 2002). From a classical conditioning perspective, if people or items are paired with other stimuli that produce positive or negative emotional responses, those people or items eventually can produce the same emotional responses. Advertisements make use of this by pairing products with stimuli that elicit positive emotions such as physically attractive or popular people. Negative racial or gender attitudes could be acquired implicitly if members of a race or gender are associated with images or words that produce negative emotional reactions. This possibility means that curricular materials need to be evaluated carefully so that students are not exposed to these types of negative associations.

This idea that school can become connected to stimuli that produce strong emotions or attitudes in students is important. It reminds teachers that they can unintentionally produce attitudes or emotional associations for school that they do not want their students to learn. This type of awareness may be particularly important for students whose life experiences are quite different from those provided by school. Think about coming to a new place where a different language is spoken, customs are unfamiliar, and maybe even the food served at lunch makes you feel nauseous. The negative feelings that these experiences create could easily become associated with school, creating negative feelings about school. As a teacher, you may be able to reduce this possibility by helping all students feel supported and welcome. For example, you could create classrooms and schools where students' various home cultures are clearly visible. You could assign other students to serve as guides and interpreters, or you could help students quickly acquire functional vocabulary in English such as the word *bathroom*.

What are the major implications of classical conditioning for the classroom?

Here are some more recommendations based on classical conditioning for creating a classroom environment that reduces the likelihood of student anxiety and discomfort.

- Emphasize improvement rather than perfection. Let students know that mistakes are a natural part of learning.
- Provide opportunities for students to redo assignments that are difficult for them.
- Maintain an orderly and predictable classroom environment. Allow students to know your expectations.
- Make sure that students who are new to the classroom are given the support they need at first. For example, spend time going over your expectations with them.

Operant Conditioning

The modern understanding of operant conditioning has developed primarily out of the work of B. F. Skinner (Skinner, 1938, 1953, 1958a, 1974; Skinner & Epstein, 1982), but operant conditioning has its historical roots in empiricism and the ideas of E. L. Thorndike and J. B. Watson among others (Thorndike, 1905, 1949; Watson, 1913, 1919). Operant conditioning is a behavioral learning model that attempts to explain learning through the effects of both antecedents and consequences on behavior. However, the focus in operant conditioning is on how consequences may be used to produce learning, so the discussion will begin there.

Consequences

Of several responses made to the same situation, those which are accompanied or closely followed by satisfaction to the animal will, other things being equal, be more

**Burrhus Frederick
Skinner (1904–1990)**

firmly connected to the situation . . . those which are accompanied or closely followed by discomfort to the animal will, other things being equal, have their connections with that situation weakened. (Thorndike, 1911, p. 244)

In this quotation, E. L. Thorndike (1874–1949) defined his original **law of effect,** which in turn formed the basis for the behavioral idea of a consequence. As we noted earlier, a consequence is a stimulus that occurs after a behavior has been emitted and that has the *effect of* making that behavior more or less likely to occur. Although Thorndike eventually revised his law of effect by dropping the potential for discomfort to make a behavior less likely, modern behavioral psychologists like B. F. Skinner (1953) have retained two types of consequences. **Reinforcements** are consequences that have the effect of increasing or maintaining the likelihood that a behavior will occur again, while **punishments** are consequences that have the effect of decreasing the likelihood that a behavior will occur again (Sulzer-Azaroff & Mayer, 1991). Behaviorists further identify two types of reinforcement and two types of punishment, positive and negative reinforcement and presentation and removal punishment.

Positive Reinforcement. With **positive reinforcement,** a behavior is more likely to occur because when the behavior does occur, a valued or satisfying consequence is provided to the learner. For example, a student comes to class on time one day and the teacher praises the student for the on-time behavior. As a result, that student comes to class on time more frequently. In this case, praise is a positive reinforcer for the on-time behavior, because it is provided to the student after the occurrence of the on-time behavior, and it has the effect of making the on-time behavior more likely to occur.

How is reinforcement different from punishment?

A number of different environmental events can serve as positive reinforcers in the classroom (Alberto & Troutman, 1999; Becker, 1986; Duncan, Kemple, & Smith, 2000; Kazdin, 1982; Schloss & Smith, 1994; Skinner, 1953). **Social reinforcers** convey affection, attention, or approval to students. They can be administered through verbal praise, teacher smiles, positive facial expressions, and gestures. This form of reinforcement is user friendly because it can be used spontaneously and with minimal planning. Also, it is a type of reinforcement that occurs as part of many naturally occurring life events, and, therefore, typically parents do not object (Kazdin, 1982).

If you use praise as a social reinforcer, certain guidelines should be followed (Brophy, 1981; Duncan, Kemple, & Smith, 2000; Good & Brophy, 2003; Harlan, 1996; McVey, 2001). First, praise should be specific to a behavior. Students need to know why they are being praised. Rather than saying, "Good job," you might say instead, "The opening paragraph does a great job of previewing key issues." Second, effective praise should be spontaneous and natural. If your praise comes across as contrived or as if you are gushing, it will not have value. Third, praise should focus on students' efforts and improvements. For example, you might praise a student's improvement by saying, "Your extra studying is really paying off!" Fourth, vary your praise statements and support them with nonverbal demonstrations of approval such as a smile or wink. Finally, praise should typically be administered privately to individuals to avoid embarrassing them or causing them problems with their peers. This is how Bernice White uses these ideas in her high school English class.

What are the guidelines for the use of praise?

➤ It's important to encourage young writers. I have my students write in journals. At least once every week, I read what they are writing and I try to pick out one area of improvement and comment on it in my written feedback.

Natural reinforcers occur without special attention or manipulation by teachers; they occur naturally in the environment (Schloss & Smith, 1994). For example, we might engage in behaviors because they are enjoyable, we feel successful at them, or they help us accomplish a goal. Young children and adolescents often play video games for hours on end. Although there are a number of reasons for this, video games do provide natural reinforcement in terms of a fun experience, and the potential for improved play with practice. Skinner (1984) has suggested that effective instructional programs in schools also have some of these same characteristics. Students become engaged in academic tasks that allow them to sense their own improvement. This is how Maria Ontiveras uses this idea.

> ➤ When I do math fact drill with my students, we play beat the clock. I set an egg timer for five minutes, and students see how many problems they can do in that time. Their goal is to improve a little each week. The kids seem to like working to beat their old score.

Feedback can function as a reinforcer by providing students with information about their performance (Kazdin, 1994). This information typically provides students with knowledge about the results of their behaviors that may not be naturally present in the academic task itself. For example, feedback may be used to congratulate students on a job well done, and to tell them what they did well.

An **activity reinforcer** is a privilege or behavior that has value to a learner, such as extra free time, additional access to the computer, and time to talk with friends. The use of activity reinforcers is based on the **Premack principle** (Premack, 1959, 1965). In general, the Premack principle states that people will engage in a less favored activity if it allows them access to a more favored activity. For example, you might tell yourself that if you read ten more pages, then you can watch a television show. This is how Marion Bellamy uses this with her junior high students.

> ➤ My junior high kids love to socialize. I tell them that if we work hard and have a good week, we will play games like social studies Jeopardy on Friday, or I may even give them some time to chat. It seems to help keep them on task during the week.

A **tangible reinforcer** is a valued object such as stickers, toys, school supplies, certificates, and ribbons that a student can earn. A tangible reinforcer might be thought of as a prize that students receive for their good behavior.

A **token** is a symbolic reinforcer that can be exchanged for tangibles, activities, and other reinforcers that students value (Cruz & Cullinan, 2001; Higgins, Williams, & McLaughlin, 2001; Martin & Pear, 1996). Classroom point systems provide an example of the use of tokens, because students can exchange the points they earn for free time, toys, or whatever back-up reinforcers are available. Your authors discuss the use of tokens more in Chapter 10. Table 2.1 summarizies the different types of reinforcers we have described.

What are the major types of reinforcers?

Positive reinforcement strategies have been found by teachers to be useful for increasing the likelihood of a number of behaviors including on-task behaviors, completion of academic tasks such as homework, and students' positive social involvement with peers (Moroz & Jones, 2002; Neef, Shade, & Miller, 1994; Sutherland, Wehby, & Copeland, 2000). However, the effective use of positive reinforcement requires consideration of the following guidelines.

- Reinforcement should typically occur as soon as possible after the response has occurred (Walker & Shea, 1995).
- When feasible, natural reinforcers and social reinforcers should be used in preference to more contrived reinforcers such as tangibles and tokens. From a practical perspective, social and natural reinforcers do not require additional resources or planning to use.

TABLE 2.1   **Types of Reinforcers**

Type of Positive Reinforcement	Definition	Examples*
Social reinforcer	Reinforcement by demonstrating approval, attention, or affection to the student	A teacher praises a student for his improvement in science.
		A teacher gives a student a thumbs up for the answer she just gave in a class discussion.
Activity reinforcer	A behavior or privilege students earn as a result of their behavior	Students earn extra computer time.
		Students are allowed a study hall if their work is done.
Tangible reinforcer	A physical object students earn through their behavior	Students earn a good behavior certificate.
		Students are given perfect attendance medals.
Token	Can be exchanged for valued reinforcers	Students earn class dollars that they can spend in a weekly auction.
		Teacher places chips in a fish bowl when students earn them. When there are enough, the students earn a class party.
Natural reinforcers	Behaviors that contain their own reinforcement	Providing students with learning activities that reflect their interests.
Feedback	Information provided to students about their performance	Writing notes to students in which you discuss their successes and improvements.

*Note: These are only examples if they increase the likelihood of the target behavior.

- When a behavior is reinforced, the effects of the reinforcement can potentially extend to behaviors that occur at about the same time, but that are not intended to be reinforced (Catania, 2000). To avoid accidentally reinforcing the wrong behaviors, tell students specifically why they are being reinforced.
- The selected reinforcers need to have **reinforcement potency** for the students, which means that students value the reinforcers (Walker & Shea, 1995). You can identify potent reinforcements for your students by having them select the reinforcers they would like to earn (Maag, 1999; McEwan & Damer, 2000; Reid, 1999).
- Over time students' preferences for reinforcers can change (DeLeon et al., 2001). A number of explanations exist, but in some cases, it is because students have satiated on the reinforcer (Reid, 1999). **Satiation** literally means to satisfy an appetite completely. When students satiate on a reinforcer, it loses its potency. Because of these changes in preference, you will want to vary the available reinforcers periodically.
  - Reinforcers typically work better if they are unexpected. Rather than promising reinforcement for a behavior, provide the reinforcement when it seems natural and appropriate to do so (Chance, 1992).
  - When students are first acquiring a new behavior, there should be ample opportunities for reinforcement (see Schedules of Reinforcement, later in this chapter).

What do the terms *reinforcement potency* and *satiation* mean?

Negative Reinforcement.   In the case of **negative reinforcement**, a behavior is more likely to occur because it allows the learner to avoid or escape an unpleasant event (Harlan, 1996; Skinner, 1953). In classrooms, students may engage in certain behaviors because these behaviors allow them to escape or avoid work demands or unwanted social interactions (Hagopian, Wilson, & Wilder, 2001). For example, a

Emilio Lopez

2.1

Barbara, our consultant, requested that I ask Sarah if she remembers when she first started feeling anxious about math. Sarah told me that she thought the feelings started in second grade when she had to take timed math tests. She couldn't work the problems quickly, and she always finished last. Because of this, the other students made fun of her. Their teasing made her feel very nervous, and eventually she actually started getting an upset stomach when it was time for math. Math continued to be hard for her, and her bad feelings about math only got worse. When she told me that, I immediately made a mental note to make extra time to show Sarah that she can learn math.

Barbara also asked some interesting questions about Robert. When I described his reactions to my praise, she asked me to talk about what Robert likes and dislikes. He likes cars and punk rock bands a lot, but he really likes it that the other kids think he is cool. He hates reading, and he often has a problem with authority. His rebelliousness, in fact, is part of what the other students like about him. She then asked me if any of this helps me understand why he reacts so negatively to my public and enthusiastic praise, and she encouraged me to think of other ways to encourage Robert.

● **How would classical conditioning explain how Sarah learned to be nervous about math? How might the guidelines for using positive reinforcement help Emilio understand why his praise is not working with Robert?**

Decision Point: What might Emilio do to try to reduce Sarah's math anxiety? Based on what you know about Robert, what might be some effective alternatives to praising him for his successes?

---

student may misbehave to avoid having to do an assignment, or a student may intentionally procrastinate when dressing for physical education to avoid some of the class period. Consider these additional examples of negative reinforcement:

- Peter observes that if he works quietly during seatwork time, he can avoid being yelled at by the teacher. He works quietly to avoid the teacher's reprimand.
- Jonathan has learned that if he lies, it often allows him to avoid being punished. He lies in situations in which he could get in trouble to avoid getting in trouble.
- Marissa learns that if she is trustworthy and keeps her friends' secrets she can avoid losing her friends.
- College students in an educational psychology class learn that if they close their notebooks and look at the clock at the end of class, the professor stops talking. Students start putting their books away every day and even a little earlier each day. Students have learned that *book putting away* behavior allows them to escape class lecture before it is over.

How are positive and negative reinforcement similar and different?

When using negative reinforcement in your classroom, you would typically establish a contingency that allows students to avoid a requirement or to take a break from an unpleasant task (Boyajian, DuPaul, Handler, Eckert, & McGregg, 2001; Kitfield & Masalsky, 2000; McComas, Goddard, & Hoch, 2002). Consider these two examples (Rose, 1999):

- Any students who get an A on a test or have turned in a specific number of homework papers get their names placed in a jar. Shortly before a spelling test, a name is drawn. That person gets to skip the test.
- If students meet an important achievement goal such as significantly improving their math test scores, they can get a Skip Homework Pass that allows them to skip one daily practice assignment. The passes are used sparingly and cannot be used for a major project.

Of the two forms of reinforcement, negative reinforcement is the one that is commonly misunderstood. Your authors have provided a discussion of some of the more common misconceptions about negative reinforcement in the Enriching Your Understanding.

ENRICHING YOUR UNDERSTANDING
Misconceptions about Negative Reinforcement

Here are some common misconceptions about negative reinforcement and explanations for why they are incorrect.

- **Misconception One: Negative reinforcement is when a teacher gives a student negative attention.**
  Although this idea seems plausible, it is really an example of positive reinforcement. The behavior is increasing because the student is receiving attention for the behavior. To be an example of negative reinforcement, the behavior must allow the student to escape or avoid.

- **Misconception Two: Negative reinforcement is when a negative behavior is increased.**
  The behavior that is negatively reinforced can be an appropriate or inappropriate behavior. For example, a teacher tells students that if they work hard, they will not need to take an assignment home. The students work hard to avoid the homework. Although the working behavior is being negatively reinforced, it is not inappropriate behavior.

- **Misconception Three: Negative reinforcement is a milder form of punishment.**
  This misconception may result from the desire to associate the word *negative* with some form of punishment. Please note that all reinforcement has the effect of increasing or maintaining a behavior. Punishment has the opposite effect on behavior.

Presentation Punishment.   Presentation punishment is when a behavior becomes less likely to occur because that behavior is followed by the presentation of an aversive or unpleasant stimulus. For example, a child misbehaves in public, and the parent reprimands the child. As a result of the reprimand, the child stops acting up. The reprimand serves as a presentation punishment for the acting-up behavior, because it is presented after the misbehavior and has the effect of stopping the misbehavior. From a behavioral perspective, the reprimand is assumed to be aversive to the child because it decreased the likelihood of the behavior.

Teachers' most frequent attempts at presentation punishment involve verbal reprimands or scoldings. Reprimands are expressions of disappointment (Harlan, 1996). They tend to more effective when they are administered in conjunction with clear nonverbal signals that the student is in trouble, and when they are administered in close physical proximity to the student (Alberto & Troutman, 1999). Scolding a student from across the room makes the interaction more public and can increase the likelihood that students will continue to misbehave because they don't want to lose face.

When using reprimands, be careful of the criticism trap (Harlan, 1996). When you reprimand a student, the misbehavior is likely to stop at least in the short run. Because of this immediate effect on students' behavior, your use of reprimands may be reinforced. As a result, you may find yourself using reprimands more frequently, and you may slip into a pattern of interacting negatively with students.

Finally, remember that teachers are only one possible source of presentation punishment in a classroom. Peers may also decrease the likelihood of certain behaviors by the aversives that they employ. If peers ridicule students for participating in class, those students may stop participating.

Removal Punishment.   Removal punishment describes a decrease in a behavior because the behavior is followed by the removal of a valued stimulus. For example, a teenager violates his curfew by coming in late, and the parents take away the use of the car. As a result of losing car privileges, the student stops coming in late. The loss of car privileges is working as a removal punishment for the behavior of coming in late. In schools, attempts at removal punishment usually involve taking away student privileges, such as free time, recess, or the right to participate in extracurricular activities.

How are presentation and removal punishment similar and different?

Focus on Learner Diversity

Student Perfectionism and Reinforcement

You may sometime in your career encounter students who hold themselves to higher standards than necessary in a situation, or who sometimes set standards that are beyond reason. For example, some students may become angry or anxious if they make one mistake on an assignment. These students are described in the literature on individual differences as perfectionists (Burns, 1980; Hollender, 1978).

Slade and Owens (1998) have proposed two subtypes of perfectionism. Positive perfectionists are motivated by the rewards that are possible through perfectionism while negative perfectionists want to avoid failure or looking imperfect. These types of perfectionism are examples of what Elliot and Covington (2001) refer to as approach and avoidance motivation, because positive perfectionists try to approach or reach positive incentives, while negative perfectionists try to avoid aversive consequences.

Negative perfectionists are of particular concern to teachers, because of the high levels of anxiety associated with this form of perfectionism. They may hold themselves to a very small margin of error. For example, they may define failure as an A minus grade on a paper. When you encounter these students, your understanding of behavioral learning theory concepts may be useful. You need to show these students that if they make mistakes, the consequences are not as terrible as they imagined, or they may not happen at all.

● **How are the concepts of positive reinforcement, negative reinforcement, and extinction relevant to this discussion? How would you help students learn that making mistakes during learning is not as bad as they may think? (For your authors' perspective on these questions, go to the text website for this chapter.)**

Guidelines for the Use of Punishment. Punishment needs to be used sparingly and cautiously because of the problems that have been associated with its use (Kazdin, 1994; Nuzzolo-Gomez et al., 2002; Papatheodorou, 2000; Sulzer-Azaroff & Mayer, 1991). Punishment can serve as a model of aggression for students, and students' negative feelings about punishment can generalize to the person administering the punishment. Additionally, the effects of punishment tend not to be maintained once the punishment is discontinued, and the effects fail to transfer to other environments in which the same behaviors occur. Finally, punishment typically teaches students what not to do, but fails to teach them what to do instead. To reduce the possibility of these issues, follow these guidelines when you decide to use punishment (Walker & Shea, 1995).

- Provide clear classroom guidelines and rules. Make sure students know what is expected of them. Clear guidelines help students know how to behave to avoid punishment.
- Be fair and consistent with your punishments. Don't establish a pattern of being more or less lenient with certain students.
- Administer punishments firmly, but in a calm and almost impersonal manner. Remember that your goal is to change a behavior, not to humiliate students.
- Try to use techniques that encourage or teach appropriate behavior in lieu of punishments. For example, if a student is inappropriately seeking attention, teach the student more acceptable ways to seek attention and reinforce her or him for using those alternatives (Fisher & Thompson, 2000).

Comparison of the Four Consequences. Figure 2.2 compares the four behavioral consequences on two key variables: the effect of the consequence on behavior and the nature of the consequence. As you can see from Figure 2.2, punishment and reinforcement differ in terms of their effect on behavior. Reinforcement increases the likelihood that a behavior will continue, while punishment decreases the likelihood that a behavior will continue. The two types of reinforcement and the two types of punishment are

What are the guidelines for using punishment?

How are reinforcements different from punishments?

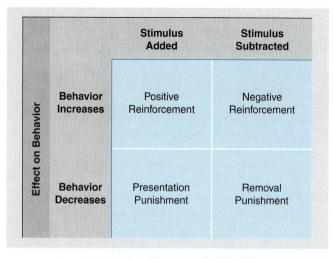

	Stimulus Added	Stimulus Subtracted
Behavior Increases	Positive Reinforcement	Negative Reinforcement
Behavior Decreases	Presentation Punishment	Removal Punishment

(Effect on Behavior)

FIGURE 2.2
Consequences of Behavior Summary Chart

different in terms of whether a stimulus is added or removed from the environment as a consequence.

Effect versus Intent. Before leaving the topics of reinforcement and punishment, one final point deserves emphasis. Often, teachers have been programmed to believe that stimuli such as praise and extra recess are reinforcers, and that stimuli such as reprimands and loss of recess are punishments. From a behavioral perspective, however, reinforcement and punishment are defined by their effect on behavior (Maag, 2001). Oddly enough, praise could function as a punishment, and a reprimand could be a positive reinforcer for some students.

For example, a teacher pulls a junior high student up in front of the class and publicly praises that student for her attentiveness and cooperation in class. Apparently, the teacher is intending to praise this student to increase the likelihood that the cooperation and attentiveness will continue. However, the effects of the praise are not as intended. The student stops being cooperative and stops paying attention. Even though the teacher's intent was to practice positive reinforcement, her praise was serving as a presentation punishment. The behavior became less likely because the student apparently perceived the praise as a punishing or painful stimulus. How could praise be painful? From a developmental perspective, many adolescents are concerned about peer perceptions, so the public praise could be embarrassing and, therefore, emotionally painful.

As a second example of this issue, consider a student in an elementary school classroom who makes noises and generally disrupts class. The teacher responds by reprimanding him in a stern voice. "I want this stopped. You are making it hard for others to learn, and I don't want to have to talk with you again." Instead of stopping the disruptions, however, the student continues to disrupt, and in fact becomes more of a disruption. In this case, the teacher's intent seems to be to provide a presentation punishment for the student. However, the effect of the reprimands seems to be operating as positive reinforcement. The disruptive behaviors are more likely to occur as a result of the reprimands being given. Why could a reprimand be a positive reinforcer? Assume that the student wants the teacher's attention. Being disruptive seems to be an effective way to get attention. That behavior, therefore, is positively reinforced by the teacher's reprimand or attention.

What is the distinction between effect and intent with consequences?

In conclusion, many of us who have taught have had the experience of accidentally reinforcing a student behavior we did not want or accidentally punishing a desired student behavior. People are different and they value or dislike different things. Understanding this point helps teachers interpret situations involving students who seem to value getting in trouble. It could be that getting in trouble is a form of attention or status for these students.

Additional Behavioral Concepts

The additional behavioral concepts of schedules of reinforcement, extinction, generalization and discrimination, and shaping and chaining are important for applying behavioral learning theory in the classroom. These ideas provide additional suggestions for teaching and classroom management.

Schedules of Reinforcement. A schedule of reinforcement is a determination of how often reinforcement will be available during operant conditioning (Ferster, 2002; Fer-

Social Influences and Behavioral Consequences

As we suggested in the discussion of effect versus intent, the same consequence may have different effects on different students. The successful use of reinforcement and punishment, therefore, depends on your understanding of your students' values. People in general possess a set of values and work for what they value (Sliwiak & Frissell, 2001). However, an individual student's values are affected by her or his experiences within her or his family and peer group, and these experiences influence the success of attempts to reinforce or punish that student.

Based on their cultural influences, students may have different criteria for success, find different forms of praise and recognition rewarding, and may differ in terms of when and how they accept criticism (Grossman, 1995). Understanding your students' cultural and family background may help you make better decisions about the use of reinforcement and punishment. For example, because of religious, family, or cultural background, some students might find teacher praise, especially public praise, embarrassing. In these cases, praise may need to be administered when you are alone with the students or through notes written to students on their papers.

The nature of peer influences in students' lives can also affect how they respond to teachers' attempts to reinforce or punish. Antiachievement attitudes can develop in students in response to peer pressure (Alderman, 1999; Brown, 1993). Peers may punish students for valuing school activities and give them reinforcement for antiachievement attitudes and behaviors. We have a number of personal labels that express this type of pressure (e.g., brown-nose, nerd, and school boy/girl). You may find that your attempts to encourage achievement attitudes and behaviors are being countered by peer-administered reinforcements for the opposite behaviors and attitudes. You may want to discuss this issue openly with students and/or find ways to encourage achievement that do not put students at risk for this negative peer pressure.

> ● How might you encourage achievement behaviors while insulating students from negative peer pressure? (For your authors' perspective on this question, go to the text website for this chapter.)

ster & Skinner, 1957; Morse & Dews, 2002; Skinner, 1938, 1953). If reinforcement is available for every occurrence of a behavior, then reinforcement is being administered on a **continuous schedule.** Continuous schedules are useful for establishing new behaviors, because new behaviors are more likely to be established quickly when they are reinforced every time they occur (Alberto & Troutman, 1999). Generally, if a new academic or classroom behavior is being established, it is helpful to provide students with frequent opportunities for reinforcement.

With an **intermittent schedule,** only some occurrences of a behavior are reinforced (Martin & Pear, 1996). The ratio and interval schedules are the two types of intermittent reinforcement schedules.

A ratio schedule is keyed to the number of responses that must occur for reinforcement to be earned. With a fixed ratio schedule, every nth response is reinforced. For example, a student may have to turn in five homework assignments before reinforcement is available, or a student may be reinforced every third time she participates appropriately in class. With a variable ratio schedule, the actual number of responses required for reinforcement will vary, but on average reinforcement is provided for the nth response. A student might be reinforced the first time he does something. The next reinforcement, however, may not occur until three responses have occurred, and then maybe only after six responses have occurred.

The focus with an interval schedule is on elapsed time. If the desired behavior occurs after a certain amount of time has elapsed, then the student is reinforced. With a fixed interval schedule, the required time interval is constant. For example, a teacher may observe a student at ten-minute intervals and if the student is behaving appropriately at that time, reinforcement is provided. With a variable interval schedule, the time interval varies. The student may be observed after one minute for the first interval, but the second interval might be two minutes.

How are an interval and a ratio schedule different?

The overall benefit of intermittent reinforcement is that behaviors become more permanent when they are reinforced intermittently (Alberto & Troutman, 1999). Also, when variable intermittent schedules are used, high rates of response or consistent rates of response are obtained. To see an example of this principle, go watch gamblers play slot machines in a casino.

In general, the information on schedules of reinforcement suggests that reinforcement be administered according to the following principle: reinforce frequently at first, and less frequently later on. This combination helps build a behavior quickly, while also helping make the behavior more resistant to extinction. This is how Marge Stuart arranges her second grade class to implement the basic idea of schedules of reinforcement when she is teaching a new skill.

> ➤ When I am teaching new reading skills, I like to work with small groups of children. That way, they get a lot of opportunities to respond and I can give feedback for each response. While I am doing this, the other students are practicing previously learned skills. My aide walks around and helps them as needed.

Here are some additional ideas to consider when deciding how to use schedules of reinforcement in your classroom.

- Be careful about accidentally placing misbehavior on an intermittent reinforcement schedule. Try to be consistent in your use of reinforcements and punishments. For example, if you laugh occasionally at misbehavior rather than ignoring it, you may be placing that behavior on an intermittent schedule. If so, that behavior will be more resistant to extinction.
- If a student works with more than one teacher, make sure to coordinate your efforts. You want to be sure that one teacher is not reinforcing or accepting behaviors others are not.

Extinction.   **Extinction** is an important concept for both classical and operant conditioning. Although there are some differences in how extinction is defined in classical and operant conditioning, both definitions seem to be connected by a single principle. That is, if the environmental support for learning is removed, the learned behavior tends to be eliminated.

In classical conditioning, the connection between the conditioned and unconditioned stimuli is supporting the learning. Consequently, if this bond is weakened, then the conditioned response can be extinguished. Extinction is accomplished, therefore, by presenting the conditioned stimulus without the unconditioned stimulus (Pavlov, 1927). For example, if the metronome or bell is sounded without the meat powder, eventually the dog should stop salivating to the sound of the metronome or bell. In the case of students who develop discomfort or anxiety about school, teachers would help them disassociate school from stimuli that elicit those feelings. This is how Gregory Pantera does this in high school biology.

> ➤ I find a lot of my high school students have developed some level of test anxiety. I try to reduce this by doing reviews, and by allowing students to be reassessed if they have trouble. I also use common, everyday examples from their lives on my tests. It's funny, but some of these students actually tell me they like my tests.

How are classical and operant extinction similar and different?

In operant conditioning, the environmental support for the behavior is the reinforcing stimulus. If that reinforcing stimulus is removed from the environment, then the behavior should be extinguished. If a teacher's attention to a behavior is the reinforcer for a behavior, then removing the teacher's attention should cause the behavior to be extinguished.

Extinction procedures have been used successfully for a variety of behaviors including swearing, tantrums, disruptive classroom behavior, obsessive-compulsive behavior, and off-task behavior (Carr & Newsom, 1985; Hall, Lund, & Jackson, 1968;

Salend & Meddaugh, 1985; Tolin, 2001; Zimmerman & Zimmerman, 1962). However, there are important considerations in the effective use of operant extinction in particular. First, the assumption is that the reinforcers can be identified and removed from the environment. Many times, behaviors have multiple reinforcers, and some of them may not be directly under the control of the teacher or even known to the teacher. This makes operant extinction difficult. For example, we have all heard teachers talk about how hard it is to extinguish a behavior if peers or parents reinforce that same behavior.

Second, with operant extinction, the behavior can actually increase in frequency or intensity before it extinguishes (Lerman & Iwata, 1996; Walker & Shea, 1995). This escalation is sometimes referred to as the **extinction burst**, and in the case of misbehavior, you will feel as if the student is testing your resolve. You need to be prepared for this escalation in the misbehavior, because if you intervene when the behavior is increasing in severity you may accidentally end up reinforcing a more severe behavior. Be aware that extinction takes time, and this approach requires patience.

Third, specific behaviors are extinguished, but the needs or motives that produce those behaviors often remain intact. If a student desires attention and you extinguish one attention-seeking behavior, that student will probably still try to seek attention some other way. You might, therefore, take the opportunity to teach the student how to get attention more appropriately, and you would reinforce the student's appropriate attention-seeking behavior. In general, extinction should be paired with the reinforcement of alternative behaviors (Catania, 2000, 2001).

Here are some additional suggestions for the use of extinction:

- Identify reinforcements for misbehaviors and try to eliminate them from the environment. Learn to ask yourself questions like, "Why is this student doing this?" or "What is the payoff for this behavior?"
- Become familiar with the types of classroom experiences that are likely to create discomfort or anxiety in the students. Try to reduce or eliminate the occurrence of those situations in your classroom. For example, with kindergartners, meet them at the door on the first day. Try to show them that you will help them get used to this new and strange experience.

Generalization and Discrimination. Generalization and discrimination occur both in classical and operant conditioning. In both types of conditioning they refer to learners' ability to determine when to produce a particular response and when not to produce that particular response. They, therefore, refer to how learners interpret different antecedent or eliciting stimuli.

Generalization occurs when students respond to similar stimuli with the same behavior (O'Donnell, Crosbie, Williams, & Saunders, 2000; Skinner, 1953). In the case of classical conditioning, this involves producing the conditioned response to stimuli that are similar to the conditioned stimulus, but that were not present in the original conditioning. In the Pavlovian experiment, dogs may salivate to a bell with a slightly different tone than the one used during the conditioning experiment. Generalization occurs if the stimulus is similar enough to the original conditioned stimulus to evoke the response.

In operant conditioning, generalization occurs when the learner understands that the consequences for responding to one antecedent stimulus are the same as the consequences for responding to another similar antecedent stimulus (Schwartz, 1989). For example, a child may find that he is praised for labeling an equilateral triangle as a triangle, and that he is also praised for labeling a right triangle as a triangle. Responding by correctly labeling three-sided objects as triangles earns the reinforcement and represents an example of generalization.

Discrimination occurs when learners identify two similar stimuli as being different, and they respond to them differently (Terrace, 1966). To carry the Pavlovian example further, the dog may not salivate to the sound of playing cards pinned to the spokes of a bicycle. The noise is distinct enough to be responded to differently by the dog.

Looking in on

Emilio
Lopez

2.2

One of our rules is that we do not accept inappropriate language or swearing in the classroom. I've found it a difficult rule to enforce, so when it was brought up during the meeting, I asked for suggestions. John Macmillan, the biology teacher, said he uses a point system in his class. Students can earn or lose points for certain behaviors. For example, students earn three points for returning homework, and they lose three earned points anytime they use inappropriate language. They need to have a certain number of points to go on the science field trips. Because students like those field trips, he says that the loss of points stops the swearing. Maggie Pearson, our most experienced teacher, says she thinks a lot of the swearing is for peer attention and to upset her. She tells her students on the first day that she is not impressed with bad language, and any student who laughs at bad language is in as much trou-

ble as the person using the language. When she and the other students don't respond to the swearing, it usually stops. Oddly enough, however, the students who are ignored usually have a streak of really bad language before they stop, almost as if they want to see if we are serious about ignoring the swearing.

● **How are the ideas of removal punishment, token reinforcement, extinction, and the extinction burst relevant to this discussion of the inappropriate language rule?**

Decision Point: Why else might students use bad language besides for attention? Why might this be an important question to ask before intervening with the inappropriate language?

In operant conditioning, discrimination occurs when the learner observes that reinforcement is associated with responding to one stimulus but not another. Using the earlier example, the child will be praised for calling a right triangle a triangle, but will not be praised for calling a square a triangle. Students' ability to discriminate between

How are generalization and discrimination different?

stimuli is an important component of many academic skills such as learning the verbal labels for different objects, knowing how to respond to different types of instructions, and concept learning such as distinguishing nouns and verbs (Green, 2001).

Generalization and discrimination form the basis for an important idea in operant conditioning called stimulus control. Stimulus control means that learners' behaviors are under the control of certain antecedents in their environment (Bower & Hilgard, 1981; Green, 2001; O'Donnell, Crosbie, Williams, & Saunders, 2000). Stimulus control develops because of learners' reinforcement history with antecedent stimuli. If a response that is given in the presence of a certain antecedent is reinforced, that response tends to be repeated when that antecedent or similar stimuli are present in

What is stimulus control?

later experiences (generalization). If a response fails to earn reinforcement when it is cued by an antecedent stimulus, then that response tends not to be given when that antecedent or similar stimuli occur in the future (discrimination). In the concept learning example given previously, students will call a three-sided shape a triangle, because they have been reinforced for this response to these types of antecedents in the past.

In your classroom, you are going to notice that some students respond better to your requests or directions than other students. How your students respond to your requests and directions depends on their learning history. If they have learned that cooperation gets consistently reinforced and that failure to cooperate earns punishment, then directions from adults are likely to have stimulus control over their behavior. They will tend to comply with those directions, especially if they see that their cooperation continues to be reinforced. For students who lack this type of stimulus control, it is important for you to develop stimulus control by reacting consistently to their cooperation or lack of cooperation. Here are some additional ideas to consider when deciding how to use stimulus control.

- Have discussions with your students about how they need to behave in different situations and give them reinforcement when they exhibit those behaviors in that situation. For example, talk to them about appropriate field trip behavior. Those who behave appropriately should be given reinforcement.
- Provide students with signals that help them determine the appropriate behavior for a situation. For example, use a zero-noise signal to let students know they are being too noisy in groups and give them reinforcement for lowering the noise level.
- Help students know how expectations may have changed. This is particularly important as students transition between elementary school and junior high, or junior high and high school.

Consider how classroom rules can be used to establish stimulus control.

Shaping and Chaining.   Shaping and chaining are ideas that are associated primarily with operant conditioning. Although there are differences between the shaping and chaining, they have evolved from the common underlying principle that learning complicated behaviors is a gradual and often step-by-step process.

Shaping.   **Shaping** is a process that involves reinforcing learners for making gradual progress toward a terminal behavioral goal (Becker, Engelmann, & Thomas,

Looking in on

Tom Pierce

2.1

Melissa was somewhat disappointed that Cynthia was still trying to avoid recess because she had worked with her all last year on this. According to Melissa, Cynthia is extremely shy and finds the somewhat noisy and less orderly world of the playground threatening. Last year Cynthia learned that if she said she was ill and requested to go to the nurse, she could miss many recesses. She started asking to go to the nurse almost every day. When I asked Melissa what I could do to help Cynthia, she suggested that we help her make some new friends so she had someone to play with at recess. Her one good friend from last year moved away during the summer. I thought I could do that by letting her work with a couple of girls she seems to like.

During the same meeting, Melissa told me that Paul's father was very abusive with him in the past, but he is no longer in the home. He hit Paul and his mother and yelled at them a lot, which is why noisy environments bother him.

Paul's mother also told Melissa that Paul gets frightened around other men, especially those who share a physical trait or mannerism with his father. Paul's mother actually requested a female teacher for Paul this year. Melissa suggested to the mother that Paul needed to learn that not all men are abusive. Melissa asked me to make a special effort to be positive with Paul, and we talked about ideas such as occasionally having lunch with Paul or going out and playing with him at recess.

● How were Cynthia's requests to go to the nurse negatively reinforced last year? How is Paul's behavior toward Tom Pierce and Melissa's recommendations to Tom related to the ideas of generalization and discrimination?

Decision Point: What ideas do you have for helping Cynthia become more comfortable with recess and for helping Tom Pierce form a personal and positive relationship with Paul?

1975; Savage, 2001). Classroom teachers typically use shaping as part of a goal-setting procedure for students. Goals are set for students, and as they achieve a goal, a higher goal is set. Consequently, shaping helps teachers focus on gradual improvement in students' behavior. A shaping procedure occurs in five steps (Zirpoli & Malloy, 1997).

How is shaping related to goal setting?

1. Identify the desired target behavior or terminal goal.
2. Identify subgoals for the terminal goal that help students move toward the terminal goal. These subgoals are **successive approximations.**
3. Identify what the student can already do in terms of the identified successive approximations.
4. Help students progress through the successive approximations by giving them reinforcement for each step they take.
5. Continue the process until the terminal goal is reached.

In this use of shaping, what assumptions are being made about the students' ability to do the homework?

Consider this use of shaping with a student who is only bringing in one math homework a week. The teacher wants the student to bring in homework every day (terminal goal). This teacher would use shaping by reinforcing the student for improving on the entry behavior. Maybe next week, the student is given reinforcement for bringing in two assignments. Once this is established, the student is given reinforcement for three assignments.

Chaining. A behavioral chain is a series of stimuli and responses that are connected in sequence (Gagné, 1985). In a typical chain, one stimulus cues a response that is reinforced. The reinforcement then serves to cue the next response in the chain, and so on. The stimuli and responses are linked together like a chain. The notion of behavioral chains has implications for both instruction and management.

How would a teacher use chaining to teach someone to read?

Chaining as an instructional design idea typically involves identifying the discrete simple behaviors that make up complicated behaviors and teaching those simpler behavior one at a time and in an appropriate sequence (Alberto & Troutman, 1999; Mayfield & Chase, 2002). For example, if a teacher wanted to teach students how to balance a chemical equation, the steps in balancing the equation would be identified, and the students would be taught to do each step correctly in sequence. The results of performing each step would now be the antecedent for the next step.

Chaining also has relevance as a classroom management idea. You may find it useful to think about misbehavior as a sequence of events that are chained together.

Shaping is the reinforcement of improvement.

For example, when one of your students leaves his chair, he usually gets in a fight with another student. When you intervene with the fight, this often leads to extreme belligerence on the part of this particular student. The fighting and out-of-seat behaviors are linked together. This understanding could be useful, because if you can intervene successfully with the out-of-seat behavior, then the number of fighting incidences could also be reduced. You also might find that you are better equipped to manage the out-of-seat behavior than the fighting and belligerence that follows. Looking for behavioral chains allows you to make choices about when to intervene with a behavior.

Here are some additional ideas to consider as you decide how to use chaining and shaping in your classroom:

- Help students set improvement goals. When they achieve a goal, increase the challenge level.
- When teaching a complicated skill with multiple steps, introduce each step separately at first. Also, make sure students have any necessary prerequisite skills for what they are about to learn.
- Be aware of curricula guides or scope and sequences that tell you what knowledge or skills your students need to be developing at this point in their education.

Our meeting on the state standards was very interesting. Joan Grayson, a sixth grade teacher, showed us a number of the sixth grade standards that were written in global and general terms such as, "Students will improve their ability to think critically with math." Although the sixth grade teachers value this goal, they all had somewhat different ideas about what it meant. That would be all right if the students didn't have to do well on a state exam that covers the standards. We decided to ask the state department of education for more specific guidance about what our students are expected to know.

After we discussed the vagueness of the standards, we also discussed how overwhelming they are in terms of a number of things that need to be taught. Maria Valencia, a third grade teacher, suggested that we prioritize them because some standards are critical for later learning. I agreed with Maria because I wanted to be sure that students learned what they needed to be successful later. Maria also suggested we have a similar discussion with the middle school faculty.

● **How does the request of the state department at least in part reflect a behavioral view of learning? How is the behavioral idea of chaining related to Maria's suggestion?**

Decision Point: Why does Maria think it's important to have this type of discussion with the middle school also?

- Look for behavioral chains in the classroom. For example, with some volatile students there are situations that predictably set them off. Try to reduce these types of situations.

Behavioral Learning Theory: The Ongoing Debate

Almost from its first applications in schools, behavioral learning theory has produced controversy. Even today, the use of behavioral techniques in classrooms continues to be debated. This debate tends to focus around both the issues with the use of reinforcement systems in classrooms, and the issues with behavioral approaches to instruction.

The Debate over the Use of Reinforcement Systems in Classrooms

Alfie Kohn (1993a, 1993b, 1995) has become one of the more outspoken critics of the use of behavioral techniques such as reinforcement in classrooms, and his criticisms include the following:

- Reward systems in classrooms are a technique for controlling students. These systems do not allow students to develop self-control and problem solving skills.
- Reward systems are ineffective. Once the rewards stop, students revert to the earlier misbehaviors. They do not lead to permanent changes in behavior.
- Reward systems may decrease students' intrinsic motivation for academic tasks. This contention is based on studies that suggest that when students are reinforced for activities they already find enjoyable, their interest in those activities can decrease. (Lepper, 1983; Lepper & Greene, 1978).

The responses to these criticisms go all the way back to J. B. Watson and B. F. Skinner, who suggested that environmental control is a natural part of the world (see, for example, Skinner, 1953). The issue is not whether environments exert control, but how that control might be used to help individuals. Also, as we discuss in Chapter 4, learners can be taught to use behavioral techniques to self-regulate their behavior.

Second, behaviorists would challenge the idea that reinforcement systems are ineffective, because this challenge fails to consider their functional definition for reinforcement (Maag, 1999). As discussed earlier in the chapter, reinforcement is defined in terms of its effect. If you went to a behavioral psychologist and said that you had tried reinforcement and it didn't work, she would most likely respond by saying, "I don't know what you did, but it wasn't reinforcement. Reinforcement by definition increases the likelihood of the behavior." From a behavioral perspective, it would be more accurate to say that your attempt at reinforcement failed. Although this may seem like a matter of semantics, behaviorists would be quick to point out that poor applications of any idea are likely not to be effective. Well-designed behavioral interventions have generally been to found to be effective interventions, especially for students with disabilities (Lloyd, Forness, & Kavale, 1998; Maag, 2001). Given the inclusion movement in this country, this is a significant finding.

The criticism that the effects of reinforcement systems do not remain once the reinforcement program has terminated is one that has been generally supported by research on behavioral interventions, specifically when these programs are used to modify problematic behaviors (Kazdin, 1977). Behaviors can be and often are extinguished once reinforcement is withdrawn (Alberto & Troutman, 1999). Additionally, the effects do not seem to easily transfer beyond the original settings where the programs were implemented (Kazdin, 1982). However, transfer of learning has been a major problem for many different approaches to instruction, not just behavioral approaches (Detterman, 1990).

The concern that reinforcement systems may damage intrinsic motivation continues to be debated today (Cameron, 2001; Cameron & Pierce, 1994; Deci, Koestner, & Ryan, 2001a, 2001b; Kohn, 1995). The damage to intrinsic motivation is more likely to occur when reinforcement is offered for compliance or task completion than when the rewards are more symbolic of students' efforts and achievements (Cameron & Pierce, 1994; Chance, 1993). It is usually better to reward students for improving their math skills than just for completing a task such as a worksheet. Also, the potential adverse effect on intrinsic motivation tends to be more likely when tangibles are used than when social and natural reinforcers are used appropriately (Deci, Koestner, & Ryan, 2001a).

How would you summarize both sides of the debate on the use of reinforcement in the classroom?

The Debate over Behavioral Instructional Techniques

Generally, behavioral instructional methods have been criticized for taking a part-to-whole approach and for focusing on teacher-directed approaches to instruction. Critics have suggested that that application of behavioral learning theory leads to drill and practice of isolated skills and limited opportunities for students to collaborate, explore, and discover knowledge (Kohn, 1993a). For example, young readers would spend considerable time practicing phonics with worksheets rather than practicing these skills in context and with other readers.

Although a complete focus on isolated skill learning may be problematic, it is also important to note that some practice of isolated skills is often useful for learners (Harris & Graham, 1996). True discovery may require lots of practice with the skills and information necessary for those discoveries (Skinner, 1984). Also, complicated behaviors such as problem solving can be taught through behavioral ideas such as cumulative practice and stimulus control (Mayfield & Chase, 2002). Consistent with a theme of this text, we take the perspective that behavioral approaches are useful for some

How would you summarize both sides of the debate on behavioral approaches to teaching?

teaching needs and not for others. Later chapters discuss how you might use behavioral approaches in your classroom.

Behavioral Learning Principles

One of the themes of this book is that appropriate application of psychological theory improves the quality of teachers' decisions. Behavioral learning theory provides a number of useful concepts for your classroom decision making. To help you apply these concepts, we have summarized them in terms of three major learning principles. In later chapters, these principles are used discuss the decisions involved in planning lessons and determining how to teach and manage classroom behavior.

Principle 2.1: Learning Is Measurable and Observable

To a behaviorist, learning is a relatively permanent change in behavior due to the effects of stimuli on that behavior. A change in behavior can be measured or observed, and stimuli that create that change can also be measured or observed. This principle has two major implications for classroom decision making.

The critical first step in planning a lesson or a classroom management strategy is to define clearly what you want your students to be able to do. This implies that teachers need clear, measurable objectives to guide their decisions. For example, if you want a student to improve how she participates in class, then you should identify observable behaviors that reflect that improvement. Maybe she will interrupt other students less or make more encouraging or positive comments to other students.

The behavioral principle that learning can be observed and measured is also clearly related to your decisions about the effectiveness of your actions. From the behavioral perspective, making decisions about the effectiveness of your actions requires a comparison between current student behavior and identified target behavior. This implies that teachers need to identify observations or measures that allow them to judge whether or not students are achieving their objectives. In the class participation example, you might count how many times this student interrupts before and after you have taken actions to help her participate more effectively.

Principle 2.2: Learning Complicated Behaviors Is Gradual and Step by Step

This second behavioral principle evolves from the belief that learning complex behaviors is a gradual process and understanding of the concepts of shaping and chaining. One implication of this principle is that teachers need to plan organized sequences of instructional activities that guide this gradual learning process. For example, students would learn certain math skills such as addition and multiplication before students learn long division.

Principle 2.2 also has an important implication for how you interact with the students in your classroom. Don't expect students to master complex behaviors all at once. Use shaping to reinforce gradual improvement in academic and classroom behaviors. A teacher might give reinforcement to students for gradually improving their performance on a math test.

Finally, Principle 2.2 implies an ongoing approach to assessment. Because learning is a gradual process, it is necessary and useful to track students' progress at each step. This approach allows you to evaluate the effectiveness of your instruction or management strategies and make changes when necessary. While presenting a skill, for example, you may ask students questions about their understanding. If some students are confused, you can correct that confusion immediately.

Principle 2.3: Learning Results from the Effects of Stimuli on Responses

Your understanding of classical conditioning, contiguity learning, and operant conditioning forms the basis for the application of this principle. This principle implies that teaching and classroom management involve the carefully planned use of stimuli to produce learning. This plan should be based on an understanding of how eliciting stimuli, antecedents, and consequences influence behavior. A skill lesson that provides modeling or demonstration as antecedents along with many opportunities for practice with feedback can be an effective use of antecedents and consequences.

Principles into Practice:
Illustrating Key Concepts

The experiences of Tom Pierce and Emilio Lopez provide examples of how the three behavioral principles apply to classroom teaching. We asked you to reflect on these applications as you looked in on Tom Pierce and Emilio Lopez. Here are our views about those opportunities to look in on these two teachers.

Looking back on

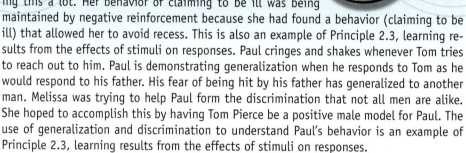

Tom Pierce is especially concerned about Cynthia and Paul, and asked Melissa, the school counselor, for help with these two students. Last year Cynthia learned that if she said she was ill, she could avoid recess. She started doing this a lot. Her behavior of claiming to be ill was being maintained by negative reinforcement because she had found a behavior (claiming to be ill) that allowed her to avoid recess. This is also an example of Principle 2.3, learning results from the effects of stimuli on responses. Paul cringes and shakes whenever Tom tries to reach out to him. Paul is demonstrating generalization when he responds to Tom as he would respond to his father. His fear of being hit by his father has generalized to another man. Melissa was trying to help Paul form the discrimination that not all men are alike. She hoped to accomplish this by having Tom Pierce be a positive male model for Paul. The use of generalization and discrimination to understand Paul's behavior is an example of Principle 2.3, learning results from the effects of stimuli on responses.

Tom Pierce also described some key events in the faculty meeting to discuss state standards. Joan Grayson initiated a conversation about how the standards were open to multiple interpretations. The teachers in this meeting wanted the state department to be more specific about what they intended. Their desire to have specific learning behaviors identified seems consistent with Principle 2.1, learning is measurable and observable. If the state is going to assess students' performance on these standards in specific ways, then the teachers wanted to know what they needed to teach. The teachers in his school also wanted to make sure that the appropriate standards were being covered at each grade level. The idea of chaining is relevant here because the teachers are trying to identify a logical sequence so that first things are taught first. Because of this desire to logically sequence the standards, the teachers are also providing an example of Principle 2.2, learning complicated behaviors is gradual and step by step. ●

Looking back on Emilio Lopez

As was the case with Tom Pierce, Emilio Lopez has concerns about two of his students, and he decided to consult with Barbara about them. Sarah seems to have acquired her math anxiety through classical conditioning. In elementary school, she was the last one done with timed math tests, and the other students made fun of her. Eventually, she associated math with being teased, and both stimuli now produce feelings of anxiety. Sarah's experience provides an example of Principle 2.3, learning results from the effects of stimuli on responses. Emilio was also trying to understand why Robert was not reacting as expected to his praise. Barbara had him think about Robert's likes and dislikes, which seems like a good way to start considering reinforcement potency. Also, Emilio might want to consider administering praise to Robert in private to reduce the chances of embarrassing Robert. Together, these experiences provide examples of the application of the guidelines for using reinforcement and Principle 2.3, learning results from the effects of stimuli on responses.

Emilio also got some ideas at a staff meeting for how to implement the inappropriate language rule. This discussion provides a number of examples of Principle 2.3, learning results from the effects of stimuli on responses. First John Macmillan's point system is an example of the use of token reinforcers. The students can exchange the points for field trip privileges. He also incorporates removal punishment into his system by taking away points for misbehavior, which has had the effect of making these behaviors less likely to occur. Maggie Pearson has decided that the bad language is mainly an attempt to get attention. She has applied the idea of extinction by providing neither teacher nor peer attention for the behavior. She has also found it necessary to live through the extinction burst as the amount of bad language often increased before it extinguished. ●

Teachers as Decision Makers

During the opportunities to look in on Tom Pierce and Emilio Lopez, we also asked you to participate in their decision making. We want to share our views of these decision points, and we also want to discuss how the three learning principles developed in this chapter inform discussions of teacher decision making in later chapters.

Tom Pierce's Decision Points

When interpreting students' behavior, it's important to consider alternative explanations for that behavior and to be willing to change one's mind about hypotheses if it's appropriate. Paul's cringing and crying behavior seem to occur when Tom Pierce tries to touch him or when the classroom is noisy. A number of hypotheses could be formulated about these behaviors. Maybe he is highly sensitive to certain forms of environmental stimulation, or maybe he associates these types of environmental stimuli with something that caused him pain in the past. Perhaps he does not do well in new situations or with people he does not know well. Later we find out that he associates the experiences with some abuse at home, but all of these initial hypotheses and others could be reasonable. Tom has done an important thing by seeking background information from Melissa to help determine which if any of these hypotheses make sense. Cynthia apparently does not want to go outside for recess. Maybe she is shy or timid, or maybe someone is threatening her during recess. It also might be that she just prefers the company of adults or to be around Tom Pierce. Once again, these are only some of the possible hypotheses, and Melissa can help Tom sort through these possible explanations.

We also asked you to consider what Tom might do to help Cynthia feel more comfortable about recess, and what he might do to form a more personal and positive relationship with Paul. He might talk to Cynthia about what she likes to do when she plays and find ways to structure those types of experiences into recess. He may even find it helpful to go out with Cynthia and help her find ways to interact with others. The counselor may need to stay involved so that she can help Cynthia develop more comfort with typical social situations. Tom has already indicated that he needs to find time to interact with Paul in positive ways. Tom could take this extra time to learn about what Paul likes and enjoys, and he could find ways to incorporate these experiences into the classroom. Tom probably also should make sure that he emphasizes positive approaches when disciplining Paul. For example, he could focus on acknowledging Paul's contributions and appropriate behavior. Perhaps he could help Paul find other supportive relationships with adult men through sports or programs such as Big Brother. In general, he should show Paul that his relationship with a man could be positive and supportive.

Tom Pierce also finds himself in a situation many teachers are experiencing. He needs to help prepare students for a state-mandated test over academic standards. By communicating across buildings, teachers can work together to make sure students are prepared. They can make sure that needed prerequisite skills are covered early and that unnecessary redundancy in curricular coverage is eliminated.

Emilio Lopez's Decision Points

Sarah's math anxiety appears to be the result of having had bad experiences in the past with math. Emilio should be aware of Sarah's sensitivity to peer criticism, and he should not allow this type of behavior in his classroom. He should also help Sarah feel more comfortable about participating in class. Perhaps at first, he could engage her in class discussions with questions she can answer comfortably. If she gets an answer wrong, he could emphasize the strengths of her answers and show her that nothing bad will happen if she gives an incorrect answer.

In Robert's case, Emilio's praise may not be having the desired effect because he is administering the praise in public. Emilio might consider administering praise in private so that Robert does not have to worry about peer reactions. Written praise statements might be a good idea because Robert can determine who gets to see the praise.

We also asked you to consider some alternative explanations for why students use bad language besides doing it for attention. For some, it just may be a habit that needs to be brought to their attention. To others it may represent how they communicate in their peer groups, while for others it may be the way they express frustration. Determining the purpose for a behavior is important because it may help you select more effective interventions. If the inappropriate language is just a habit, maybe you can make students aware of the importance of language for seeking and keeping employment. This type of intervention, however, may not work if the language serves another purpose for the student.

Looking Ahead: Learning Principles and Decision Making

One of the themes of this book is that teachers' decision-making process is improved through the application of principles from psychological theory. In Chapter 1 we identified these three broad categories of teacher decisions that provide opportunities to apply psychological theories.

- Decisions made when planning a lesson
- Decisions made when teaching and managing in the classroom
- Decisions made when assessing the effectiveness of their actions

In Chapters 7 through 10, the principles developed in this chapter are used to discuss applications of behavioral learning theory to the decisions teachers make in instructional design, instructional delivery, classroom management, and assessment of learning. Table 2.2 allows you to look forward and see the implications of these principles for the types of decision making discussed in those later chapters.

TABLE 2.2   **Principles into Practice: Looking Forward**

Decision Area	Implications for Practice	Looking Ahead
Principle 2.1: Learning is measurable and observable		
Planning	Teachers need specific goals and objectives for their academic and behavioral interventions.	Chapters 7, 9, and 10
Assessing effectiveness	Teachers need to identify measures or observations that allow them to assess changes in students' behavior.	Chapters 9, 10
Principle 2.2: Learning complicated behaviors occurs gradually and step by step		
Planning	Complicated behaviors should be broken down into component steps, and instruction should be planned to teach these steps in sequence.	Chapter 9
Teaching and classroom management	Teachers should reinforce gradual improvements in students' behavior.	Chapters 7 and 10
Assessing effectiveness	Assessments should occur throughout the learning process and should monitor learners' progress toward the terminal learning goal.	Chapters 7, 10
Principle 2.3: Learning results from the effects of stimuli on responses		
Planning	Classroom environments need to be planned to provide the stimuli needed to produce the desired learning.	Chapters 7, 8, and 9
Teaching and classroom management	Effective teaching and classroom management involve providing appropriate antecedents and consequences for the desired learning.	Chapters 7, 8, 9, and 10

Name _____ Date _____

Chapter 2 Study Guide

Use this Study Guide to review and test your knowledge of key concepts introduced in this chapter and to search out further information on issues and topics raised in this chapter.

 **Key Terms**   

Review the following key words from the chapter and then connect to Research Navigator (www.researchnavigator.com) either directly or through this book's Companion Website to explore research on the topics as they relate to education today.

Activity reinforcer (p. 33)   Classical conditioning (p. 29)   Consequence (p. 27)
Antecedent (p. 27)   Conditioned response (p. 30)   Contiguity learning (p. 28)
Chaining (p. 44)   Conditioned stimulus (p. 30)   Continuous schedule (p. 39)

Chapter 2 Study Guide continued

Discrimination (p. 41)
Eliciting stimuli (p. 26)
Extinction (p. 40)
Extinction burst (p. 41)
Feedback (p. 33)
Generalization (p. 41)
Intermittent schedule (p. 39)
Law of effect (p. 32)
Natural reinforcers (p. 33)
Negative reinforcement (p. 34)

Operant conditioning (p. 31)
Positive reinforcement (p. 32)
Premack principle (p. 33)
Presentation punishment (p. 36)
Punishments (p. 32)
Reinforcement potency (p. 34)
Reinforcements (p. 32)
Removal punishment (p. 36)
Response (p. 26)
Satiation (p. 34)

Schedule of reinforcement (p. 38)
Shaping (p. 43)
Social reinforcers (p. 32)
Stimulus (p. 26)
Stimulus control (p. 42)
Successive approximations (p. 44)
Tangible reinforcer (p. 33)
Token (p. 33)
Unconditioned response (p. 30)
Unconditioned stimulus (p. 30)

Alternative Response Items

1. Which one of the following statements regarding the behaviorist view of learning is most accurate?
   a. Behaviorists explain learning in terms of internal mental processes such as thinking and memory.
   b. Behaviorists explain learning in terms of the effects of stimuli on responses.
   c. Behaviorists believe that learning can occur without a change in a person's behavior.
   d. Behaviorists put their emphasis on ideas such as self-esteem or self-concept.

2. The first part of the law of effect says that if a behavior is followed by a pleasant event, that behavior tends to be repeated. This is similar to the definition for what other concept?
   a. Positive reinforcement
   b. Negative reinforcement
   c. Presentation punishment
   d. Removal punishment

3. A reasonable description for the learning process in classical conditioning would be:
   a. Learning through the law of effect
   b. Learning through active mental involvement
   c. Learning vicariously
   d. Learning through stimulus association or connection

4. For which one of the following learning outcomes would contiguity learning be the most appropriate process?
   a. Learning the correct way to respond when a teacher calls roll
   b. Overcoming a fear of high places
   c. Improving students' creative problem-solving abilities
   d. Helping improve students' self-esteem

5. Billy has learned that if he sits in the back of the class and slumps down in his chair, he can avoid being called on in class. He does not like to partici-

pate, so he is now using the slumping behavior more and more regularly. From a behavioral perspective, we would say that his slumping behavior is being:
   a. Positively reinforced   c. Punished
   b. Negatively reinforced   d. Shaped

6. John has a reputation as a school bully, but he is also very artistic. One day, Mr. Olivera praises John's artwork in front of other students, and this humiliates him. From then on, John will not do art for Mr. Olivera. What consequence is changing his art behavior?
   a. Positive reinforcement
   b. Negative reinforcement
   c. Presentation punishment
   d. Removal punishment

7. Which of the following is an example of shaping?
   a. Billy is able to throw a football correctly the very first time he tries.
   b. Sam buys himself a more expensive car when he gets a raise at work.
   c. Sally tells herself that she must do her homework before she goes out to play.
   d. Mary is reinforced for improving her spelling scores each week.

8. Often when teachers plan their curricula, they take an area such as social studies and break it into small units. They then teach each unit in a logical sequence. This approach to instructional design is an example of:
   a. Chaining   c. Shaping
   b. Negative reinforcement   d. Contiguity learning

9. For which one of the following situations would it be most appropriate for a teacher to reinforce almost every occurrence of the behavior?
   a. Sally is just beginning to learn how to do a front somersault correctly.
   b. A teacher is reviewing addition facts with fourth graders.
   c. John has gotten to the point at which he is bringing in his homework every day.

10. Mary developed a fear of Mr. Olsson, her last year's teacher. Her new teacher is also a man, and when she first meets him, she also feels fear. Her fear reaction to the new teacher would be an example of:

    a. Discrimination
    b. Extinction
    c. The law of effect
    d. Generalization

Constructed Response Items

Short Answer/Completion Items

1. What type of reinforcer is implied in the statement, "The reward for doing a job well, is a job well done?"

2. The observation that students emit different behaviors for a fire alarm bell than for the end of the class period bell is an example of _____.

3. A student self-manages her studying by saying, "If I study fifteen more minutes, then I'll go out with my friends." What type of positive reinforcer is she using? What behavioral principle is she using?

4. A teacher is complaining about his seventh period class. "I yell and yell at them, and they keep getting worse and worse!" How would a behavioral psychologist explain this increase in students' misbehavior?

Essay Items

1. How are contiguity learning, classical conditioning, and operant conditioning similar and different?

2. How would you teach someone to divide fractions using the idea of chaining?

3. Using a concept or concepts from operant conditioning, explain why is it important for teachers to go over their classroom rules with their students and to make sure they are consistent in enforcing the rules?

Practicing Your Decision Making

Based on where you envision yourself teaching, how will behavioral ideas be useful to you as a classroom teacher?

INTASC in Action

Use the following activities to think about how behavioral learning theory concepts and principles relate to the INTASC standards.

Standard 2: Student Development. A theme of this text is that no single theory can account for the range of decisions that teachers must make. Using the experiences of Tom Pierce and Emilio Lopez that you periodically looked in on as you read, for what types of learning goals or outcomes would operant and classical conditioning be most applicable?

Standard 3: Diverse Learners. The idea of reinforcement potency implies that students differ in terms of what they find reinforcing. Focus on Learner Diversity boxes provide examples of how personal and social characteristics influence both how teachers provide reinforcement and what they provide as reinforcement.

What other personal or social characteristics of learners might influence your decisions about how to provide reinforcement?

Standard 5: Motivation and Management. How might operant conditioning concepts be used to promote positive social interaction? Active engagement in learning? Self-motivation?

Standard 7: Planning. Principle 2.3 states that learning complicated behaviors occurs gradually and step by step. Why would this principle be supportive of K–12 teachers planning math or reading curriculum together?

Standard 9: Reflective Practice and Professional Growth. The debate over the use of behavioral approaches in classrooms is only one of many controversies that exist in education today. With many of these debates, both sides have valid points. What can you do as a teacher to ensure that you consider different points of view carefully before making your decisions?

 **Web Resources**

To read more about theories of learning, visit the following site:

Theory into Practice Database
http://tip.psychology.org/

TIP is a database of brief summaries of fifty major theories of learning and instruction and is intended to make learning and instructional theory more accessible to educators.

Understanding Cognitive Learning Theory

Standards in This Chapter

Although learning the concepts and associated principles presented in this chapter will contribute to your mastery of all of the INTASC standards, the material presented in Chapter 3 is most strongly related to those standards listed below.

● **Standard 2:** Student Development

● **Standard 3:** Diverse Learners

● **Standard 4:** Multiple Instructional Strategies

● **Standard 9:** Reflective Practice and Professional Growth

In this chapter, cognitive learning theories and how cognitive learning principles may be applied to teaching decisions are discussed. We use the plural term *cognitive theories* because there is no single cognitive theory, but rather a family of theories that all explain learning by describing the nature of knowledge and the processes through which knowledge is acquired and used.

When you have finished this chapter, you will be able to use cognitive learning theory concepts to analyze and make decisions about various classroom situations. As in the previous chapter, the concepts presented in this chapter have been incorporated into a series of learning principles that will guide later discussions about instructional design and delivery.

● Principle 3.1: Meaningful learning occurs when new knowledge is connected to existing knowledge.

● Principle 3.2: Effective instruction encourages learners to coordinate their various basic mental processes.

● Principle 3.3: The limitations of students' working memory must be accounted for in instruction.

● Principle 3.4: Learning is an active, goal-directed process.

Close-ups on the Classroom

Sheila Gutierrez Selects a New Text

This is my third year teaching fifth grade, and I think I am finally getting the hang of it. I guess my building principal thinks so too, since she has asked me to be on the district's textbook committee. The committee is composed of teachers and administrators from several of the schools in our district, so I will have an opportunity to meet some of my colleagues from around the district and learn how what I'm doing fits in with the bigger picture. Our budget for next year allows for the purchase of new mathematics texts for all the elementary grades, so this year we are reviewing several mathematics series so that we can place the orders next July. Even though the committee meets late Friday afternoons, I am really looking forward to this assignment.

We need new textbooks, because the current books are very old and worn. The pictures and story problems are out of date, and the kids call them lame. Also, the old textbooks are difficult to use with some of our new technology. Last year we received a grant to purchase computers along with some software for our classrooms. I would like to find a mathematics series that provides more challenge to the kids and allows them to take advantage of our new software. Our first meeting is next Friday, and I am anxious to hear what my colleagues have to say and to see what other textbooks have to offer.

Decision Point: What sort of questions would you ask if you were buying a textbook series for an entire school district?

Before proceeding with Chapter 3, be sure you read the Close-ups on the Classroom features about Sheila Gutierrez and Charles Elliot. At various points in the chapter, you will revisit both teachers in their classrooms and follow their decision-making progress. Their classroom experiences are closely integrated with the key concepts of this chapter and serve as important models for understanding Cognitive Learning Theory.

The Cognitive View of Learning

The behavioral learning theories discussed in Chapter 2 are attempts to explain learning by focusing on observable environmental events in the form of stimuli and responses. In contrast, cognitive learning theories describe and explain learning in terms of internal mental events. As a result, the definition of learning, and the explanations for how learning occurs are different for cognitive theorists and behaviorists.

How does the cognitive view of learning differ from that of behavioral learning theory? What are the implication of these differences?

From a cognitive perspective, learning involves the transformation of information in the environment into knowledge that is stored in the mind. For our purposes, **information** is defined as patterns of energy present in the environment. Energy is any aspect of the environment that can produce a sensation and is primarily in the form of light, sound, and pressure. A **sensation** is just a signal from the senses to the brain that occurs whenever a particular kind of energy is present in the environment. **Knowledge** is created when the information contained in sensations is represented in a meaningful manner in the mind of the learner. From a cognitive perspective, learning occurs when new knowledge is acquired or existing knowledge is modified by experience. Cognitive learning theories explain how knowledge is acquired and/or modified.

Cognitive learning theory does not describe a single theory, but rather a family of theories with many branches. Information processing is one branch of cognitive learning theory that has proven to be useful for thinking about how learners acquire knowledge in classrooms. The information-processing branch itself has many different branches and the remaining sections of this chapter describe a hybrid version of information-processing theory that incorporates the major elements of various branches of information-processing theories.

The New York Times
expect the world®
nytimes.com

THEMES OF THE TIMES

Expand your knowledge of the concepts discussed in this chapter by reading current and historical articles from the New York Times by visiting the "Themes of the Times" section of the Companion Website.

Secondary

Charles Elliot's Chemistry Class

This is my tenth year teaching science at New Freedom High School; however, it is my first year teaching the eleventh grade chemistry class. My chemistry students are all hard-working motivated kids who see themselves as college bound; so I was surprised to find that they were having trouble following some of the lab safety procedures. I have also discovered that many of the students have difficulty adjusting the concentration of the solutions we use in our labs. The procedure is a relatively simple application of proportions, and I know they've had this in their mathematics classes.

In spite of a few minor problems, I expect these students to do well; however, I do have some concerns about one student, Ralph. When he was in my general science class, he did well in his lab group, but his scores on my unit tests were the lowest in the class. He didn't participate voluntarily in class discussions. When I called on him his anxiety was just too painful to watch, so I stopped asking him questions in class. I have known Ralph since he was in ninth grade and I know he is not normally shy, but when it comes to talking in class he just clams up. He barely passed general science, so I need to do a better job with him this time.

Decision Point: What hypotheses might you propose for the difficulties experienced by some of the students in Charles Elliot's chemistry class?

Information-Processing Theory

Information-processing theories of learning are a product of the relatively new field of study called *cognitive science*. Cognitive science is the systematic study of the mind and is concerned with answering questions about the nature of knowledge, how knowledge is acquired and modified, and how knowledge influences mental and physical performance. Information-processing theories of learning try to answer these questions by constructing models of how the mind works.

A model is a concrete representation of mental events that can be used to guide the understanding of those events. Historically, models of mental events have been developed using available technology as a metaphor. As an early example, Socrates likened the mind to the blocks of wax that were used at the time to write notes and send messages. Wax was melted and placed in a shallow frame. Letters were scratched into the wax and the sepia (ink) was wiped over the letters to give them distinction. In the Platonic Dialog, Theaetetus (translation by Robin Waterfield, 1987), Socrates discussed the mind using this metaphor and noted that a brittle mind would not carry an accurate representation of information, just as brittle wax would not allow a message to be imprinted. Also, like wax that is too soft, a soft mind would allow the information to fade too quickly.

Learning occurs when learners add to or modify existing knowledge.

Modern information-processing psychology uses the computer as a metaphor for human mental events. Computers take input from the environment, process it using programs stored in memory, and then create output based on the processing of the input. By analogy, the information-processing model describes how people input information into their central processor (brain), and how they process that information within various memory systems until appropriate output or responses can be generated.

In both the case of the computer and the human information processor, the knowledge stored in memory is going to greatly impact the types of processing that can occur. Information-processing theorists have understood this and have put considerable effort into describing the nature of knowledge and how it is acquired, stored, and used. The discussion of the information-processing theory begins by examining the nature of knowledge. This is followed by a look at the information-processing model as a tool for explaining how knowledge is acquired, stored, and used. The information processing model you will learn about has been referred to as a multi-store model of memory, because it proposes different memory stores, each with different characteristics (Atkinson & Shiffrin, 1968). The actual model presented in this chapter combines aspects of the original multi-store model of memory with key ideas from Anderson's (1993) adaptive control of thought or ACT model.

Knowledge as the Representation of Information

If cognitive theories are going to explain learning, then they need to be able to describe the nature of knowledge and how it is stored and represented in memory. This is a complex task because human memory is so complex; however, cognitive theorists have focused on three capabilities of human memory in developing their ideas about the nature of human knowledge:

- Knowledge can represent different types of information.
- Knowledge can represent information in different ways.
- Knowledge can represent isolated pieces of information or the perceived relationships among many pieces of information.

Cognitive psychologists use these three basic capabilities to explain the variety of ways humans learn, remember, and apply knowledge. In the rest of this section, these three capabilities serve as organizer for a discussion of knowledge.

Types of Information.   People are able to remember a great variety of things, specific events they've experienced, as well as facts and ideas that they've read or heard about. In addition, people are able to remember how to perform many tasks skillfully. Consider the kind of information that is implied by the following examples:

➤ Reminiscing with her friends, Alex says, "I can picture in my mind the dress I wore to my first dance."

➤ When the science teacher asks what the students know about the Periodic Table of Elements, Samuel answers, "The atomic number tells us the number of protons and electrons in an atom of an element."

➤ George is going fishing with some friends after school. He rides his bicycle to the store to meet his friends before they all go to the lake.

➤ Carol and her friends are painting their clubhouse. She uses the formula for the area of a rectangle to calculate how much paint they will need to buy.

The statements of Alex and Samuel exemplify our ability to store and remember important events and facts. Such memories are an important part of who we are and affect our ability to deal effectively with the world around us. Memories of facts and ideas we have encountered or experiences in our lives allow us to recognize, categorize, and reason about events, objects, and ideas. The actions of George and Carol are examples of our ability to remember how to do things, such as riding a bicycle or doing a mathematical calculation.

Types of Representations.   The human mind is capable of representing information in different ways, and the way information is represented determines its influence on behavior (Anderson, 1983). This means we may infer the nature of someone's knowledge by observing their behavior. Many people have made the observation that sometimes people are able to explain or describe an action, but are unable to do it themselves; and other times people are able to perform some act, but are unable to explain how they did it. This observation has led cognitive psychologists to propose two separate ways in which knowledge is represented in the mind. Knowledge that allows us to describe or recognize objects and events is called declarative knowledge, whereas knowledge that allows us to actually perform some physical or mental action is called procedural knowledge (Anderson, 1983; Ryle, 1949).

Declarative knowledge is the way our mind represents facts, ideas, and concepts. It gets its name because it is knowledge we can declare orally or in writing. Your authors hope that you gain some declarative knowledge from reading this text. Some examples of the things your new declarative knowledge should allow you to do might include:

- State how cognitive learning theorists define learning.
- List the learning principles of this chapter.
- Discuss the difference between cognitive and behavioral views of learning.

Declarative knowledge is important because it allows us to interpret our experiences by recognizing how they are similar to past experience. Also, declarative knowledge combined with our powers of deduction and inference allow us to understand the present and predict the future.

Procedural knowledge is *how to* knowledge that guides the performance of physical and mental skills. Procedural knowledge allows us to do things such as bake cookies, do a front somersault, or solve a long division problem. An important characteristic of a skill represented by procedural knowledge is its automaticity. **Automaticity** refers to the degree to which a skill can be performed without consciously thinking and deciding about each step of the performance. This occurs when a skill is well practiced. For example, if you are taking notes while you are reading, you really don't have to concentrate on the skills involved in letter formation or writing. Thankfully, those skills have reached a level of automaticity that allows them to be performed without your conscious attention. Some psychologists estimate that only 5 percent of our learned behaviors are consciously controlled; the other 95 percent function without conscious control (Bargh & Chartrand, 1999).

The distinction between declarative and procedural knowledge is important for teachers, because it roughly corresponds to the types of information that define an academic domain. For example, a science curriculum might include certain facts, such as the values of natural constants such as the speed of light, as well as concepts such as the conservation of energy and matter. These facts and concepts are examples of information that would be represented as declarative knowledge by the learner. There are also likely to be science skills included in the curriculum. Examples of these skills might include analytical techniques, techniques for the preparation of specimens, or the operation of special equipment. The skills would need to be represented in students' memories as procedural knowledge. Teachers, therefore, need to understand these different types of knowledge and how they are learned.

What kinds of declarative and procedural knowledge might you want your students to learn?

Representations of Declarative Knowledge in Memory. Whenever we think about what people know, it seems natural to think in terms of the amount of information or knowledge they possess. Thinking about knowledge this way implies that there is some basic unit of measure that may be used measure how much knowledge someone has. Information-processing theories propose that declarative knowledge may be thought of as being composed of basic cognitive units sometimes called chunks (Anderson, 1996; Miller, 1956). A **chunk** may be thought of as a packet of declarative knowledge representing some information people have learned. For example, we may have a chunk that contains our understanding that humans are mortal, and another chunk may contain our knowledge of the sequence of events at the beginning of World War II.

Looking in on

Sheila Gutierrez

3.1

Our first meeting was very interesting and educational. Besides myself, two teachers from the other elementary schools in the district, one teacher from the middle school, a teacher from the high school, and Mrs. Halstrom the curriculum coordinator were there.

The meeting didn't go as I expected; I had thought we would have a stack of textbooks that we could begin reviewing, but instead Mrs. Halstrom opened the meeting by asking each of us briefly to discuss our ideas and concerns for the district's mathematics curriculum. I was asked to go first and fortunately in the days before our meeting I had been thinking about some of the shortcomings of the old texts. I began by noting how out of date the texts were. I also expressed my concern about redundancy in the texts across the grade levels and my disappointment that the old texts don't provide much in the way of what I would call *real* problem-solving activities. Most of the exercises required

the kids to simply practice math facts or at most solve simple word problems. I stated that I thought that most of my students could handle more advanced work. Many of the other teachers expressed similar concerns with the old textbooks.

After each of us had a chance to voice our opinion, it was getting late. Mrs. Halstrom passed out a copy of the standards developed by the NCTM. She explained that she wanted us to become familiar with these standards before the next meeting.

● **What types of knowledge do you think children need to acquire to be able to use mathematics to solve real-world problems?**

Decision Point: Imagine you were asked to pick a textbook for your future students. What would your ideal textbook look like and how would you use it in your class?

Declarative knowledge can represent information in a variety of ways. As an analogy, think of the ways information is represented in this textbook. Some of the information is in the form of text; while other information is presented in a graphic form, such as diagrams, photographs, or charts; and sometimes the information is presented both textually and graphically. Human memory has a similar capability; we seem to be able to remember some things using a language-based code, such as a verbal description of some event or the definition for a term. Alternatively, we may store information and recall it in the form of a mental image, as when we recall the look on a friend's face when he was surprised on his birthday. Anderson (1983, 1993) proposes three different types of chunks, each storing a different type of information: (a) temporal strings, (b) images, and (c) proposition. Figure 3.1 provides an example of each type of chunk.

Why is some information in a text presented verbally while other information is presented in a graphic format?

A **temporal string** is a chunk that preserves our perception of the timing or order in which things occur (Anderson, 1983). In Figure 3.1 the notes on the scale might be represented in memory as a specific sequence of sounds and pauses that create a melody. In addition to the rhythm of a melody, temporal strings may represent the sequence of letters or sounds of a word, the words of a poem, or the sequence of items

FIGURE 3.1 Three Types of Chunks for Representing Declarative Knowledge

	Proposition	Image	String
Type of information preserved	Temporal (time) relationships among events, the order in which things occur	Spatial relationships among objects	Meaningful relationships among words, ideas, and concepts
Example			Square is checkered

appearing on a shopping list. Whenever order is an important characteristic of an experience, we are likely to store that the information as a temporal string. If information is stored as a temporal string, the information will be most easily recalled starting from the beginning. If we need to retrieve the information in an order different from the way it was stored, retrieval is likely to be difficult. For instance, when doing a crossword puzzle, retrieval of a word is easier if you have the beginning letters as a clue than if you have the same number of letters from the middle of the word.

An **image** is a chunk that represents information about the way objects are arranged in space (Anderson, 1983, 1993). Images are closely related to our visual perception, and we tend to store information as an image when we perceive that the important aspect of an experience is the spatial relationships. For instance, if you ask someone for directions to the nearest public telephone, you will often find that there is a considerable pause before they answer. If you ask them what they were doing during that pause they are likely to say they were trying to visualize the location of the phone. Information about where things are is frequently stored as images like a mental map that can be recalled when we need to find something. Sometimes a picture is worth a thousand words and an image can actually contain a great deal of information. To test this, try to write a complete description of the example of an image presented in Figure 3.1. As teachers, you will find it useful from time to time to have students create images to understand and remember complicated information.

A **proposition** is a language-based representation that stores information about the semantic relationship between at least two elements of a chunk (Anderson, 1983, 1993). While propositions are frequently described using words, it is important to remember that a proposition represents an idea, not a specific collection of words (Gagné, Yekovich, & Yekovich, 1993). This means that propositions store information about the meaning of experiences based on our interpretations of those experiences. This allows us to eliminate information that is not meaningful, resulting in a more compact memory unit. These more compact units may be more easily manipulated and combined as we think about and reason through our experiences. Propositions allow us to store information about things that may not be easily stored as a temporal string or image, and are often an interpretation of some experience. However, there is a disadvantage to storing information as a proposition, because if our interpretation is incorrect, the information stored is also incorrect.

Learners tend to code information from reading or listening as propositions (Kintsch, 1977), and propositions have been important in research on how students process text or a lecture. As a first step in such a study, the researcher frequently determines how many propositions are contained in the material to be learned. This is done using the type of shorthand shown in Figure 3.1 to represent each proposition in the material to be learned. In the example shown in Figure 3.1, the proposition is represented by the *dot* with arrows pointing to the elements and relationship contained in the proposition. In this example there are two elements, square and checkered. The relationship between square and checkered is expressed by the verb *is*. The proposition is, "The square is checkered." Propositions may be organized into a propositional network that shows how the ideas in a text are related. Figure 3.2 is an example of a propositional network for the sentence, "The quick red fox jumped over the lazy brown dog." As you can see, this simple sentence contains five propositional chunks of information. Analyzing text or speech in this way can give us an idea of how much information people can process in a short period of time.

What determines the most efficient type of representation for storing declarative knowledge?

Representations of Procedural Knowledge in Memory. Skills, mental as well as motor, are stored as procedural knowledge. The ability of musicians to play their instruments or athletes to perform in an event is possible because of information stored as procedural knowledge. Likewise, the expert mathematician's skillful performance of mathematical operations is possible because of his or her procedural knowledge. Many of the abilities that we rely on daily, such as the ability to drive a car, write a

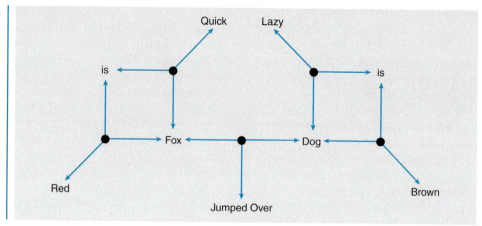

letter, or comprehend text, are only possible because large portions of those abilities are represented in long-term memory as procedural knowledge.

The basic unit of procedural knowledge is a **production** (Anderson, 1983), each composed of two parts: (a) a condition and (b) an action. The condition portion of the production stores information about the environment and mental conditions that trigger the action. The action portion of the production stores information that guides a mental or physical action that is triggered when a person recognizes the existence of the conditions. Consider the following example of a production.

Conditions

1. If my goal is to go to town, and
2. I am driving on Camp Townsend-Winona Road, and
3. I am approaching the intersection with State Route 89, and
4. The traffic light is green, and
5. There is no traffic in the intersection.

Actions

1. Then remove my foot from the accelerator to slow the car, and
2. Then turn left and enter the right-hand lane of Route 89 South, and
3. Apply pressure to the accelerator and resume speed.

Notice the condition specified the physical surroundings appropriate for the action, being the driver in a car, being at a particular intersection, the state of the light, and the actions of other drivers, as well as my mental state, having the goal of going to town. If all of the physical and mental conditions are met, the action automatically follows, otherwise some other action will be taken. The automaticity of the action means that I need not consciously control each step of the production.

Interconnections of Knowledge.   The third and maybe most important capability of human memory is the ability to interconnect and organize knowledge into larger integrated wholes. Information-processing theory proposes different mechanisms for integrating and organizing declarative and procedural knowledge. Declarative knowledge may be organized into schemata, or in ACT theory into declarative knowledge networks. In addition, ACT theory proposes that procedural knowledge may be organized into production systems.

Schema and Declarative Knowledge.   Schema and related ideas such as frames and scripts are concepts used by cognitive theorists as an explanation for how declarative knowledge is organized in memory (Minsky, 1975; Rumelhart & Ortony, 1977; Schank & Abelson, 1977). In our discussions, we use schema as a generic term to represent these related ideas. A **schema** (pl. schemata) is a memory structure that contains the organized and interconnected declarative knowledge people have in a particular domain or area. Schemata form as learners abstract the common elements of their multiple experiences with similar events, forming a representational category described by those common structural elements. For example, after multiple experiences with eating in restaurants, learners often form a schema for restaurant eating that captures the general nature of that event. Their schema contains ideas such as you need to be seated, you need to order, and you need to pay. Similarly, after multiple experiences with mathematical story problems, a schema or schemata may form for the types of problems that occur frequently. Additional characteristics of schema include the following:

- Schemata may be as small as a single idea or as large as several interconnected ideas (Marshall, 1995). For example, you may have a schema for your pet cat or for cats as a general category of animals that includes house cats, tigers, lions, leopards, and so on.
- One schema can become part of another schema, and schemata can interconnect (Schallert, 1982). As you learn more about teaching, your schema for lesson planning may include or be connected to your schema for classroom management or for assessing students' learning.
- As we have more and more experiences with the same event, our schema for that event becomes richer and more detailed (Schallert, 1982).
- Schemata are flexible. Because they store the general nature of an event, they can be applied to understanding varying examples of that event (Marshall, 1995). For example, if we form a schema for eating in a fast food restaurant, we understand what to do in any fast food restaurant.

Several variety of schemata have been proposed. Schemata that store information from our experiences with naturally occurring objects are called **natural categories** (Gagne, Yekovich, & Yekovich, 1993). Natural categories are often hierarchically organized with other schemata and store information about perceived regularities in our experiences with members of the category (Rosch, Mervis, Gray, Johnson, & Boyes-Braem, 1976). Our schemata (concepts) for plants and animals are typically natural categories derived from our personal experiences. Teachers can help learners acquire natural categories for either concrete or abstract ideas by providing them with many examples from a category as part of a lesson. Consider how Margaret Howe helps her students develop a natural category for geometric shapes.

➤ I begin my unit on geometric shapes with the concept of polygons. First, I give them a definition, and then show them a variety of examples, such as squares, triangles, and pentagons. For each example we discuss how it fits the definition. I also provide the students with some nonexamples such as circles or ellipses and ask them to explain why they don't fit the definition.

Schema for events are called **scripts** (Schank & Abelson, 1977). As with natural categories, we form these scripts with repeated experiences with various categories of social interactions. Scripts influence our expectations and guide our actions in many situations. For instance, students may have one script that guides their actions on the playground, another that represents their experience at lunch, a script that is activated for regular class, and another script that guides behavior when they have a substitute teacher. How might an understanding of scripts explain Judy Forester's experience in her art class?

➤ For most of my students this is their first real art class, and they really don't know what to expect. To help them adjust, I take the first few class periods doing simple art exercises, so they can get used to the materials and routines of the class, before they begin work on any complicated projects.

A third important type of schema is the text schema. **Text schemata** store information about the different types of organizing structures that appear in text (Ceck &

Meyer, 1988; Kitao & Cross, 1990; Richgels, McGee, Lomax, & Sheard, 1987). The knowledge of the structure of texts improves our ability to comprehend and recall what we have read (Bartlett, 1967; Meyer, 1975). Text schemata may be organized into two broad categories, narrative (or stories) and expository text (McNeil, 1987). Children seem to be more naturally adept at comprehending stories, possibly because stories are such a natural way for people to communicate. However, many school texts fall into the expository text schema category, and to improve students' comprehension of these texts some explicit instruction about the text organization may be needed. Helen Kruger applies this idea in her geography class.

➤ Many of my seventh graders are actually very good readers but they still have trouble with our geography textbook. I take some time at the beginning of the year to teach them how to use the textbook's headings and subheadings to create an outline of the information in the text. It seems to help the students remember and understand what they have read.

What are the three categories of schemata, and how do they affect learners' ability to learn?

Schemata influence several key learning processes. They allow us to recognize when something is or is not an example of an object or event and allow us to make inferences when we are supplied with incomplete information. They also can affect where we focus attention and how we store information in memory (Anderson & Pearson, 1984; Marshall, 1995; Schallert, 1982). Consider a how a young reader might use her schemata as she reads a Sherlock Holmes novel:

➤ Helen finds an old book on her parents' bookshelf. The title is *The Treasury of Sherlock Holmes* by Sir Arthur Conan Doyle. She recognizes that the name of the author and Sherlock Holmes are associated with mystery novels. Because she has a schema for how mystery novels are organized, she begins looking for specific types of information as she begins reading the first story: descriptions of the characters, the mystery they face, as well as information that may turn out to be important clues. A passage early in the story has Holmes and Watson taking a Hansom to the scene of a crime. While she was unfamiliar with the term *Hansom*, she infers from the context of the sentence that it is some type of transportation. She knows from watching Sherlock Holmes on television that he frequently travels in horse-drawn cabs and conjures an image of such a cab clattering down foggy cobblestone streets.

Helen's recognition of the names of the main character and the author cause her to activate her schema for mystery stories. Her schema causes her to focus on specific details of the story that experience has told her will be important to understanding the plot and solving the mystery, and her schema for Sherlock Holmes' world (nineteenth-century London) allows her to decipher new words and to enrich her understanding and experience of the story.

What type of schemata does Helen activate as she reads the Sherlock Holmes mystery?

Schema abstraction is a natural process and has been observed in children as young as three years of age (Loewenstein & Gentner, 2001). However, the process needs to be supported by teacher actions. When presenting new concepts or activities you can help your students develop accurate schemata by pointing out similarities and differences or by explaining relationships among the elements of experienced objects and events.

Declarative Knowledge Networks. ACT theory proposes that chunks of declarative knowledge are stored in memory as declarative knowledge networks (Anderson, 1983, 1993). A declarative knowledge network is a model of how information is stored in memory. Chunks of declarative knowledge are represented as nodes connected by associations to form a network of temporal strings, images, and propositions. Figure 3.3 is an example of how a part of a student's declarative knowl-

When children learn how books or stories are organized, their ability to read with comprehension is enhanced.

edge of a science topic might be modeled as a network. The chunks of declarative knowledge (propositions, images, and sequences) are connected by lines that represent associations among the chunks. Given this model of the knowledge stored in a person's memory, learning can be represented as adding a new chunk to the net, adding a new association between chunks of information, or changing the nature or strength of an association.

Interconnections among Procedural Knowledge. Units of procedural knowledge may be organized into complex sequences of actions called production systems. Production systems contain a series of productions that fire sequentially to complete

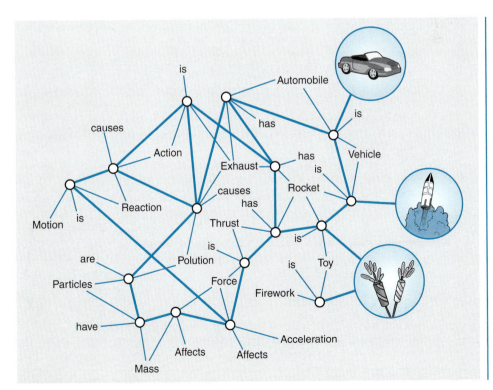

FIGURE 3.3 Network Model of Long-Term Declarative Memory

Focus on Learner Diversity

Diversity and Differences in Prior Knowledge

From the perspective of information processing, the influence of prior knowledge cannot be overestimated. Prior knowledge influences what we attend to, our perceptions, and the way we store and recall experiences. So it should not be surprising, from the perspective of information processing, that the individual difference most likely to influence learning is that among individual students' knowledge bases.

Students' knowledge bases may differ in both size (the amount of information) and content (the type of information stored). In general, the sizes of learners' knowledge bases are positively related to their ages (Kail & Bisanz, 1995). Older children have experienced more and therefore know more. Knowing more results in children's perceptions becoming more conceptually driven as they get older. As children come to know more, they are able to formulate goals that influence their ability to focus their attention and ignore distractions. As children become more knowledgeable, they are better able to use context to find the meaning in text, films, and conversations. Finally, as children experience more learning situations, they become more aware of learning strategies and more sophisticated in their application of learning strategies.

In addition to concepts and skills, a person's habits, values, and beliefs are also a reflection of their knowledge base (Rogoff & Chavajay, 1995; Rogoff & Morelli, 1989). The individual's knowledge base develops as a result of their interaction with their environment. Culture is an important aspect of that environment. The differences in individuals' knowledge bases, associated with their cultural experiences, have been associated with the perception and recall of events described in text (Bartlett, 1958, 1967; Tyler, 2001), and it seems likely that all cognitive processes are affected by such differences. This suggests that teachers need to be sensitive to how cultural differences might influence students' knowledge bases and how these differences are likely to affect students' perception and encoding of instructional content.

● How might your students' cultural backgrounds affect the way they process information in your class? (For your authors' perspective on this question, go to the text website for this chapter.)

a complicated action. The results of the first production in the series act as the condition for the next production. Consider the following example:

Condition 1 — If your goal is to enter your house, you are at the front door,
Action 1 — Then try to open the front door.
Condition 2 — If your goal is to enter your house, you are at the front door, and the door is locked,
Action 2 — Set the goal to find your keys and look for your keys.
Condition 3 — If your goal is to enter your house, you are at the front door, the door is locked, and you've found your keys,
Action 3 — Then unlock the door and enter the house.

What idea from behavioral learning is similar to the concept of the production system?

The activation of each production leads to a change in the perceived conditions, which then result in the activation of the next production. The activation of a production system results in a chain of discrete actions that run in a smooth and relatively automatic way until the main goal is achieved or a new goal is established.

A Comparison of Declarative and Procedural Knowledge. Both declarative and procedural knowledge are important for success in any endeavor. For example, teachers need both theory and applications to succeed in the classroom. Table 3.1 compares and contrasts declarative and procedural knowledge. As you can see, while the units of knowledge are different, both declarative and procedural knowledge may be organized into more complex cognitive structures. Each type of representation has its own advantages and disadvantages. Declarative knowledge is learned quickly and is flexible, allowing people to understand and adapt to new situations. Procedural knowledge allows people to respond efficiently and automatically to situations they repeatedly encounter. Procedural knowledge takes longer to acquire, but once learned is less likely to be forgotten.

	Types of Knowledge	
Characteristics	**Declarative Knowledge**	**Procedural Knowledge**
Basic unit	Chunks (propositions, images, and sequences)	Productions (condition/action pairs)
Integration	Schema/network	Production system
Application	Flexible: can be used in a variety of contexts	Use specific: used in limited contexts
Effects on behavior	Inefficient: Behavior requires conscious control; is slow and prone to errors	Efficient: Behavior is automatic (does not require conscious control); is fast and has few errors
Learning	Fast: New chunks can be acquired relatively quickly	Slow: Acquiring new productions often requires the effort of many trials
Forgetting	May be forgotten quickly	Relatively slow to forget

TABLE 3.1 Comparison of Declarative and Procedural Knowledge

An Information-Processing Model

The information-processing models are designed to explain how declarative and procedural knowledge are acquired and how knowledge influences subsequent learning and performance. These models describe human thinking and memory in terms of mental structures and basic cognitive processes. The structures are memory stores where information or knowledge is held. Each memory store is unique in terms of:

- The way information is stored
- The capacity, or amount of information that may be stored at one time
- The duration, or the amount of time the information is retained in the memory store

The basic cognitive processes are those mental activities used to manipulate information within a memory store and to move information from one memory store to another. It is important to note that information-processing models are tools to help us understand and predict how people learn and are not meant to describe the anatomy of the brain. Figure 3.4 provides a schematic overview of the information-processing model used in this chapter. Subsequent sections contain discussions of each structure and the relevant mental processes for that structure in sequence.

FIGURE 3.4 An Information-Processing Model

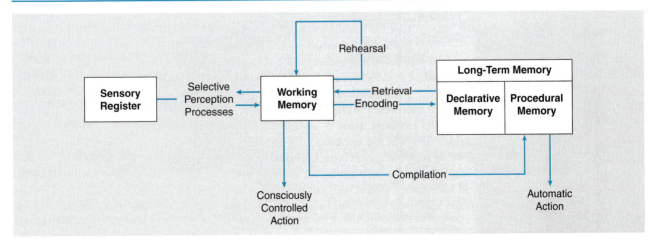

Sensory Register

Information first enters the information-processing model in the form of sensations from our various sense organs (i.e., eyes, ears, nose, and so forth). These sensations are transferred to the particular **sensory register** that is specialized for that type of sensory information (e.g., sensory register for vision or hearing). A sensory register is a large-capacity store where all sensations are held briefly. The duration of a sensory register varies by the nature of the stimulus, but the typical duration is from a fraction of a second to a few seconds, with many sensations never reaching a conscious level of awareness. In the brief time that these sensations are retained, only some are identified and marked for further processing. The cognitive processes that accomplish this initial screening of information are referred to as **selective perception processes** (Gagne, Yenkovich, & Yenkovich, 1993). Selective perception includes the processes of perception and attention.

Attention is the cognitive process of selecting information from the sensory register for further processing. Another way to say this is that we focus our attention on particular sensations but not on others. At times, this selection or focusing process is under voluntary control and at other times it is not. Attention that is under voluntary control is called *selective attention* (Howes, 1990). Learners intentionally select some information to attend to because that information is important for achieving their goals. Teachers can assist learners in this process by helping them identify the information that is important. Teachers might emphasize certain points in a presentation by writing them on the board or repeating them.

> **How might students' personal goals affect how they focus their attention?**

It is also the case that sometimes external events cause an automatic shift in attention. Changes in our surroundings, such as a loud noise or movement within our peripheral field of vision, often draw, at least momentarily, our attention. This automatic selection is referred to as an **orienting response,** and the stimulus that automatically draws our attention is called an **orienting stimulus** (Howes, 1990). Suppose that a general science class is engaged in a lab activity. One student accidentally drops a piece of glassware that makes a loud noise as it shatters. The attention of other students is diverted from the lab activity as they all search for the source of the noise. In this case the loud noise was an orienting stimulus and the students looking up was an orienting response.

Highly chaotic environments are likely to affect students' attention processes by providing a variety of orienting stimuli or distractions. In a later chapter your authors discuss the importance of maintaining a predictable classroom environment. This discussion provides a theoretical justification for providing that type of environment.

Perception is the process of identifying meaningful patterns of information in the sensations present in the sensory register. Perception is heavily influenced by the interaction of stimulus context with the prior knowledge of the person perceiving the stimulus. Stimulus context refers to the stimuli that surround or are associated with the stimulus being perceived. Compare how the symbol 13 looks when it appears in the sequence, 12, 13, 14. Compared with its appearance in the sequence A, 13, C. Typically, the identification of this symbol is heavily influenced by the surrounding stimuli (the other symbols) you identify as context. The middle symbol, 13, can be a 13 or the letter B. Use of context is important, therefore, because it helps you identify appropriate prior knowledge to use in perceiving the stimulus.

Selective perception is the critical first step in processing information. What is learned depends on what is attended to, processed, and stored in memory. A classroom experience that is similar to this perceptual activity is reading decoding. If you encounter the word *lead* in isolation on an index card, could you decode it? As presented, there are actually two potentially correct responses. The only way to determine the correct response is place the word in context. Try this instead, "The fishing weight was made of lead." By providing this context, you can select the correct decoding from memory. The general implication for teachers is to make sure that students have sufficient context to understand the information presented or the problem to be solved. If terms are going to be used in specialized ways that are unfamiliar to students, students need to know that these terms are used differently in this context.

Students' ability to recognize and apply context is dependent on their prior knowledge. Try this sentence: "The man standing in the bows, tossed the lead and shouted, 'By the deep six.' " In this situation, unless you know something about ships and sailing, you may not be able to interpret the pronunciation or meaning of the word *lead*. When the context activates relevant prior knowledge, learners perception is guided by **top-down processing**. When the context does not activate relevant prior knowledge from the learner's memory, perception occurs through **bottom-up processing**. Top-down processing is in general faster and more efficient than bottom-up processing. For this reason teachers should ensure that learners are reminded of relevant prior knowledge at the beginning of a lesson.

What is the difference between attention and perception?

Working Memory

The next memory store in the information-processing model is the working memory. **Working memory is a memory store where information is temporarily maintained while it is being used** (Baddeley, 1990). The information stored in working memory may come from the selective perception of the outside world or through the retrieval of information stored in long-term memory (Anderson, 1983). The working memory is extremely important because it is where all the various processes that may be considered *thinking* occur. For example, the comprehension processes you are using to read this sentence are operating in working memory. In general, information that has been selected from the sensory register for additional processing enters the working memory where it can be analyzed using existing knowledge from long-term memory. It is at this point that we consider information to be represented as knowledge, specifically declarative knowledge.

The characteristics of the working memory pose some interesting limitations on our abilities to think and problem solve. First, the duration of time that information can remain in working memory is variable. As long as the information is being consciously attended to, it remains active in working memory. However, if the information is not consciously attended to, it disappears quickly. Suppose you are trying to remember a phone number that you have just looked up. As you walk across the room to the phone, you are able to keep it active in working memory by saying it over and over. However, halfway to the phone, a friend engages you in conversation. You concentrate on what your friend is asking, and soon find the number is no longer available to you. Your attempt to listen to your friend caused you to divert attention from the numbers, and they are forgotten.

In addition to duration, working memory is also limited in terms of its capacity for information and thought processes. The amount of information that can be contained in working memory at one time is limited, and there are limitations on the number of complicated mental processes that can be consciously attended to at one time. The **working memory load** of a task refers to the amount of information that must be simultaneously maintained and processed to accomplish a task. Working memory can be overloaded by too much information at one time or by trying to perform complicated mental processes. Working memory overload can result in an error due to forgetting a critical piece of information or skipping an important step in the process.

By directing students' attention to the important aspects of a lesson, teachers can support students' learning.

CHAPTER 3 Understanding Cognitive Learning Theory **69**

Historically, working memory capacity for information has been demonstrated by giving people lists of numbers, letters, or pictures to recall in sequence (e.g., 6, 8, 7, 9, 1, 4, 5). With each trial, the length of the list increases. At some point, the person being tested can no longer remember the entire list. The typical finding is that the adult capacity of working memory is about 7 ± 2 chunks of information (Miller, 1956). As discussed previously, a chunk can be thought of as a packet or piece of information stored as declarative knowledge.

The limits of processing capacity become important as the complexity of the learning task increases. Increasing the amount of information in a visual presentation seems to overload working memory and adversely affects recall (Kemps, 2001). Complexity is also increased when learners are required to perform multiple complicated processes simultaneously. Our conscious attention to one or more of these processes adversely affects how well we can attend to the other processes. For example, beginning readers often have to expend considerable cognitive effort to decode the text on a page (i.e., translate the letters on the page into sounds or words). This emphasis on the decoding processes often has an impact on their ability to comprehend or get meaning from the text. Available working memory capacity is dedicated to decoding, and this adversely affects the comprehension processes needed to develop meaning (Laberge & Samuels, 1974).

How might the pace of instruction affect students' working memory load?

Enhancing the Efficiency of Working Memory. The processing limitation of working memory is a serious problem for learners. However, the processing efficiency of working memory can be enhanced. One way that learners can enhance working memory efficiency is to use memory strategies. Memory strategies are techniques that can be used to improve a cognitive performance. Two strategies that can be used to improve the efficiency of working memory are maintenance rehearsal and chunking. If information is not kept active in working memory, it is lost. Maintenance rehearsal is the process of repeating information over and over to keep it active in working memory. This is a common strategy for remembering some piece of information for a short period of time. For example, you may have had the experience of looking up a phone number and then walking to a different room to use a phone. In this situation many people repeat the number over and over until they are able to dial the number.

Chunking is a second memory strategy that can have the effect of enhancing working memory efficiency and involves grouping information into larger meaningful pieces of information. As you may recall from our discussion of working memory, the capacity of working memory is limited to approximately seven chunks of information. However, the actual amount of information in a chunk may vary. For example, to a learner reading a textbook, a prefix could be a chunk, an entire word could be a chunk, or a phrase could be a chunk. Teachers of beginning readers often make use of this idea by having these readers memorize sight words. These are words that can be recognized on sight and that do not have to be decoded sound by sound (e.g., *the, and, was*). Each sight word, therefore, is a chunk, and knowledge of sight words reduces the number of words that have to be sounded out by the reader. The net effect is to reduce the amount of working memory capacity needed for decoding. Consider how this idea is used by Ella Milos.

> ➤ I always have a prereading exercise in class before we begin reading a new story. I begin by providing the students with a list of three or four words and their definitions that I think are likely to be unfamiliar to the children. Then the children complete an exercise in which they use the words to complete a set of sentences. Finally, they write sentences of their own using each of the words on the list.

In addition to the use of memory strategies, another way learners deal with the limited processing capacity of working memory is to develop appropriate procedural knowledge representations. Procedural representation is appropriate for routine mental or physical skills that are likely to be used consistently in specific circumstances to accomplish specific goals. The automaticity that is characteristic of procedural

Learning Disabilities and Information Processing

The persistent academic difficulties of some adults and children are difficult to explain. These individuals score in the average range on measures of general intelligence, but do poorly on tests of reading and mathematics. Their difficulties are not related to a lack of opportunity, mental retardation, emotional disorders, or physical impairment. The individuals who display these characteristics are often diagnosed as having a learning disability (Swanson & Seigel, 2001). Information-processing theory provides a useful way to study learning disabilities, with research currently focused on resolving the differences between two competing explanations.

One perspective is that learning disabilities are caused by a general deficit in the working memory of learning disabled persons (Swanson & Seigel, 2001; Keeler & Swanson, 2001). This deficit, thought to be neurobiological in origin, degrades performance in situations that place heavy demands on the working memory, such as reading comprehension and the solving of mathematical problems. Other researchers support similar conclusions (Cornoldi, Carretti, & De Beni, 2001;

Daneman, 2001; Hambrick, Wilhelm, & Engle, 2001; Wolters, 2001). An alternative perspective is that the difficulties of individuals diagnosed with learning disabilities are actually related to differences in the information they have stored in long-term memory (Torgesen, 2001; Vellutino, 2001). Persons with learning disabilities lack the skills and knowledge necessary for effective encoding of information and so have difficulty retrieving information from long-term memory to working memory when it is needed.

While some may view the disagreement among researchers as weakness, in reality it is the strength of the scientific method. Eventually, the evidence will allow a resolution to the competition of ideas, with the best explanation winning. This might mean better diagnosis and treatment for those students with learning disabilities.

● **What are the implications of the previous discussion for helping students with learning disabilities be successful in your classroom? (For your authors' perspective on this question, go to the text website for this chapter.)**

knowledge allows these skills to be performed without consciously attending to the performance in working memory. For example, if certain subskills such as reading decoding become automatic, then they do not pose a processing load in working memory, and other reading skills can operate more efficiently. To achieve this level of automaticity, students need practice using the skills. If the skills are complicated, they may need a considerable amount of practice over a fairly lengthy time period. For example, building fluency with reading decoding requires that students are given numerous opportunities to read over their first few years as readers.

By being sensitive to the limitations of working memory, teachers can maximize learning by helping their students optimize their working memory. Teaching your students appropriate memory strategies and reminding them when to use the strategies will improve your students' ability to learn new information. Avoid overloading your students' working memory by managing the pace and complexity of information presented in your lessons. Finally, teach your students how to use make appropriate use of note taking, calculators, check lists, or other external memory aids.

What type of knowledge is affected by strategies that improve working memory performance?

Long-Term Memory

Long-term memory is the third and final memory structure, and it is where all the knowledge we have learned is stored (Baddeley, 1990). As shown in Figure 3.4, long-term memory is divided into declarative and procedural components (Anderson, 1983). The knowledge in declarative long-term memory represents the concepts and ideas, organized into schemata or knowledge networks. Procedural knowledge representing an individual's skills are represented in procedural long-term memory. The duration of information in long-term memory is long and is potentially available for retrieval for as long as we live. The capacity of the long-term memory seems to be virtually unlimited. In fact, it seems to be the case that the storage of knowledge in long-term memory actually increases the capacity to add new knowledge.

Encoding, Compilation, and Retrieval

Encoding and compilation processes allow us to modify the contents of long-term memory, and retrieval allows us to make use of the knowledge we have stored there. **Encoding** is the process of preparing information to be stored in declarative long-term memory. **Compilation** is the process that uses declarative knowledge in working memory and creates new procedural knowledge in procedural long-term memory. **Retrieval** is the process of activating or recalling knowledge from long-term memory. For declarative knowledge, retrieval makes the knowledge active in working memory. For procedural knowledge, retrieval results in the automatic performance of some action. Successful learning depends on encoding or compiling knowledge so that it can be retrieved when it is needed. As a teacher, therefore, you will want to create learning environments that help your students successfully encode, compile, and retrieve information.

General Guidelines.   Information-processing theory provides three general guidelines that are useful for thinking about maximizing your students' encoding and retrieval processes. These guidelines are:

- Active learning enhances encoding and compilation.
- Aligning learning activities with the conditions under which knowledge is to be used enhances retrieval processes.
- Providing repeated opportunities to review and practice newly acquired knowledge reduces the chances that it will be forgotten.

Active Learning.   Students are more likely to be successful at encoding, compilation, and retrieval if they are active in their own learning. An active learner is one who engages in thought processes that result in meaningful understanding of the material (Simons, 1993). Active learning, therefore, is seeking meaning from experience. Active learners pursue understanding rather than waiting for understanding to be given to them. It is important to note that the activity we are referring to is mental activity and not necessarily physical activity. Teachers are often advised to provide hands-on learning experiences. The cognitive view of active learning would suggest that teachers should strive instead to provide *minds-on* activities (Schamel & Ayres, 1992). Teachers can engage students in active learning by designing thought-provoking activities that encourage students to apply reasoning to their learning. Consider how the following teachers encourage their students to engage in minds-on learning:

> As a prelude to a science lesson on air pressure, an elementary schoolteacher demonstrates how an inverted test tube floats in a large jar of water. A rubber membrane is stretched over the mouth of the jar. When the teacher presses on the membrane, the test tube sinks.

> As a final activity to a unit on graphing, Mr. Collins challenges his prealgebra students to each write a word problem that can be solved using graphing techniques.

Providing the students with an unexpected situation, as exemplified by the floating and sinking test tube is likely to stir the students' curiosity. It is hoped they will then engage in the rest of the lesson with the goal of solving this mystery. In the second example the teacher challenges the students to set appropriate goals by giving them a novel and difficult task. Both cases illustrate the importance of the learners' intentions and motivation to active learning. Cognitive learning theories, such as information processing, recognize the importance of motivation in learning and provide ways to think about what types of motivation might result in the most effective learning. Your authors discuss the process of motivation more fully in Chapter 6.

Aligning Learning and Performance.   **Alignment** refers to the degree to which a learning situation is similar to a specific performance situation. Students are more likely to be successful if they align their encoding and compilation processes with the way they will be expected to retrieve and use the knowledge. In the late 1960s and early 1970s, Tulving and his associates first found that if the encoding task was similar to the retrieval task, students were more likely to remember what they had encoded (Tulving, 1974; Tulving & Osler, 1968). Tulving referred to this phenomenon as **encoding specificity.** The concept of encoding specificity highlights the importance of having students encode knowledge in a way that is similar to the way in which students will be asked to recall and use the knowledge. Similar findings have emerged from the study of transfer.

Transfer is applying what is learned to other related situations. Transfer is often more likely to occur if the learning and transfer situations are similar (Detterman, 1993). For instance, learners are more likely to recall and apply a problem-solving strategy to problems that are similar to those they have already solved. As new problems become less like previously solved problems, problem-solving performance is degraded. This is the idea behind the concept of **transfer-appropriate processing,** proposed by Morris, Bransford, and Franks (1977). The idea is that retrieval of information from long-term memory is to some degree a reconstruction process, and when the processes of a task are similar to the processes that occurred at the time of learning, retrieval is improved (Baguley & Payne, 2000).

For teachers this means that the best method of teaching students facts or skills depends on the way learners will be expected to use the information. As a teacher, you must think of how your students will need to use the knowledge they are learning and create encoding opportunities matched to those uses. Consider how teachers might be applying this concept in the following examples:

➤ Mr. Sanders, a geometry teacher, asks the shop teacher, the physics teacher, and the calculus teacher for examples of the kinds of problems students might encounter in their classes that would require the use of geometry knowledge. Mr. Sanders then uses the information to create problems for his students to solve.

➤ Ms. Kellogg, an elementary teacher, wants her students to be able to use their reading skills to help them solve problems. She designs reading activities around examples of operating instructions for interesting electronic devices, rules for games, and directions for simple science projects.

What basic cognitive processes must students perform to transfer what they've learned to a new situation?

In both of these cases the teachers have anticipated the context in which their course content might be useful to their students. They then used this knowledge to design learning activities that provided a context similar to the anticipated future uses.

A key concept that is related to both active learning and alignment is metacognition. **Metacognition** is the knowledge students have about learning and their ability to use that knowledge to self-regulate their learning (Duell, 1986; Schneider, 1998). As is implied by this definition, metacognition requires both declarative knowledge and procedural knowledge. Students' knowledge about the nature and limitations of their memory, the memory requirements of certain tasks, and strategies for learning and remembering information are stored as declarative knowledge. Students' ability to set goals and to automatically monitor progress relative to these goals is represented as procedural knowledge. Students who self-regulate their learning are taking an active role in guiding and controlling their own learning. Self-regulation involves setting appropriate goals, selecting effective learning approaches, and monitoring progress toward these goals. The goal of helping your students to become *life-long learners* means helping your students develop their metacognitive knowledge so they can be active in their own learning. Metacognition is discussed further in later chapters.

How does metacognition influence the way learners study for different types of tests, e.g., multiple choice versus essay?

Review and Practice. The third and final guideline is that when students are encouraged to review and practice what they have learned, the information tends to be remembered longer and better. This finding has emerged for both declarative and procedural knowledge. For example, in the case of procedural knowledge, there is a

Looking in on

Charles Elliot

3.1

Yesterday I went to visit the mathematics teacher, Steve Carlson, to discuss ways to help the chemistry students with some of the mathematics they encounter in my class. When I explained the problems the kids were having with adjusting the concentration of different solutions, he was surprised. He noted that these were really simple proportion problems, and the students should have been solving similar problems since sixth grade. Most of these students are in his precalculus class and although they hadn't worked any proportion problems in his class, he was sure they knew how to do them.

He suggested that maybe students were having difficulty because of the context surrounding the problems or by the way the problems were stated. We decided to walk down to the lab and take a look at some of the texts from my students' previous mathematics curriculum classes. We discovered that proportion problems were presented and reviewed in both algebra I and algebra II. Steve suggested that maybe if I reminded them that they had solved similar problems before, they would be able to solve these problems. I decided to plan a review of relevant math concepts and procedures during the next class meeting.

After we got back from the library, Steve asked how the year was going so far and what kind of things the kids were doing. As I described the class I realized how complicated it must seem to these students. They are trying to master chemical symbols and use unfamiliar lab equipment to perform complex experiments; it must seem overwhelming at times. It is really no wonder that they forget the safety procedures. I've decided to step back and schedule a couple of class periods to teach lab safety. I can organize the procedures into categories according to the situation and rationale behind each. I have also decided to place posters with the safety rules around the lab to remind them of the most relevant safety points before each lab.

● **How do the concepts of alignment and transfer-appropriate processing explain Mr. Elliot's students' difficulty in applying the math skills in his chemistry class?**

● **Do you think the techniques that Mr. Elliot has decided to use to improve lab safety will be helpful? Explain your answer using the concepts from information-processing theory.**

Decision Point: What techniques and strategies might you use in your class to help your students remember important concepts and procedures?

---

predictable relationship between the amount of practice a person has had with a skill and the proficiency or fluency with which they are able to perform the skill. Increased practice leads to increased fluency with the skill. This observation has been called the power law of practice, and it has been observed for a wide variety of skills (Haberlandt, 1997). **Distributed practice** or the **spacing effect** are two concepts related to the effectiveness of review and practice. Students are more likely to remember material if the opportunities to encode that material are distributed over time. Reviewing material that was studied previously improves the quantity and quality of what students remember (Dempster, 1991). The importance of review and practice implies that you should be incorporating such activities as a regular part of your lesson planning.

What does the concept of distributed practice imply about the effectiveness of cramming?

Encoding and Retrieval of Declarative Knowledge.   Declarative knowledge is more likely to be understood and remembered if it is meaningful to the learner. Information can be made more meaningful at encoding in two ways. First, the meaning of new information may be expanded by the process of elaboration. **Elaboration** is defined as the association of new information with knowledge already stored in long-term memory. Referring to the declarative knowledge network model of memory (see Figure 3.3), elaboration is adding new chunks of knowledge to the net by making connections between the new knowledge and knowledge already stored in memory. For instance, a student learning about the planets of the solar system learns that Venus is closer to the sun than the Earth. Then the student remembers that it feels warmer closer to an electric heater than farther away and thinks that it is probably hotter on Venus. Figure 3.5 provides a model of the propositions that result from the student's elaboration. Notice that by elaborating on the new information, the student is adding to the meaning of the presented information and actually increasing the information stored in his or her memory.

Second, new information may be made more meaningful by placing that information within a category or sequence of related ideas. This process is called **organization** and is similar to elaboration in that the process results in the creation of new connections or associations in long-term memory. For example, learners find it easier to remember a list of objects if the list is grouped into a finite number of categories. The information in each category is linked by shared attributes or relationships. To continue the previous example, the student might create a category for inner planets (i.e., those that are small and rocky, such as Mercury, Venus, Earth, and Mars). Figure 3.6 provides a model of the propositions that result from this student's organization.

The retrieval of declarative knowledge from long-term memory to working memory occurs through a process called the **spread of activation** (Anderson, 1983). Declarative knowledge that is active in working memory cues or activates associated units of declarative knowledge in long-term memory. As the activation spreads, new chunks of declarative knowledge become active in working memory and the activation spreads to a new set of chunks as the process continues. The process of retrieval is determined by the associations among the chunks of knowledge in long-term memory. An important implication of this explanation of retrieval is that the likelihood of recalling a specific chunk of declarative knowledge is related to the number of associations with other chunks. In other words, the more associations that lead to a chunk of declarative knowledge, the more likely it is to be recalled. Note that both elaboration and organization result in the creation of more associations in the

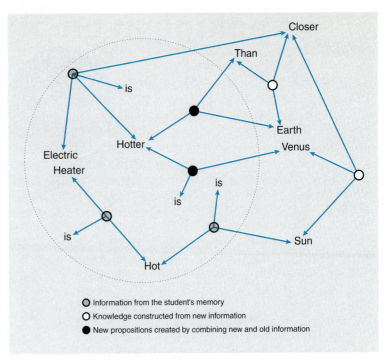

FIGURE 3.5 Elaboration: Connecting New Ideas with Ideas Already Stored in Memory

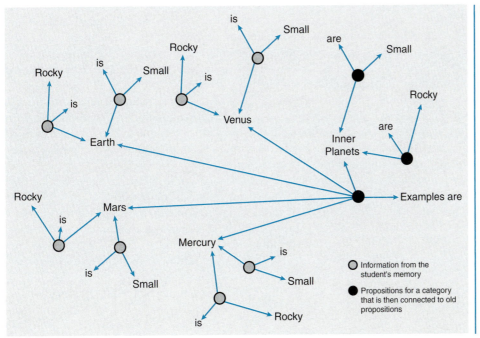

FIGURE 3.6 Organization: Placing Information Stored in Memory into Categories

Before coming to today's meeting, I looked over the NCTM standards that we were given at the end of last week's meeting. There were many objectives, some referring to specific mathematical skills and some referring to conceptual knowledge, but I was gratified to see that problem solving was prominent on the standards list. Today's meeting was a little more focused than the last, and Mrs. Halstrom explained that we were required by district policy to use the NCTM standards as a guide for developing mathematics curriculum; therefore, we were going to use these standards to compare different texts.

The majority of the committee seemed to be familiar with the standards, but Mrs. Halstrom had us go over them anyway and to discuss those text characteristics that would help us address the standards for our different grade levels. She plans to use our input to develop a rubric to evaluate the different texts that are available. As we discussed the standards

I began to appreciate even more how interconnected the mathematics curriculum was, how my students' achievement is affected by what they've learned in earlier grades, and how what they learn in my class affects their achievement in later grades. Mrs. Halstrom took notes and promised to have a draft rubric ready for our next meeting.

● **From the perspective of information processing, why should a teacher in one grade level be concerned with what teachers in other grade levels are doing?**

Decision Point: To what extent should curriculum in mathematics or other subject areas be guided by national standards such as those developed by the NCTM. (A copy of the NCTM standards can be found on the Web at http://standards-e.nctm.org/previous/CurrEvStds/)

declarative memory network, and so assist later retrieval because the information can be recalled by using these connections.

This description of encoding and retrieval explains the effectiveness of learning strategies such as mnemonics. A **mnemonic** is a memory support that connects unfamiliar information to students' prior knowledge (elaboration). They also can help students organize information or make sequences of events more memorable such as the acronym FACE in music, to remember the note spaces on the treble clef. Some examples of mnemonics would include the following:

- **First Letter Strategies.** As the name implies, first letter mnemonics use the first letters of items on a list or events in a sequence to produce an acronym or an acrostic. *HOMES* is an example of an acronym for the names of the Great Lakes (Huron, Ontario, Michigan, Erie, Superior). "My very educated mother just served us nine pizzas" is an acrostic phrase for the order of the planets from the sun (Mercury, Venus, Earth, Mars, Jupiter, Saturn, Uranus, Neptune, Pluto).
- **Keyword Mnemonic.** Developed by Atkinson (1975), the keyword mnemonic employs both sound links and imagery to connect two parts of a pair together. For example, the word *Pato* in Spanish means duck. If English speakers are trying to connect the terms, they get a keyword or sound link to the unfamiliar word that can be visualized. For example, the syllable *pat* sounds like the English word *pot*. The students then visualize the sound link interacting with the other word, such as an image of a duck cooking in a pot.
- **Link Systems.** With link systems, a concept, word, number, or idea is associated with another object, word, sound, touch, smell, or picture (Master, Mori, & Mori, 1993). For example, if students had to remember the words *bear, window,* and *table* in order, they could be linked together into the sentence, "The bear jumped through the window and landed on the table."
- **Method of Loci.** The **method of Loci** is a variation of the **link system** that uses a sequence of familiar locations to remember a sequence of information. For example, students might visualize the first room they enter in a house and have the first item interact with the location, and so on until all items are connected to a location.

ENRICHING YOUR UNDERSTANDING
Less Is Sometimes More

A major idea in cognitive psychology is that learning is made meaningful if students connect new learning to existing knowledge. These connections are formed through elaboration. However, the research on elaborations does not consistently support their effectiveness. In some cases elaborations that are provided to students have no effect on their learning, and in other cases they may have an adverse effect on students' learning (Dempster, 1987; Stein, Littlefield, & Bransford, 1984). Like many things in life, it's not what we do, but how we do it that matters.

According to Dempster (1993), in order for elaborations to help students, they must meet four necessary but occasionally insufficient conditions. First, the elaborations must be personally meaningful to the learners. They must connect to knowledge that the learner in fact possesses. Second,

elaborations should be relevant and should not take students' attention away what they are supposed to learn. Some elaborative activities may be so complicated that students may focus on the activity and not the intended point. Third, the elaboration should be related precisely to the point it is elaborating. Learners should be able to infer the main point from the example. Finally, elaborations should be used when they are needed. Some points are clear without elaborations.

● **How might these ideas help you do a better job of selecting elaborative activities that are likely to be effective? (For your authors' perspective on this question, go to the text website for this chapter.)**

The actual processes of elaboration and organization occur in working memory where new associations are formed among chunks of declarative knowledge created by selective perception processes or retrieved from long-term memory. Since the capacity of working memory is limited, the amount of information that students can elaborate or organize in a given period of time is also limited. You should keep this in mind as you plan your lessons. Avoid giving students too many new ideas at once and allow them time to elaborate and organize what they are learning.

As a final point, it is important to remember that the way knowledge is organized and elaborated has a powerful impact on how the knowledge will be retrieved and used. Declarative knowledge is organized and elaborated into schemata. Schemata have profound effects on where attention is focused, what is understood and remembered,

TABLE 3.2   Elaboration Examples

The acronym TACE is useful for understanding the types of thought processes involved in elaboration. It stands for **T**ransform, **A**pply, **C**onnect, and **E**xtend. Here are some examples of TACE.

Transform
Have students summarize text they have just read in the form of a chart.
Have students put ideas and concepts into their own words.

Apply
Have students make use of information they just learned to solve a problem.
Have students teach what they have learned to someone else.

Connect
Have students compare and contrast ideas they are learning.
Have students create maps that show the relationships among ideas they have been studying.

Extend
Have students think of new examples of concepts they have just learned.
Have students think of questions they would like to ask the author of something they just read.

SQ3R is an acronym that stands for a series of steps in a textbook studying strategy developed by Francis Robinson (1961). Each letter in the acronym stands for a step in the strategy. A brief description of each step is listed here.

- **Survey.** Learners preview or survey the reading selection. The goal is to identify the five or six main ideas around which the chapter is structured.
- The next three steps are repeated for each section of the text.
- **Question.** Learners turn topic headings into questions that can be answered while they are reading.
- **Read.** Students read to answer the questions they have posed.

- **Recite.** Once students have read a section, they look away from the book and try to answer the question(s) in their own words.
- **Review.** Students review any notes they have taken or test their memories for the main points from each section.

⬤ From the perspective of information-processing theory, what is the purpose of each step of this strategy? (For your authors' perspective on this question, go to the text website for this chapter.)

---

and learners' ability to problem solve (Anderson & Pearson, 1984). Using terminology from earlier in the text, key processes such as perception, attention, encoding, and retrieval are all going to be influenced by the schemata that are activated to guide those processes.

Compilation.   Unlike declarative knowledge, procedural knowledge is not directly encoded into long-term memory. As previously defined, compilation is a process that creates and organizes new procedural knowledge in long-term memory as the skill is performed. The compilation process is made up of two parts, proceduralization and composition.

Proceduralization is the cognitive process that creates new productions from declarative knowledge active in working memory. When we are first learning a skill, we represent the skill as declarative knowledge. We are likely to form declarative knowledge representations about the types of goals that can be reached by applying the skill, the conditions under which the skill should be used, and the actual mental or physical steps involved in executing the skill. To execute the skill using this declarative knowledge, we have to think about each step of the performance. For example, consider a young basketball player who is practicing a skill she has just been shown. At first, she has to think about what she has to do. This is slow and inefficient. How many of us have heard a coach say, "Stop thinking so much, and just do it." With some practice, these thoughts are converted to productions through proceduralization. Rather than having to think consciously about the skill, if the conditions exist for the action, we just do it. A production for a basketball player may look like this, "If she comes down the side, then move into a position that keeps her on the side." Productions contain actions that will be taken immediately if the conditions for the action are present. Automatic action replaces deliberate thought about the skill.

Composition is the process of combining two or more productions into a single more efficient production representing a more complex skill. The result of composition is a more integrated and fluid performance of the series of actions that make up the skill. In the case of the basketball player, she may combine several productions into her production sequence for defending her opponent for the full length of the court.

Compilation is a natural consequence of practicing a new skill. As the production system for a new skill is formed, the learner passes through three stages: (a) cognitive,

(b) associative, and (c) autonomous (Fitts & Posner, 1967). In the **cognitive stage,** the learner must form a declarative representation of the new skill that accurately represents the goals, conditions, and actions of the skill (Anderson, 1983, 1987; Jitendra, DiPipi, & Perron-Jones, 2002; Sweller, 1989). Effective instruction for learners in this stage would involve providing students with explanations, models, and guidance as they attempt to perform the skill. At this stage of skill learning, all of the instructional actions a teacher might take to help students elaborate and organize their understanding of the skill and manage their working memory load are appropriate.

The learners' early practice allows them to proceduralize portions of the skill and they enter into the **associative stage** (Fitts & Posner, 1967; Anderson, 1987). At this stage, the skill is represented by declarative knowledge and by the productions that resulted from earlier proceduralization. The existence of these first productions results in opportunities to combine productions through the composition process. Providing learners with informative feedback is necessary to prevent learners from developing inappropriate production systems (Singley & Anderson, 1989). Guided practice, or seat work, in which the teacher observes the learner's progress and corrects any errors is an appropriate instructional activity. In addition, learners should practice the skill in as many variations of appropriate context as possible so as to maximize their ability to transfer the skill appropriately.

The final stage is the **autonomous stage** and is defined by the completion of the compilation process (Anderson, 1987; Fitts & Posner, 1967). Further practice at this stage serves to maintain the strength of the production. Opportunities for independent practice, such as homework, are appropriate.

The activation (or retrieval) of procedural knowledge depends on the information that has been stored in the condition portion of a production. A production is activated only when the knowledge in working memory matches the pattern stored in the conditions portion of the production. This accounts for some of the difficulties learners have in appropriately applying skills they've learned. If the pattern of information stored in the conditions of a production is too general, then an action may be taken even when it is inappropriate. Conversely, when conditions of a production are overly specific, the match only occurs in a limited set of circumstances. In other words, sometimes an action might not be taken, even when it would have been appropriate to do so. For this reason, the conditions that are stored as part of the production are critical in determining the ultimate usefulness of a skill. This is why it is important that a skill be practiced in as many appropriate contexts as possible.

When introducing a new skill, be sure that students have a clear understanding of how the skill is performed and when it may be useful.

Why would you not assign homework to learners in the cognitive stage of learning a skill?

How might the concepts of generalization and discrimination be used to describe the activation of procedural knowledge?

$\mathcal{L}$evels of Processing: An Alternative to the Multi-Store Model

You have just finished reading about a version of the information-processing model or multi-store model of memory. The term *multi-store model of memory* refers

Looking in on

Sheila Gutierrez
3.3

We've been meeting all through the fall, using Mrs. Halstrom's rubric to evaluate several textbook series. The rubric was divided into three parts. The first part was a comparison of the text content with the appropriate standards. The second part dealt with text characteristics such as reading level, photos, diagrams, examples, and exercises. The third part of the rubric evaluated the instructional materials available for the teacher, such as classroom activities, exercises, bulletin board materials, and software. After evaluating various textbook series, we've finally decided that the district could buy either one of two series. The final decision will be made by the school board.

Both series cover the same concepts and skills and address all of the standards, and each had very similar characteristics. Both series also provided exercises and problem-solving activities that were appropriate for learners at that grade level. We all agreed that the students would be more likely to benefit from these features because they incorporated knowledge and situations familiar to the students. Each of the series provided the teachers with activities that could be assigned for in-class practice and a different set of problems that could be assigned as homework. Both series provided quizzes, concept introductions, and classroom activities that provided support for reviewing previously learned concepts and skills throughout the year. Finally, each series provided specific suggestions for how to use commonly available software to enrich the students' learning experience. I've learned a lot through this experience, and all in all I will be happy with either one of these texts. Many of my concerns were addressed, and I think I have a better understanding of where my instruction fits into the larger curricular goals of the district.

● **How might different features in a textbook help students process the information presented in the text, and can the text features described be justified using information-processing theory? Explain your answer.**

Decision Point: Would the same kind of features be appropriate for other textbooks for other subject areas?

to the different memory structures or locations where processing and storage of knowledge occur (sensory register, working memory, long-term memory). This view has not been without its critics, and one important alternative that has been proposed is **levels of processing** (Craik & Lockhart, 1972).

In the levels of processing view, the permanence or duration of a memory is a function of the level at which the information has been processed. Levels of processing can range from shallow to deep. At a shallow level, the information is analyzed in terms of sensory or physical characteristics such as brightness, contour, pitch, and so on. At a deep level of processing, information is analyzed in terms of its meaning, particularly its relationship to other knowledge the learner possesses. In general, information that is processed at a deeper level is more likely to be retained and understood. For example, maybe recently you have had the experience of sitting down to read a few pages of text, and at some point you realize that you don't remember anything you just read. You really were not concentrating on the reading, and you remember looking at words and pictures, but little more than that.

Maybe on another occasion you memorized a textbook definition so that you could write it down on a test. When the test questions asked for application or understanding, you became aware that you did not understand the definition. Levels of processing theorists would suggest that in both of these situations, you failed to process the information deeply. You did not process the information in a way that would make it meaningful.

Although levels of processing was proposed as an alternative to the multi-store model, a general implication of both seems to be similar. If students are going to understand and retain what they are trying to learn, then they must analyze what they are learning in terms of its meaning. Another way to think of this is that if students

Charles Elliot

3.2

A few weeks ago during study hall, I asked Ralph if he felt he was doing his best in chemistry, and he seemed a little embarrassed by the question. When I asked him if he was doing the reading and homework, he said he did the reading every night, but was having trouble with his homework, and that his older brother was giving him some pointers.

I asked to see his notes from class, and when he showed me his notebook it was clear that he had been listening in class. It looked as if he had tried to copy down everything that was said, but couldn't keep up and so missed quite a bit. He even copied down things that the other students had said. When I asked Ralph if this was the normal way he took notes, he told me it was. I pointed out that each lesson only has one or two main ideas, to which all the other information is related. Then I asked Ralph to look at his notes from the previous day and pick out the main ideas of the lesson. After some discussion and prompting he was able to identify two important concepts. Then I began to teach him an outlining strategy for taking notes. I demonstrated the strategy by rewriting a portion of his notes using the main ideas he had identified as headings. Then I helped him as he rewrote the rest of the notes. By the end of the session, he seemed to be getting the hang of it.

During the next study hall I asked Ralph about the reading for today's class. He knew a few specific details but didn't seem to understand the gist of what he had read. I decided that I would first try to teach Ralph the SQ3R reading strategy. I explained what SQ3R stood for, the psychology behind the strategy, and its effect on reading comprehension. After I demonstrated the technique on one section of our text, I coached Ralph while he applied the strategy to the next section of the text. After he had completed the strategy, I asked Ralph to explain what he had just read. He was a little hesitant, but finally gave a pretty good summary. When I told him so he seemed surprised. I told Ralph that learning a new reading strategy was just like learning a new wrestling move, and that if he practiced he would improve.

Ralph has been stopping by every day during my planning period and giving me a summary of the day's reading. On each occasion I have given him feedback and praise for his obvious improvement. He is participating more in class discussions, asking appropriate questions, and volunteering answers. His quiz scores are improving also.

● **How do techniques like note taking and SQ3R (see Enriching Your Understanding) improve students' abilities to comprehend and remember what they are learning?**

Decision Point: What suggestions would you give a future student to help the student become a better learner in your class?

are going to process information at a deep level, they need to engage in processes such as elaboration and organization and they need to be active in their own learning.

Cognitive Learning Principles from Information-Processing Theory

In keeping with the theme of this book, the concepts presented in this chapter have been synthesized into four general learning principles. In this section each principle is presented and discussed in terms of some of the general implications. In later chapters, these principles are used to organize discussions of the selection of instructional goals, the sequencing of instructional activities, and the assessment of students' learning.

Principle 3.1: Meaningful Learning Occurs When New Knowledge Is Connected to Existing Knowledge

One of the most important findings derived from research in cognitive learning theories in general and information-processing theory in particular is that students' prior knowledge has a powerful impact on the quality of their learning. The existing knowledge that students activate during learning affects where they focus their attention, how they interpret the meaning of new information, and how they encode or compile new information.

This principle has important implications for lesson planning. When planning instruction, you must be sensitive to your students' existing knowledge. Successful lessons provide any relevant knowledge your students lack, correct their misunderstandings, and help them connect new information to relevant prior knowledge. For instance, you may want to familiarize yourself with the curriculum of other grades and classes or administer pretests to better understand what your students know. In addition, when planning on a larger scale you should consider how to sequence lessons so that the knowledge gained in one lesson becomes a foundation for later lessons.

Principle 3.2: Effective Instruction Encourages Learners to Coordinate Their Various Basic Mental Processes

Learning is a complex mental event that results from the coordination of a number of basic processes. Teachers should try to create learning environments that encourage students to engage in the processes necessary for successful learning. Here are a few key processes for successful learning of declarative and procedural knowledge.

Selective Perception. Within the information-processing model, the concept of selective perception processes highlights two important aspects of learning. The first is that for any new information to be stored as knowledge it must first be attended to by the learner. As a teacher you may make use of orienting stimuli to initially attract your students' attention. But maintaining that attention will also be influenced by the students' goals.

The second important implication has to do with your students' perceptions. What is learned from a situation depends on how a learner perceives the situation. Students' perceptions may be influenced by the materials being presented and by their relevant prior knowledge.

Elaboration and Organization. The ability of students to understand and apply their declarative knowledge depends on how they encode the information. Successful encoding is facilitated when new knowledge is integrated with existing knowledge through organization and elaboration. Teachers should help their students to make associations between what they are learning and what they already know and to organize what they know into appropriate categories.

Students also need to organize across types of knowledge representations (i.e., declarative and procedural knowledge). Although procedural knowledge and declarative knowledge may be represented separately, students will be able to maximize the benefit of their learning if teachers find ways of helping students connect their declarative and procedural knowledge. For example, understanding math principles may help students better determine when to use a math procedure.

Compilation. Students' performance of skills is enhanced if they form appropriate procedural knowledge representations of those skills. The way skills are represented is affected by the conditions under which the skill is practiced and the type of feedback provided during practice. When teaching a skill, be sure the students understand the goal of the skill, what information or materials are required to perform the skill, as well as the specific actions that make up the skill. As they practice, you should carefully observe their performance and provide information about what they are doing correctly, where they are making mistakes, and how to correct their mistakes and improve their performance. Whenever possible, you should vary the context in which the skill is practiced.

Principle 3.3: The Limitations of Students' Working Memory Need to Be Accounted for in Instruction

The concept of working memory has many implications for teaching. The limited capacity of working memory will influence your decisions about the rate at which new information is presented to the students, how much time you will allow for the completion of in-class assignments or tests, and the degree of complexity of your lessons, labs, projects, or other learning activities. In addition, you may wish to take the time to teach your students content-appropriate strategies for managing their working memory, such as note taking or mnemonic techniques.

Principle 3.4: Learning Is an Active and Goal-Directed Process

Successful encoding and retrieval depend to a great extent on aligning these processes with the intended learning goals. Teachers may improve the learning of their students by helping them identify the appropriate learning goals and by providing learning experiences that will help students reach those learning goals.

Students should also be asked to take an active role in their own learning. Teachers should help students develop the knowledge, dispositions, and skills necessary to self-regulate their own learning. The development of students' metacognitive abilities is an important educational goal. Teaching students to set appropriate goals, how and when to apply specific learning strategies to reach those goals, and monitor their progress toward their goals are all actions that advance learners' metacognitive abilities and dispositions.

Principles into Practice:
Illustrating Key Concepts

An examination of the experiences of Sheila Gutierrez and Charles Elliot demonstrate how these principles might guide decision making in the classroom. Review these two cases and examine the decisions from the perspective of specific learning principles developed in this chapter.

Looking back on

When we first met Sheila Gutierrez, she was assigned to work with the district curriculum committee that was to make recommendations for a new district-wide mathematics series of textbooks. Sheila saw this as an opportunity to address some of the concerns she had with the textbooks she was using in her own class. This case provides an example of the multiple levels of complexity that typify the decision making in educational settings, and we can see the importance of several cognitive learning principles in Sheila's growing awareness of how the curriculum is integrated across grade levels.

At the first meeting, each member of the committee shared some of their concerns and hopes for the next math textbook series. As Sheila noted, the teachers on the committee developed a better idea of what their colleagues were trying to accomplish and how the instruction at one grade level was related to that at another. Principle 3.1, meaningful learning occurs when new knowledge is connected to existing knowledge, explains the importance of the interconnectedness of the curriculum. The relevant concept from cognitive learning theory is transfer. In other words, what the students learn in one grade affects their learning in later grades.

Principle 3.4, learning is an active goal-directed process, was recognized by the teachers and curriculum coordinator at the end of the meeting, when the teachers were given a set of standards that were to be used to guide their selection of a text series. In addition, the consideration of common standards also highlights the interconnectedness of curriculum and that the teachers in the district are all part of a team working toward the same goals.

At the second meeting, the committee members were discussing the mathematics standards and those text characteristics that would help them reach the standards they were given at the previous meeting. Principle 3.2, effective instruction encourages learners to coordinate their various mental processes, can be seen in the desire of the committee that realistic problem-solving activities be provided in the text materials. Problem solving and other complex tasks encourage students to coordinate all of the basic cognitive processes. In addition, these types of activities encourage transfer-appropriate processing, in that the mental processes required by the learning tasks are similar to those that allow the students to apply what they've learned outside of the classroom. This same principle is present in the decisions of the National Council of Teachers of Mathematics (NCTM) as they developed their standards and the textbook companies as the developed their textbook series.

Finally, the committee developed and applied a rubric, or set of guidelines, based on the NCTM standards and their discussion, that was used to evaluate the textbook series. Once again, the importance of Principle 3.1, meaningful learning occurs when new knowledge is connected to existing knowledge, is seen in the committee's desire to pick a text that allows teachers at each level of instruction to fulfill their responsibility to helping the learners reach the same goals. The description of the evaluation rubric and the books highlights the importance of Principle 3.2, effective instruction encourages learners to coordinate their various mental processes. From Sheila's description, we learn that the books in each series include materials and activities that are intended to help the learners encode the declarative knowledge and compile the procedural knowledge that are implied in the NCTM standards. ●

Looking back on *Charles Elliot*

Although Charles Elliot had been teaching for ten years, this was his first year teaching chemistry and he was concerned about lab safety and puzzled by his students' apparent inability to perform what he thought would be routine lab procedures. In addition, he was concerned with one of his students who is having difficulty with the course material.

During a conversation with the school's mathematics teacher, Charles was reminded that the lab is a new and complex environment and that the students may simply have forgetten what they were supposed to do. This realization is related to the working memory load of the students in a new and unfamiliar environment. In keeping with Principle 3.3, the limitations of students' working memory must be accounted for in instruction, Charles decided to use several strategies to help the students. First, he decided to take time to help his students effectively encode the procedures. Then he decided to provide the students with reminders to help them retrieve the information from their long-term memory when it is needed. As part of his lab safety instructions Charles decided to organize the lab rules into categories. This is an example of chunking and will help reduce the students' working memory load while they are encoding the new information.

The difficulty Charles' students are having with mathematical procedures is an example of failing to transfer the skills they learned in math class to solving problems in the chemistry class. This problem highlights the importance of Principle 3.1, meaningful learning occurs when new knowledge is connected to existing knowledge. The learners' inability to connect the context of the chemistry class with the information acquired in mathematics is adversely affecting their learning. Charles decided to take some time to review some relevant procedures with his class. By helping the students apply their mathematics procedures in the chemistry lab, it is likely that their overall ability to transfer their mathematics skill will be improved.

Ralph is a student who is having difficulty in Charles' chemistry class. Ralph's difficulty seems to be related to his difficulty comprehending the reading assignments and poor note-taking skills. Mr. Elliot decided that Ralph can do several things to improve his learning. He began by helping Ralph with his note-taking skills. The effectiveness of good note-taking skills is explained by Principle 3.3, the limitations of students' working memory must be accounted for in instruction. Notes serve as an auxiliary memory, so that things that are not encoded when they are first encountered may be reviewed when there is more time. This allows a more efficient use of working memory. Teaching Ralph to focus on the main ideas of the lesson also reduces his working memory load during class discussion, allowing him more cognitive resources for participation in class discussions. Charles decided to address Ralph's reading difficulty by teaching him the SQ3R reading strategy. This strategy exemplifies several of this chapters principles. In keeping with Principle 3.2, effective instruction encourages learners to coordinate their various mental processes, the entire strategy is designed to encourage learners to read for a purpose and to think about and monitor their progress in meeting that purpose. More specifically, Principle 3.4, learning is an active, goal-directed process, explains the importance of the initial steps of scanning and developing questions. The questions are the reader's goals that can guide their metacognition as they read. ●

Teachers as Decision Makers

A major theme of this text is that teachers are decision makers. To give a you feel for how cognitive learning theory and information processing can guide decision making, you were asked to think about questions and issues as you read about and looked in on the teachers presented in two cases. In this section your authors present their perspectives on the cases and then discuss how the learning principles of this chapter may be connected to applications in later chapters.

Sheila Gutierrez's Decision Points

When considering what questions you would ask if you were buying a textbook, it might be useful to remember the tetrahedral model presented in Chapter 1. Consider the nature of the learners in your class, the types of criterial tasks the learners will be expected to perform that would indicate successful learning, what types of learning activities you will use to help the learners be successful, and how the text will be used with other class materials in those learning activities. When thinking about the nature of the learners, you might want to ask if the learners have the necessary reading skills and background knowledge to comprehend the text. From the information processing perspective, when considering the criterial tasks, you need to ask yourself what type of knowledge, declarative or procedural, you expect your students to acquire. When choosing a textbook, or other instructional material, you should ask, does this text support the types of processing (elaboration, organization, or compilation) required to acquire this type of knowledge? You should also ask if this text supports or benefits from other available instructional materials.

Note that Sheila was concerned that the books be integrated with the available computer software. Answering the questions to describe the ideal textbook was the first decision point for Sheila. The second time you looked in on Sheila you were asked to what extent should teachers be guided by external standards when making decisions in their classrooms. Currently, considerable controversy surrounds this issue. However, standards developed by qualified experts allow for the articulation of curriculum across grade levels. As a teacher you are really part of a team that educates children from the time they enter the school system until they graduate. The standards can give you some idea of where you fit, what you can expect from students who have completed earlier grades, and what obligations you have to the those who will be teaching your students when they leave your classroom.

Charles Elliot's Decision Points

After initially presenting Charles Elliot's case, you were asked to make some hypotheses about the causes of the difficulties experienced by his students. Not having yet read the information about cognitive learning theory and information processing you might still have come up with some commonsense hypotheses. For instance, the students might be forgetting lab safety procedures because they were overly excited. From the perspective of information processing, information must be stored in long-term memory before it can be remembered and used later. Several things must happen for this to occur. The information must be attended to. Then the information must be keep active in working memory long enough to be encoded into long-term memory. The information must be encoded in such a way that it is likely to be retrieved in situations for which the information will be useful. Finally, the information should be retrieved from long-term memory and reviewed periodically. Good learning strategies encourage and guide students as they complete the various cognitive tasks.

In Ralph's case you might have guessed that he had some reading or communication difficulties that detracted from his performance in the class. As you read the chapter, you should have been able to refine your hypotheses. If students are having trouble with reading, you might suggest a strategy such as SQ3R. Students who are having difficulty remembering the contents of discussion and lecture may be taught note-taking techniques. Students who are having difficulty with tests may be taught study strategies that are appropriate for the type of tests they must take or strategies for how to take specific types of tests. Younger students typically have no or few simple study strategies. Taking time with these students to teach one or two techniques that are especially appropriate for what they have to learn may pay big dividends later. More mature high school students are more likely to have developed effective strategies, in which case teaching them more strategies is unlikely to improve their performance. However, it may be that some students in high school have not developed effective strategies and would benefit from such instruction. It might be more efficient to handle these students on a case-by-case basis, providing one-on-one instruction when it seems appropriate.

Looking Ahead: Cognitive Learning Principles and Decision Making

One of the themes of this book is that teachers' decision making is improved through the application of principles from psychological theory. In Chapter 1 your authors identified three broad categories of teacher decisions that provide opportunities to apply psychological principles:

- Decisions made when planning a lesson
- Decision made when teaching and managing in the classroom
- Decisions made when assessing the effectiveness of their actions

In later chapters, the principles developed in this chapter are used to organize discussions of applications of information-processing theory to these three types of decisions. Table 3.3 allows you to look forward and see the implications of these principles for the types of decision making discussed in those later chapters.

TABLE 3.3 — Looking Ahead: Cognitive (Information-Processing) Learning Theory Principles and Decision Making

Decision Area	Implications for Practice	Looking Ahead
Principle 3.1: Meaningful learning occurs when new knowledge is connected to existing knowledge		
Planning	Teachers should help students make meaningful connections by cueing retrieval of relevant information from their long-term memory and by encouraging and assisting students to elaborate and organize new information.	Chapters 7, 8, 9
Principle 3.2: Effective instruction encourages learners to coordinate their various basic mental processes		
Planning	When planning lessons, teachers should consider how the elements of the lesson affect attention, retrieval, encoding, and compilation.	Chapters 7, 8, 9
Teaching and classroom management	Teacher should develop and apply communications skills and skills with media that help students direct the selective perception processes, retrieve relevant knowledge from long-term memory, and elaborate and organize new information.	Chapters 7, 9
Principle 3.3: The limitations of students' working memory must be accounted for in instruction		
Planning	Teachers should be sensitive to limitations in learners' abilities to process information when making decisions about how many new concepts to cover in a lesson.	Chapters 7, 8, 9
Principle 3.4: Learning is an active, goal-directed process		
Planning	When planning lessons, teachers should include activities that encourage students to develop strategic knowledge.	Chapter 8
Assessment	Meaningful assessment of instructional effectiveness requires alignment between content and processes of assessment tasks with those of the learning tasks.	Chapter 9

Name _____ Date _____

Chapter 3 Study Guide

Use this Study Guide to review and test your knowledge of key concepts introduced in this chapter and to search out further information on issues and topics raised in this chapter.

 ## Key Terms

Review the following key words from the chapter and then connect to Research Navigator (www.researchnavigator.com) either directly or through this book's Companion Website to explore research on the topics as they relate to education today.

Alignment (p. 72)	Automaticity (p. 59)	Chunk (p. 59)
Associative stage (p. 79)	Autonomous stage (p. 79)	Chunking (p. 70)
Attention (p. 68)	Bottom-up processing (p. 69)	Cognitive stage (p. 79)

Compilation (p. 72)
Composition (p. 78)
Declarative knowledge (p. 59)
Declarative knowledge network
   (p. 64)
Distributed practice/spacing effect
   (p. 74)
Elaboration (p. 74)
Encoding (p. 72)
Encoding specificity (p. 73)
Image (p. 61)
Information (p. 56)
Knowledge (p. 56)
Levels of processing (p. 80)
Link systems (p. 76)
Long-term memory (p. 71)

Maintenance rehearsal (p. 70)
Memory strategies (p. 70)
Metacognition (p. 73)
Method of Loci (p. 76)
Mnemonic (p. 76)
Natural categories (p. 63)
Organization (p. 75)
Orienting response (p. 68)
Orienting stimulus (p. 68)
Perception (p. 68)
Procedural knowledge (p. 59)
Proceduralization (p. 78)
Production (p. 62)
Production systems (p. 65)
Proposition (p. 61)
Retrieval (p. 72)

Schema (p. 63)
Scripts (p. 63)
Selective perception process (p. 68)
Sensation (p. 56)
Sensory register (p. 68)
Spread of activation (p. 75)
Temporal string (p. 60)
Text schemata (p. 63)
Top-down processing (p. 69)
Transfer (p. 73)
Transfer-appropriate processing
   (p. 73)
Working memory (p. 69)
Working memory load (p. 69)

Alternative Response Items

1. After some thought, a student is able to match dates to important events in colonial America. According to information-processing theory, what type of knowledge does the student have?

   a. Declarative
   b. Procedural
   c. Temporal
   d. Factual

2. What characterizes a performance that is guided by procedural knowledge?

   a. Frequent errors
   b. Conscious control
   c. Automaticity
   d. High working memory load

3. According to the information-processing theory, what type of basic unit of declarative knowledge stores information about spatial relationships?

   a. Temporal strings
   b. Images
   c. Propositions
   d. Productions

4. After several encounters with dogs in the neighborhood, a child develops a basic understanding about dogs that includes their general physical characteristics and typical behavior. What type of schema most likely represents this child's understanding of dogs?

   a. Natural category
   b. Script
   c. Text schema
   d. Concrete

5. According to the information-processing theory presented in this chapter, what type of knowledge representation is acquired most easily and quickly?

   a. Productions
   b. Chunks
   c. Text schemata
   d. Natural categories

6. Students who elaborate or organize new information are more likely to be able to remember the information later. What concept from information-processing theory explains this finding?

   a. Spread of activation
   b. Maintenance rehearsal
   c. Proceduralization
   d. Metacognition

7. A teacher has learned that her students do better on tests that use terms and phrases that are similar, or identical to, those in the text. What cognitive learning theory concept best explains this observation?

   a. Chunking
   b. Orienting response
   c. Encoding specificity
   d. Automaticity

8. What concept from cognitive learning theory refers to students' ability to use what they know about themselves and a specific learning situation to improve their learning?

   a. Encoding specificity
   b. Transfer-appropriate processing
   c. Metacognition
   d. Spread of activation

9. Imagine you are preparing for a test of your knowledge of cognitive learning theory and information processing. According to cognitive research, which of the following study strategies is likely to result in your best performance on the test?

   a. Study for thirty minutes each night for a week before the test.
   b. Study for thirty minutes the night before the test.
   c. Study for three hours the night before the test.
   d. Study for six hours the night before the test.

10. During which stage of skill learning is it most appropriate for the teacher to help the students elaborate on the conditions and goals that define the context in which the skill should be applied.

a. Cognitive stage
b. Associative stage
c. Autonomous stage
d. None of the above

Constructed Response Items

Short Answer/Completion Items

1. According to the information-processing model presented in this chapter, how is knowledge represented in working memory?

2. Elaine is asked to write down the months of the year in alphabetical order. Even though she can normally say the months in under ten seconds, it takes her many minutes to comply with the request. How might a cognitive learning theorist explain Elaine's difficulty?

3. A teacher habitually begins class by reviewing the main concepts presented in the previous day's lesson. How might this technique improve the students' learning?

4. Which of the basic cognitive processes are likely to be involved when someone is learning a new skill?

5. Which memory store is most likely to limit what a person is able to learn in a fifty-minute class period?

Essay Items

1. Give two examples of content you will be teaching; one example that your students are likely to represent by declarative knowledge and one that is likely to be represented as procedural knowledge. Explain your reasoning for each example.

2. Using the information-processing model, explain why a person from another culture would have trouble understanding American situation comedies.

3. What are some examples of metacognitive self-regulation activities you engaged in to understand this chapter? Explain each example using concepts from information-processing theory.

Practicing Your Decision Making

1. Consider the kinds of things you would like your students to learn in your class, for example, reading and computation skills, comprehension of the causes and consequences of important historical events, and so on. What kinds of knowledge (declarative or procedural) correspond to these learning objectives?

2. Given the instructional goals you've identified in number 1 above, give some examples of the learning activities that you would design. Use the concepts from information-processing theory to explain why these learning activities are likely to be effective.

INTASC in Action

Use the following activities to think about how behavioral learning theory concepts and principles relate to the INTASC standards.

Standard 2: Student Development. Think about trying to teach a new learner how to perform a complicated skill such as playing the piano or driving a stick shift car. How would an understanding of the information-processing model help you teach this skill more effectively?

Standard 3: Diverse Learners. From a cognitive perspective, differences in learners' existing knowledge is an extremely important source of individual differences. Describe how differences in existing knowledge could affect students' performance in these areas.

1. Knowing what's important to study from a text-book
2. Being able to learn new information in a content area
3. Being able to problem solve

Standard 4: Multiple Instructional Strategies. Observe students working on complicated problems that are unfamiliar to them such as decoding unknown text, solving complicated algebraic problems, or even learning to master a new video game. What signs if any of working memory overload did you observe? What supports if any were present to manage the potential overload?

Standard 9: Reflective Practice and Professional Growth. In many cases, the skills you will be teaching are at an automatic level for you. How might that make it difficult for you to teach that skill to a beginner? How will you monitor your teaching to ensure that you are aware of any issues your automaticity is creating for your learners?

 # Web Resources

Cognitive Psychology Tutor
http://teach.psy.uga.edu/CogPsychTutor/default.htm
This online resource presents an opportunity to test your understanding and ability to apply concepts from cognitive psychology.

University of Minnesota-Duluth Study Strategies Homepage
www.d.umn.edu/student/loon/acad/strat/
This website provides information about SQ3R and other learning strategies.

4

Understanding Social Cognitive Theory

In this chapter, the major ideas and principles of social cognitive theory are presented. Specifically, the chapter describes the ideas of Albert Bandura, the psychologist given credit for having originated the key ideas of current social cognitive theory. These ideas and principles are particularly useful for understanding the types of issues teachers Daleesha Goodwin and Ann Guiter are trying to resolve in the Close-up on the Classroom feature on the following pages. You will look in on them occasionally to see how social cognitive theory informs their practice.

As was the case with Chapters 2 and 3, the concepts in this chapter have been summarized in terms of a few key learning principles. The principles are listed here, and they are also discussed at the end of the chapter in terms of their application to Daleesha Goodwin's and Ann Guiter's classroom experiences.

- Principle 4.1: Learners acquire important knowledge, behaviors, and dispositions through their exposure to models.
- Principle 4.2: Learners' self-belief systems guide their learning and their behavior.
- Principle 4.3: Learners have the potential to self-regulate their own learning processes.

Standards in This Chapter

Although learning the concepts and associated principles presented in this chapter will contribute to your mastery of all of the INTASC standards, the material presented in Chapter 4 is most strongly related to the following standards:

- **Standard 2:** Student Development
- **Standard 3:** Diverse Learners
- **Standard 4:** Multiple Instructional Strategies
- **Standard 5:** Motivation and Management

Daleesha Goodwin and Dropout Prevention

My job as the dropout specialist for Lincoln High School is to provide counseling, family outreach, and tutorial services for students who are at risk of dropping out. Today I will be making a number of visits to local businesses to meet with potential mentors for our students and to arrange new partnerships for our work-study program. Also, I will also be running three different counseling groups with students who have been identified by teachers as potential dropouts.

I am worried about a number of students, but right now I am particularly worried about Louis. He's really at a critical point, and I think the next few months might determine whether or not he stays in school. Louis is a very quiet ninth grader who is the third of six children in his family. None of his older siblings have finished high school. Neither parent is a high school graduate, and according to Louis' teachers, his family doesn't provide much encouragement to Louis when it comes to school.

Louis' main problem right now is that he is not coming to school regularly. As a result, he is now failing two classes. Louis does not have a lot to say during group counseling, so I feel that I need to meet with Louis individually to see what's going on with him.

Decision Point: What information should Ms. Goodwin collect initially to help her with Louis?

Before proceeding with Chapter 4, be sure you read the Close-ups on the Classroom features about Daleesha Goodwin and Ann Guiter. At various points in the chapter, you will revisit both teachers in their classrooms and follow their decision-making progress. Their classroom experiences are closely integrated with the key concepts of this chapter and serve as important models for understanding Social Cognitive Theory.

Social Cognitive View of Learning

How are cognitive learning theory and social cognitive theory related?

From a social cognitive perspective, learning is the process of converting information from the environment into mental representations that guide behavior (Bandura, 1986). This definition of learning should sound familiar, because it is similar to the cognitive definition of learning provided in Chapter 3. Current social cognitive theory can be thought of as an example of a cognitive learning theory that focuses primarily on how people come to understand their world by observing others in their environments and how they learn to achieve personally meaningful goals.

Albert Bandura and his colleagues make some key assumptions about the nature of learners that provide a conceptual framework for their discussions of learning and teaching. These assumptions can be organized around two key questions. First, what is the nature of the relationship between learners and their environments? Second, what personal and social factors affect the nature of the learning process?

Learners and Their Environments

Bandura's concept of reciprocal determinism describes the social cognitive perspective on the relationship between learners and their environments. **Reciprocal determinism** is the idea that learners' behaviors are determined by the reciprocal or mutual influence of these three key factors: the learners' internal mental representations (e.g., thoughts, expectations, and beliefs); the learners' behavior and its outcomes; and the learners' environmental influences (Bandura, 1986, 1999; Zimmerman, 1999). A mutual or reciprocal influence means that each factor influences the other factors and is

Elementary

As a Chapter I reading specialist for my district, I work with students who are well below grade level in reading. My job consists mainly of providing supplemental reading instruction to small groups of students and consulting with teachers on how to improve their students' performance in reading. I have consultations scheduled with two teachers today, one in the morning and one in the afternoon.

My afternoon consultation is with Ernest Franklin, one of our fifth grade teachers. He is concerned about Ellen's performance in science and social studies. Ellen is a student I exited from my program last year because she was doing so well. However, Ernest told me that she has trouble with textbook reading and really needs to develop better study strategies. For example, he gives his students quite a bit of time to read their textbooks. Then he asks them questions about what they have read. Ellen seldom if ever can answer these questions, and he thinks she cannot read well enough to do the work in his class. Also, he has observed that she doesn't do simple things such as taking notes while she is reading. I think Ellen should be able to handle the assigned reading, but I also know that many of my students run into difficulties when they are asked to read textbooks in the upper grades. I hope we can work something out to help Ellen when we meet this afternoon.

Decision Point: What types of data would be helpful in deciding how to help Ellen?

---

also influenced by the other factors. In general, reciprocal determinism means that people are affected by their environments, and that they also exert influence on their environments. Reciprocal determinism is represented visually in Figure 4.1. The double-headed arrows represent the idea of a mutual influence.

As an example of reciprocal determinism, consider your role as a decision maker in the classroom and how your decision making both affects the teaching environment and is affected by the teaching environment. When you begin teaching, you come equipped with knowledge and beliefs about teaching and the nature of people that you have acquired over your lifetime. Your choices of goals for your students, instructional strategies, and classroom management approaches are all influenced by your beliefs. Your students and potentially your overall school environment can be affected by these beliefs and accompanying decisions. However, you won't teach in a vacuum. The beliefs and behaviors of students, parents, administrators, colleagues, and members of the community are all potentially powerful environmental influences on your behavior and beliefs. For example, the cultural and life experiences of your students might make some teaching behaviors more or less effective. You may find yourself changing your teaching behaviors or maybe even ultimately your beliefs. Consider the experience of Tim Johnson, a first-year teacher.

> ➤ I started out believing that students need to do homework every night. I thought homework taught students responsibility. As you can imagine, I was very disappointed that so many of my students did not do the homework. I teach in a rural environment, and my students have lots of chores to do in the morning and at night. I'm not sure my view of homework makes much sense for these students.

Reciprocal determinism, therefore, highlights the importance of understanding human behavior in terms of the complex interactions between personal and environmental

FIGURE 4.1 Reciprocal Determinism
(*Source:* Adapted from Bandura (1986). *Social foundations of thought* (p. 24). Upper Saddle River, NJ: Prentice Hall.)

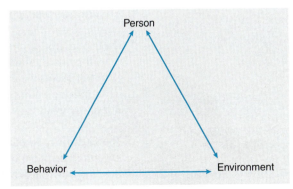

How can community standards affect your decisions as a teacher?

influences. It is helpful to remember that while you are teaching and managing your students, you are also being taught and managed by your students. Teachers need to be aware of these mutual influences as they make their decisions.

Learners' Social and Personal Characteristics

Bandura identifies a set of personal and social characteristics of learners that help define the nature of key learning and teaching processes. These characteristics include the following (Bandura, 1986, 1999, 2001).

- Learners have the capability to represent their experiences symbolically.
- Learners have the capability to learn vicariously.
- Learners have the capability to self-regulate.

Symbolic Representation. Symbolic representation is the process of translating experiences into mental models that guide behavior (Bandura, 1986). As such, symbolic representation is the basic process involved in all learning. According to Bandura (1974), learners have two representational systems, the imaginal and the verbal systems. Imaginal representation allows learners to translate experiences into enduring mental images of those experiences. For example, you may have a mental picture of how to change a flat tire in your memory. The verbal representational system translates our experiences into verbal codes. For example, you may also have the list of steps for changing a flat tire stored in memory. Verbal codes are extremely important for our ability to organize and retrieve what we have observed.

The ability to represent experiences symbolically provides learners with a mechanism for using past experiences to guide current behavior. Bandura (1974, 1977) referred to this ability as delayed matching or delayed modeling. People determine how to behave based on the knowledge and expectations that they have stored from previous learning. They make predictions about the likely outcomes of their behavior, and then select their behaviors accordingly. Consider this classroom example.

➤ John likes students who try hard. He praises them for their hard work. His students learn that if they want praise in the future, they need to try hard.

Symbolic representation provides a foundation for one of the important assumptions that social cognitive theorists make about learning. Bandura and the social cognitivists distinguish between learning and performance. As noted earlier, learning is the acquisition of mental models that guide behavior. Performance, on the other hand, is what people actually do in a given situation (Mischel & Mischel, 1994). One important implication of the distinction between learning and performance is that people can acquire mental models without actually having to engage in overt behaviors. For example, you may learn how to divide fractions by watching someone demonstrate how to divide fractions. A second important implication of the distinction between learning and performance is that students' performances may not reveal what they have learned. People may self-censure their behavior if it violates moral principles or if the behavior is socially unacceptable (Bahn, 2001). For example, it's not always socially desirable to be the student who answers teachers' questions. Peers may call these students *brown-nosers* or *school boys/girls* or *teachers' pets*. Given these potential aversive consequences, some students may not show what they know.

In general, therefore, performance can be an imperfect indicator of learning. When students do not do something, you need to be cautious in assuming that they cannot do something. There can be many personal and social reasons why people do not show what they know.

The Capability to Learn Vicariously. Bandura (1977) acknowledges that people can and often do learn through their own experiences, and he refers to this type of learning as **enactive learning**. However, Bandura also believes that acquiring complicated

As a classroom teacher, it is likely that you will have students in your classroom for whom English is a second language. You will need to understand how to help these students succeed. The silent period and the affective filter are two ideas from the research on second language learning that are related to the social cognitive theory.

The silent period occurs for many students following their initial exposure to a second language. During the silent period, which can last for several months, students mostly listen to the new language without speaking much in the second language (Ovando & Collier, 1998). There can be many reasons for the silent period, including students' comfort level with their environment and their personal feelings of confidence with the new language. Teachers would be mistaken, however, if they believed that no language learning is oc-

curring during the silent period. Students who listen without speaking tend to progress as well as their more verbal peers in acquiring a second language (Allwright & Bailey, 1991).

One implication of the silent period is that your second language learners should be given the opportunity to be involved in class experiences that require the use of the second language, but you should not require them to speak unless they feel comfortable doing so. Their observations of the class interactions provide them with important information about the second language they are learning.

● **Why is the silent period an example of the social cognitive distinction between learning and performance?** (For your authors' perspective on this question, go to the text website for this chapter.)

---

cognitive and social understandings through direct experience would be highly inefficient. As an alternative, Bandura proposes **vicarious learning,** which is learning by observing the experiences of others. Vicarious learning provides a useful explanation for how people often learn complicated social behaviors from each other. For example, children may acquire aggressive behavior by watching people in their daily lives or models in the media act aggressively (Anderson & Bushman, 2001; Bandura, 1973).

The Capability for Self-Control. From a social cognitive perspective, people have the capabilities to be proactive, self-organizing, and self-regulating. They are active agents in their own psychosocial development (Bandura, 1997, 1999; Bandura, Barbaranelli, Caprara, & Pastorelli, 2001). This potential for self-control or personal agency has the following features (Bandura, 2001).

- Learners have the capability to act with intent.
- Learners have the capability for forethought.
- Learners have the capability for self-reactiveness.
- Learners have the capability for self-reflectiveness.

An **intention** is a representation of a future course of action, and it reflects people's ability to be proactive in their lives (Bandura, 2001). People can make plans about how to behave to produce certain outcomes, which means that they are active agents in their own development.

Forethought is the ability to take a future orientation by setting goals and making plans to achieve those goals (Bandura, 1986). Forethought is an important capability because it allows people to use potential future consequences as current motivators of their behavior (Bandura, 1977, 2001). If people have

Children can learn important social skills vicariously.

The famous Bobo studies done in the 1960s are still one of Bandura's most interesting demonstrations of vicarious learning. In one of these studies, preschool children watched one of two films. In one film, an adult played very aggressively with a Bobo doll, an inflatable plastic doll with a weighted bottom that bounces back when hit. In the second film, an adult plays calmly with Tinkertoys, a children's construction toy. Later the preschool children were allowed to play with a variety of toys, including a Bobo doll and Tinkertoys. Before the children were allowed to play, however, the experimenters tried to induce frustration by not allowing the children to play with their favorite toys. Bandura and associates found that the children who had observed the aggressive adult model tended to be much more aggressive in their play than those who had watched the calm adult model (Bandura, Ross, & Ross, 1963). This study replicated findings achieved in an earlier study with *live* models (Bandura, Ross, & Ross, 1961). Later research has tended to confirm the finding that observing aggressive models can induce heightened aggression in some learners (Anderson & Bushman, 2001; Farver & Frosch, 1996; Liebert & Sprafkin, 1988).

● **What do see as the relevance of Bandura's research for your role as a classroom teacher today? (For your authors' perspective on this question, go to the text website for this chapter.)**

clear, achievable goals, then they can determine appropriate courses of action. Also, their long-term goals may help them deal with the day-to-day frustrations that occur as they try to meet their goals by helping them to think beyond immediate experiences. Goals can also help them judge improvement and progress. For example, as you pursue your goal of becoming a master teacher, you will encounter occasional setbacks. Perhaps you may have to reduce the number of classes you take in a semester, or quit for a year to pay for your education. Being able to focus on your ultimate goal may help you deal with these setbacks.

Self-reactiveness involves setting personal standards for success, self-evaluating progress toward those standards, and using self-administered consequences and guidance to regulate behavior (Bandura, 1986, 2001). This capability evolves both from direct and vicarious learning experiences (Grusec, 1992). People learn through direct experience that some behaviors will be successful in achieving goals, while other behaviors will not. They also have the opportunity to observe the self-standards that others set for themselves and the consequences that accompany those standards. They do not automatically internalize the standards that others set for themselves. Instead, they evaluate these various observations and select personal standards based on their evaluation of what they observed. Consider this example.

➤ In high school, I had a close relationship with my football coach, John Rayburn. He had played college football, so he knew what it took to succeed at that level. Even at age 50, he did everything he asked us to do during conditioning drills. My work ethic in football and life came from being around John.

Self-reflectiveness is the ability to think about our own thought processes and to analyze our own experiences. Through these self-reflective activities, people can develop beliefs and expectations about their environments and themselves. Cognitive learning theorists refer to these types of self-reflective processes as metacognitive activities, and they are important if students are going to be able to control their own learning processes (Flavell, 1979).

How are metacognition and self-reflectiveness related?

According to social cognitive theorists, self-efficacy is an extremely important component of self-reflection. Bandura (1993, p. 118) defined **self-efficacy** as ". . . people's beliefs about their capabilities to exercise control over their own level of functioning and over events that affect their lives." In other words, self-efficacy is a person's belief about how likely it is that she or he can perform a task successfully. If learners have high self-efficacy, they believe they can succeed if they try. Low levels of self-efficacy would mean that learners doubt their ability to succeed if they try. Self-efficacy beliefs are important because they influence how people "think, motivate themselves, and behave" (Bandura, 1993, p. 118).

It should be noted that self-efficacy is not the same as self-concept. Self-efficacy involves personal judgments about the likelihood of success for a particular task (Gaskill & Woolfolk Hoy, 2002; Pajares, 1997). Self-concept is more general and consists of a variety of different self-beliefs. Consequently, self-efficacy can be viewed as a part of self-concept.

Social Cognitive Theory and the Teaching/Learning Process

The assumptions that social cognitive theorists make about learners form the basis for their discussions of classroom teaching and learning. First, symbolic representation is important for understanding the role of consequences in learning. Second, vicarious learning provides an extremely useful process for acquiring complicated cognitive and social behaviors and attitudes. Third, the potential for self-regulation has important implications for how you might think about classroom management and motivation issues.

The Role of Consequences in Learning

As you learned in Chapter 2, consequences have a central role in a behavioral explanation of learning. From a traditional behavioral perspective, behavior is controlled directly by its immediate consequences. People acquire new behaviors because of the effects of reinforcement and punishment on that behavior.

Based on his views of learners, Bandura modified the behavioral view of consequences for a number of reasons. First, although he acknowledged that consequences could play an important role in regulating learners' existing behaviors, he also suggested that they provide a poor explanation for how new and complicated behaviors are learned. For example, it would be difficult to learn to speak if children could only produce words that they had been reinforced for using (Bandura, 1977).

Second, Bandura differed with the behaviorists in terms of an explanation for how consequences operate. He rejected the radical behavioral idea that consequences affect behavior "automatically without conscious involvement" (Bandura, 1977, p. 19). According to Bandura, consequences affect behaviors because they create expectations for the future. Because of the ability to represent experiences symbolically, people can develop the expectation that the same behavior will produce similar outcomes in the future (Bandura, 1986). Consequences, therefore, provide information that learners can use to guide and self-regulate their future behavior. For example, a young child may have learned that if he whines about taking a bath, he will get in trouble. He uses this information to determine what he will do at bath time in the future.

Third, Bandura broadened the view of how consequences can be experienced by learners. He agreed that people's behavior could be influenced by direct experience with environmental consequences. He also suggested, however, that consequences can be experienced vicariously, and they can be self-administered. **Vicarious consequences** refer to changes in learners' behaviors that result from observing the reinforcement or punishment that a model receives for the modeled behaviors. For example, a junior high school student observes that a peer receives a lot of attention for dressing a certain way. The student decides to dress that same way. In another situation, a young child sees a brother get in trouble for behaving a certain way and decides not to behave that way. Vicarious consequences are observed and interpreted rather than being experienced directly by the learner. Here are some ideas for using vicarious reinforcement in your classroom.

How are vicarious consequences related to peer pressure?

- Develop ways of publicly recognizing good student efforts as both a direct incentive for the students who did the work, and a vicarious incentive for others who observe the recognition. For example, you might post good student work on a bulletin board. In doing this, be sensitive to personal and developmental issues. For example, for some adolescents, the risk of embarrassing them might outweigh the potential vicarious and direct benefits of public recognition.
- Arrange to have successful former students return to discuss what they are doing or have done to be successful.

Consequences can also be self-administered. Bandura (1977, 1986) suggested that learners internalize their experiences with environmental consequences. As a result, they establish personal standards, self-evaluate their progress toward meeting those standards, and administer self-reinforcement and criticism. Learners, therefore, are not entirely dependent on immediate environmental experiences to modify their behavior. Consider Octavio Ramirez's approach to learning.

➤ I try to study a little bit each night for about a week before a test. Each night after I study, I have my parents ask me questions about what I just studied. If I do well, I let myself watch television. If I don't do well, I go back and review what I missed.

Vicarious Learning

As discussed earlier in the chapter, vicarious learning is learning through the experiences of others. In describing vicarious learning, Bandura and his associates use a specialized vocabulary. As many of their terms are not used the way we might use them in our in day-to-day conversations, your authors begin by defining some key terminology. We then describe the basic nature of vicarious learning in terms of its potential effects on learners and the variables that affect the success of modeling.

Model.   Vicarious learning occurs through the observation of models. According to Bandura and his colleagues, "a **model** is any stimulus array so organized that an observer can extract and act on the main information conveyed by environmental events without needing to first perform overtly" (Rosenthal & Bandura, 1978, p. 622). There are three types of stimulus arrays that can serve as models (Bandura, 1971). **Live models** are people with whom the learner has direct contact. Parents, teachers, and peers would be examples of live models. **Symbolic models** are pictorial models. Print and electronic media are the common ways in which symbolic models are made available to learners. A **verbal description** is the third type of model, and it consists of directions on how to perform a behavior. For example, a teacher might prepare a poster board with the steps in long division. This poster would be provided so that students could refer to it as a model.

Modeling.   **Modeling** is a transmission process that involves interactions between learners and models, and that results in changes for the learners. According to Bandura (1986, p. 47), ". . . modeling has always been acknowledged to be one of the most powerful means of transmitting values, attitudes, and patterns of thought."

When Bandura categorizes types of modeling experiences, he does so in terms of the potential effects of modeling on learners. Generally, modeling can have either performance or learning effects. Modeling can influence learners' decisions about what previously learned behaviors are appropriate or useful in a situation, or it can result in new behaviors, knowledge, or dispositions for learners.

Performance Effects.   By observing models, people can determine which behaviors are likely to be successful, appropriate, or valued in a situation. This understanding of how to behave results from one of these three modeling effects: the inhibitory effect, the disinhibitory effect, or the facilitating effect.

I'm glad I decided to meet with Louis alone, because this is the most he has ever opened up to me. When I asked him why he was not coming to school, he told me an interesting story. He said that he started having trouble in school in fourth grade and nothing seemed to help him. He started feeling "stupid." The more he thought he was stupid, the less he tried. After all, why try if you can't do it? Because he didn't try, he got further behind, and he thinks this made his teachers believe he was stupid too. They started treating him as if he was stupid by giving him easy work or putting him in what he called the "dummy" classes. He started to feel even worse, so he just stopped coming. He then told me that the school doesn't do anything but have people talk to his parents. He just comes back for a while to get people off his parents' back, and then he just stops coming again. As soon as he can, he's not coming back at all.

I asked him what he would do if he dropped out. He said all his brothers dropped out and got jobs. One was a waiter, another worked as a laborer for a construction site. They had money to spend and no one on the job hassled them because they hadn't finished school. That's what he would do so he could buy a car and hang out. All that bad stuff that is supposed to happen to you if you dropped out of school was a lie. School couldn't help him get what he wanted; it was just a waste of time.

● **How is the concept of self-efficacy relevant to what Louis has to say about school? Why is Louis' experience with school an example of reciprocal determinism? How does the disinhibitory effect relate to Louis' decision to drop out of school?**

Decision Point: Given this information provided by Louis, what might Daleesha do to try to change his attitudes toward school?

Inhibitory and Disinhibitory Effect. Inhibitions are the mental restrictions we place on our behaviors. For example, most of us would not yell "fire" in a crowded theater. We inhibit that behavior for our own welfare and the welfare of others. According to Bandura (1965, 1986), inhibitions can be strengthened or weakened by what people observe happening to others.

The **inhibitory effect** occurs when a modeling experience serves to strengthen inhibitions for a behavior because the learner observes a model receiving aversive consequences for that behavior. For example, a young girl answers a question in class, and other students make fun of her. Her participation behavior will be affected directly by this. However, other students who observe her experience might be less likely to participate also. They have learned vicariously that there are unpleasant consequences for participating. They strengthen their inhibitions for that behavior, and they choose not to participate.

The opposite of the inhibitory effect is the **disinhibitory effect.** Disinhibitory effects occur when learners engage in a previously inhibited behavior because a model is observed engaging in that behavior without the anticipated aversive consequences. The models are either not punished for engaging in the behavior, or they may even receive reinforcement. For example, students in a speech class are terrified to be the first person to give a speech because they anticipate all forms of personal humiliation. As it turns out, however, the first one or two students to give their speeches have nothing bad happen to them. Some students may have their inhibitions weakened by this experience, and they now volunteer to give their speeches. Their behavior has been disinhibited.

How are the inhibitory and disinhibitory effects different?

The disinhibitory effect is useful for understanding certain classroom management issues. Some misbehaviors are highly contagious. If some students engage in these behaviors with no apparent consequences, other students are likely to engage in those behaviors. For example, if one student makes animal noises without moving his lips and *gets away* with it, that behavior is likely to spread. From a social cognitive view, the other students' misbehavior is disinhibited. For highly contagious behaviors, you should intervene quickly to prevent the disinhibitory or spreading effect (Kounin, 1977).

Response Facilitation.   Bandura (1986) refers to the third performance effect as the response facilitation effect. **Response facilitation** occurs when a model's behavior serves as a social cue or reminder for the learners to engage in the same behavior. With response facilitation, there are no observed consequences for the behavior. The model's behavior just prompts the same behavior from the learner. For example, one student puts her name on the top of a paper, and others who observe this do the same because of what they observed. Their responses have been facilitated. Children have just completed a play for their parents, and a few parents stand up and applaud. Pretty soon, the whole audience is standing. Although some of the last parents to stand might do so in part because of mild social pressure, many of the parents stand because they have been cued to do so. Their behavior has been facilitated.

Here are some ideas for using the performance effects of modeling in your classroom.

- Target social behaviors you want to facilitate in students, and then model these behaviors consistently. For example, if the goal is to facilitate love of reading, you should show how much you enjoy reading.
- Make sure that your discipline actions match your stated rules and consequences. Students often attend more to what you do than what you say. If you do not follow through on what you have said to students, others may observe this and disinhibit their misbehaviors.

Learning Effects.   **Observational learning** is Bandura's term for modeling experiences that result in learners acquiring new behaviors, cognitive processes, judgmental standards, or rules that allow learners to generate new behaviors (Bandura, 1977, 1986). Observational learning can produce completely new understandings, or it can result in new ways of organizing and combining existing understandings (Bandura, 1986). A wide variety of behaviors and understandings can be acquired through observational learning. For example, students can acquire basic literacy skills, classroom discourse patterns, aggressive tendencies, and health-related knowledge through observational learning (Cox, McKendree, Tobin, Lee, & Mayes, 1999; Foshee, Bauman, & Linder, 1999; Horner, 2001; Lee, Dineen, McKendree, & Mayes, 1999; Tripp, Herrmann, Parcel, Chamberlain, & Gritz, 2000).

Observational learning can also occur in different ways. It can occur as a result of the intentional efforts of teachers or parents to teach new skills or standards of behavior through modeling. For example, a biology teacher may use the processes of observational learning to teach students how to use the scientific method in their problem solving. Observational learning can also occur in more incidental or unintended ways. For example, parents often worry about the new negative behaviors that children will learn from other students at school.

One important result of observational learning can be the acquisition of general rules or principles. Bandura uses the term **abstract modeling** to describe this possibility. Through abstract modeling, learners can create a generalization or principle that connects several related but different experiences (Bandura, 1971, 1977, 1986). This principle or generalization allows learners to produce novel behaviors that they have not observed. Consider this example.

➤ Mary Paulson has watched several different third grade teachers' approaches to classroom management. Her somewhat novel approach to classroom management has developed by combining what she has seen in ways that fit her own personal style of working with students.

Observational Learning Process.   The process of observational learning is defined in terms of four types of activities that need to occur for people to learn through modeling. These four activities or components are attention, retention, production, and motivation (Bahn, 2001; Bandura, 1977; Ferrari, 1996).

The introduction of a model into an environment does not guarantee that students will learn from that model. Successful observational learning depends in part on learners' ability to pay **attention** effectively to the model. Observational learning may be unsuccessful because learners do not attend to the model at all, they fail to focus their attention on the key components of the modeling, or they may not interpret the modeling appropriately (Bandura, 1971).

Students' prior knowledge and experience level influence where they focus their attention. Young and inexperienced learners, for example, often have difficulty determining where to focus attention during learning, and consequently they may fail to focus on the critical elements of the learning situation (Broderick & Blewitt, 2003; Maccoby & Hagen, 1965). Because of this, models often need to include specific guidance on what is important to focus on during learning. When you are providing the modeling, you can focus students' attention with statements such as, "The next part is really important." When using verbal directions as a model, you could place stars by key components or highlight them in a different color. These alerting cues are particularly important if the modeling is complex or unfamiliar to the learners (Bandura, 1986).

> **Why would prior knowledge and experience influence where students focus attention?**

Retention involves creating and storing knowledge representations that guide behavior. A knowledge representation might be a mental picture of how to do something, or a set of directions that guide behavior. In order to profit from modeling, students need to develop and retain these knowledge representations. Ideas discussed about encoding and retrieval in Chapter 3 are relevant here.

First, modeling can be complicated and contain multiple steps or components. To reduce working memory load, complicated procedures may need to be broken down into steps or components and modeled one at a time. You can also help your learners by displaying the steps in a complicated procedure on a poster or on an overhead that they can refer to until they have encoded the steps.

Second, modeled events are more effectively retained if they are likened to well-known experiences of the learner (Gerst, 1971). As you may remember from Chapter 3, this is a form of elaboration. For example, teachers may be asked to think of the stages in direct instruction as stages in gardening. Before planting a seed, the soil must be prepared because it increases the likelihood that the seed will grow. In the same sense, the first steps of direct instruction involve preparing learners by helping them engage in activities such as activating relevant prior knowledge.

> **Practice with feedback is important for acquiring observed skills.**

Third, students' retrieval of learned material is improved if they have retrieval cues. Consequently, providing a mnemonic for the steps in a modeled procedure might be helpful. For example, students might be taught the acronym PROWL for the steps in an approach for writing an essay question (Plan, Read, Outline, Write, Look over). The mnemonic gives them an additional retrieval cue.

The **production** component of observational learning deals with converting the mental representations to motor activity. For example, once students have acquired the mental representation PROWL for writing an essay test, they then need to put that knowledge to use. When students are practicing what they have seen modeled, they need feedback on how they are doing. The implication for teachers is that students need some opportunity to practice what they have learned with supervision.

In some cases, the processes you are teaching through observational learning are not readily observable. For example, a learning strategy may be executed through a series of thought processes that cannot be observed directly. If you are going to provide feedback to your students, you will need to make their internal mental processes observable. You may request that they verbalize their thought processes so you can provide feedback to them. For example, you might ask students to talk through the processes they used to solve a math problem.

From a social cognitive perspective, students may learn something but decide not to demonstrate that learning. According to Bandura (1986), this is most likely to occur when there are few if any incentives for performing a behavior, or if the behavior carries a high risk of punishment. This is where the **motivation** subprocesses become important. You can help by showing students the benefits of what has been modeled and by managing the risks involved in performing a new behavior.

How do teachers encourage students to try the behaviors they model for them?

The benefits of a modeled behavior can be established through direct, vicarious, and self-reinforcement opportunities (Bahn, 2001). For example, if students are reinforced directly for a behavior or see others being reinforced for a behavior, they are more likely to engage in that behavior. Students can also self-reinforce by monitoring the positive effects of their behavior. For example, they might keep track of their own progress in learning a new skill.

Remember that learning something new or different can be hard at first. Also, learners' first attempts at applying what they are learning are likely to be awkward and unskilled. Support learners at these times by providing encouragement such as, "It is hard right now, but with practice it will get easier." You might also schedule class time so that students can share their experiences as they try to implement what they are learning. Beyond providing the aforementioned opportunity for feedback, these discussions may help students understand that it is possible to get better with practice, and that their difficulties are not necessarily unique or the result of a lack of ability.

Here are some additional ideas for incorporating observational learning into your classroom.

- Use role-playing to teach social behaviors to students. For example, young children might role-play how to approach others to ask them if they can play with them.
- When presenting content, also consider demonstrating to students any strategies or techniques you use to help you learn this type of content.

Review of Modeling Effects.   In review, modeling can influence both performance and learning. The inhibitory effect, the disinhibitory effect, and the facilitating effect are the three types of performance effects. Observational learning is the term reserved for acquiring new understandings through modeling. Table 4.1 provides a summary and comparison of these modeling effects.

Variables That Influence the Success of Modeling.   As you can see from Table 4.2, the success of modeling is influenced by the characteristics of the model, the characteristics of the learner, and the characteristics of the modeled behavior (Druckman & Bjork, 1991; Ferrari, 1996). Even though your authors discuss these categories separately, so-

TABLE 4.1   A Comparison of Modeling Effects

Modeling Effect	Learning or Performance Effect	Nature of the Influence	Example
Observational learning	Learning	New behaviors, dispositions, or knowledge are acquired	A child learns to color within the lines by observing an older sibling
Inhibitory effect	Performance	The inhibitions for enacting a behavior are strengthened	A model gets detention for a behavior; other students don't do that behavior
Disinhibitory effect	Performance	Learners' inhibitions for a behavior are weakened	A student isn't punished for throwing food at lunch; other students throw food
Facilitating effect	Performance	Behaviors are cued by a model's behavior	A parent buckles a seat belt; the child buckles up too, without being told

Looking in on

Today I started teaching Ellen some strategies for taking notes from a textbook. I began by telling her that these note-taking techniques have worked well for me and for other students. I taught her these techniques by putting a page of text on an overhead projector and by showing her how I would take notes on this page of text. To help Ellen follow what I was doing, I also provided her with a list of the key note-taking techniques I would be demonstrating. I tried to keep the list down to four or five important strategies, because I didn't want to give Ellen too many ideas to think about at one time. Also, I demonstrated one strategy at a time and gave her time to ask questions. Over the next couple of weeks, we'll both take our own notes from her reading assignments from class, and I will compare her notes with mine. That way I can give her suggestions for improvement. I hope I will be able to show her tangible results if her class grades improve. I'm also thinking about having her work occasionally with two other students who are using these techniques successfully. They are doing quite a bit better on tests, but I am still continuing to work with them to help them be better learners.

● **How has Ann Guiter used her understanding of the attention, retention, production, and motivation components of an observational learning lesson in the note-taking lesson?**

Decision Point: Why is Ann Guiter thinking about having Ellen work in a group with other students she is teaching?

cial cognitive theorists believe that these variables mutually influence each other. For example, if a student has a high level of self-efficacy, she may be willing to try harder behaviors, and succeeding at these harder behaviors can elevate her self-efficacy.

Characteristics of the Model.   Learners are likely to attend to models that appear to have competence, power, or prestige (Bandura, 1971, 1986; Sasso & Rude, 1987; Schunk, 1987). In part, this is because these models have achieved some success through their behaviors. Interestingly, learners' perceptions of models' prestige can often extend beyond their areas of demonstrated competence (Rosenthal & Bandura, 1978). For example, young children may think that their parents can do anything.

Model similarity is another important model characteristic, especially for helping learners judge the appropriateness of a behavior and for helping learners develop certain belief systems (Schunk, 1987). For example, young boys and girls may look to their peers to determine if their behavior is age or gender appropriate.

Important self-belief systems such as self-efficacy are also influenced by exposure to peers of similar age and competency level (Brown & Inouye, 1978). This idea is reflected in the distinctions made between coping and mastery models (Braaksma, Rijlaorsdam, & van den Bergh, 2002; Schunk, 1995; Schunk, Hanson, & Cox, 1987; Thelen, Fry, Fehrenbach, & Frautschi, 1979).

A **mastery model** is one who performs a behavior flawlessly and with great confidence. A mastery model can demonstrate how a performance can be done eventually. For example, a master teacher can show beginning teachers what highly skilled teaching looks like.

TABLE 4.2   Variables That Influence Modeling

Model Characteristics	Learner Characteristics	Modeled Behavior
Power	Developmental status	Complexity
Prestige	Goals	Unfamiliarity
Competence	Self-efficacy	Functional value
Similarity	Outcome expectations	

Successful athletes or musicians often are models for students.

Coping models demonstrate what people go through when they are first learning. They demonstrate less confidence than mastery models, and they make the errors or missteps common when people are first learning. However, they also demonstrate how to manage frustration and how improvement is possible with effort. For example, you may learn how to cope with the day-to-day frustrations of being a beginning teacher by watching another new teacher who has figured out how to improve. Coping models may be particularly beneficial for the self-efficacy and skill development of students who have little familiarity with the demands of an academic task and who have had difficulties learning in the past (Schunk, 1995). However, the effects of any model seem to be influenced by model and learner similarity (Braaksma et al., 2002).

Learner Characteristics. Learners' developmental status and prior experience influence their ability to profit from modeling in a number of ways. First, young and experienced learners may have difficulty selecting and attending to the important aspects of modeling. Second, young and inexperienced learners may have underdeveloped strategies for encoding new learning and for managing working memory load (Berk, 1996). Third, very young learners also have less capability to use verbal representational systems, which influences the speed with which they learn and also the generalizability of what they have learned (Bandura, 1971, 1977). Finally, young learners may lack the prerequisite motor and cognitive skills needed for the required learning or performance. This final issue became painfully obvious to one of your authors as he tried to teach his two-year-old son to pitch and catch a baseball. This parent's enthusiasm clearly exceeded the child's ability to reproduce the required physical behaviors.

Learners' willingness and capability to profit from modeling are also influenced by their goals. Learners are more likely to attend to modeling that helps in their progress toward their goals (Bandura, 1986). For instance, student teachers are likely to pay close attention to what their supervising teachers do and say.

Learners' self-efficacy beliefs and their outcome expectations also affect their ability to profit from modeling. For example, self-efficacy influences their beliefs about the likelihood that they can succeed at the modeled behavior (Schunk, 1987). **Outcome expectations** are learners' beliefs about the possible outcomes for engaging in a behavior. Learners are more likely to learn and engage in behaviors that will help them achieve desired outcomes. For example, a learner may believe that if she can learn to use a particular strategy, it will help her read better. If this is a desired outcome, the learner is more likely to engage in the learning process.

Characteristics of the Modeled Behavior. Some modeling stimuli are more complex than others. Also, learners differ in terms of how familiar they are with the information conveyed by the model. Both of these factors influence the outcomes of modeling. In general, complex and unfamiliar behaviors are harder to learn. You may find that you need to do a number of things to assist your learners in those situations. You may need to provide more guidance and practice time for the learner; you may need to break down the modeling stimulus into more manageable parts; or you may need to slow down the pace of the lesson.

Learners are more likely to learn and perform behaviors that have functional value (Bandura, 1971; Schunk, 2001). **Functional value** means that the modeled behavior is clearly linked to positive outcomes for the model. The learner anticipates that the behavior will have the same consequences for them. Consider this example.

➤ John has learned that students who act up in class get a lot of positive attention from other students, and the teacher doesn't seem to stop them. He starts acting up also.

You want your students to be aware of the functional value of appropriate behaviors. For example, if you only attend to misbehaviors, students may observe that the only way to earn your attention is through misbehavior, and these misbehaviors then have functional value in that classroom. To avoid this, you should frequently and consistently reinforce desirable behaviors, while being consistent in the punishment of inappropriate behaviors.

How is the idea of outcome expectations related to the idea of functional value?

Here are some ideas to guide your application of factors that influence the success of modeling.

- Post your rules and consequences so that students know what are the likely outcomes of certain behaviors. Also, be consistent in your application of the rules and consequences so that students get clear, unambiguous information about behavioral outcomes.
- Help students think about long-term outcomes for certain behaviors. For example, teachers may need to help students understand the benefits of particular courses for career goals.
- Involve your students in setting rules or explain to students the reasons for your rules and consequences, so they can understand why it is to their benefit to follow the rules.
- Assess students to determine if they have the prerequisite knowledge or skills for what you are trying to teach through observational learning.
- Remember that young learners and inexperienced learners have difficulty knowing where to focus attention. Provide prompts or signals to identify the critical aspects of the model.
- Manage working memory load issues for inexperienced and young learners by breaking complicated behaviors into steps or parts.
- Try to demonstrate to students why a modeled behavior is important to learn and use. For example, have students self-report on how a strategy is helping them in the classroom.
- Use groups of heterogeneous ability in your class so that students have access to both student mastery and coping models.
- Use peer tutors in the classroom to provide access to models that are similar to the learners.

*S*elf-Regulated Learning

Helping learners develop the ability to self-regulate their own learning is an important goal for many cognitive theories including information-processing theory and the cognitive developmental theories discussed in the next chapter. Social cognitive theory is no exception. In 1993, Bandura wrote, "A major goal of formal education should be to equip students with the intellectual tools, self-beliefs and self-regulatory capabilities to educate themselves throughout their lifetime" (p. 136).

Social Cognitive Definition of Self-Regulated Learning

Learners who are effective at self-regulating their own learning processes tend to achieve better than students who are not (Biemiller & Meichenbaum, 1992;

Meichenbaum & Bielmiller, 1998). From a social cognitive perspective, learners self-regulate through these three activities.

- Learners set challenging but achievable goals for themselves (intention and forethought) (Schunk, 1990).
- Learners select and employ effective strategies to achieve their goals (intention and forethought) (Zimmerman, 1999).
- Learners employ self-regulation strategies such as self-observation, self-judgment, and self-administered consequences to motivate and guide their learning (self-reactiveness and self-reflectiveness) (Bandura, 1977; Bandura & Cervone, 1983).

An important determining factor in learners' ability to engage in these self-regulation activities is their self-efficacy (Grusec, 1992; Zimmerman, 1999). Self-regulatory efficacy refers to students' beliefs that they can engage in the behaviors necessary to self-manage their learning.

Self-Efficacy.   As noted earlier in the chapter, self-efficacy is learners' personal sense that they can have some control over experiences that affect them (Bandura, 1977, 1995, 1997; Bong & Skaalvik, 2003; Zimmerman, 2000). In classrooms, self-efficacy involves learners' personal assessment of their ability to succeed at academic tasks. Self-efficacy, along with learners' ability to set goals, have been found to be two key motivational variables in achievement (Zimmerman, Bandura, & Martinez-Pons, 1992).

Sources for Determining Self-Efficacy.   Learners' self-efficacy beliefs develop from their own direct experiences with success and failure, vicarious experiences, verbal persuasion, and their physiological reactions (Schunk, 1996; Zimmerman, 2000). Learners cognitively evaluate each of these experiences to determine their personal meaning for them. As a result, the same experience may affect different learners in different ways.

Learners' own direct experiences with success and failure are a highly influential source of information about self-efficacy because they provide personally relevant information about the likelihood of future successes and failure (Bandura, Adams, & Beyer, 1977; Pajares, 2003; Wise & Trunnell, 2001). There is an old saying that if all things are equal, past experience is a good predictor of future experience. Students who continually try and fail or continually try and succeed both have powerful evidence of the likelihood of future success.

How is the idea of a coping model relevant here?

Vicarious experience can also influence self-efficacy. Observing the successes or failures of people who are similar to us is likely to affect our sense of self-efficacy (Bandura, 1986).

Verbal persuasion is an attempt by others to influence a person's self-efficacy through what they say to that person. For example, you may tell students that you think they are great math students to try to increase their sense of self-efficacy. The impact of verbal persuasion on self-efficacy depends on the believability of the verbal message (Lackey, Miller, & Flanigan, 1997). Also, the effects of verbal persuasion are usually short-lived, especially if the verbal message is countered by direct experience (Bandura, 1993). Students who are told that they can learn may have trouble believing that message if they continue to fail. Consequently, the verbal message should be supported by success experiences students have earned through their efforts.

Certain physiological responses are associated with the anticipation of success and failure (Lackey, Miller, and Flanigan, 1997; Schunk, 1996). Sweating, blushing, fatigue, and anxiety are often associated with the anticipation of failure. If these physiological responses occur, they provide further data to students about the likelihood of their success. Teachers should create classroom environments in which students feel emotionally supported.

In today's schools, the goal is to include students with special needs as much as possible in the regular education classroom. This means that you are likely to have students in your classroom with mental retardation, learning disabilities, and other special learning needs. You need to be prepared for the learning and motivational needs of these students.

Students with special learning needs typically have had a history of school or social failures. Because of these failure experiences, they may develop a motivational belief system called *learned helplessness* (Hallahan & Kaufmann, 2000; Marks, 1998; Settle & Milich, 1999; Valäs, 2001). Learned helplessness is students' belief that no matter what they do, they are likely to fail (Seligman, 1992). Helpless students believe they do not control their behavioral outcomes (Nurmi, Onatsu, & Haavisto, 1995). In social cognitive terms, these learners develop very low self-efficacy for classroom learning. Students with learned helplessness often reduce their effort at school because they believe that effort will not matter. This results in more failure experiences that reinforce the learned helplessness beliefs while also preventing them from learning needed skills (Borkowski, 1992).

Teachers' attempts to break this motivational cycle are often complicated because these students also lack knowledge of effective learning strategies and a sense of when and how to use these strategies. (Hallahan & Bryan, 1981; Torgesen, 1977). One place to start, therefore, is to teach your students learning strategies, while helping them develop a more optimistic view of themselves as learners.

● **Using what you have read about topics such as self-efficacy and goal-setting, explain how you might help these students develop more positive self-efficacy beliefs. (For your authors' perspective on this question, go to the text website for this chapter.)**

Self-Efficacy Effects on Achievement. Self-efficacy beliefs influence thought processes, emotions, and behaviors. More specifically, students' perceived self-efficacy can influence their choice of activities, the quantity and quality of their efforts, their persistence in the face of adversity, and their emotional responses.

Students' self-efficacy beliefs influence their choices of activities in a number of ways. First, students tend to engage in tasks that they feel confident about and to avoid tasks for which they lack confidence (Pajares & Schunk, 2002). Second, levels of self-efficacy are correlated with levels of intrinsic interest in tasks (Zimmerman & Kitsantos, 1997, 1999). Students tend to be interested in activities at which they can succeed and are more likely to engage in activities that interest them (Pajares & Schunk, 2001; Schraw, Flowerday, & Lehman, 2001). Third, self-efficacy beliefs can influence the level of challenge students choose for themselves. Students with higher levels of self-efficacy are likely to select harder goals for themselves (Pajares & Schunk, 2001; Zimmerman, Bandura, & Martinez-Pons, 1992). Fourth, self-efficacy beliefs have been found to be an important factor in students' career choices (Bandura, Barbaranelli, Caprara, & Pastorelli, 2001; Betz & Hackett, 1997; Hackett, 1995; Panagos & Dubois, 1999; Sullivan & Mahalik, 2000). Students are likely to avoid course work and occupations for which their self-efficacy is low.

Self-efficacy beliefs also affect the amount and type of effort students expend on an academic task. Students with high levels of self-efficacy are more likely to believe that they can succeed with additional effort (Alden, 1986). Self-efficacy beliefs also influence students' willingness to use effective learning strategies and to discard faulty strategies that aren't working (Linnenbrink & Pintrich, 2003; Schunk, 1996; Walker, 2003; Zimmerman & Martinez-Pons, 1990).

Persistence is students' willingness to continue to try in the face of adversity. Students with high levels of self-efficacy tend to continue to expend effort when they encounter adversity (Jinks & Morgan, 1999; Lackey, Miller, & Flanigan, 1997; Pajares, 1997; Schunk & Pajares, 2002; Zimmerman, 2000). This willingness to persist is important when students are engaged in learning new and complicated skills.

Finally, self-efficacy is related to a number of important emotional responses. High levels of self-efficacy are associated with decreased levels of stress, anxiety, and depression (Bandura, 1997; Pajares & Kranzler, 1995). Also, people who have high self-efficacy for their ability to cope with emotional challenges are more likely to take on emotionally threatening situations (Bandura, 1998). In general, students who believe they can succeed tend to develop more positive emotional reactions about learning.

How to Enhance Self-Efficacy.   Given the importance of self-efficacy as a motivational factor, classroom environments need to facilitate high levels of student self-efficacy. Higher levels of student self-efficacy can be encouraged in a number of ways (Bandura, 1993; Fall & McLeod, 2001; Schunk, 1987, 1996; Walker, 2003; Zimmerman, 2000).

- Help students develop the idea that ability can be acquired and improved. This can be accomplished in general by making sure that students are working toward achievable improvement goals, and by providing students with the help they need to achieve those goals.

Why might teachers allow students to get help and redo assignments that were difficult for them?

- Downplay social comparisons and academic competition. Instead, emphasize self-comparisons. For example, have students chart their own improvement or use evaluation approaches such as portfolios that show improvement.
- Help students believe that they can succeed through effort. Teach students cognitive and metacognitive strategies that will help them improve their performance.
- Provide frequent feedback to students about their progress.
- Provide instructional materials and experiences that are moderately challenging, but that are at the students' instructional level.

What ideas might enhance students' self-efficacy?

- If students are discouraged, stress improvement in small increments. Start with tasks students can succeed at and gradually increase task difficulty.
- Provide students with some choice in what and how they learn to promote a sense of personal control over their learning.

How is goal-setting related to the concept of metacognition?

Goal Setting.   Goals are important for self-regulation because they specify standards for success. They also prompt learners to monitor their progress toward their goals and to modify their efforts to increase the likelihood of reaching their goals (Bandura, 1991). Helping learners to be effective goal setters can improve both their sense of self-efficacy and their achievement (Bandura & Schunk, 1981).

Goals are likely to be more useful to learners if they meet certain criteria (Locke & Latham, 1990; Ridley, Schutz, Glanz, & Weinstein, 1992). First, the goals should be specific. Vaguely conceptualized goals are hard to monitor and evaluate. It is better to specify the types of improvements that are desired. For example, rather than setting a goal to be a better student, a student might focus on reading the assigned material for tomorrow's class.

Second, goals should be reasonably challenging. They should not be set so high that failure is guaranteed, but they should not be set so low that minimal effort is required to accomplish the goals. If goals are both specific and reasonably challenging, students often can improve their motivation to perform (Locke & Latham, 1994).

How does this relate to the idea of shaping from Chapter 2?

Goals should be proximal, which means that learners should think in terms of short-term goals that lead eventually to their long-term goals (Bandura & Schunk, 1981). For example, you could talk to students about what they would like to accomplish today or this week that will help them accomplish their long-term goals.

Selecting Effective Strategies.   To be successful, learners need to possess appropriate learning strategies, and they need to apply them when it would be useful. We have referred to these activities previously as metacognitive activities. It is insufficient to

Looking in on

After I listened carefully to Louis describe his beliefs about school, I told him I thought he was very smart and really understood himself and others well. I also reminded him that state law would not let him drop out now. Since he needed to be here, I wanted him to give me a chance to show that school could be helpful. For example, we have some special computer programs and tutors that are designed to help students catch up in school. A number of his classmates have used them and done very well, and I would be glad to ask some of them to talk to him about them. Also, I would like to get him involved in our work-study program next semester when he is old enough. As long as he is making progress in school, he can have a part-time job with one of our partner companies. When he finishes school, they will enroll him in a job-training program. At the end of the training, he will have a better paying job than he could get without the training, and there is a chance to be promoted to a better job. However, for all of this to work, he has to come to school now. I told him we would just focus on next week. His goal would be to attend class every day next week. We will worry about the following weeks later. He said that would be hard, and he might not be able to do a whole week. We decided to take it one day at a time. We put a calendar up, and I asked him to put a mark on it each day he came to school.

Daleesha Goodwin

4.2

● **How are the social cognitive ideas of vicarious learning, outcome expectations, and goal setting relevant to this situation.**

Decision Point: What else could Daleesha do to encourage Louis to stay in school?

---

teach learners how to study and learn, unless teachers also help them develop the beliefs that strategies will help them and the understanding of when to use particular strategies. For example, Rebok and Balcerak (1989) taught elderly adults to use a mnemonic to help their memory performance. Although the mnemonic helped, the training did not necessarily create a sense of memory efficacy, which was defined as the belief that memory can be improved. As a result, only 39 percent of the adults who were trained generalized the strategy to other settings. Learners need both knowledge of strategies and a sense that they can improve their performance. We revisit strategic learning in Chapter 8.

Why would self-efficacy affect students' willingness to try a strategy they just learned in another setting?

Self-Regulating Behaviors. Self-regulation involves self-observation, self-judgment, and self-administered consequences (Bandura, 1971, 1986). Self-observation includes activities designed to help learners develop an awareness of their own behavior by observing it. Self-judgment is when learners assess their behavior in terms of its functional value and its relationship to the learners' goals. For example, students might pick what they consider to be their best artwork for a student show. Self-administered consequences are reinforcements and punishments that learners administer to themselves. Typically, learners also determine when they have met the criteria for these consequences. These three activities have been translated into three intervention approaches: self-monitoring, self-reinforcement, and self-instructional programs.

Self-monitoring involves procedures that require learners to observe and record their own behavior systematically (Kanfer & Goldstein, 1986; Kazdin, 1982; Mace, Belfiore, & Hutchinson, 2001; Reid, 1996). Typically, learners are asked to make a mark on a recording form every time a behavior occurs, answer questions about their behavior, or complete a checklist. For example, a shy learner might put a mark on the card every time she participates in class, or she might answer a series of yes or no questions about how she participated in class. Self-monitoring programs have been developed for a variety of purposes including improving students' on-task behavior, academic production, strategy use, and social skills (Allsopp, Santos, & Linn, 2000; Carr & Punzo, 1993; Hallahan, Lloyd, Kosiewicz, Kauffman, & Graves, 1979; Jitendra, Hoppes, & Xin, 2000; Peterson, Young, West, & Peterson, 1999; Reid, 1996; Shimabukuro, Prater, Jenkins, & Edelen-Smith, 1999).

Looking in on

Ann Guiter

4.2

As we were working together, Ellen told me that she can understand the words she is reading in the textbook, but that she is prone to daydream when she reads. Usually, she is unaware of this, and she gets frustrated because she spends a lot of time in front of a book with no payoff for her as a learner. Once she understood the note-taking techniques, I decided to teach her another strategy that might help her. I told her to write, "What did I just read?" on an index card and to put the card in the book as a bookmark for how far she wanted to read. I suggested at first that she set the goal of reading a couple of pages. I told her when she came to the bookmark, she should try to answer this question for the section she just read. If she can answer the question, she congratulates herself on being a successful reader and she continues to read. If she can't answer the question, then I want her to ask these questions:

(1) Was I paying attention? If not, I need to re-read this. (2) Do I need to look up some words? If so I have my dictionary with me. (3) Do I need to ask my teacher questions about what I didn't understand? If so, I should write them down so I don't forget them. Ellen told me that she had seen someone use this strategy in one of her classes. The other students noticed the card and started making fun of that student. She didn't think she wanted to try this.

● **How has Ann Guiter incorporated opportunities for self-monitoring, self-reinforcement, and self-instructional statements into the reading strategy? How is the concept of an inhibitory effect relevant to this situation?**

Decision Point: How might Ann Guiter modify this strategy so that Ellen will be more willing to use it?

Self-reinforcement programs involve four basic components (Graham, Harris, & Reid, 1992).

- Determining the standards for earning a reward
- Selecting the reinforcer to be earned
- Evaluating performance
- Self-administering the reinforcer

How could you use self-reinforcement in your own learning?

Teachers may meet with students to set classroom goals. Students would then identify reinforcements they want to earn for meeting the goals. When students determine they have met the goals, they reinforce themselves. One concern that teachers have with an approach such as this is that students may not set challenging enough goals, or they may be lenient in their self-assessments. There is some evidence that this can occur (Felixbrod & O'Leary, 1974), so you will want to work cooperatively with students in establishing goals and standards of performance.

Self-instructional programs involve providing students with a set of written or verbal prompts they can use to guide their thinking and problem solving (Bambara & Gomez, 2001; Meichenbaum & Goodman, 1971). There are six basic forms of self-instructions that can be used in combination or in isolation (Graham, Harris, & Reid, 1992).

- **Problem definition instructions.** Students may ask, "What is my problem?"
- **Focusing attention and planning instructions.** Students might tell themselves, "I need to concentrate. What distractions need to be removed?"
- **Strategy instructions.** Students talk themselves through the steps in a strategy. Students might say, "The first step in solving a story problem is to draw a picture."
- **Self-evaluating and error correcting instructions.** Students evaluate their performance to catch mistakes or deviations from their strategy. A student might say, "I forgot to provide the units for my math answer," or "I need to check for spelling errors."
- **Coping and self-control instructions.** Students help themselves cope with frustration or negative emotions such as anxiety. A student might say, "I can do this. I just need to follow my plan."

- **Self-reinforcement instructions.** A student might say, "I did that one just right."

A number of different self-instructional programs have been developed for use in the classroom. For example, *Think Aloud* is a classroom program that makes extensive use of self-instruction to help students manage their impulses (Camp, 1977; Camp & Bash, 1978; Camp, Blom, Hebert, & van Doornick, 1977). As part of this program, students are taught this four-step self-instructional program for problem solving.

- What is my problem?
- What can I do?
- Am I using my plan?
- How did I do?

The three-step self-instructional program of cover, copy, and compare is a second self-instructional approach, and it has been taught to students to help them study for tests in a number of academic areas (McLaughlin & Skinner, 1996; Struthers, Struthers, & Williams, 1983). For example, when studying for a spelling test, students would look at a word, cover it, try to copy it, and then compare to see how they had done.

Here are some additional ideas for encouraging your students to self-regulate their learning.

- Use written and oral contracts with students to set reasonably challenging goals.
- Have students write about what they would like to be doing in five or ten years and have discussions about how to realize those goals.
- Do goal-setting conferences with student as part of report card process. Have them self-evaluate progress and set goals for the next grading period.
- Introduce students to a variety of problem-solving and learning strategies at different times and in different contexts. Teachers in a school could identify a series of learning strategies and introduce them in different content areas.
- Help students identify the appropriate times to use the strategies they have learned. Talk to students about when a memory strategy such as a mnemonic should be used.
- Allow students some input into the grades they earned. For example, students could present their ideas about the grade they think they deserve.
- Have students select the portfolio work samples that they think best represent their learning.
- Videotape students' performances and allow them to assess their own performance.
- Have students work as peer tutors in lower grades, so they can assess what they have learned.
- Have students write down their major class accomplishments for a grading period.
- Teach students to talk themselves through difficult problems.
- Teach students to use simple work-checking routines such as reversing math operations to check their accuracy.

HAVE YOU PROOFREAD YOUR WORK?

1. Use a red pen or pencil.
2. Check for spelling. Use the dictionary.
3. Check for punctuation.
4. Look for run-on sentences.
5. Do you have a good introduction?
6. Does your ending summarize your discussion?
7. Do you have a title?

Self-instruction helps guide students' behaviors.

Social Cognitive Learning Principles

One of the themes of this book is that appropriate application of psychological theory improves the quality of teachers' decisions. Social cognitive learning theory provides a number of useful concepts for your classroom decision making. To help you apply these concepts, we have summarized them in terms of three major learning principles. In later chapters, these principles are used to organize discussions about the decisions involved in determining how to teach and how to manage classroom behavior and how to assess learning.

Principle 4.1: Learners Acquire Important Knowledge, Behaviors, and Dispositions through Their Exposure to Models

Bandura's social cognitive theory explains how learning occurs through modeling. Bandura's ideas about vicarious consequences, performance effects of modeling, observational learning, and variables that influence the success of modeling are all important concepts for implementing this principle.

Principle 4.1 has an important implication for classroom teaching and classroom management. Skills, social behaviors, strategies, and attitudes in particular are often learned directly or indirectly through modeling. Consequently, the effective use of observational learning is an important tool for enacting some of your decisions about how to teach.

Principle 4.2: Learners' Self-Belief Systems Guide Their Learning and Behavior

According to social cognitive theory, two key learner belief systems are outcome expectations and self-efficacy. In particular, students' self-efficacy impacts on the types and amount of effort students expend in classrooms. Chapter 6 on motivation theory discusses how other self-belief concepts from value x expectancy theory can help support your understanding and application of self-efficacy. For example, you will learn how students' motivational goals are influenced by their expectations for success.

The major implication of Principle 4.2 for your decision making is the need to consider students' self-beliefs when selecting goals and learning experiences for students. Whenever possible, try to create classroom environments that promote a positive sense of self-efficacy among students.

Principle 4.3: Learners Have the Potential to Self-Regulate Their Own Learning Processes

Bandura believes that students self-regulate by setting goals, selecting appropriate strategies to achieve those goals, and by using the self-regulation processes: self-monitoring, self-reinforcement, and self-instruction. The application of Principle 4.3, therefore, is important for achieving the goal of encouraging students to become self-regulating learners.

Principle 4.3 has specific implications for decisions about what to teach. Students often need to develop self-management and learning strategies to succeed. Our classrooms need to be places where these strategies are developed through teaching and approaches to classroom management. Principle 4.3 also has implications for how you assess students' learning. Students need the kinds of experiences that teach them how to self-evaluate their progress as learners.

Principles into Practice:
Illustrating Key Concepts

The experiences of Daleesha Goodwin and Ann Guiter provide examples of how the three social cognitive principles apply to classroom teaching. We asked you to reflect on these applications through a series of questions we asked you when you looked in on these two professionals.

Looking back on

Louis provided Daleesha Goodwin with important insights about his attitudes toward school. Louis revealed low self-efficacy as a student when he told Daleesha that he was "stupid," and that it wouldn't help if he tried. Louis' beliefs about himself as a learner seemed to develop as a result of complex interactions that provide an example of reciprocal determinism. His self-efficacy was influenced by his lack of success in school, which caused him to behave in ways that affected how teachers treated him. His teachers' reactions resulted in him feeling even less capable as a student. Louis' experiences provide a clear example of Principle 4.2, learners' self-belief systems guide their learning and behavior.

Louis' reasons for dropping out provide an example of the disinhibitory effect because he has learned from observing his brothers that you can drop out and nothing bad happens in the short run. In fact, his family models provide evidence that there may even be benefits for dropping out. This interaction with Louis provides an example of Principle 4.1, learners acquire important information, behaviors, and dispositions through their exposure to models.

Later, Daleesha tried to modify Louis' outcome expectations for staying in school by showing him how he could work and go to school and eventually get an even better job through the work-study program. She was trying to connect staying in school with some outcomes Louis desired for himself. She also wanted Louis to improve his school attendance so that he could profit from the work-study program. They engaged in goal setting and were able to identify short-term, achievable goals for Louis. These interactions provide examples of Principle 4.2, learners' self-belief systems guide their learning and behavior, and Principle 4.3, learners have the potential to self-regulate their own learning processes.

Finally, Daleesha wanted Louis to talk to students who had used the computer and tutorial programs successfully. She hoped that Louis could learn vicariously from these students' experiences with these programs. Daleesha is applying Principle 4.1, learners acquire important information, behaviors, and dispositions through their exposure to models. ●

Looking back on

Ann Guiter's note-taking lesson demonstrates all four component processes of observational learning. She focused Ellen's attention on key parts of the lesson by providing Ellen with a list of the note-taking techniques she would be learning. To help Ellen with retention of the note-taking techniques, Ann Guiter presented them systematically and a step at a time, and she restricted the number of ideas she presented. Ellen could also refer to the list of note-taking ideas later if necessary. When Ellen practiced the strategy, she had a chance to compare her efforts with Ann's as a way to provide her with feedback, an important part of the production process. Motivation for the strategy was built by showing Ellen how the strategy helped her do better in class. This use of observational learning demonstrates an important application of Principle 4.1, learners acquire important information, behaviors, and dispositions through their exposure to models.

Later on, Ann Guiter wanted to help Ellen with her tendency to daydream when she was reading. The question, "What did I just read?" was a cue to help Ellen self-monitor. If Ellen could answer this question, she self-reinforced by praising herself. If she could not answer the monitoring question, she was provided with an additional set of monitoring questions and some self-instructional statements to help her read more effectively. This approach is another example of the application of Principle 4.3, learners have the potential to self-regulate their own learning processes. It's interesting that Ellen had noticed what happened to another student who used the note card technique in class. That student got made fun of by other students. As a result, Ellen does not want to use the note card technique. Ann

Guiter will need to address this example of the inhibitory effect. Ellen's behavior provides another example of Principle 4.1, learners acquire important information, behaviors, and dispositions through their exposure to models. ●

Teachers as Decision Makers

During the opportunities to look in on Tom Pierce and Emilio Lopez, you participate in their decision making. Your authors want to share their views of these decision points, and they also want to discuss how the three learning principles developed in this chapter inform discussions of teacher decision making in later chapters.

Daleesha Goodwin's Decision Points

Daleesha is trying to work with Louis, a potential dropout. As we have mentioned before, it's important to make sure you have the information you need to make effective decisions. Louis' most pressing issue is attendance. Because there can be multiple reasons for an attendance problem, Daleesha needs to talk to Louis about why he is missing school. It's easy to make assumptions based on what she knows about him, but she could also be misled by what she knows. Also, he is at risk for failing at least two classes. Daleesha needs to talk to his teachers to see if it's possible for him to pass his courses, and what he will need to do.

When Daleesha met with Louis, he provided valuable information about his attitudes toward school. The attendance issue seems to be connected to his low self-efficacy and the modeling that is being provided by his brothers. This modeling is potentially powerful because his brothers have a number of characteristics of effective models. They are similar to Louis and are likely to have power and prestige for Louis. Her intervention needs to address both of these issues. Her general plan should involve seeking the cooperation of Louis' family and providing academic support for Louis.

Daleesha has a very ambitious plan for helping Louis, but it is worthwhile to consider what else might need to be done. For example, students may be more interested in school if they have personal connections with other students and teachers. Daleesha can provide some of this, but it might be useful to involve other teachers and to consider continuing Louis in one of her groups. One possible benefit of this approach is that Louis has more than one person to go to for help or support. Also, Daleesha is doing something important by involving the community through the work-study and mentoring programs. She may want to extend those efforts. For example, adult education classes may be useful for students who have dropped out and their families.

Ann Guiter's Decision Points

As you remember, Ann Guiter was trying to help Ellen be more successful with textbook reading and studying. Once again, it's important to remember that students can struggle with an academic task such as textbook reading for different reasons. For example, the textbook may be written at too high of a reading level, or Ellen's interest level, prior knowledge, and vocabulary development in the content areas could be partly to blame.

Ann has decided to begin by helping Ellen learn more effective techniques for taking notes. Currently, she is working with Ellen individually, but Ann is considering having Ellen work with other students who are also learning the strategy. Ann could have a number of reasons for wanting to do this. First, these students are similar to Ellen in important ways, and they are starting to improve by using what Ann is teaching them. Consequently, they can serve as powerful coping models for Ellen.

Eventually, we find out that Ellen is reluctant to use the note card strategy because another student got made fun of for using it. Ann has a number of possible ways she could address this. One way is to make the strategy less observable to others. For example, Ellen could just put a hand a few pages back in the book and use her hand as a cue, or maybe Ellen could use the strategy without a physical cue to do so. Having Ellen practice the techniques with a group of other students might also help. She won't feel that she is the only one doing this. Finally, Ann may want to work with the entire class on developing study strategies. That way, Ellen is doing what everyone else is doing.

Looking Ahead: Social Cognitive Principles and Decision Making

One of the themes of this book is that teachers' decision-making processes are is improved through the application of principles from psychological theory. In Chapter 1 your authors identified these three broad categories of teacher decisions that provide opportunities to apply psychological theories.

- Decisions made when planning a lesson
- Decisions made when teaching and managing in the classroom
- Decisions made when assessing the effectiveness of their actions

In later chapters, the principles developed in this chapter are used to organize discussions of applications of social cognitive theory to the decisions teachers make in the areas of instructional delivery, classroom management, and assessment of learning. Table 4.3 allows you to look forward and see the implications of these principles for the types of decision making discussed in those later chapters.

TABLE 4.3	Looking Ahead: Social Cognitive Principles and Decision Making	
Decision Area	**Implication for Practice**	**Looking Ahead**
Principle 4.1: Learners acquire important information, behaviors, and dispositions through their exposure to models		
Teaching and classroom management	Teachers can use what they know about modeling and observational learning to help understand students' social behaviors and to teach new information, behaviors, and dispositions.	Chapters 7, 10
Principle 4.2: Learners' self-belief systems guide their learning and behavior		
Planning	Teachers need to design instruction and classroom environments that promote self-efficacy for learning.	Chapter 8
Teaching and classroom management	Teachers need to understand how self-efficacy and other self-belief systems affect students' motivation to learn.	
	Teachers need to use teaching approaches that encourage students to believe they can succeed.	Chapters 7, 8
Principle 4.3: Learners have the potential to self-regulate their own learning processes		
Planning	Teachers need to create classroom environments that encourage students to self-regulate their learning and behavior.	Chapter 10
Teaching and classroom management	Students need to learn the strategies necessary to self-regulate their learning and behavior.	Chapters 8, 10
Assessment	Students need to learn how to self-assess their own learning.	Chapter 10

Chapter 4 Study Guide

Use this Study Guide to review and test your knowledge of key concepts introduced in this chapter and to search out further information on issues and topics raised in this chapter.

💻 Key Terms

Review the following key words from the chapter and then connect to Research Navigator (www.researchnavigator.com) either directly or through this book's Companion Website to explore research on the topics as they relate to education today.

Abstract modeling (p. 100)
Attention (p. 101)
Coping models (p. 104)
Disinhibitory effect (p. 99)
Enactive learning (p. 94)
Forethought (p. 95)
Functional value (p. 105)
Inhibitory effect (p. 99)
Intention (p. 95)
Live models (p. 98)
Mastery model (p. 103)

Model (p. 98)
Modeling (p. 98)
Motivation (p. 102)
Observational learning (p. 100)
Outcome expectations (p. 104)
Production (p. 101)
Reciprocal determinism (p. 92)
Response facilitation (p. 100)
Retention (p. 101)
Self-efficacy (p. 96)
Self-instructional programs (p. 110)

Self-monitoring (p. 109)
Self-reactiveness (p. 96)
Self-reflectiveness (p. 96)
Self-reinforcement (p. 110)
Symbolic models (p. 98)
Symbolic representation (p. 94)
Verbal description (p. 98)
Vicarious consequences (p. 97)
Vicarious learning (p. 95)

Alternative Response items

1. A kindergarten teacher knows that if she praises one student publicly, other students who see this often mimic the praised behavior. The impact on the other students is an example of:

   a. Enactive learning
   b. Self-efficacy
   c. Vicarious learning
   d. Reciprocal determinism

2. Rhonda times herself each time she runs a mile to see if she is making progress toward her ultimate goal of a five-minute mile. From a social cognitive perspective, this is an example of:

   a. Forethought
   b. Self-reactiveness
   c. Self-reflectiveness
   d. A performance effect

3. Learned helplessness exists when learners believe there is no connection between their efforts and what happens to them. How would social cognitive theorists describe learned helplessness?

   a. A person with learned helplessness has very low self-efficacy.
   b. A person with learned helplessness is overly self-reactive.
   c. A person with learned helplessness cannot learn vicariously.
   d. A person with learned helplessness has been negatively reinforced.

4. Ben posts a list of steps for editing a paper so that his English students can refer to it when they edit. What type of model is he using?

   a. Live model
   b. Symbolic model
   c. Verbal description
   d. Enactive

5. A child learns to throw temper tantrums from watching another child. Which modeling effect is this?

   a. Inhibitory effect
   b. Disinhibitory effect
   c. Response facilitation
   d. Observational learning

6. While demonstrating a math problem, Ms. Begay says to students, "Be careful here. It's very important to do this next step correctly." Which observational learning process is she trying to influence?

   a. Attention
   b. Retention
   c. Production
   d. Motivation

7. John believes he is a good student because he has always done well, and his teachers have told him he is a good student. What two sources for determining self-efficacy is he using?

   a. Vicarious and direct experiences
   b. Physiological responses and direct experiences

c. Verbal persuasion and vicarious experiences
d. Verbal persuasion and direct experiences

8. Gregory places a mark on an index card every time he raises his hand before speaking. What self-regulation activity is this?

a. Self-reinforcement
b. Self-instruction
c. Self-monitoring

9. When Gregory solves math problems, he begins by asking himself, "What type of problem is this? Does it look like one I've done before?" What form of self-instruction is this?

a. Problem definition
b. Focusing attention
c. Coping and self-control
d. Self-reinforcement

10. Paul sees his friends break the rules and leave the playground during recess. They don't get in trouble, so he joins them the next time. What is this an example of?

a. Response facilitation effect
b. Disinhibitory effect
c. Inhibitory effect
d. Observational learning effect

Constructed Response Items

Short Answer/Completion Items

1. Bandura's idea that people and their environment mutually influence each other is _____.

2. The ability to take a future orientation by setting goals and making plans is referred to by Bandura as_____.

3. Sally works hard at her job because she believes that if she works hard she will get raises and a promotion. This is an example of the effects of _____ on behavior.

4. What are the three criteria for effective motivational goals?

Essay Items

1. How would reciprocal determinism explain how two children from the same family might have quite different experiences growing up in the family?

2. Even though there are potential vicarious learning effects, why might teachers want to be reluctant to punish students in front of their classmates?

3. How might teachers' self-efficacy beliefs affect their teaching?

Practicing Your Decision Making

1. Assume that you have a student in class who has trouble paying attention when you are explaining things to your class. How would you use the self-regulation ideas in this chapter to help this student be better at paying attention?

2. How would observational learning be useful to you as a teacher?

INTASC in Action

Use the following activities to think about how social cognitive concepts and principles relate to the INTASC standards.

Standard 2: Student Development. Peer pressure is an important influence on students' social development. How could concepts such as the facilitating effect, the inhibitory effect, and functional value be used to explain how peer pressure operates?

Standard 3: Diverse Learners. Self-efficacy is an important source of individual differences. You will have students with different levels of self-efficacy for what you have to teach. Assume that you have students who believe they never will be successful in your classroom. How would you work with them to improve their self-efficacy?

 Web Resources

Read more about social cognitive theory and related issues by visiting the following websites:

Albert Bandura Bio
www.ship.edu/~cgboeree/bandura.html

Read a biographical sketch of Albert Bandura, the leading theoretician and researcher in the area of social cognitive theory, as presented by Professor George Boeree of Shippensburg University.

Theory into Practice Database
http://tip.psychology.org/

TIP is a database of brief summaries of fifty major theories of learning and instruction and is intended to make learning and instructional theory more accessible to educators.

Cognitive Developmental Theories and Constructivism

Standards in This Chapter

Although learning the concepts and associated principles presented in this chapter will contribute to your mastery of all of the INTASC standards, the material presented in Chapter 5 is most strongly related to the following standards:

● **Standard 2:** Student Development

● **Standard 3:** Diverse Learners

● **Standard 4:** Multiple Instructional Strategies

Cognitive developmental theories provide descriptions of typical developmental changes in mental capabilities and explanations for how and why these changes occur. For teachers, they provide important information about the nature of people's thought processes and how these thought processes are likely to change with age, as well as important perspectives on classroom teaching and learning. In this chapter, your authors focus on the connections between cognitive developmental theories and classroom learning. You will explore the ideas of Piaget, Vygotsky, and Bruner and learn how these theories are reflected today in constructivism.

To facilitate your understanding of these ideas and how they relate to classroom decisions, the key ideas in this chapter have been summarized in terms of these three general principles of learning:

● Principle 5.1. Learning is more powerful if learners actively construct their own understandings.

● Principle 5.2. Learning experiences are more effective if they take into account the cognitive developmental levels of the learners.

● Principle 5.3. Students' knowledge construction is assisted by the nature of their interactions with people and objects in their environments.

This year I'm serving as chair of our district-wide committee to revise our K–12 social studies curriculum. Our superintendent has asked us to develop a coordinated curriculum that emphasizes a finite number of key themes and that reflects current thinking about social studies learning. We're also supposed to identify materials and classroom activities that can be used to implement the curriculum.

I'm always amazed how hard it is to get a group of professional educators to agree on what needs to be taught. We have some goals in common, but we also differ on a lot of key points. A major challenge of this committee is to make sure that all curricular areas are fairly represented, and that elementary and middle school curricula support our overall goals for our graduates.

Already, it is clear that we also have some interesting differences of opinion about how to teach social studies. Although most of us describe ourselves as student-centered educators, we don't all agree on what a student-centered classroom looks like. It will be interesting to see what comes out of this committee.

Decision Point: What existing curricular resources might this committee want to make use of in their work?

Before proceeding with Chapter 5, be sure you read the Close-ups on the Classroom features about Greg Urlacher and Molly Costas. At various points in the chapter, you will revisit both teachers in their classrooms and follow their decision-making progress. Their classroom experiences are closely integrated with the key concepts of this chapter and serve as important models for understanding Cognitive Development and Constructivism.

According to Seifert and Hoffnung (1994, p. 6), cognitive development "involves changes in reasoning and thinking, language acquisition, and the ways individuals gain, store, and remember or recall knowledge of their environments." Cognitive developmental theorists, therefore, are interested in topics such as the stages of language acquisition, how children's strategy use changes with age, or why four-year-old children use different problem-solving approaches than ten-year-old children. Cognitive developmental theories provide descriptions of typical developmental changes in mental capabilities and explanations for how and why these changes occur.

Theories of cognitive development serve two major functions for teachers. First, they provide teachers with important information about the nature of people's thought processes and how these thought processes are likely to change with age. Second, cognitive developmental theories provide important perspectives on classroom teaching and learning. Although both functions of cognitive developmental theories are important, the connections between cognitive developmental theories and classroom learning are of primary concern. To explore these connections, this chapter begins with the theoretical ideas of Piaget, Vygotsky, and Bruner, three developmental theorists whose ideas have provided important perspectives on classroom learning.

Piagetian Theory

Piaget's writings span approximately seventy years and provide a rich and complicated theory for how people acquire knowledge and how thought processes change with age. Although some of his ideas are criticized heavily today, his historical importance for psychology and education cannot be denied. He is clearly one of the most influential thinkers of the last century.

Molly Costas and the Parent Workshops

As part of our parent outreach program for our district's preschool and kindergarten programs, we provide a series of workshops for our parents on young children's development. I've been asked to provide workshops in the areas of cognitive development and developmentally appropriate teaching for young children. These workshops are very well attended, and they give us a wonderful opportunity to work with our parents and to explain why we have structured our programs in certain ways.

Although parents generally are very positive and supportive of our efforts, we do have parents every year who have significant concerns about our programs. Mr. Tsosie, one of our new parents, told me at the beginning of the year that developmentally appropriate teaching sounds like code for not challenging students enough. He intends to be at our workshops, and I'm sure he will keep me on my toes.

I also know we have a lot of young, first-time parents. In the past they have asked a lot of questions about what is *normal*. My colleague, Maria, has already had to field a number of those questions in the areas of language development and social-personal development. I expect more of the same in my meetings also.

Decision Point: How might Molly Costas identify potential topics that would be useful for her students' parents?

Piagetian theory can be organized into two main parts. The first part of his theory consists of his ideas about the purpose and nature of intelligence. Piaget concerned himself mainly with identifying the major goal of intelligence and how people acquire the knowledge structures necessary for intelligent behavior. The second part of this theory provides a stage theory perspective on human cognitive development that describes how people's intellectual capabilities change with age.

Piagetian View of Intelligence

When you hear the word *intelligence,* you may tend to think about it in terms of the types of performances measured by standardized intelligence tests. Piaget, however, took a broader view of intelligence (Ginsburg & Opper, 1988). According to Piaget (1950, 1952), intelligence is a set of cognitive capabilities that allows people to adjust to the demands of their environments. These cognitive capabilities consist of learners' knowledge structures, the cognitive functions they use in acquiring their knowledge structures, and their ability to self-regulate their cognitive functions.

Knowledge Structures. The basic Piagetian knowledge structure is the scheme or schema as it is sometimes called. A **scheme** is an organized pattern of thought or action that people use to understand and interact with their world. Schemes can be thought of as concepts, categories of knowledge, or as a card in an index file (Wadsworth, 1996). Although some schemes are present at birth or shortly after, other schemes develop as a result of our experiences. These experiences create schemes that are ". . . the structure or organization of actions as they are transferred or generalized by repetition in similar or analogous circumstances" (Piaget & Inhelder, 1969, p. 4). In other words, a scheme represents the knowledge that has been abstracted from the common elements of different but related experiences. For example, children might observe that all of the cats in the neighborhood meow. Their scheme or understanding of cats will probably contain the generalization that cats meow. The implication is that people tend to organize knowledge about their experiences into categories.

How does the Piagetian idea of a scheme compare with the information-processing idea of a schema discussed in Chapter 3?

Cognitive Functions. According to Piaget, people are born with two cognitive functions that they use to develop and refine their schemes. These functions are organization and adaptation, and they account for and regulate cognitive growth (Nurrenbern, 2001).

Organization is the general tendency of biological organisms to combine structures into more complicated structures or systems (Ginsburg & Opper, 1988; Nichols, 2000). For example, the heart and lungs combine with other biological structures to form the circulatory system. These more complicated biological structures coordinate the functions of several different structures, which results in our increased capabilities to adjust to the changing demands of a complicated environment. Similarly, cognitive structures or schemes also tend to combine to form more complicated and sophisticated schemes. For example, children may combine their scheme for birds and their scheme for bats into a larger scheme for all animals that fly. Organization provides learners with new and more sophisticated ways to understand their environments.

How might organization of your schemes for classroom management and classroom instruction help you become a more efficient teacher?

Adaptation is the second major cognitive function, and it involves the processes used to develop and refine schemes to adjust to our environments (Cohen & Younghee, 1999; Piaget, 1962). Adaptation occurs through the two complementary subprocesses of assimilation and accommodation.

Assimilation is the act of interpreting environmental events in terms of existing schemes (Jonckheere, Mandelbrot, & Piaget, 1958; Piaget & Inhelder, 1969). For example, a mother is pushing her fifteen-month-old infant in a stroller. As the child passes various unknown men, the infant smiles, points, and exclaims loudly, "Daddy!" The child is interpreting these new men in terms of the child's existing knowledge that tall, two-legged men are called daddy. Piaget's infant daughter, Lucienne, and her first experience with a pack of cigarettes provide another example of assimilation (Piaget, 1962). Because Lucienne did not have a scheme for cigarettes, she responded to them in terms of her existing schemes for exploration. She stuck the cigarette pack in her mouth and she banged it on a table. These are actions she had previously internalized as ways of exploring new objects. In both cases, the child's actions would be seen as examples of assimilation, because an experience was related to or interpreted in terms of the child's existing schemes.

It should be noted that assimilation is an active process during which an environmental stimulus is interpreted in terms of existing knowledge in a person's schemes (Thomas, 2000). Assimilation can be likened to the biological act of digestion (Ginsburg & Opper, 1988; Wadsworth, 1996). Food is taken into the digestive structures, and the digestive processes modify the food into a form that is more usable to the biological organism. In the case of cognitive assimilation, experiences may also be modified so they fit better with the schemes that are used to interpret those experiences (Cohen & Younghee, 1999). Knowledge is not simply reproduced or copied from experience. Instead, it is constructed by transforming environmental information into knowledge that fits with existing schemes. Consider the following example.

➤ Mrs. Rayburn, a junior high science teacher, is amazed how resilient her students' belief systems are. She shows them a science demonstration that contradicts their beliefs, and the students find a way to make the demonstration fit with their beliefs. "I guess that's one reason why it is hard to change students' misconceptions about science."

Accommodation is when environmental experiences cause a person to change the nature of a scheme (Piaget & Inhelder, 1969). For example, the mother in the previously described situation wants the child to understand that not all men should be called daddy. In this case, accommodation would involve modifying the contents of the daddy scheme. Other adjustments can take the form of creating new schemes to handle experience better or more efficiently. In either case, existing schemes are inadequate to adapt to the environment, so changes are

How is accommodation different from assimilation?

Exposure to different points of view can provide a starting point for accommodation.

made to the available schemes. Note the role of accommodation in the following classroom example.

➤ Mrs. Pantera's sixth grade science students often have developed some misunderstandings of physical science concepts such as heat and gravity. "I often need to assess students' understanding of these concepts before I introduce them. I can then try to create experiences that allow them to confront and hopefully *change* their particular misunderstandings."

Self-Regulation. From a Piagetian perspective, people are motivated to make sense of the world so that they can adapt to its demands. To accomplish this, people must self-regulate and maintain a sense of balance among the many factors that influence their ability to understand and adapt to our environments. Piaget (1977) referred to this cognitive balance as equilibrium. He used the term **equilibration** to refer to self-regulating activities people engage in to achieve cognitive balance.

Equilibration involves assessing current understanding in terms of how well it explains experiences and maintaining an appropriate balance between assimilation and accommodation in making sense of those experiences. The general implications for classroom teaching are that learners are intrinsically motivated to have the world make sense, and learners need to self-regulate their own learning to make sense of the world. Both of these implications have become cornerstone ideas in constructivist approaches to classroom learning.

> What similarities are there between the Piagetian idea of equilibration and the information-processing idea of metacognition?

Piagetian Stage Theory

Piagetians apply a stage theory perspective to cognitive development both for the overall course of cognitive development and for the development of particular cognitive structures (Thomas, 2000). In general, development occurs through the series of four stages that are presented in Table 5.1. Piagetians tend to make the following assumptions about the nature of these four stages.

• Each stage is defined by the development of cognitive structures or capabilities that are qualitatively different from those of earlier stages. Development is not simply a matter of acquiring additional information, but is also a matter of developing different ways of understanding the world.

TABLE 5.1	An Overview of Piagetian Developmental Stages	
Piagetian Stage	**Typical Age Range**	**Key Concepts from Each Stage**
Sensorimotor stage	Birth to 2	Intentionality; object concept
Preoperational stage	2–7	Semiotic function; irreversibility; egocentrism; centration
Concrete operational stage	7–11	Various concrete operations including seriation, classification, conservation, negation, identity, and compensation
Formal operational stage	Unclear at this point	The ability to formulate and systematically test hypotheses; propositional logic; the ability to reason about hypothetical situations

- The sequence of the stages is the same for all children and adolescents, but the timing of the stages can vary. This means that although typical age ranges can be specified for stages, these ages may not apply to every child.
- Development is cumulative in that development in later stages has its basis in development that occurred in earlier stages.
- Children and adolescents may demonstrate characteristics of two developmental stages simultaneously. Piaget refers to this as **horizontal décalage** (Ginsburg & Opper, 1988; Nurrenbern, 2001). Horizontal décalage implies that children and adolescents may demonstrate a cognitive understanding in one situation, but fail to show the same level of cognitive understanding in a related but different situation. Piagetians usually credit children and adolescents with their highest demonstrated level of development.

Sensorimotor Stage. The *sensorimotor stage* is the period of cognitive development that occurs during the first two years of life. The term **sensorimotor** is descriptive of the nature of cognitive development during infancy because infants think and develop schemes through their motor responses to stimuli in the environment. For example, by hitting crib mobiles and making them move, infants develop basic understandings (schemes) about cause and effect. Although a lot happens during these first two years, the development of intentionality and object permanence are particularly important to Piagetians (Wadsworth, 1996).

Why is the first Piagetian stage called the sensorimotor stage?

Intentionality. Intentionality develops gradually during the sensorimotor stage, and it consists of consciously acting in certain ways to achieve goals (Thomas, 2000). At first, newborn infants' motor responses consist mainly of neonatal reflexes. For example, if you place your finger a few millimeters into a newborn infant's mouth, your finger should initiate a sucking reflex. If you place your finger in a newborn's hand, the infant should demonstrate the palmar grasp reflex by closing the hand around the finger. All neonatal reflexes are initiated by an environmental stimulus, and the infant responds automatically to the stimulus.

By the time infants exit the sensorimotor period, however, they develop the understanding that they can achieve goals through their behavior. This understanding is reflected in the development of circular reaction. A **circular reaction** is when an infant's behavior creates an environmental effect that motivates the infant to repeat the behavior (Piaget, 1927). One of your authors recently observed a circular reaction at a local restaurant. A waiter placed drawing paper and a crayon on the high chair tray in front of an infant girl. The infant picked up the crayon and dropped it on the floor, and the young father promptly returned it to the tray. The infant picked it up and dropped it again, and the father picked it up again. This cycle went on for quite a while. From the infant's perspective, this was a great game because she was initiating an experience through her behavior. She was acting with the intent of repeating an experience, and the adults had the privilege of witnessing a circular reaction.

Object Permanence.   **Object permanence** is infants' understanding that objects continue to exist even when they are out of sight (Piaget, 1954; Piaget & Inhelder, 1969). Infants demonstrate object permanence by continuing to search for objects that are partially or completely hidden. Piaget believed that a complete understanding of object permanence did not develop until eighteen to twenty-four months of age, but other research suggests that object permanence may be present as early as two-and-one-half months of age (Carey & Xu, 2001). Consider this young mother's experience with object permanence.

➤ Mary remembers a few months ago when she could cause Sally to lose interest in a toy by putting the toy behind her back. Now, Sally points and tries to look behind Mary.

Object permanence is important to Piagetians because it means that infants are starting to make the transition from thinking through their actions to thinking symbolically with mental representations such as images and ideas. They can use these symbols to think about objects that they are no longer experiencing directly, and the development of object permanence provides the basis for the rapid development of symbolic thought in the next stage.

Why is the development of object permanence important to the Piagetians?

Preoperational Stage.   The **preoperational stage** begins at the end of the sensorimotor stage and typically continues until approximately age six or seven. Children's thinking during this period is characterized by rapid increases in their ability to think symbolically and by a series of characteristics that make their thought processes quite different from those of older children and adults.

How would social cognitive theorists such as Bandura describe deferred imitation?

Symbolic Thought.   Piagetians refer to the ability to think symbolically as the **semiotic function** (Piaget & Inhelder, 1969). The semiotic function means that children are not restricted to thinking through their immediate and direct sensorimotor experiences with their environments. They now can manipulate mental symbols that represent those experiences. The development of the semiotic function is observable in a number of children's behavior patterns including deferred imitation and the capability for symbolic play.

Deferred imitation is the ability to imitate a model that is no longer present. Deferred imitation involves storing and using symbolic representations of past experiences in future situations. For example, a young child observes another child throw a tantrum to get a desired toy. Later that child imitates the same behavior when trying to get a toy she wants.

Symbolic play or pretend play occurs when children use themselves or objects in their environment to represent other experiences or objects in their environment. Consider these observations of three- to five-year-old children during free-play time in a preschool.

➤ One young boy has tied a blanket around his neck and is running around the room making flying noises. Another child is in a corner having a battle with two action figures she brought to school. A third child has turned a large cardboard box into a car and is sitting in the box and driving.

Symbolic play is an excellent example of assimilation because children use their understanding of their experiences to create novel uses for objects in their environment.

As babies, we learn the concept object permanence, which is the recognition that an object continues to exist when out of sight.

Also, symbolic play can enhance children's knowledge of objects, actions, and symbols that in turn is important for later language development (Lyytinen, Poikkeus, Laasko, Eklund, & Lyytinen, 2001).

Characteristics of Preoperational Thought. An **operation** is an internalized cognitive action that allows children to reason logically about their experiences (Wadsworth, 1996). Children in the preoperational stage have not developed operational logic, but rely instead on intuition and perception. Their reasoning is characterized by the Piagetians as having the limitations of irreversibility, egocentrism, and centration.

Irreversibility is the term used to describe the observation that preoperational children do not have reversible operations. A logical operation is reversible if the child realizes that the effects of one operation can be nullified by the effects of another operation, or that an operation can be readily inverted into its opposite (Beard, 1969; Thomas, 2000). For example, mentally combining blue and red beads together to form a group of red and blue beads can mentally be undone by separating the beads into a red and blue group. Pouring the juice back into the pitcher can reverse pouring a pitcher of juice into several cups. According to the Piagetians, preoperational children lack these types of understandings. For example, a four-year-old girl is asked if she has a sister. She replies that she does and her sister's name in Maria. However, when asked if Maria has a sister, the four-year-old says no. The four-year-old apparently is having trouble readily inverting her relationship with her sister into the opposite relationship.

Preoperational thought is also egocentric. **Egocentrism** is the tendency of preoperational children to judge everything from their point of view (McDonald & Stuart-Hamilton, 2002; Piaget, 1924). Egocentrism has two important consequences for preoperational children's thinking. First, they have difficulty taking a point of view that is different from their own. For example, a preschooler plays hide and seek by standing in full view of others with her hands over her eyes. She apparently feels hidden because she cannot see the others. If she cannot see them, it follows that they cannot see her.

The second consequence of egocentrism is that preoperational children do not perceive a need to justify their thinking to themselves or others. If there is only one point of view, which is the child's, there is no need to justify this point of view to others. Perhaps this is why young children are comfortable answering "why" questions with "just because" or a shrug of the shoulder. From a Piagetian perspective, they don't feel compelled to have an explanation.

Centration is the tendency of preoperational children to limit their perception to one aspect of a complicated stimulus rather than to all aspects of the stimulus (Craig, 1999). When children are able to consider multiple aspects of a stimulus they are able to decenter. For example, a preoperational child may pick a tall skinny glass as having more water in it than a shorter and wider glass, even though the same amount of liquid has been poured into each glass. They center or focus only on the height of the water in the glass, rather than also considering the shapes of the glasses.

Stage of Concrete Operations. The **stage of concrete operations** begins at the end of the preoperational stage and continues at least to age twelve and perhaps longer. You may notice that the prefix *pre* is now removed. Children in this stage are operational, which means they are less susceptible to egocentrism, irreversibility, and centration in their thought. The descriptor *concrete* has been added to help define the types of operations that are available. Concrete operations are those mental actions that operate on physical objects and are how the child comes to understand the nature of physical reality (Piaget & Inhelder, 1969). Conservation, seriation, and classification are important examples of these concrete operations.

What is egocentrism according to the Piagetians?

Use the ideas of irreversibility and centration to explain why sharing might be a difficult idea for some young children.

Looking in on

Molly Costas

5.1

During our parent meetings I try to leave time for our parents to ask questions about their children. Very often, they want to know if something is normal, or they want a reason why their children do some things that strike them as cute or unusual. For example, one of our mothers was concerned that her fifteen-month-old infant was becoming a brat. He goes to the trash can and drops forks, toys, even watches into the garbage. When she pulls it out, he throws something else in and laughs. She said that he seems to enjoy making more work for her. Another parent thought it was funny that her three-year-old child would answer her grandparents' questions on the phone by nodding her head. Her grandparents kept on having to ask if she was still on the phone. The best one so far is the three-year-old boy who asked for a lot of cookies when there was only one left. The dad broke the one cookie in half in front of the child and handed him a *cookie* for each hand. The three-year-old boy was thrilled that he got more cookies.

● **How might Piagetian concepts be used to explain these observations to these parents?**

Decision Point: If the parent asked you what to do about the child who was throwing things in the trash, what would you recommend?

Conservation. **Conservation** is children's understanding that quantity is unrelated to the arrangement and physical appearance of an object (Feldman, 2000; Shimoff, 1998). With a conservation task, the appearance of a task situation is changed, but the amount or quantity of the object remains constant. Children who can conserve understand that a change in appearance does not necessarily change the amount. Figure 5.1 provides some examples of different conservation tasks. As you can see from Figure 5.1, conservation tasks are classified in terms of the quantity or amount that does not change. For example, a conservation of number task is one in which the physical stimulus changes appearance, but the number of objects remains unchanged. A conservation of length task is one in which appearances change but length does not change.

According to Piaget, the best criteria for determining if children are in the concrete operational stage is how they perform on conservation tasks (Fraisse & Piaget, 1963). To be considered in the concrete operational stage, children must immediately recognize that the change in appearance has not changed quantity or amount, and they must also use one or more of the following operations to support their judgment (Fraisse & Piaget, 1963). The first of these operations or arguments is **identity**, which is the understanding that if nothing is added or taken away, nothing changes. For example, on the conservation of number task described in Figure 5.1, a child would say that there is no change because no coins had been added or taken away. A second operation or argument is **negation** or reversibility. Negation is the understanding that for a particular operation or action, there is an action or operation that undoes the effects of the first operation. In the conservation of number task, a child would say that if you mentally push the coins back together, you can see nothing has changed. The third operation or argument is **compensation**, which is a form of decentering. The compensation argument is that changes in one dimension can explain the observed change in another. With the conservation of number task, the one row is longer, but that is because the spacing between items is larger.

Seriation and Classification. Seriation and classification are two additional operations that figure prominently in Piagetian discussions of the stage of concrete operations (Piaget & Szeminska, 1941; Piaget & Inhelder, 1969). **Seriation** is the operation that allows children to arrange objects in terms of increasing or decreasing size. Consider this example of seriation.

➤ Sally, a seven-year-old, is cleaning her room. She has decided to put her stuffed animals on her shelf in order from tallest to shortest. "The big ones are first, then the medium-sized ones, and then the tiny ones."

Conservation Task	Description	Examples of Identity, Compensation, and Negation Arguments
Conservation of number	Lay out two rows of objects (e.g., coins). Each row has the same number of objects, and the objects in each row are aligned with each other. Ask the child, "Which row has more in it or are they the same?" Have the child verify the equality. Then in full view of the child, spread out the bottom row, and repeat the earlier question. 	Identity Argument: "They are still the same because you did not add or take away any objects." Negation Argument: "They are still the same because if you put the bottom row back, you can see that nothing has changed." Compensation Argument: "They are still the same. The bottom row looks like it has more because it is longer, but that is because the spaces between the objects are bigger."
Conservation of length	Lay out two identical pencils, rods, or sticks side by side. Ask the child, "Which pencil, rod, or stick is longer or are they the same?" Have the child verify the equality. In full view of the child, take one pencil and slide it over. Repeat the question. 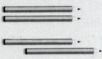	Identity Argument: "They are still the same because you did not add or take away any length." Negation Argument: "They are still the same because if you push the bottom row back, you can see that nothing has changed." Compensation Argument: "They are still the same. The bottom one looks like it is longer because it sticks out on this end more, but that is because it starts further in that direction."
Conservation of liquid	The child is shown two identical glasses with equal amounts of liquid in each, and asked if the amounts are the same or not. In front of the child, the first glass is poured into a tall, skinny glass. The second glass is poured into a short, wide glass. The child is asked if the amount of the liquid in the two new glasses is the same or not. 	Identity Argument: "They are still the same because you did not add or take away any liquid." Negation Argument: "They are still the same because if you pour them back, you can see that nothing has changed." Compensation Argument: "They are still the same. The water level in the tall skinny one is higher, but that is because the glass is tall and skinny."

FIGURE 5.1 Examples of Piagetian Conservation Tasks

Classification is the operation that allows us to place objects into categories on the basis of shared characteristics. For instance, a child's ability to categorize different examples of triangles, squares, and circles correctly would be the result of the classification operation. For the Piagetians, both seriation and classification are important for children's development of mathematical and scientific logic.

Stage of Formal Operations.   The **stage of formal operations** theoretically begins at the end of the concrete operational stage, and it is the final of the four Piagetian

Looking in on

Greg Urlacher

5.1

Today, our attention turned to our general goal of helping our students become more effective thinkers and problem solvers. We wanted to decide what this goal means, and we wanted to brainstorm different ideas for teaching students to be critical and analytical thinkers. Joan, a high school American and world history teacher, said that she wants her students to be able to analyze historical events in terms of their effects on current events. One way she does that is to have students imagine how life would be different today if history was changed. For example, what would America be like if the South had won the civil war? She also likes students to study their own community and to develop and test hypotheses about the historical basis for what they see around them. For example, one student is very interested in why the train tracks run through the middle of town, because he always has to stop and wait for trains to go by when he drives home. He was surprised to find out that the reason actually dated back to the early 1900s. Many of us liked Joan's approach, but we were worried about how to evaluate these types of activities fairly. Some of us have used student exhibitions that require students to present their research and to answer questions from students and other teachers as an evaluation approach. However, these can be time-consuming and hard to grade objectively and can affect our ability to cover the material in the curriculum. Also, some students don't do well talking in front of others.

● **What Piagetian formal operations are present in Joan's approaches to teaching thinking skills?**

Decision Point: What suggestions do you have for addressing the issues brought up at the end about the use of student exhibitions?

stages. Formal operations act on ideas rather than on objects, and there are a number of important differences between formal and concrete operational reasoning (Gruber and Vonèche, 1977; Piaget & Inhelder, 1969; Wadsworth, 1996).

Hypothetico-Deductive Reasoning. The first and most important change that marks the advent of formal operational thinking is the ability to reason from hypotheses. Piagetians refer to this type of logic as **hypothetico-deductive reasoning.** During the stage of formal operations, adolescents become capable of forming theories or hypotheses and of developing systematic ways to test or prove their hypotheses. Mr. Farley makes use of this potential in his high school world history class.

➤ Rather than telling my students the reasons for historical events, I start by explaining the event. Students then try to guess at possible causes of events. They then talk about how they would research the causes of this particular event if they were alive when it first happened.

Propositional Logic. The second important change that occurs in the stage of formal operations is the ability to engage inpropositional logic. With the advent of **propositional logic,** adolescents become capable of determining the truth or fallacy of propositions that may or may not have a basis in experience. For example, consider the following propositions. All Freebies are Noogies and all Noogies are Bozos. Consequently, Freebies are Bozos. Propositional logic allows you to determine whether the conclusion is true or false, regardless of the content of the propositions. Concrete operational children might say that they don't know whether the conclusion is true or false because they don't know any Freebies.

Ability to Consider the What-Ifs. The third important change is an extension of the second. Formal operational structures allow the adolescent to go beyond the content of the logic they are evaluating. They can consider the *what-if* question, which allows them to deal effectively with

From a Piagetian perspective, why would formal operations be important in activities such as critical thinking?

hypothetical situations. They are not restricted to situations they have experienced or can imagine.

Current Status of Piagetian Theory

Piaget's ideas about the nature of intelligence continue to be influential today in discussions of classroom learning. For example, schemes, organization, adaptation, and equilibrium are important concepts in a view of learning called *psychological constructivism*. In fact, psychological constructivism is often referred to as Piagetian constructivism (Vadeboncoeur, 1997). Psychological constructivism is discussed later in this chapter.

The current status of Piagetian stage theory, however, is somewhat different. Over the last twenty to thirty years, Piagetian stage theory has been researched thoroughly, and this research has raised the following concerns.

- Piagetians have tended to underestimate the capabilities of infants and young children. Their logic is not as limited as the Piagetians claim (Cole & Cole, 1993).
- Children's performance on Piagetian tasks appears to be influenced by a number of factors other than cognitive development (see Enriching Your Understanding box) (Gelman & Baillargeon, 1983; Siegel & Hodkin, 1982).
- As many as 40 to 60 percent of adolescents and young adults do not fully achieve formal operational reasoning (Cole & Cole, 1993; Feldman, 2000). Also, cross-cultural studies of formal operational thinking in adolescents have found that formal operational thought is not a universal stage across cultures (Laboratory of Comparative Human Cognition, 1983; Rogoff, 1981).
- Development within stages is so gradual that two people within the same stage can be very different in terms of their cognitive development. Also, movement from one stage to another occurs gradually. Consequently, a four-stage model may not accurately reflect the gradual nature of cognitive development.

ENRICHING YOUR UNDERSTANDING
The Competence/Performance Relationship

How do we determine whether or not someone has reached a particular stage of cognitive development or, in the case of classroom teaching, has succeeded as a learner? What are the criteria for success, and what assessment tasks will be used so that an accurate estimate of learners' competence is developed? In developmental psychology the answers to these questions determine the competence/performance relationship (Chandler & Chapman, 1991).

Critics of Piagetian tasks (e.g., conservation) have raised serious questions about the validity of these tasks for measuring cognitive development. Researchers have found that performance on Piagetian tasks can be influenced by children's language development, motivation, perceptual development, memory, and social development (Siegel & Hodkin, 1982). For example, some children do better if conservation tasks are pre-

sented nonverbally or if more familiar materials are used. If performance on these assessments is influenced by so many different variables, then interviewers should not assume that task success or failure is due only to cognitive development. Interviewers especially need to be careful when interpreting task failure. They need to consider the multiple possible reasons for why students do not succeed at any assessment task, and that performance on an assessment task may not always reveal learners' competence or ability to do those tasks.

● In what ways is an understanding of the competence/ performance issue important for classroom teachers' classroom assessments of their learners? (For your authors' perspective on this question, go to the text website for this chapter.)

- A single, global theory of cognitive development may not be the most effective way to explain all the different types of cognitive development and the differences observed among individuals and groups of people.

Alternatives to Piagetian Stage Theory. The observation that children become more sophisticated in their thinking and problem solving as they grow older is empirically validated and important. However, the Piagetians only provide one theoretical explanation for this observation, and there can be alternative explanations (Caroff, 2002). Information-processing theory and neo-Piagetian theories provide two important alternative explanations.

Information-processing views of cognitive development are based on the multistore model of memory described in Chapter 3. Students' cognitive development is explained in terms of the following improvements in their ability to process information more efficiently.

- As children develop during the elementary school period, they become better able to sustain attention and resist distractions, and they become better able to focus attention on the important parts of a task (Hagen & Stanovich, 1977; Ruff & Lawson, 1990).
- As children develop during the elementary school period, they tend to develop automaticity for important basic skills such as reading decoding and basic math calculations. As discussed in Chapter 3, automaticity reduces working memory load and allows for more complicated problem-solving approaches.
- During elementary school, children acquire more knowledge in long-term memory, and that knowledge becomes more integrated. These developments allow students to be more efficient in learning new knowledge (Bjorklund, 1987; Eacott, 1999).
- As students develop during the elementary school period, they tend to develop more effective strategies for memorization and learning (Bjorklund & Coyle, 1995; Kail, 1990; Plumert, 1994). For example, preschool children are much less likely to use strategies such as rehearsal and organization than are older elementary school students.
- During the elementary school period, students improve their metacognitive knowledge and self-regulation skills (Schneider, 1998). For example, upper elementary school students have a better sense of their memory capabilities, are more accurate in their judgments of whether or not they know something, and are more likely to allocate attention to difficult or unknown material when studying (Nelson & Narens, 1994; Schneider, 1998).

Neo-Piagetian theories retain some of Piaget's key assumptions, but they also differ from Piagetian theory in key ways (Case, 1987, 1992; Cole & Cole, 1993; Pascual-Leone, 2000; Siegler, 1998). First, neo-Piagetians reject the idea of general laws or stages of development and believe instead that development can occur differently in different areas or domains or in different ways for different children. Second, Neo-Piagetians theorize a different mechanism for development. Cognitive development results from increases in processing or working memory capacity, rather than qualitative changes in mental structures such as schemes.

One advantage of these alternatives to Piagetian theory is that they often focus on the developmental sequences for specific skills such as number sense or spelling (Henderson & Beers, 1980; Siegler, 1998). These theories can be particularly useful for teachers because they identify the types of strategies and understandings you are likely to observe as children's knowledge of an academic skill increases. For example, by age four, many children use counting to solve simple addition problems. By the time these children are first graders, many of them start using the *min* strategy for single-digit addition problems (Rittle-Johnson & Siegler, 1998). With the min strategy, children say the name of the larger number and count up from there. For example, if asked to add eight plus two, the child would say "eight," and then count up two (nine and ten).

Educational Implications of Piagetian Theory

Piaget did not set out to explain school learning, and there is no Piagetian dogma on education (Bunce, 2001; Gruber & Vonèche, 1977). He did on occasion discuss education, but for the most part specific recommendations for applying his theory to school-based learning was not of interest to him and have come from others (Bunce, 2001; Elkind, 1976; Fischbein, 1999; Furth, 1970; Furth & Wachs, 1974; Herron, 1975; Hooper & DeFrain, 1980; Kamii, 1985; Schwebel & Raph, 1973). These educational recommendations have focused on teaching students to think and problem solve and typically are some variant of the following core ideas from Ginsburg & Opper (1988) and Hooper & DeFrain (1980).

What do Piagetians mean by the idea of an active learner?

- Learners need to be engaged in active learning experiences that allow them to invent or construct understanding through their own spontaneous research activities, rather than having ideas transmitted to them through teacher-directed instruction (McCarthy Gallagher & Reid, 1981).
- Teachers should be aware of their students' cognitive developmental level and design learning experiences that are developmentally appropriate for those students. According to Furth and Wachs (1974), a developmentally appropriate activity is one that challenges a student's thinking, but that is not so difficult that the student is likely to fail. This idea has been referred to as *optimal mismatch* (Kuhn, 1979).
- Children, especially young children, learn best from concrete learning experiences (Ravanis & Bagakis, 1998).
- Social interaction is important for fostering development. During social interactions, children can complement and also compensate for the thinking of others. Also, when younger learners are exposed to points of view that are different from their own, it helps them confront their egocentrism. Also social interactions help older students become more reflective about their thinking.

A number of these ideas have been incorporated into the constructivist views of classroom learning, as discussed later in this chapter.

Vygotsky's Sociohistorical Theory

Lev Semenovich Vygotsky was born in Russia in 1896 and died in 1934 from tuberculosis at age thirty-eight. Over his relatively short professional career, L. S. Vygotsky developed the theoretical basis for a view of development and education that is very influential today. A major emphasis in Vygostsky's work was the importance of understanding cognitive development in terms of the social and cultural contexts in which it occurs (Luria, 1979; Moll, 1990; Vygotsky, 1962, 1978, 1981, 1987).

The Role of Cultural Tools in Cognitive Development

Vygotsky believed that as students engage in activities within their social environments they create their understandings of their worlds (Thomas, 2000). Each environment provides cultural tools to support or mediate students' activities (Miller, 2002). A tool is an extension of a person that allows that person to go beyond his or her physical or mental limitations (Greening, 1998). Vygotsky (1981) identified two types of cultural tools that are specialized for different types of actions. Technical tools are cultural tools that are used to act on objects in the environment. For example, a hammer and a nail allow us to transform two separate pieces of wood into two connected pieces of wood.

Psychological tools or signs are cultural tools that guide or mediate thoughts and behaviors. Psychological tools extend people's mental capabilities and they support their thinking and problem solving. For example, language is an important psychological tool that allows people to establish social contact, influence others, and eventually guide their thinking and problem solving. Memory systems such as mnemonics are another example of a psychological tool that is used to improve memory for ideas. Theoretical frameworks are tools that can mediate problem solving and decision making in a professional domain (Hedegaard, 1990). (Please note that the development of theoretical knowledge as a tool for decision making is a major goal of this text.)

How are technical and psychological tools different?

The nature and goals of social environments determine the types of psychological tools that are available, and how those psychological tools are used. For example, studies of people's math reasoning as they weigh food for the Weight Watchers diet suggest that math problem solving in these types of *real-world* contexts employ different psychological tools than is the case for math reasoning in the math classroom (Lave, 1988). For example, when faced with the problem of measuring out three-quarters of two-thirds of a cup of cottage cheese, one dieter used the elements of the setting to solve the problem. He patted two-thirds of a cup of cottage cheese into a circle on a cutting board, marked it into fourths, and took three of those portions. In a classroom, both the nature of the problem-solving activity and the available psychological tools would likely be different, and call forth different problem-solving approaches.

Development of Higher Order Mental Functions

Although he wrote about a variety of developmental issues, Vygotsky tended to focus on how people acquire their higher mental functions. For Vygotsky, a function is a mental process such as attention, perception, memory, and thinking. These mental functions first appear in their elementary form. Elementary functions develop naturally, are present both in animals and humans, tend not to be voluntary, can occur without conscious awareness, and are not assisted by psychological tools (Cole, 1985; Thomas, 2000; Wertsch, 1985). In its elementary form, memory would involve the automatic formation of an association between two events that have occurred together, such as the cat that associates the sound of the can opener with food. In its elementary form, attention would involve some automatic change in how attention is focused. For example, both people and many animals react automatically to an unexpected loud noise by looking in the direction of the noise.

A computer can be an example of a psychological tool.

Higher mental functions are unique to humans, and although they develop out of the elementary functions, they differ from them in several ways. Higher mental functions are under the control of the person, social in origin, and are assisted by psychological tools (Vygotsky, 1978; Wertsch, 1985). Memory as a higher mental function would involve elaborative activities such as connecting two events through the use of psychological tools such as analogies or mnemonics. Attention as a higher mental function would involve deliberate regulation of attention, as when we make conscious choices about where to focus attention based on prior knowledge.

Vygotsky's General Genetic Law of Cultural Development

Vygotsky's general genetic law of cultural development is that any higher mental function exists first on a social level before it occurs within the person as a psychological process (Vygotsky, 1981). Vygostsky described this as the transition from the intermental to the intramental plane (Wink & Putney, 2002), and the gradual development of higher mental functions from social interactions is **internalization** (Duveen, 1997). For example, the ability to think critically would originate in social interactions such as Socratic questioning or debate. From these interactions, people would internalize psychological tools such as the ability to understand different points of view or the ability to critique claims made in an advertisement.

The Vygotskian view of the role of egocentric speech provides another important example of how mental functions originate in social interactions (Emerson, 1997; Vygotsky, 1962, 1978; Wertsch, 1985). Children's first experience with speech is as a means to socially interact with others, but at approximately age three, egocentric speech makes its first appearance. **Egocentric speech** is when children are talking aloud, but they are talking to themselves (Feldman, 2000). Vygotsky believed that children used egocentric speech to guide and regulate their problem solving. Support for his position was provided by the observation that the amount of egocentric speech tends to increase as problem difficulty increases for young children (Berk, 1985; Duncan, 1991; Schimmoeller, 1998).

How does Vygotsky's view of egocentric speech relate to the social cognitive idea of self-instruction presented in Chapter 4?

Around age seven, egocentric speech pretty much disappears, although even older children and adults talk aloud occasionally while solving some problems. However, Vygotsky believed that self-talk did not really disappear, but instead became internalized as inner speech or self-regulation. Egocentric speech represented the middle ground between social speech and the use of internal speech to monitor and guide the problem-solving process. Consider this classroom application of self-regulating speech by Sally Jenkins.

➤ Sometimes it gets noisy in my classroom. I encourage my children to talk to themselves and each other as they solve story problems. For example, my students will ask, "What is the problem here?"

Zone of Proximal Development. The zone of proximal development is Vygotsky's concept of how social interactions can be most productive for helping learners internalize mental functions (Mahn, 1999). Vygotsky (1978) defined the **zone of proximal development** as the distance between what a learner can accomplish independently in a domain, and what that same learner can accomplish while working with a more skilled adult or peer. This distance or zone defines an area of immediate potential for the learner, because what the learner can do with assistance today is likely to be what the learner will soon be capable of doing independently. Cognitive growth is maximized if social interactions occur within the learner's zone of proximal development. The implication of the zone of proximal development is that students benefit from instruction that is moderately challenging.

Development Is an Historical Process within Cultural Contexts

Vygotsky and his associates believed that a complete theory of human development must take into account changes that occur at four historical levels including the development of the species (phylogeny), the history of human beings since becoming a distinct species, the history of individual children (ontogeny), and the history of the development of psychological processes during an experimental task (Cole, 1990). These historical analyses have practical implications for teachers in at least two ways.

First, Vygotsky believed it was important to understand ontogeny or the personal developmental history of learners. Without this type of analysis, Vygotsky suggested that it is possible to describe people's functioning, but not possible to explain the causes of that functioning (Wertsch, 1985). Of particular interest to Vygotsky were children whose development had been disrupted. The Vygotskians noted that two children could both be failing at school, but the causes of their failure and their potential to learn could be quite different because of their personal histories (Luria, 1961). Joann Gregory, a special education teacher, has had this experience.

➤ We collect a developmental history on all students who have been referred for special education services. Just this last week, the parents of a second grader who had been referred told us that the child had missed almost half of first grade due to illness. This put the child's problems in second grade in a different light.

Second, Vygotsky thought it was also important to understand individual development in terms of the history of that individual's cultural or social group (Vygotsky, 1981). To the extent that cultures differ, it is reasonable to expect that the cultural tools that are developed would differ. If cultural tools differ from one society to another, then people's ways of thinking and knowing could also differ. People's cognitive development would have to be understood in terms of its cultural contexts. This viewpoint has come to be known as a contextualist view of cognition. Contextualist views of development explain human development in terms of the complex interactions between people and their various environmental contexts (Rogoff & Morelli, 1989; Steenbarger, 1991; Sue, 1991).

Educational Implications of Vygotskian Theory

Vygotsky's theoretical ideas have implications for both instruction and assessment. The zone of proximal development provides a mechanism for providing strategy and skill learning. Vygotsky's view of the role of culture in development has led to the consideration of classrooms as cultural contexts. For example, how do classroom participation structures promote or constrain learners' interactions within those classrooms? The goal has been to develop classroom cultures that support students' active learning within their zones of proximal development. Finally, the zone of proximal development provides a structure for assessing students' learning potential.

The Zone of Proximal Development and Strategy and Skill Learning.   Students' skill and strategy learning within their zones of proximal development can be conceptualized in two ways. Teaching within the zone of proximal development can be conceptualized as a tutorial or as an opportunity for collaborative problem solving.

Tutoring within the Zone of Proximal Development.   In a tutorial approach, learners interact with more skilled peers or adults to perform a task that those learners cannot perform independently. The adults or more skilled peers in these situations guide or support the performance of the learners with the goal of helping them internalize important skills or strategies. The guidance provided by more skilled learners is often referred to as scaffolding (De Guerrero & Villamil, 2000; Wood, Bruner, & Ross, 1976). However, it also has been referred to as guided participation (Radziszewska & Rogoff, 1991) and responsive teaching (Gaskins, Anderson, Pressley, Cunicelli, & Satlow, 1993). Scaffolding is also important in cognitive apprenticeship approaches (Brown, Collins, & Duguid, 1989).

Scaffolding usually follows a three-step sequence. At first, the adults or more skilled learners assume most of the responsibility for completing the task. For example, they may model and explain what they are doing. Second, the learner and the adult or peer guide share responsibility for task completion. The guide gradually relinquishes control to the learner as the learners' skills increase. Finally, the learner takes full responsibility for completing the task. This final step represents a transition

An important theme in both Vygotsky's and Bruner's writing is that cognitive development needs to be understood in terms of the cultural and social contexts in which that development occurs. This viewpoint is sometimes referred to as a *contextual view* of development, and it has implications for teachers' understanding of cognitive development in a number of important ways.

First, contextualists recommend that we are cautious about our interpretations of what *normal* development looks like. It can be easy for members of a dominant culture to consider their behavior as the norm and to consider the behavior of other groups as a variation of the norm (Rogoff & Morelli, 1989). This can be particularly problematic when the variation is further seen as a deficit. For example, from a deficit perspective, children's knowledge of a second language would be seen as a factor that could interfere with learning English. The contextual view of cognitive development would warn against viewing a cultural difference as a deficit. Instead these differences would be viewed as positive variations that need to be understood in terms of the cultural environment of the learner.

Second, when interpreting cognitive development within a cultural context, teachers also need to remember that cultures are dynamic and prone to change and evolution. The cognitive skills and the ways in which cultures facilitate cognitive development also can change over time (Greenfield, 1999). Therefore, teachers need to understand that changes in cultural contexts can create quite different experiences and worldviews for different generations of people from the same culture.

Finally, the contextual view provides important cautions when assessing cognitive development across cultures. As noted earlier in the chapter, there are variables that can affect performance and consequently mislead us in our judgments about children's competence. Specifically, children and adults from other cultures may not interpret the testing situation as intended by the person administering the test (Miller-Jones, 1989). One of the more striking examples of this comes from Glick's (1975) research on classification with the Kpelle. The Kpelle subjects sorted twenty items into functional categories rather than the groupings intended by the researchers. For example, they put a hoe with a potato and a knife with an orange. When asked about their approach, they told the researchers that this is how wise people would do the task. When asked how a *fool* might do it, the Kpelle used the categories perceived by the researchers as correct (e.g., tool with tool, food with food). The point is that we need to judge capabilities in terms of the culture in which those capabilities are developed and used.

● **How might the implications of a contextualist view of development affect how you assess students' learning? (For your authors' perspective on this question, go to the text website for this chapter.)**

---

from socially supported performance to independent performance. From a Vygotskian perspective, a new zone of proximal development has been created.

Collaborative Problem Solving and the Zone of Proximal Development. Collaborative problem solving is a second way to conceptualize skill and strategy learning within the zone of proximal development. In this case, the idea of scaffolding by a more skilled learner is replaced by the ideas of two learners collaborating together to accomplish a goal (Wells, 1999). For example, two students may work together as partners to help each other understand the meaning of a text. Through their interactions, they help each other develop new understandings or skills. This type of interaction is referred to as mutual or collective scaffolding (De Guerrero & Villamil, 2000; Donato, 1994).

Classrooms as Sociocultural Contexts. Earlier in this chapter, Vygotsky's view of development as the internalization of cultural tools and how the nature of a society or culture determines the types of cultural tools that develop were presented. This perspective has been extended to classrooms (Cobb, Wood, & Yackel, 1993; Engeström, 1996; Moll & Whitmore, 1993; Palincsar, Brown, & Campione, 1993). Classrooms can be viewed as communities or cultures, and learning can be viewed as enculturation. The ways in which classrooms are structured can affect the types of interactions students have and the types of psychological tools they internalize. For example, Brown and

Molly Costas

5.2

Tonight's meeting was very challenging and interesting. Mr. Tsosie was able to attend for the first time and he wanted an explanation of our developmentally appropriate preschool curriculum. His main concern, as I mentioned before, was that he thinks it may be code for playing with the children and not challenging them. He's particularly concerned about his daughter, who is very advanced in a number of areas. I explained to him that a developmentally appropriate curriculum should challenge children by having them work at a level just above where they are as a learner. We try to engage children in these types of learning situations while we gradually help them develop the necessary skills and strategies to meet these challenges; our job is to guide their learn-

ing. We hope that our instruction pushes students to do their best. Although Mr. Tsosie said he likes that idea, he was curious how that's possible with fifteen children, many of whom are at different levels. I told him we use a lot of approaches including one-on-one instruction, collaborative learning, small group instruction, and individual learning projects.

● **How is the concept of the zone of proximal development related to the instruction in this preschool?**

Decision Point: What might this preschool do to help parents understand their program better and to help their teachers deliver more individualized instruction?

Campione (1994) have described a model of classroom teaching called *community of learners*. The classroom is structured like an effective research community in which students conduct research, consult with peers and adult resources, and present their findings to the community for review. The classroom is structured to help students acquire a number of learning and research tools that help them become lifelong learners.

How is the community of learners' culture different from more traditional classroom cultures?

The Zone of Proximal Development and Assessment. Interpreters of Vygotsky's ideas have generally agreed that he intended the zone of proximal development as both an assessment and an instructional idea (Campione, 1996; Campione, Brown, Ferrara, & Bryant, 1984; Daniels, 1996; Phillips, 1977; Wertsch, 1985). When Vygotsky was the Director of the Institute of Pedagogy, he became concerned about the use of standardized ability tests to assess students' potential to learn (Griffin & Cole, 1984). Although these tests were useful for assessing students' independent functioning level, they were inadequate for differentiating between students who had achieved the same independent functioning level but who had different learning potentials (Luria, 1961). For example, imagine that two students have achieved the same score on an individually administered standardized test. One student has had limited access to formal schooling, whereas the other has had full access to formal schooling. Their scores on the standardized test may reveal what they accomplished under these circumstances, but may not accurately assess their potential to learn when they are both provided with similar access to instruction.

To assess learning potential more accurately, Vygotskians suggested that standardized ability tests should be supplemented with measures of a learner's zone of proximal development. In this case, evaluators would *scaffold* learners as they attempted problems that were slightly above the assessed independence level. Measures of learning potential would either be how much improvement learners showed during the zone of proximal development procedure, or how much help it took to achieve a certain level of performance.

The interpretation of a zone of proximal development assessment procedure can be different depending on how the zone of proximal development is conceptualized (Allal & Ducrey, 2000; Minick, 1987; Van der veer & Valsiner, 1991). The zone of proximal development can be viewed as a characteristic or trait of the learner. In this case, measurements of the zone of proximal development would reveal learners' generalized potential to learn and could be useful for making predictions about students' potential for academic progress. However, the zone of proximal development may

Scaffolding and the Interactionist View of Second Language Learning

The interactionist view of second language learning suggests that students who are acquiring a second language will benefit from learning environments that provide comprehensible input (Krashen, 1982). To create comprehensible input for second language learners, native speakers adjust the complexity of their language and provide cues in their communications. These cues help second language learners understand what's being communicated, and they also help them improve their skills in the second language. Because comprehensible input is an attempt to guide and support learning, it can be viewed as a form of scaffolding. Teachers can scaffold language learning in their classrooms in a number of ways (Lapp, Flood, & Tinajero, 1994).

- Initially, accept language with grammatical errors and provide modeling of appropriate language usage.
- Use simple, well-formed sentences of limited length and complexity, while modeling appropriate grammar and intonation.

- Frequently repeat key words or ideas.
- Provide context clues such as simple diagrams or illustrations.
- Use a semantic elaboration technique in which you take what the student said and add to it.
- Use nonverbal cues such as gestures and body language to help support the meaning of oral language.
- Help students apply language in physical activities such as role-playing.

● **Which of these ideas provide examples of the scaffolding behaviors described in Figure 5.1? (For your authors' perspective on this question, go the text website for this chapter.)**

only exist when it is created by the interactions between a learner and an evaluator. This view implies that a learner's zone of proximal development could be different depending on the academic domain and who is providing the scaffolding; learners could have multiple zones of proximal development. In this latter case, the goal might be to identify what forms of scaffolding help this learner with particular tasks. It is possible to make the case that Vygotsky intended both uses for the zone of proximal development, but insufficient data exist to support the idea that the zone of proximal development is stable enough across situations to warrant general predictions about learning potential across all cognitive tasks (Allal & Ducrey, 2000).

Jerome S. Bruner's Cognitive Developmental Theory

Jerome Bruner provides a third cognitive developmental theory that has definite implications for instruction. In fact, Bruner defined instruction as "an effort to assist or shape growth" (Bruner, 1978, p. 1). Bruner's theory of cognitive development focuses on how knowledge representation systems develop and how culture influences cognitive development.

Knowledge Representation

What similarities are there between Bruner's idea of knowledge representation systems and Piaget's idea of the scheme or schema?

According to Bruner (1964), an important factor in the development of an intelligent mind is the ability to represent knowledge. Knowledge representation systems allow learners to store rules or generalizations that can organize and explain recurrent themes in their experience (Bigge & Shermis, 1999). Bruner thought that people have three systems for representing knowledge, the enactive, iconic, and symbolic representational systems (Presno, 1997). He further believed that these representational systems develop in sequence, starting with the enactive system, followed by the iconic system, and ending with the symbolic system. By the time people reach adolescence, they typically have all three representational systems.

Enactive Representation.   The first representation system to develop is **enactive representation** or the representation of knowledge through motor responses. People know something by doing it. When knowledge is represented or stored in an enactive mode, it is often represented as a habit or pattern of motor activity for accomplishing a task (Bruner, 1978). For example, the series of actions for tying a knot may be represented in an enactive mode. When working with very young children, teachers need to remember that they may know how to do things they cannot explain verbally because their knowledge is represented in an enactive rather than symbolic mode.

Iconic Representation.   The second representational system to develop is **iconic representation**. Iconic representation is the use of mental images to represent knowledge. According to Bruner, this capability develops relatively early in life and can be observed during infancy. An example of iconic representation is when a young child represents his understanding of circles by a mental picture of circles. Bruner (1978) noted that even adults are sometimes better able to understand verbal information if it is transformed into a picture or image. For example, it is sometimes useful to draw maps or diagrams of text to help students understand the relationships among the ideas in the text.

Symbolic Representation.   The final representational mode to develop is **symbolic representation**. Symbolic representation involves the use of arbitrary symbol systems such as language or mathematical notation. For example, a student could represent a rule such as, "I need to invert and multiply when I divide fractions" as a set of verbal propositions. According to Bruner (1978), the ability to use language to represent knowledge is very important in the development of logic, the ability to deal with events outside of our experience, and the ability to reflect on our own thinking.

> **What similarities are there between Bruner's symbolic representation systems and Piaget's semiotic function?**

Culture and Cognitive Development

Earlier in this chapter, we discussed Vygotsky's ideas of cultural tools and cognitive development as the internalization of those tools. Bruner tends to view cognitive development in a similar manner. He believed that cultural systems assist cognitive development by helping learners acquire the amplification systems of the culture. There are amplifiers of actions such as hammers and shovels, amplifiers of the senses such as microscopes and pictures that stop the action, and amplifiers of thought such as logic systems and language (Bruner, 1964, 1965). Like Vygotsky, Bruner believed that amplifiers of thought are the most powerful amplification systems.

> **Compare Vygotsky's idea of psychological tools with Bruner's idea of amplifiers of thought.**

Another point of similarity with Vygotsky is that Bruner believed that learners acquire amplification systems by interacting with the social, physical, and cultural resources of their environments (Bornstein & Bruner, 1989). Like Vygotsky, Bruner believed that the nature of these instructional interactions differ based on the goals that a cultural group has for its members. For example, in his analysis of Laurence and Lorna Marshall's films of the hunter and gathering society of the !Kung Bushmen of the Kalihari, he noted that instruction in amplification systems tended to occur continually, always in a situation in which the amplification system would be used, and more through showing than through telling (Bruner, 1965). Bruner noted that these interactions are quite different from how formal schooling occurs in industrialized countries, a point also endorsed by Vygotskians. To some extent, classrooms should be cultures of learning that allow students to develop the tools needed to function in their societies (Bruner, 1996).

One particular form of an instructional interaction that interested Bruner is the interaction between adults and children in problem-solving situations. In these problem-solving situations, adults guide or support learners as they solve problems together. As suggested earlier, the term **scaffolding** is used for this type of guidance and support (Wood, 1989; Wood, Bruner, & Ross, 1976; Wood & Middleton, 1975). The shared usage of scaffolding by Vygotskians and Bruner provides one more example of the connections that exist between the two theories. Table 5.2 contains the types of instructional support that Wood, Bruner, and Ross (1976) first labeled as scaffolding behaviors.

Bruner and Classroom Instruction

Bruner perceived a close relationship between his theory of cognitive development and his theory of instruction. Discovery learning, the psychology of the discipline, and the spiral curriculum are Bruner's three main contributions to a theory of classroom instruction.

Discovery Learning.   Bruner (1961) believed that knowledge students discover for themselves is the most uniquely personal knowledge they have. His definition of discovery learning would "include all forms of obtaining knowledge for oneself by use of one's own mind" (Bruner, 1961, p. 22). As an approach to classroom instruction, **discovery learning** is an inductive process that allows learners to discover important principles, relationships, or concepts through their own experiences. According to Bruner (1995) the discovery process can occur in a number of ways, including the use of Socratic questioning, problem examples that allow students to find patterns, and activities that encourage students' willingness to take risks in their learning. Consider this example of discovery learning in Mary Hartley's class.

➤ I provide my students with circles of different sizes, a ruler, and a piece of string. My students use the ruler and string to get measures of circumference

TABLE 5.2	**Types of Scaffolding Behavior**	
Scaffolding Behavior	**Description**	**Examples**
Recruitment	The teacher enlists the learners' interest and adherence to task requirements	A teacher might help learners understand how their participation can improve their competence
Reducing the degrees of freedom	The teacher simplifies the task requirements for the learner	A teacher might break a task down into a series of steps, or the teacher might complete some parts of the task, while allowing learners to participate at their own levels
Direction maintenance	The teacher encourages the student to focus on the task, and encourages the learner to take the next step	A teacher would manage environmental events that are distracting; the teacher lets student, know when they are on the right track
Marking critical features	The teacher identifies the important components of a performance for learners, and teachers help students perceive discrepancies between their performance and their goal	Teachers might alert students to problem areas that need to be avoided; they might identify the one or two key things to remember; they might also help learners compare what they are doing to their goals
Frustration control	The teacher helps students work through frustration and provides increased levels of assistance if necessary	A teacher might acknowledge that a task is difficult, but also let students know it is going to get easier; they may take more control of the interaction if learners are very frustrated
Demonstration	The teacher models and explains how to approach the learning task	A teacher might tell learners, "This is how I do this and why"

Adapted from Wood, D., Bruner, J., & Ross, G. (1976). The role of tutoring in problem solving. *Journal of Child Pyschology and Pyschiatry, 17,* 89–1000.

and diameter for each circle. They are asked to divide each measured circumference by its diameter and to tabulate the results. With measurement error factored in, they are going to observe that for each circle, the result turns out to be about 3.14 or pi.

Bruner advocated for discovery learning because he felt it took advantage of learners' natural curiosity, and that it helped them develop their thinking capabilities. He, however, also noted that "discovery, like surprise, favors the well-prepared mind" (Bruner, 1961, p. 22). Students who lack relevant background knowledge and skills are less likely to be successful at discovery, a point that has been supported by later research on inductive learning (Kuhn, Black, Keselman, & Kaplan, 2000). He also supported forms of discovery that were scaffolded or guided by more expert learners, rather than completely unstructured or open forms of discovery. Bruner's supported or scaffolded form of discovery is called **guided discovery**.

How are scaffolding and guided discovery related?

Bruner and Curriculum Design. Bruner's views on curriculum design or developing a "course of study" were organized around two key ideas. First, he believed that the focus should be on helping students understand the psychology of a subject matter. Second, he believed that curriculum should be spiraled.

The Psychology of a Subject Matter. The **psychology of a subject matter** includes both the key organizing principles or ideas of a discipline and the characteristic ways in which practitioners of that discipline solve problems (Bruner, 1965). For example, when students study environmental science, they would focus on understanding major concepts such as biological interdependence rather than memorizing a large number of facts, because these important ideas provide a structure for organizing subsequent knowledge.

Also, students need to engage in the research and inquiry methods of the discipline. Bruner wanted students to acquire knowledge, but he also wanted them to learn to think and solve problems. In the environmental science example, therefore, students would learn ideas through the application of the scientific method. In history, they would learn history through the research methods used by historians.

One important implication of organizing a curriculum around the psychology of a subject matter is that teachers would have to make decisions about what to include in a course of study. This approach tends to replace breadth of coverage with depth of coverage, an idea referred to as *less is more* (Dempster, 1993).

Spiral Curriculum. A **spiral curriculum** involves periodically revisiting key organizing ideas in a discipline throughout a curriculum (Bruner, 1960). Each time an idea is revisited it is done at a higher level of complexity and sophistication that is consistent with learners' increasing prior knowledge and representational abilities (Harden & Stamper, 1999; Parry, 2000). For example, the idea of biological interdependence could be introduced to young children through their observations at local ponds. In later grades, interdependence would be reintroduced at a higher level of complexity. For example, students might study the idea in terms of the impact of reduced numbers of predators on their prey.

Constructivism

Constructivism is somewhat difficult to define succinctly because it means so many different things to different people. It has been referred to as an epistemology or explanation of how knowledge is acquired (Simpson, 2001), a theory of classroom learning (Bevevino, Dengel, & Adams, 1999), or a worldview or an ideological position (Matthews, 2000). Also, constructivism has connections to many different philosophies, including Dewey's progressivism, postmodernism, and critical theory

Today we got down to the main charge of this committee, developing the new curriculum. Some of us want to identify a finite number of important concepts or principles that we would revisit periodically in the social studies curriculum. These would be so-called big ideas that students can use to organize their understanding of social studies. This is a difficult task because we are trying to work across all the grade levels and across content areas at the high school level. One idea that I think has potential is the conflict between the rights of the individual and the rights of society. Some of our elementary school teachers think they could integrate this idea into their discussions of fairness, citizenship, and even their beginning of the year discussions about classroom rules. I think it's a wonderful organizing topic for students' research and de-

bates on issues such as censorship, and it's a topic that easily can be approached at different levels of complexity throughout the curriculum. Some colleagues thought that identifying a list of ideas we would all teach would restrict teacher creativity. Instead, they thought each teacher or grade level should select their own ideas. Students would then get exposed to a number of key ideas.

● **How is Bruner's idea of the spiral curriculum related to this discussion?**

Decision Point: What do you see as the strengths and weaknesses of the two alternatives these teachers are discussing for selecting organizing ideas?

among others. In terms of the social sciences, there are connections to cultural anthropology and sociology.

For purposes of this discussion, constructivism is restricted to those aspects that have significantly influenced classroom learning and instructional design. Matthews (2000) refers to these as educational constructivisms. In schools, the influence of educational constructivism has been particularly strong for curricular areas such as math and science. However, the constructivist view has influenced almost all curricular areas. For example, whole language approaches to reading instruction are typically considered as examples of constructivist approaches.

Educational Constructivism

Educational constructivism can be thought of as a cognitive perspective on learning with strong connections to the cognitive developmental theories of Piaget, Vygotsky, and Bruner. At the heart of educational constructivism is the idea that learners actively construct their knowledge rather than passively receiving knowledge from their environments (Bodner, Klobuchar, & Geelan, 2001; Paris & Byrnes, 1989; Simpson, 2001). When educational constructivists refer to knowledge, they typically are referring to the types of knowledge required in activities such as critical thinking, reasoning, and problem solving (Driscoll, 1994).

Although educational constructivists would agree with the basic idea that knowledge is constructed rather than copied from experience, there are theoretical disagreements within educational constructivism about the nature of knowledge and the knowledge construction processes. Two of these different perspectives, psychological constructivism and social constructivism, have been particularly important in translating constructivist ideas into classroom applications.

Psychological constructivism is a form of constructivism with strong connections to Piagetian theory. Psychological constructivists believe that knowledge exists in the mind of the learner in the form of mental structures, and that knowledge is constructed individually through the processes of assimilation, accommodation, and organization. **Social constructivism** has strong connections to the social interactionist ideas of Vygotsky and Bruner. Social constructivists tend to believe that knowledge consists of cultural tools that exist in the social world before they are internalized, and that knowledge is internalized as a result of interactions with the social environment.

Constructivist View of Classroom Learning

By combining the implications of both psychological and social constructivism for classroom learning, it is possible to develop an integrated list of constructivist suggestions for classroom learning. All constructivists may not endorse every idea on this list, but the list provides an overview of how constructivist ideas have been translated into educational practice.

- Classrooms need to provide opportunities for students to engage in the discovery of new knowledge through problem-solving experiences.
- Classrooms need to provide complex learning experiences that allow students to integrate knowledge and to view knowledge from different perspectives.
- Classrooms need to provide opportunities for students to think collaboratively with teachers and other students.
- Students need to learn to be self-regulated learners who can take an active role in designing their own learning experiences.
- Students need to be engaged in authentic learning experiences that allow them to enculturate into communities of practice.

One way to think about these classroom implications is that modern educational constructivists have extended the earlier cognitive developmental ideas in interesting and creative ways. Table 5.3 presents the relationship between this list of constructivist suggestions for classroom learning and the related ideas from the cognitive developmental theories of Piaget, Vygotsky, and Bruner.

What connections are there between these ideas and the theoretical ideas of Piaget and Bruner?

Discovery of New Knowledge. Constructivists tend to agree that traditional transmission models of teaching (e.g., lecture) do not typically provide the types of interactions with knowledge that lead to deep understanding of that knowledge (Marlowe & Page, 1998; Richardson, 1997). Students need to be actively investigating and experimenting to develop meaningful understandings. Consequently, constructivists tend

TABLE 5.3 Constructivist View of Teaching and Cognitive Developmental Theory

Constructivist Suggestions for Teaching	Piaget	Vygotsky	Bruner
Classrooms need to provide opportunities for students to engage in the discovery of new knowledge through problem-solving experiences.	Learners need to be engaged in spontaneous research activities.	Higher mental functions are generated from learners' actions.	Discovery learning results in meaningful understanding.
Classrooms need to provide complex learning experiences that allow students to integrate knowledge, and to view knowledge from different perspectives.	New cognitive structures develop from existing structures.		Students should learn the psychology of the different subject matters.
Classrooms need to provide opportunities for students to think collaboratively with teachers and other students.	Social interactions allow learners to confront their egocentrism.	Development follows the general law of cultural development.	Learners acquire amplification systems through social interactions.
Students need to learn to be self-regulated learners who can take an active role in designing their own learning experiences.	Learners seek equilibrium.	Higher mental functions are mediated and controlled by learners.	The goal of education is to teach learners to think and problem-solve.
Students need to be engaged in authentic learning experiences that allow them to enculturate into communities of practice.		Different cultures provide different cultural tools.	Different cultures provide different amplification systems.

to support inductive approaches to teaching such as inquiry learning and discovery. Mr. Davidson, a high school history teacher, implements this idea in the following way.

> ➤ I occasionally lecture, but I prefer to describe briefly an historical event so that my students can generate research questions to answer about an event.

Integration of Knowledge.   As stated earlier, constructivists are primarily interested in the types of knowledge that are involved in activities such as problem solving and critical thinking. Consequently, they are in favor of methods that stress understanding of principles and concepts rather than rote memorization of isolated pieces of information. For constructivists, meaningful understanding results from relating new learning to prior learning, from integrating concepts within and between disciplines, from being able to represent knowledge in different forms, and from reflecting on the nature of their own knowledge (Brooks & Brooks, 1999; Spiro, Coulson, Feltovich, & Anderson, 1988; Ward, 2001). Consequently, they would tend to support approaches that integrate curriculum and that organize learning around conceptual themes or complicated problems. Mr. Davidson implements this idea in the following fashion.

> ➤ I find that students can get a good feel for different perspectives on a historical event from reading the popular literature of the time and by studying the available technology of a period. My colleagues in science and English are collaborating with me so that students also study historical events in terms of the science and literature of the day.

Social Construction of Knowledge.   The idea that knowledge can be socially constructed is typically associated with social constructivism, but Piaget also acknowledged the value of social interactions for knowledge construction (Smith, Dockrell & Tomlinson, 1997). This idea can be implemented in a number of ways. Students can collaborate to solve problems, or they can interact with more skilled learners, or they may share responsibility for learning and understanding. Situated cognition and distributed cognition are two examples of how instruction might facilitate the social construction of knowledge.

Situated Cognition.   **Situated cognition** can take many forms and names including cognitive apprenticeships, situated learning, and legitimate peripheral participation (Hendricks, 2001). In general, situated cognition approaches claim that both knowledge and learning cannot be separated from the contexts in which they are learned and applied (Brown, Collins, & Duguid, 1989; Fenwick, 2000; Greeno, 1993; Kirshner & Whitson, 1997; Lave, 1993). Learning is the process of enculturation during which learners acquire the concepts, ideas, theories, beliefs, values, and appropriate actions required by members of a community or practice (Lauzon, 1999; Lave & Wenger, 1991). For example, students learn the knowledge required of scientists by becoming a member of a scientific community.

An important implication of situated cognition approaches is that if knowledge is to be usable, it needs to be acquired through authentic learning activities (Basden, 2001). **Authentic learning activities** involve an emphasis on higher level thinking skills, substantive conversation among community members, social support for learning, an emphasis on depth of knowledge, and connections to the world outside the classroom (Gross & Kientz, 1999; Newmann & Wehlage, 1993). Typically, authentic learning activities are similar to, or in some cases, identical to real-world situations that require the use of what is being learned. For example, Griffin (1995) found that students were better able to execute map-reading skills if instruction included map-reading practice on the actual land that corresponded to the map, rather than as a set of skills taught only within the classroom.

We continue to discuss a wide range of options for our social studies curriculum. Today, Fred Waring, a high school government and economics teacher, started the meeting by saying that he thinks we really haven't addressed an important part of social studies learning. Each year he gets his senior government students involved in community learning projects that pair his students up with legislators, judges, and political leaders. The students help frame legislation, collect polling data, and generally get involved in applying what they have learned about our political system in real-world contexts. His students get the added benefit of interacting with experts in the field of government. Fred says all too often students don't internalize what we are teaching, but instead just memorize information for a test. He says social studies should lead to practical knowledge and a deeper understanding of our society. Although we like what Fred has to say, many of us are starting to worry that we may try to do too many things. We want to see if we can integrate what we have heard into a reasonable and coherent experience for our students. We don't want a bunch of powerful but isolated learning experiences for our students.

● **How does the idea of situated cognition apply to what Fred Waring is discussing?**

Decision Point: How might the discussion for organizing themes and Fred's suggestion for real-world learning be combined or integrated?

According to Brown, Collins, and Duguid (1989), a way to provide more authentic learning situations is to use cognitive apprenticeship models of teaching. A **cognitive apprenticeship** involves having students develop their concepts through authentic (realistic) applications of their concepts while collaborating with more skilled learners. For example, students might learn science by collaborating with scientists on research projects, as in the following example from Rob Mackenzie's geology class.

> ➤ To help my students better visualize contour maps, I have them work with college students and professors from the local university as they work to produce a contour map of the university.

Distributed Cognition.   **Distributed cognition** is the idea that "people appear to think in conjunction or partnership with others and with the help of culturally provided tools and implements" (Salomon, 1993, p. xiii). Knowledge and the tools for processing that knowledge are located both within the mind of the learner and within the social-historical environment of the learner (Cole & Engeström, 1993). For example, as a cultural tool, the computer allows the learner to engage in problem-solving activities that would be nearly impossible without the support of the computer. The computer in this case becomes a tool for distributing cognition (Perkins, 1993).

The distributed cognition perspective is that the collective knowledge of a society cannot be completely understood by one individual, but is distributed among the individuals in a society. The same may be said of classrooms in which students and teachers may possess different parts of the distributed knowledge in that environment. From a distributed cognition perspective, therefore, the goal is to create communities of practice in which students and teachers interact actively with each other and with the available cultural tools. Note the following example from Joanne Lawson's sixth grade classroom.

> ➤ Students in my classroom have developed expertise with different available computer programs. They then serve as teachers and resources for other students. They will eventually learn something about every program, but they will be class experts on at least one.

Authentic learning typically involves real-world experiences.

Self-Regulated Learners. According to Simons (1993) constructive learning is self-regulated learning. Constructivist learning environments engage students in experiences that teach them how to set goals, reflect on their own learning, and help them become independent problem solvers. Teachers might implement this suggestion by allowing students to have a voice in selecting their learning goals, how they will meet those goals, and how their progress will be evaluated. Mr. Peterson tries to encourage self-regulated learning in the following manner.

➤ Students often come to me unprepared to be researchers. I try to spent time at the beginning of the year helping them learn basic research strategies such as differentiating fact from opinion, and so forth. I want them to be able to apply these skills to guide their own research later.

Cognitive Developmental/Constructivist Learning Principles

The major ideas that have been discussed in this chapter can be summarized in terms of three general learning principles. These principles are discussed here, and they serve as organizers in later chapters for discussions of constructivist approaches to teaching, instructional design, and classroom management.

Principle 5.1: Learning Is More Powerful If Learners Actively Construct Their Own Understandings

Piaget, Vygotsky, Bruner, and the constructivists believe that learners develop a more meaningful understanding if they are active participants in their own learning. Although traditional approaches to instruction have their uses, they often do not create the levels of learner activity necessary for deep conceptual understanding. This principle implies that students should be allowed to learn by forming and testing their own hypotheses, by physically interacting with their environments, and by learning

Given that we've had so many questions from parents about our teaching approaches and philosophy, we've decided to create an informational pamphlet for parents. Our teaching philosophy is summarized in these bulleted points.

- We believe that students need to be full participants in their own learning. To do this, we must help them develop the skills they need to be self-directed learners.
- We believe that young children learn best when they actively explore their own environments. Learning should provide multiple opportunities for hands-on experiences.

- We believe that children often learn better from other children. We endeavor to provide multiple opportunities for students to work together to learn.
- We believe children are motivated when the learning situation challenges them. We are here to guide them through those challenges.

● **What constructivist ideas are present in this preschool's philosophy of teaching?**

Decision Point: Given the diverse nature of classrooms, what practical issues will these teachers need to consider in helping students' parents get the most from their pamphlet?

to reflect on their own learning processes and outcomes. Classrooms should be places in which students seek connections among ideas, and major organizing principles and concepts are stressed.

Principle 5.2: Learning Experiences Are More Effective If They Take into Account the Cognitive Developmental Levels of the Learners

This principle relates to Piaget's cognitive developmental stages, Vygotsky's notion of the zone of proximal development, and Bruner's ideas of knowledge representation systems. This importance of learners' developmental levels or prior knowledge for new learning is a key idea in constructivist views of learning also. Here are some implications of these principles.

- Adults should understand the nature of cognitive development in children and adolescents, and they should use that understanding in designing learning experiences for children and adolescents.
- Young children or novices in an academic domain profit from concrete experiences with new learning. Eventually, teachers should help students link those experiences to more abstract or symbolic experiences.
- Try to assess students' current levels of understanding and design instruction that is moderately challenging for those students.
- Try to understand learners' mental models that guide their thinking. Provide activities that help them expand or challenge those models.
- When working with young children, assume there is an underlying logic to what they say, even if it is not the same as yours.

Principle 5.3: Students' Knowledge Construction Is Assisted by the Nature of Their Interactions with People and Objects in Their Environments

Students' interactions with their environments influence the types of understandings they develop, especially their interactions with other people. This principle is reflected in the importance that Piaget, Vygotsky, and Bruner place on social interactions for children's development. The principle also relates to Vygotsky in terms of his ideas of cultural tools, the impact of the social-cultural history of the learner, and his general law of development, and to Bruner in terms of his ideas on amplification systems. Finally, this principle is present in constructivism in terms of the idea of social constructivism and authentic learning experiences. Here are some general implications of this principle.

- Students should be allowed to debate different points of view on issues.
- Students need to develop technological competencies that can extend their capabilities as problem solvers.
- Students need to engage in collaborative problem-solving activities, particularly those that require students to bring different forms of expertise to the problem.
- Learning experiences should extend out into the students' community.

Principles into Practice:
Illustrating Key Concepts

The experiences of Greg Urlacher and Molly Costas provide examples of how the three cognitive developmental/constructivist principles can be applied to classroom teaching. You were asked to reflect on these applications through a series of questions about their decisions. Here are your authors' views on the answers to those questions.

Looking back on

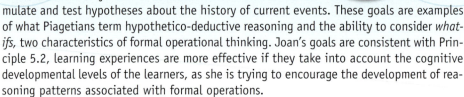

Greg Urlacher's social studies curriculum committee has turned its attention to the thinking skills they want included in their curriculum. Joan wants high school students to predict the impact of hypothetical changes in the outcomes of history on current events and to be able to formulate and test hypotheses about the history of current events. These goals are examples of what Piagetians term hypothetico-deductive reasoning and the ability to consider *what-ifs*, two characteristics of formal operational thinking. Joan's goals are consistent with Principle 5.2, learning experiences are more effective if they take into account the cognitive developmental levels of the learners, as she is trying to encourage the development of reasoning patterns associated with formal operations.

Greg Urlacher's committee also wants to identify some *big ideas* that would be revisited periodically throughout the curriculum at higher or deeper levels of understanding. This committee is planning a spiral curriculum as a way of providing sufficient time for students to construct a meaningful understanding of key ideas. In combination with their earlier expressed desire for students to form and test hypotheses about social studies topics, they are applying Principle 5.1, learning is more powerful if learners actively construct their own understandings.

Fred Waring wants students to develop a meaningful and practical understanding of social studies by working on authentic problems with mentors in the community. Fred seems to be suggesting a cognitive apprenticeship approach and providing the opportunity for situated cognition. His recommendations are an application of Principle 5.3, students' knowledge construction is assisted by the nature of their interactions with people and objects in their environments. ●

Looking back on

The parents in Molly Costas' workshop have raised some interesting questions about their children's development. Although any observation can be interpreted in a different way, the parents' experiences can be explained through Piagetian concepts. The infant who is making a game out of repeatedly throwing objects in the trash and having mom retrieve them could be an example of a circular reaction. The parent who thought it was funny that her three-year-old child would talk on the phone by nodding her head may be observing an example of egocentrism. The child knew she was nodding her head, so others should know that also because people see the world in the same way. The child who thought he had more cookie after one cookie was broken in half, was failing to demonstrate conservation. The change in appearance fooled the child about the amount of cookie. By using Piagetian theory, Molly might be able to help her parents understand these behaviors and how they might respond to them. She is applying Principle 5.2, learning experiences are more effective if they take into account the cognitive developmental levels of the learners.

As anticipated, Mr. Tsosie raised a concern about the level of challenge provided by developmentally appropriate practice. Molly explained that developmentally appropriate instruction actually has children working at challenging tasks with the guidance and support of adults. Molly's discussion seems very close to one possible application of Vygotsky's zone of proximal development, and reflects an effort to factor students' developmental levels into teaching decisions. Consequently, this is an application of Principle 5.2, learning experiences are more effective if they take into account the cognitive developmental levels of the learners. The guidance provided to students is an example of scaffolding and Principle 5.3, students' knowledge construction is assisted by the nature of their interactions with people and objects in their environments.

Molly's proposed informational pamphlet for parents contains a number of philosophical statements. They want students to actively explore their environments and to be self-directed learners. They also want children to learn by interacting with each other and to provide social support and guidance as their students attempt challenging tasks. Taken together these ideas seem to reflect a constructivist view of learning that incorporates elements of both psychological constructivism and social constructivism. Also, these ideas as a group represent the application of all three cognitive developmental/constructivist principles. ●

Teachers as Decision Makers

At numerous points in this chapter, you were asked to participate in the decision making of Greg Urlacher and Molly Costas. First we will share our views on those decision points.

Greg Urlacher's Decision Points

Greg Urlacher's committee has the challenging task of revising the K–12 social studies curriculum. With this type of task, it is important to use any existing resources that can inform the decision making. Certainly, he wants his committee to have any memo or letter describing the scope and charges of the committee, and he would want his committee to have the current social studies curriculum. Finally, any relevant state standards or state curriculum and similar information from professional organizations for the teaching of social studies might be useful also.

Greg's committee also discussed how to evaluate student exhibitions fairly. Although these types of assessments are discussed later, here are some preliminary ideas.

Teachers should have a pretty good idea of what they are hoping to evaluate with the exhibition. Is it content knowledge, presentation style, or a lot of different outcomes? Appropriate checklists and rating scales should be developed and provided to the students. Also, more traditional assessments may need to be developed to address outcomes not addressed through the exhibitions or to help students prepare for state-mandated exams. Finally, the time-consuming nature of these activities can be addressed by having some part of the work or presentations done outside of the class and by recruiting and training additional evaluators.

Greg Urlacher's committee is considering a common dilemma for teachers. How do they balance the need for a common curriculum with the need to honor teacher creativity and individuality? In this situation, the intent of common themes is to allow for a spiraling effect and the opportunity for each teacher to build on previous work. By individualizing themes, these possibilities may be lessened significantly. However, prescribing the themes may reduce teacher creativity. Usually, these situations require a compromise. This compromise can be facilitated if the strengths and limitations of each approach are identified so that a reasonable synthesis can occur that maximizes strengths and minimizes weaknesses. For example, two key themes can be identified for a curricular area, and teachers can add a third theme of their choice. Perhaps teachers could discuss how to integrate other important ideas into the teaching of the key themes.

In a similar fashion, the identified conceptual themes can be used as a structure for having students reflect on the experiences they have during the authentic learning experiences that occur outside the classroom, or even as an evaluation structure for the exhibitions. In that case, students would show what they have learned about those themes from their classroom and community experiences.

Molly Costa's Decision Points

Molly Costa needs to select topics for her parent meetings. A number of options are possible for selecting topics such as surveying the parents or identifying topics that the teachers think would be helpful based on their experiences with the parents. Allowing the parents to have some input seems useful, however, because it might create more interest among the parents for the meetings.

If a parent asks Molly for a recommendation for her child who throws things into the garbage, Molly should consider the purpose or meaning of the behavior. If the Piagetian interpretation of this behavior is accurate, then this behavior represents important cognitive development for the child. Perhaps the parent could provide an alternative such as a box into which a child could place geometric shapes. Rather than discouraging the behavior, the goal would be to find a more acceptable outlet for the behavior.

If Molly's preschool wants to help parents understand their program better, and they also want to provide more individualized instruction to her students, then they might consider how to involve the parents more effectively. One solution that could address both issues is to initiate a parent volunteer program. This volunteer program could be connected to the parent meetings in that Molly could use those meetings to help parents develop knowledge and skills that would be useful both at home and in the classroom.

Finally, given the diverse nature of classrooms, a number of concerns become important in the design of the informational pamphlet. First, what are the home languages of the children? A pamphlet in English may not be useful to parents who only read Spanish, for example. Interestingly, this observation has implications for how Molly structures her parent meetings. She may need to offer meetings in different languages. Also parental literacy levels and backgrounds may need to be considered. Is the pamphlet written in a way that is accessible to parents? For example, is it full of educational jargon? She may need to consider alternatives in addition to the pamphlet such as a slide show presented in different languages.

Looking Ahead: Cognitive Developmental/Constructivist Principles and Decision Making

One of the themes of this book is that teachers' decision-making process is improved through the application of principles from psychological theory. In Chapter 1, we identified these three broad categories of teacher decisions that provide opportunities to apply psychological theories.

- Decisions made when planning a lesson
- Decisions made when teaching and managing in the classroom
- Decisions made when assessing the effectiveness of their actions

In later chapters the principles developed in this chapter are used to organize discussions of applications of the cognitive developmental/constructivist theories to the decisions teachers make in the areas of instructional delivery, classroom management, and assessment of learning. Table 5.4 allows you to look forward and see the implications of these principles for the types of decision making discussed later.

TABLE 5.4   Looking Ahead: Cognitive Developmental/Constructivist Principles and Decision Making

Decision Area	Implication for Practice	Looking Ahead
Principle 5.1: Learning is more powerful if learners actively construct their own understandings		
Teaching and classroom management	Students need to be engaged in learning through exploration and discovery with the goal of acquiring meaningful, interconnected understandings of knowledge.	Chapters 7, 9
	Students need to be actively involved in classroom management decisions and procedures.	Chapter 10
Planning	Teachers need to design learning environments that support active exploration, problem solving, and social construction of knowledge.	Chapter 9
Assessment	Teachers need to design assessments that ask students to apply their knowledge in problem solving situations.	Chapters 7, 9
Principle 5.2: Learning experiences are more effective if they take into account the cognitive developmental levels of the learners		
Planning	Teachers need to design developmentally appropriate instruction.	Chapter 9
Teaching and classroom management	Classroom management and teaching strategies should be developmentally appropriate.	Chapters 8, 9, 10
Principle 5.3: Students' knowledge construction is assisted by the nature of their interactions with people and objects in their environments		
Planning	Teachers need to design environments that allow students to collaborate as they solve authentic problems.	Chapters 7, 9
Teaching and classroom management	Students need to be engaged in learning experiences that emphasize exploration, invention, and collaboration.	Chapters 7, 9, 10
	Students should collaborate with teachers in establishing and implementing classroom management procedures.	Chapter 10
Assessment	Students need to be engaged in authentic assessments that are guided by more skilled learners.	Chapters 7, 8, 9

Name _____ Date _____

Chapter 5 Study Guide

Use this Study Guide to review and test your knowledge of key concepts introduced in this chapter and to search out further information on issues and topics raised in this chapter.

💻 Key Terms

Review the following key words from the chapter and then connect to Research Navigator (www.researchnavigator.com) either directly or through this book's Companion Website to explore research on the topics as they relate to education today.

Accommodation (p. 122)
Adaptation (p. 122)
Assimilation (p. 122)
Authentic learning activities (p. 144)
Centration (p. 126)
Circular reaction (p. 124)
Classification (p. 128)
Cognitive apprenticeship (p. 145)
Compensation (p. 127)
Conservation (p. 127)
Deferred imitation (p. 125)
Discovery learning (p. 140)
Distributed cognition (p. 145)
Egocentric speech (p. 134)
Egocentrism (p. 126)
Enactive representation (p. 139)
Equilibration (p. 123)

Guided discovery (p. 141)
Higher mental functions (p. 133)
Horizontal décalage (p. 124)
Hypothetico-deductive reasoning (p. 129)
Iconic representation (p. 139)
Identity (p. 127)
Internalization (p. 134)
Irreversibility (p. 126)
Negation (p. 127)
Neo-Piagetian theories (p. 131)
Object permanence (p. 125)
Operation (p. 126)
Organization (p. 122)
Preoperational stage (p. 125)
Propositional logic (p. 129)
Psychological constructivism (p. 142)

Psychological tools or signs (p. 133)
Psychology of a subject matter (p. 141)
Scaffolding (p. 140)
Scheme (p. 121)
Semiotic function (p. 125)
Sensorimotor (p. 124)
Seriation (p. 127)
Situated cognition (p. 144)
Social constructivism (p. 142)
Spiral curriculum (p. 141)
Stage of concrete operations (p. 126)
Stage of formal operations (p. 128)
Symbolic play (p. 125)
Symbolic representation (p. 139)
Zone of proximal development (p. 134)

Alternative Response Items

1. Sally is able to combine her ability to scan the environment with her ability to grasp objects. This creates the more complicated behavior pattern of looking for and grabbing desired objects. From a Piagetian perspective, this is an example of:

   a. Organization   c. Accommodation
   b. Assimilation   d. Equilibration

2. John, a four-year-old boy, believes air does not have weight. He learns through science demonstrations that he was wrong. As a result he now believes that air does have weight. This change in understanding is an example of:

   a. Assimilation   c. Organization
   b. Accommodation   d. A scheme

3. Ramona believes that everyone likes dogs because she likes them. What characteristic of preoperational thought is she demonstrating?

   a. Egocentrism   c. Centration
   b. Irreversibility   d. The semiotic function

4. How is formal operational thought different from concrete operational thought?

   a. Formal operational thought is more egocentric than concrete operational thought.
   b. Formal operational thought is more abstract and hypothetical than concrete operational thought.
   c. Formal operational thought develops in children before concrete operational thought.
   d. Formal operational thought tends to be more intuitive than concrete operational thought.

5. Which one of the following educational recommendations is most *inconsistent* with Piagetian theory?

   a. Young children learn most effectively when lessons are presented primarily through lecture.
   b. Children should work with other children to solve problems.
   c. Learning activities for young children should involve concrete experiences.
   d. Learning experiences should be designed to challenge students' misunderstandings.

6. Which one of the following is an example of a psychological tool?

   a. A gardening hoe
   b. A word-processing program
   c. An electric saw
   d. Microwave oven

7. Which one of the following is an example of Vygotsky's general genetic law of development?

   a. A student acquires the reading strategies of a more skilled reader by interacting with that more skilled learner.
   b. Students change their opinions about an idea based on their own private experiences with that idea.
   c. Students must represent knowledge physically before they can represent that same knowledge symbolically.
   d. Students may have difficulty in complicated problem-solving activities because they are overwhelmed by the complexities.

8. Vygotsky referred to the distance between what a learner can accomplish alone and what that same learner can accomplish with the help of a more skilled learner as the:

   a. General law of development
   b. Zone of proximal development
   c. Internalization

9. Bruner's idea of thought amplifiers is similar to Vygotsky's idea of:

   a. Egocentric speech
   b. The general law of development
   c. Psychological tools
   d. The zone of proximal development

10. The constructivist idea that learning needs to occur in authentic or real-world contexts with the guidance of others is:

    a. Psychological constructivism
    b. Distributed cognition
    c. Metacognition
    d. Situated cognition

Constructed Response Items

Short Answer/Completion Items

1. An infant's understanding that items continue to exist even when they are out of the infant's sight is _____.

2. You have two identical beakers with the same amount of liquid in each. After having an eight-year-old child verify the equality, you pour the contents of one beaker into a third beaker that is taller and skinnier than the first two. You ask if this beaker has more water or the same amount as the first two. This child says they are the same because no water was added or removed. This child has used _____ to explain the answer.

3. In guided discovery, teachers help students develop their own understanding by prompting and guiding students' thinking. This type of teaching is an example of _____.

4. What form of constructivism is most closely associated with Vygotsky's theory of cognitive development?

Essay Items

1. What are the similarities and differences between Piagetian and Vygotskian theory?

2. Why might students find it hard to engage in accommodation?

3. Provide an example of something you learned through scaffolding.

4. What examples of constructivist teaching have you observed in classrooms?

Practicing Your Decision Making

Based on your experiences as a teacher and a learner, what do you see as the strengths and limitations of a constructivist approach to classroom learning?

INTASC in Action

Use the following activities to think about how cognitive developmental concepts and principles relate to the INTASC standards.

Standard 2: Student Development. The ideas of optimal mismatch and the zone of proximal development both suggest the importance of providing students with learning experiences that challenge their thinking, but that are not too far ahead of their cognitive development. What are the challenges of applying an idea such as this in a typical classroom? What might you do to overcome these challenges?

Standard 3: Diverse Learners. Whenever you take on the responsibility of teaching, ask yourself the following question. For the goals that I have for my students, what is the range of student preparation for meeting those goals? Use this question to remind yourself that even though students may be similar in chronological age, they can differ widely in terms of maturity and background experiences.

Standard 4: Multiple Instructional Strategies. How can the ideas presented in this chapter help you think about ways to encourage your students to be problem solvers?

Web Resources

For more information on concepts in cognitive developmental theories and constructivism, visit the following websites.

Jean Piaget Society (JPS)
www.piaget.org/

The JPS provides an open forum for the discussion of issues related to human knowledge and its development. It also encourages the application of advances in the understanding of development to education and other domains. The site provides a special listing of suggested readings for students.

Massey University: Virtual Faculty
www.massey.ac.nz/~alock//virtual/project2.htm

Read about the teachings of Lev Vygotsky through numerous postings of papers and web links to other sites on Vygotsky.

Selected Readings on Constructivism
carbon.cudenver.edu/~mryder/itc_data/ constructivism.html

This centralized site, hosted by the University of Colorado at Denver, provides connections to numerous links on numerous subjects as they relate to constructivism.

Motivating Students to Learn

Chapter 6 explores the nature of motivation and its causes, as well as the psychological factors that affect students' motivation to learn. This chapter presents information about how learner characteristics are related to motivation and how those characteristics are related to these key motivational principles:

- Principle 6.1: Learners are more motivated when they believe their actions will result in successfully completing challenging tasks.
- Principle 6.2: Learners are more motivated by activities that appeal to their personal needs, motives, and interests.
- Principle 6.3: Learners are more motivated when they have specific near-term goals that they believe are important.
- Principle 6.4: Learners are more motivated when appropriate levels of variety, choice, and surprise are incorporated into lessons.

Standards in This Chapter

Although learning the concepts and associated principles presented in this chapter will contribute to your mastery of all of the INTASC standards, the material presented in Chapter 6 is most strongly related to the following standards:

- **Standard 2:** Student Development
- **Standard 3:** Diverse Learners
- **Standard 4:** Multiple Instructional Strategies
- **Standard 5:** Motivation and Management

Karen Hilderbrand's Fifth Grade Class

I've been teaching fifth grade at General Arnold elementary school for fifteen years. General Arnold is a suburban school, the student population is growing rapidly and becoming more diverse. So when the other fifth grade teacher retired last year we hired a new teacher to take her place as soon as we could. The new teacher's name is Alfred O'Conner and he is fresh out of teacher college. My building principal has asked me to be Mr. O'Conner's mentor this year.

I remember when I started my first year of teaching I was very nervous. I think my experiences in college and student teaching were very good, but when you have your own class things are different. Looking back on it I realize that I actually had all of the information I needed to plan and execute good lessons, but at the time I felt so overwhelmed by demands of the job that I didn't have time to even think. I wish the district had a mentor-teacher program back then, because I thought that if I asked one of the other teachers they would think I didn't know how to do my job. I made a lot of mistakes that could have been avoided if I would have had someone to mentor me.

As a new teacher, one of my biggest concerns was motivating the students to participate in various learning activities. For instance, I knew it was important that the students practice applying the skills they were learning in mathematics, reading, and writing, but the exercises were so tedious that they would do just about anything to get away from them. Occasionally, I lost my temper and became very strict with the students. When this happened, it seemed everybody's motivation and performance suffered, even my own.

I hope I'll be able to help Alfred avoid some of the mistakes I made. I've scheduled a meeting with him on the Monday before school starts, so we can get to know one another, and I can get an idea of what kind of help I might be able to provide.

Decision Point: Why is student motivation such a critical issue for teachers?

Intuitively, people sense that motivation is related to learning in important ways. In Chapters 1 through 5 the major psychological theories of learning were examined and principles were developed that explain how variations in classrooms and instruction influence learning. However, it is impossible to predict precisely how an instructional activity will affect individual students. This is because, to a large degree, learning depends on the intentions of the learner. In other words, learners' motivation influences how they interact with instructional materials and the teacher. Psychologists and teachers agree that meaningful learning requires the active participation of the learner. This means that, as a teacher, you must understand what motivates your students to become actively engaged in their own education. Then you must use this understanding to guide the design and delivery of instruction in your classroom.

Before proceeding with Chapter 6, be sure you read the Close-ups on the Classroom features about Karen Hilderbrand and Josef Amir. At various points in the chapter, you will revisit both teachers in their classrooms and follow their decision-making progress. Their classroom experiences are closely integrated with the key concepts of this chapter and serve as important models for understanding Motivation Theory.

The Study of Motivation

What is motivation? Most people have naive theories about what motivates themselves and others, and tend to talk about motivation in relatively vague ways. The first step in improving your understanding of, and decision making about motivational issues is to develop a clear definition of motivation. **Motivation** is a mental

Josef Amir's Algebra II Class

I teach three sections of general science and three sections of algebra I, two sections of algebra II, and a section of geometry in a small rural school district. Three years ago the state began to require that all students take a standardized test before graduation. The test is based on the standards mandated by the State Board of Education, including a mathematics section that requires some pretty sophisticated algebra. This new policy has had a big effect on my classes. Before, when students were only required to take algebra I to graduate, only those students who planned to go on to college took algebra II and geometry. Now nearly all of our students take algebra II.

One of the biggest effects of this change has been in the nature of the students in the class. Specifically, there is more variation in the students' attitudes and interest in mathematics. I still have the students who are just interested in mathematics or who see algebra as a stepping stone to college, but now I also have many students, mostly seniors, who are not interested in mathematics and don't believe it will help them get ahead. This second group sees my class as just another hoop they have to jump through and often seem unhappy or even resentful about being in my class. This has caused me to rethink the way I teach algebra II.

The new policy hasn't just affected mathematics, my colleagues in English, history, and science are experiencing similar problems with the students in their upper level classes. We had our first staff meeting yesterday at which we were to recommend topics for this year's in-service program. After a pretty short discussion, we requested that we have some workshops on how to improve motivation in the classroom. The district superintendent said he would contact the faculty at the local university to see if they would be willing to help set up a series of in-service workshops on classroom motivation for the district's teachers.

Decision Point: What topics would you recommend for the in-service workshops that the district is planning?

---

process that activates, directs, and maintains behavior (Alderman, 1999; Pintrinch & Schunk, 2002; Reeve, 1996). This definition suggests that there are three aspects to a learner's motivation:

- The direction or goal of the motivation
- The relative strength of the motivation
- The duration of the motivation

Psychologists and teachers who are interested in students' motivation can gain valuable insights by looking at four types of learner behaviors or behavioral characteristics: (a) the choices they make, (b) the effort they invest in achieving a goal, (c) the frequency with which they take certain actions, and (d) the persistence with which they pursue an objective (Graham & Weiner, 1996). These four aspects of behavior provide clues about the direction, strength, and duration of people's motivation. For instance:

How might choice, effort, frequency of learning behaviors, and persistence affect the success of students in your class?

➤ Erik's chooses an advance placement astronomy course rather than another year of French. Erik's choice provides a clue about his personal educational goals. Perhaps his goal is to pursue a college degree in science.

➤ Alice spends many hours in the public library and courthouse researching historical and biographic information to complete a family history. Alice's effort suggests how strongly she is motivated to complete this project.

➤ Having received a low grade on the last history test, Jimmy is studying twice as hard for the next history test. Jimmy's persistence in the face of perceived failure suggests that his motivation to do well in history is an enduring characteristic.

These four aspects of behavior, choice, effort, frequency, and persistence, are important because they influence the quality of students' learning. Erik's choice of an elective course, in addition to providing his teachers with a clue about the direction of his motivation, will also affect his academic success. As will be discussed later in the chapter, the choices learners make and the goals they set have an important influence on their ultimate level of achievement. In Alice's case, her actions provide evidence of both the direction and strength of her motivation. It is also likely that her effort will have an important effect on the quality of her project. Jimmy's persistence suggests that he has an enduring motivation to succeed, and his persistence will make it more likely that he will eventually reach his goals.

Intrinsic and Extrinsic Causes of Motivation

What causes learners to become motivated to learn in the first place? Psychologists have investigated three possible categories of causes: (a) motivation results from internal mental and physical states, (b) motivation results as a response to our environment, or (c) motivation results from an interaction of the environment with internal states.

When motivation is directed toward achieving and maintaining a pleasant internal psychological state, the resulting motivation is called an **intrinsic motivation.** The basic idea behind intrinsic motivation is that the reward for completing or engaging in some activity is inherent to the activity itself (Spence & Helmreich, 1983). This inherent reward is often a pleasant feeling or emotion. Students are intrinsically motivated when they have some control over their learning, are engaged in moderately challenging tasks, when curiosity is stimulated by the learning task, or when they engage in fantasy or make believe activities (Lepper & Hodell, 1989; Melone & Lepper, 1987). Consider how the following students' thoughts and emotions are related to their motivation:

> ➤ Sally is happiest when she is talking with her friends. They talk about everything, school, play, brothers, and sisters. When the bell rings for recess, she runs to meet her friends and continues the discussion they were having before school started.

> ➤ Erik is fascinated by rockets and space travel. He reads everything he can find about rockets, including their history, use, and design. He even builds model rockets at home in his spare time.

In Sally's case she is motivated to seek out and talk to her friends because the activity is fun. In other words talking with her friends is its own reward. Erik is interested in rockets, and his interest motivates him to seek out information about rockets and engage in activities related to the area of interest. For Erik, learning more about rockets is rewarding because it matches his interests.

Extrinsic motivation is a motivation that arises from an external reward (Alderman, 1999; Reeve, 1996). Learners become extrinsically motivated when they recognize a relationship between their actions and receiving some external reward. In other words the learner realizes that, "If I do A, then B will happen." Examples of external rewards include money, peer approval, or public recognition. In schools, external rewards may include grades or praise from parents, the teacher, or classmates. These rewards are frequently public and under the control of others.

The relationship between intrinsic and extrinsic motivation in education has been the subject of much controversy and debate. Some argue that the use of extrinsic rewards is an attempt to manipulate students' behavior that ultimately results in a decrease in their natural intrinsic motivation to learn (Kohn, 1993b). Others argue extrinsic consequences, such as praise, are a form of feedback necessary to let students know that their efforts are effective (Chance, 1992, 1993) and that these extrinsic signs can actually enhance intrinsic motivation (Covington, 2000).

This argument is difficult to resolve in part because it is often hard to determine to what extent a person is motivated intrinsically or extrinsically. In many cases, a good performance, even if intrinsically motivated, results in attainment of extrinsic rewards. Consider, the case of Mr. Andersen's science students:

➤ As part of a unit on machines, Mr. Andersen assigned his students to teams, and each team had the task of designing a vehicle. The vehicle had to be powered by rubber bands and be capable of transporting a payload of one pound for at least six feet. The students were given access to a variety of materials and were also allowed to use materials that they could find at home. Each team demonstrated the operation of their vehicle in class. The students measured how far and how fast each vehicle transported its payload. Then the students collectively selected a machine to represent their class in a statewide competition. Mr. Andersen observed that the students appeared to be very interested in the project and that they seemed to be having fun designing and building their machines. He also noted that the students were spending a great deal of their free time on the project, with some even arriving early and staying late to test and refine their designs.

Many of these students are probably intrinsically motivated by the project. However, these same students are likely to be aware of the potential extrinsic consequences, such as a good grade for completing the project or the potential admiration of their teacher and peers if their machine is selected to represent the class or wins an award in the state competition.

In this case, Mr. Andersen provided an environment that presented his students with an opportunity, but how individual students respond to such an opportunity depends on each individual's physical and psychological characteristics. This explanation is in line with the view of motivation as resulting from an interaction between people's internal mental characteristics and the environment in which they find themselves. This is the perspective presented in this chapter.

The implication of the interactionist perspective is that to understand how to motivate your students, you must learn about those mental characteristics that influence motivation and how those characteristics interact with the environment. This chapter considers three categories of mental characteristics and how they affect students' response to classroom situations: (a) needs and motives, (b) emotions, and (c) cognitions.

How is intrinsic motivation different from extrinsic motivation?

Students' Needs and Motives

Two important characteristics influencing learners' motivation are their needs and their motives. A **need** is a physical or psychological condition that a person must maintain to stay healthy (Maslow, 1987). **Motives** are habits or tendencies to seek out and enjoy certain activities or accomplishments (Atkinson, 1957; McClelland, Atkinson, Clark, & Lowell, 1953; McKeachie, 1961). The learners who enter your classroom will each have their own unique set of needs and motives. They will be motivated to the extent that the classroom climate you establish and learning activities you plan allow them to meet and gratify these personal needs and motives.

Needs

One important and influential view of human needs and their effects on motivation was that proposed by Abraham Maslow (1987), whose theory comes from a humanist perspective. Maslow believed that all humans are motivated by the same set of basic human needs. He proposed that these basic needs could be arranged in a hierarchy

All people need to establish and maintain supportive relationships with others.

In what ways might the gratification of intellectual and aesthetic needs contribute to satisfying the basic human needs?

FIGURE 6.1 Maslow's Hierarchies of Needs

Basic Human Needs

Cognitive Needs
Aesthetic Needs
Intellectual Needs

Self-actualization Needs

Esteem Needs

Belonging Needs

Safety Needs

Physiological (Survival) Needs

in order of their importance to survival and the maintenance of physical and psychological health. In addition to these basic needs, Maslow also proposed that humans possessed a set of intellectual needs that formed a separate hierarchy. He suggested, that while these hierarchies were separate, they were related in important ways.

Maslow's hierarchy of needs has frequently been represented as a pyramid, and Figure 6.1 provides a graphic example of this interpretation. **Physiological needs** such as food, water, and shelter are the most basic to survival and so form the base of the pyramid. The need for a stable and predictable environment, referred to as **safety needs,** forms the next level of the pyramid. **Belonging needs** form the third level and refer to the need to form supportive or cooperative relationships with other people. The forth level are **esteem needs** and refer to the need for status within a group as well as a positive self-concept. At the top of the pyramid is the need for **self-actualization.** This is the need for each individual to develop his or her own unique abilities and talents to the highest level possible. The hierarchical organization implies that those needs at the bottom of the pyramid are more critical to our physical and mental well-being than those needs at the top.

Cognitive needs include intellectual needs and aesthetic needs. **Intellectual needs** describes the human tendency to try to understand and explain the world. **Aesthetic needs** are exemplified by the human desire to experience beauty and to find or create symmetry and completeness. Maslow believed that the cognitive needs supported the basic needs in important ways (Maslow, 1987; Rowan, 1999). In Figure 6.1 this idea is expressed by showing the intellectual needs as connected to all of the basic human needs.

To get a better idea of the relationship between intellectual and basic needs, consider the situations described below:

➤ When Edward first started school a few months ago he was anxious and even cried when his mother left. Now he is familiar with the classroom routine. He is no longer anxious about school and even looks forward to seeing the teacher and his new friends each day.

➤ The conversations of Maria's friends are typically about the members of the most popular band or the plots of popular television shows. Her knowledge of these subjects allows her to easily participate in and contribute to these conversations.

➤ Kathy is recognized as an excellent writer by her classmates and teachers. She seems to be able to express any idea in a way that is easily understood by the reader. Now she has been asked by the journalism teacher to edit the school newspaper.

Notice how satisfying intellectual and aesthetic needs contribute to the gratification of the students' basic human needs. In Edward's case, understanding of the school routine reduced his anxiety about school. Being able to predict what would happen day to day contributed to the satisfaction of his safety needs. Maria's knowledge of popular music and television shows provides an opportunity to interact with her peers and so helps her gratify her belonging needs. Kathy's writing skill combines both the intellectual and aesthetic needs and contributes to her ability to gratify her esteem needs as well as her self-actualization needs.

Needs and Motivation.   According to Maslow (1987) motivation results from the drive to satisfy the needs represented in the hierarchies of basic needs and intellectual needs presented in Figure 6.1. The conscious goals people select are actually means for satisfying their basic needs. Consider the case of Gail, a high-school sophomore:

➤ Gail is a typical teenager faced with many new opportunities, but also many new problems. This is her first year in senior high, and she's not happy in her new surroundings. She is doing average work, but doesn't especially enjoy her classes. She doesn't have many classes with her old friends, she's unfamiliar with the teachers, and even has difficulty finding her way around the school. Things aren't like they used to be at home either. Gail has been feeling isolated from her family. Since becoming a teenager, she has become more assertive, and this is causing friction between her and her parents. The one bright spot was the coach's suggestion that she try out for the cheerleading squad. She has decided to take advantage of this opportunity and has been practicing the routines she knows are part of the tryouts.

Gail's decision to try out for the cheerleading squad may be seen as a means to satisfy her belonging need. By joining a group made up of people her own age with similar interests, she may be able to form supportive relationships with others.

Maslow (1987) suggested that people from different cultural backgrounds may appear motivated to achieve different goals, but that the different goals just reflect different ways of satisfying the same core set of basic human needs. For instance, because different cultures value different things, people from different cultures can be expected to set different goals to acquire status within their culture and the esteem of their peers. Consider the cases of Eleanor and Feona:

➤ Eleanor lives in a small rural community in Montana and has decided she wants to be a champion barrel racer. Her goal reflects the values of the rural community in which she lives.

➤ Feona lives in Silicon Valley, California. She has decided to get a college degree in computer technology and business to pursue a career in computer programming.

For both Eleanor and Feona, the values of their culture influence the goals they set. By satisfying these goals they satisfy their basic needs for esteem. In Eleanor's rural community, horsemanship is an important skill, much admired by her peers. On the other hand, Feona comes from an urban community where status is derived from your job.

Maslow also proposed that conscious goals were often under the influence of multiple needs. In other words, sometimes people set goals that allow them to gratify two or more needs at the same time. Consider the case of Isaac:

➤ Isaac began wrestling in junior high and is now on the varsity wrestling team. Many of Isaac's abilities are respected by his friends on and off the team, by the coaches, and by his teachers. Isaac is confident that if he works hard he can continue to earn the support and respect of his teammates and others in the school.

By joining the wrestling team and working hard, Isaac has been able to satisfy three basic needs at the same time. By forming meaningful relationships with his teammates and the coaches Isaac satisfies belonging needs. Being on the team also wins him the respect of the other students in the school, thereby helping to satisfy his esteem needs. Finally, the stability of the wrestling team and the school help satisfy his safety needs.

Deficiency Needs and Growth Needs. Maslow also divided his list of needs into two categories, deficiency needs and growth needs (Maslow, 1955). **Deficiency needs** operate on the principle of homeostasis. **Homeostasis** refers to the maintenance of an optimal state, condition, or balance. To stay healthy, humans must maintain certain biological and social conditions in a more or less constant state, a state of homeostasis. Deficiencies in any of these conditions result in a motivation to remedy the situation. Once the deficiency no longer exists, the motivation associated with that particular need disappears. Consider the following examples:

➤ Billy is thirsty after recess and stops at the water fountain for a drink, then returns to his classroom.

➤ When Janet moved to town she didn't know anybody. She joined the school choir and now has many friends. When asked to join the school spirit club, she declines.

In the case of Billy, his thirst represents the basic physiological need to maintain a healthy amount of fluids in his body. He satisfies this need by drinking water. Once the need for fluid is satisfied he is no longer motivated to drink. Janet was motivated by her belonging needs to join the choir. Her action resulted in the formation of many friendships and gratified her need to form meaningful relationships with others. Her belonging need being gratified, she was not motivated to join the school spirit club.

Maslow (1987) referred to the need for self-actualization and the cognitive needs as higher needs and believed that under certain conditions these higher needs become independent of the lower basic needs. When this happens the influence these needs exert over an individual's motivation actually increases or grows each time the need is gratified (Maslow, 1955). For this reason these needs are labeled **growth needs.** Consider the following examples:

How is the motivation to fulfill a growth need different from the motivation to fulfill a deficiency need?

➤ Over the years Emily's parents and teachers provided her with many opportunities to hear performances of the local orchestra, and so she has come to appreciate and enjoy orchestral music. Now she regularly attends concerts and even supports the local orchestra with her donations.

What type of need, deficiency or growth needs, is most likely to cause persistent motivation in students? Why?

➤ Jovita was encouraged by her parents to ask questions and to answer her own questions through exploration and experimentation. Jovita has now decided to take an advance placement science class as an elective course in her senior year.

ENRICHING YOUR UNDERSTANDING
Development of Needs through Childhood

Hampden-Turner (1981) provides an interesting interpretation of Maslow's theory of needs as it relates to human development. In this view, the relative influence of different needs changes across the lifespan. Figure 6.2 provides a graphic illustration of this perspective.

For instance, in infancy a child is aware of little else than immediate needs and the presence of the primary caregiver. At this age physiological needs are most important. As the child gets older and becomes better able to imagine the future, the stability and predictability of the environment become more important and in terms of general influence, safety needs supersede physiological needs. As children continue to mature, the social aspects of life assume greater importance and belonging needs supersede safety needs in general importance. Finally, in young adulthood, esteem needs become most influential. The growth needs, self-actualization, and the cognitive needs become stronger with each opportunity for gratification. These needs may eventually become so influential that a person may sacrifice everything else, esteem, relationships, safety, and even health to achieve self-actualization or intellectual or aesthetic growth.

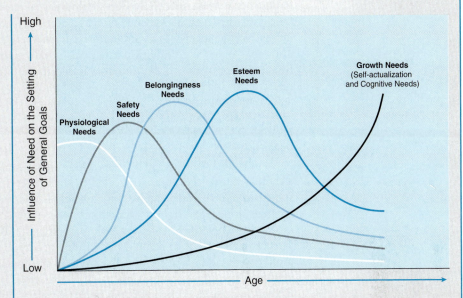

FIGURE 6.2 The Developmental Progression of Maslow's Needs
(Adapted from C. Hampter-Turner (1981). *Maps of the mind,* New York: Macmillan.)

● **What needs are most likely to influence the motivations of the children in your future classroom? (For your authors' perspective on this question, go to the text website for this chapter.)**

In the case of both Emily and Jovita, the opportunity to gratify their aesthetic and intellectual needs has caused them to set goals and take actions that will allow them to continue to gratify these needs.

Motives

Motives are considered relatively stable individual characteristics or *traits* that influence a person's performance in a wide variety of situations. As previously defined, motives are habits or tendencies to seek out and enjoy certain activities or accomplishments (Atkinson, 1957; McClelland, Atkinson, Clark, & Lowell, 1953; McKeachie, 1961). An important implication of this definition is that motives are different from needs, in that motives are learned rather than innate (Atkinson, 1957). This means that learners have different motives because they have had different life experiences.

How are motives different from Maslow's needs?

Atkinson (1957, 1964) proposed that a partial list of these motives would include motives (a) for achievement, (b) to avoid failure, (c) for affiliation, and (d) for power and control. McKeachie (1961) studied the influence of these motives on the academic performance of college students. He found that students with different motives responded to classrooms and instructors in different ways.

The **achievement motive** is defined as a desire to complete challenging tasks successfully. For an individual with a strong achievement motive, the amount of pleasure experienced when successful depends on the perceived level of challenge. In other words, as the level of challenge increases, the pleasure experienced with success also increases. The **motive to avoid failure** is a disposition to avoid the shame or humiliation associated with failure. Individuals with a strong motive to avoid failure prefer situations in which the outcome is certain and are made especially anxious by uncertainty. Individuals' motive to avoid failure seems to be negatively related to the achievement motive; that is, when one is strong, the other is weak (Atkinson, 1957, 1964; Murry, 1955). Stable differences in the way learners respond to challenges has been observed in children as young as five years of age (Ziegert, Kistner, Castro, & Robertson, 2001).

The difference between learners with a strong achievement motive and those with a motive to avoid failure is revealed by their preference for challenge and their response to failure. Individuals with high achievement motives prefer moderately challenging situations. In practical terms, this means that these students are most motivated when they perceive a task is challenging, but achievable. In this situation, learners feel justified in being proud of their accomplishments. Learners with a strong motive to avoid failure are more focused on the uncertainty and so try to avoid challenging tasks. They are most attracted to situations in which the outcome is certain. Rather than face a challenging, but uncertain situation, these learners prefer situations for which the probability of success is very high (almost certain to succeed) or very low (almost certain to fail).

Persistence in the face of failures and setbacks is another way in which learners with a strong achievement motive differ from learners with a strong motive to avoid failure. When they fail to achieve their objective, learners with a high achievement motive are likely to persist, whereas learners with a strong motive to avoid failure are more likely to give up.

Consider how preference for challenge and persistence is revealed in the cases of Gerald and Kevin, two boys considering their selection of an elective mathematics course. Each must choose between calculus II, viewed by most students as very challenging, and a practical problem-solving course reputed to be very easy.

➤ Gerald took calculus I last year, and in spite of working very hard, received a grade of C+. Gerald is accustomed to receiving A's but he thinks that given the difficulty of calculus I he did okay. He sees the C+ as an accurate indication of how much he's learned and how much more there is to learn. Gerald believes that calculus II will be difficult, but that it will be more worthwhile than the practical problem-solving course. Gerald elects to take calculus II.

➤ Kevin also took calculus I last year and received a C+. Kevin typically receives A's and he views the C+ as a failure. Kevin was actually embarrassed when he saw his score on the final exam. Kevin sees calculus II as a threat to his overall grade point average and to his ego. He elects to take the practical problem-solving course instead.

Why might someone who has a motive to avoid failure prefer to take a course they are sure to fail instead of a course they might fail if they don't master the material?

Both boys worked hard in the calculus I course and received the same grade. Gerald exhibits an achievement motive in that he is focused on opportunities to improve his skill in mathematics and actually prefers challenging tasks. Kevin has focused on the potential threat to his ego or self-esteem, and his motive to avoid failure is revealed by his choice of a class in which he is certain to succeed.

Learning is most likely to occur when learners attempt challenging tasks. This puts learners with a strong need to avoid failure at a disadvantage. Think of the relative differences in mathematics skills between

Gerald and Kevin after each has completed their elected course. Atkinson (1957) maintained that for all persons the maximum motivational strength occurs at moderate levels of challenge. This means that when learners with a strong motive to avoid failure are forced to accept a moderately challenging task, they may be motivated to perform, but they won't like it. However, it is important to remember that you must challenge your students even if they would prefer that you do not.

The **affiliation motive** is defined as a desire to establish, maintain, or restore effective relationships with other people (Atkinson, 1964; McKeachie, 1961). These students are more motivated in the classroom when they perceive the instructor as warm and friendly. It is also likely that these students would prefer classroom activities such as cooperative learning or group work to independent or competitive situations.

Students with high levels of motivation to achieve prefer challenging tasks and persist when they experience failure.

The **power motive** is defined as a desire to control the means for influencing others (Atkinson, 1964; McKeachie, 1961). Students with a high need for power enjoy leadership, may be argumentative, and seem to enjoy trying to persuade others to accept their point of view. These students seem to prefer classrooms where they are encouraged to assert themselves by voluntary participation in class discussions.

What need proposed by Maslow is similar to the affiliation motive?

$\mathcal{E}$motions and Classroom Motivation

Students' emotional responses to your classroom and instructional activities also affect their motivation to learn. Emotions are an automatic physical and mental response to a perceived situation (James, 1918). The physical component is the level of physiological arousal, as indicated by things such as heart rate or respiration. The level of arousal is associated with the strength of the emotion and with the strength of the resulting motivation (Brehm, 1999). The cognitive component is the conscious interpretation and labeling of the situation, in other words, what people think of the situation. This component of an emotion is most closely associated with the direction or goal of the resulting motivation.

Pekron, Goetz, Titz, and Perry (2002) have found that students experience a variety of emotions in anticipation of and response to people and events in classrooms. These emotions have an important effect on how students interpret and react to teachers, classmates, and classroom activities (Weiner, 1985; Linnenbrink & Pintrich, 2002). Three emotions of particular interest to educators are interest, curiosity, and anxiety. Understanding the nature of these emotions helps you understand your students' behavior.

Interest

What is it that makes a class, learning activity, or project interesting to students? Interest is an emotion that arises from the interaction of a specific situation or task with the unique needs, abilities, skills, and values of an individual (Krapp, Hidi, & Renninger, 1992; Reeve, 1996). This means that what one person finds interesting, another person may find of no interest at all. In spite of the idiosyncratic nature of interest, it is important for teachers, because interested students are more likely to be actively engaged in their own learning (Schiefele, 1992; Snow & Jackson, 1994).

Students often become interested in a topic or activity because they have extensive background knowledge relevant to the situation or because the topic or activities appeal to the internalized values of the students (Reeve, 1996). Interest derived from the specific knowledge, beliefs, and values of the student is called **individual interest** (Renninger, 1992). Such individual interest is characterized as being a stable enduring characteristic of the learner (Snow & Jackson, 1994). Consider the comments of these two students discussing an assignment to write a short expository paper on any topic they choose:

➤ Eddie says, "I'm going to write about soccer, because I've been playing since I was in first grade. Maybe I'll write about the off-side rule."

➤ Susan responded, "That's okay for you, but I don't know anything about soccer. Anyway, I'm more interested in nature. Yesterday I saw a Lewis woodpecker in our backyard. I think I'll write about how to attract birds to your backyard."

In this case, both Eddie and Susan are writing about what they know and value. A student who has extensive knowledge or values relevant to a topic or activity is likely to set goals to explore and find out about such topics or activities.

Sometimes, it is the task itself that learners find interesting. This may occur when they find a task enjoyable because it's challenging or allows them to satisfy some need. The type of interest generated by such tasks is called **situational interest** (Hidi & Anderson, 1992; Reeve, 1996). It is possible that teachers can manipulate classroom activities to stimulate this type of interest; however, when the learners' needs have been satisfied, or when they've mastered the challenge of the task, they will lose interest. Consider the experience of Mr. Carlyle.

➤ Mr. Carlyle looks at the computer sitting unused in the back of the class. When he first brought it in, the students couldn't wait to get free time to play with the math games on the computer. Mr. Carlyle noticed that as students' math performance improved, they spent less time on the computer; and yesterday he heard several students complain that the computer games were too easy. He makes a mental note to put in a request for some new software, something that's more challenging.

At first, Mr. Carlyle's students found the arithmetic drills on the computer challenging and were motivated to practice math facts and operations to improve their skills. However, once these skills were mastered, the computer program was no longer challenging and offered no further opportunity for growth or improvement, so the children lost interest.

> **What's the difference between motivation that results from a situational interest and motivation that results from an individual interest?**

Curiosity and Anxiety

What students know can affect their interest in a subject, but their emotions are also affected by what they don't know. Consider a student who is reading a mystery novel, not knowing how the book will end. The student may be driven by curiosity to read nonstop until she reaches the end. However, the unknown does not always cause students to engage in exploratory behaviors. Sometimes the unknown causes them to become worried or afraid. In this case, they may try to withdraw from or otherwise avoid the situation. Consider the cases of Ramon and Gene:

➤ Ramon watches as his third grade teacher Ms. Ash places a piece of stone she calls pumice in a pan of water. He and his classmates are amazed when this piece of rock floats. Immediately he raises his hand to ask, "Where did this rock come from?"

➤ Gene is normally an outgoing and friendly six year old. But everything about this new place is strange, the adults, the kids, even the smells are unfamiliar. He watches anxiously as his mother finishes talking to the teacher, then leaves. His first day of school is overwhelming and he doesn't speak all day.

Ramon is faced with the unknown in the form of a puzzling event. In this case Ramon's action suggests that he is experiencing what is usually thought of as curiosity. **Curiosity** is a cognitively based emotion that causes us to engage in exploratory behaviors (Spielberger & Starr, 1994). **Exploratory behaviors** are behaviors directed toward seeking out new experiences or gathering additional information and include asking questions, looking up information in books, experimentation, thinking, and other activities that we generally associate with learning.

In Gene's case, too many things are unfamiliar to deal with all at once. His

Curiosity motivates students to explore a situation and to work toward gathering additional information.

reaction is subdued and withdrawn. Gene is experiencing anxiety. **Anxiety** is an emotion that causes students to try to withdraw from or avoid the person or situation causing their anxiety. Notice that both curiosity and anxiety both seem to be related to learners' uncertainty (Lader, 1975; Spielberger & Starr, 1994).

Curiosity and Anxiety in Classrooms.   What is the relationship between anxiety and curiosity and how are these emotions related to classrooms? Two theoretical approaches have attempted to explain curiosity (Reeve, 1996; Spielberger & Starr, 1994). One explanation is that whenever students detect a gap in knowledge or experience an event that violates their expectations, they are motivated to fill the gap or explain the contradiction. An alternative approach to explaining curiosity is that each person acts to maintain an optimal level of arousal or excitement (Berlyne, 1967). From this perspective, when students' arousal level is too low, they are motivated to seek out a more stimulating environment.

Spielberger and Starr (1994) have proposed a model that reconciles these two perspectives on curiosity and explains the relationship between curiosity and anxiety. They propose that as a situation becomes more exciting, people are simultaneously influenced by two conflicting impulses: (a) the impulse to explore and find out, and (b) the impulse to avoid the unknown. The emotional experience and behaviors associated with different levels of arousal result from the balance between the opposing impulses to explore and avoid a situation.

How exciting people find a particular environment is dependent on the arousal potential of that environment. The **arousal potential** refers to how stimulating or exciting students find the environment to be. The arousal potential of a classroom is increased by the novelty, complexity, or uncertainty perceived by individual students (Berlyne, 1967; Reeve, 1996). The model proposed by Spielberger and Starr (1994) proposes that the impulses to explore and to avoid change as the arousal potential increases. This model is based on the assumption that everybody has an optimal or preferred level of arousal and will try to maintain that level of arousal by engaging in exploratory or avoidance behaviors.

Student Boredom.   In situations in which the arousal potential is low and does not result in an optimal level of arousal, the person's goal is to increase the arousal potential. In other words, if the situation is perceived as boring, people take action to make the situation more exciting and thereby relieve the boredom. In such situations a person's impulse to explore is stronger than the impulse to avoid, and the exploratory behavior is described as diversive. **Diversive exploration** consists of exploratory

How is Berlyne's view of curiosity similar to Piaget's concept of equilibrium presented in Chapter 5?

behaviors that relieve the boredom by increasing the arousal potential of the situation. The goal of relieving boredom is pretty general, and so the actual nature of diversive exploratory behaviors is likely to be idiosyncratic and difficult to predict. Consider these examples of diversive exploratory behavior observed during a study hall:

➤ Hillary takes out her math book and begins her homework assignment.

➤ Sam takes an encyclopedia from the shelf and begins to scan the contents.

➤ Judy takes the ink cartridge from her pen. She then uses the empty pen as a pea shooter to shoot paper wads at her friend across the room.

As you can see, this type of exploratory behavior is not always beneficial to students' learning. In fact some of the behaviors that result from boredom may be disruptive to the learning of other students.

Student Curiosity.   In situations in which the arousal potential of a situation results in arousal that is above the person's optimal level, the individual's goal is to reduce the arousal potential of their environment. When the person's arousal is only moderately higher than their optimal level, the impulse to explore is still stronger than the impulse to avoid. But now the purpose of exploration is to reduce the arousal potential to the optimal level, by gathering specific information that will reduce the complexity or uncertainty of the situation. **Specific exploration** consists of actions directed toward understanding a specific situation, thereby reducing the complexity or uncertainty of the situation and returning the arousal potential to the individual's optimal level. The emotion experienced in such situations describes what most people think of as curiosity. Consider the students who observe their science teacher's demonstration at the beginning of class.

➤ As the students enter the classroom, the teacher is setting up a demonstration. A hot plate in the front of the room is heating an aluminum can. Next to the hot plate is a pan of ice water. The bell rings and the students are still talking when the teacher picks up the can with a pair of tongs and places it upside down in the ice water. There is a loud pop and the can is immediately crushed. The students stop their talking and look to the front of the room. Then they all start asking questions at once.

The unusual behavior of the can motivates the students to engage in specific exploratory behaviors in an effort to understand this event. These behaviors might include

What is the difference between diversive exploratory behaviors and specific exploratory behaviors?

asking the teacher or another student to explain what happened, consulting a science book to find information to help explain the event, or using the kitchen stove and materials at home to conduct experiments with aluminum cans and other containers.

Student Anxiety.   When the arousal potential of a situation results in levels of arousal that are far above a person's optimal level, the person is likely to experience anxiety. The goal is still to reduce the arousal potential, but now the impulse to avoid is stronger than the impulse to explore and the individual takes action to escape or avoid the situation. Skipping class, misbehaving in order to be expelled from class, or procrastination may all be attempts to temporarily avoid an anxiety-producing situation. Perceptions of risk and ambiguity often increase the arousal potential of a situation to an uncomfortable level. Consider the reactions of the students in the following situations:

➤ Eleanor is required to complete a twenty-page term paper by the end of the semester. She finds the whole thing overwhelming and just doesn't know where to start. It's the end of the semester and she hasn't even picked a topic.

➤ Today is the day of the big test that will determine whether or not students will be allowed to graduate. Clifford's misbehavior ensures that he will be sent to the principal's office instead of taking the test with the rest of the class.

Looking in on

My first meeting with Alfred went well. It turns out he and I went to the same college and even had some of the same professors. Al said he was really happy to have landed this job, but confessed that he was also a little anxious. He really likes working with kids this age and is really looking forward to his first year, but he knows how energetic kids are and is a little concerned about keeping his kids on task.

I told him that I had similar concerns. I want the students on task, but I don't want the fun to go out of learning. I told him he had a natural advantage: Being new to the school, many of the students would be curious to see what kind of teacher he would be. I suggested that he might be able to use the children's curiosity by introducing new material with some kind of discrepant event. I explained that a discrepant event was something surprising or unexpected that was related to the day's topic. It gets the kids to look at the lesson as a puzzle or mystery to be solved. Sometimes it doesn't take much to make kids curious, almost anything unexpected or out of the ordinary works. I also warned him against overusing the technique. Too many surprises are not surprising, but if he did it once in a while the students would see the class as interesting and fun, and that is half the battle.

Al noted that presenting students with a discrepant event seemed likely to work when he was introducing new ideas, but might really require a lot of work to think of new surprising things to do, especially when he just wanted them to practice a skill or review some material that was already covered.

I agreed that the technique was not appropriate for some objectives. As for reviews and practice, I told him that over the years I had developed exercises for the different content areas in the form of games. Some of the games use individual competition, some allow the kids to form teams, and others have the kids working to improve their own records. We discussed this idea for a while, and I told Alfred he was welcome to make copies of my game materials and use them in his class if he liked. However, I cautioned him that he should be careful to keep his objectives in mind when he was developing his games. It is easy for the kids, and the teacher, to become so involved in a game that the instructional objective of the lesson becomes lost.

● **How do discrepant events and games affect students' motivation to learn?**

Decision Point: When would you consider using a discrepant event to motivate students in your classroom? When would you consider using a game? What cautions should you observe when using this approach?

In Eleanor's case, she sees the term paper as an ambiguous assignment. She doesn't know what she needs to do or even how to begin. To avoid the unpleasant feelings caused by this assignment, she has been putting off starting the assignment. Clifford is faced with a high-risk situation. His misbehavior in class resulted in his being sent to the office, allowing him to avoid the situation temporarily.

Perception of Arousal Potential. As previously defined, arousal potential refers to how stimulating or exciting students find the environment to be. This means that different students in the same classroom may differ in their perceptions of how exciting or threatening the situation is. Consider two students, Elliot and Marta, each taking the same standardized test.

➤ Elliot has taken many standardized tests. He understands the rules and has never experienced any negative consequence associated with his performance. Elliot thinks the test items themselves are fun. They are like puzzles or the trivia games he plays with his family. When his teacher tells the group to begin, Elliot immediately starts to read and answer the test items.

➤ Marta attended an alternative school before transferring to the public middle school and has had no experience with standardized tests. When the test booklet is placed on her desk all she can think about is what her friends, the teachers, and even her parents will think about her if she does poorly. She is so distracted and worried, she can't concentrate on the test items. Finally, just to get away from the situation, she answers the items as quickly as she can.

Elliot has had a lot of experience with standardized tests and views them as a sort of game. He is familiar with the testing procedures, the consequences, and even the nature of the test items. He may even be a little interested or curious to see the items on this new test. For Elliot the arousal potential of the test situation is close to optimal. In Marta's case, standardized tests are a new experience. She is unfamiliar with the test format or the potential consequences. For her the arousal potential of the situation is too high and has a negative effect on her performance. She answers the test items quickly in an effort to escape the anxiety of the immediate situation.

Students' response to a classroom or learning activity depends on their perception of arousal potential of the situation. If they see the classroom environment as not sufficiently arousing, there is a good chance that the students will not be focused on learning and eventually engage in behaviors that are disruptive. Teachers can increase students' perceived arousal potential by providing students with appropriate levels of novelty, complexity, or surprise. This increases the likelihood that students will try to understand the material being taught. However, teachers must use caution, since too much novelty, complexity, or surprise may cause students to perceive the classroom as ambiguous, uncertain, and risky. Such perceptions may cause students to try to withdraw or escape, physically or psychologically.

How do teachers' decisions affect the arousal potential of their classrooms?

Students' Cognition and Classroom Motivation

Psychologists have researched the effects of cognition on motivation from a variety of perspectives. Much of this research has focused on one or a combination of the following factors:

- Student beliefs
- Student value placed on tasks
- Student goals

The discussion of the various lines of research is situated within the framework of an expectancy-value theory of motivation.

FIGURE 6.3 An Expectancy-Value Model (Adapted from Eccles et al. (1983). Expectancies, values and academic behaviors. In J. T. Spence, ed. *Achievement and achievement motives*. San Francisco: W. H. Freeman and Co.)

An Expectancy-Value Theory of Motivation

Expectancy-value theories focus on the motivation to engage in achievement-oriented behaviors, such as learning new concepts or mastering new skills. The basic idea is that this kind of motivation is the result of the interaction of two psychological constructs, expectancy and value of the task. Figure 6.3 presents a version of an expectancy-value model adapted from Eccles et al. (1983) original model.

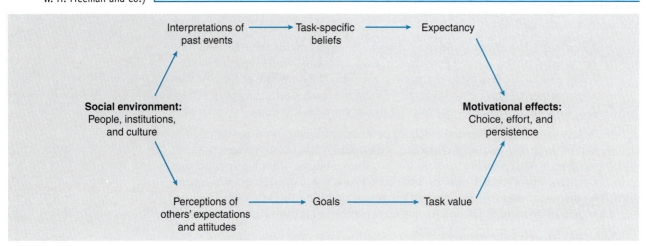

Looking in on

Josef Amir

6.1

Today was our first in-service workshop. Clara Yost and Rich Espanoza from a nearby regional university led the workshop. The workshop began with a presentation and large group discussion of the concept of student needs. As the professors were presenting Maslow's hierarchy of needs, it occurred to me that the recent changes in graduation policy may affect the basic needs of many of our students. For instance, the sudden change may affect their sense of safety. Last year these students were looking forward to finishing their course work and graduating; now their futures are no longer certain. Students faced with a new graduation requirement may feel their esteem needs are also threatened. Many of these students took algebra I in ninth grade; now they are seniors and required to take algebra II. Many are having a hard time keeping up with younger students who just took algebra I last year. Many of these seniors miss class quite often. Perhaps they are just trying to avoid being embarrassed.

As I thought about how my students needs were affected by the new graduation requirements, Clara and Rich introduced something called the expectancy-value theory of motivation. The central idea of this theory seemed to be that motivated students need to believe that what we have to teach is worthwhile and that they can learn it. Perhaps there was a way to make my class more valuable to my students by showing them how learning algebra might help them satisfy their needs and reach their own goals. But the students also needed to believe that they could be successful. It seemed that a technique that would help my students build their confidence while learning algebra would allow them to gratify their esteem and safety needs and increase their confidence in their ability to succeed. Perhaps I could do this when presenting new concepts by starting out with problems that have few steps and small numbers and then gradually increasing the complexity. This way the students could develop confidence and experience success.

● **How would you evaluate Mr. Amir's plan to increase his students' success in class?**

Decision Point: How might an understanding of students' needs and expectancy-value theory help you make better decisions?

One way to think of an expectancy is as a person's judgment about how that person's actions will influence future outcomes. This rather commonsense idea is that people's motivation to act is influenced by their belief that the action will result in their achieving some desired end. For example, Josh sees some of his classmates choosing up sides for a game of kickball. Josh likes to play kickball, but he thinks the other boys don't like him and won't let him play, even if he asks. Josh decides not to ask to join a team and instead plays by himself on the swings. Because Josh believes that the boys playing kickball don't like him, he expects his request to join a team will be rejected, so he doesn't ask.

How does the idea of expectancy compare with the concept of self-efficacy presented in Chapter 4?

Various psychologists and theories have proposed some version of the concept of expectancy as part of an explanation of individual motivation (Atkinson, 1957; Bandura, 1982, 1989; Eccles et al., 1983). Learners' expectation of success in a given situation will be influenced by their beliefs about themselves and about the nature of the task or situation. These beliefs will in turn be primarily influenced by their previous experiences of success or failure with similar tasks.

Learner expectancies may be divided into specific expectancies and general expectancies. **Specific expectancies** are defined as a person's expectation for successfully performing or completing a specific task. Specific expectancies are thought to be determined by past experiences of success or failure with similar tasks. **Generalized expectancies** are defined as a person's expectation of success in general categories of endeavor. Generalized expectancies are especially important when the learner is facing a situation that is new or unfamiliar.

The value a person attaches to a task is based on the person's assessment of the task's value and its cost. The **task value** is the anticipated reward associated with the successful completion of a task. Task value may take into account both intrinsic and extrinsic rewards, for example, feelings of accomplishment as well as an A on a report card. In considering the cost of a task, the learner may consider the amount of effort or other resources required to successfully complete the task. The value of a task is also influenced by the goals that students set for themselves. The goals that learners set are influenced by the attitudes and expectations of the people who are important in their lives.

How do students' expectancies and the values they attach to activities work together to affect their motivations?

In expectancy-value theory it is important to note that students' experiences are subjective in nature. That is to say, it is not the actual event that matters, but how the event is interpreted. The interpretation of events and the perception of others' attitudes and expectations are colored by the social environment of the learner. This environment is composed of the people, institutions, and culture to which the learner is exposed.

Learner Beliefs and Motivation

Learners' beliefs play an important role in their motivations to learn. The general expectancy-value model suggests that learners' expectancy is directly related to their beliefs about the adequacy of their own skills and abilities relative to a particular task. One way to think of this is in terms of learner confidence. When learners are confident, they expect to be successful; when they lack confidence, then they see success as uncertain. Variation in learners' expectations across subject areas may be explained by looking at what they believe about themselves and what they believe about specific subject areas or activities with which they are faced (Eccles et al., 1983).

Task-Specific Beliefs and Expectancy.   Individuals' expectancies are influenced by their task-specific beliefs. Learners' task-specific beliefs result from an interaction between the learners' beliefs about their own abilities and their perceptions of the difficulty of a task (Eccles et al., 1983; Eccles & Wigfield, 1995). Consider two students' expectations with regard to writing assignment in their tenth grade history class.

➤ In Mr. Ross' tenth grade history class, 40 percent of the grade for the six-week grading period will be based on a twenty-page term paper. Sheila doesn't consider herself to be a good writer; her grades in English composition were always low no matter how hard she works. She is resigned to getting a grade of C, or an even lower grade this time on her report card.

➤ Eva believes she is a good writer. She has always done well in her English classes and regularly contributes articles to the student newspaper. She expects the term paper will take some time, but she's confident she can do it and receive a good grade.

Self-Concept of Ability.   According to Eccles et al. (1983), "**Self-concept of ability** is defined as the assessment of one's own competency to perform specific tasks or to carry out role-appropriate behaviors." You can think of a learners' self-concept of ability as their confidence that they can master a skill or learn the content in a specific academic domain. Consider what these two learners' statements say about their self-concept of ability:

➤ While working on an art project, Todd says, "I hate all this handicraft stuff. It's all a bunch of girl stuff anyway. I just can't do it and it makes me feel stupid."

➤ The teacher is dividing the class into teams and assigning positions for a game of kickball. Siobhan says, "I hope the teacher lets me play first base today. Then I can be the first batter and get a turn at the plate before the period ends."

> The history teacher has just announced that Friday there will be a multiple choice test of important names and dates. Randy thinks to himself, "I'm doomed: There's no way I can memorize all this stuff by Friday."

For each of these students what they believe about themselves affects their motivation toward the specific tasks they encounter. Self-concept of ability is similar to the concept of self-efficacy presented in Chapter 4; however, it seems to include a strong emotional component, based on social comparison and self-evaluation (Bong & Clark, 1999).

How would you describe these students' self-concept of ability with regard to the tasks they are performing?

How is self-concept of ability similar or different to the concept of self-efficacy presented in Chapter 4?

Perception of Task Difficulty.   The **perceived task difficulty** refers to students' beliefs about the amount of effort they will need to invest to perform some task successfully. A task may be perceived as hard because the task is complex, requires special skills, requires a lot of effort, or is judged by a high standard. Consider the following student statements about difficulty. In each of these, the students perceive that an activity or course is difficult for a different reason.

> Sara is looking over a chemistry lab procedure and says, "Lab 3 looks like a tough one; look at all the steps." (Perceived difficulty due to complexity)

> Arnold is talking about basketball practice with a friend and says, "Basketball is really hard for me. I never learned to do lay-ups." (Perceived difficulty due to a lack of special skills)

> Elliot is looking over the syllabus for an English composition class. Seeing the requirement for a two-page paper every week he says, "Wow, this class will require a lot of work." (Perceived difficulty due to required effort)

> Jackie is discussing her course assignment with a friend and says, "I have three hard courses this year; the teachers are Jones, Ekman, and Story, and they are all hard graders. (Perceived difficulty due to high standards)

Often the perception of task difficulty interacts with learners' self-concept of ability. Brookhart and DeVoge (1999) found that third grade students' perceptions of assessment tasks as well as their self-efficacy were related to the interpretation of previous experiences with similar assessment tasks. In other words, students who are confident they possess the skills to complete a task successfully are likely to evaluate the task as less difficult than students who do not have confidence in their abilities. Consider two students assessing the difficulty of a course in English composition:

> Gerald says, "I've always been a good writer. This English composition course will be easy."

> Sylvia says, "My spelling is terrible, and I've always had trouble with all those punctuation rules. I know that I'm going to have a hard time with this English composition course."

Gerald is confident in his ability to write and therefore does not see the writing assignments of the English composition course as making the course difficult. Conversely, Sylvia believes that she has problems with elementary writing skills and that this will make the writing assignments difficult.

Sources of Learners' Task-Specific Beliefs

In the expectancy-value model presented in Figure 6.3, learners' task-specific beliefs are influenced by their perception and interpretation of their experiences. As noted in the previous section, these task-specific beliefs can be understood as an interaction between the learners' self-concept of ability and the beliefs about the difficulty of the task. But where do these specific beliefs come from? Part of the answer is that learners' beliefs result from the interpretation of past experiences. Attribution theory

How you respond to your students' successes and failures will influence their attributions.

provides a systematic way of understanding how people interpret their experiences and how these interpretations affect their task-specific beliefs (Weiner, 1985).

Attributions.   Because understanding cause is so important, people are innately driven to explain the cause of events. An explanation of the cause of an event is called an **attribution.** Attributions, once formed, affect thinking, emotions, and behavior (Heider, 1958; Weiner, 1985, 1992, 1994). It is important to remember that an attribution is subjective; it is the perception of a cause, not the actual cause, that influences the psychological and behavioral responses. Often, people make mistakes in their understanding of causes and then suffer because they apply the misunderstanding to the choices they later make.

Forming Attributions.   In the course of a day, learners have many interactions with teachers and peers. A student may take a test, receive a grade for a paper turned in the day before, be coached by the teacher on the proper application of a skill, work with another student on a science project, receive or provide assistance, make an important play in a pickup game on the playground, or attempt to make a new friend. In each of these situations students may interpret the results of the interaction as a success or a failure and try to understand the causes behind the experience.

Any number of explanations may be generated for a single event. The exact attribution students settle on will be influenced by what students believe about themselves, the task, observations of others' performances on the same or similar tasks, and the reactions of others to his or her performance. Consider the case of Erik who has just received his grade on a mathematics exam:

> ➤ As Ms. Foreman returned the first mathematics test of the year, Erik waited with confident anticipation. Last year, math was his best subject. Erik was shocked when he saw the large C– on his test paper. "Wow!" he thought, "This test was harder than I thought."

Past experience has led Erik to think of himself as good in math, and a good grade would have confirmed this belief. The situation became more interesting (psychologically) when he received a bad grade on the examination. People are reluctant to change their beliefs about themselves, especially if it means devaluing some ability or personal characteristic. In Erik's case, a cause other than low math ability must be found (after all he knows he is good in math). Perhaps he will attribute the low grade to the extreme difficulty of the test questions.

The performance of others on the same or similar task provides clues that affect the formation of an attribution. Let's return to Erik's case:

> ➤ Erik thinks to himself, "I'll bet everyone got a low grade on this test." Looking around at the expressions on the faces of his classmates, Erik tries to confirm this conclusion. Finally, he asks his friend Joey, "What did you get on the test?" "I got a B," responds Joey.

If Erik would have observed that his peers received similar scores on the exam, then the explanation that the low grade was caused by the extreme difficulty of the test would have been confirmed. However, this was not the case. For Erik, the difficulty of the exam problems is no longer a viable explanation.

Learners' knowledge of the task also influences the attributions they will form. Once again let's consider Erik's situation:

➤ Erik thinks to himself, "Math problems are pretty straightforward. You either get them wrong or right. There's no way Ms. Foreman could have messed up on grading my exam."

Erik believes that mathematics exams are objective measures of a performance. This being the case, the chance that teacher bias was a factor in the low grade is small. At this point Erik may begin to reassess his belief that he has a natural talent for mathematics. How the teacher and the rest of the class react to a performance also provides cues that affect the attribution process. Consider how Ms. Foreman's reaction to Erik's performance might influence Erik's beliefs.

➤ Erik remembers the expression on Ms. Foreman's face when she passed him his paper. During a break, he approaches Ms. Foreman to see if maybe she made a mistake. Her tone of voice as she responds to Erik's questions makes it clear she expected him to do better and that she thinks his low grade was his own fault. As he returns to his desk, Erik thinks to himself, "I should have studied last night instead of going to the video arcade."

Ms. Foreman's response leads Erik to assume that she thought he could do better, and that the cause of his low grade was his own fault. How do you think Erik would have responded if the teacher displayed pity toward Erik's math performance?

In addition to beliefs about the task and environmental cues, attributions may also be affected by the personality of the learner. These personality characteristics reveal themselves in stable patterns or biases in the types of attributions that learners make. A natural human tendency is to take credit for success whenever possible. This contributes to a healthy positive self-image. On the other hand, people tend to blame their failures on external causes. Such an attribution spares their egos and protects their self-images. This pattern is called the **self-serving bias** (Weiner, 1992). While such a bias ensures that students experience the maximum amount of emotional pleasure and the minimum amount of emotional pain, there is a danger in such an attribution pattern. It is possible that this pattern of attribution will cause us to make serious mistakes for which we may suffer in the future.

➤ Sam looks at the large red A on the top of his science quiz, and thinks, "I knew I would get an A; I'm just good in science."

➤ Frankie looks at her D+ on her science quiz and thinks, "These tests aren't fair, my answers are OK; Mr. Valence just doesn't like me."

In Sam's case the A confirms his self-concept that he is good in science. Taking credit for this performance allows him to feel proud of himself. Frankie protects her ego by blaming her grade on Mr. Valence's tests and his attitude toward her. However, as was discussed previously, what people believe affects how they behave. If Sam believes his good grade was the result of some innate talent, he may not study for the next examination. Likewise, Frankie's belief that her poor performance had nothing to do with her own behavior will not lead her to study harder or differently for the next examination. In both cases the students' performance on future quizzes is likely to deteriorate.

Another important attributional pattern is that of learned helplessness. Students display **learned helplessness** when they internalize the cause of failure and externalize the cause for success. Whenever learners experience a successful event, they attribute that success to someone or something else. Whenever learners experience failure, they attribute the failure to a lack of ability or some negative characteristic they believe they possess. This is just the opposite of the self-serving bias. This pattern of attributions usually leads students to give up; they do not persist or try to think their way through their difficulties. These types of behaviors will have serious negative consequences for learner achievement. Additional failures serve to confirm the negative self-concept.

Development of Self-Concept of Ability and Attributions. Self-concepts, especially those that relate to perceptions of ability have been shown to be related to academic performance (Marsh, 1984; Marsh, Cairns, Relich, Barnes, & Debus, 1984). Children's perception of ability and effort change in predictable ways from early childhood to adolescence (Kun, 1977; Nicholls, 1978). Nicholls identified four levels of reasoning about ability, effort, and outcomes. In level 1 reasoning, ability and effort are not distinguished. Children at this level believe that children who try harder are smarter. In level 2 reasoning, children focus only on effort. Children expect that if two people invest equal effort they will achieve equal outcomes. Ability is not typically recognized as a cause at this level. In level 3 reasoning, children begin to intermittently attribute performance to ability and understand the concept of compensation. The idea is that effort can compensate for a lack of ability, and that ability can compensate for lack of effort in the determination of outcomes. The idea here is that effort and ability can combine in an additive way to cause a particular level of outcome. In level 4 reasoning, ability is seen as something that may limit or enhance the effects of effort. At this level, students begin to make inferences about ability level from information about effort and outcome, that is, higher effort indicates lack of ability.

In a review of the research on the perception of children with learning problems, Licht (1991) suggests that experiencing failure in the early years of life may result in lowering of evaluation of ability. Since children with learning problems are more likely to experience failure, they are more susceptible to the development of low self-evaluations. The low self-evaluation, or self-concept of ability, is then likely to prevent the child from achieving the child's full potential. The development of these low self-concepts is mediated by the home environment, the relative ability of their classmates, and how much emphasis is placed on social comparison in classrooms. Teachers can help students with learning problems make appropriate attributions and thereby reduce the possibility that these learners will develop negative self-evaluations.

Dimensions of Attributions. The causes identified by students as explanations for their performances typically fall into one of four categories: effort, ability, task difficulty, and luck. If we look at these four categories of explanations, we find that each can be understood in terms of the same three characteristics or causal dimensions. These three causal dimensions are locus of causality, causal controllability, and causal stability (Graham, 1994; Weiner, 1992, 1994). The **locus** of an attribution has to do with the learner's perception of who or what is responsible for an outcome. If the learner takes responsibility for an event, then the attribution is said to have an internal locus. If the learner believes that someone or something else is responsible, then the attribution has an external locus. The **controllability** of an attribution refers to the person's perception that he or she has control over the situation. The **stability** of an attribution refers to the perception of the cause's constancy over time; in other words, the likelihood that the same cause will affect similar situations in the future.

What are the characteristic attributional dimensions of luck, task difficulty, ability, and effort?

The attributions that students make to explain the events they experience in school may be analyzed with regard to these three dimensions. Often the attributions that students make can be placed in one of the four broad categories: luck, task difficulty, ability, or effort. Table 6.1 provides examples of attributional statements from these four categories and summarizes the likely dimensions of attributions that students might make for their successes and failures.

Effects of Attributions. The attributions learners make for events in the classroom affect what they believe and feel about themselves, teachers, and different school subjects and classes. These emotions and beliefs affect students' motivation when they face similar situations in the future.

In general, perceptions of success result in a positive emotional response, while perceptions of failure result in a negative emotional response. The focus of a learner's emotion is determined by the locus of the attribution the learner makes. If the locus

TABLE 6.1 — Attributional Dimensions of Students' Attributions

Attribution	Examples	Locus	Stability	Controllability
Luck	**Success:** "It's a good thing the teacher didn't ask about Boyle's law." **Failure:** "I would have gotten a good grade if my dog hadn't eaten my homework."	External	Unstable	Uncontrollable
Task difficulty	**Success:** "Essay exams are easy; I can always write enough to get a good grade." **Failure:** "I just can't understand this language; why didn't Shakespeare write in normal English?"	External	Stable	Uncontrollable
Innate ability	**Success:** "I know I'd make the audition for band; I've always been musically talented." **Failure:** "I expected this grade; my visual learning style is just not compatible with her lectures."	Internal	Stable	Uncontrollable
Effort	**Success:** "It's a good thing I stayed home and studied last night; it really paid off." **Failure:** "I spent too much time studying names and dates and not enough studying causes."	Internal	Unstable	Controllable

is internal, the learner's emotion will be directed inward. In the case of success, the emotion might be pride; in the case of failure, the emotion experienced may be guilt or shame (Hareli & Weiner, 2002; Turner, Husman, & Schallert, 2002; Weiner, 1985). If the locus is external, the emotion will be directed outward, possibly toward a person, or persons, that have been identified as the cause. If the experience was interpreted as a success, the emotion may be one of gratitude, but if the experience was interpreted as a failure, then the emotion is often anger or frustration.

The dimension of controllability has an important influence on the exact nature of the emotional response, especially in situations that the learner perceives as a failure. An attribution that is internal and controllable is likely to result in a feeling of guilt; but in the case of an internal and uncontrollable attribution the resulting emotion is likely to be feeling of shame. Consider two elementary students who are considering their low grades on an English grammar work sheet.

➤ Agnes feels bad about her low grade because she believes she didn't try hard enough. She hurried through the assignment and made many careless errors, and she thinks she should have done a better job.

➤ James also feels bad when he sees his low grade. He doesn't know what he did wrong or how he could have improved his performance. He believes that he did his best, but that his best just wasn't good enough.

In Agnes' case she has identified a controllable cause and feels guilty that she didn't do a better job. James' attribution indicates that he doesn't know what he could have done to improve his score. He feels shame at his perceived lack of ability. The feelings of guilt and shame are distinguished as having different effects on the future performance (Weiner, 1994). Feelings of guilt are associated with an increase in the quality of later performances. For instance, in Agnes' case she is likely to be more careful on future assignments and therefore improve her performance. Shame, on the other hand, is associated with a decrease in the quality of later performances. James, believing he lacks ability, is likely to give up. Not trying is almost certain to result in poorer performances in the future.

In general, an external locus is associated with a lack of control. But when the external cause is someone else, the perception of that person's control influences the emotional response to that person. If people believe that a person had control of and caused a negative consequence, they are likely to think of them as deserving of punishment, but if they believe the person did not have control, then they are less likely to believe the person deserved punishment (Weiner, 1994). This logic affects the inferences we draw from others' reactions to performances (Graham, 1994). Consider the way the teacher's reaction might affect these learners' attributions.

➤ Daniel's English teacher has a conference with each student to review student portfolios and discuss their progress. During the conference, the teacher tells Daniel, "I'm very disappointed in your work lately; I know you can do better."

➤ As Sandra is struggling with an algebra problem, her teacher stops and says, "I know you have a tough time with this stuff; let me show you how to do those kinds of problems again."

When people react to a learner's failure with anger or disappointment, the learner is likely to infer that the others believe the learner had control over the situation. When others react to a learner's performance with sympathy or pity, then the learner will infer that the others thought the cause of the failure was not under the control of the learner.

The stability of learners' attributions affects the learners' expectations for the future. If an attribution is stable, then the learner expects similar results to similar situations. When a learner's attribution is unstable, then there is a degree of uncertainty about the future. In the case of a perceived failure, this means that there is hope that the future may bring success. If this sense of uncertainty is combined with the feeling of control, then the learner will be motivated to try a new strategy or invest more effort on future occasions. Table 6.2 summarizes the effects of typical student attributions.

Ideally, teachers want to encourage students to attribute their successes and failures to causes that are intrinsic, unstable, and controllable. If students see the cause as intrinsic, then they are taking responsibility for the outcomes they've experienced; and since the cause is unstable but controllable, learners may hope for improved re-

TABLE 6.2 Effects of Various Attributions from Experiences of Failure

Attribution	Emotional Response	Expected Response from Others	Expectation for the Future	Effect on Behavior	Likely Effect on Achievement
Luck	Negative but probably unfocused	Sympathy	Uncertain	Uncertain	Decrease in achievement
Difficulty	Frustration or anger that may be directed toward a person seen to be responsible for the failure	Sympathy	Repeated failure in similar situation	Attempt to avoid similar situations in the future	Decrease in achievement
Ability	Shame and feelings of inadequacy or devaluation of self-concept	Pity	Repeated failure in similar situation	Attempt to avoid similar situations in the future	Decrease in achievement
Effort	Guilt for having made a bad choice	Anger or disappointment	Improvement if different choices and actions are taken in similar situation	Invest more effort or try a different strategy in similar situation in the future	Increase in achievement

Looking in on

Karen Hilderbrand

6.2

Today when Alfred and I met he seemed somewhat subdued. When I asked him what was wrong he said he was having trouble getting through to one of the students. His problem student was Jimmy, a young boy whose family had just moved into the area. Jimmy was having trouble with most of his work, but Al believed that it was all related to his poor reading skills. Al's suspicions were confirmed when he spoke with the school psychologist, who informed him that Jimmy had been evaluated for a learning disability at his last school, but that the tests turned up nothing except poor reading comprehension skills. Earlier in the day Al had talked to Jimmy, who told him that he was just a visual learner and that he never did well on anything that required him to read or write.

Al thought Jimmy's attitude was self-defeating and was determined to do something about it. After talking with Jimmy, Al was sure that Jimmy had the ability to do the work, and he was going to work with him until he started showing some improvement. He decided to start working with Jimmy during recess to improve his reading comprehension. I agreed that that was a good idea, but suggested that he check with the principal and Jimmy's folks before proceeding. I told Al that it would be important for Jimmy to be able to see the improvement in his reading for himself. I suggested that Al develop a record-keeping system that both he and Jimmy could use to track his progress. Eventually, Jimmy should learn to set his own goals for improvement and learn to track his own progress.

● **What are the characteristics of Jimmy's attribution, and how might Al's reaction to Jimmy's performance affect his attribution?**

Decision Point: How will your response to your students' performances affect their attributions?

sults in the future if they make the right choices and invest the necessary effort. To encourage students to make such attributions, teachers need to:

- Communicate high expectations for their students' performances
- Provide students with explicit suggestions for how to improve their learning
- Direct students' to notice personal improvement rather than comparisons with other students.

Goal Orientation. Learners' goal orientation is another factor affecting students' task-specific beliefs. A **goal orientation** is the habitual way in which a person perceives and sets goals when faced with an achievement task (Ames, 1992). In the classroom this means that a learner's goal orientation affects the kinds of goals the learner sets when faced with learning and assessment activities (Ferguson, 2000).

Traditionally, two distinct goal orientations and associated goal types have been identified in the literature (Dweck, 1992); however, Elliot (1999) has suggested that the pattern of data from various studies can be more adequately explained with three types of goals and associated goal orientations. Elliot's suggestion is based on a general tendency of people to approach or seek out pleasant events and to avoid or try to escape from unpleasant events. **Mastery goals** are approach goals that have as an objective some level of mastery or competence. **Performance approach goals** are approach goals that focus on demonstrating a level of competence relative to other people. **Performance avoidance goals** are avoidance goals that focus on not appearing incompetent relative to other people. Research investigating the validity of different measures of learners' goal orientation seems to support these three types of goal orientations (Smith, Duda, Allen, & Hall, 2002).

Students who approach a learning situation with the intention of understanding a concept or acquiring new skills are said to have mastery goals, and students who habitually set such goals are said to have mastery goal orientation, which is associated with many desirable outcomes in the classroom (Elliot, 1999). Students with a mastery goal orientation seek out and enjoy challenging situations and believe that if they work hard, they will ultimately be successful. These learners see intelligence as a characteristic that can be improved by experience and the application of effort. This perspective is an incremental view of intelligence. Mastery goal–oriented learners are more likely to define success by comparing the results of their efforts with their own previous performances. Recent research confirms the relationship between mastery goal orientation and learners' attitudes toward intelligence and has also found that these students tended to be more optimistic and to explain failures in ways that allowed them to maintain their motivation to learn (Eppler, Carsen-Plentl, & Harju, 2000).

What types of needs, motives, and attributions would you associate with learners who set mastery goals?

Because they are focused on improvement of skill and mastery of a task, these students are said to be task involved. Somuncuoglu and Yildirim (2001) found that with regard to learning tasks, students with mastery goal orientation were more likely to report that they employ learning strategies that result in deeper learning, such as summarizing and synthesizing material from texts, lectures, and other learning activities. These students were also more likely to report that they monitor their learning and spontaneously take remedial action when they experienced confusion.

Learners who approach a learning situation with concern for how their performance will be judged by others are said to have **performance goals** (Dweck, 1998). In keeping with Elliot's (1999) classifications, these learners may have either performance approach goal or performance avoidance goal orientations. These learners are especially worried about how their performance on a given task will affect their own and others' perception of their abilities. The response of these learners to challenge and difficulty depends on their confidence in their ability to succeed. If they are confident in their abilities to perform as well or better than others, then they are likely to set performance approach goals. If, however, they are not confident of success, they set performance avoidance goals. In other words, they seek to avoid the situation or give up quickly in response to failure. Learners with a performance goal orientation tend to believe that if one has the ability, then a task ought be easy, and if a person has to work hard to succeed, then that person lacks ability. These learners also see ability, or intelligence as fixed. This is an entity view of intelligence. Performance–goal oriented students tend to define success by comparing their performance with the performance of those around them. Doing better than those around them maintains or enhances their self-image or ego; therefore, these learners are said to be *ego involved*.

What types of needs, motives, and attributions would you associate with learners who set performance goals?

Students' goal orientation is reflected in their pattern of beliefs and of behaviors related to school achievement. Table 6.3 compares the differences between learners with mastery goal orientation with those with a performance goal orientation.

Research suggests that the goal orientations of students may be affected by the instructional activities in classrooms. After reviewing the literature in mathematics education, Middleton and Spanias (1999) noted that an inquiry approach to mathematics that included a focus on the development of conceptual understanding of mathematics was related to a decreased likelihood that students would develop performance goal orientation. The goal orientation of students with regard to reading and writing was studied by Meece and Miller (1999). Their finding indicated that instructional activities that provide students with choice, challenge, and complexity resulted in a decrease in students' performance goal orientation toward reading and writing assignments. Patrick, Anderman, Ryan, Edelin, and Midgley (2001) conducted a study that compared high and low-mastery oriented classrooms. These researchers found that teachers in high-mastery classrooms shared a number of characteristics, including:

- Not associating students' performance with ability
- Stressing the importance of student involvement in the learning process
- Providing support and showing concern for students' learning

	Goal Orientation	
Characteristic Beliefs	Mastery	Performance (Approach and Avoidance)
Beliefs about intelligence	Incremental view: intelligence and mental ability can be enhanced by experience and learning from one's mistakes	Entity view: intelligence is fixed and will not change
Beliefs about effort	Effort leads to success	Effort indicates a lack of ability
Beliefs about success	Success referenced to personal standards	Success defined by comparison with others' performances
Motivational Patterns		
Typical goals	Seeks to improve competency or skill in some area, to understand and master the application of concepts	Seeks to appear better than others in some area, to receive public recognition of superior performance, avoid risks of failure
Response to challenge	Seeks challenging tasks	If confidence in ability is high, seek challenging tasks; if confidence in ability is low, avoid challenging tasks
Response to difficulty	Engages in effective problem solving; response to failure is adaptive, i.e., learners display more persistence	If confidence is high, engages in effective problem solving; if confidence is low, has a negative emotional response and does not engage in effective problem solving

After reviewing the research on goal orientation and student learning, Ames (1992) made specific recommendations for encouraging mastery goal orientation in students. First, when planning instruction and assessment tasks teachers should reduce the emphasis on social comparison by providing an appropriate variety of activities and deemphasizing the public aspects of students' performance. Second, teachers should encourage intrinsic motivation by reducing the emphasis on grades and other extrinsic signs of performance. Finally, Ames recommended that teachers help their students develop a sense of autonomy by providing students with choices whenever possible.

Motivation and the Perceptions of Value

In the expectancy-value model presented in Figure 6.3, the values that students attach to performing a specific task or achieving some goal has a strong influence on their motivation. Students' perceptions and beliefs about the potential payoff as well as the cost of attempting some task is another important cognitive factor affecting their motivation to learn.

Perceptions of Task Value. Eccles et al. (1983) proposed that tasks might be valuable to learners in three ways. Learners may find an activity valuable because of the attainment value, interest value, or utility value they attach to the task. The **attainment value** of a task is the value learners attach to a task, because they believe that it is important to do it well. Learners perceive a task as having attainment value to the extent that completing the task allows them to attain some extrinsic or intrinsic reward (Eccles et al., 1983).

The attainment value that is attached to a task may be different from one learner to another. For instance, suppose a high school teacher has assigned the class the task of writing an essay on the characteristics of Shakespeare's tragedies. For some students, it may be important to do a good job on the assignment, because it confirms something they believe about themselves, e.g., "I'm a good student," or "I'm a good writer." Other students may find it important to do a good job on the essay, because it gains them access to a particular group of students, perhaps a group of students

The **goal structure** of a learning or assessment activity refers to the relationship, with respect to achieving success, among the students engaged in the activity. In situations with competitive goal structures, the relationship among the students is negative. If one student wins, others must lose. In situations with cooperative goal structures, the relationship among the students is positive. The level of achievement of one student contributes to the success or failure of the others. In situations with an individualistic goal structure, the relationship, with regard to achievement, among the learners is neutral.

From the standpoint of learner motivation and academic performance, which type of goal structure, competitive or cooperative, is better? The quick response that many teachers and researchers give is that a cooperative goal structure is always better. However, Ingelhart, Brown, and Vida (1994) suggest that the answer is not as simple as many might think. According to these researchers, it depends on how one views the competition. Some people view competitive situations as a challenge and may value such situations as an opportunity for self-assessment and to show what they can do. Other people see competitive situations negatively and experience a great deal of stress in these situations. There are two possible explanations for this second response. First, it may be that the person views a competitive situation as presenting an unacceptably high chance of failure. Second, the competitive goal structure is at odds with the goals of establishing and maintaining friendly relationships.

Inglehart, Brown, and Vida (1994) were concerned with the effects of competition on the achievement of men and women. They suspected that competitive situations caused women to experience more stress, thereby preventing them from achieving their full potential. To investigate this idea, they conducted research that looked at how peoples' attitude toward competition (positive or negative) affected their level achievement in a competitive medical program at the University of Michigan. They had two hypotheses. The first was that people who had a positive appraisal or attitude toward competition would do better in the program than those who did not view competition positively. The second hypothesis was that more men than women would have a positive attitude toward competition. Both of these hypotheses were supported by their research findings.

On average, men had higher levels of achievement than did women; however, it should be noted that the determining factor was each person's attitude toward competition, not their sex. Women who attached a positive value to competition did as well as men with the same attitude, while men who viewed competition negatively performed the same as women with similar attitudes.

● **How would expectancy-value theory explain the differences in people's reaction to competitive situations? (For your authors' perspective on this question, go to the text website for this chapter.)**

interested in Shakespeare. Still others may be motivated by the prospect of receiving a good grade.

A learner may find a task valuable because there is some inherent enjoyment associated with the performance of the task. This is called the intrinsic or **interest value** (Eccles et al., 1983) of the task. For instance, with regard to the essay assignment, some students may find enjoyment in writing or perhaps in any activity that has to do with Shakespeare or the theater.

Finally, a task may be valuable because the learner believes that completion of the task will help them reach some other valued goal. This is referred to as the **utility value** of the task and is determined by how important the current task is to the attainment of some future goal. Referring once again to the assignment of writing an essay on Shakespeare's tragedies, a student may see this as leading to a good grade in the course, thus contributing to a high grade point average, which in turn contributes to the student's goal of being accepted to a particular college.

You frequently hear students discussing the relevance of a lesson, homework assignment, or course. How is the concept of relevance related to task value?

It is likely that students may find a task valuable for a variety of reasons. For a single task, it may be important to do a good job to maintain their self-images; the task may be intrinsically interesting and completing

Culture may be defined as a system of values or a set of beliefs about how the world works. Values and beliefs combine to influence the types of goals members of a particular culture set for themselves and the actions they take to achieve these goals. Some researchers have suggested that cultural values influence the nature of achievement motivation of the members of the culture (McClelland, 1967). The idea is that learners internalize the values of their culture that in turn influence their motivation toward specific tasks. The dominant culture in the United States places a high value on achievement and sees academic accomplishments as an important achievement goal. However, the United States includes many cultural and ethnic groups, and if culture affects values, then other cultural groups within the United States may value other goals more highly or may define achievement differently. To what extent is this hypotheses true?

Hérbert and Reis (1999) have investigated this question by analyzing the cases of culturally diverse high-achieving students in urban settings. As is typical of qualitative research, interviews were conducted with a small number of students and their parents, siblings, peers, teachers, counselors, and other people with whom these students frequently interacted. These high-achieving students were found to have a strong belief in their ability to achieve their goals. Their goals were similar to those of successful students from the dominant culture and included academic success and attainment of professional degrees and careers. The authors suggested that the belief in their own abilities exhibited by these students was developed over time through supportive interactions with peers and adults. Peers are especially influential on the intrinsic value students place on school and academic achievement and the goals that students set (Arfanirromo, 2001; Ryan, 2000, 2001).

Psychometrics offers an alternative approach to assessing the effects of culture on motivation. Psychometrics involves the development and use of instruments (tests, surveys, and questionnaires) to identify common dimensions of human abilities and dispositions. Evidence from the psychometric approach suggests that differences in cultural values do not explain the different academic performances across culturally diverse populations (McInerney, 1995; McInerney, Roche, McInerney, & Marsh, 1997). The psychometric research is consistent with the conclusions drawn from the qualitative investigation reported by Hérbert and Reis (1999) that students' beliefs in their own abilities are good predictors of school success, regardless of culture.

● **What actions should a teacher take to help motivate students from different or minority cultures? (For your authors' perspective on this question, go to the text website for this chapter.)**

the task may contribute to the accomplishment of their long-range goals. These different types of task values may be additive in nature, with each type of value contributing to the overall value of a task (Eccles et al., 1983).

Perception of Costs.   In addition to the value learners assign to a task, the overall value of a task is also affected by the perceived cost of performing the task (Eccles et al., 1983). The idea is that the overall value of a task is actually the value attached to the task, minus the cost of completing the task. This means that as the perceived cost goes up, the overall value of the task decreases. If the cost exceeds the value, then students will not be motivated to engage in the task and may even be motivated to avoid participation.

Three factors have been identified as contributing to learners' perception of the cost of some activity: (a) beliefs about the required effort, (b) loss of valued alternatives, and (c) the cost of failure. The perception of effort is based on the task-specific beliefs of the individual and their expectancy. The expected effort required to complete a task successfully takes into account perception of self-ability and task difficulty.

The idea of the loss of a valued alternative is based on the fact that when a person chooses to do one thing, that person is also choosing not to do something else. It is often the case that accomplishing anything worthwhile requires that the pursuit of other objectives be postponed. Those postponed objectives have value also. Not

Looking in on

Josef Amir

6.2

After our last workshop, several of the teachers decided to meet during our planning periods to try to put some of what we learned into practice. Our group included Elena Clauswicz, who taught general science and physics, and Kelly Murry, the business math teacher. One of the items we wanted to discuss was how to help the students see the value in what we were all teaching. The workshop made it clear that one way we could help our students see the value of our classes was by coordinating our course content as much as possible and making explicit references to what was being covered in other classes. We decided to work on sample problems in our class that allowed the students to see how similar math techniques could be applied in different content areas. In addition, we decided that our examples should make explicit connections to the kinds of things the kids encountered in their lives outside of school.

As we talked, Elena expressed a concern that we were focusing too much on what the learners might do with what we taught them and forgetting about learning for learning's sake.

We all agreed with this point, but recognized that putting the fun back in learning might be difficult because many of the students felt pressured to pass the graduation examination. I suggested that if the students in our classes experienced some success with the content they might enjoy it more and stop worrying so much about the coming exam. Elena pointed out that we would have to ensure that the tasks were still challenging; otherwise the college-bound students would be bored and the other students would be insulted. Elena suggested that we help our students learn to deal with the occasional failure by focusing on what actions can be taken to improve.

● **How might the concepts of utility value, attainment value, and interest value be used to explain these teachers' concerns?**

Decision Point: How might your decisions about planning instruction affect the balance between your students' attainment value and the level of challenge in your classroom?

---

gaining these values is the cost of not pursuing the objective. Consider Alice as she considers whether or not to enroll in an advance placement astronomy class.

> ➤ Alice thinks to herself, "Astronomy sounds like an interesting class, and if I took this course it would help fulfill my science requirement. But, Eddie says that we will have to complete five big projects with papers. It sounds like there is a lot of work involved and I'd probably have to quit the cheerleading squad."

For Alice, taking an advance placement astronomy class to satisfy her science requirement is attractive. The course content may be personally interesting, and successful completion of the course may improve her chances of acceptance into college programs that will contribute to her career goals. However, she believes she may have to give up her spot on the cheerleading squad and give up other extracurricular activities as well. This means that she will lose the value associated with these activities (i.e., fun, prestige, and status).

When the learner is uncertain of success, the psychological cost of failure becomes another important factor in cost assessment. As the perceived risk of failure increases, the reward of participating in the task is devalued. This means that the probability of success, associated with a learner's expectancy, influences the perception of costs. Consider Alice as she works through her decision.

> ➤ Alice thinks, "I've always been pretty good at science, but Mr. Fenton is a hard grader. Julie only got a C in his class last year."

Alice may find participating and doing well in science valuable because it confirms her self-concept of being smart and good in science. However, Alice believes the

Gender and Motivation in Science and Mathematics

The underrepresentation of women in careers associated with mathematics (i.e., chemistry, physics, and engineering) is of concern to many educators and policymakers in the United States. Is the disproportionately low representation of women in these careers indicative of differences in women's abilities compared with men or to differences in their motivations? After reviewing the research literature, Hyde (1994) found that differences in the men's and women's performances on standardized mathematics tests are typically very small. She concluded that these differences may be the result of women having taken fewer electives in mathematics and courses related to mathematics (i.e., science). In other words, the small difference between men's and women's performances are the result of motivation, not innate ability. This conclusion is consistent with research reported by Eccles et al. (1983) who found that the female subjects in a longitudinal study (a) placed less value on mathematics achievement and (b) were more likely to attribute failure to a lack of ability, than were the boys in the study.

Farmer, Wardrop, and Rotella (1999) reported the results of an investigation of the factors that affect the choices of men and women to pursue careers in science. Their research found that one of the best predictors for women choosing a science career was valuing mathematics and science. Additionally, these researchers found that both men and women who chose science careers had aspirations for a prestigious career, were intrinsically motivated to take more high school science courses, and were similar in their attributions for success and failures in mathematics. These findings are similar to those reported by DeBacker and Nelson (2001), who found that high-achieving students (boys and girls) were more goal directed and valued science more that low-achieving students.

It should be remembered that when the performances of people from different groups are compared, a great deal of overlap exists, and that large-scale programmatic changes in the ways mathematics and science are taught may have an adverse effect on motivation of those students (male and female), who are currently successful. Certainly, the research seems to indicate that boys and girls who do well in mathematics and science and who go on to choose careers in science are more alike than different. As teachers we must be sensitive to the needs, motives, goal orientations, and other dispositions of individual students and use our understanding of individual students to help them maintain their motivations to learn.

● **How might your interactions with students affect their motivations to continue to learn? (For your authors' perspective on this question, go to the text website for this chapter.)**

---

teacher is an especially tough grader, and that there is a significant risk of not getting an A. Alice may think that not getting an A may lower her chances of being accepted at the college of her choice. In addition, she may see a potential for a lower grade as a threat to her view of herself as someone who is smart and good in science.

Taking everything into account, Alice chooses not to enroll in the astronomy class. Taking into account the possibility of not getting an A, the value of taking this interesting course is outweighed by the value of the things she would have to give up and by the risk to her ego.

Goals

In the model of motivation presented in Figure 6.3, task value is influenced by the goals that people set for themselves. **Goals** are the objectives that people consciously intend to pursue (Locke & Latham, 1990, 1994). Your students' goals will influence how they approach learning in your classroom, how much effort they will invest in learning, and ultimately their level of achievement. The actual goals your students set will be the result of an interaction of the students' characteristics and the conditions you establish in your classrooms.

The Nature of Goals. To understand how your students' goals will affect their performance in your classroom, you must understand the nature of goals. Goals have two characteristics that affect motivation and achievement. These characteristics are the goal content and the goal intensity (Locke & Latham, 1990, 1994; Pintrich & Schunk, 2002).

"**Goal content** refers to the object or result being sought" (Locke & Latham, 1990, p. 25). The content of students' goals may vary in terms of completion deadlines, degree of specificity, and degree of difficulty. Consider the following list of goals:

- Get an A on a test
- Obtain a college degree
- Master a list of spelling words
- Write a poem to express deep feelings

Look at the goals presented. Compared with the other goals, getting a college degree is a long-term goal, i.e., the deadline may be far in the future or even nonexistent. These goals also differ in terms of their specificity. Mastering a list of spelling words is a more specific goal than the other three. The actions required to master a list of spelling words are probably more clearly understood than the actions required to reach the other goals. Difficulty of a goal refers to the amount of effort required to reach a goal or level of excellence defining the goal (Locke & Latham, 1994). For instance, mastering a spelling list or getting an A on a test may be easier than getting a college degree or writing a poem. Researchers have found that these three characteristics of goals are related to behaviors associated with motivation (i.e., effort, persistence, and strategic thinking) and ultimately the level of achievement. In general, high-achieving students are likely to be the ones who have goals that are (a) difficult but achievable, (b) specific, (c) short-term, and (d) related to long-term goals.

Goal intensity refers to the mental effort that the person setting the goal is willing to expend in the pursuit of a goal. Intensity is indicated by the person's commitment to accomplishing the goal. Goal commitment is an expression of the importance that a person attaches to the achievement of the goal. When a person is committed to achieving a goal, the person is willing to expend more effort and to persist in the face of adversity.

Goals and Achievement.   Locke and Latham (1994) have identified three ways in which goals affect performance and achievement. First, goals affect performance by directing and focusing action. When learners set effective goals, they are more likely to focus their efforts on actions directed toward the accomplishment of the goal. They don't waste time and effort engaged in activities unrelated to the accomplishment of the goal. Goals also affect the amount of effort learners are willing to expend. In general, people adjust their level of effort to match the goal's difficulty and level of challenge. Finally, goals affect persistence in the pursuit of the goal. These effects are most likely to occur when goals are specific, short-term, and challenging (difficult) and when they are important to the learner.

Goal Setting.   Ideally, students should learn to set appropriate learning goals for themselves. However, sometimes learners are simply unable to do this, and you will have to step in and help your students set goals. The need for teachers to set goals for their students may vary with the ability of the students to set appropriate goals for themselves. Learners' abilities to set appropriate goals depend on their general level of maturity and the experience within the area of instruction. Older, more experienced learners are better able to set appropriate goals for themselves, whereas younger, less experienced learners are unlikely to be able to set their own goals.

What actions might a teacher take to help students set effective goals?

While the research suggests that receiving goals from a recognized authority (such as the teacher) is as effective as self-generated goals, it may be necessary to explain the rationale behind the goals established by the teacher (Locke & Latham, 1990, 1994). While many students may perceive the interest value in some goals, it may be necessary to provide your students with information that will help them find the attainment value or the utility value associated with accomplishing certain goals. Teachers frequently do this by pointing out which concepts or skills are especially important for success in upcoming tests or other performances or by explaining how achieving the stated goal may contribute to other types of accomplishments in the future.

From the perspective of the expectancy-value theory, setting and achieving worthwhile goals cause learners to develop a healthy self-concept of ability and to value challenging situations more highly. Helping your students set appropriate goals will ensure they experience the motivational benefits of succeeding. Teachers can help their students set appropriate goals by telling what their goals should be, coaching students as they set goals for themselves, or by demonstrating how to use long-term goals to set intermediate goals.

Motivational Principles and Their Application to Classrooms

As with previous chapters, the concepts presented in this chapter have been used to derive four principles that you may use to guide your decisions as you plan lessons, manage your classroom, and develop and administer assessments of your students' learning. In later chapters these principles are used to explain the effectiveness of specific instructional techniques and to justify the application of these techniques to specific situations.

Principle 6.1: Learners Are More Motivated When They Believe Their Actions Will Result in Successfully Completing Challenging Tasks

A consistent finding reported by Locke and Latham (1990, 1994) is that setting more difficult or challenging goals results in higher levels of achievement. However, the difficulty or challenge associated with an objective is only part of the story. Learners' motivations are also affected by their belief that they can successfully reach the goals. Atkinson's (1957) principle of motivation predicts that learners will be most motivated by learning activities and assignments when the level of challenge is moderate. This idea was expanded by the general expectancy-value theory with the concept of task-specific beliefs and self-perceptions of ability.

This principle has implications for how you plan instruction and how you interact with your students as they participate in the learning activities that you've designed. Designing instruction that is appropriately challenging for your students requires that you have some idea of their current levels of understanding and ability. If an instructional goal is too challenging for the students, you may need to establish some subgoals by breaking the task down into a more appropriately challenging sequence of tasks.

An important part of your students' beliefs about their abilities results from their interpretations of the causes of success or failure on similar performances. As the students attempt various instructional tasks, it is inevitable that sometimes some students will fail. How students explain their failures has serious consequences for their continued motivation (Hareli & Weiner, 2002; Turner, Husman, & Schallert, 2002; Weiner, 1985). Your response to students' failures and successes is likely to affect the types of attributions they make. Avoid making comments that focus on ability. Ideally, you want to help your students to recognize the relationship between their own effort, strategic choices, and actions and the outcomes they experience.

Principle 6.2: Learners Are More Motivated by Activities That Appeal to Their Personal Needs, Motives, and Interests

Learners are motivated by a variety of needs, desires, and interests. As a teacher, you should consider these student characteristics when planning your lessons. Some needs and interests may be fundamental and important to all people. This was the idea behind lower level needs in Maslow's hierarchy of basic needs and the concept of situational interest. Additionally, individual experience results in idiosyncratic growth needs, motives, and interests.

Once again successful application of this principle starts with observing your students to discover and understand their needs, motives, and interests. You can then use this knowledge when planning lessons to help students make connections between the content and their interests and to select learning activities that provide the students with opportunities to gratify their needs, motives, and interests. It is unlikely that a single activity will allow the gratification of each student's needs. Also a single activity that is often repeated may loose its potency in this regard. Therefore, you should plan variety in your lessons.

One of the key deficiency needs identified in Maslow's (1987) theory is the safety need. All people need to feel safe, physically and psychologically. This sense of safety is an essential part of the ideal classroom climate. Consistency and predictability contribute to your students' sense of safety. This suggests that the variations in your instructional activities should not be too extreme. Your students' sense of safety is also affected by the development and enforcement of the rules for your classroom. Finally, your interactions with your students affect their trust in you and therefore their feelings of safety in your class. Use a positive emotional tone when providing feedback to your students, and let them know that it's acceptable to take risks and make mistakes because they are opportunities to learn.

Principle 6.3: Learners Are More Motivated When They Have Specific Near-Term Goals That They Believe Are Important

Locke and Latham's (1990, 1994) work has indicated the importance of goals in achievement situations. In general, learners' goals are more likely to influence motivation when they are specific and proximal and when the learners believe that achieving the goal is important. Here are some classroom techniques that take advantage of these relationships. Beginning a lesson in a way that explicitly or implicitly establishes a goal enhances the motivation of your students. Modeling goal setting and coaching students as they set their own learning goals helps them become more effective at setting goals for themselves.

Principle 6.4: Learners Are More Motivated When Appropriate Levels of Variety, Choice, and Surprise Are Incorporated into Lessons

Variety, complexity, and surprise contribute to the arousal potential of the environment. As pointed out in the discussion of interest and anxiety, an optimal level exists for the arousal potential for your classroom. If the arousal potential is too low, the students will become bored and be motivated to make the class more exciting (often in ways you won't like). If the classroom environment becomes too stimulating, the students attempt to reduce the stimulation by trying to escape mentally or physically from the situation. The former situation is a more common problem in classrooms. Your classroom will be more exciting and interesting by planning demonstrations and activities that are surprising, complex in interesting ways, or that provide students with choices.

Principles into Practice:
Illustrating Key Concepts

The experiences of Karen Hilderbrand and Josef Amir provide examples of how teachers deal with motivational issues in their classrooms. How teachers deal with these issues may be seen as an application of specific principles of motivation. An analysis of these separate cases provides an example of how these principles may be applied.

Looking back on

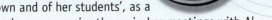

Karen Hilderbrand

When you first met Karen Hilderbrand, she had been assigned to mentor a new teacher, Alfred O'Conner, in his first year as a third grade teacher. As Karen reflected on her role as a mentor, she recalled her own first year and identified motivation, both her own and of her students', as a main concern. Student motivation became a major theme in her meetings with Al.

Karen's first meeting with Al was concerned with keeping the kids on task without letting the fun go out of learning. Karen suggested that Al might try introducing new material with a discrepant event. Discrepant events are demonstrations or statements that violate students' expectation or challenge their preconceived ideas. These activities are intended to increase the arousal potential, causing students to become curious and engage in specific exploration. This is an example of the application of Principle 6.4, learners are more motivated when appropriate levels of variety, choice, and surprise are incorporated into a lesson.

Karen also suggested that perhaps Al could incorporate some games into his class exercises and volunteered the use of activities she had already developed. Games often pique students situational interest and exemplify an application of Principle 6.2, appealing to learners' personal needs, motives, and interest. Variations of game-like exercises may also allow students to gratify their motives for achievement, affiliation, and control. It may also be possible to vary the difficulty of games so that all students experience some level of success at a challenging task. This is an application of Principle 6.1, learners are more motivated when they believe their actions will result in successfully completing challenging tasks.

When Karen next met with Al, they discussed a motivational problem with a specific student named Jimmy. Jimmy believed that he was a visual learner and therefore could not do well on tasks that required reading. Jimmy's explanation for his difficulty may be evaluated using the dimensions of attribution theory. Jimmy's explanation has a stable, uncontrollable internal locus of causation. To help Jimmy improve, Al must first change his beliefs about the causes of his poor performance. By working with Jimmy, Al is communicating that Jimmy's cause of his poor performance is something that can be changed (i.e., is unstable) and is something over which Jimmy has control. Helping students make appropriate attributions is another example of the application of Principle 6.1. Karen also suggested that Al develop a method to track Jimmy's progress and suggested that eventually Jimmy will learn to set goals and track his progress on his own. By initially providing Jimmy with a structured set of goals, Al is providing a model from which Jimmy may learn to set his own goals. Principle 6.3, learners are more motivated when they have specific near-term goals that they believe are important, highlights the importance of goals. Focusing on personal improvement is likely to have two beneficial effects on Jimmy's motivation. First, by focusing on his own progress rather than comparing himself with others, he is more likely to set approach goals (mastery or performance) rather than avoidance goals. Second, teaching Jimmy to track his progress allows him to focus on and experience personal success and to enhance his self-concept of ability. ●

Looking back on
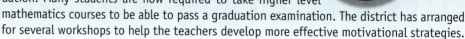
Josef Amir

Motivating high school students taking a required course presents several problems that most teachers face at some point in their careers. Josef Amir is struggling with problems caused by changes in his state's requirements for graduation. Many students are now required to take higher level mathematics courses to be able to pass a graduation examination. The district has arranged for several workshops to help the teachers develop more effective motivational strategies.

You looked in on Josef after his first workshop. The presentation of Maslow's theory of needs has provided Josef with a way of understanding how the changes in the state's graduation requirements might be affecting his students. Josef realizes that he must re-think the way he is teaching to address these students' needs (Principle 6.2, learners are more motivated by activities that appeal to their personal needs, motives, and interests). Josef notes that the new requirements may be affecting the deficiency needs of some students. The new requirements were unexpected and the uncertainty may threaten some students' safety needs, while being forced to enroll in a class for which their self-concept of ability is low may be threatening their esteem needs.

The concept of expectancy-value theory provided Josef with another way to think about motivating his students to learn. The idea is to increase the task value, and more specifically, the utility value of academic subjects for the students by showing them how they might satisfy their long-term goals, including passing the graduation examination, by learning the content of his courses. By tying course content to the students long-term goals, Josef is applying Principle 6.3, learners are more motivated when they have specific near-term goals they believe are important. One of the leaders of the workshop suggested that they also look at students' expectations of success on the graduation examination. Principle 6.1, learners are more motivated when they believe their actions will result in successfully completing challenging tasks, highlights the importance of students' beliefs that they can be successful. If their expectancy is low, then their motivation will also be low. Josef believes he can increase the odds of his students experiencing success by carefully organizing the learning activities and exercises to start easy and gradually increase in difficulty. He believes that by doing this the students might come to enjoy the subjects being taught. Success results in positive emotions that may be seen as a form of intrinsic attainment value. In addition to increasing the students' perceived task value, success is likely to affect the students' expectancy of success when faced with similar content on the graduation examination.

After the workshops had concluded, Josef and several of his colleagues decide to continue to meet to find ways to apply what they've learned. One suggestion is that they find ways to make explicit connections between the content of the various courses they teach. By showing students that the material in one class might help them achieve in other classes, the teachers are increasing the potential utility value of each class. This is another application of Principles 6.3, learners are more motivated when they have specific near-term goals that they believe are important, and 6.2, learners are more motivated by activities that appeal to their personal needs, motives, and interests.

One of Josef's colleagues, Elena, reminded the group that they didn't want to lose sight of the intrinsic attainment values associated with learning. This requires that the level of challenge be maintained at an appropriate level. Elena notes that if there is not an appropriate level of challenge, the students may become bored or insulted. With challenge comes the possibility of occasional failure, and the teachers need to learn to help the students think about these occasions in a positive adaptive way. This means helping students make appropriate attributions for their successes and failures. The effectiveness of the attributional coaching will affect the learners' expectations for success on future performances, and so represents an application of Principle 6.1, learners are more motivated when they believe their actions will result in successfully completing challenging tasks. ●

Teachers as Decision Makers

Throughout this chapter you looked in on Karen Hilderbrand and Josef Amir as they dealt with specific issues. In each instance, you were presented a decision point and asked to think about the decisions that these teachers faced. In this section we discuss our perspectives on these decisions and explain how the principles developed in this chapter are applied to decision making in later chapters.

Karen Hilderbrand's Decision Points

In the opening vignette, Karen Hilderbrand had been assigned as a mentor for a new teacher and was thinking about what she could do to help. Karen began by reflecting on her own first year and identified student motivation as a major concern. She noted that as a beginning teacher she seemed overwhelmed and lamented that keeping the students on task and enjoying learning was one of her biggest challenges. Student motivation is a common concern of both beginning and experienced teachers, and the concern is justified, because it is related to teachers' effectiveness both directly and indirectly. Motivation is directly related to student learning because of the relationship between motivation and effort. People only expend effort if they are motivated, and meaningful learning is effortful. Paying attention, taking notes, asking questions, participating in discussions, completing assignments, and thinking are all activities that require effort and depend on the learners' motivations. The more motivated learners are, the more effort they will expend and the more they will learn.

Motivation also has an indirect effect on teacher effectiveness because of its relationship to classroom management. When awake, people are always motivated to do something; even someone who turns off the morning alarm clock and rolls back under the covers is motivated to stay in a nice warm bed. When students are not motivated to learn what you have to teach, it is likely they will be motivated to do something else, frequently something disruptive.

When we first looked in on Karen she had just met Alfred, the new teacher she had been assigned to help. Alfred was concerned about keeping kids on task and maintaining a positive classroom climate. Karen suggested that he might try to begin his lessons with a discrepant event. The decision here involves deciding when and how to incorporate a discrepant event into a lesson. This technique is especially useful when introducing new material to students with little background knowledge. Discrepant events may also help when you wish to challenge students' misconceptions to encourage conceptual change. You should be judicious in applying this technique. Overuse may weaken the potency of the technique and in some cases may cause some students to become overanxious.

Alfred was concerned about a specific student, Jimmy, who was making maladaptive attributions about his poor performance. Jimmy doesn't believe that he can do anything about his poor performance. As a teacher you need to be aware that your interactions with students will affect their explanations for their successes and failures. Remember that you want to encourage students to make attributions that will enhance their persistence. Explanations that focus students' attention on their effort and strategic choices are most likely to help students in this regard. This is especially critical when the students believe they have failed. Students need to see the relationship between their choices and the outcomes they experience and accept the responsibility for their choices. Communicating your expectation that they can do better, and when necessary providing explicit guidance for improvement is critical to developing your students' self-concept of ability.

Josef Amir's Decision Points

Josef is experiencing new motivational concerns related to changes in policy at the state and district level. He and his colleagues had called for a series of workshops on motivation. What topics would be appropriate for these kinds of workshops? Obviously teachers need specific techniques that they can apply in their classrooms. The problem is that differences in content and students' characteristics from class to class mean that no motivation technique is likely to be effective in every classroom or with every group of students. In other words, teachers need to know about techniques, but they also need to know how to match techniques to specific classroom circumstances. Teachers need theories of motivation that connect specific techniques, learner characteristics, and instructional objectives.

The first workshop presented Maslow's hierarchy and expectancy-value theory. How might an understanding of your students' needs and expectancy-value theory help you make a better decision? By understanding your students' needs you will have a better idea of what they will find valuable in subject area or a learning activity. Your students will be more motivated to the extent that you are able to plan lessons that allow students to gratify their various needs. However, you must be careful not to focus too much on deficiency needs. Remember, helping students gratify their intellectual and aesthetic needs may actually increase the influence such needs have on the choices they make and the effort they expend toward learning in your class.

As teachers plan learning and assessment activities, they need to consider how their lessons and the way they assess students' learning affect their expectancy for success. Good instructional planning considers learners' level of knowledge and skill in order to provide learning experiences that provide a balance between challenge and learners' expectations of success. When learners have doubts about their ability to be successful, you may want to provide less challenging tasks initially and then gradually increase the level of challenge as the students develop confidence in their abilities and appropriate attributions for the performances.

Looking Ahead: Learning Principles and Decision Making

One of the themes of this book is that teachers' decision-making processes are improved through the application of principles from psychological theory. Chapter 1 identified three broad categories of teacher decisions that provide opportunities to apply psychological theories.

- Decisions made when planning a lesson
- Decisions made when teaching and managing in the classroom
- Decisions made when assessing the effectiveness of their actions

In later chapters, the principles developed in this chapter are used to organize discussions of applications of motivation theory to the decisions teachers make in the areas of instructional design, instructional delivery, classroom management, and assessment of learning. Table 6.4 allows you to look forward and see the implications of these principles for the types of decision making discussed in those later chapters.

TABLE 6.4 Principles into Practice: Looking Forward

Decision Area	Implication for Practice	Looking Ahead
Principle 6.1: Learners are more motivated when they believe their actions will result in successfully completing challenging tasks		
Planning	Teachers need to consider learners' ability level when planning lessons to ensure an appropriate level of challenge	Chapters 7, 9, and 10
Teaching and classroom management	Teachers should encourage students to make appropriate attributions when providing learners with feedback	Chapters 7, 8, and 9 (feedback)

continued >

TABLE 6.4 *continued*

Decision Area	Implication for Practice	Looking Ahead
Assessing effectiveness	Assessment tasks should be aligned with instructional content and processes	Chapter 9

Principle 6.2: Learners are more motivated by activities that appeal to their personal needs, motives, and interests

Decision Area	Implication for Practice	Looking Ahead
Planning	Teacher should consider students' needs, motives, and interests when planning lessons and selecting instructional activities	Chapters 7, 9, and 10
Teaching and classroom management	When interacting with students, teachers should consider individual students' needs and motives and help students make connections between classroom activities and their individual interests	Chapters 7, 9, and 10
Assessing effectiveness	Teaches should consider students' needs and motives when selecting assessments tasks	Chapter 9

Principle 6.3: Learners are more motivated when they have specific near-term goals that they believe are important

Decision Area	Implication for Practice	Looking Ahead
Planning	Lessons should have clear objectives	Chapter 9
Teaching and classroom management	Instructional objectives should be clearly communicated and when possible related to students' personal and long-term goals	Chapter 9
Assessment	Assessment activities should be clearly related to instructional objectives	Chapter 9

Principle 6.4: Learners are more motivated when appropriate levels of variety, choice, and surprise are incorporated into lessons

Decision Area	Implication for Practice	Looking Ahead
Planning	Teachers should use a variety of instructional techniques and strategies and use their knowledge of their students to plan for novelty and surprise	Chapters 7, 9, and 10
Teaching and classroom management	Teachers should reduce students' anxiety by providing rules and procedures and being consistent in the dealings with students	Chapter 7
Assessment	Teachers should reduce students' anxiety by designing assessments that are equitable and fair	Chapter 9

Name _____ Date _____

Chapter 6 Study Guide

Use this Study Guide to review and test your knowledge of key concepts introduced in this chapter and to search out further information on issues and topics raised in this chapter.

 Key Terms

Review the following key words from the chapter and then connect to Research Navigator (www.researchnavigator.com) either directly or through this book's Companion Website to explore research on the topics as they relate to education today.

Achievement motive (p. 164)
Aesthetic needs (p. 160)
Affiliation motive (p. 165)
Anxiety (p. 167)
Arousal potential (p. 167)
Attainment value (p. 181)
Attribution (p. 174)
Belonging needs (p. 160)
Controllability (p. 176)
Curiosity (p. 167)
Deficiency needs (p. 162)
Diversive exploration (p. 167)
Esteem needs (p. 160)
Exploratory behaviors (p. 167)
Extrinsic motivation (p. 158)
Generalized expectancies
  (p. 171)
Goal content (p. 186)

Goal intensity (p. 186)
Goal orientation (p. 179)
Goal structure (p. 182)
Goals (p. 185)
Growth needs (p. 162)
Homeostasis (p. 162)
Individual interest (p. 166)
Intellectual needs (p. 160)
Interest value (p. 182)
Intrinsic motivation (p. 158)
Learned helplessness (p. 175)
Locus (p. 176)
Mastery goals (p. 179)
Motivation (p. 156)
Motive to avoid failure (p. 164)
Motives (p. 159)
Need (p. 159)
Perceived task difficulty (p. 173)

Performance approach goals
  (p. 179)
Performance avoidance goals
  (p. 179)
Performance goals (p. 180)
Physiological needs (p. 160)
Power motive (p. 165)
Safety needs (p. 160)
Self-actualization (p. 160)
Self-concept of ability (p. 172)
Self-serving bias (p. 175)
Situational interest (p. 166)
Specific expectancies (p. 171)
Specific exploration (p. 168)
Stability (p. 176)
Task value (p. 172)
Utility value (p. 182)

Alternative Response Items

Multiple Choice Items

1. What concept from Maslow's theory describes the human need for a stable and predictable environment?

   a. Physiological needs   c. Belonging needs
   b. Safety needs   d. Esteem needs

2. Which of the following phrases best describes learners with a strong need to avoid failure?

   a. They prefer situations that present a moderate degree of challenge.
   b. They prefer situations with an uncertain outcome.
   c. They prefer situations with a certain outcome.
   d. They have no strong preferences with regard to the level of challenge.

3. What type of goal is most closely associated with curiosity?

   a. Approach goals   c. Long-term goals
   b. Avoidance goals   d. Performance goals

4. What pattern of attribution is associated with the self-serving bias?

   a. Failure is attributed internally, and success is attributed externally.
   b. Success is attributed internally, and failure is attributed externally.
   c. Both success and failure are attributed internally.
   d. Both success and failure are attributed externally.

5. When a learner experiences failure, what are the characteristics of an attribution of a student who is most likely to be motivated to try harder in the future?

   a. Internal, stable, and uncontrollable
   b. Internal, unstable, and controllable
   c. External, stable, and uncontrollable
   d. External, unstable, and uncontrollable

6. What dimension of an attribution is most closely associated with a learner's expectations for future performances?

   a. Locus
   b. Controllability
   c. Stability

7. What term best describes the goal set by a student who has a mastery goal orientation?

   a. Approach goals   c. Diversive goals
   b. Avoidance goals   d. Attainment goals

8. What view of intelligence is most closely associated with a mastery goal orientation?

   a. Incremental   c. Multiple
   b. Entity   d. Triarchic

9. What type of value best describes a learner who engages in a task because success on the task will make the learner feel proud?

   a. Attainment value
   b. Utility value
   c. Interest value

10. What type of learner is most likely to give up after a first failed attempt to perform some skill?

    a. A student who has a mastery goal orientation
    b. A student who has a performance approach goal orientation
    c. A student who has a performance avoidance goal orientation

Constructed Response Items

Short Answer/Completion Items

1. What type of goal orientation is most likely to result in the student setting an approach goal?

2. What type of needs from Maslow's theory are examples of growth needs?

3. What type of motive is most closely related to Maslow's belonging need?

4. What factors contribute to the arousal potential of a lesson?

5. What type of goal orientation is most closely associated with the motive to achieve?

Essay Items

1. Describe how the needs and motives of students are likely to change as they mature.

2. Identify the attributional dimensions (locus, controllability, and stability) of the following students' statements and explain your answers.

   a. Jerome: "I could have done better on that test, but I just couldn't get interested in studying last night."

   b. Ellie: "I think my paper deserves a better grade than this; I think the teacher just doesn't like my style."

   c. Franco: "I should have worked harder on my science project, instead of messing around with my dad's car last week."

Practicing Your Decision Making

1. Given the content that you are likely to teach, describe some ways that you might incorporate surprise, choice, and variety into your lessons.

2. In this chapter we have discussed various factors that affect learners' motivations. Discuss how the factors might affect your decisions with regard to motivating your students to learn.

   a. Level of student maturity
   b. Required versus elective courses and activities
   c. Summer school classes

INTASC in Action

Use the following activities to think about how motivational concepts relate to INTASC Standards 2, 3, 4, and 5.

Standard 2: Student Development. Consider the age range of the students you are likely to be teaching. Make a list of those students' characteristics and experiences that is likely to influence their:

a. Perception of the level challenge associated with learning activities in your class,
b. Expectancy of success, and
c. Perception of the value associated with participation in learning activities in your class.

You may want to review Chapters 2 through 5 as you consider your answers.

Standard 3: Diverse Learners. Discuss how you modify your lessons to motivate a student with learned helplessness.

Standard 4: Multiple Instructional Strategies. Discuss how you might use critical thinking and problem-solving activities to increase students' motivation in your future classroom.

Standard 5: Motivation and Management. Discuss how learning about your students' family and cultural backgrounds might be used to increase students' interest in your lessons.

Web Resources

For more information on concepts in motivational theory, visit the following websites.

Peak Performance

www.glencoe.com/ps/peak/selfassess/
motivation.html

This site provides an example of an inventory that may be used to conduct a self-assessment of your own motivation. What does the inventory tell you about your own motivation?

Abraham Maslow Bio

www.ship.edu/~cgboeree/maslow.html

Read a biographical sketch of Abraham Maslow, an important theoretician and researcher in the area of personality and motivation, as presented by Professor George Boeree of Shippensburg University.

National Education Association

www.nea.org/parents/tools/motivate.html

Read this special resource provided by the National Education Association discussing how parents can help with classroom motivation.

Engines for Education

www.engines4ed.org/hyperbook/nodes/
NODE-62-pg.html

Engines for Education, a nonprofit organization dedicated to educational reform, offer ideas for curricula and environments that make learning fun and vital. This site provides specific ideas for enhancing motivation in the classroom.

Motivating Students

www.virtualsalt.com/motivate.htm

This site provides ideas and tips for enhancing classroom motivation.

Using Effective Instructional Techniques, Strategies, and Technology

Standards in This Chapter

The concepts presented in this chapter will contribute to your mastery of all of the INTASC standards; however, the material presented in Chapter 7 relates most strongly to the following standards:

- **Standard 2:** Student Development
- **Standard 3:** Diverse Learners
- **Standard 4:** Multiple Instructional Strategies
- **Standard 5:** Motivation and Management
- **Standard 6:** Communications and Technology
- **Standard 9:** Reflective Practice and Professional Growth

Your decisions about how to teach will be influenced by many factors including the nature of your students, the requirements of your curricula, and the necessity to prepare students for high-stakes testing. As a result of these influences and others, you are likely to need a variety of instructional techniques and strategies to be successful. The main goal of this chapter, therefore, is to familiarize you with instructional techniques and strategies from different theoretical perspectives. In addition, technology applications that can be used to support these different instructional techniques and strategies are discussed. This discussion is organized around the theoretical principles presented in Chapters 2 through 6. When you have completed this chapter, you should be able to do the following:

- Identify teaching techniques and a teaching strategy for implementing behavioral learning principles,
- Identify teaching techniques associated with social cognitive principles,
- Identify teaching techniques and a teaching strategy for implementing information-processing learning principles,
- Identify teaching techniques and a teaching strategy for implementing constructivist learning principles,
- Explain how principles of motivation theories influence your selection and use of instructional techniques and strategies, and
- Identify technology applications to support the techniques and strategies from each theoretical perspective.

Close-ups on the Classroom
Middle School

Jacy Winston and the Teaching Observation

I have been a junior high math teacher for the last ten years, and I really enjoy the challenges of working with this age student. Today after school I have an appointment with my new principal Lawrence to go over the results of his first observation of my teaching. In our district our principals are required to observe us twice a year and to have conferences with us about those observations. Even though I'm an experienced teacher, I'm a little nervous. Different principals expect to see different things from teachers. I hope he just wants me to do what I do best as a teacher.

The lesson he saw did turn out to be fairly representative of daily life in my classroom. The first twenty minutes was spent showing students how to use a graphing program on the computer. They'll use this program several times during the year, and it's an important analytical tool for a unit I do with the social studies department that requires students to analyze population data and make predictions based on the data. This unit is an example of our new principal's desire to find ways to integrate learning experiences across curricular areas.

For the remainder of the class period, my students worked in groups, helping each other understand how to use the graphing program on some sample problems I provided. During this time I walked around and answered questions and listened to the students' discussions. This is typical for me because I use a lot of small group work in my classroom. Students at this age appreciate some time to talk together, and if I structure it well, they actually can learn a lot from each other.

This afternoon, I will also be discussing my professional growth goal for the year. I have a number of students with disabilities in my classes, and I'd like to learn more about how to help these students.

Decision Point: What factors are influencing Jacy's decisions about how to teach?

Before proceeding with Chapter 7, be sure you read the Close-ups on the Classroom features about Jacy Winston and Marsha Van Pelt. At various points in the chapter, you will revisit both teachers in their classrooms and follow their decision-making progress. Their classroom experiences are closely integrated with the key concepts of this chapter and serve as important models for understanding various instructional techniques and uses of technology.

Instructional Principles, Techniques, and Strategies

As stated previously in Chapter 1, a theoretical principle is a general guideline that evolves out of the beliefs of a particular theory and that helps connect that theory to classroom practice. For example, behaviorists tend to believe that learning is an incremental process. Consequently, one of their principles is that classroom learning needs to occur gradually and step by step.

An **instructional technique** is a specific action taken by teachers during the instructional process and can be thought of as a single component of the teaching process. Consider the different instructional techniques used by the following teachers.

- Manny Garcia pauses after he asks a thought-provoking question to give his students time to think.
- Joanne Marino writes specific feedback on her students' English compositions.
- John Woodall writes measurable objectives for his special education students.

Instructional techniques are usually associated with learning theories that analyze teaching into its component parts such as behavioral learning theory and information-

Marsha Van Pelt and the Tutoring Program

My district has started an after school tutoring program and decided to staff the program with classroom teachers on a volunteer basis. I volunteered right away because I appreciated the opportunity to earn extra money, and it's a nice change of pace to work with students one on one or in small groups. Although it's an enjoyable experience, it's not without problems. For example, originally it was recommended that we not tutor our own students, but this created some controversy among teachers. This issue continues to be debated, and it's possible that we will change that recommendation.

One of my duties in this tutorial program is to review computer software in different curricular areas. We are primarily looking for tutorial software that we can use to increase students' basic knowledge and skills. I just recently got a program in social studies that I am going to review after school.

The students I am tutoring have a wide variety of learning problems. Marcus is a second grader who is having trouble with reading. When he comes to a difficult word in a passage, he tends to omit it or substitute a word that doesn't make sense. He is also a very slow reader and that discourages him. Some days it's really hard to get him to try. He broke my heart the other day when he told me he was stupid because he stumbles over words as he reads.

Lonnie, Marilyn, and Brandon are struggling in math. A big part of their problem is that they don't understand what they are doing. I've decided to work with them as a group even though they have different strengths and weaknesses in math. I hope they can help each other. I'm excited about this group because I am going to try some things I've been reluctant to try with my class of fifth graders.

Robin and Sarah are sixth graders who were referred for some help with their writing. In part, they have trouble because their writing tends to be disorganized and hard to follow. The writing samples I read also seem to leave out important information for the reader. It's almost like they are assuming the reader knows what they know.

Decision Point: What do you think the arguments are for allowing teachers to tutor their own students? What do you think the arguments are for recommending that teachers do not tutor their own students?

processing theory. Consequently, the majority of the techniques described in this chapter are typically associated with these two theoretical perspectives, but they are used in one form or another by many different approaches to teaching.

An **instructional strategy** combines several principles and techniques to create an overall approach for teaching a lesson, or in some cases, a way to organize and structure classrooms for learning. Often, an instructional strategy is associated with a particular theory, but the same strategy can be connected to more than one theory. Mastery learning, direct instruction, and problem-based learning are examples of instructional strategies that are presented in this chapter.

How are instructional strategies and instructional techniques different?

Educational Technology

Roblyer, Edwards, and Havriluk (1997) define **educational technology** as teaching tools and the processes necessary to apply those tools. Examples of technology tools are computers and computer software, audiovisual equipment, and technologies used to accommodate the needs of learners with disabilities. The processes involved in the use of educational technology are your decisions about how best to use technology to support your students' learning.

Research on Educational Technology and Classroom Learning. Research on the effects of educational technology on classroom learning has yielded inconsistent results and a variety of opinions about the usefulness of educational technology (Clark, 1983, 1994; Clark & Sugrue, 1995; Hefzallah, 1999; Kent & McNergney, 1999). One explanation for the inconclusive research findings is that any evaluation of educational technology is also an evaluation of the instruction being supported by technology (Coley, Cradler, & Engel, 2000). If a teaching strategy is not used well, then the technology used with the lesson is likely to be ineffective also (Driscoll, 2001). The selected technology application may be less important for successful learning than factors such as the nature of the instructional activity and the characteristics of the learners (Abrami, 2001). Educational technology, therefore, is more likely to be beneficial when it is used in thoughtful ways to support teachers' goals for their students (Bloome & Kinzer, 1998; Clements & Sarama, 1998; Shrock, 1994).

How would you summarize the research findings about the effectiveness of educational technology for improving classroom learning?

What does the thoughtful use of technology involve? How can you avoid just using technology for technology's sake? The following questions are useful in making effective decisions about the uses of educational technology discussed in this chapter.

- What are the capabilities of a particular technology application, and what types of learning outcomes are supported by the technology? For example, is it a drill and practice program or intended for other uses?
- Does the technology application fit well with the overall goals I am trying to accomplish, the type of classroom learning environment I have established, and the nature of my students?
- What are the time requirements and financial costs of using a particular technology application and are the possible outcomes worth the time and money invested?
- What are the potential unintended negative effects of the use of a particular technology? For example, will the use of a technology application isolate students from each other?
- Is the selected application a well-designed example of this type of application?

*B*ehavioral Learning Theory and Teaching

In general, behaviorists view classroom learning as a step-by-step process that is guided by measurable objectives. The effective use of behavioral teaching techniques and strategies requires answers to the following questions.

- What specific behaviors do my students need to learn and to what level of proficiency?
- What instructional experiences will best help my students learn the desired behaviors?
- How will students' progress toward learning the desired behaviors be measured?

The skills and knowledge necessary to answer these questions are presented over the next few chapters. In this chapter, the focus is on how Principles 2.2 and 2.3 generate teaching applications that can help your students learn specific behaviors.

Principle 2.2: Learning Occurs Gradually and Step by Step

Behaviorists take a part-to-whole perspective on learning, which means that complicated or unfamiliar behaviors need to be learned gradually or step by step. As you remember from Chapter 2, Skinner's (1953) techniques of shaping and chaining are used for this purpose.

Shaping as an Instructional Technique.   Shaping is defined as reinforcing gradual improvement toward a terminal goal. It can be used to teach brand new behaviors or to improve the quality of existing behaviors (Zirpoli & Melloy, 1997).

In some cases, students may not be able to produce a desired behavior, but may be able to produce some precursor or approximation of a behavior. For example, a young student with a severe speech delay may not be able to say his name, "Tom," but he can make a *t* sound. The speech therapist might shape this behavior by initially accepting *t* for the student's name and then gradually expecting the child to get closer to the complete pronunciation.

More typically, students may be able to produce a behavior, but need to improve the accuracy, frequency, duration, or speed of the behavior. For example, one of your students may make a number of mechanical errors in writing. You could shape this student's editing behavior by requiring this student to reduce the number of his mechanical errors to earn full grade credit in this area. In an elementary school, you might use a shaping procedure to set speed goals for simple math calculations. In this case, students need to increase gradually the number of simple addition problems they solve correctly in a given amount of time to meet their goals.

Chaining as an Instructional Technique. A behavioral chain is a series of behaviors that need to be executed in sequence (Zirpoli & Melloy, 1997). Chaining as an instructional technique involves teaching students to execute a behavioral chain, such as teaching students to execute the sequence of steps in long division. In teaching through chaining, you have three major choices of how to sequence the instruction: total task presentation, forward chaining, and backward chaining (Alberto & Troutman, 1999; Martin & Pear, 1996; Spooner & Spooner, 1984).

Total task presentation involves teaching all the steps in a chain at one time. For example, you might demonstrate all the steps in long division and ask students to learn all those steps at once. This approach tends to be effective with simple behavioral chains.

Forward chaining involves teaching the first step or task of a chain until students have mastered it. Then the second step or task is taught until it is mastered, and this process is followed until all the steps or tasks have been taught. For example, you would teach the first step in long division until it's mastered, then the second step, and so on until all steps have been taught.

Backward chaining begins by teaching the last step or task in a complicated behavior. Then each component is taught one step at a time in reverse order until the first step or task is reached (Alberto & Troutman, 1999; Hagopian, Farrell, & Amari, 1996). For example, someone might be taught the game of golf by starting with putting and then working backward to driving from the tee (Simek & O'Brien, 1981). If you are teaching a learning strategy to your students, you might do the first steps with students, and then ask them to complete the last step on their own. Next time, they would do the last two steps on their own, and this approach would be followed until students are executing the strategy independently.

Although backward chaining may seem odd at first glance, there can be benefits. First, students start with the successful completion of a task, which can increase their motivation for learning previous steps (Killian, 1988). Also, exposure to later steps may help students understand the importance of executing earlier steps more carefully. For example, Earl (1982) described a demonstration film for showing students how to conduct an experiment measuring the effects of chemical and electrical stimulation on a frog's heart. By first seeing later steps in

How are backward and forward chaining different?

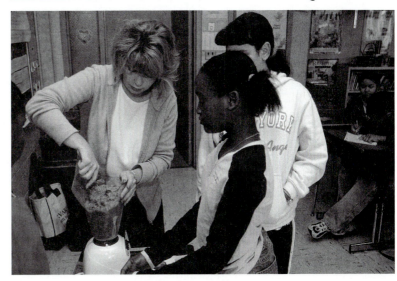

Total task presentation is modeling all the steps of learning a skill.

the procedure, students were less likely to make critical mistakes in the first incisions they were asked to make.

Research comparing the effectiveness of these approaches has provided mixed results (Spooner & Spooner, 1984). To a large extent, your decision about which approach to use should be based on your experience. You'll need to determine which approach works best for your learners and the skills you need to teach.

Principle 2.3: Learning Results from the Effects of Stimuli on Behavior

In order for learning to occur, behaviorists suggest that students must successfully practice the behaviors they need to learn. They have developed some instructional techniques that are designed to help students practice more effectively.

The General Nature of Effective Practice. According to behaviorists, effective practice has two main characteristics. First, practice activities should directly support the learning objectives. For example, if you want students to learn to add two numbers together, then they should practice adding two numbers together. Second, students need to practice behaviors correctly. Behaviorists believe that if students practice a behavior incorrectly, that is the way they will learn it. Instructional prompts and feedback are two instructional techniques that can be used to promote correct practice.

Instructional Prompts. An **instructional prompt** is an antecedent stimulus that encourages correct responses from students (Gropper, 1987). Prompts help students avoid errors when they are first learning, or they provide support so students can produce a correct response when they are first learning. For example, highlighting the ones column in green as a reminder to start here when adding two-digit numbers is using a prompt to help students avoid a common error. Here are some other examples of prompts.

- Guidance provided to students about format, content, and scoring in the directions for a paper (Shiland, 2000)
- An alphabet train or number line taped to students' desk to promote correct letter or number formation
- Pencil holders that guide young children's fingers to the correct way to hold a pencil
- Partially worked out math problem on the top of a practice sheet when students are first practicing a new math skill
- A worksheet with editing marks that students can refer to when they are first learning to edit their papers

How does prompting help students practice correctly? Behaviorists recommend that teachers provide considerable environmental support in the form of prompts when students are learning a new behavior. As learners become more comfortable with a behavior, the prompts should be faded or removed gradually so that students do not become dependent on the prompts.

Feedback. **Feedback** is evaluative data provided to students to improve or maintain their level of performance (Schloss & Smith, 1994). To a behaviorist, feedback can be reinforcement for correct responses or a mild aversive stimulus for incorrect responses. For example, a computerized drill and practice program might respond with, "Good job!" when students give a correct answer, or "Not quite right. Try again!" when students give an incorrect answer. Because behaviorists emphasize the reinforcing effects of feedback, their guidelines for effective feedback are similar to their guidelines for effective use of reinforcement.

First, behaviorists believe that feedback should immediately follow the occurrence of the target behavior. A number of studies have supported this belief (Dihoff, Brosvic,

& Epstein, 2003; Dihoff, Brosvic, Epstein, & Cook, 2004; Kulik & Kulik, 1988). Other research, however, has provided support for delaying feedback (Brackbill, Bravos, & Starr, 1962; Kulhavey & Anderson, 1972; Surber & Anderson, 1975). The delay-retention effect (DRE) is one hypothesis for the value of delaying feedback (Kulhavey & Anderson, 1972). According to the DRE hypothesis, delayed feedback is thought to be preferable because it reduces the likelihood that the incorrect answer will compete with the correct answer in memory. Although this debate is likely to continue, there are some general recommendations your authors can make. Teachers' feedback minimally needs to be timely. Students should receive feedback in time for that feedback to help them improve their next performance. Also, if you want students to receive immediate feedback, technology can help you with the practical issues involved in providing feedback in a classroom of thirty learners (Hall et al., 2001; Price, Martella, Marchand-Martella, & Cleanthous, 2002).

Second, feedback should be scheduled like reinforcement. Learners should have ample opportunity for feedback when they are first learning; then the opportunities for feedback can be reduced once the behavior is established. This is essentially an application of the schedules of reinforcement idea from Chapter 2.

How is this guideline for using feedback similar to the guidelines for using prompting?

Instructional Feedback as Information. Subsequent research on instructional feedback also suggests that feedback is more effective when it provides information to students that can guide their learning (Bangert-Downs, Kulik, Kulik, & Morgan, 1991; Deci & Ryan, 1987). Consequently, feedback should be specific and informational about what students have done well and about what they need to improve. This view of feedback is more consistent with a cognitive or social cognitive view of learning, but it provides additional important guidance on how to provide students with effective feedback. Consider these examples of specific, informational feedback.

- Your introductory paragraph does an excellent job of identifying the key points you will address in your paper. You may want to review your coverage of these main points in your paper's summary.
- You have written a clear and researchable hypothesis for your science fair project. However, you need to consult the points I wanted you to cover in your discussion of your method. For example, how long will the study take?

Mastery Learning as an Instructional Strategy

As stated earlier in the chapter, instructional principles and techniques can be combined to create a teaching strategy. Very often, the result is a strategy that reflects how a particular theory would structure and organize a classroom for learning. Although mastery learning did not originate primarily out of behavioral theory, it is an example of a teaching strategy that can be used to implement a behavioral view of teaching.

Common Elements of Mastery Learning. **Mastery learning** is a strategy for organizing classroom instruction that is based on the idea that if students are given the time and the help they need to learn, they can learn (Bloom, 1968; Carroll, 1963). Although there are different forms of mastery learning, all of the various forms share these common elements (Becker, 1986; Guskey, 1997, 2001).

- Teachers divide curriculum into a sequence of units.
- Teachers establish clear and measurable standards of mastery for those units.
- Teachers teach to the objectives and assess mastery of the objectives.
- Students who do not master objectives are given additional time and the help they need. These students are retaught and retested with alternate forms of the test until they reach mastery.
- Students who demonstrate mastery of unit objectives are provided with enrichment activities or allowed to progress to the next unit.

Looking in on

It should be emphasized that teachers may use a variety of teaching approaches with a mastery learning format. For example, mastery learning can easily be combined with cooperative learning approaches (Laney, 1999). However, mastery learning is well suited to a behavioral approach to classroom teaching because it focuses on the teaching of specific objectives in a sequential manner, and students are encouraged to learn initial skills correctly before they progress to later skills.

Effectiveness of Mastery Learning.   Classroom research on mastery learning has generally supported mastery learning as an effective instructional strategy (Block & Burns, 1976; Guskey & Pigott, 1988; Kulik, Kulik, & Bangert-Downs, 1990a, 1990b). Supporters of mastery learning suggest that mastery learning increases the number of students who master course objectives, reduces the tendency to move students on before they are ready, helps teachers focus on important objectives, and provides a structure for identifying and assisting students who need help.

Mastery learning, however, also has its critics. Slavin's (1989a) review of mastery learning provides a much less positive picture of its effectiveness. His synthesis of research on mastery learning suggests that effectiveness can vary depending on the age of the students, length and type of mastery learning, and the way that researchers measure achievement. Teachers have also expressed the concern that mastery learning is too much of a sequential view of learning and may be less suitable for courses with nonsequential content (Postlethwaithe & Haggarty, 1998). Given the issues with mastery learning, you need to consider carefully when to use this strategy. You could, for example, identify critical foundational objectives in your curricula and use mastery learning approaches primarily for those objectives.

What are the overall findings on the effectiveness of mastery learning?

Educational Technology and Behavioral Approaches

Behavioral psychologists, especially B. F. Skinner, were among the first to see the potential of educational technology. This interest in the use of technology to support learning was reflected initially in the development of programmed learning, beginning in the 1950s and 1960s, and later in the design of drill and practice programs.

& Karge, 1996). For example, you might compare the structure of the atom to the structure of the solar system, or the information-processing model to a computer. Teachers can provide instructional analogies or students can generate their own. Either way, the goal of an instructional analogy is to help students relate the unfamiliar to the familiar.

It is important to note that inexperienced learners and children are susceptible to misrepresenting the intended relationship in the analogy (Spiro, Feltovich, Coulson, & Anderson, 1989; Vosniadou & Brewer, 1987). If you generate analogies for your students, they may have difficulty differentiating the parts of the analogy that are relevant from the parts that are not (Zook, 1991). For example, the hard drive of a computer is a useful analogy for long-term memory only in the sense that both computers and humans have semipermanent storage capabilities. However, the way that information is stored on a hard drive is an incomplete analogy for our complex abilities to interrelate knowledge in memory.

K-W-L helps students activate prior knowledge.

Analogical reasoning is also a fairly abstract ability. Young students and inexperienced students may have difficulty with these complicated processes (Zook, 1991). Also, if students are asked to generate their own analogies, they may have trouble identifying familiar knowledge that can serve as a useful analogy.

Instructional variables such as the content of the analogy, its complexity, and available instructional supports will affect students' ability to use analogies effectively (Zook & Maier, 1994). Students can benefit from instructional supports such as prompts that provide explicit knowledge of the goal for using the analogy, or spatial/semantic organizers such as tables or diagrams that highlight important relationships in the analogy (Bulgren, Deshler, Schumaker, & Lenz, 2000; Zook & Di Vesta, 1991). Whether you supply analogies for the students or have your students generate their own, you will want to help guide your young and inexperienced students' use and interpretation of those analogies.

From a Piagetian perspective, why would young children have trouble forming analogies?

Coordinating Basic Mental Processes

From an information-processing perspective, your students need to engage successfully in certain basic mental processes in order to learn. For example, they need to focus their attention on the important parts of what they are learning, and they need to organize the information they are learning. Information-processing psychologists have identified instructional techniques that can influence those key mental processes. However, it is important to remember that how a technique actually affects learners' thought processes depends on a number of factors including the characteristics of the learners and how a technique is used. For example, learners' interest level for a lesson and their prior experiences with similar lessons can influence how they respond to a technique. Also, you need to remember that the same technique can be designed to influence more than one basic process.

Techniques to Focus Learners' Attention. At times, you have specific information or skills that you want your students to learn. It may, however, not always be readily apparent to your students what those are. A number of instructional techniques have been identified that can help students know where to focus their attention.

Providing Learning Objectives. Providing your students with learning objectives is one way to help them identify the important information in a lesson or reading assignment. Consider this example.

> ➤ Sally Ord likes to begin her lessons by identifying the key points that need to be learned from her lesson. She says things like, "When we are done, you should know the following things, or be able to do the following."

Generally, research in this area suggests that providing students with specific objectives helps them focus on information and skills that are relevant to the objectives, but not on information or skills that are less relevant to the objectives (Faw & Waller, 1976; Klauer, 1984; Zumbach & Reimann, 2002). This effect is stronger for information that students wouldn't normally identify by themselves as being important (Duell, 1974).

Adjunct Questions. Textbook authors often use adjunct questions as a way of helping students focus their attention. **Adjunct questions** are questions that are inserted in text (Peverly & Wood, 2001; Rothkopf, 1966, 1970). They may be provided before students read the text during reading or after students read the text. The questions in the margins of this text are an example of adjunct questions.

When adjunct questions are provided before a reading selection, students focus to a large extent on information that is relevant to the questions. When adjunct questions are placed at the end of the reading selection, students focus on information related to the questions, but they are more likely to recall information that is not directly related to the questions (Boker, 1974; Faw & Waller, 1976; Rothkopf, 1966).

Why would it be useful to turn topic headings into questions before reading sections of text?

Additional research on adjunct questions provides the following results (Anderson & Biddle, 1975; Boker, 1974; Hamaker, 1986; Hamilton, 1985; Mayer, 1975; Rickards & Divesta, 1974).

- Adjunct questions typically facilitate learning regardless of placement.
- Questions provided after text are preferable to questions provided before text for typical classroom learning situations.
- Meaningful questions promote more complete learning than rote questions.
- Frequent use of questions provided after the text may be preferable to less frequent use.

Learners Need to Organize Information. Encoding and understanding of information is improved if students perceive how that information is organized. Mayer (1987) has referred to organization as developing internal connections, because the connections are among ideas within the lesson, rather than to existing knowledge. Signals, graphic organizers, and outlines are instructional techniques that can help students form internal connections.

Signals. **Signals** are text devices that highlight important ideas or the structural organization of ideas in text without conveying additional content (Lorch & Lorch, 1996; Meyer, 1985; Meyer, Talbot, Stubblefield, & Poon, 1998). For example, authors may also use number signals so that readers know where they are in a series of ideas or a sequence of steps. "The first idea is . . ." and "Our last of four points is . . ." are examples of number signals. Authors may also signal text organization with an introductory or summary paragraph that discusses the organization of the reading, or they may put key ideas in bold or italic print to help students know that those ideas are important. The paragraph heading for this section is an example of a signal, because it helps you follow the structure of this chapter.

Although signals are typically thought of as device used in written text, they may also be useful in your presentations or lectures. For example, you may stop after a major section of a presentation and review key points for students, or you may use signals to help mark transitions within your presentation. This is how Consuela Archuleta applies this idea in her high school biology course.

> ➤ When I lecture, I like to alert students to transitions between topics. For example, I might say things like, "We are done with this topic and ready to move on to the next topic, which is. . . ."

Outlines and Spatial/Semantic Organizers. You can help your students understand how information is organized in a text or a lecture by providing them with an outline or a spatial/semantic organizer for that information. You are probably already familiar with outlines as a way of representing a linear organization of ideas. **Spatial/semantic organizers** are instructional tools that represent the organizational structure of information in a visual/spatial manner (Chmielewski & Dansereau, 1998). Visual/semantic organizers go by many names and can take many forms including concept and knowledge maps (Bahr & Dansereau, 2001; Chang, Sung, & Chen, 2001; Novak, 1990), Venn diagrams and webs (Camp, 2000), structured overviews (Barron, 1969; Bassoppo-Moyo, 1997), and graphic organizers (Kirylo & Millet, 2000; Merkley & Jefferies, 2000/2001). Here is how John Gregorio uses Venn diagrams in his teaching.

> ➤ I use Venn diagrams to help students compare and contrast key ideas. The similarities between the two ideas are written in the part where the circles overlap. The differences between the two ideas are written in the nonoverlapping parts of each circle.

One commonly used spatial/semantic organizer is the concept or knowledge map. These maps consist of nodes and labeled links that reflect the interrelationships of ideas. Ideas or concepts are placed at the nodes and labeled lines or links are drawn between concepts to reflect how they are related or interconnected. Figure 7.2 provides an example of a concept map.

Concept and knowledge maps have been used across academic domains and grade levels and for various purposes. Concept maps have been used to help students plan their writing, build vocabulary knowledge, and improve reading comprehension (Sturm & Rankin-Erickson, 2002). They also have been used for curriculum design and for assessing students' knowledge structures (Edmondson, 1995; Ruiz-Primo & Schavelson, 1996). Research supports concept mapping as an effective intervention for improving students' organization and cohesion in writing, their ability to develop meaningful understandings, and their ability to reflect on their own misunderstandings (Sturm & Rankin-Erickson, 2002; van Boxtel, Linden, Roelofs, & Erkens, 2002).

When implementing spatial/semantic organizers in your classroom, there are some recommendations to consider (Baroody & Bartels, 2000; Katayama & Robinson, 2000; Merkley & Jefferies, 2000/2001).

- Start small at first. Use a single topic with a few concepts to interconnect.
- Consider using technology designed for creating concept maps. They make it easier to produce and edit concept maps.
- Actively involve students in the creation and use of maps. For example, provide incomplete maps that students are asked to complete as they take notes. Have students identify and reflect on the relationships that are portrayed.
- Consider having students interact as they develop and interpret maps. If they develop separate maps for what they have read, have them compare and contrast their maps.

Limitations of Working Memory and Instruction

As you remember from Chapter 3, the working memory is a limited capacity processor that can be overloaded by too much information at one time or the requirement

FIGURE 7.2. Sample
Concept Map
(*Source:* Adapted from Holly, C. D.
and Dansereau, D. F. (1984). The
development of spatial learning
strategies. In C. D. Holly and D. F.
Dansereau (Eds.), *Spatial learning
strategy: Techniques, applications
and related issues,* pp. 3–19. New
York: Academic Press.)

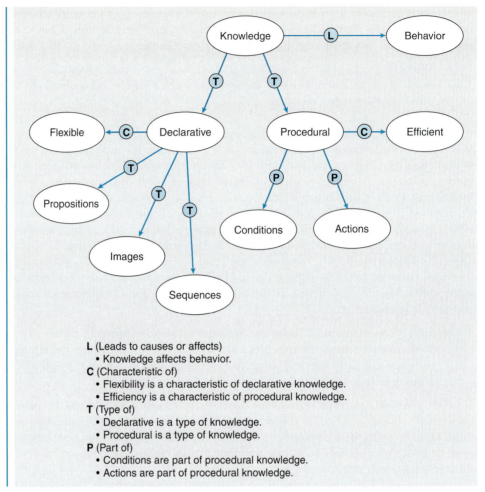

L (Leads to causes or affects)
   • Knowledge affects behavior.
C (Characteristic of)
   • Flexibility is a characteristic of declarative knowledge.
   • Efficiency is a characteristic of procedural knowledge.
T (Type of)
   • Declarative is a type of knowledge.
   • Procedural is a type of knowledge.
P (Part of)
   • Conditions are part of procedural knowledge.
   • Actions are part of procedural knowledge.

to execute too many complicated mental processes at once. Cognitive load theory provides a framework for understanding how the limited capacity of working memory can influence instruction. According to cognitive load theory, instruction poses three different types of cognitive load on working memory (Bannert, 2002; Sweller, 1999).

• **Intrinsic cognitive load** derives from the material to be learned and is determined by the complexity of the material to be learned and learners' prior knowledge about that material. Intrinsic load is high for complex and unfamiliar material.
• **Extraneous cognitive load** results from inadequately designed instruction. Typically, this occurs when extraneous information or unneeded processes for the learning goal are included in the instruction.
• **Germane cognitive load** results from the additional cognitive effort learners expend to create deeper constructions of information or automatize schemata.

In general, teachers should try to eliminate extraneous load and should help novice students cope with the demands of intrinsic and germane load. For example, novices might benefit from instruction that first presents the individual elements of a complicated task and then provides a whole task presentation (Pollock, Chandler, & Sweller, 2002). Also, students may need time during instruction to consolidate what they are learning. Here are some additional ideas for managing cognitive load.

• When presenting information, pause periodically to allow students time to process what you are saying.
• Provide students with slot outlines for note taking. A slot outline is an outline with some of the ideas omitted. Students fill in the missing ideas.

- Provide students with cue cards when they are practicing a new skill and ample practice with new skills.
- Limit the number of important points you include in a presentation.
- When providing complicated definitions, present them in pieces or chunks.
- Repeat key information more than once. (This also helps focus attention on these ideas.)

Direct Instruction as an Instructional Strategy

Direct instruction is a highly structured and interactive form of teacher-directed instruction that derived from behavioral learning theory as a highly scripted method for teaching basic reading and math skills (Carnine & Silbert, 1979; Englemann & Bruner, 1974; Mac Iver & Kemper, 2002). Beginning in the 1970s and 1980s, a form of direct instruction became associated with process-outcome research and information-processing theory. **Process-outcome research** refers to a series of studies that attempted to link teacher behavior to students' learning (Brophy & Good, 1986). The process-outcome research identified different teacher behaviors that seemed to be associated with students' success as learners. Some of these have already been presented to you as instructional techniques that can be used to implement information-processing theory into the classroom. The Enriching Your Understanding contains additional findings from this research.

The Three-Step Sequence of Direct Instruction. Hunter's (1982, 1984) mastery teaching and Rosenshine's (1987) explicit teaching are two examples of direct instruction strategies. Although there are differences between ITIP and explicit teaching, both strategies occur in this same three-step sequence: lesson introduction, lesson

ENRICHING YOUR UNDERSTANDING
Process-Outcome Research on Teacher Questioning

As you have already read, process-outcome research attempted to link teachers' behaviors to student achievement by examining what effective teachers did. This research provided a number of recommendations for both teaching and classroom management. For example, here are selected findings from that literature on teachers' question-asking behaviors (Good & Brophy, 2000).

- Teachers should use a sequence of higher level questions and factual questions that are well matched to their objectives. In some cases, teachers might ask factual questions first to focus students' attention on key information, and then follow up with questions that ask students to integrate or apply that information. In other cases, you might want to reverse that sequence.
- Avoid simple yes or no questions, because they typically require follow-up questions and may waste instructional time. Also, avoid leading questions such as, "This is important, don't you agree?"
- Questions should be clear, brief, aligned to the lesson intent, and phrased in language that is appropriate for the

level of students. If new or unfamiliar words are used, they should be defined.
- Questions should typically be addressed to the whole class and distributed across students. At times, however, teachers may identify a student to respond before asking a question. For example, a student may be identified before a question is asked to refocus that student's attention on the lesson.
- Teachers should provide appropriate wait time for their questions. **Wait time** is an intentional pause to allow students to think about the question. The length of wait time should be adjusted based on the level of the question. Longer wait time should be provided for complex or involved questions.
- Teachers should provide feedback to students when questions have correct or incorrect answers.

● How might these ideas for asking questions be applied during direct instruction? (For your authors' perspective on this question, go to the text website for this chapter.)

TABLE 7.1 Explicit Teaching and Instructional Theory into Practice

Step	Explicit Teaching	Mastery Teaching
I. Introduction	1. Begin the lesson with a short statement of goals. 2. Review relevant prerequisite knowledge.	1. Provide an anticipatory set by focusing learners' attention and by activating relevant existing knowledge. 2. Inform learners of the objectives of the lesson.
II. Presentation	3. Present the lesson one point at a time, with opportunities for student practice after each step. 4. Give clear and detailed explanations. 5. Provide a high level of active practice for students. 6. Check for understanding. 7. Provide guided practice. 8. Provide feedback.	3. Provide clear instructional input with varied and specific examples. 4. Provide modeling if appropriate. 5. Check for understanding frequently. 6. Provide for opportunities for guided practice.
III. Ending	9. Provide students with clear directions for independent work. 10. Review as needed.	7. Provide students with independent practice.

presentation, and lesson ending. Table 7.1 lists the sequence of steps for ITIP and explicit teaching and their relationship to this three-step sequence.

Lesson Introduction.   The lesson introduction of a direct instruction lesson is designed to prepare students for what they are about to learn. During this step teachers help students coordinate various mental processes. For example, teachers help their learners focus their attention on the key information in the upcoming lesson presentation by using techniques such as stating objectives or by helping students understand why the lesson is important. Teachers also help learners activate relevant prior knowledge for what they are going to learn. This could be accomplished through techniques such as a review of prior learning, advance organizers, or the K and W steps of K-W-L. Here are some sample statements from the introduction of a direct instruction lesson.

What learner mental processes are teachers trying to influence with these statements?

- "Before we begin today's lesson, can someone tell me what we learned about cells in yesterday's lesson?"
- "When we are finished today, I would like you to be able to answer the following questions."
- "You will want to concentrate on these points today, because you will need them to understand them for your work in lab tomorrow."

Lesson Presentation.   Behavioral learning theory and the process-outcome research have heavily influenced the lesson presentation step in direct instruction. Here are the key characteristics of a direct instruction presentation.

- Each direct instruction lesson should focus on a finite amount of information.
- Information should be taught in a logical sequence. For example, teachers should begin by teaching prerequisite skills for later skills. Additionally, teachers should employ techniques such as spatial/semantic organizers, signals, and outlines to help students follow the organization of a particular lesson.
- During the presentation, teachers should provide students with frequent opportunities to respond and to receive feedback on their learning. This is called *checking for understanding*. For example, a math teacher may have students work problems on small white boards at their desks. Each student can then show her or his work.
- Teachers should provide students with opportunities for guided practice. **Guided practice** is when teachers supervise students by providing feedback, prompts, and

Looking in on

Marsha Van Pelt

7.2

Today I am going to teach Robin and Sarah a strategy for improving the organization of their writing. I decided to begin by asking them how they felt when they were given confusing directions to follow. They both said that it bothered them because they couldn't understand what they were being asked to do. They also said that directions were confusing if they were given out of sequence, or the person assumed you knew what they knew, or if the person told you a lot of things that really weren't necessary. I told them that those same feelings can happen if our writing isn't well organized, and by the end of this lesson they would have a way to organize their writing better.

I showed them a way to organize writing that began with drawing a circle with spokes coming out of it. They said it looks like a picture of the sun. We put the words, "My Morning Routine" in the circle because it was our topic. I selected it because it was familiar to them. I then had them suggest details about their morning routine that we placed on the spokes. We next worked together to turn the topic into a topic sentence and to decide what details from our spokes we wanted to include and in what order. Working together we wrote a paragraph on an overhead. Then I had them plan a paragraph on a topic of their choice using our strategy, while I answered their questions and gave them feedback. Tonight they will take their plan home and finish their paragraph. This was a lot to get done in the hour I had with them.

● **What components of direct instruction are present in this lesson?**

Decision Point: What do you think of Marsha's decision to use direct instruction here?

---

encouragement as students practice what they have just been taught. For example, an English teacher might give students some sample writing to edit while the teacher circulates around the room providing guidance.

Lesson Ending. Direct instruction lessons should end with a review of the key points in the lesson and with opportunities for independent practice. **Independent practice** is when students practice what they have learned on their own, as in the case of homework or a test. Here is how Stan Pierce uses homework when he uses direct instruction with his high school geometry class.

What behavioral principles and techniques are included in direct instruction?

➤ I like to work a few problems together with the class. I allow them to ask questions to make sure they understand. I then assign some problems for homework. I use the homework to introduce the next lesson. We review the homework and talk about how it relates to today's lesson.

By using guided practice, teachers encourage students and give them feedback.

Effectiveness of Direct Instruction. Direct instruction has both its critics and supporters. Critics claim that direct instruction is antithetical to student-centered approaches and reduces learning to acquiring information (Berg & Clough, 1991; Weinert & Helmke, 1995). Supporters note that a large number of classroom and laboratory studies have supported the effectiveness of teacher-directed instruction, particularly if teachers are sensitive diagnosticians of students' learning needs and adjust their teaching

to those needs (Weinert & Helmke, 1995). Also, teacher-directed instruction provides students with access to teachers' expertise through their presentations (Baines & Stanley, 2000).

Research findings on the effectiveness of direct instruction vary. Research on Madeline Hunter's direct instruction approach generally failed to support a strong relationship between training in this program and significant improvement in students' achievement (Mandeville, 1992; Mandeville & Rivers, 1991; Slavin, 1989b; Stallings & Krasavage, 1986). Research on behavioral versions of direct instruction such as the *Reading Mastery* curriculum (Englemann & Bruner, 1995), however, has generally found it to be an effective instructional program for developing students' basic math and reading skills (Adams & Englemann, 1996; Carlson & Francis, 2002). Also, instructional models that incorporate basic components of direct instruction and cognitive strategy instruction are effective interventions for the reading comprehension difficulties of students with learning disabilities (Swanson, 1999). In general, direct instruction can be an effective approach for teaching well-defined basic skills and information, especially if students have limited background knowledge (Rosenshine & Stevens, 1986).

Information-Processing and Technology

The development of cognitive learning theories and advances in technology have historically been closely related. For example, the advent of the computer served as a useful concrete model for human information-processing, and research continues today on the use of computers to model human intelligence and problem-solving capabili-

Focus on Learner Diversity

Direct Instruction and the Linguistically Diverse Student

English language learners can find themselves in classrooms where they are expected to learn academic content that is being presented in English while they learn English. These dual expectations can be challenging for both the teacher and the student. In response to this issue, sheltered English instruction or specially designed academic instruction in English approaches have been developed (Echevarria, Vogt, & Short, 2000). The intent of these approaches is to accommodate students' language needs while developing their academic and English language competencies simultaneously. A number of ideas from sheltered instruction seem particularly useful when considering how to meet the needs of these students during direct instruction. Here are some suggestions for you to consider (Echevarria, Vogt, & Short, 2000; Kottler, 1994).

- For each of your lessons, develop both content and language goals for your students. For example, if you are teaching about photosynthesis, teach students about the meaning of the morpheme *photo* and how it can help them with other complicated vocabulary such as *photogenic* (Echevarria, Vogt, & Short, 2000; Kottler, 1994).
- Connect lesson content whenever possible to students' backgrounds and life experiences.

- Review or preteach key vocabulary for the upcoming lesson.
- When presenting content, make sure that you enunciate clearly, and that the pace of the presentation and the vocabulary used in the lesson are appropriate in terms of your students' language skills.
- Provide appropriate levels of wait time that allow your English language learners the time they need to process questions.
- Encourage English language learners to expand on their answers for additional language development. For example, ask students to tell you why they believe their answer makes sense.
- Structure guided practice around concrete activities that allow students with different language levels to interact with each other.
- Make sure that the directions for homework assignments are clear. If appropriate, consider doing a few of the homework items together as a class.

● **How can these suggestions be connected to the three major parts of a direct instruction lesson? (For your authors' perspective on this question, go to the text website for this chapter.)**

ties. Technology can support the application of cognitive learning principles in the classroom in a number of ways.

Technology as a Knowledge Source.   Technology tools such as the Internet can be used to provide students with background knowledge and in some cases to update existing classroom sources for background knowledge. Consider how these teachers are using the Internet in their classrooms.

➤ When Toni Yazzie uses K-W-L in the classroom, she begins by assigning small groups of students to work with designated websites. The students use the websites to locate current interesting ideas or facts for the "What do you know?" step of K-W-L. It seems to help motivate them to participate because they have information to share.

➤ Sally Ornstein has some of her students use computer tutorials to learn basic science information they lack. It helps ensure that students have needed background knowledge for problem solving.

The amount of information available to learners on the Internet has grown exponentially over the last few years (Norton & Wiburg, 1998). However, this rapid growth has occurred in a generally unregulated environment (Newby, Stepich, Lehman, & Russell, 2000). By now you probably are aware that some websites contain images and information that school districts do not want to make accessible to students. You need to familiarize yourself with your district's policies regarding the use of the Internet in the classroom. The rapid, unregulated growth of the Internet poses other challenges for educators. Websites can contain inaccurate information, and it can be difficult to identify the sources for the information being provided or even the authors of the website (Cooke, 1999; Norton & Wiburg, 1998). Both students and teachers need to be critical consumers of the information they receive from websites. Because of these issues, here are some simple guidelines for the use of the Internet in classrooms.

• Teachers should check out websites carefully before designating them for use. Look at the accuracy of the information and verify the authors of the site.
• Schools should develop acceptable use policies for the Internet and appropriate controls on the technology. As a new teacher, you should familiarize yourself with these policies.
• Students should be taught to validate information by using a cross-media check (additional websites) and an intermedia check (different resources) (Norton & Wiburg, 1998).
• You may need to teach your students how to search the Internet strategically for information. If they are not strategic, they often end up with much more information than they wanted or needed.

Technology and Managing Working Memory Load.   Educational technology can help your students manage the working memory load in instruction by taking over some of the processing tasks. Consider this example from John Saraguso's biology class.

➤ My high school biology students investigate the effects of different levels of four variables on the survival of plants and animals in a small ecosystem. I use a computer simulation that keeps track of how changes in the four variables affect different species. My students can concentrate on interpreting what is happening, rather than focusing on record keeping and graphing.

John Saraguso's application of technology is similar to allowing math students to use calculators during complicated problem-solving activities. In both cases, students can concentrate on the mental processes involved in problem solving rather than on calculations or record keeping. These types of applications can improve students' performance by offloading some task requirements to the technology and by supplementing the capabilities of working memory (Baylor, 2000; Kumar & Wilson, 1997).

Working memory load can also be managed by helping students develop behavioral fluency for certain simple skills such as math calculations. Students have achieved **behavioral fluency** when they can perform a skill quickly and with minimal or no errors (Spence & Hively, 1993). As you may remember from Chapter 3, information-processing theorists refer to behavioral fluency as automaticity. Although there certainly is some controversy about the need to build behavioral fluency, there are data to suggest that fluency with basic skills can help students with later learning and application of those skills (Binder, 1993; Spence & Hively, 1993). For example, Haughton (1972) found that children who could solve single-digit arithmetic problems at a minimum of fifty to sixty correct per minute were more successful at later parts of a math curriculum. As a teacher, you have to determine if you want students to develop behavioral fluency for some skills, and how much time this goal merits in your classroom.

When you select computer software to help students develop behavioral fluency, there are some characteristics to look for in the software. First, the program should

Why might it be useful to show students their progress across practice sessions?

provide students with both error data and rate data. For example, a program designed to build reading decoding fluency would report students' decoding errors and their reading rate. Effective behavioral fluency programs should also provide students with knowledge of their progress by charting their improvement over practice sessions (Binder, 1993; Spence & Hively, 1993). In the reading decoding example, students can track their improvement in reading rate over time.

Cognitive Theory and Intelligent Tutors.   Many early forms of computer-assisted tutorials were unable to provide the type of tailored instruction that is provided by effective tutors. As both technology and cognitive theories of learning and performance evolved, tutorials were designed that could be more responsive to students' learning needs. These tutorials became known as **intelligent tutors** (Newby et al., 2000; Polson & Richardson, 1988).

Intelligent tutors differ from the earlier tutorial programs in terms of the knowledge that is encoded in the program (Burns & Capps, 1988; Kumar, Smith, Helgeson, & White, 1994; Steele & Steele, 1999). Intelligent tutors contain expert knowledge about the academic content to be taught, but they also store information about students' performance with the program and make decisions about how students need to be taught. An intelligent tutor assesses the differences between students' understanding of a domain and the expert knowledge base it has stored. Then based on a model of students' understanding, the intelligent tutor provides assistance that is tailored to students' understanding.

Discover is an example of an intelligent tutor for teaching secondary students and adults how to solve story problems (Steele & Steele, 1999). Through *Discover*, students learn the following steps for solving story problems.

- Read and say the question.
- List important information.
- Make a picture.
- Choose the operation.
- Estimate the answer.
- Write the equation.
- Solve the equation.
- Check your answer.

Discover is based on the Strategic Interventions Model for strategy learning (Lenz, Ellis, & Scanlon, 1996). Students are assessed to determine their initial level of expertise, and then they are exposed to a series of teaching modules based on their existing knowledge and performance within the program. As a result, the tutoring is tailored more directly to students' needs.

Social Cognitive View of Teaching

Principle 4.1, learners acquire important knowledge, behaviors, and dispositions through their exposure to models, has direct implications for classroom teaching. Modeling or teaching through demonstration plus explanation is an important technique for teaching skills and strategies.

Modeling of Academic Skills and Strategies

Modeling is an important component of many approaches for instructing academic skills and strategies (Duffy, Roehler, & Rackliffe, 1986; Murphy, Weil, & McGreal, 1986). This is because modeling provides students with examples of how a skill or strategy is performed successfully and helps students develop the expectations that a skill or strategy can be learned (Bandura, 1997). Obviously, modeling can be useful when teaching a physical skill such as swinging a tennis racket, but it also can be useful for teaching cognitive or mental skills such as how to design a study in science or how to use a reading comprehension strategy.

When you are teaching complicated mental procedures such as long division, it is helpful to make your thought processes accessible to your students. You can do this through **cognitive modeling**, which is thinking aloud as you demonstrate a skill or strategy (Manning, 1991; Meichenbaum & Biemiller, 1998).

What are some examples of cognitive skills you have learned?

Cognitive modeling can take the form of self-questioning or self-instructional directive statements (Meichenbaum & Biemiller, 1998). "What is the next step?" or "What is my goal?" are examples of self-questioning. Examples of self-instructional directive statements would include statements such as, "I need to go back and check my answer," or "I need to slow down when I reread a passage." Self-questioning and self-instructional directive statements can be used for the following purposes during cognitive modeling (Meichenbaum & Biemiller, 1998).

- *Summaries of important information and planning statements.* "What should I do first?" "This is what I have done so far."
- *Accessing relevant prior knowledge.* "What did I learn yesterday that can help me?" "This is like the problems we practiced Tuesday."
- *Self-monitoring.* "Did I do that right?" "I didn't understand what I just read, so I need to read it again."
- *Accessing help.* "Who should I ask for help?" "The encyclopedia should have what I need."
- *Self-reinforcement.* "I did that pretty well." "I think that's a good way to do this."

If you decide to use cognitive modeling in your classrooms, some factors should be considered. Typically, cognitive modeling should be in the form of an interactive dialogue between the model and the learners, rather than a monologue on the part of the model. For example, during cognitive modeling, a teacher might ask students what they think needs to be done next, or the teacher could begin a step in a process and invite students to finish it.

Also, remember that other students or symbolic models such as characters in a story can provide cognitive modeling. For example, in an early application of cognitive modeling to teach problem solving, Bloom and Broder (1950) allowed students to compare their problem-solving processes with those modeled by more successful students. In the Productive Thinking Program (Covington, Crutchfield, & Davies, 1966), cognitive modeling is provided and critiqued by characters in a series of stories that students read.

Today I'm teaching Marcus what to do when he comes to an unknown word by showing him what I do when I can't decode a word. To start, I read a passage while he follows along. Occasionally, I'll stop at a difficult word and talk aloud while I try to decode it. For example, I'll say things such as, "This is a hard one but I know some things I can try," or "Does this have any smaller words in it that I know how to read?" When I finish decoding a word, I ask myself things such as, "Does this word make sense in this sentence?" I also like to congratulate my-self by saying things such as, "I got that one!" Although my approach seems to be working, Marcus occasionally drifts off and stops paying attention. I need some ideas about how to keep his attention while I model.

● **What general categories of cognitive modeling statements are present in this lesson?**

Decision Point: Based on your reading about cognitive modeling, what recommendation could you make to help Marcus stay involved in the lesson?

Social Cognitive Theory and Technology

As you may remember from Chapter 4, Bandura was one of the first to study the effects of televised models on young children's aggressive behavior, a topic of continuing interest to educators and psychologists. Social cognitive theorists have continued to investigate the role of technology in providing models for learners.

Technology and Modeling. The potential of technology to provide instructional models to students has long been recognized. For example, you may have purchased self-instructional tapes that employ models to show you how to improve your golf swing or how to use software packages. This potential has also been incorporated into some intelligent tutor systems. For example, *Wordmath* is a computer-assisted cognitive apprenticeship for teaching nine- to twelve-year-old students to solve story problems (Looi & Tan, 1998). This system supplies modeling to students through its Model Solution module. This module provides examples of expert or teacher problem solving. As each step of the problem-solving strategy is demonstrated, the rationale behind the step is displayed in a *pop-up*. As is the case with all cognitive modeling, the procedure is demonstrated, while students get access to the model's thought processes.

Technology can also provide self-modeling opportunities for students. **Self-modeling** is an intervention that uses visual images of a student engaged in adaptive behavior to strengthen or teach that behavior (Dowrick, 1999). Self-modeling typically involves having students watch taped segments that have been edited or produced to show them only engaged in the appropriate or adaptive behavior. Students repeatedly view these tapes over a period of days as an intervention (Creer & Miklich, 1970).

Self-modeling has been found to be an effective intervention for a number of behaviors such as increasing appropriate classroom participation (Hartley, Bray, & Kehle, 1998), increasing cooperative classroom behavior (Lonnecker, Brady, McPherson, & Hawkins, 1994), improving parenting skills (Reamer, Brady, & Hawkins, 1998), and reducing aggressive/disruptive behaviors (McCurdy & Shapiro, 1988). Additionally, self-modeling has been used with preschoolers through adults (Buggey, 1999).

A number of possible explanations can account for the effectiveness of self-modeling. First, students tend to profit more from modeling that is delivered by models who are similar to them (Bandura, 1986). Using a student as her or his own model provides the greatest degree of model/learner similarity. Second, self-modeling may positively affect self-efficacy (Kehl, Bray, Margianon, & Theodore, 2002). By showing students tapes of themselves successfully performing a behavior, students are provided with concrete evidence that they can be successful at that behavior. From a cognitive perspective, self-modeling could also operate by replacing memories of inappropriate or maladaptive behaviors with memories of successful behavior (Kehle et al., 2002).

What are the theoretical explanations for the effectiveness of self-modeling?

Technology and Self-Regulation.   Technology also can provide support for students' self-monitoring and evaluation and can be used to teach self-instructional approaches (Campbell, 1985; Osborne, Kiburz, & Miller, 1986). For example, Lonnecker, Brady, McPherson, and Hawkins (1994) videotaped two second-grade students with learning and behavior problems. Using a form of a self-modeling approach, these tapes were edited to provide examples of these students behaving in socially appropriate ways, and of these same students behaving inappropriately. Students watched themselves on tape and identified the behavior they were doing. If the behavior was inappropriate, students were asked to suggest an alternative behavior. Later, students rehearsed or role played their alternatives. This combination of treatments was effective for increasing students' socially appropriate behavior.

Constructivist View of Teaching

Constructivists tend to focus on the design of classroom environments that support students' construction of their own knowledge. Consequently, their contributions are more in the nature of instructional strategies than instructional techniques. As we discuss these instructional strategies, notice that constructivists have adopted and modified instructional techniques and strategies that were presented earlier in the chapter. For example, they prompt or cue students as they scaffold their learning. However, rather than prompting a particular behavior, they tend to prompt students' thinking and problem-solving processes. Also, from a constructivist perspective, teachers are viewed as guides or facilitators of student learning rather than as deliverers of instruction. This is an important difference with the behavioral and information-processing view of teaching presented earlier in this chapter.

As you learned in Chapter 5, educational constructivism has its basis in the developmental theories of Piaget, Vygotsky, and Bruner. In Chapter 5 the following learning principles for constructivism were developed. They guide the discussion of constructivist teaching approaches.

- Principle 5.1: Learning is more powerful if learners actively construct their own understandings.
- Principle 5.2: Learning experiences are more effective if they take into account the cognitive developmental levels of the learners.
- Principle 5.3: Students' knowledge construction is assisted by their interactions with people and objects in their environment.

Learners Actively Construct Their Own Understandings

As noted in Chapter 5, constructivists generally agree that transmission models such as direct instruction cannot provide the type of experiences necessary for students to construct a meaningful understanding (Richardson, 1997). Instead, students need to be involved in activities that encourage them to invent or formulate their own understandings. A number of instructional strategies have been developed that are consistent with this intent. In general, these strategies are referred to as inductive or student-centered strategies.

Inductive Teaching Strategies.   Inductive teaching strategies initiate learning through students' experiences. Sometimes these experiences occur naturally and sometimes teachers provide them. Students' goal is to construct an understanding of these experiences by analyzing and interpreting those experiences. Through their attempts at analysis and interpretation, students should also improve their skills as researchers and investigators. Discovery learning and inquiry training are two examples of inductive teaching strategies.

Discovery Learning. You may remember from Chapter 5 that discovery learning is a key instructional concept in Bruner's cognitive developmental theory. According to Bruner (1961), discovery is the process of translating experiences into new understandings. A number of different discovery teaching strategies have been developed (Weimer, 1975). Two of these, guided discovery and open/free discovery, provide a sense of the range of teaching strategies that can be labeled as discovery learning.

Guided discovery is structured or led by the teacher. Teachers typically begin by providing examples and nonexamples of concepts or principles, or they provide experiences that can be used to induce a generalization. Students then hypothesize about the concept rule, principle, or nature of the generalization. Students are provided with additional experiences, prompts, or questions so that they can test their hypotheses. This process continues until students arrive at the rule for the concept or the nature of the generalization. Figure 7.3 provides a guided discovery lesson for a simple concept.

Open/free discovery is a discovery teaching approach with minimal teacher guidance and supervision. In its extreme form, open/free discovery involves putting students in an environment full of potential experiences and asking them to select from these experiences and learn. In this extreme form, the learners make all decisions about instructional goals, pacing, learning method, and evaluation. The teacher is available as a learning resource only at the discretion of the student (Rogers & Aston, 1992). It's highly unlikely that you would see this extreme form of open/free discovery as the primary teaching strategy in public schools because it is a highly inefficient strategy when compared with guided discovery and direct instruction. On occasion, however, teachers may allow unguided investigation and exploration. This is how Mary Howe does it in her first grade math class.

> ➤ I like to give students free time to play with the manipulatives we are going to use that day. It's interesting to see what they do. In some cases, they invent what I was planning to show them later.

Suchman's Inquiry Training. Developed originally for science learning, Suchman's (1962) **inquiry training** begins with the presentation of a discrepant event. A discrepant event is something that does not seem to make sense and that intrigues the students. For example, you could place a peeled, hard-boiled egg in the mouth of a milk bottle and have your students observe that the egg will not fit through the open-

Earlier in the chapter guided practice was discussed. Why do you think the term *guided* appears both in guided practice and guided discovery?

How are guided discovery and open/free discovery similar and different?

FIGURE 7.3 A Sample Guided Discovery Lesson for a Concept

Step One: The teacher provides examples and nonexamples of the concept.
"Today we are studying triangles. Let me show you what they look like. Try to notice what they have in common." The teacher shows varied examples. "These are not triangles. Try to notice how they are different from triangles. The teacher decides to show ovals and circles.

Step Two: Students hypothesize about the rule for the concept.
One child offers the rule that triangles have three sides.
Another child suggests that they are shapes with points. (Note: The teacher set this up with the choice of nonexamples.)

Step Three: Teachers provide additional examples and nonexamples to test the hypotheses.
This time the teacher includes rectangles, and so forth, as nonexamples.
Students use these new examples and nonexamples to test hypotheses.

Step Four: Students invent or discover the rule or generalization.
Students come to a consensus that triangles are three-sided shapes.

Lonnie, Marilyn, and Brandon need to learn how to divide fractions. I gave them a fraction pre-test and they can multiply fractions, reduce fractions, and invert a number. I've decided to give them groups of problems that yield a pattern. Later I'll give them a choice of algorithms and have them find the one that yields the various patterns they have observed. For example, I started out by giving them a number of problems that involve dividing 1 by a simple fraction (e.g., 1 divided by $\frac{1}{5}$). I also gave them whole circles and the same size circles cut into three, four, five, or six equal parts. I told them that when we divide 1 by $\frac{1}{5}$, we are asking how many $\frac{1}{5}$ths are there in 1. I asked them to suggest a way to use the circles to answer

Marsha Van Pelt

7.4

these types of questions. Lonnie and Marilyn came up with covering the whole circle with the circle cut into five pieces and counting the parts. Once they decided to use that approach, I had them solve other similar problems and to look for a pattern. Brandon noticed that the answer is always the denominator, so he said whenever you divide by a fraction, the answer is always the denominator. Now I have to figure out what to do with Brandon's misunderstanding.

● **How is the idea of guided discovery relevant to this example?**

Decision Point: What would you do next to help Brandon discover his misconception about dividing fractions?

ing in the bottle. You would then remove the egg from the bottle and heat the bottle. When you quickly replace the egg in the opening, it falls into the bottle. The desire to understand this discrepant event becomes the motivation for students to engage in inquiry learning.

Inquiry training teaches students to use the scientific method to understand the discrepant event they have just witnessed. Students begin by forming a hypothesis about the discrepant event. They then collect data to test their hypotheses, analyze the data, and draw conclusions. The goal is to help them understand the discrepant event through the application of scientific reasoning.

The discrepant event, or anomalous data as it is sometimes referred to, plays an important role also in conceptual change teaching. Students may have personal theories about the world that are flawed or inaccurate. For example, one of your authors asked his four-year-old daughter if air weighs anything. When she could not feel any weight pushing down on her palms as she moved them skyward, she theorized confidently that air does not weigh anything. Conceptual change teaching is designed to help students adjust these types of incomplete or flawed conceptions, and often begins by exposing students to discrepant events in terms of their personal conceptions. However, it should be noted that exposure to a discrepant event by itself is often not enough to cause conceptual change (Chinn & Brewer, 1993; Tsai, 2003). Also, students can be quite devoted to their personal theories, and their willingness to change is affected by a host of personal, motivational, social, and historical factors (Pintrich, Marx, & Boyle, 1993). Generally, conceptual change teaching needs to create certain conditions to be effective (Posner, Strike, Hewsen, & Gertzog, 1982). First, students need to become dissatisfied with their existing conception. This is when the discrepant event can be useful. Second, the new conception must be intelligible or make sense. This typically implies a deep level of understanding. Third, the alternative conception should seem plausible. Finally, the new conception must be fruitful or open to new areas of inquiry.

Knowledge Construction through Social Interactions

In implementing Principle 5.3, teachers would need to create situations that provide opportunities for students to work together with adults or peers to construct understanding. One way to do this is to create problem-solving or learning situations with adults or peers by providing scaffolding as students learn or problem solve. Another way is to create group learning situations such as cooperative learning.

Scaffolding. As noted earlier in this chapter, constructivist teachers typically function as guides or facilitators of students' learning. **Scaffolding,** as you remember from Chapter 5, is the general term typically used for this type of teaching (Wood, Bruner, & Ross, 1976). Scaffolding is descriptive of teachers' roles in a number of approaches, including guided discovery (Bruner, 1961), assisted performance (Gallimore & Tharp, 1990), and cognitive apprenticeships (Collins, Brown, & Newman, 1989). In Table 7.2 we have listed a number of ways in which teachers can provide scaffolding or guidance. As you can see from Table 7.2, scaffolding involves a full range of instructional techniques including cueing, modeling, and providing emotional and cognitive support.

Cooperative Learning. **Cooperative learning** is when students work together to accomplish shared goals that both benefit the group as a whole and the individual members of the group (Johnson, Johnson, & Holubec, 1994). It can be viewed as both an

TABLE 7.2 Strategies for Providing Guidance to Learners

Type of Support Offered by the Teacher	Scaffolding Behavior*	Assisted Performance**	Cognitive Apprenticeship†
Teachers model and explain how to approach the learning task	Demonstration	Modeling	Modeling
Teachers simplify task for learners	Reducing degrees of freedom		Scaffolding
Teachers enlist learners' interest and adherence to task requirements	Recruitment		
As students perform the task, teachers provide cues, corrective feedback, and reinforcements for correct performances		Feeding back contingency management	Coaching
Teachers have students explain what they are doing and why			Articulation
Teachers encourage students to focus on the task and to take the next step	Direction maintenance		Exploration
Teachers identify important components of a performance for learners, and teachers help students perceive discrepancies between their performance and their goals	Marking critical features	Feeding back	Reflection
Teachers help students work through frustration and provide more guidance if needed	Frustration control		
Teachers help students identify for themselves additional situations in which their skills will be useful			Exploration
Teachers provide directions to students or ask questions that guide their performance		Instructing, questioning	
Teachers provide cognitive structures for students' learning		Cognitive structuring	

*Wood, Bruner, & Ross, 1976; **Gallimore & Tharp, 1990; †Collins et al., 1989.

instructional strategy and as a way to build a shared sense of community among students (Adams & Hamm, 1996). As an instructional strategy, cooperative learning can be used to implement the principles of many different learning theories. However, the idea of community building through cooperative learning seems particularly well matched to the social constructivist idea of distributed expertise that was presented to you in Chapter 5.

Characteristics of Effective Cooperative Learning. According to Johnson and Johnson (1994), effective cooperative learning approaches have five characteristics in common.

- In effective cooperative learning, students are involved in small groups that work together in face-to-face interactions to achieve both the goals of the individuals and the groups.
- Effective cooperative learning promotes a sense of positive interdependence. Students believe that must help each other to succeed.
- Effective cooperative learning includes individual accountability. Each student needs to believe that she or he will be held responsible for learning. Teachers can create individual accountability by testing students individually or by holding them accountable for their part of a project.
- In effective cooperative learning, students learn to use appropriate social skills when interacting with other people. When you implement cooperative learning, you are not only helping students achieve academic goals, but you are also helping them learn how to interact more effectively in groups.
- Effective cooperative learning allows students time to discuss their group processing skills. Students are given time to reflect on how well they are working together and how they might improve in the future.

Types of Cooperative Learning. A large number of cooperative learning structures are available for classroom use. Student Teams Achievement Divisions, Jigsaw, and Group Investigation, however, are commonly used examples.

Student Teams Achievement Divisions (STAD) is a cooperative learning strategy developed at Johns Hopkins University (Slavin, 1986). STAD begins with a teacher presentation of a skill or informational lesson. Students then work in teacher-selected groups to master the information or skill that has been presented. These teacher-selected groups are designed to be heterogeneous in terms of achievement, gender, and ethnicity. Students are tested individually and those who improve over previous test scores or who do well can help their group earn recognition. STAD is well matched to the goal of learning new information or skills (Arends, 1997).

How might you integrate STAD into a direct instruction model?

Jigsaw is cooperative learning strategy that was designed by Aronson and his colleagues (Aronson, Blaney, Stephan, Sikes, & Snapp, 1978). Students are assigned to groups of four or five, and the material that needs to be learned is divided into a number of parts that equals the number of students in each group. Each member of the group is assigned a part of the information to learn. Members from each group who have the same assigned material meet as expert groups to learn the assigned material. They then return to their group to teach what they have learned. Students are individually tested on all of the material. Jigsaw gets its name because each group member only has a part of what she or he needs to know. Jigsaw is designed to help students acquire academic information (Arends, 1997).

How does Jigsaw build positive interdependence?

Group investigation is designed to help students acquire complex academic information and inquiry skills (Sharan et al., 1984). Students are grouped into five- or six-member research teams and select a topic for their group to research. These teams work with their teacher to design a research plan for their topic, they carry out the research plan under the teacher's supervision, and they report their findings to the rest of the class. Students' learning is evaluated as well as their contributions to their group.

Looking in on

Lawrence wanted me to discuss how I set up my group work. When I'm teaching new skills or information, I usually start by presenting the skill or information. Then my students work in their assigned groups to practice and understand the skill or information. At the end of the lesson, I assess each student individually, and students who do well or improve on their past test scores can earn points that can be exchanged for a group incentive. I hope that they learn to help each other, because it helps the group. Lawrence said it must work because my students work together well. I told him it didn't start out that way. We spent a lot of time at first talking about and even role playing social interaction skills. For example, my students needed help with how to confront someone politely who wasn't helping the group, so I taught them the I-message (see Chapter 10). Even though they've been doing group learning for a while, I still set aside time for them to evaluate how their group is doing. In fact, I occasionally appoint a member in each group to administer a group-process checklist to the group so they can talk about how their group is doing. Although I'm happy with how this approach is working, I think we'll have to use a different group learning structure for our problem-solving unit. I think we need something better suited for helping students learn research skills.

● **What type of cooperative learning is Jacy using? What characteristics of effective cooperative learning can you identify in her approach?**

Decision Point: Why does Jacy think they may need a different group structure for the problem-solving unit? What would you suggest from what you have read?

Research on Cooperative Learning. Research on the effects of cooperative learning have suggested that well-designed and executed cooperative learning can be effective for achieving a range of academic and social outcomes (Ellis & Fouts, 1993; Stevens & Slavin, 1995). These outcomes include improved social development, more positive relationships among students, and equal or superior academic achievement in many cases when compared with other instructional strategies (Johnson, Johnson, & Holubec, 1994).

Successful implementation of cooperative learning, however, requires a great deal of skill on the part of the teacher. A number of variables including group composition, the nature of assigned task and materials, students' status, personalities, and students' interpersonal skills can influence the success of cooperative learning (Cohen, 1994; Cohen, Lotan, & Catanzarite, 1990; Tudge, 1990; Webb & Farivar, 1994). For example, teachers need to assign learning tasks that can be better accomplished by working with others than by working alone (Cohen, 1994). If the assigned learning tasks could be best accomplished working alone, students may see no reason to develop positive interdependence in their groups. Also, students' personalities need to be considered in forming groups. Tudge (1990) found that highly confident but less competent students can convince less confident but more competent students to accept a less sophisticated perspective on a problem.

Getting Started with Cooperative Learning. Cooperative learning is a complicated instructional strategy. At the end of the chapter, web resources are presented for gaining additional information about this strategy. Also, the En-

> Cooperative learning can build positive relationships among students.

riching Your Understanding provides some examples of informal cooperative learning strategies. In addition, here are some general guidelines for getting started with cooperative learning (Freiberg & Driscoll, 2000).

- Prepare your students for cooperative learning. Do team building activities and help students develop the interpersonal and group process skills they are likely to need.
- Begin with small groups of two or three students. Smaller groups are easier for students to manage.
- Use teacher-selected heterogeneous groups rather than student-selected groups. This helps with classroom management issues and provides opportunities for students to work with a variety of peers.
- Keep groups together long enough for them to build unity, but do eventually change groups to broaden students' experiences.
- Be clear about your goals and how students will be assessed.
- Provide specific feedback both for the academic learning and group process.

Problem-Based Learning: A Constructivist Instructional Strategy

Problem-based learning is an instructional strategy that incorporates a number of constructivist learning principles. Current forms of problem-based learning began in medical schools in the late 1960s and early 1970s as a way of helping students better understand and apply knowledge (Barrows, 1996; Dolmans et al., 2002). Although there are various forms of problem-based learning, they tend to share some common elements. Learning and problem solving are organized around a problem, case, question, or project (Jonassen, 1999). Learning and problem solving typically have a multidisciplinary focus, occur through collaboration with adults and students,

ENRICHING YOUR UNDERSTANDING
Informal Cooperative Learning Structures

Cooperative learning methods such as jigsaw and group investigation are potentially powerful strategies, but they also are complicated to implement. However, a number of informal cooperative learning structures have been developed that are somewhat less complicated to implement (Baloche, 1998; Kagan, 1992; Lyman, 1992). In addition, they can be used as part of other instructional strategies such as direct instruction or discovery learning. Here are a few examples.

Think pair share begins when the teacher poses a thought-provoking question or problem. Students are told not to answer immediately, but to just think about the question. Then they pair up with another student and discuss their ideas. Finally, students are asked to share their ideas with the class. One potential benefit of think pair share is that it provides students with time to think before they discuss ideas as a class.

Numbered heads together begins by having students number off in their groups of three or four. The teacher then poses a problem or question, and the students think about it by themselves. The students then discuss the question or problem in their groups. Finally, the teacher calls out a number at random, and that student must report on the group discussion. It is similar in some ways to think pair share, with the added benefit of encouraging individual accountability. Students do not know who will be called on to report to the class.

Pens in the middle typically involves groups of three or four students and also begins when a teacher poses a question. The students think about the question by themselves, and then they share their thoughts with their group. When a student shares an idea, she or he puts a pen in the middle. That student cannot share a second idea until each student in the group has a pen in the middle. The intent is to encourage all students to participate.

● **How could you use think pair share in a direct instruction lesson and discovery learning lesson? (For your authors' perspective on this question, go to the text website for this chapter.)**

and are assessed through artifacts or exhibitions. Communities of Learners (Brown, 1994; Brown & Campione, 1990), Roots and Wings (Slavin, Madden, Dolan, & Wasik, 1994), and Learning Expeditions (Rugen & Hartl, 1994) are all examples of problem-based learning.

How does the authentic question or problem component of problem-based learning relate to situated cognition?

Authentic Question or Problem. In problem-based learning, students' knowledge construction efforts are organized around real-world questions or ill-defined problems (Hmelo & Evensen, 2000; Maxwell, Bellisimo, & Mergendoller, 2001; Ryan, 1997). Opportunities for learning and problem solving develop as the problem unfolds (Edens, 2000). For example, in the problem-based learning model Roots and Wings, students participate in simulations that require them to make decisions (Slavin et al., 1994). In one scenario, they are playing different roles in a debate over environmental legislation, and they need to learn the necessary knowledge and research skills to participate in an informed manner. Learning Expeditions requires students to investigate questions such as, "How can we tell if a community is thriving?"

Multidisciplinary Focus. Although a problem may be centered in a particular discipline, students learn to use skills and knowledge from a number of disciplines to solve their problem or answer their questions (Arends, 1997). Their goal is to connect

Focus on Learner Diversity
Inclusion and Constructivism

Inclusion is based on the belief that students with disabilities should be educated to the maximum extent possible in regular education settings. For inclusion to be successful, classroom teachers need to modify their instruction so that students with disabilities can participate fully in the classroom. Also, regular and special education teachers need to collaborate to make sure that students with disabilities learn the basic academic competencies they may lack. Successful inclusion, therefore, requires teachers to understand how their curriculum and instructional methods interact with characteristics of students with disabilities (Mastropieri & Scruggs, 2000).

Full participation in a constructivist classroom often requires learners to be self-regulating, to employ effective learning and study strategies, and to work successfully with other students. Although students with disabilities are a diverse group, they often possess characteristics that make this type of learning challenging. They are more likely than students without disabilities to have deficits in verbal and nonverbal communication skills, to have difficulty with reading and writing, to have difficulty learning new knowledge, and to have less effective interpersonal skills (Maheady, Harper, & Mallette, 2001; Wolford, Heward, & Alber, 2001). This does not mean that constructivist practices are completely inappropriate for students with learning disabilities. In fact, some evidence exists that students with disabilities can profit from constructivist learning experiences that require them to think for themselves and to reason through to their own conclusions

(Scruggs & Mastropieri, 1994). However, teachers need to be prepared to make appropriate accommodations.

Accommodations for learners in constructivist classrooms need to be based on an understanding of each student's needs. For example, students with lower IQs may have trouble drawing inferences from data and may require certain accommodations (Mastropieri, Scruggs, Boon, & Carter, 2001). They may need more practice, support from trained peers, or teaching that uses a more deductive approach. Other students with disabilities may need help with the interpersonal skills necessary to learn from other learners. For example, they may need to learn how to recruit help or assistance from their peers (Wolford, Heward, & Alber, 2001).

One additional point needs to be made about educating students with disabilities in constructivist classrooms. You need to remember that students with disabilities often lack basic academic competencies in reading, math, and writing. Because of this, you need to make sure that exploration and problem-solving activities are combined with opportunities for specific skill development (Harris & Graham, 1996).

> ● **Constructivist learning experiences can require students to use technology such as computers and to be engaged in hands-on or physical learning activities. Why might these activities need to be modified for some students with disabilities? (For your authors' perspective on this question, go to the text website for this chapter.)**

knowledge and skills from different academic areas. For example, in Ann Brown's (1994) Communities of Learning, students research science or social studies questions, but in the process of that research they improve their reading comprehension and ability to use technology. Roots and Wings requires students to integrate concepts and skills from science, social studies, reading, math, technology, and the fine arts.

Collaboration. Problem-based learning usually includes opportunities for students and adults to work together in small groups to answer questions or solve problems. Often the teacher takes the role of a tutor who helps students make connections and who monitors their learning, manages their group work, facilitates discussion, and challenges students' thinking (Dolmans et al., 2002; Ngeow & Kong, 2001). However, students may also take the role of tutors or content experts for their groups.

Artifacts or Exhibits. Students are asked to demonstrate their learning through presentations or exhibits. For example, in Roots and Wings students demonstrate their learning through public debates, concrete models, and technology-assisted projects. In Community of Learners, students are often cast in the role of teacher or presenter for the information they are learning. They hold dialogues with other students and the teacher to help improve their understanding, and they learn their material in such a way that they can convey it effectively to the community.

Technology and the Construction of Knowledge

As has been discussed, constructivists want teachers to create complex learning environments that encourage students to explore, invent, and discover. Technology can help establish and manage these types of learning environments in a number of ways.

Authentic Learning Environments and Technology. Technology-based simulations can create authentic learning environments by allowing students to apply knowledge in ways that may not be possible or economically feasible with more traditional classroom approaches. Microworlds provide one example of this use of technology. *Microworld* is a term coined by Papert (1980) that usually refers to computer-generated models that can be manipulated by students to help them understand key principles or ideas. For example, *Interactive Physics* is a microworld that allows students to conduct physics experiments related to motion (Roth, 2001). Here are some other examples of microworlds or contexts for exploration of principles.

- *Jasper Adventures* (Cognition and Technology Group at Vanderbilt, 1992) uses interactive video to engage students in simulations that require them to apply important mathematics ideas as they problem solve. For example, in one simulation, students need to use their math and problem-solving skills to rescue a wounded bald eagle.
- *Archaeotype* was created by New York's Dalton School as a way of introducing students to history and archaeology. This multimedia computer simulation involves students in a collaborative archaeological dig in which they discover artifacts and research what is known about ancient cultures (Dimaraki, Black, & Brown, 1998).
- *The Space Shuttle Commander* (Rieber, 1992) is a software simulation that teaches Newtonian laws of motion to elementary and middle school students as they attempt to steer a space shuttle in space.

What would a microworld application look like for helping teachers learn about classroom management?

Technology as an Information Source. One major reason why students have difficulty discovering new knowledge is that they lack appropriate prior knowledge (De Jong & von Joolingen, 1998). This includes both academic content knowledge and knowledge of how to conduct an experiment. For example, students may not know how to frame a hypothesis or how to design an experiment that matches their hypothesis.

Students can use CD-ROM technology, computer programs, and appropriate websites to help them gather necessary academic content knowledge. In fact, some applications provide links to websites where students can immediately access information they need for their problem solving when they need it (Williams et al., 1998).

Support structures designed into software can also increase students' knowledge of the scientific method (e.g., hypothesis formation and research design). For example, *Smithtown*, a computer simulation to teach microeconomics to students, provides a hypothesis menu that helps students learn to write more effective hypotheses. This menu prompts students to write their hypotheses in terms of the relationships among variables and even suggests appropriate language for hypotheses (Shute & Glaser, 1990).

Technology to Enhance Problem-Solving Capabilities.   Technology can be designed to enhance your students' capabilities as researchers and to support their cognitive and metacognitive processes. For example, a number of general-purpose technologies can be used to help students with some of the more labor-intensive and repetitive aspects of inquiry. Computer programs can be used in data collection, data entry, and data analysis. Students can also use graphing programs or spreadsheets to enter data and to observe trends in their data as they are experimenting. This is how Robin Osprey does this in her middle school science class.

> ➤ I have my students use a graphing tool as they are collecting data. Occasionally, I have them look at trends in their graphs and make predictions about how the graph is going to look later. I find it helps to have them write a brief explanation of why the graph is turning out the way it is.

Technology to Present Findings.   Students can use technology to summarize and report their findings to others. General-purpose applications such as multimedia presentation software, word processing programs, spreadsheets, and databases can be used for students to exhibit what they have learned. Additionally, programs such as *SemNet* for Macintosh computers and *Visimap* for Windows provide students with visual and verbal screen tools for constructing concept maps. These concept maps provide a visual/spatial representation of students' understanding of concepts and their relationships (Jonassen, Peck, & Wilson, 1999). This is how Octavio Moreno uses technology to have his students exhibit their learning in his fifth grade classroom.

> ➤ We have a class web page that my students have helped design. As they complete a research project, they post brief summaries of their findings on the web page. As the year progresses, we develop our own on-line research database.

For some constructivists, the creation of a product that can be shared with others is more than just a culminating activity. The process of creating these products can help students clarify and even deepen their understanding. For example, **constructionists** design learning environments in which students are engaged in explorations that lead to an external product that can be exhibited, examined, and evaluated by others (Papert, 1990; Tucker & Gunn, 1998). Through the process of externalizing their thinking through a product, students can receive feedback and information that clarifies and extends their thinking.

Technology and Cooperative Learning.   A growing body of literature suggests that students find that cooperative work is easier to accomplish and more motivating when supported by technology (Roblyer, Edwards, & Havriluk, 1997). General-purpose software can be used to support cooperation in a number of ways (Denning & Smith, 1997). For example, students can use computers to keep records of their work in a central location. Spreadsheets can be used to keep a tally of group improvement points or for other record keeping. Telecommunications applications such as electronic mail and teleconferencing can help connect students from different geographical locations for cooperative group work. This is how Eliza Carmichael connects her students to students in other cities.

➤ My sixth graders are doing a cooperative project with sixth graders from another city. Each group is collecting data for their own cities and sharing that information electronically. The combined data will be used to show differences between their communities.

How could Eliza Carmichael turn her city project into a cooperative learning exercise?

Some computer and video simulations are designed specifically for cooperative learning or can easily be adapted for that purpose (Dockterman, 1998). For example, *Biology Sleuth* engages students in the problem-solving task of diagnosing a patient's medical condition. Students are provided with information they need to solve this type of problem, and they work in groups of two or three at a single computer to solve the problem. Students work together to learn, but later they are assessed individually about their learning (Albanese & Jacobs, 1990).

Technology and Scaffolding.   Constructivist ideas such as situated cognition and anchored instruction suggest that students' learning needs to be situated in realistic and complex problem-solving environments. As students work on these complex problems, more skilled learners scaffold their learning. This role of the more skilled learner can be fulfilled by support structures programmed into computer simulations (Guzdial, 1998; Krajcik, Soloway, Blumenfeld, & Marx, 1998; Nicaise, 1997). Computers, for example, can be programmed to provide scaffolds for students by modeling and coaching, reducing task complexity for the learner, and providing feedback and encouragement. For example, a computer could provide a prompt when students give an incorrect answer or show a possible solution for a problem. These types of functions have been referred to as **software-realized scaffolding** (Guzdial, 1998). Software-realized scaffolding functions can also be supplemented with human scaffolding provided by teachers or other students. This combination can help students acquire scaffolding behaviors for use with their interactions with teachers and other students (Kozma & Shank, 1998).

Broadening the Learning Community with Technology.   It is common for constructivists to use the metaphor of a community to describe the types of learning environments they envision. For example, constructivists write about a community of learners, or a community of practice, or discourse communities (Brown & Campione, 1994; Lauzon, 1999; Woodward-Kron, 2004). Technology could be useful for creating broader communities for learning. On-line communication systems such as electronic mail, listservs, and chat rooms can give students access to a larger number of resources for scaffolding their learning. For example, the *CoVis* project provides students with a collaborative notebook (O'Neill & Gomez, 1994). Students can pose questions and receive answers from people from all over the country.

Some Cautions Concerning Constructivist Instructional Approaches

Constructivist approaches to classroom learning can be exciting, and they are often innovative. However, many of these classroom approaches are relatively new and have not been systematically evaluated over time (Airasian & Walsh, 1997; Harris & Graham, 1996). Additionally, there are reasonable issues that can be raised about constructivist approaches. For example, it may be the case that some students do much better with these approaches than other students (Mastropieri, Scruggs, Boon, & Carter, 2001). Also, constructivist approaches are not well suited to all the various types of learning required by a curriculum. For example, in addition to opportunities to construct conceptual understanding, math students need considerable practice on the basic skills of math (Hamm & Perry, 2002; Harris & Graham, 1996). Discovery approaches to learning may not result in the ability to simply recall a math fact when presented with a problem (Steel & Funnell, 2001). Because of these types of concerns, you want to provide a variety of learning experiences in your classroom.

*M*otivation Principles and Classroom Teaching

In Chapter 6, four general principles were developed from theories of motivation that can inform your use of instructional techniques and strategies. They are:

- Principle 6.1: Learners are more motivated when they believe that their actions will result in successfully completing challenging tasks.
- Principle 6.2: Learners are more motivated by activities that appeal to their personal needs, motives, and interests.
- Principle 6.3: Learners are more motivated when they have specific near-term goals that they believe are important.
- Principle 6.4: Learners are more motivated when appropriate levels of variety, choice, and surprise are incorporated into lessons.

Successful Completion of Challenges

Principle 6.1 suggests that students will be more motivated if they believe a relationship exists between their effort and their success on challenging tasks. In terms of attribution theory, students need to attribute their successes to their ability and/or effort and attribute their failures to the nature of their effort.

Students use multiple cues from their environment in forming their attributions for their successes and failures (Reeve, 1996; Ruble, 1983; Stipek & Hoffman, 1980). For example, they use their prior performance history and their perceptions of how they compare with other students. They are also influenced by attributional feedback from teachers. **Attributional feedback** links students' successes and failures to the causes of those successes and failures (Schunk, 1989). In general, when your students do not succeed, you want them to attribute those failures to the nature of their effort. For example, "You are starting to get it. You just need some more practice." When they succeed, you want to help them attribute the success to their ability and efforts. For example, "I knew you could do it. You usually do well when you have taken your time."

Why would students have more confidence in their abilities to succeed in the future if they succeed at moderately challenging tasks?

Teachers can also communicate their beliefs about students' ability through subtle and unintentional cues when they provide feedback and praise (Barker & Graham, 1987; Dweck, 1999; Meyer, 1982; Weiner, Graham, Taylor, & Meyer, 1982). For example, if you provide overly enthusiastic praise to students for the accomplishment of relatively easy tasks, students who observe this may believe that the praised student has low ability (Barker & Graham, 1987). Teachers who provide pity to students who fail, tend to communicate their belief that the pitied student has low ability (Graham, 1984).

Students' Personal Needs, Motives, and Interests

Principle 6.2 suggests that students have needs and motives that affect their ability to profit from teaching. For example, Maslow's basic safety need implies that students want to learn in a secure and emotionally supportive environment. Students can feel at risk during instruction when they request help from the teacher or other peers. Studies done at the elementary, secondary, and postsecondary level suggest that students who have low self-esteem or perceive themselves as lacking ability, often regard seeking help as a risky endeavor (Karabenick & Knapp, 1991; Newman, 1990, 1991). When they seek help, they believe others will perceive it as a sign that they have low ability. Consequently, you need to help students feel more comfortable about requesting help. For example, students tend to feel more comfortable about requesting help if activities are introduced as ways of building competence, rather than as measures of students' ability.

As discussed in Chapter 6, one way to conceptualize student interest is to divide it into individual (personal) and situational interest (Hidi & Anderson, 1992; Hidi &

Looking in on

As we finished the conference, Lawrence told me he liked what I am doing. He asked if there was anything he could do to help with my professional growth goal. I told him I think I was learning a lot about how to adapt my teaching to students with special learning needs, but I am really concerned about the motivation of these students. So many of them have failed so often in the past that they honestly believe they can't learn math or how to read better. In fact, some of them almost seem depressed to me. I want them to believe that they can learn. Lawrence asked me what I'm doing now. I told him that I make sure that I give my students assignments that are neither too hard nor too easy. When they do well, I talk to them about what they did that is helping them succeed. When they don't do well, we talk about a different approach they could take next time. Sometimes, however, it's hard to get them to try. For example, I need some ideas for how to encourage them to answer questions during class discussions. They often know an answer but are afraid they will look *stupid* if they say something wrong.

● **How is Jacy applying the idea of attributional feedback in her classroom?**

Decision Point: How might think pair share help Jacy with her students who are reluctant to participate?

Haracklewicz, 2000; Renniger, 1998; Schiefele, 1991). Individual interest is a relatively stable personal disposition that develops over time and is connected to particular knowledge or activities. For example, your authors have developed personal interest in the study of psychology over their lifetimes. Personal interest in a learning topic is associated with increased attention, persistence, and learning (Asher, 1980; Schiefele, 1991). In contrast, situational interest results from aspects of the environment that elicit an immediate affective response that may not last. For example, a teacher may generate situational interest in the multiplication table by teaching it through games.

How are individual and situational interest different?

It should be noted that there are challenges involved in trying to connect to students' personal interests. First, in a large classroom personal interests can vary enough to make it extremely difficult to incorporate everyone's personal interest into a lesson (Hidi & Anderson, 1992). Also, students' interest in a topic does not guarantee improved performance or learning (Garner, Brown, Sanders, & Menke, 1992; Hidi, Renniger, & Krapp, 1992). Students may attend to interesting but unimportant details in what they are learning, or their interest may give them an inflated sense of what they really know about a topic. Consequently, teachers will need alternative ways of generating value for their lessons such as stimulating situational interest. Interestingly, over time situational interest can change into something more intrinsic for the learner (Hidi & Harackiewicz, 2000). One of your goals could be to increase the number of topics that students find personally interesting. Also, teachers could stress the instrumental value of a lesson for helping students achieve their goals (Deci, 1992).

Specific Near-Term Goals

In applying Principle 6.3 it is important to remember that learners tend to do better when they understand the goals of the instruction and why those goals are important (Burden & Byrd, 1999). Also, proximal or near-term goals provide students with more opportunities to receive feedback about their learning over time, and they can be used to encourage their efforts toward meeting long-term goals (Alderman, 1999). You can specify your objectives or goals at the beginning of lessons and provide information to students about the value of the objectives. Students' progress toward meeting these objectives might be assessed by having students answer the "What have I learned?" question from K-W-L at the end of a lesson or unit.

You can also stress the value of the learning activities in your classroom. You can stress utility value by teaching knowledge in terms of its use. For example, students who are learning how to count change might do so in terms of a school store or bartering system. You can stress the value of strategy learning by including task value statements in the cognitive modeling of a strategy. Raul Jacobs does this with his special education students.

> ➤ When I introduce a new strategy, I usually do it when students are engaged in a task for which that strategy is useful. I say, "I used to have trouble with this. Let me show what I learned that helps me. . . ."

Appropriate Levels of Variety, Choice, and Surprise

Principle 6.4 has a number of implications for teaching. From a motivational perspective, variety is important for maintaining students' enthusiasm for learning and also your enthusiasm for teaching. Your ability to use teaching techniques and strategies from different theoretical perspectives will help you maintain that enthusiasm.

Students' engagement with learning is higher when they have some choice in the learning activities (Malone & Lepper, 1987). This can be done in a number of ways. During guided practice, for example, students can select whether they want to work alone or with other students. You could also provide a variety of learning stations or centers for students to practice what they are learning. In problem-based learning, students can select the part of a problem they want to research, or the method they would like to use to communicate their results.

Suchman's idea of the discrepant event can be used effectively to generate surprise and curiosity and can be used both with direct instruction and inquiry approaches. For example, you could introduce your lesson with a discrepant event and then inform students that today's lesson will help them make sense of what they have just observed.

Principles into Practice:
Illustrating Key Concepts

The experiences of Jacy Winston and Marsha Van Pelt provide examples of how theoretical principles can be translated into teaching techniques, teaching strategies, and supporting technology applications. Both teachers found it necessary to use techniques and strategies from different theories to accomplish their goals. We believe that this will be your experience also. As you read about these teachers' experiences you were asked to reflect on their use of teaching techniques and strategies through a series of questions. Here are our perspectives on those questions.

Looking back on Jacy Winston

Jacy Winston's lesson on the graphing program provides numerous examples of the components of effective practice. First, her practice problems were similar to the problems her students would encounter later. The program itself provided immediate feedback, which was supplemented by feedback from the teacher and other students. She also provided her students with a prompt in the form of a handout that listed the steps in using the program. Her teaching provides an example of an application of Principle 2.3, learning results from the effects of stimuli on responses.

Jacy's structure for group work provides examples of several key aspects of cooperative learning. She was basically using a STAD approach because she presented a skill, and then her students worked together to understand that skill. Also, each member of the group could help their group earn an incentive if they did well or improved on previous performances. Her students worked together to achieve individual and group goals, and positive interdependence was encouraged by the group incentive. Students were individually held accountable for learning how to use the graphing program, and Jacy made time to teach her students social interaction skills and for her groups to reflect on their group processes. Jacy's use of STAD provides an application of Principle 5.3, students' knowledge construction is assisted by their interactions with people and objects in their environment.

Jacy asked for help with her extremely discouraged students. She already is using a form of attributional feedback to help her students connect their successes with their efforts. She does this by making sure the learning tasks are at the right level of challenge, and by specifically telling them how they are achieving their successes. She is applying Principle 6.1, learners are more motivated when they believe that their actions will result in successfully completing challenging tasks. ●

Looking back on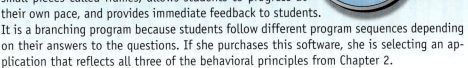

The social studies tutorial software is an example of programmed instruction because it has specific content objectives, presents that content in a logical sequence of small pieces called frames, allows students to progress at their own pace, and provides immediate feedback to students. It is a branching program because students follow different program sequences depending on their answers to the questions. If she purchases this software, she is selecting an application that reflects all three of the behavioral principles from Chapter 2.

Marsha Van Pelt used a form of direct instruction to teach Robin and Sarah an organizational strategy for writing. She introduced the lesson by activating relevant prior knowledge about confusing directions. She also used this as an opportunity to provide a motivational set for the lesson. She ended the introduction by stating her objective for the lesson, so her students knew where to focus their attention. During her lesson she modeled the strategy and actively involved her students in that modeling. She reduced working memory load by choosing a familiar topic that allowed her students to concentrate on the strategy rather than the content of the writing. Students practiced the strategy under her supervision for guided practice and were given a homework assignment for independent practice. Her direct instruction lesson represents an application of Principle 3.1, meaningful learning occurs when new knowledge is connected to existing knowledge; Principle 3.2, effective instruction encourages learners to coordinate their various basic mental processes; and Principle 3.3, the limitations of students' working memory need to be accounted for in instruction.

Marsha used cognitive modeling to teach Marcus some strategies for decoding unknown words. The examples she provided of her cognitive modeling included attempts to access relevant prior knowledge (e.g., "Does this have any smaller words in it I know how to read?"). She monitored her use of her strategies through questions such as, "Does this word make sense in the sentence?" She also self-reinforced through statements such as, "I got that one!" Her one planning statement was to remind herself that she knew what to do. Her lesson is an application of social cognitive Principle 4.1, learners acquire important knowledge, behaviors, and dispositions through their exposure to models.

Marsha also used a form of guided discovery to help her students understand why we invert and multiply when we divide fractions. She exposed her students to patterns of answers, and eventually they will be asked to select the algorithm that would yield the different patterns of answers they were observing. At one point, she even asked students to invent a way of using some manipulatives to solve a problem. She was applying Principle 5.1, learning is more powerful if learners actively construct their own understandings. ●

Teachers as Decision Makers

As you looked in on Jacy Winston and Marsha Van Pelt, you were asked to participate in their decision making. First we will share our views of these decision points.

Jacy Winston's Decision Points

In Jacy's brief overview of her teaching day, she mentioned a number of factors that were influencing her teaching decisions. First, she was hoping that her approach to teaching would be acceptable to her new principal. In response to his desire to integrate learning experiences across the curricula, she was already collaborating with social studies teachers on a unit. Finally, her group work activities, in part, were an attempt to address the needs and interests of her students. As you can see from Jacy's example, decisions about how and what to teach are influenced by many factors.

Jacy had decided not to use a discovery approach in her graphing lesson. She appears to have based her decision on her belief that discovery lessons have the potential to take more time to complete than teacher-directed lessons, and that her students may lack necessary prior knowledge and experiences to make discovery learning effective in this case. Like many teachers, Jacy probably has a lot to cover in this class. Consequently, she needs to consider when it makes most sense to engage students in discovery and when a teacher-directed approach makes sense given her goals and her students.

In your authors' experience, when young teachers are asked why they need to teach in different ways, they typically focus on a learner characteristic such as learning style. An equally important or even more important reason is that different learning objectives might be better reached through different teaching approaches. In Jacy's case, STAD seems well matched to skill or informational learning. For their problem-solving unit, a group investigation or a modification of jigsaw might make more sense. In the case of jigsaw, students could research different aspects of an issue and share their findings with their group.

Finally, Jacy might find think-pair-share to be helpful with her reluctant learners because it gives these students time to prepare an answer, and they can discuss their ideas with someone else before answering in front of the whole class. This is a case in which a teaching technique can help with a motivational issue.

Marsha Van Pelt's Decision Points

Marsha Van Pelt's faculty is discussing whether or not teachers should tutor their own students. With this type of decision it's often helpful to consider the strengths and weaknesses of both recommendations. By doing this, you may find a way to synthesize both recommendations to create a more effective option. For example, tutoring their own students allows teachers to make use of the rapport they may have with those students, and it may make it easier to transfer what they learn from tutoring these students to the classroom. On the other hand, if another teacher tutors the students, they may see things the classroom teacher missed or try approaches that wouldn't occur to the classroom teacher. Also, maybe they can establish a higher level of rapport with a student. Perhaps the better recommendation is to select tutors on the basis of what would be best for a particular student.

At the beginning of this chapter you were provided some questions for evaluating a technology application that Marsha might find useful. This particular software is designed to provide drill and practice on basic history information. Whether or not a particular software is useful would depend on teachers' goals and beliefs about teaching. Whether this program is time or cost effective would depend on how much time students need to spend with the program and its overall cost. For example, would it be necessary to buy multiple copies of this program? One of the potential unintended consequences of a program such as this is that it can isolate students from each other. Could teachers find a use for this program that avoids that potential problem?

Later, you considered Marsha Van Pelt's decision to use direct instruction to teach a strategy. Certainly different teachers will make different choices in these types of situations. Given the limited time she has to work with these students and the complexity of the new strategy she is teaching, your authors think her choice to use direct instruction here seems reasonable.

Later in the chapter, you were asked to provide ideas for how to get Marcus more involved in the cognitive modeling lesson. As mentioned in this chapter, cognitive modeling is more effective if it is interactive. Marsha could involve Marcus by asking for his suggestions about what to do, by having him show what he would do, or perhaps by having him complete some of the steps in the strategy.

Marsha Van Pelt has encountered an important issue in complex learning situations. How should she confront a student's misconception about dividing fractions? When using guided discovery, the teacher tries to be more of a guide than a presenter of knowledge if possible. She would provide other experiences or questions that would allow Brandon to discover his misconception. For example, she could give him some other problems that do not produce the same pattern of answers that he observed in the first set.

Name _____ Date _____

Chapter 7 Study Guide

Use this Study Guide to review and test your knowledge of key concepts introduced in this chapter and to search out further information on issues and topics raised in this chapter.

 **Key Terms**

Review the following key words from the chapter and then connect to Research Navigator (www.researchnavigator.com) either directly or through this book's Companion Website to explore research on the topics as they relate to education today.

Adjunct questions (p. 210)
Advance organizer (p. 207)
Attributional feedback (p. 232)
Backward chaining (p. 201)
Behavioral fluency (p. 218)
Branching program (p. 205)
Cognitive modeling (p. 219)
Comparative advance organizer (p. 208)
Constructionists (p. 230)
Cooperative learning (p. 224)
Direct instruction (p. 213)
Drill and practice programs (p. 206)
Educational technology (p. 199)
Expository advance organizer (p. 207)
Extraneous cognitive load (p. 212)
Feedback (p. 202)

Forward chaining (p. 201)
Frames (p. 205)
Germane cognitive load (p. 212)
Group investigation (p. 225)
Guided discovery (p. 222)
Guided practice (p. 214)
Independent practice (p. 215)
Inquiry training (p. 222)
Instructional analogy (p. 208)
Instructional prompt (p. 202)
Instructional strategy (p. 199)
Instructional technique (p. 198)
Intelligent tutors (p. 218)
Intrinsic cognitive load (p. 212)
Jigsaw (p. 225)
K-W-L (p. 208)
Linear program (p. 205)
Mastery learning (p. 203)

Numbered heads together (p. 227)
Open/free discovery (p. 222)
Pens in the middle (p. 227)
Problem-based learning (p. 227)
Process-outcome research (p. 213)
Programmed learning (p. 205)
Scaffolding (p. 224)
Self-modeling (p. 220)
Signals (p. 210)
Software-realized scaffolding (p. 231)
Spatial/semantic organizer (p. 211)
Student Teams Achievement Divisions (STAD) (p. 225)
Think pair share (p. 227)
Total task presentation (p. 201)
Wait time (p. 213)

Alternative Response Items

1. Some math books provide sample worked problems so that students can remind themselves how to do a problem correctly. These worked problems are an example of _____.

a. Prompting
b. Backward chaining
c. Cognitive modeling
d. Mastery learning

2. Which one of the following is an example of an important characteristic of feedback for behaviorists?

   a. Mary assigns nightly homework for practice but does not return it until the end of a unit.
   b. Fred doesn't like to give a lot of feedback during new learning because he doesn't want students to become dependent on it.
   c. Joanne provides self-checking templates with explanations for in-class assignments so that students can check their work right when they finish.
   d. Rashad doesn't like to be too specific with his feedback because he wants students to figure out things for themselves.

3. Marilyn Mayer has a tutorial program in which a problem is presented, students type in an answer, feedback is given, and the next problem is provided. What type of programmed instruction is this?

   a. Linear program
   b. Branching program
   c. Recursive program

4. Ramona begins her lesson on the human cell by discussing what students know about communities. Later she will relate cell structures to similar community structures. What technique is she using?

   a. Expository advance organizer
   b. Comparative advance organizer
   c. Signal
   d. Prompting strategy

5. Mark wants his students to focus on certain information in their reading assignments. Which of these techniques is best matched to this intent?

   a. Expository advance organizer
   b. Comparative advance organizer
   c. Adjunct question
   d. Instructional analogy

6. Some ideas in a presentation are complicated and unfamiliar to students and require additional concentration from learners. What type of cognitive load is this?

   a. Intrinsic load
   b. Extraneous load
   c. Germane load
   d. Long-term memory load

7. One explanation offered for the effectiveness of self-modeling is that it provides visual confirmation that a learner can improve with effort. How would a social cognitive theorist explain this?

   a. The learners' outcome expectations have been altered.
   b. The information is more powerful because it is in a symbolic mode, which is a powerful way to represent information.
   c. The students' self-efficacy beliefs may have been strengthened by observing themselves being successful.
   d. The modeling is different enough from what the learner typically does to make it interesting.

8. A common lesson format is to present content and then to have the students practice that content with support or supervision. Which form of cooperative learning uses this structure?

   a. STAD
   b. Jigsaw
   c. Group investigation

9. Which of these are components of problem-based learning?

   a. An authentic question or problem
   b. A multidisciplinary focus
   c. Collaboration
   d. All of the above

10. Which one of the following is an example of attributional feedback?

    a. "You really do a good job when you slow down and concentrate."
    b. "Your answer to question 3 is very good."
    c. "Good job!"
    d. "This paper is better than your last one."

Constructed Response Items

Short Answer/Completion Items

1. A specific action taken by the teacher during instruction is a(n) _____.

2. Mastery learning suggests that if people are given the help they need and the _____ they need, they can learn.

3. In K-W-L what happens at the *K* step?

4. Teachers' talking aloud as they demonstrate a mental skill to their students is _____.

5. Suchman's inquiry training begins with the presentation of a _____.

Essay Items

1. This textbook has certain features. For each of the features listed below, try to identify its purpose or purposes from an information-processing perspective?

   End of chapter questions
   Key Terms (end of chapter)
   Paragraph headings
   Terms in boldface
   Chapter cases

2. Arrange these teaching strategies and models on a continuum ranging from least teacher-directed to most teacher-directed approach.

   STAD
   Mastery learning

   Open/free discovery
   Inquiry training

3. Using what you learned in this chapter and Chapter 5, try to connect these ideas to problem-based learning.

   Situated cognition
   Distributed cognition
   Authentic learning

4. In what ways could technology be useful in support of problem-based learning?

Practicing Your Decision Making

1. In this chapter, we have suggested that we need to vary how we teach. Think about how these factors would affect your choice of teaching strategies and models.

   a. Students' prior knowledge
   b. State competency exams for students
   c. Community standards
   d. Your level of teaching experience
   e. Time

2. For the level and content you plan to teach, is there a time when mastery learning would be a useful model? Explain you answer.

3. How would you determine if a technology application is appropriate for your goals?

INTASC in Action

Use the following activities to think about how concepts and principles from this chapter relate to the INTASC standards.

Standard 2: Student Development. Helping students link new information to their existing knowledge is an important goal of teaching. Select a teaching technique from this chapter that is designed for this purpose, and describe how you would use it in a lesson (advance organizer, review, and so on).

Standard 4: Multiple Instructional Strategies. The recommendation that teachers should present information in different ways can be supported from a variety of perspectives. How would the following ideas from educational psychology lend support to this recommendation?

   Differences among learners (prior knowledge, development, and so on)
   Motivational theory
   Levels of processing (Chapter 3)

Standard 5: Motivation and Management. Reflect back on your time in school. Can you identify a personal interest that actually began as a result of something you did in school? If so, what happened to create that interest? How might a strategy such as problem-based learning help create personal interest in students?

Standard 6: Communications and Technology. Identify a local classroom teacher and interview that teacher using the following questions.

1. How do you use technology in your classroom for instruction?
2. How do you use technology to assist you with administrative tasks such as *taking* role?
3. What do you see as the primary values of technology for teaching? What issues or problems do you perceive with the use of technology in classrooms?

Web Resources

Instructional Design Models
http://carbon.cudenver.edu/~mryder/itc_data/idmodels.html

Read more information on various instructional techniques and strategies including advance organizers, concept mapping, discovery learning, and problem-based learning. Prepared by Martin Ryder of the University of Colorado at Denver.

Core Competencies
www.aicpa.org/edu/teachstrat.htm

This page includes examples of teaching strategies and classroom techniques that may be used to teach core competencies or elements of core competencies.

Glossary of Instructional Strategies
http://glossary.plasmalink.com/glossary.html

This special glossary of instructional strategies provides brief descriptions of numerous instructional strategies

with links to essays and samples that provide further discussion and application examples.

SCIMAST
www.sedl.org/scimast/

Visit the homepage for the Southwest Consortium for the Improvement of Mathematics and Science Teaching and explore the various resources available to teachers of math and science. Conduct a search for constructivism *and see examples of lessons set up using constructivist approaches.*

Adventures of Cyberbee: Web Evaluation
www.cyberbee.com/guides.html

Created by Karen McLachen, the media specialist at East Knox High School, Ohio, this site contains some easy-to-use forms for your students to evaluate the technical adequacy and content of websites.

Teaching for Transfer and Problem Solving

The purpose of this chapter is to provide you with an understanding of transfer to help you make decisions that enhance your students' ability to use what they've learned in your classroom. The chapter begins by elaborating the definition of transfer and by discussing why transfer is a pivotal concept in your decision making about teaching. This discussion examines how the theoretical principles developed in Chapters 2 through 6 may be applied to enhance transfer in your classes. When you have completed this chapter, you should be able to do the following items.

- Define transfer as a psychological process and describe different types of transfer.
- Explain the relationship between transfer and students' ability to solve problems and their ability to learn more effectively.
- Explain the characteristics of instruction that contribute to students' ability to transfer what they learn.
- Use the instructional principles developed in Chapters 2 through 6 to understand how to teach for transfer.

Close-ups on the Classroom

Middle School

Maly Nuth and the Curriculum Articulation Committee

I am currently teaching sixth grade reading at Frost Middle School. Frost is one of two middle schools in a small rural district. I've been teaching at the middle school level for three years, and before that I taught third grade for five years at East Hill Elementary. I guess that my experience at both the elementary and middle school levels is why the district curriculum coordinator asked me to chair the curriculum articulation committee. The committee's task is to find ways to improve student learning by coordinating what and how we teach across grade levels and between buildings.

The committee will be composed of teachers selected by their colleagues at a series of meetings held by the district administration before the beginning of the school year. Each of the district's four elementary schools will select one teacher to represent the school at the meeting and to report back to the teachers in the buildings. The middle school and high school teachers selected representatives for the various subject areas: mathematics, science, language arts, social studies, vocational education, and physical education.

I think it is a good idea. It is easy to become so involved in the day-to-day activities of your own classroom that you lose track of what your colleagues are doing. As teachers we sometimes forget that we are part of a team, and in the end we are all trying to accomplish the same thing. When I first moved to the middle school, I was certain that I would be able to use my experience at the elementary school as a guide to planning lessons that built on the students' elementary experience. But I found that even with this experience I often made inaccurate assumptions about what students could and couldn't do. If nothing else, this committee will help us develop an appreciation for what our colleagues are doing throughout the district.

One issue that we need to address as a committee is a concern that has been expressed by members of the high school curriculum articulation committee. They are concerned that students are not being taught key concepts and skills that they need to succeed in high school. Interestingly, when they provided specific examples to us, we were all confused because most if not all of those skills and concepts were being taught. We wondered if our students are not remembering what we taught them, or if they are not applying what we have taught them.

Decision Point: When you have your own classroom, which of your decisions are likely to be influenced by the actions of your colleagues, and how will your decisions affect other teachers' decisions?

Before proceeding with Chapter 8, be sure you read the Close-ups on the Classroom features about Maly Nuth and Keith Randich. At various points in the chapter, you will revisit both teachers in their classrooms and follow their decision-making progress. Their classroom experiences are closely integrated with the key concepts of this chapter and serve as important models for understanding how to teach for transfer and problem solving.

School Learning and the Importance of Transfer

The New York Times
nytimes.com
expect the world®

THEMES OF THE TIMES
Expand your knowledge of the concepts discussed in this chapter by reading current and historical articles from the New York Times by visiting the "Themes of the Times" section of the Companion Website.

Chapter 3 defined transfer as the process whereby the results of previous learning influence learning or performance in a new situation. Enhancing students' ability to transfer what they have learned is widely recognized as an important goal of schooling (Brooks & Dansereau, 1987; Cornfold, 2002; Mayer & Wittrock, 1996; Yamnill & McLean, 2001). This is because transfer is critical to success in many situations. Reading a book, balancing your checking account, writing a paper, and successfully solving novel problems are all tasks that are affected by the concepts and skills you transfer to these tasks. Transfer is also often a critical component of successful learning. Consider Bryan Salvido's experience with his students in his first-year Spanish class.

Keith Randich's Alumni Survey

My name is Keith Randich, and I teach American history at John Adams High School. John Adams High School is in a blue-collar community not far from Washington, DC. The opportunities for our graduates are quite diverse. A number of good colleges and universities are nearby, as well as several good two-year institutions offering vocational and technical programs. In addition, the proximity of Washington provides many of our graduates the opportunity for a job on graduating from JAHS.

In order to determine if our school is preparing our students to take advantage of these opportunities, we are conducting a self-evaluation. As part of the evaluation we are conducting surveys of teachers, students, and recent graduates. The administration formed separate committees to analyze the responses from each of these groups, and the committees will present summaries of their analyses at a meeting at the end of May.

I have been asked to chair the committee analyzing the responses from our alumni. The committee is composed of three other teachers besides myself: Martha Bowman, who teaches business and accounting classes, Charles Brouseau, who teaches several mathematics classes, and Clara Alport, who teaches English.

At our first meeting each member of the committee received a complete set of survey responses for the alumni group. All of the names and other identifying information had been removed from the survey responses. The survey itself has respondents use a scale to indicate their level of agreement with specific statements such as, "I would send my children to JAHS," and some fairly open-ended questions such as, "How well did your experience at JAHS prepare you for what your are doing now?" Our job was to try to identify some trends in responses that would help us identify things we were doing well and areas in which we could improve. To make the task more manageable, we decided to sort the responses into three categories based on where people went immediately after they graduated: college, vocational/technical training, or work.

Decision Point: Given that students will follow quite different career and life paths after high school, how could schools help prepare students for the varied choices they will make?

> I've found that students who have better English skills also do better with first-year Spanish because there are many Spanish words that are similar to English words. If the students know the English word, then they learn the Spanish word more easily. For instance, the Spanish word *barco*, which means boat, is similar to the English word *Barque*, which is a kind of boat. Students who have this word in their English vocabulary learn the Spanish word more quickly than those who don't.

Bryan's observations illustrate the benefit of previously learned concepts and skills to the understanding of new material. Bryan's example illustrates that transfer depends on what students have learned previously and may also explain some of the variations in students' performances. Students who lack relevant prior knowledge are likely to perform less well compared with their more knowledgeable peers.

What might Bryan do to help those students with weaker vocabularies?

There is also wide agreement that sometimes transfer is difficult for students and occurs less often than desired (Alexander & Murphy, 1999; Detterman, 1993; Stark, Mandl, Gruber, & Renkl, 1999). People frequently miss opportunities or make mistakes because they fail to transfer what they've learned. Consider the experience of Bob Kennedy with the students in his ninth grade industrial arts class.

> One project my students must complete is to use a blueprint for a shed to create a parts list. For some of the materials, such as shingles, sheathing, and paint, the students need to use basic geometry to determine the area to be covered. I know they've all learned how to calculate the areas of squares, rectangles, triangles, circles, and other shapes in their math classes, but for some reason many of the students just don't use these skills until they're reminded.

How might you design
a lesson to help your
students remember
relevant prior knowledge?

Bob Kennedy's observation is not uncommon. People frequently just don't notice that a previously learned concept or skill might be useful in a new situation until they are reminded. Much of the research on transfer has been directed at determining the factors that influence whether or not someone will transfer what he or she knows at an appropriate time. By understanding these factors, you can make it more likely that students will take advantage of what they know.

It should also be noted that the effects of transfer on learning are not always beneficial. Sometimes people attempt to apply an inappropriate concept or skill, resulting in slower performance or outright mistakes. Consider Mary Eddistone's experience teaching sixth grade mathematics.

➤ Many of my students have trouble with negative numbers. Specifically, when they are asked to subtract a larger number from a smaller number they get the sign wrong. When I ask them to explain how they got their answer, it was clear that they are so used to subtracting the smaller number from the bigger number that they don't even pay attention to how the problem is written.

You may have noticed in each of the preceding examples that the learners were dealing with a problem situation. Transfer is a key factor in learners' ability to solve problems both in and out of the classroom.

Transfer and Problem Solving

Problem solving involves taking the physical or mental actions necessary to solve a problem (Andre, 1986). To make this definition meaningful, the concept *problem* must be defined. Most psychologists identify three characteristics that are shared by all problem situations (Mayer, 1992). First, problem situations always include a goal or objective. Second, problem situations have givens. Givens are defined as the information, materials, and tools that are available when the problem is first perceived. Finally, a problem situation has obstacles that prevent the problem solver from immediately reaching the goal. Students' problem solving is affected by how they perceive or understand the various components of a problem-solving situation.

Perception and Problem Space.   In the case of problem solving, the term **problem space** is applied to learners' mental representations of a problem situation (Newell & Simon, 1972). The problem space that learners create is based on their perceptions of the problem situation, and the prior learning experiences that are applied or transferred to the problem situation influence how that problem situation is perceived. The problem space is critical because it influences the problem-solving activities of the learner. Consider how Sandra's and Billy's previous experiences influence the way they approach the mathematics problem presented in Figure 8.1.

How does previous
experience affect perception
of the problem space?

➤ Sandra is in tenth grade. "Okay, I need to figure out how tall the flagpole is. Well, I remember from my earth science class that the rays of the sun are parallel at the Earth's surface. This means that the angle between the top of the shadow and the top of an object will be the same for all objects at the same time of day. . . .Oh, this is a geometry problem!"

➤ Billy is in third grade. Billy notices the numbers in the problem statement and thinks, "This must be an arithmetic problem. That means I'll have to add, subtract, multiply, or divide some of these numbers to get the right answer." Looking at the picture, Billy thinks, "Hmmm, the flagpole has to be taller than the mailbox, so I'll probably have to add or multiply."

For both Sandra and Billy, the goal of the problem situation seems to be the same, find the height of the flagpole, but their perception of the givens is different. For

Sandra, important givens include the lengths of both shadows, the height of the mailbox, and that the shadows occur at the same time of day. She recognizes that the relationships among these elements are described by the angles they form. For Billy, the important givens are the numbers. Recognizing that the relationships between objects and their shadows are described by angles, Sandra identified the problem as one requiring geometric reasoning and operations. On the other hand, Billy's focus on numbers and his understanding of word problems as being solvable by the application of arithmetic, causes him to classify the problem as a situation requiring arithmetic operations. In both cases, how the problem is conceptualized is dependent on the knowledge the learner brings to the problem situation. In other words, the creation of the problem space depends on the process of transfer.

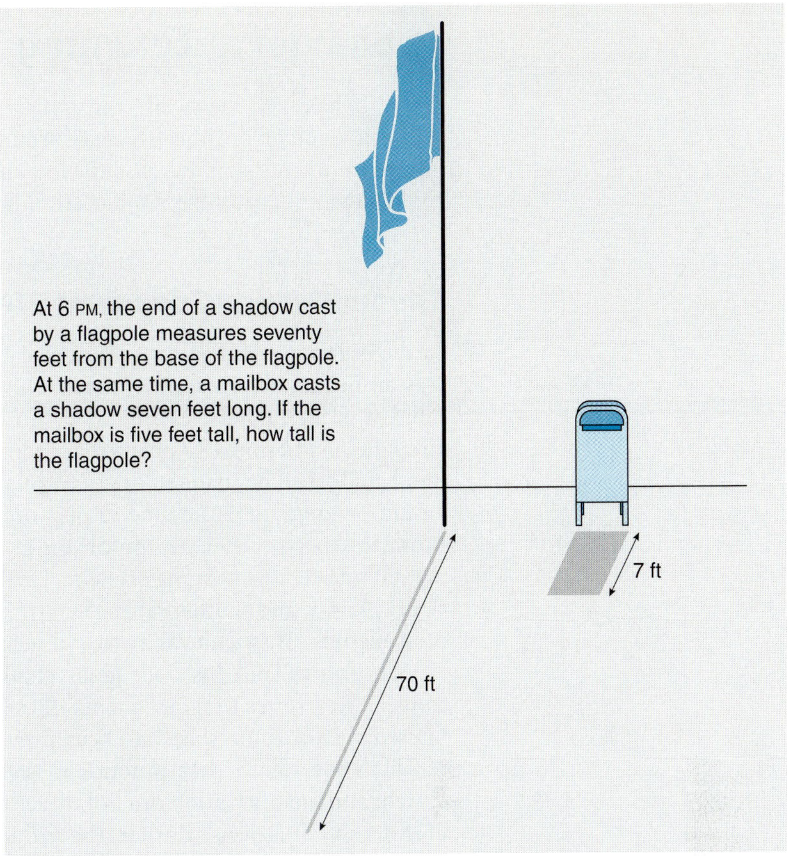

At 6 PM, the end of a shadow cast by a flagpole measures seventy feet from the base of the flagpole. At the same time, a mailbox casts a shadow seven feet long. If the mailbox is five feet tall, how tall is the flagpole?

7 ft

70 ft

FIGURE 8.1 Sample Math Problem

Learning as an Example of Problem Solving

Classroom learning can be viewed as an extremely important problem-solving activity for students. Thinking about classroom learning as an exercise in problem solving highlights the importance of transfer to the learning processes. As with all problem situations, the students' perception of the goals and givens of the learning activity will be influenced by their previous experience with similar activities. For instance, students' knowledge of how they will be assessed may influence how they perceive the goal of a learning activity and, therefore, what they actually think about and do while engaged in that learning activity. Learners who believe they are going to be assessed by a multiple-choice test may approach the particular learning activity differently than learners who believe they will be assessed by an essay examination. Likewise, learners' knowledge of learning techniques and strategies influence how they study. To learn successfully, learners must transfer what they know about themselves as learners, learning strategies, classroom dynamics, and the special requirements of various learning tasks to the current learning experience. Helping learners succeed requires that students acquire and transfer the types of metacognitive knowledge necessary to learn how to learn.

To summarize, transfer affects performance in many situations. As people complete mundane, day-to-day activities, their performance is affected by the concepts and skills they have previously learned. When novelty or complexity causes them to categorize a situation as a problem, a successful solution typically depends on their ability to transfer knowledge and skills acquired from previous experiences. Finally, when people are faced with a learning task, the way they approach the task and how well they learn is also determined by their ability to transfer and apply their prior knowledge. In the remainder of this chapter, we will discuss how the theoretical principles presented in Chapters 2 through 6 may be applied to enhance transfer in and out of your classroom.

In what situations are students' performances likely to be influenced by their ability to transfer what they've learned?

Behavioral Learning Theory and Transfer

Behavioral views of transfer are primarily an application of Principle 2.3, learning results from the effects of stimuli on responses. The goal is to create learning environments that increase the likelihood that students will emit a behavior when environments containing similar stimuli are encountered.

Thorndike and Identical Elements

At the beginning of the twentieth century, the doctrine of **formal** (or **mental**) **discipline** was an influential view of transfer. This perspective was based on the idea that the mind was like a muscle. Just as a muscle, with proper exercise, the mind can be strengthened to improve performance in a variety of tasks; so it was believed that the mind could also be made stronger through exercise, and the increased mental strength would enhance performance in any number of mental activities (Kolesnik, 1958). From this perspective, an important goal of education was to strengthen learners' mental muscle by engaging students in the rigorous study of difficult subjects such as Greek, Latin, and mathematics (Lemire, 2002). These difficult courses were thought of as mental calisthenics that would help students develop a strong, flexible mind.

Thorndike and his colleagues challenged the formal discipline perspective of transfer. In a series of experiments, these researchers found that transfer was a more limited phenomenon than had been previously supposed (Thorndike & Woodworth, 1901). They found that practice in such basic mental tasks as estimation, visual search, and memorization did not directly increase the ability to perform similar tasks in different situations. Rather, the influence of training in one situation on performance in a second situation was related to the similarity between the two situations. This observation prompted Thorndike and Woodworth to speculate that the influence of training was only likely to extend to those functions that shared identical elements with the training situation. **Identical elements** are the aspects or activities (e.g., stimuli and responses) that are common to two different situations. In other words, the likelihood that transfer will occur depends to a large extent on the similarities between one situation and another. Consider the following situation:

> ➤ While on her senior trip with her French club, Mary has an opportunity to travel to some other European countries. Mary purchased travel guides with common phrases in various languages. As she traveled, she noticed that it seemed easier for her to read the signs and understand the people in Spain and Italy than in Germany.

How might the concept of identical elements explain the differences in Mary's ability to understand different European languages? The grammar and vocabulary of French are more similar to that of Italian and Spanish than to German. In other words, French shares more identical elements with Spanish and Italian. Mary's ability to read and understand other languages is influenced by the languages she already knows.

The contrast between the view of transfer proposed by Thorndike and Woodworth with the formal discipline view of transfer helped draw attention to some important questions about transfer. What actually will transfer, and what impact do environmental similarities have on transfer? Advocates of the formal discipline approach were suggesting that it was possible for learners to acquire general mental abilities that would transfer across situations (Mayer & Wittrock, 1996). This form of transfer has come to be known as **general transfer,** or sometimes nonspecific transfer, because it refers to the application of general skills and knowledge to apparently dissimilar situations. For example, a student who is able to transfer a general problem-solving strategy such as visualization to different problem situations would be demonstrating general transfer. In contrast, Thorndike (1903) argued that transfer is more specific. Transfer involves the application of specific behaviors learned in one situation to a new situation. This type of transfer is referred to as **specific transfer** because it involves the transfer of specific behaviors learned in one situation to a new similar situation. For example, the student who can add two plus two in algebra and in statistics is demonstrating specific transfer of this addition behavior.

Thorndike also argued, on the basis of his data, that transfer is much more likely to occur if the learning and transfer environments are more similar. In contrast, advocates for the formal discipline approach seemed to be arguing that the training of the mind that occurs in Latin should transfer to quite different environments or academic areas. Transfer that occurs between similar environments is referred to as **near transfer,** while transfer between dissimilar environments is referred to as **far transfer** (Gick & Holyoak, 1987). For example, transferring the ability to drive a manual transmission from a Datsun to a Toyota is an example of near transfer. Being able to recognize that the scientific principle of a lever learned in physics might help you design a pop-top soda can is an example of far transfer.

How are the educational implications of identical elements different from the implications of formal discipline?

Additional Research on Similarity and Transfer

Further research into the transfer phenomenon revealed that the relationship between the similarity of situations and transfer was not so straightforward. While it is often the case that experiences in similar situations can facilitate performance, sometimes these experiences can actually inhibit people's ability to perform. When a previous experience results in improved performance in a new situation, it is called **positive transfer.** When previous experiences actually interfere with performance in a new situation, it is called **negative transfer.** For example, some of what you learn to do while teaching one group of students may positively transfer and help you with the next group. Other things you learn may negatively transfer and create a problem working with a different group.

What is the relationship between jokes, riddles, and brain teaser-type puzzles and negative transfer?

To help resolve the inconsistent effects of similar experiences on transfer, Osgood (1949) suggested that the actual similarity between two situations had to be looked at more closely. Behavioral learning theorists study learning by observing the effects of stimuli on students' responses. Osgood suggested that to understand transfer researchers had to look at the similarity between both the stimuli and responses involved in the learning and transfer situations. Figure 8.2 shows a flow chart summarizing Osgood's reasoning. First, researchers must consider if the person perceives similarity between the stimuli presented in the learning and performance situations. If no similarity is perceived, no transfer occurs. If similarity is perceived, then transfer can occur. Next, they must consider whether the response learned is appropriate for the performance situation. If the learned response is appropriate, then positive transfer is likely, but if the

FIGURE 8.2 Effects of Stimulus and Response Similarity on Transfer

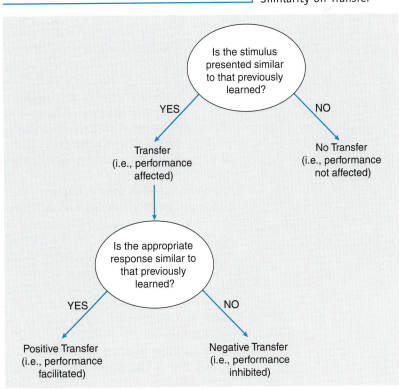

learned response is inappropriate, then negative transfer will occur. Consider Mary's situation again as she visits Madrid, Spain, with her French club.

> ➤ While in Madrid, Mary and her friends are invited to a party at the home of some friends of their chaperone. Mary is excited to meet and speak with some Spanish kids her own age, so armed with her travel guides she practices her Spanish phraseology and vocabulary. At the party Mary is excited by how much of the conversation she is able to understand. However, when she tries to speak, she finds that she keeps inserting French words into the conversation, even when she knows the correct Spanish words. One of her new Spanish friends even remarks that she speaks Spanish with a French accent.

How might Osgood's description of the causes of positive and negative transfer be used to explain Mary's experience? The answer to the first question on the flow chart of Figure 8.2 is yes. The stimuli, French and Spanish share many similarities. However, the answer to the second question is no. Mary's automatic responses, the sounds she attaches to letters and the way she pronounces words, are inappropriate.

In summary, Thorndike's ideas about teaching for transfer seem most helpful for teaching behaviors that have specific and probably limited applications. He would suggest that teaching students the specific behaviors they will need to apply in the transfer situations, and that teachers try to make learning environments as similar to transfer environments as possible. For example, when teaching a business computing course in high school, the teacher should teach students how to use a spreadsheet with examples they are likely to encounter in the workplace. Also, the programs and machines they are exposed to in the classroom should be the ones they are likely to use at work. Osgood's work implies that students practice a behavior with specific information about when that behavior is useful and when it is not and that students should be reinforced for using a behavior correctly.

Generalization, Discrimination, and Transfer

In the terminology of behavioral learning theory, appropriate transfer could be viewed as a balance between the processes of generalization and discrimination. In Chapter 2 *generalization* was defined as making the same response to similar situations; *discrimination* was defined as making different responses to similar situations. Positive transfer occurs when learners are able to generalize a response appropriately from the learning situation to transfer situations. Negative transfer could occur if the learner fails to discriminate between the learning and transfer situation and emits a response that is inappropriate in the transfer situation. When teaching for transfer, you need to help students establish this balance (Butterfield, Slocum, & Nelson, 1992). This is accomplished by providing students with experiences with various eliciting stimuli and consequences so as to promote an appropriate balance between generalization and discrimination.

How are generalization and discrimination related to transfer?

Inductive Learning from Examples. One way to help learners to generalize and discriminate appropriately among different stimuli is to provide them with opportunities to respond to a variety of related experiences, demonstrate correct responses for the learners, and provide them with feedback as to the correctness of their own responses. Gradually, learners learn to distinguish among and make appropriate responses to different situations. Learning about a category of objects or events in this way, by experiencing the similarities and differences of separate examples, is called inductive learning. The process of inductive learning is very natural and accounts for much of what people learn in our day-to-day dealings with people and things.

Consider how a child learns about classrooms. Each day in school the child notes what is similar and what is different. The child comes to understand that there are some common characteristics of classrooms such as the types of furniture and equipment available, and routine activities such as roll taking. She or he will expect to see these every time she or he goes to school. The child also comes to recognize that there are some characteristics that are not important defining characteristics of the category such as the color of a teacher's dress or tie.

When the child is learning about schools and classrooms, each experience of each school day is called a positive example while experiences with other types of events and institutions, youth groups, church, and sporting events are negative examples. In behavioral terms a **positive example** is an example for which a specific response or responses may be appropriately applied; and a **negative example** is an example in which the same responses would be inappropriate. Teaching someone to respond appropriately to different situations by providing a set of positive and negative examples with appropriate feedback is the basis of inductive teaching. Here, the term *response* is used in a broad sense to include actions such as:

- Correctly identifying examples of a category of objects or events
- Applying appropriate mathematical operations
- Making an appropriate pass on the basketball court
- Knowing when to use encyclopedias or dictionaries to find the answer to a question

Each of these objectives may be taught by providing the learner with appropriate positive and negative examples. By observing the differences and similarities among the examples, a learner is able to learn when different types of actions are required.

What is the difference between positive and negative examples?

Composing Sets of Examples. The process of providing sets of examples that may be compared and contrasted is called **juxtaposition.** Engelmann and Carnine (1991) have compiled a list of five juxtaposition principles to be used as a guide in preparing sets of examples:

1. **Wording principle:** To make the sequence of examples as clear as possible, use the same wording on juxtaposed examples.
2. **Set-up principle:** To minimize the number of examples needed, juxtapose examples that share the greatest number of possible features.
3. **Sameness principle:** To show sameness across examples juxtapose examples that are greatly different and indicate that the examples have the same label.
4. **Difference principle:** To show difference between examples, juxtapose examples that are minimally different and treat the examples differently.
5. **Testing principle:** To test the learner, provide examples that have no predictable relationship to each other.

These principles have been used to construct the set of examples in Figure 8.3 for teaching students the concept of *parallel*. Now take a closer look at how these principles are used by examining the set of examples presented in Figure 8.3.

The Wording Principle. Notice the similarity of wording on examples one through five. Each example in Figure 8.3 is clearly labeled as positive (these lines are parallel) or negative (these lines are not parallel) with the least possible variation in the phrasing. This application of the wording principle reduces the possibility of confusion on the part of the learner due to differences in the words used or the structure of the sentence.

The Set-up Principle. By following the set-up principle, the number of examples needed to communicate the concept is keep to a minimum. Imagine if Figure 8.3 had been composed of examples of parallel lines, parallel strings of beads, or airplanes flying in parallel formation. To avoid confusion and clearly communicate the concept parallel, positive and negative examples of parallel lines, beads, and airplanes in various orientations would be needed. By using one common set of objects (lines) teachers are able to keep the number of examples to a minimum.

FIGURE 8.3 A Sequence of
Examples for Teaching the
Concept *Parallel*

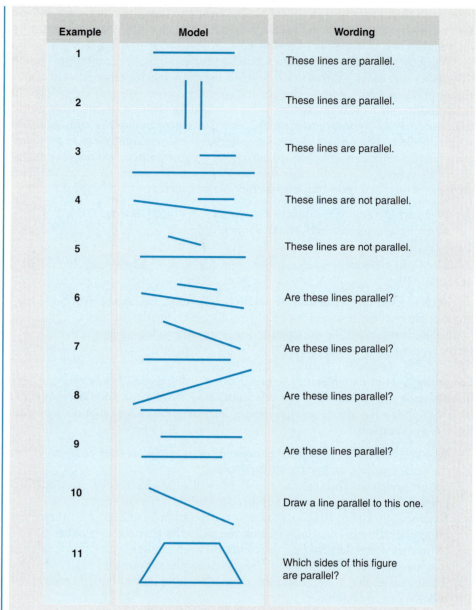

Example	Model	Wording
1		These lines are parallel.
2		These lines are parallel.
3		These lines are parallel.
4		These lines are not parallel.
5		These lines are not parallel.
6		Are these lines parallel?
7		Are these lines parallel?
8		Are these lines parallel?
9		Are these lines parallel?
10		Draw a line parallel to this one.
11		Which sides of this figure are parallel?

The Sameness Principle. Examples one through three in Figure 8.3 show the use of the sameness principle. Comparing examples one and two, the parallel lines are rotated from horizontal to perpendicular. By labeling these two examples as the same the learner understands that the overall orientation doesn't matter. By using the maximum possible difference in orientation, the learners come to understand that any example with a lesser amount of rotation will also be a positive example. Comparing examples two and three, the students learn that the lines need not be the same length to be parallel. The purpose of the first three examples is to show the range of possible variations that can still be labeled parallel. In other words, the learners are learning to generalize across positive examples.

The Difference Principle. Application of the difference principle is represented in examples three through five of Figure 8.3. The only difference between examples three and four is that one line has been rotated slightly so that the lines are no longer parallel. By showing that only this slight change transforms a positive example to a negative example, the learner expects that more drastic changes in the same dimension will also result in a negative example. Comparing example five with example four shows that changing the orientation of either line results in a negative example. Applying the difference principle helps learners discriminate negative examples from positive examples.

The Testing Principle. Examples six through eleven of Figure 8.3 show the testing principle. Note that the first example tested, example six, is also only minimally different from the negative example presented in example five. Each example tests learners' ability to generalize (transfer) the concept to different situations.

From the examples presented in Figure 8.3 you might think that this technique is only useful when teaching simple

Children learn inductively when they are presented positive and negative examples of a concept.

concepts, but examples may also be used to teach cognitive problem-solving routines and complex factual relationships (Engelmann & Carnine, 1991). Typically, problem-solving and reasoning activities can be organized as a sequence of steps. The objective then becomes to teach each step of the sequence. As the learners achieve a degree of mastery for separate steps, the steps are combined with others until the entire sequence is mastered.

Information-Processing Approaches to Enhancing Transfer

Review the concept of chaining presented in Chapter 2. How is it applicable here?

From a cognitive perspective, transfer involves the application of previously learned knowledge to new situations. As noted previously in this chapter, problem solving and learning can be seen as very similar processes. The same basic cognitive processes described in Chapter 3, are involved in both activities. In addition, Chapter 3 stressed the importance of prior knowledge to a person's ability to process new information meaningfully, and this observation applies to both learning and problem-solving situations. According to the information-processing theory presented in Chapter 3, information may be represented in the form of declarative knowledge or procedural knowledge. Each type of knowledge plays a unique role in a person's ability to solve problems or learn. Considering the potential contributions of each type of knowledge provides a useful tool for making decisions when planning lessons or helping students deal with problems during learning activities. The two types of knowledge potentially provide these four possible forms of transfer (Brooks & Dansereau, 1987; Singley & Anderson, 1989).

1. Students could transfer previously learned declarative knowledge to help them acquire new declarative knowledge in a meaningful way. In schools this often involves the application of content learned earlier in a course or in a previous course to the learning of new declarative knowledge. For example, students might apply their knowledge of the Bill of Rights in learning about censorship
2. Students could transfer previously learned declarative knowledge to help them apply or learn procedural knowledge. This would happen when concepts or information students have previously learned help them acquire or apply a skill, such

Looking in on

We held our first meeting on curriculum articulation today. After the committee members had each introduced themselves, I asked the committee to consider what they thought the major benefit would be from articulating the curricula across different subjects and grades levels. After some discussion, the committee agreed it was knowing they would be able to better help their students learn if they knew what they had already mastered and would be expected to master in the future.

Next, we tried to define what it meant to articulate a curriculum. This seemed to be a more difficult question for the committee to resolve. Everyone quickly agreed that articulation meant a logical progression of concepts and skills, but there seemed to be more to it. Further discussion revealed that, not only was it important to consider what was covered, but to also be aware of what the students did to master the material. Apparently, simple variations in instructional or assessment procedures were enough to confuse many of the students.

As a result of the brainstorming session, we identified several areas in which increasing the consistency of our teaching might improve our students' learning and performance. One area that was noted by several participants was

in mathematics instruction. Variation in the way mathematics exercises and problems were presented or discussed seemed to have a negative effect on the students' learning and performance. To a lesser extent similar observations were made in other subject areas.

As we discussed this phenomenon, one of the first suggestions was that we standardize the format and vocabulary used to present and discuss mathematics. However, several members of the committee said that standardizing in this way might actually handicap our students later. It seems that the variety wasn't the problem, but rather, that the students weren't learning which variations were important and which were not. After further discussion, the committee decided that we all needed to provide students with experience in all of the variety of ways that exercise and problems within different subject areas are presented.

● **How might the concepts of similarity and transfer be used to explain the characteristics and potential advantages of an articulated curriculum?**

Decision Point: How would information about how your students had been taught or assessed by previous teachers aid your own decision making?

---

as knowledge of place value helping students develop a meaningful understanding of math procedures.

3. Students could transfer previously learned procedural knowledge to the learning or application of new procedural knowledge. For example, students may use previously learned math skills in a higher level math course.

4. Students could transfer previously learned procedural knowledge to the acquisition of new declarative knowledge. Typically, this would involve the application of cognitive and metacognitive learning strategies, such as using a previously learned note-taking procedure to help learn information from a textbook.

Principle 3.1: Meaningful Learning Occurs When New Knowledge Is Connected to Existing Knowledge

A key cognitive learning principle is that new knowledge is more understandable and memorable if it can be connected to prior knowledge. This principle provides a theoretical rationale for the types of transfer listed previously.

Declarative Knowledge and Meaningful Learning. Information-processing theory proposes that information that is learned thoroughly in a meaningful way is more likely to be recalled when it is needed. This being the case, it should be no surprise that the degree of learning (or meaningfulness) is an important factor affecting students' ability to transfer declarative knowledge to additional situations (Gick & Holyoak, 1987).

When students are first exposed to new information, their understanding is likely to be incomplete. They may focus only on the surface attributes of the information being learned without understanding the information in meaningful ways. In this case, no transfer would be expected or possibly even negative transfer could occur. As students gain more experience with information, they begin to comprehend the relationships between the new information and previously learned knowledge. The effect is that the new information gradually becomes more meaningful, and it is more likely that positive transfer of the information will occur.

What this implies for you as a teacher is that for declarative knowledge to be useful to your students, they must learn information in a meaningful way. This means that you must encourage your students to be active learners and help them to elaborate and organize the information you present in class. There are a number of techniques to help students connect new learning to prior knowledge (see Chapters 3 and 7 for examples). Analogies and derived structural schemata are two examples of these techniques that are useful for helping students transfer declarative knowledge. These techniques are useful because they help students focus on the structural similarities between new and old knowledge. Encouraging learners to focus on structural similarities is likely to increase the degree of meaningful learning and, therefore, improve the chances that the newly learned information will be applicable in some future situation.

Teaching with Analogies. Instructional analogies were introduced in Chapter 7 as a technique for helping students connect new information to existing knowledge. Analogies, therefore, provide a structure for transferring existing declarative knowledge to the learning of new declarative knowledge. For example, when students are studying the topics of electricity and electric circuits in general science classes, they are often invited to compare an electric circuit with a plumbing system. This is an example of teaching with analogies. Pairs of situations, objects, or events are analogous if they share some degree of structural similarity, but on the surface appear dissimilar (Gentner, 1989). Consider the analogy of electric circuits with plumbing systems. On the surface, the two systems are dissimilar because electrons, wires, batteries, and switches are different from water, pipes, tanks, and valves. However, the relationships among the various elements of these two systems are similar:

- Pipes carry the water from one place to another; wires carry electrons from one place to another.
- Tanks store water, batteries store electrons.
- Valves direct the flow of water, switches direct the flow of electrons.

Helping students see the similarities among the relationships of the two systems promotes meaningful learning by encouraging students to use what they know about one system to think about and organize what they are learning about the new system. An additional benefit of teaching with analogies is that the students may get into the habit of looking for relationships. This habit may transfer and enhance the meaningfulness of students' learning of other materials.

Case-based reasoning provides an example of how analogies can support problem solving (Kolodner, 1997; Schank, Berman, & Macpherson, 1999; Schank & Cleary, 1995). Case-based reasoning suggests that people use their past experiences or the experiences of others to guide their thinking in new situations. Consequently, one way to support students problem solving in complex and unfamiliar situations is to provide students with cases that describe how others have responded to similar problems. These cases provide the informational base for applying past experience to current experience.

Research on the use of analogical problem solving suggests that using analogies to understand and respond to problems is not a simple process. Using an analogy requires that the similarities in relationships, what Gentner (1989) refers to as **structural similarity**, be recognized. Simply being presented with, or remembering a potentially useful analogy, is not enough (Anolli, Antonietti, & Cantoia, 2001). For example, teaching about electricity using a plumbing analogy assumes that the learners are sufficiently familiar with structural relationships of plumbing systems to recognize and organize the relevant information in the new system. This assumption may not be justified for some, or even most of the students in a class. This means that if you plan to use analogies in your classes you must ensure that the students have the necessary prior knowledge to benefit from the introduction of the analog, and you may have to explicitly help students find the structural similarities between the two situations. If students lack knowledge of these structural similarities, the analogy is unlikely to help them understand the new information and may even make learning more difficult or cause students to form misconceptions about what they are learning.

Derived Structural Schema.   Dansereau (1995) refers to schemata that preserve structural relationships of a category of events or objects as **structural schema.** Chapter 3 described a schema as a type of memory structure representing information in a person's long-term memory. People's schemata define their understanding of categories of objects or events. This abstract structural information is important to our ability to apply our knowledge in new situations. The performance of expert problem solvers is typically attributed to the structural relationships represented in experts' schemata (Chi, Feltovich, & Glaser, 1981).

Dansereau (1995) further distinguishes between two types of structural schema, natural and derived. A **natural structural schema** preserves the structural relationships among the elements of a category of objects or events, but this understanding is acquired gradually across many experiences. Learners naturally come to acquire schema from experiencing many similar episodes through the process of inductive learning. This means that in the natural course of events, the structural characteristics of situations are learned gradually and over a long period of time. A **derived structural schema** is similar to a natural schema in that it preserves structural relationships, but is different in being consciously derived or produced by an expert. Presenting students with a derived structural schema helps them to learn deductively.

Dansereau (1995) refers to derived structural schemata as "generic analogs," (p. 107) and suggests that their use shares many of the advantages of teaching with analogies, while avoiding some of the disadvantages associated with variation in the learners' prior knowledge.

Figure 8.4 provides an example of a derived structural schema applied to the familiar electric circuit and plumbing analogy. The idea is that the teacher, acting as the expert, creates a derived structural schema that represents a class of concepts or procedures that will be taught. The teacher then presents the derived schema to the learners as a concept map, list of questions, outline, or whatever form seems most appropriate for the subject being taught. The learners can then use the derived structural schema as a guide to organize and elaborate new information in a variety of learning activities.

The derived structural schema presented in Figure 8.4 identifies five categories of structurally similar information that can be found in a variety of distribution systems. The five categories of information are what, activators, routing, problems, and systems and can be remembered by the acronym WARPS. Figure 8.4 also shows two examples of the kind of information that might be placed in the categories for two different types of distribution systems. This same structural schema might be used to study transportation systems, information systems, or market economies. Dansereau (1995) identifies these five characteristics of good structural schema:

In what way is a derived structural schema like an advance organizer?

1. Clear identification of important structural characteristics of the category to assist learners in identifying analogous attributes in new examples of the category.
2. The organization of the derived structural schema should be tailored to the anticipated uses to make it as easy to use as possible.
3. Keep the number of characteristics of the derived structural schema to seven or fewer to avoid overloading working memory.
4. The characteristics should be labeled in a meaningful way to aid the recall of the characteristics.
5. Memory aids such as acronyms should be used when possible to help learners remember the characteristics of the category.

FIGURE 8.4 Sample of a Derived Schema for Distribution Systems

WARPS
(Distribution Systems)

What: What is distributed and what is its source?

Activators: What is the moving force of the distribution system?

Routing: What is the nature of the routes of distribution? What is the nature of storage? How is distribution controlled?

Problems: What are the potential obstacles to distribution?

Systems: What other systems affect or are affected by distribution?

Electric Circuits

What: Electrons from chemical reactions or machines

Activators: Electric potential, the difference between the number of electrons at two points

Routing: Electrons travel on metal wires, may be stored in batteries or capacitors; distribution is controlled by switches

Problems: Shorts to ground cause electrons to drain from the system

Systems: Mining, power production facilities, manufacturing electric appliances, society, and ecosystems

Water Distribution Systems

What: Water from rivers, lakes, and wells

Activators: Water pressure caused by pumps or differences in elevation (gravity)

Routing: Water flows through canals, aqueducts, or pipes made of various materials. It may be stored in tanks of reservoirs. Distribution is by valves

Problems: Leaks may cause water to drain from the system

Systems: Ecosystems, social institutions, manufacturing, and society

Declarative Knowledge and Learning Skills.   In 1908, Judd summarized an experiment that assessed the effects of principled understanding of a situation on performance. Figure 8.5 shows the general setup of the experiment. Two groups of boys practiced throwing darts at an underwater target. One group had been given an explanation of the concept of refraction of light through water, and how refraction distorts the apparent position of underwater objects, while the other group received no explanation of the refractive qualities of water. Initially, both groups were able to learn to hit the underwater target; however, when the depth of the water was changed, which changed the apparent position of the target, the participants who had the conceptual explanation were able to adjust their performance to the new situation more quickly. These results suggest that conceptual knowledge can influence people's acquisition of a skill.

Conceptual information is stored as schemata in long-term memory. An important aspect of this type of knowledge has to do with understanding relationships stored in the schemata. When faced with a problem or novel situation, understanding the relationships among the various aspects of a situation allows a person to take more effective actions. The schemata individuals bring to bear on a task affects their perception and understanding of the task. Differences in these schemata account for many of the observed differences in individuals' performance in these situations. In other words, how a task is understood affects the actions a person is likely to take when dealing with the task (Chi, Feltovich, & Glaser, 1981; Chi et al., 1989; Sweller, 1989).

How would you describe the learning process of persons who do not have a conceptual understanding of a situation?

Experts versus Novices.   One approach to investigating the role that declarative knowledge plays in transfer has been to study the differences between the performances of novices and experts in problem-solving situations. An expert is a person who has acquired special skills and knowledge through learning and experience

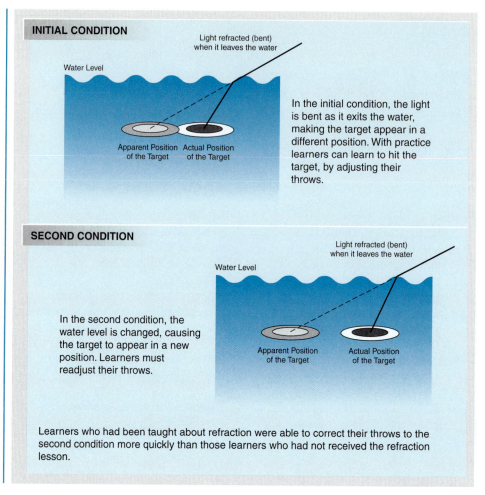

INITIAL CONDITION

Light refracted (bent) when it leaves the water

Water Level

Apparent Position of the Target Actual Position of the Target

In the initial condition, the light is bent as it exits the water, making the target appear in a different position. With practice learners can learn to hit the target, by adjusting their throws.

SECOND CONDITION

Light refracted (bent) when it leaves the water

Water Level

In the second condition, the water level is changed, causing the target to appear in a new position. Learners must readjust their throws.

Apparent Position of the Target Actual Position of the Target

Learners who had been taught about refraction were able to correct their throws to the second condition more quickly than those learners who had not received the refraction lesson.

(Ericsson & Charness, 1994). In general, this research reveals that the more skilled problem solving of experts is not primarily a difference in intelligence or general problem-solving strategies, but is more a difference in the amount and quality of domain-specific knowledge (Bransford, Brown, & Cocking, 2000). Domain-specific knowledge is knowledge that is pertinent to a particular performance or content area. For example, domain-specific knowledge in physics would include the knowledge a person has accumulated in physics. The performance of experts and novices has been compared in a variety of domains (Bransford, Brown, & Cocking, 2000; Chi, Feltovich, & Glaser, 1981; de Groot, 1965; Ericsson & Simon, 1993; Glaser, 1984; Peskin, 1998; Zeitz, 1994). A summary of the findings includes:

- Because of their extensive and well-organized knowledge base, experts are more likely than novices to recognize meaningful patterns in problem-solving situations rather than having to abstract or infer those patterns.
- The knowledge base of experts tends to be organized around major principles or ideas, which helps them classify problems more accurately in terms of the relevant principle. This type of organization is particularly important for high-road transfer (Johnson, 1995; Perkins & Salomon, 1989). **High-road transfer** refers to the thoughtful transfer of knowledge based on the recognition of abstract principles that govern both situations, such as recognizing two physics problems as being based on the same principle. It contrasts with **low-road transfer,** which is when prior learning is automatically and directly transferred, such as transferring how to drive a stick shift car from one car to another or the application of a multiplication fact.

Exceptional learners are those students who require special instructional considerations. Exceptional learners include learners with disabilities, or students with academic gifts. For students with disabilities, the focus has been on providing instruction in learning strategies that will allow these learners to be more academically successful. Some successes have been reported in a wide variety of academic areas, from spelling (Fulk & Starmont-Spurgin, 1999), to community college algebra classes (Feigenbaum, 2000), to the preparation of adults with learning disabilities to pass their GED exams Westberry, 1994).

The problem has been that learners with disabilities often do not spontaneously transfer the strategies they learned to new situations (Lupart, 1995; Troia & Graham, 2002, Fuchs, Fuchs, Hamlett, & Appleton, 2002). This has caused some researchers to include an emphasis on strategies aimed at developing propensities for self-regulation and metacognition as well as specific learning strategies (Lupart, 1995; Vaidya, 1999). In addition to a need for self-regulation, researchers have come to realize that a learning strategy that may work for an average learner may not be appropriate for learners with disabilities (Montague, 1993). Therefore, the specific nature of each learner's disability must be considered when deciding what learning strategies to teach.

One of the characteristics associated with students with academic gifts is their spontaneous use of self-regulation and metacognition during learning (Risenberg & Zimmerman, 1992; Lupart 1995). However, these students are not a homogeneous group (Lupart, 1995; Freeman, 1999), and many of these students may be at risk for academic failure. Manning and Glasner (1996) suggest that many students with academic gifts may benefit from explicit instruction in metacognition and self-regulation strategies also.

> ● **How might the concepts of near and far transfer be used to explain how learners who are learning disabled or mentally retarded perform in transfer situations? (For your authors' perspective on this question, go to the text website for this chapter.)**

- Experts' knowledge is more sensitive to context, which means they are more likely to be able to identify the part of their knowledge base that is most relevant for a problem.

A number of potential implications from the expert novice research exist for helping students develop a meaningful knowledge base that can be transferred to different situations. First, it should be noted that the development of an expert knowledge base is a lengthy and often effortful process, Students need multiple exposures to a knowledge domain over time. Also, teachers should help students identify key principles and concepts, their relationships to each other, and their relationships to various types of problems. Information should be taught in terms of its connection to previous learning and its application in multiple settings.

Situational Similarity and Transfer. The transfer of declarative knowledge can influence skill learning and problem solving. Success, however, depends on activating appropriate declarative knowledge. Gick and Holyoak's (1987) concepts of surface and structural similarity help explain how students' perceptions of situations determine the knowledge that is activated and, consequently, the type of transfer that occurs. Surface similarity refers to the degree to which the elements describing two situations are identical. Structural similarity refers to the degree to which the two situations share analogous relationships among the elements that describe the situations. Figure 8.6 provides a graphic illustration of their reasoning. The analysis of a transfer task begins by asking two questions. Does the current situation (transfer situation) share surface similarity with previous experiences (learning situations)? Does the transfer situation share structural similarity with the learning situation? The answer to the first question determines the likelihood that some types of transfer will occur because the likelihood of retrieving prior knowledge is directly related to the degree of surface similarity shared by the transfer situation and experiences stored in long-term memory. The answer to the second question determines how prior knowledge

FIGURE 8.6 The Effects of Surface and Structural Similarity on Transfer

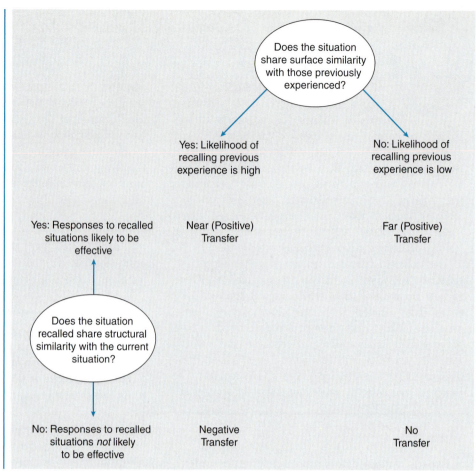

will affect performance in the transfer situation. When the transfer situation shares a high degree of structural similarity with the recalled learning situation, then positive transfer is likely. However, if the recalled learning situation isn't structurally similar to the transfer situation, then negative transfer is the likely result.

In addition to positive and negative transfer, Figure 8.6 also makes a distinction between near and far transfer. When there is a high degree of surface and structural similarity between two situations, then the learner is attempting near transfer. In a near transfer situation, successful (positive) transfer is likely. When the degree of surface similarity between two situations is low, but there is a high degree of structural similarity, then the issue is far transfer. The low surface similarity means that people often do not remember facts and procedures that would be useful in dealing with the new situation. For this reason, cognitive psychologists expect far transfer to be a relatively rare event. Can you use the description of transfer presented in the preceding paragraph and Figure 8.6 to explain the following situations?

➤ Allen is on the varsity baseball team and is taking his first golf lesson. As he places his ball on the tee, he thinks, "How hard can this be? Both baseball and golf have a stick and a ball." On his first attempt his ball only putters a few feet from the tee. On his next try he makes good contact with the ball, but it hooks sharply and flies deep into the woods along the fairway.

➤ Emily's cooking class has been given the assignment of baking one dozen chocolate chip cookies. The problem is that the recipe is for making thirty cookies. She quickly calculates that 12/30th is the same as 2/5th and adjusts the recipe accordingly. She thinks to herself, "This is just like what we do in chemistry class when we mix up solutions with different concentrations." As she looks around the room at her classmates, she is surprised to see that many are having difficulty.

In Allen's case his perception is that baseball and golf are similar because they both have a ball and a stick. He is focusing on the surface features of the situation. The structural relationships, the way the golf club is held compared with a baseball bat, the motion involved in a proper swing are different for the two situations. Therefore, Allen is experiencing negative transfer.

Emily's classmates are focusing on the surface features of the cooking task, resulting in their failure to remember the appropriate information about proportions. However, Emily's focus on the similar underlying relationships between chemistry and cooking class allows her to make an appropriate response to her cooking assignment, even though the similarity between the surface features of the two activities is low. Emily's response is an example of far transfer, and is more typical of an expert response.

How might the concepts of surface and structural similarity used to explain transfer be applied to the examples presented earlier in the chapter?

Transfer of Procedural Knowledge.   Meaningfulness is also important when learning transferable skills. When students learn skills in a rote fashion they are less likely to use those skills in appropriate situations and are more likely to apply the skills in inappropriate situations (Singley & Anderson, 1989). A number of considerations can help students learn skills in a meaningful fashion.

Initial Learning Stages.   With regard to transfer, the early (cognitive) stages of learning a skill are especially critical (Singley & Anderson 1989; Sweller, 1989). According to information-processing theory, learning a new skill begins with the acquisition of declarative knowledge (Anderson, 1983; Fitts & Posner, 1967). It is during the cognitive stage that the learners form a schema representing not only the nature of the skill, but also when and why the skill should be applied. The development of this declarative representation or schema is critical to the learner's ability to later apply the skill (Chi et al., 1989). For this reason, it is important that learners focus on understanding the skill when it is first presented (Sweller, 1989). The learners' initial understanding of a new skill should include information about:

- Why is the skill performed? In other words, what are the goals that the successful performance of the skill will accomplish?
- When is it appropriate to apply the skill, and what information or materials are required to perform the skill?
- How is the skill performed? What sequence of actions leads to the attainment of the goal? This includes knowing the intermediate products or subgoals that will allow the learner to monitor his or her performance

Two instructional techniques that are appropriate for this stage of learning are goal-free problems and analogical problem construction.

Sweller (1989) noted that the traditional approach to teaching problem-solving skills, such as those presented in mathematics classes, was to provide learners with a worked example of a problem, and then provide learners with practice solving similar problems. Sweller suggested that this approach forced the learners to have two simultaneous goals: (a) understanding the nature of the problem, that is, forming a problem schema, and (b) finding an answer to a specific problem. Attempting to do both placed a heavy load on learners' working memory, resulting in poorly constructed and incomplete problem schema. In other words, traditional instruction may violate Principle 3.3, the limitations of students' working memory must be accounted for in instruction, preventing students from elaborating and organizing the information presented in the problem statement.

Sweller (1989) suggested that using goal-free problem statements might alleviate the load on learners' working memory. **Goal-free problem statements** are statements that do not require learners to work toward a specific solution, but allow them to focus on relationships within a problem. Figure 8.7 provides an example of a standard and a goal-free problem statement for the same geometry problem. Notice that the standard statement requires the learner to focus on finding the area of the triangle. To solve this problem the learner may have to work backward by asking and answering a series

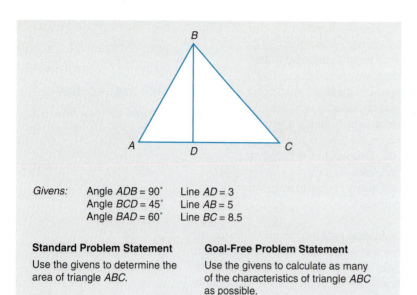

Givens:
Angle *ADB* = 90° Line *AD* = 3
Angle *BCD* = 45° Line *AB* = 5
Angle *BAD* = 60° Line *BC* = 8.5

Standard Problem Statement
Use the givens to determine the area of triangle *ABC*.

Goal-Free Problem Statement
Use the givens to calculate as many of the characteristics of triangle *ABC* as possible.

FIGURE 8.7 Standard versus Goal-Free Problem Statements

of questions such as, "I need a height and a base of the triangle. But these are not available, so what do I need to find the base?" In contrast, the goal-free statement does not set any final goal, instead the learner is invited to explore the problem and solve for as many unknowns as possible. Sweller believes that this approach allows the learner to focus on relationships within the problem, resulting in better understanding.

Transfer of a solution from one problem to another often depends on the problem solver recognizing the analogical relationships between a previously solved problem and the new problem (Ross, 1989). As discussed, the recall and use of analogies often depend on learners recognizing the structural relationships among problem types. Bernardo (2001) suggests that learners' ability to recognize such relationships is enhanced by the use of an **analogical-problem construction** strategy. With this approach, learners are provided with a worked example of a problem, then asked to write a problem of their own that is similar to the example. Bernardo's research has shown that learners who apply this strategy are better able to transfer their problem-solving skills to new problems.

> **What can teachers do to ensure that practice occurs within an appropriate cognitive context?**

Appropriate Practice. Practice is essential to the development of a skill, and the skill is more likely to transfer if practice occurs within an appropriate cognitive context (Carlson, Khoo, & Elliot, 1990). **Cognitive context** refers to the learners' beliefs about why they are practicing a skill. An appropriate cognitive context requires that learners be aware of why, when, and how the skill will be used as they practice the skill. This means that when learning a new skill, students should be made aware of this information early and be reminded of it as they practice the skill. One approach to providing students with this awareness is to demonstrate the application of the skill in as many appropriate contexts as possible early in the learning sequence.

> **Students can use computer simulations to practice with an appropriate cognitive context and feedback.**

Transfer of Procedural Knowledge to Procedural Knowledge. In many situations, previously learned skills serve as components of skills that are learned later. For example, students need to multiply and subtract during long division. In some cases, these component skills need to be learned first. In the long division example, it would be useful for students to have learned how to subtract before beginning to learn long division. Consequently, the important instructional issue is making sure that skills are taught in a logical sequence. Chapter 9 discusses how to analyze skills for their prerequisites.

In other cases, it may be useful to engage students in the more complex skill and have them learn component skills as necessary. For example, students might be engaged in a complicated problem-solving task in environmental science that requires component skills such as topographic map reading or the use of certain laboratory procedures or equipment. Instructional modules could be created to teach these skills when students need them in their problem solving. The underlying assumption is that these skills may seem more understandable when taught in terms of their use or purpose. This is discussed further in the context of constructivism and transfer.

Principle 3.4: Learning Is an Active and Goal-Directed Process

As you remember from Chapter 3, cognitive theorists view learners as having an active role in regulating their own learning. Self-regulating learners engage in a series of metacognitive activities such as identifying their goal, selecting appropriate strategies for their goal, and monitoring their progress on a learning task. These types of activities require learners to transfer previously learned procedures (strategies) to the acquisition of new declarative knowledge. The ability to transfer strategies effectively is a component of the extremely important problem-solving task of learning how to learn.

Cognitive Strategy Instruction.   Cognitive strategy instruction is the overall process of helping students to develop appropriate ways to solve problems. Our discussion focuses on the development of cognitive strategies for improving students' ability to learn in classrooms. This discussion is organized around six key questions:

- What is a cognitive strategy?
- Why is cognitive strategy instruction important?
- Do my students need strategy instruction?
- What type of classroom environments supports strategic behavior?
- How do I identify strategies to teach?
- How do I teach a strategy?

What Is a Cognitive Strategy?   A **cognitive strategy** is a plan of action that is relevant for solving problems (Reid, Hresko, & Swanson, 1996). It helps students know what to do to manage a range of activities better (Perkins, Simmons, & Tishman, 1990). A cognitive strategy may be as specific as creating a diagram of a story problem or as complicated as a multistep process for studying for a test. Also, strategies should not be equated with skills or algorithms, but instead should be considered examples of heuristics (Duffy & Roehler, 1989; Rosenshine & Meister, 1992).

An **algorithm** is a rule or procedure for solving a problem that when properly applied always solves the problem. The term typically applies to mathematical procedures, but may also include routine operations or skills in other areas of performance. Some examples of algorithms are:

- The Pythagorean theorem
- Medical tests to detect the presence of antibodies associated with a specific disease
- Computer diagnostics performed by a mechanic on a modern automobile

The disadvantage of algorithms is that typically they are only applicable to a narrow range of specific types of problems. For instance, learning to use a computer to diagnose an automotive problem will not work if you are trying to repair a 1964 Chevy. Algorithms may improve students' performance when faced with a specific type of problem, but will not improve the learners' general reasoning or problem-solving ability.

Why might algorithms not aid in general transfer?

A **heuristic** is a flexible problem-solving approach that must be adapted to the demands of the problem-solving situation. For example, the skillful use of the scientific method requires flexibility in the application of the basic steps to solve different types of problems, or a particular textbook reading strategy may need to be used differently for different types of text. When experts are faced with novel or atypical problems, they resort to the use of heuristics (Perkins & Salomon, 1989). Examples of some of the heuristics used by experts include:

- Find a problem that you know how to solve that is analogous to the novel problem.
- Simplify the novel problem by breaking it into parts or simplifying some to the variables.
- Draw a picture of the situation that shows the important relationships among the elements of the problem.

Why Is Cognitive Strategy Instruction Important? To be effective, self-regulating learners need to have a variety of strategies and a good understanding of how, where, and why to use these strategies (Wood, Willoughby, & Woloshyn, 1995). Some students may intuitively develop an effective understanding of cognitive strategies as they try to learn or problem solve. However, less effective students may fail to develop successful strategies or fail to apply the strategies they know in an effective manner (Ritchie & Karge, 1996; Troia & Graham, 2002). Even more successful learners could benefit from learning how to learn more efficiently. Knowing how to teach cognitive strategies, therefore, is an important tool for teachers.

Do My Students Need Strategy Instruction? It is important to note that students may be unsuccessful as learners and problem solvers for a number of reasons and that strategy instruction by itself will not address all these various reasons for not succeeding. For example, successful problem solving not only requires knowledge of cognitive strategies, but also a well-developed fund of world and domain knowledge and motivation to apply what is known (Snyder & Pressley, 1995). Students may be unsuccessful because they lack strategies, because they lack basic skills and background knowledge, because they lack self-confidence, or some combination of these and other factors. You need to assess why students are not being successful, and then determine what would be most helpful to your students. For example, if a student lacks necessary prerequisite skills or knowledge, then the missing skills or knowledge will need to be learned, and the relevant strategies may be those that help the students acquire the needed background knowledge.

Also, remember that students will come to you with different levels and types of strategic knowledge. Allocate class time to talk to your students about what they already know about how to learn and problem solve. For example, you could ask them for some strategies for approaching an assignment you have just given them. These discussions may help you determine your students' needs for cognitive strategies.

What Type of Classroom Environment Supports Strategic Behavior? The point has been made that unless an environment supports or requires students to think, it is unlikely that students will see the need to learn how to think (Beyer, 1998). Students may have limited need to learn cognitive strategies if they can succeed without them.

What is the relationship between learning strategic behaviors and students' zone of proximal development?

Consequently, at least some classroom tasks must be challenging enough to require strategic behavior. You may find it useful to review Vygotsky's idea of the zone of proximal development as a guiding concept (Vygotsky, 1978). Also, teachers need to create environments that value the successful use of strategies (Robertson, Priest, & Fullwood, 2001). Students should be reinforced for their problem solutions, but they also should be reinforced for using effective strategies to produce those solutions.

How Do I Identify Strategies to Teach? The first step is to determine where your students may need help. Begin by asking if there are learning tasks that your students struggle with because they don't have a good method for approaching those tasks. Once you identify the area of need, you need to identify strategies that might address that need. There are a number of useful books and articles that describe different types of strategies. (O'Shea, O'Shea, & Algozzine, 1998; Pressley & Woloshyn, 1995; Wood, Woloshyn, & Willoughby, 1995). In addition, a website resource section is included at the end of the chapter that provides a description of various learning strategies.

Why would you create a strategy for your students?

On occasion, however, you may also find it useful to create your own strategies, possibly because you want to tailor a strategy to your specific context or because you can't locate a relevant strategy. These references may help you think through this process (Babkie & Provost, 2002; Lambert, 2000). When your authors have helped teachers develop cognitive strategies, we begin by brainstorming what successful learners do with the task of interest. We next try to sequence and group that knowledge into a manageable series of steps. We follow that by selecting words to describe the steps that can be used to create an acronym for the steps in the strategy. Figure 8.8 provides an example of teachers' use of this process to create a strategy for helping students write answers to essay questions.

How Do I Teach a Strategy? To apply a cognitive strategy effectively, students need to acquire considerable knowledge about their strategies. For example, they need to learn how to execute a strategy, when and why to use a strategy, how to coordinate different strategies, and how to monitor their use of a strategy (Snyder & Pressley, 1995; Wood et al., 1995). Both explicit strategy instruction models and collaborative and interactive models of strategy instruction such as reciprocal teaching are designed to help students acquire the necessary knowledge for effective strategy use.

Explicit-strategy instruction involves the direct explanation and modeling of cognitive strategies, and the opportunity for students to receive coaching and guided practice with the strategy (Bos & Vaughn, 2002; Deshler, Ellis, & Lenz, 1996; Lambert, 2000; Pressley, Goodchild, Fleet, Zajchowski, & Evans, 1989; Rafoth, Leal, &

FIGURE 8.8 Creating a Cognitive Strategy

To create a cognitive strategy, you can begin by analyzing the learning task in terms of what successful learners do. You could accomplish this with a series of questions.

1. **What is the task of interest?**
   Students are having difficulty writing an essay test. They know the material, but fail to communicate effectively when they answer the essay questions. The goal is to create an information-processing analysis for answering essay questions effectively.

2. **What do good learners do with a task like this?**
   The task for this example is to brainstorm a list of techniques learners use to answer essay questions effectively.

   They read the question carefully and underline what they are to do.

   They overview the test and think about which questions to answer first.

   They create a time schedule for taking the test. For example, if the questions are equally weighted and there are four of them, take allotted time and divide it into fourths.

   They write down key ideas they want to address or if time allows they outline.

   They make sure that they answer the question that has been asked.

   They proofread their answers if time allows.

3. **Order the techniques into a logical sequence and, if possible, combine some techniques into a single step.**

   Planning
   Overview the questions
   Select the order in which they will be written
   Create a time schedule

   Read
   Read for what the question is asking

   Outline
   Write down key words
   Outline if time allows

   Write
   Keep the question in mind
   Make sure to touch on key ideas that have been listed

   Look over
   Proofread and correct
   Did I answer the question?

4. Create an acronym to help students remember the steps (PROWL).

Cultural and language differences need to be considered in terms of impact on transfer. Teachers should always take their students' prior knowledge into account when planning and delivering instruction, and teachers may do this intuitively when working with students who are similar to them. However, when working with learners with backgrounds different from their own, teachers should not assume that their examples and analogies will be useful (Nashon, 2003). Teachers must become good observers to gain insights into the way their students are thinking and use these insights in reflecting on and planning instruction.

Language has also been linked to learners' ability to transfer. Bernardo (1998) reports a language compatibility effect, whereby bilingual problem solvers had difficulty transferring information learned in one language to transfer problems presented in a different language. Following a series of studies, he concluded that although the learners were able to learn equally well in both languages, they had difficulty when they tried to transfer what they had learned in one language to the other. Bernardo explained these findings by suggesting that knowledge learned in one language may be difficult to access for problems presented in a second language.

● **What concepts from the study of transfer may be used to explain differences in what learners from different cultures learn from the same classroom activity? (For your authors' perspective on this question, go to the text website for this chapter.)**

Defabo, 1993; Roehler & Duffy, 1984; Snyder & Pressley, 1995). In general, explicit strategy instruction involves the following components.

- The teacher describes the strategy and models its use for students.
- The teacher informs students of when and why to use the strategy.
- Students are provided with guided practice and coaching as they apply the strategy.
- Students are asked to reflect on the use of the strategy, which might involve assessing the effectiveness of the strategy or considering how to modify the strategy for future use.
- Students are provided with independent practice opportunities.

When implementing these components, you should also consider the following factors that influence strategy learning. First, it takes considerable experience with a strategy for students to become adept at applying that strategy (Duffy & Roehler, 1989). Consequently, it may be better to acquaint students thoroughly with a finite number of strategies than to provide cursory experiences with a large number of strategies (Snyder & Pressley, 1995). For example, a team of secondary teachers could identify three or four strategies that will be taught in all their different classes. Students will get extended exposure to the strategies in different contexts, which should also facilitate transfer.

Second, learning cognitive strategies can pose significant cognitive load, especially when the strategy is new or unfamiliar (Perkins, Simmons, & Tishman, 1990). You

What factors should you consider when teaching a strategy to your students?

can manage this load by providing students with retrieval cues such as a list of the steps in the strategy or a mnemonic that cues the steps in the process. Also, only a small number of strategies should be introduced at one time. Finally, you could introduce strategies with previously learned content or familiar problems so that students can focus on the strategy rather than the newness of the content or problem. Introducing a cognitive strategy with previously learned content also provides an opportunity for distributed practice, and an opportunity for students to compare their success with and without the strategy.

Reciprocal teaching is an approach for teaching students cognitive strategies through a collaborative and interactive learning structure (Palincsar & Brown, 1984; Palincsar & Herrenkohl, 2002). Reciprocal teaching and other interactive structures

Maly Nuth

8.2

At today's meeting we reviewed the list of vocabulary, phrases, exercises, and assessment formats used across grade levels. The list seems to be complete, but we want to send it around to all the teachers who teach arithmetic or mathematics to see if we've missed anything.

Mrs. Chow, the middle-school mathematics teacher, expressed her concern that while this sort of standardization is helpful, it might give us a false sense of security. Mrs. Chow noted that the children really needed to develop a meaningful understanding of the concepts they were learning if they were to be able to use concepts outside of the classroom. Mrs. Chow suggested that we should discuss techniques that might help our students develop more meaningful understanding of what we are teaching.

We then began to discuss various techniques and strategies we have employed to help our students increase the meaningfulness of what they are learning. As this discussion proceeded, it became clear that we were really discussing techniques or study strategies that the students could employ themselves to increase their own learning efficiency.

As our discussion continued, it became apparent that note taking was the most commonly listed learning strategy at the secondary level, but few teachers at either the ele-

mentary or secondary level spent any time providing explicit instruction on how to take notes. Several of the committee members stated that they have seen a variety of note-taking systems used by our students. Everything from word-by-word transcription to well-developed outlining techniques. After some discussion we decided that our students would benefit from learning a standard outline form of note taking as early as it was feasible. In addition, the committee recommended that teachers demonstrate the outlining technique by using the technique with lectures, discussions, and other instructional activities for which it may be practical to do so. The committee also recommended that teachers create the outlines as the lesson progresses, rather than presenting overheads or handouts of outlines prepared in advance, in order to provide an model of how outlines are developed.

● **From the perspective of information-processing theory, how might learning strategies such as note taking increase the meaningfulness of what students learn?**

Decision Point: Learning how to learn is an important instructional objective. How will you help your students reach this goal?

such as Transactional Strategies Instruction (Brown, El-Dinary, Pressley, & Coy-Ogan, 1995) and Collaborative Strategic Learning (Bos & Vaughn, 2002; Vaughn & Klinger, 1999) allow students to gain the meaning of written text through their interactions with other class members, including the teacher.

In the case of reciprocal teaching, students are engaged in a discussion of the meaning of a text that is structured around the use of these four comprehension strategies: prediction, clarification, questioning, and summarization (Palincsar & Herrenkohl, 2002). At first, the teacher leads a discussion of a piece of text everyone has read and models and explains the comprehension strategies. The teacher would also explicitly tell students where and when these strategies will be useful (Pressley & Wharton-McDonald, 1997). Next, students take turns leading a discussion on subsequent text segments, while the teacher provides guidance and scaffolding as students apply the strategies. Eventually, control is transferred to the students and they lead the groups on their own. Reciprocal teaching gradually transfers control of the reading process to the students (Slater & Horstman, 2002). As such, it represents an example of Vygotsky's idea of internalization that was described in Chapter 5, because social interactions involving strategies eventually become internalized as cognitive strategies for the individual student.

Research on reciprocal teaching has generally supported it as an effective instructional approach for improving students' text comprehension (Palincsar & Brown, 1984; Rosenshine & Meister, 1994). Some data suggest, however, that the effectiveness of reciprocal teaching can be improved by explicitly preteaching the strategies before engaging students in the reciprocal teaching experiences (Rosenshine & Meister, 1994).

Social Cognitive Theory and Teaching for Transfer

Chapter 4 presented Bandura's social cognitive learning theory. The principles, concepts, and strategies that have developed out of social cognitive theory provide important additional perspectives on how students learn and transfer strategies to self-regulate their learning.

Principle 4.1: Learners Acquire Important Knowledge, Behaviors, and Dispositions through Their Exposure to Models

Both social cognitive theory and information-processing theory provide support for teaching students transferable cognitive strategies. As mentioned in previous sections, having access to successful models of those strategies is an important component of different approaches to strategy instruction (Lapan, Kardach, & Turner, 2002; Snyder & Pressley, 1995). Because cognitive strategies are mental processes, the type of modeling that is well matched to strategy instruction is cognitive modeling. Teachers would implement cognitive modeling by talking aloud as they execute a strategy (Oster, 2001). They might also include statements that help students focus their attention on important information about the strategy by alerting students to common mistakes in implementing a strategy.

Principle 4.2: Learners' Self-Belief Systems Guide Their Learning and Behavior

Students' self-beliefs influence their motivation to perform, to learn cognitive strategies, and to transfer or apply what they have learned (Pressley et al., 1989). From a social cognitive perspective, self-efficacy is an extremely important self-belief. As you remember from Chapter 4, self-efficacy is students' beliefs about the likelihood of success with effort. Self-efficacy and cognitive strategy instruction mutually influence each other. First, successful strategy instruction can help students develop more positive self-beliefs (Casteel, Isom, & Jordan, 2000). If strategies lead to successful performance, then students' self-efficacy for those tasks may be enhanced.

Also, students' willingness to learn and apply cognitive strategies is influenced by their self-efficacy. For example, self-efficacy beliefs affect students' willingness to use effective learning strategies and to discard faulty strategies that aren't working (Schunk, 1996; Zimmerman & Martinez-Pons, 1990). Also, self-efficacy can affect students' attributions for success (Bandura, 1993). In turn, students' attributions can impact on their willingness to be strategic. Students with high self-efficacy are more likely to attribute lack of success to insufficient effort, and cognitive strategies are likely to be seen as useful for improving effort. If self-efficacy is extremely low, students may not see the value in adjusting their effort because they may believe they lack the ability to succeed. The implication is that students should develop the belief that if they use a more effective strategy, they can be successful (Alderman, 1990; Protheroe, 2002a, 2002b). This means that teachers need to help students identify effective strategies and reinforce students for using those strategies effectively.

Principle 4.3: Learners Have the Potential to Self-Regulate Their Own Learning Processes

From a social cognitive perspective, students self-regulate by establishing goals for their performance and by engaging in self-regulatory behaviors such as monitoring and evaluating their performance. One source of the difference between successful and less successful learners is the ability to self-regulate (Biemiller & Meichenbaum, 1998; Protheroe, 2002a, 2002b; Zimmerman, 2000). In order for students to transfer strategies appropriately, they need to identify the goal for an activity, select the appropriate strategy, and monitor their progress toward meeting their goal. In other words, they need instruction on how to self-regulate the use of that strategy (Belmont, Ferretti, & Mitchell, 1982). Teachers can describe when and why a strategy can be used, provide students with ways of monitoring their progress, and allow students to reflect on their strategy use through classroom discussions or journals.

Learners can acquire learning strategies and dispositions by observing their teachers.

Constructivism Applied to Transfer

Both constructivists and information-processing theorists would agree that knowledge is more likely to be transferred if that knowledge has been learned meaningfully. The constructivists, however, offer somewhat different suggestions for how to facilitate the meaningful learning of knowledge for the purposes of transfer. Their ideas can be organized around theoretical principles developed in Chapter 5.

Principle 5.1: Learning Is More Powerful If Learners Actively Construct Their Own Understandings

From a constructivist perspective, learning is more meaningful if students invent or discover key relationships or principles for themselves, rather than having principles or relationships explained to them by someone else. According to constructivists, invented knowledge is personally meaningful, more memorable, and more easily transferred to novel situations (Cobb, 1999; Gesi & Massaro, 1992; Ward, 2001). Research findings on the effectiveness of inductive learning methods for producing meaningful learning and transfer provide a somewhat mixed picture (De Jong & van Joolingen, 1998; Gesi & Massaro, 1992; Land, 2000; Solter & Mayer, 1978). However, it is possible to conclude that when discovery learning is done well, it can produce the type of meaningful understanding that leads to transfer. There are, however, a number of factors that influence the success of discovery learning.

First, all forms of discovery learning are not equally effective in producing meaningful understanding and transfer. In general, guided discovery methods tend to be more effective than open or free discovery methods (Kittel, 1957; Mayer & Wittrock, 1996). Students may fail to discover the intended relationships and principles without guidance and support.

Second, students' prior knowledge clearly affects what they will learn from instruction (Dochy, Segers, & Buehl, 1999). Constructivists seem to acknowledge this when they suggest that students can better understand the concepts they are learning if they connect them to previously constructed knowledge (Ward, 2001). However, it has also been suggested that the perils of having students construct their own knowledge are as apparent as the advantages (Cobb, 1999). In particular, students may construct misconceptions that can be difficult to change. In the case of transfer, these misconceptions could make it difficult to transfer knowledge when appropriate and possibly even result in negative transfer. The construction of knowledge by students needs to be supervised carefully because of these potentials.

Students can also differ in terms of the skills required to construct knowledge successfully (De Jong & van Joolingen, 1998; Kuhn, Black, Keselman, & Kaplan, 2000). In the area of science discovery learning, for example, students could differ in terms of how skillfully they can manage and execute key components of discovery such as formulating hypotheses, designing experiments that provide tests of hypotheses, and interpreting data generated from these experiments.

The prior knowledge and prerequisite skills issues may be more pronounced for some populations of students than for others. For example, Mastropieri and Scruggs (1997) found that students with mild disabilities were less likely to reach a correct induction during a guided inquiry lesson than were their peers without disabilities. Teachers may find it helpful to teach key concepts, skills, and necessary terms that are necessary for successful discovery (Gersten & Baker, 1998).

The general implication is that learners may vary in their ability to learn meaningfully from discovery learning lessons and consequently to transfer what they have learned. Teachers may adapt to these differences in a number of ways including providing more explicit guidance or support during discovery or by combining teacher-directed and discovery lessons together.

Principle 5.3: Students' Knowledge Construction Is Assisted by the Nature of Their Interactions with People and Objects in Their Environments

Developmental and constructivist theoreticians have added another important dimension to our understanding of transfer. They point out that context is an important factor that influences quality of learning and consequently students' ability to transfer what they have learned. When constructivists talk about context, they are discussing a social context that is defined by participation in particular social practices (Cobb & Bowers, 1999). For example, a research team is defined by certain social roles and practices. The importance of social context figures prominently in the idea of situated cognition, which was first introduced in Chapter 5.

Situated Cognition.   Situated cognition exists in different forms and is described by different terms such as situated learning, cognitive apprenticeships, and legitimate peripheral participation (Hendricks, 2001). Its relevant definitions, benefits, and issues continue to be debated (Anderson, Reder, & Simon, 1996, 1997; Cobb & Bowers, 1999; Greeno, 1997). However, some frequently mentioned elements of situated cognition should be reviewed before discussing transfer of learning from this perspective.

First, researchers who work from a situated cognition perspective suggest that it is useful to think of knowledge as being analogous to the tools people use to solve problems and make things (Brown, Collins, & Duguid, 1989). Knowledge and tools have three characteristics in common:

- Both tools and knowledge can only be completely understood when they are used in a meaningful way.
- Using a particular tool or bit of knowledge changes the way a person understands a problem or situation.
- The specific uses for tools or knowledge are embedded within cultural contexts.

This implies that knowledge cannot be separated from the context in which that knowledge is acquired and applied. From a situated cognition perspective, formal schooling can be criticized for failing to recognize this by trying to teach knowledge outside of its context. From a situated cognition perspective, teaching knowledge out of context leads to incomplete and underdeveloped understanding of that knowledge (Choi & Hannafin, 1997).

Looking in on

Keith Randich

8.1

For this first meeting, we decided to review the survey results of those graduates who went directly into the workforce or into vocational-technical training. This represented about 50 percent of those surveyed. About half of this group went straight into the workforce, finding work in local retail business and the construction trades or clerical or service-industry positions in the city. The other half of this group typically enrolled in a two-year program at the local community college before going to work. Each of the committee members had reviewed this batch of surveys the week before, and our goal was to discuss and summarize what we had found.

Martha Bowman began by noting that she was somewhat surprised by this group's responses. She had expected that those graduates who went to clerical positions would have found the computer training they received at JAHS to be one of the more applicable parts of the curriculum. Instead this group listed accounting, general mathematics, and English (especially letter writing and grammar) as being most helpful. She discussed this with one of her former students who was visiting home and was informed that the computers and software they found at their new jobs were more up-to-date than what they had worked with at school, and that while the keyboarding skills and general information about how computers worked was useful, most people had to learn software capabilities and commands from scratch. In some cases, the old habits they developed when working with the school computers actually got in the way of learning the new systems.

Clara Alport thought there might be more to this than just obsolete computers and software. She noted that many of the surveys had comments that made reference to specific examples and activities that they had completed in their classes at JAHS. A common statement began with the phrase, "It was just like that project . . ." or "It was just like those exercises. . . ." Reflecting on her own instructional activities, she noted that she had put a great deal of emphasis on writing and grammar, but because of her students' interests she frequently had them practice these skills in the context of writing a letter. When she looked back at the surveys, she noted that many of the students had noted that their writing skills help with some type of letter-writing activity.

The question was raised as to whether the kind of examples we used were appropriate given the kinds of things our students were doing after graduation. We agreed to review the surveys again with this in mind.

● **How does the concept of situated learning explain observations made by Clara Alport?**

> **Decision Point:** How can you plan class projects that contribute to your students' ability to transfer what they've learned to situations outside of the classroom?

In a situated cognition approach learning occurs through enculturation (Hendricks, 2001). Enculturation is the process of acquiring knowledge of participation structures for a social context through prolonged activity within that context. For example, you will learn the structure of participation for a given classroom setting when you student teach in that setting. Such enculturation is most likely to occur when learners act as apprentices to more skilled learners as they collaborate on authentic or real-world tasks (Brown, Collins, & Duguid, 1989; Griffin, 1995; Hendricks, 2001). To achieve this goal, Campione, Shapiro, and Brown (1995), suggest that classrooms should be designed so that:

- Students are encouraged to engage in metacognition by making them aware of the potential to use what they learn in a wide variety of situations.
- The social context of learning is emphasized by encouraging discourse with teachers, outside experts, and among the learners themselves.
- Learners explain what they are learning to others.
- Topics and materials provide opportunities for extended analysis, and instruction occurs in authentic contexts.

Situated Cognition and Transfer. Somewhat distinct perspectives on transfer can be associated with situated cognition (DeCorte, 1999). One possible perspective that is attributed to situated cognition is that skills cannot transfer because they cannot be separated from their context of use. This perspective has been critiqued on the grounds of both research and anecdotal evidence to the contrary. Multiple examples exist of knowledge being transferred outside of the situation in which it was acquired (Anderson, Reder, & Simon, 1997; Moore, 1998).

A second perspective on transfer is that situating learning in context enhances the possibility of teaching students transferable cognitive strategies and skills (Hendricks, 2001). From this perspective, it would be argued that because students are actively learning by doing and because the classroom imitates real-world application settings, transfer of the learned strategies or skills to real-world settings is more likely. However, one of the concerns with situating the learning of skills and strategies in a particular context is that the learning may become too closely associated with that context. The potential problem is that if the learning is overly contextualized, learners may fail to transfer that learning to relevant but somewhat dissimilar contexts (Bransford, Brown, & Cocking, 2000; Griffin, 1995). If strategies are associated with the solution of a particular problem in a particular setting, they may not transfer to different settings or to related but different problems. One of the ways to address this issue is to vary the problem contexts used to introduce strategies to students so that they can see how these strategies can transfer.

A third perspective is that situating cognition allows students to understand the structures of participation for a particular social context that may transfer to other contexts (Greeno, 1997; Greeno, Moore, & Smith, 1993). For example, students may acquire understandings of the routines of collaborative work or how information is accessed during collaborative scientific research. As a result, students learn to be more successful participants in that context. These understandings would transfer to the extent that they are generally applicable to other contexts, or to the extent that they can be modified successfully for other contexts (Greeno, 1997).

How do proponents of situated cognition view transfer?

Both the goal of teaching transferable learning strategies and patterns of participation are present in the design of the communities of learners model, which is an example of both situated and distributed cognition. It provides a reasonable example of how transfer might be addressed from this perspective.

Communities of Learners and Transfer. A community of learners is defined by a distribution of expertise among the community members (Brown & Campione, 1994). In other words, no one member of a group has all the knowledge and skills necessary to reach the group's objectives. Learners and teachers must also acquire the necessary participation activities and structures to collaborate as problem solvers. Additionally, another purpose for situating and distributing cognition in this model is to help students acquire transferable learning-how-to-learn strategies.

The community of learners model has a number of participation structures that define its social context (Brown & Campione, 1994). First, the learners must feel and act on a sense of responsibility to the others in the class. Since no one person in the community has all of the expertise, each member of the community must be responsible to the other members, and share his or her expertise in collaborative learning activities. Second, there must be activities that encourage productive interaction among community members. Finally, the members of the community of learners must engage in constructive discussion. The members must be willing to make statements, ask questions, and make critical comments to further the learning experiences of the group. The implied transfer goal is that these ways of participating are useful in any collaborative research community.

The participation structures listed previously are regularized to allow the community members to become familiar and comfortable with the activities and thereby further facilitate their participation (Brown & Campione, 1994; Campione, Shapiro, & Brown, 1995). This is accomplished through the incorporation of four characteristics that distinguish the communities of learners' classroom: (a) the use of

reciprocal teaching, (b) use of authentic tasks, (c) cooperative learning and production activities, and (d) use of benchmark lessons. Support for these components comes from the theories presented in Chapters 3 through 5.

As mentioned earlier in this chapter, reciprocal teaching is a method for helping students acquire reading comprehension strategies. This instructional approach is consistent with Principle 4.1, learners acquire important knowledge, behaviors, and dispositions through their exposure to models, and Principle 5.3, students' knowledge construction is assisted by the nature of their interactions with people and objects in their environment. In a community of learners, students need transferable reading strategies to allow them to research topics independently. In this sense, the community of learners addresses the teaching of transferable strategies.

The idea of authentic tasks is found in Chapter 5 and comes from the constructivist perspective. In authentic learning activities, learners learn new material by participating in activities that are as close as possible to the real-world activities in which the material would be used. This approach is supported by Principle 5.1, learning is more powerful if learners actively construct their own understandings.

Cooperative learning and production activities are designed so that learners are dependent on one another for the accomplishment of their goals. The community of learners model relies on the jigsaw method, a cooperative learning technique discussed in Chapter 7. Each learner researches and develops expertise in some aspect of a topic being learned and is responsible for explaining what they've learned to the other members of their group. Cooperative production tasks are group activities that focus on producing something, a report, a paper, or some other artifact. The jigsaw approach to instruction is supported by Principle 5.3, students' knowledge construction is assisted by the nature of their interactions with people and objects in their environment.

A benchmark lesson is an activity in which the teacher or some outside expert introduces a new topic or idea. The introduction of new information via an organized presentation of an expert provides the learners with a framework within which to organize their subsequent experiences. This approach is consistent with Principle 3.1, meaningful learning occurs when new knowledge is connected to existing knowledge.

Looking in on

The final group of survey results that we analyzed were from those graduates who went on to a four-year program at a college or university. Once again, we found that many of the responses mentioned the value of mathematics and English. In addition, these students also noted that their preparation in specific subject areas related to their majors in college was helpful. However, the committee noted a third trend in this group. Many of these students credited various classes and teachers with instilling in them habits that helped them make it through freshman year. The responses from this group of graduates credited specific classes with helping them develop skills and confidence to be successful students. The committee found several themes that indicated the common characteristics of these classes.

Classes that were cited as providing the critical disposition to get through college were frequently described as incorporating real-world problems and issues. These classes were also described as instilling a sense of responsibility and obligation to the other students in the class, often through the use of cooperative projects and activities. Finally, these classes were described as providing a safe environment to express and critically analyze ideas.

Looking at the curriculum for JAHS and the classes available, it seemed that these opportunities were most often available in upper level courses in science, social studies, and history classes. Only a few exceptions to this observation were noted, and we discussed how the qualities noted in the responses of the graduates might be incorporated more broadly across the curriculum.

● **How are the characteristics of communities of learners expressed in the comments noted by the committee?**

Decision Point: What factors might you want to consider if you wish to incorporate techniques to develop academic dispositions into your classroom?

Motivation and Transfer

Commitment and motivation are required by students to learn something well enough to transfer it. Also, learners need to be motivated to apply what they have learned for transfer to occur. Consequently, it is appropriate to think about how motivational principles might be useful for creating those types and levels of motivation in students (Yamnil & McLean, 2001). It is also possible, however, to consider how activities designed to promote learning for transfer might enhance students' motivation to learn. For example, the types of problem-solving and thinking activities that are associated with far and general transfer could possibly increase students' engagement in the learning processes. The principles developed in Chapter 6 provide a useful context for discussing these motivational issues.

Principle 6.1: Learners Are More Motivated When They Believe Their Actions Will Result in Successfully Completing Challenging Tasks

One of the major implications of this principle is that students are motivated by succeeding at moderately challenging tasks and by attributing that success to their ability and effort (Pintrich & Schunk, 2002). It is good to remember that students may find requests to transfer what they have learned extremely challenging. Teachers should make sure that they provide sufficient guidance and scaffolding to make transfer obtainable with appropriate effort. For example, transfer often requires a meaningful understanding of what has been learned. You need to schedule sufficient time for this to occur, and your choice of learning activities needs to engage students in meaningful processing of information. Also, providing students with guidance about when they will use what they have learned may make it more likely that they will successfully transfer that knowledge.

Students' motivation to apply a strategy depends in part on their belief or expectancy that the strategy will be effective. To help students develop this awareness, Snyder and Pressley (1995) suggest that learners be taught and encouraged to monitor their performance generally and while applying learning strategies. In addition, teachers need to encourage students to make appropriate attributions by pointing out that effective academic performances are the result of the correct selection and performance of learning strategies. Also, you could reinforce students for the strategic transfer of prior learning (Alexander & Murphy, 1999). When students apply prior learning in effective ways, you may want to tell them what they did well.

Principle 6.2: Learners Are More Motivated by Activities That Appeal to Their Personal Needs, Motives, and Interests

Students' interest in what they are learning is related to their willingness to engage in meaningful learning activities (Pintrich & Schunk, 2002; Schiefele, 1991). This is important because the active, meaningful learning often required as a prerequisite for transfer can be extremely demanding and requires a commitment on the part of the student. However, some attempts to create situational interest in a learning task may actually undermine students' ability to learn for transfer. For example, the term **seductive details** is used to describe details that are added to a text to increase interest, but that are not related to the intended meaning of the text. These types of details have been found to have an adverse effect not only on learning but on transfer (Harp & Mayer, 1997, 1998; Mayer, Hieser, & Lonn, 2001). The seductive details may cause students to impose an inappropriate theme or schema onto the text. The interest that teachers generate in a learning task should be tied to the important ideas or meaning of what is being learned.

In terms of task value, teaching for transfer can help teachers establish the utility value for their lessons. Utility value is the usefulness of learning for students' future goals (Wigfield & Eccles, 1992). As mentioned earlier, teachers should include clear guidance about where knowledge can be used to increase the likelihood of transfer. By helping students learn how knowledge can be applied both in and out of school, teachers are demonstrating utility value for the learning.

Principle 6.3: Learners Are More Motivated When They Have Specific Near-Term Goals That They Believe Are Important

Goals are important for student learning because they help students envision desired outcomes, and they help them monitor their progress toward those outcomes. If the goal is to have students apply what they have learned, then that needs to be made explicit to students so that they can learn in ways that are best matched to those outcomes. Helping students know when and where a strategy can be used can help them understand what the goal is for learning the strategy.

What is the relationship between motivation and transfer?

General Suggestions for Teaching for Transfer

This chapter has presented various theoretical perspectives on transfer and application of those perspectives into instructional techniques and strategies. While each theory presents an unique perspective on the nature of transfer, a number of themes seems to cut across theoretical boundaries. Keeping these general themes in mind as you plan and execute instruction will enhance your students' ability to transfer what they learn in your class in appropriate and useful ways.

- When possible, have students practice skills in the way they will need to use them. For example, have students practice decoding skills as they are reading for meaning.
- When teaching for transfer, provide students with multiple examples of how a concept or skill applies in varying contexts For example, talk to your teaching colleagues and identify skills or strategies that can be used in different content areas. All of the involved teachers should introduce those skills or strategies in their content area.
- Help students understand when and why they can apply what they are learning. For example, provide students specific guidance about when they should and when they should not use a cognitive strategy.
- Make sure students understand knowledge at a deep conceptual level. Use the ideas discussed in this and previous chapters for encouraging meaningful processing of knowledge. Limit the use of rote learning approaches.
- Distribute practice or learning experiences across time. For example, revisit knowledge you introduced earlier in the year, and if possible vary the practice context. Give students multiple opportunities to learn key knowledge.

Principles into Practice:
Illustrating Key Concepts

In this chapter you looked in on Maly Nuth and Keith Randich as they considered various issues related to the topic of transfer. In each instance, you were asked to answer a question related to the particular situation that they faced. This section presents the authors' perspectives on these questions.

Looking back on

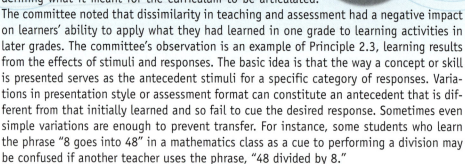

Maly Nuth

The first time you looked in on Maly Nuth, she had just convened a committee that was to consider ways to articulate the curriculum across grade levels and buildings. The first task of the committee was to clarify their job by defining what it meant for the curriculum to be articulated.
The committee noted that dissimilarity in teaching and assessment had a negative impact on learners' ability to apply what they had learned in one grade to learning activities in later grades. The committee's observation is an example of Principle 2.3, learning results from the effects of stimuli and responses. The basic idea is that the way a concept or skill is presented serves as the antecedent stimuli for a specific category of responses. Variations in presentation style or assessment format can constitute an antecedent that is different from that initially learned and so fail to cue the desired response. Sometimes even simple variations are enough to prevent transfer. For instance, some students who learn the phrase "8 goes into 48" in a mathematics class as a cue to performing a division may be confused if another teacher uses the phrase, "48 divided by 8."

The key to avoiding this state of affairs is to provide learners with an appropriate variety of examples of the types of situations in which concepts or skills might be usefully applied. Remember, an appropriate set of examples helps learners distinguish those characteristics of a concept that are relevant from those that are irrelevant. In mathematics students may easily focus on the form of presentation, such as addition and subtraction problems always presented in a vertical format, and come to consider this as a relevant characteristic of the addition and subtraction process. To counteract this, learners must be provided examples that display all of the ways a concept may vary and still be considered the same concept. By providing this type of variety during instruction we improve the chances that our students will focus on the appropriate dimensions of similarity and not be distracted by irrelevant similarities or differences.

When you next looked at Maly's committee, Mrs. Chow expressed concern that the children were not learning concepts in a meaningful way, and that this might be due to the failure of the learners to apply effective learning strategies, including note taking. This observation is related to several of the principles from cognitive learning theory. Principle 3.1, meaningful learning occurs when new knowledge is connected to existing knowledge. The purpose of many instructional and learning strategies such as derived structural schema or analogies is to help learners make meaningful connections among the concepts they are learning and with information they already have learned. Principle 3.3, the limitations of students' working memory must be accounted for in instruction, is especially relevant to note-taking strategies. Notes serve as an external memory that allows students to take time to actually encode conceptual information later, rather than at the time it is presented. Students who do not know how to take notes, or who have not developed the skill sufficiently must encode any material as it is presented and run the risk of overloading their working memory. Finally an extension of Principle 3.4, learning is an active and goal-directed process, is that by teaching students to employ appropriate learning techniques teachers can help them take control of and direct their own learning. ●

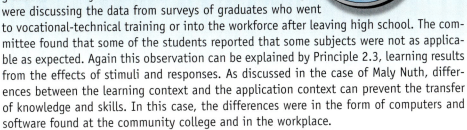

Looking back on
Keith Randich

Keith Randich is the chairman of a committee that is looking for ways to improve the programs at their high school by evaluating survey data collected from recent graduates. When you first looked in on this committee they were discussing the data from surveys of graduates who went to vocational-technical training or into the workforce after leaving high school. The committee found that some of the students reported that some subjects were not as applicable as expected. Again this observation can be explained by Principle 2.3, learning results from the effects of stimuli and responses. As discussed in the case of Maly Nuth, differences between the learning context and the application context can prevent the transfer of knowledge and skills. In this case, the differences were in the form of computers and software found at the community college and in the workplace.

The committee proposed an explanation for the survey results that was consistent with Principle 5.3, students' knowledge construction is assisted by the nature of their interactions with people and objects in their environment. This principle is at the heart of situated learning approaches. The hypothesis seemed to be confirmed by one of the committee members' observation that students reported that many tasks at the community college or on the job reminded them of specific projects and activities in which they had participated at high school.

When the committee looked at their former students who went on to college, they found that the reports from these graduates seemed to be different compared with those who went into the workforce. The college students reported that what was most helpful to them were habits or dispositions toward academics that they had developed while in high school. While the outcome seems to be different it also can be explained by Principle 5.3. Dispositions such as those reported by the college students may be most effectively developed by the establishment of a community of learners that encourages and supports the development of these types of general dispositions. ●

Teachers as Decision Makers

As you read through the chapter, you participated in the decision making of the teachers presented in the opening vignettes and cases. This section presents the authors' perspective on these decision points.

Maly Nuth's Decision Points

The goal of Maly Nuth's committee, to articulate the district curriculum across grade levels, can be seen as optimizing students' ability to transfer what they learn in one grade to their learning in later grades. You were to consider how information about your students' previous school experiences or the requirements they would face later in school would aid your own classroom decision making. Knowledge of your students' past experience and needs allows you to make better decisions when selecting instructional objectives and planning learning activities. Learning as a process depends to a large extent on students' ability to transfer. Learning new concepts is aided when students can make connections between the new concept and concepts they've previously learned. Learning a new skill is easier if it incorporates skills that have already been mastered. Given this, knowing what concepts and skills your students have already mastered will allow you to make better decisions about what objectives your students are ready for, to select effective examples, and guide your students' recognition of relevant relationships.

Likewise, knowing what your students will need to accomplish in the future is also a valuable guide to the selection objectives and planning of learning activities. When selecting among potential instructional objectives, the contribution that the concept or skill will make to future learning should be considered. Students also need to learn those skills associated with specific instructional activities and assessment techniques. Introducing your students to the types of activities they will face in the future will enhance their participation in those activities in the future.

You are next asked to consider the importance of learning how to learn. Academic skills such as note taking, preparing flash cards, and the use of mnemonics have been found to enhance learning. Unfortunately, these skills may not be taught in an explicit manner. Teaching your students how and when to apply these techniques can enhance their learning throughout their academic careers.

Providing students with these skills may be accomplished in a variety of ways. Learning strategies and techniques may be directly taught, demonstrations of techniques can be incorporated into lessons, or a combination of direct instruction and demonstrations can be used. In either case you must also provide your students with opportunities to practice the techniques and strategies. Practice allows the learner to proceduralize some of the skills involved in the techniques and strategies and also serves as an important motivation function by allowing the learners to develop confidence or self-efficacy with academic tasks.

Motivation is a key aspect of transfer. Applying learning strategies and techniques often requires the learner to expend significant amounts of effort, especially when they are first learning and have not proceduralized the necessary skills. You must establish an environment in which learners feel that their skills are up to the task and their efforts will result in success. You must carefully select exercises that provide an appropriate level of challenge and when necessary provide your students with instructional and emotional support. Your learners must also learn how to respond to failure. The example you provide when faced with a difficult task or even failure can be a critical influence on how your students respond to adversity.

Keith Randich's Decision Points

When you were introduced to Keith Randich he was reflecting on how information from students who had graduated from his school might be used to improve the school's programs. You were asked to consider how your decision making in the classroom might take into account the variety of futures faced by your students. Accounting for the variety of learner needs is always difficult, and there is no single correct way to do this. To answer this question you must speculate about those situations in which learners will find what you are teaching useful. To ensure that your speculations are as accurate as possible, you must find out about your students and the kind of futures they imagine for themselves, and combine that knowledge with your knowledge of academic content and with what you know about your students' community and the world in general.

When you first looked in on Keith the committee was examining the effect of class projects and exercises on students' ability to transfer what they've learned. You were asked that you consider how answering this question might affect instructional decisions you make. Class projects and exercises can provide an important bridge between the classroom and the outside world. Such activities allow learners to apply the concepts and skills they learn in an environment that simulates, as nearly as possible, the complexity of the real world. The skills developed in working with and adapting to these complex tasks may make transfer more likely. However, teachers must be careful to avoid introducing too much complexity before learners are ready. When a concept or skill is first learned, learners tend to focus on the surface attributes of the situation and are unlikely to understand the important relationships. At this stage learners' susceptibility to misconception is increased by too much complexity, and misconceptions can result in negative transfer in future situations.

In the final opportunity to look in on Keith Randich, you considered what you might do to help students in your class develop dispositions that help them in future academic activities. Dispositions have to do with the general goals that students will be motivated to achieve in a variety of situations. The development of such dispositions is likely the result of observing these dispositions and practicing them over a relatively long period of time in many situations. Supporting the development of such dispositions is likely to be influenced by the combined efforts and support of many people including teachers, school administrators, parents, and other students.

Name _____ Date _____

Chapter 8 Study Guide

Use this study guide to review and test your knowledge of key concepts introduced in this chapter and to search out further information on issues and topics raised in this chapter.

 ## Key Terms

Review the following key words from the chapter and then connect to Research Navigator (www.researchnavigator.com) either directly or through this book's Companion Website to explore research on the topics as they relate to education today.

Algorithm (p. 261)	Cognitive context (p. 260)	Far transfer (p. 247)
Analogical-problem construction (p. 260)	Cognitive strategy (p. 261)	Formal discipline (p. 246)
	Derived structural schema (p. 254)	General transfer (p. 246)
Case-based reasoning (p. 253)	Explicit-strategy instruction (p. 263)	Goal-free problem statements (p. 259)

Heuristic (p. 261)
High-road transfer (p. 256)
Identical elements (p. 246)
Juxtaposition (p. 249)
Low-road transfer (p. 256)
Mental discipline (p. 246)
Natural structural schema (p. 254)

Near transfer (p. 247)
Negative example (p. 249)
Negative transfer (p. 247)
Positive example (p. 249)
Positive transfer (p. 247)
Problem solving (p. 244)
Problem space (p. 244)

Reciprocal teaching (p. 264)
Seductive details (p. 273)
Specific transfer (p. 247)
Structural schema (p. 254)
Structural similarity (p. 253)

Alternative Response Items

1. A science teacher is teaching the concept of solutions by showing his students a series of positive and negative examples of solutions. For each example he performs a series of tests and provides the students with the results. Finally, he asks the students to describe the characteristics of the concept he is teaching. What type of learning is the teacher trying to encourage?

   a. Algorithmic
   b. Heuristic
   c. Inductive
   d. Deductive

2. In preparing this lesson (Refer to item 1 above) the teacher carefully selected positive examples that appeared very different, but possessed critical characteristics of solutions, and negative examples that appeared similar to the positive examples except that they lacked one critical characteristic. What concept best describes the teacher's selection of positive and negative examples?

   a. Juxtaposition
   b. Deductive learning
   c. Inductive learning
   d. Derived structural schema

3. What term refers to a *rule of thumb* or general approach to solving certain problems?

   a. Algorithm
   b. Heuristic
   c. Inductive reasoning
   d. Deductive reasoning

4. A student, who has just upgraded to the latest version of software for her word processor, keeps making mistakes because the cut and paste function have been switched to different keys. What concept best describes the student's difficulty?

   a. General transfer
   b. Near transfer
   c. Far transfer
   d. Negative transfer

5. What is the difference between a derived structural schema and a natural structural schema?

   a. Derive structural schema store information about relationships; natural structural schema do not.
   b. Natural structural schema store information about relationships; derived structural schema do not.
   c. Derived structural schema are created by experts; natural structural schema are not.
   d. Natural structural schema are created by experts; derived structural schema are not.

6. What instructional technique is designed to encourage learners to focus on developing a schema while practicing a new skill, rather than focusing on finding an answer to a problem?

   a. Inductive teaching
   b. Deductive teaching
   c. Natural structural schema
   d. Goal-free problems

7. What instructional technique is based on an apprenticeship model of learning?

   a. Reciprocal teaching
   b. Derived structural schema
   c. Goal-free problem statements
   d. Inductive learning

8. What type of transfer is most closely associated with learning algorithms?

   a. General transfer
   b. Specific transfer
   c. Far transfer
   d. Negative transfer

9. What type of transfer is most closely associated with overgeneralization?

   a. General transfer
   b. Specific transfer
   c. Far transfer
   d. Negative transfer

10. What type of transfer is most closely associated with the concept of formal discipline?

    a. General transfer
    b. Specific transfer
    c. Near transfer
    d. Negative transfer

Constructed Response Items

Short Answer/Completion Items

1. A teacher begins instruction by defining the concept that the students are to learn, and then providing the students with many positive and negative examples of the concept. What type of learning will occur?

2. A student who has mastered Spanish is able to quickly master the Latin names for the plants in her biology class. What concept from the study of transfer best explains the ease with which this student was able to learn biological terms?

3. A psychology teacher develops a list of important attributes shared by all psychological theories and uses the list to create a chart for the students to fill as they read about new theories. What term best describes the teacher's technique?

4. What learning process is most likely to result in a natural structural schema?

5. What concept from transfer might best be used to explain why a person who learns a new language later in life will always have an accent?

Essay Items

1. What is the relationship between the perception of similarity across experiences and transfer?

2. What is the difference between inductive and deductive learning?

3. Use the concepts of transfer to compare the advantages and disadvantages of learning algorithms with learning heuristics.

4. What's the relationship between analogies and derived structural schemata?

Practicing Your Decision Making

1. Consider the students you are likely to be teaching in the future: What knowledge, skills, or dispositions do you want them to transfer?

2. Given your answer to the previous question, what instructional techniques and strategies do you think will be effective?

INTASC in Action

Use the following activities to think about how motivational concepts relate to INTASC Standards.

Standard 1: Content Pedagogy. Many states have developed academic standards that serve as guidelines of the teachers of the state. These can typically be found on the web under the department of education. Find the standards for your state. Select one standard for the grade level and subject that you are likely to be teaching, and then list the knowledge and skills that would help the learners in your class master the objective. How well is your list reflected in the standards for previous grade levels?

Standard 3: Diverse Learners. Consider your own personal history. How have experiences in your family, community, and culture provided you with skills or knowledge that helped you learn? Have there been any experiences at home or in your community that made it more difficult for you to learn?

Standard 4: Multiple Instructional Strategies. Consider the objective you identified for Standard 1 in this section. What knowledge or skill is associated with the standard? List situations outside of your classroom, where this skill or knowledge will transfer.

Standard #7: Planning. Consider the objective you identified for Standard 1 and your response for Stan-

dard 4 of this section. What instructional methods would most likely help the students apply what they've learned to real-life situations?

 Web Resources

Center for the Advancement of Learning
www.muskingum.edu/~cal/database/genpurpose.html

The Learning Strategies Database offers students and instructors practical information to identify appropriate learning strategies for students and to plan effective learning activities.

The Thinking Classroom
http://learnweb.harvard.edu/alps/thinking/

This page, sponsored by Project Zero at Harvard, provides teachers with suggestions for improving student learning and thinking.

Study Strategies
www.d.umn.edu/student/loon/acad/strat/

This section of a special online student handbook created by the University of Minnesota at Duluth provides a guide for study skills and competencies that aid learning.

Utilizing Instructional Design

Standards in This Chapter

The concepts presented in this chapter will contribute to your mastery of all of the INTASC standards; however, the material presented in Chapter 9 relates most strongly to the following standards:

- **Standard 2:** Student Development
- **Standard 3:** Diverse Learners
- **Standard 4:** Multiple Instructional Strategies
- **Standard 5:** Motivation and Management
- **Standard 7:** Planning
- **Standard 9:** Reflective Practice and Professional Growth

Chapter 9 begins with a discussion of the overall nature of the instructional design process because there are certain instructional design considerations and techniques that are relevant regardless of your theoretical approach to instructional design. Then, different views of instructional design that have their basis in learning and motivation theories are presented. As in previous chapters, you will be shown how these instructional design approaches can be connected to key theoretical principles developed in earlier chapters. By the end of this chapter you should be able to do the following.

- Understand the role and nature of educational objectives,
- Understand the importance of instructional alignment and task analysis for instructional design,
- Understand the role of learner characteristics in instructional design,
- Understand the key elements of Gropper's behavioral approach to instructional design,
- Understand the key elements of Gagné's conditions of learning,
- Understand the components involved in the design of a constructivist learning environment, and
- Understand the relevance of ARCS for designing motivating instruction.

Close-ups on the Classroom

Mona Carrie and State-Mandated Testing

I'm student teaching with a wonderful third grade teacher, Karen Whitehorse, but to be honest, teaching isn't exactly what I thought it would be. I'm a little disillusioned. Almost everything seems to be about state testing and state standards. It seems that whenever I want to do something really creative, Karen and I have to figure out how to make it fit with the state standards and the state-testing program. Karen is also worried about how much time things take, because there is a lot to do in a limited amount of time. I understand her concerns, but I got into teaching to share the joy I get from great literature and art, not to prepare students for a test. Oddly enough, Karen actually feels the standards and the test may have made her a better teacher. She says her teaching is more focused, and she still can do a lot of things she and the children enjoy. We are planning the next literature unit together, and Karen says she will help me incorporate key academic standards into the unit.

We both agree that the biggest challenge is helping all our students meet the standards. For example, we have three students in the classroom who do not speak English as their first language, but the state test is given only in English. I think that's unfair, but we are one of those states with so-called English only laws. Also, a number of students in our classroom qualify for special education services. They are making progress, but I don't think the progress is happening quickly enough.

Decision Point: What environmental variables are influencing these teachers' decisions about what and how to teach?

The teachers in the opening vignettes are involved in practical issues related to the instructional design process. As a teacher, you will be involved in the instructional design process when you plan lessons, units, or instructional programs for your students or when you evaluate the design of prepackaged instructional programs. Consequently, instructional design is one more example of your role as a decision maker.

As you can tell from the opening vignettes, your instructional design decisions will be influenced by a number of variables including the nature of your students, the existence of mandated testing programs, and the values and beliefs of parents and other members of your community. Effective instructional design, therefore, requires not only the skilled use of design principles and techniques, but also your ability to consider your teaching context in making decisions.

Before proceeding with Chapter 9, be sure you read the Close-ups on the Classroom features about Mona Carrie and Marisol Hernandez. At various points in the chapter, you will revisit both teachers in their classrooms and follow their decision-making progress. Their classroom experiences are closely integrated with the key concepts of this chapter and serve as important models for understanding instructional design.

The General Nature of the Instructional Design Process

The instructional design models presented in this chapter can be placed in one of two broad categories. Instructional design models in the first category operate from the assumption that there are specific behaviors, knowledge, and beliefs that must be learned, and that there are different instructional strategies or conditions that work best for each type of knowledge and behavior (Reiser, 2001; Spector, 2000; Willis, 1998). For example, these models might specify the components of an effectively designed lesson for teaching a specific skill or concept. Both behavioral and cognitive learning theories have provided examples of these models (Gagné, 1985; Gropper, 1983; Merrill, 2001). Also, the ARCS model for applying motivation theory to instructional design fits in this category (Keller & Litchfield, 2002).

Marisol Hernandez and Problem-Based Learning

At Harding High School we endorse a constructivist view of science learning. We want our students to learn through the investigation of meaningful problems, and we want to focus on helping students discover a few key scientific principles. Consequently, we are in the middle of changing our instruction over to a problem-based learning approach. As you can expect, there have been some challenges in making this type of change.

First, the current district science curriculum includes a large number of science concepts and terms. We want to rewrite the curriculum, but we've heard that the new state standards for science are due to be released. We have decided to work with the current curriculum for now.

Another major challenge is that our students are underprepared for the types of learning experiences we want them to have. For example, a number of our students struggle with reading and even basic algebra calculations. Also, our students have only had limited experience with inquiry learning and collaborative problem solving in the elementary and middle schools. Our success is going to depend to a large extent on our ability to collaborate with other teachers in this high school and in the elementary and middle schools.

Another interesting challenge has been identifying problems for our students to research. Very often, the problems we identify have public policy and social implications. We have spent a lot of time discussing the appropriateness of certain problems in terms of cultural, community, and family standards. We don't want to avoid controversy, but we want to make sure that we are being appropriately sensitive to families and other community members. We will continue to meet as a team to resolve all of these issues. We think the efforts will be worthwhile for students.

Decision Point: What environmental variables are influencing these teachers' decisions about what and how to teach?

Instructional design models in the second category provide recommendations for structuring learning environments that support students as they solve problems and invent their own understandings. These types of models are usually associated with constructivist views of classroom learning such as problem-based learning (Jonassen, 1999).

Given the complexity of classroom learning, your authors support, as have others, an eclectic view of instructional design (Mukhopadhyay & Parhar, 2001; Reigeluth, 1997). No single model or category of instructional design will be most effective for the wide range of learning outcomes and learners in today's classrooms. For example, students who are constructing their own understanding may at times need to be directly taught a needed skill or concept that they have not learned previously. Consequently, your goal should be to acquaint yourself with a variety of instructional design approaches that can support the various types of decisions you will need to make as you design instruction.

Regardless of the approach to instructional design, the process is typically organized around these four questions (Kemp, Morrison, & Ross, 1994).

1. What do you want your students to learn?
2. What types of instructional experiences will best accomplish the objectives?
3. What types of evaluation procedures will best demonstrate whether your students have learned?
4. What are the characteristics of your learners?

Legally mandated testing is one of several contextual variables that affect instructional design decisions.

Your answer to the first question should result in the educational objectives for your instruction. The answers to the second and third questions should help you design instructional activities and assessments that are matched or aligned to your objectives. The fourth question is a reminder that learner characteristics need to be considered as you identify objectives, learning activities, and assessments.

Educational Objectives

The various theoretical approaches to instructional design share the common assumption that instructional design is a goal-directed process; instruction is designed to accomplish a purpose or intent. Therefore, developing statements of those intentions or purposes is an important component of instructional design. These statements go by a variety of names including goals, aims, intents, objectives, competencies, proformas, and learning outcomes (Cohen & Manion, 1977; Langdon, 1999). For purposes of this discussion, statements of the intent or purpose of instruction are referred to as **educational objectives**.

Behavioral Theory and Educational Objectives.   Behaviorists recommend that objectives should specify the desired learning outcome in measurable terms. Their recommendation to write objectives in measurable terms is present in a number of discussions of the instructional design process (Dick, Carey, & Carey, 2001; Kemp, Morrison, & Ross, 1994). In the early 1960s, Mager (1975) developed a commonly used format for writing specific instructional objectives, which is consistent with the behavioral recommendation.

A **Mager-style instructional objective** has three components. First, it specifies what students will be able to do. Second, it identifies the conditions under which that behavior will be performed. Third, it specifies the criterion for success, which is usually stated in terms of desired levels of accuracy or speed. Consider the following example.

What are the components of a Mager-style objective?

- **Conditions:** Given a worksheet with fifty single-digit addition problems
- **Behavior:** Students will be able to write the correct answer
- **Criterion:** 90 percent of the time

Objectives written in this format can help with lesson planning because the expected student performance is specified. The previous example provides clear guidance about the type of practice students should be doing, and how students' progress will be assessed. However, this approach to writing objectives has been criticized for encouraging teachers to focus on isolated, easily measured skills rather than on broader, more complicated cognitive outcomes such as improved critical thinking or creativity (Linn & Gronlund, 2000). Additionally, these types of objectives have been criticized for being inconsistent with the goals of constructivist approaches to learning (Choi & Jonassen, 2000; Johnson, 2000).

Cognitive Theory and Educational Objectives.   Measurable objectives have a role in cognitive theory, particularly in terms of the learning of specific procedural skills or facts. However, specific behavioral objectives may be less suitable for more complicated or higher level cognitive outcomes. In lieu of these specific objectives, your objectives could be more generally stated such as, "Students will become more creative." Although this objective addresses more complicated cognitive activities, it also makes instructional design more complicated because the objective is relatively vague and open to multiple interpretations. For example, what does it mean to be creative, and how is that assessed? Gronlund's (2000) **cognitive objectives** resolve this issue by supporting these types of objectives with lists of more specific behaviors that indicate that the broader objective is being met. Consider this example.

- **Instructional Objective:** Students will improve their ability to reason critically about a science argument.

- **Behavioral Indicators:** Students will be able to list the strengths and weaknesses of an argument. Students will decide how well the evidence that is provided meets the criteria for effective evidence.

Constructivism and Educational Objectives. General or more broadly stated cognitive objectives are suitable for some applications of constructivism. However, constructivist approaches often encourage students to take a great deal of responsibility for their own learning. An alternative to teacher-generated objectives, therefore, is to allow students to select some or all of the objectives for their learning (Choi & Jonassen, 2000; Kozma, 2000; Willis, 1998). In this case, objectives emerge out of students' attempts to learn, rather than being prespecified by teachers. For example, as students are investigating an area, they might collaborate with other students or teachers to identify what they need to learn or accomplish to be successful.

A potential benefit of student-generated objectives is that they may better reflect students' needs and interests. Also, as discussed earlier in this text, goal setting is an important component of student self-regulation of learning, and this can provide one more opportunity to learn to self-regulate. However, it is important to note that a process like this often has to be integrated into an environment that requires teachers to address certain academic standards.

Criteria for Evaluating Objectives. You will find as a teacher that there are almost an infinite number of learning objectives that could be identified for your students. However, your objectives need to be appropriate and useful for your students. Here are some questions to ask in determining whether or not your objectives are appropriate for your course and your students (Linn & Gronlund, 2000).

- Do your objectives represent the full range of outcomes envisioned for your students? For example, do your objectives reflect different levels of understanding, and both important cognitive and affective outcomes?
- Are your objectives aligned to state standards or district and school curricular goals?
- Are your objectives consistent with sound principles of learning and motivation? For example, do you take students' needs and prior knowledge into account? Are your objectives likely to lead to long-term retention of meaningful information?
- Are your objectives realistic given the nature of your students and the time you have to accomplish those objectives? Can you differentiate between essential objectives and useful but optional objectives?

Instructional Alignment

Instructional alignment occurs when the decisions concerning instructional activities and evaluation support the achievement of desired learning outcomes (Cohen, 1987, 1995; Walker, 1998). Once objectives or desired learning outcomes are identified, lessons or learning environments are designed that have the best chance of producing those outcomes and evaluations are selected or designed that tell whether or not the objectives have been met. Instructional alignment implies that different types of learning outcomes are likely to need different lesson designs and evaluation approaches.

As an example of alignment decisions, assume that your objective is to teach students how to prepare a microscope slide. What types of instructional experiences are aligned to that simple objective? Your students would probably find it useful to see the process demonstrated in some way and to be given a chance to practice what they have learned with feedback. An aligned assessment for preparing a microscope slide would involve something such as giving the students the necessary equipment and seeing if they can prepare a slide.

Although instructional alignment originates from a behavioral view of learning, it is an important consideration in almost all instructional design approaches. For

If you wanted to make sure students knew the parts of a microscope, what would be an aligned assessment to that objective?

example, if your goal is to have students transfer what they have learned to real-life situations, then the instruction should provide experiences with real-world or authentic applications (Walker, 1998). If your goal is to create self-directed learners, then environments need to be developed that support that goal, and evaluation methods should be developed to assess students' levels of self-directedness.

It is also important to note that current discussions of alignment are often framed in terms of meeting district and state objectives or standards (Downey, 2001; Wilson, 2002). This view of alignment is important because students are held accountable for these standards and goals on high-stakes testing such as graduation examinations (see the Enriching Your Understanding).

Why is it important to begin lesson alignment by considering what students need to learn?

As a final observation, effective instructional alignment requires careful consideration of what your students need to learn, because it is possible to develop well-aligned lessons for trivial or unimportant objectives. Also, alignment requires a pretty thorough understanding of what an objective requires from students.

Learner Characteristics and Instructional Design

When designing instruction, teachers need to consider the characteristics of their learners. The nature of their learners can affect the objectives they select, how they teach, and how they assess. In this discussion of learner characteristics, the assump-

ENRICHING YOUR UNDERSTANDING
No Child Left Behind

The **No Child Left Behind Act (NCLB)** is the 2001 reauthorization of the Elementary and Secondary Education Act (Igo, 2002). It is sweeping educational reform legislation that is based on these four principles: stronger accountability for results, increased flexibility and local control, expanded options for parents, and dependence on proven teaching methods (Stallings, 2002). NCLB targets a variety or areas including character education, early reading programs, parent involvement, and technology development (Cradler & Cradler, 2002; Igo, 2002; Lewis, 2002; McLester, 2003; Paige, 2002). However, the emphasis on research-validated instructional methods and the accountability components of NCLB are likely to have the most pronounced effects on your decisions about how and what to teach.

According to NCLB, states are to develop "challenging state standards" that will be measured by state tests. These standards and tests need to be in place first for reading and mathematics by the 2005–2006 school year, and students in grades three through eight will be required to take these tests. Standards in science are to follow later. The National Assessment of Educational Progress will be used with some students in each state to validate the state test (Linn, Baker, & Betebenner, 2002). In addition, schools are required to set measurable improvement objectives and to show sufficient annual yearly progress such that all students will be able to

meet state standards at the end of twelve years. Schools who fail to show adequate annual yearly progress may have a series of increasingly severe interventions or sanctions applied ("The New ESEA," 2002). Supporters of NCLB suggest that it holds teachers accountable for students' learning, and that the mandated testing provides information that helps schools identify what needs to be improved (Paige, 2002).

Arguments against mandated testing programs in general include concerns that these tests may adversely affect minority and economically disadvantaged students, increase the number of students who drop out, create dissatisfied professionals because of their lack of control over key teaching decisions, and restrict the focus of teaching to preparing students for these tests (Darling-Hammond & Wise, 1983; Linn & Gronlund, 2000; Pearson, Vyas, Sensale, & Kim, 2001; Perreault, 2000; Schmidt, 2000). The state tests currently in existence have been criticized for creating an uneven playing field because some tests yield higher pass rates than others (Linn, Baker, & Betebenner, 2002). Although this debate will continue, test accountability is one contextual variable that will influence your decision making.

● **How might the No Child Left Behind Act affect your instructional design decisions? (For your authors' perspective on this question, go to the text website for this chapter.)**

Karen has selected *Amelia Bedelia* books for our next literature unit. I looked these over and they are kind of neat. The main character, Amelia, takes everything that's said to her literally. For example, when she is asked to dust the furniture, she actually spreads dusting powder on the furniture. I told Karen that I thought our students would like these books, and I thought this unit would be a great time to try out something I read about in a teacher magazine. The author of the article recommended having students pantomime their favorite scenes as a way to assess their comprehension. I thought this activity would be effective with some of our second language learners and students who have trouble reading. Karen agreed that this sounded like an interesting idea, but she also said that it might be premature to talk about evaluation until we thought about our objectives. One of her goals was for students to understand what they had read, but she also had other goals in mind. For example, she thought that *Amelia Bedelia* books were good for teaching about idioms, one of the language forms our students are expected to know. Also, she was interested in teaching students how to write better organized paragraphs. She asked me to plan my lessons with those goals in mind and to see if I could fit my interesting assessment idea into what we needed to teach.

● **Why is this a discussion about instructional alignment?**

Decision Point: What role could Mona's assessment idea play in a unit such as this?

tion is made that teachers often have a common set of objectives that they need to accomplish with all of their students. For example, all students need to learn to solve algebraic equations or to read. The issue in this case is how can teachers provide instruction that allows students who differ from each other in significant ways to meet those objectives?

A **learner analysis** is one way to consider your learners' characteristics in the instructional design process (Dick, Carey, & Carey, 2001). Although some of Dick, Carey, and Carey's recommendations for conducting a learner analysis are more relevant for instructional design professionals, a number of their questions are useful for classroom teachers to ask about their learners.

- What entry behaviors, prerequisite skills, or prior knowledge are required by this lesson, and which students possess that needed background? Historically, this question has been addressed by consulting records of previous performance or by pretesting.
- What are my students' attitudes toward the content and potential delivery modes? Your answer to this question can influence your choice of content and delivery mode. However, you may have to teach content or use delivery modes that your students may not like. In those cases, you would pay closer attention to motivational issues in your design decisions.
- What are the key academic motivation issues that need to be addressed? Later in the chapter this issue is discussed in more detail.
- What are the educational and ability levels of the students? In today's inclusion classrooms, this would include an analysis of the needs of your students with disabilities.
- What are my students' general learning preferences? This is when you would consider students' learning styles and whether it's more useful to match instruction to style or have students develop new ways of learning.
- What are the group characteristics of my learners? Are they relatively homogeneous or heterogeneous in terms of variables such as gender, ethnicity, and culture? This is when you would consider how to accommodate the diverse backgrounds of your students.

A learner analysis helps you identify what modifications you may need to make to accommodate the needs of your learners. It does not, however, provide specific

Universal design is a concept that originated in architecture (Story, Mueller, & Mace, 1998). Architects who work from the perspective of universal design create structures that can accommodate a broad range of potential users (Rose, 2000). The same general principle when applied to instructional design has been called **universal design for learning (UDL)** or universal instructional design (Rose, 2000; Silver, Bourke, & Strehorn, 1998). This approach to instructional design emphasizes flexible instruction with options for broad access to learning.

UDL begins with an analysis of the instructional objective or standard to determine what students are supposed to learn. Individualized learning goals are identified if possible, and instruction is designed with multiple options for accomplishing the learning goals (Rose, Sethuraman, & Meo, 2000). Although the actual options depend on the characteristics of the learner, some general guidelines can be abstracted from the UDL literature (Pisha & Coyne, 2001; Rose, 2000, 2001; Shaw, Scott, & McGuire, 2001).

- Instruction should provide perceptible information that takes into account learners' sensory capabilities. For example, students with visual impairments or severe reading disabilities may benefit from text readers or recorded text.
- Instruction should provide options to account for differences in students' learning rates. For example, self-paced mastery learning programs can be designed to accommodate varying rates of learning (Brothen, Wambach, & Hansen, 2002).
- Teachers should vary their presentation modes to account for differences in how students learn best.
- Physical environments should be designed to accommodate participation by learners with different mobility needs. For example, is their adequate space for students to move around and meet with each other?
- Simplified and clarified instructional messages should be available. For example, shorter and less complicated text could be made available.
- Instruction should include strategic support for learners who need it. For example, you can provide models of expert performance or hints on how best to approach a task.

The goal is to provide flexibility in terms of how students learn and demonstrate that learning to others. Flexibility, therefore, might extend to both the learning and assessment of learning. Your decision about when to provide flexibility will depend on what students are expected to learn and how they are expected to demonstrate that learning.

> ● **How might the requirement that students pass a mandated test in a particular test format influence your decisions about UDL? (For your authors' perspective on this question, go to the text website for this chapter.)**

guidance on how to design instruction to meet the needs of various learners. The discussion of universal design of instruction contained in the Focus on Learner Diversity may provide some initial recommendations in this area.

Task Analysis

Task analysis is an important instructional design tool that can help you with the decisions you need to make in answering the four instructional design questions introduced at the beginning of this section. **Task analysis** is the process of explicitly identifying the subtasks, information flow, inputs, and decisions required by learners to perform a learning task (Seels & Glasgow, 1998). In general, task analysis is the process of identifying the component parts of a complex task (Alberto & Troutman, 1999; Wolfe, 1998). Although task analysis is also usually associated with behavioral learning theory, it may be the single most important process of any approach to instructional design (Jonassen, Tessmer, & Hannum, 1999).

Behavioral Learning Theory and Task Analysis.   The behavioral view of chaining is that complicated behaviors consist of a sequence of discrete behaviors that are linked or chained together. The effective teaching of complicated behaviors requires teachers to identify the individual behaviors in a chain. Procedural analysis and learning hierarchy analysis are two forms of task analysis that can be used to identify the links in behavioral chains. Together, they help you decide how a particular behavior is performed and the required prerequisite behaviors for the target behavior.

Procedural Analysis.   **Procedural analysis** results in a sequence of steps for completing a particular task. To complete a procedural analysis, simply list the component skills or steps of a complicated behavior in a sequence that leads to successful execution of that behavior (Parsons & Reid, 1999). For example, a sequence of steps for multiplying fractions or the steps for changing a flat tire would be procedural analyses for those tasks.

The goal of a procedural analysis is to gain an understanding of how a particular learning task is done. By identifying the component parts of a complex task, you can make sure that important components or steps are not left out of instruction (Wolfe, 1998). Also, a procedural analysis can help you plan assessments to determine which component parts students have mastered or still need to learn (Reeves & Stein, 1999).

Learning Hierarchy Analysis.   In general, a **learning hierarchy analysis** is the process of identifying the sequence of prerequisite skills and knowledge for a particular learning task (Dick, Carey, & Carey, 2001; Gagné, 1985; Jonassen, Tessmer, & Hannum, 1999). Prerequisites are knowledge or skills that should be learned before the skills or knowledge in the current lesson are learned. For example, dividing fractions requires several prerequisite math skills such as subtraction, multiplication, and division. A learning hierarchy analysis is useful, therefore, for sequencing instruction for a series of behaviors, as is required in planning a series of units or a curriculum. Learning hierarchy analysis can help you avoid teaching a lesson for which your students are unprepared.

You can identify prerequisites for a learning task in a number of ways (Yelon, 1996). For simpler lesson goals, it may be sufficient to examine the objective for prerequisites. For example, if you want students to add two-digit numbers together without regrouping, students should already know how to add single-digit problems. For more complicated tasks, you can create a task description or procedural analysis for that task. Then, for each step in the procedural analysis, you would identify the prerequisites. For example, assume that as part of a complicated project students need to use the Internet to research a topic. Using the Internet successfully implies a number of prerequisites such as knowing how to log on to a computer, how to use a search engine, and how to critique information provided in a website. Once these prerequisites are identified, you would determine whether your students possess these required prerequisites before you teach your lesson.

> **How are procedural analysis and learning hierarchy analysis different?**

An information-processing analysis begins by having learners talk about their thought processes.

Cognitive Theory and Information-Processing Analysis.   An **information-processing analysis** is a procedural task analysis of the mental processes involved in an activity such as composing a story or analyzing a story problem (Jonassen, Tessmer, & Hannum, 1999; Smith & Ragan, 1993). For example, an information-processing analysis of how students write revealed that they engage in planning, translating, and reviewing as they compose and write (Flower & Hayes, 1981; Hayes, 1996; Hayes & Flower, 1980).

An information-processing analysis begins by having learners describe how they think through a complicated mental

task, or by having them think aloud as they perform that complicated mental task (Brandt & Uden, 2002; Swanson, 1993). These self-reports are converted to a flow chart or a list of steps that describe how learners typically complete a cognitive task. Information-processing analyses have not only been used to understand how learners accomplish complicated mental tasks, but also to identify the strategies of more successful or expert learners that can be taught to less successful or novice learners. This is how Marion Woo applies this idea.

➤ When I am trying to think of some learning strategies to teach my students, I begin by asking myself what I would do to succeed, or what some of my more successful students have done.

Constructivism and Task Analysis. Constructivist approaches to instructional design are typically based on the assumption that learning needs to occur in authentic, problem-solving contexts. To design instruction that situates learning in authentic contexts, you would need to understand those contexts. Task analysis could be used in a number of ways to understand learning contexts.

First, task analysis could be used to develop a meaningful understanding of the activity structures that define a context of practice (Jonassen, Tessmer, & Hannum, 1999). In essence, this is an understanding of the types of problems that need to be solved in a particular context, and how practitioners operate within a context to solve those problems. You would analyze the context in terms of the goals of an activity within a context; the tools used in accomplishing those goals; and the motives, characteristics, problem-solving strategies, and required knowledge of practitioners in that context. For example, if the goal were to design learning contexts that simulate the problem solving of geologists in the field, then the problem-solving activities of geologists in the field would need to be analyzed and understood.

Task analysis could also be used to index the stories that practitioners tell about their problem solving (Jonassen & Hernandez-Serrano, 2002). These stories or cases can then be used to scaffold students' problem solving by helping clarify theoretical or conceptual ideas, providing a problem to be analyzed or solved, or as a source of advice from practitioners on how to solve problems in a domain.

Finally, a form of task analysis called **environment analysis** can help you understand the contextual factors that enhance or reduce the likelihood of success of an instructional design (Tessmer, 1990; Tessmer & Richey, 1997). You will find that an instructional design approach is more likely to succeed if it is modified to your teaching context. Constructivist approaches pose some special challenges in this regard. For example, a constructivist teacher would need to balance coverage of prescribed content or standards with the need for students' self-directed learning. Also, the noise that is generated by active exploration would need to be considered in terms of its effects on other teachers.

What is environment analysis?

Behavioral Learning Theory and Instructional Design

Charles Gropper (1974, 1975, 1983, 1987) has developed an approach to instructional design based on behavioral learning theory that describes how instructional treatments (stimuli) can be designed to produce the learning of specific behaviors (responses). As in previous discussions of the application of behavioral theory, Gropper's work is described in terms of the behavioral learning theory principles developed in Chapter 2.

Principle 2.1: Learning Is Measurable and Observable

Gropper's approach to instructional design begins with a thorough performance analysis of the objectives selected for instruction. When you conduct a **performance** analysis of your objectives, you specify the behaviors students are to learn, and the conditions under which they must demonstrate those behaviors (Gropper, 1983). A performance analysis should yield specific, measurable objectives.

How would a performance analysis help you write behavioral objectives?

Principle 2.2: Learning Is Gradual and Step by Step

Gropper (1983) suggests that complicated behaviors such as learning to read can be broken down into component behaviors. Gropper's (1983) analyzes behaviors through a skill analysis. A **skill analysis** is a form of procedural analysis used to analyze complicated behaviors into these component behaviors.

How is Gropper's idea of a skill analysis similar to the idea of a procedural task analysis?

- **Discrimination:** Students can distinguish between related stimuli or responses. For example, they can differentiate between fungi and algae.
- **Generalization:** Students are able to respond in the same way to a class of stimuli. For example, a student recognizes that right triangles and equilateral triangles are both triangles.
- **Association:** Students can connect a response with a stimulus. For example, students know that the letter *t* makes the *tuh* sound.
- **Chain:** Students can connect a number of stimulus-response units together. For example, students know how to decode a word by combining the sounds of the different letters.

Principle 2.3: The Effects of Stimuli on Responses

In general, Gropper (1983) views instruction as the process of establishing stimulus control. As discussed in Chapter 2, stimulus control occurs when students learn that if they emit a behavior in the presence of a particular antecedent, they will be rewarded. In establishing stimulus control, both criterion stimuli and cues need to be identified.

Criterion stimuli are the stimuli that must gain control over a response by the time instruction is finished. These stimuli are established as part of the performance analysis of a goal, and they represent how students will be asked to demonstrate their learning. Examples might include students being able to respond to a particular type of test question, being able to write an essay, or being able to construct a birdhouse with provided materials.

A **cue** is an instructional stimulus that helps establish stimulus control for the criterion stimulus. Cues are instructional applications such as lectures, demonstrations, hints, directions, and visual aids. For example, dotted letters on a penmanship paper are cues that help students form letters correctly until they are able to form the letters correctly on their own. Instructional design is the process of arranging cues into instructional treatments that are most effective for establishing stimulus control for the criterion stimulus.

How do criterion stimuli and cues differ?

Instructional Treatments. For Gropper (1983) instructional treatments are cues that are effective for teaching a particular type of behavior. **Routine treatments** are the generic formats for teaching facts, skills, or concepts. **Nonroutine treatments** are modifications and extensions made to routine treatments if the behavior to be learned is especially complicated or difficult.

Treatments for Learning Facts. A **fact** is a statement of association between two things (Kemp, Morrison, & Ross, 1994). The learning of facts requires students to learn multiple S-R connections and to recall those connections at a later date. For example, young children may need to memorize the capitals of the fifty states, or the formula for finding the circumference of a circle. Older students might be asked to memorize important historical events and dates or definitions for terminology.

CHAPTER 9 Utilizing Instructional Design **291**

The routine treatments for teaching facts consist of the following two components. Students need to be told or shown what the facts are, and they need to practice and review the facts either by stating or applying the facts, or both. These routine treatments can be done in a number of ways. For example, students can read about facts in a text, see them in a movie or on a website, or have them explained in a lecture. The practice and review can also occur in a number of ways (Kemp, Morrison, & Ross, 1994). Students could covertly rehearse the facts by saying them to themselves, they could write the facts, or they could respond to questions about the facts. Paul O'Neill likes to use games to rehearse facts with his high school history classes.

> ➤ I actually have constructed a game board with lights and light switches. The students compete as members of a team to answer questions first. They try to be the first one to turn on their light and get a question right.

Nonroutine treatments are planned when you anticipate that the factual learning will be difficult for students. The learning of facts can be complicated by a number of factors. In general, the number of facts to be learned affects difficulty. Also, competition between new and old S-R connections influences difficulty. For example, learning the definition of negative reinforcement can be difficult because of prior associations students form for the word *negative*. Finally, similarity among facts may provide additional difficulty. For example, the formulas for the area and circumference of a circle can easily be confused.

These issues can be addressed through nonroutine treatments such as presenting a few facts at a time and designing a practice that draws students' attention to the differences between similar facts. For example, you could include cues in your lesson design such as different color chalk for different ideas, or you could underline or otherwise highlight key differences between definitions. You could present two easily confused facts at different times and make sure the first fact is learned well before presenting the next. You could also provide students with mnemonics (strategy) for facts that are difficult to remember (Mastropieri & Scruggs, 1991; Raschke, Alper, & Eggers, 1999).

When should you plan nonroutine treatments for factual learning?

Treatments for Concept Learning. A **concept** is a categorical idea that is used to represent a group of items, ideas, or relationships that share common attributes (Kemp, Morrison, & Ross, 1994). For example, a triangle is a concept that includes geometric shapes with three enclosed sides, and a mammal is a concept that includes animals that possess certain characteristics such as being warm blooded. Above is a concept that represents a particular spatial relationship. According to Gropper (1983), concept learning requires that students learn the concept's definition, that they are able to use that definition to discriminate nonexamples from examples of the concept, and that they are be able to use that definition to identify all encountered examples as fitting in the concept category (generalization).

In the case of a concept lesson on triangles, students would need to learn that triangles are geometric shapes with three sides, and they would need to be able to differentiate triangles from rectangles and ovals. Also, they would need to be able to recognize that although right triangles, acute triangles, and equilateral triangles are somewhat different in appearance, they are all still examples of triangles.

The routine treatments for a concept lesson consist of the following.

- The lesson should contain a definition of the concept and possibly some guidelines to help students distinguish between related concepts. For example, "A *noun* is a part of speech that indicates person, place, thing or idea. It is different from a verb because. . . ."
- Students need to be provided with examples and nonexamples of the concept. In the case of a concept lesson on nouns, they would be shown various examples of the different categories of nouns, and nonexamples would be selected from other parts of speech such as verbs.

- Students should be given practice that requires them to state the definition and to categorize or produce examples of the concept correctly. For example, they may be asked to circle the nouns in their own writing.

The selection of examples and nonexamples is an extremely important part of a concept lesson for helping students avoid misconceptions. Overgeneralization and undergeneralization are two common errors students make in concept learning if examples and nonexamples are not selected carefully (Smith & Ragan, 1993). Students overgeneralize when they include nonexamples as examples. For instance, they classify a diamond as a triangle. Students undergeneralize when they fail to categorize an example of a concept. For example, they do not classify whales as mammals. The examples and nonexamples must be selected so that the boundaries of the concept category are clear.

What does it mean to overgeneralize a concept?

The difficulty of concept learning is affected by a number of variables. First, examples and nonexamples of a concept may be difficult to distinguish. For instance, examples of punishment and negative reinforcement can be difficult to differentiate. Second, some concepts include examples that are not very similar to each other, as in the case of bat and dog as examples of mammals. Third, some concepts may be very broad or abstract such as democracy.

These issues can be addressed through nonroutine treatments such as providing students with maps or diagrams that help them distinguish related concepts. For example, a Venn diagram could help students visualize areas of overlap and differences between concepts. Examples and nonexamples can be presented in pairs that allow students to focus on key similarities and differences. For example, Bible and book can be presented together as examples of proper and common nouns. Finally, examples can also be presented in a sequence of graduated difficulty, which means that typical examples are presented before less typical examples are presented (Tennyson & Cocchiarella, 1986). For example, if you were teaching the concept of adverbs, you might start with the *ly* examples before dealing with examples such as *well* as in, "He did that well."

Treatments for Procedural Rules.   With **procedural rule learning**, students are asked to perform a task according to rules or a set of prescribed steps for a procedure (Gropper, 1983). For example, students learning how to divide fractions or how to mount a microscope slide are learning procedural rules. Students must learn the series of steps for the procedure and also when the procedure should be applied. To accomplish this, Gropper recommends the following routine treatments.

- The steps in a procedure need to be identified. This is when procedural task analysis is useful. For example, you could use procedural task analysis to identify the steps in long division.
- The steps need to be demonstrated or modeled. For example, you could work a few long division problems at the board.
- Students would be provided with the rules or rationales for each step. For example, you would tell students how to determine if they have divided by the largest possible number.
- Students need to practice in varied contexts and with the opportunity for feedback. For example, students would be provided with guided practice with different applications for long division.

The difficulty of learning to follow a procedural rule is determined by the number of steps in a procedure, the difficulty in determining when similar but different procedures should be applied, or the complexity of the rules for applying a step in a procedure. Nonroutine treatments include breaking the procedure into parts and teaching one part at a time, or providing students with a checklist or job aid to help them as they are learning (Spaulding & Dwyer, 1999). For example, you could create a poster as a visual display for the sequence of steps in a procedure. You also could provide a verbal prompt that focuses students on a critical component of a performance such as "Meet the ball at the front foot" for teaching students to hit a tennis ball (Konukman & Petrakis, 2001). You can also teach the common or general rules for applying a procedure before introducing the exceptions.

It should be noted that Gropper (1983) views the teaching of problem solving as an additional example of learning procedural rules. The complexity involved in learning and transferring problem-solving strategies such as the scientific method would, however, require the use of numerous nonroutine treatments.

Information-Processing Theory and Instructional Design

Although a number of instructional design approaches reflect the influence of cognitive learning theory, Robert Gagné (1985) has developed one of the more widely used instructional design theories from a cognitive perspective (Smith & Ragan, 1993). Gagné's theory can be conceptualized as consisting of these three main components (Driscoll, 2002).

- A classification system for types of knowledge or learning outcomes
- General events of instruction
- Specific conditions of learning for the different types of learning outcomes

As with other applications of cognitive theory, your authors show how these components reflect the cognitive learning principles from Chapter 3.

Principle 3.4: Learning Is an Active Goal-Directed Process

Gagné's (1985) approach to instructional design begins with a goal analysis that typically includes a procedural task analysis and learning hierarchy analysis of the goal and a determination of the type of learning outcomes contained in the instructional goal (Dick, Carey, & Carey, 2001; Gagné, 1985; Gagné, Briggs, & Wager, 1988; Smith & Ragan, 1993). Identifying the type of learning outcome is a key component of Gagné's theory because instruction is designed that aligns to a particular type of learning outcome.

Gagné's Categories of Learning Outcomes. Gagné's system for categorizing learning outcomes is one of several attempts to develop classifications systems for types of knowledge (Anderson, 1983; Bloom, Englehart, Furst, Hill, & Kratwohl, 1956; Merrill, 1983). However, Gagné's (1985) categories are probably the most widely used by instructional designers, and to some extent other categorical systems share important similarities with Gagné's system (Reigeluth & Moore, 1999). Gagné's five categories of learning outcomes are verbal information, intellectual skills, attitudes, psychomotor skills, and cognitive strategies. The intellectual skills category is further divided into a hierarchy of five subcategories.

Verbal Information. **Verbal information** consists of the facts, lists, names, and organized information that students are expected to learn (Gagné, 1985; Gagné & Driscoll, 1988). It is also what information-processing theorists refer to as declarative knowledge. At the end of instruction, the learner is expected to state, list, or describe something (Dick, Carey, & Carey, 2001). Knowing the parts of plants, the first ten amendments to the constitution, and key events in the Civil War are all examples of verbal information.

Verbal information, especially learning of facts, can be perceived as low-level or even unimportant learning. However, students' knowledge of verbal information can be important in a number of ways (Gagné & Driscoll, 1988). First, it may provide important prerequisite knowledge for interpreting other learning experiences. For example, knowing what colors litmus paper turns in the presence of acids or bases can help students interpret the results of an experiment concerning acids and bases. Second, some verbal information has practical, even day-to-day uses. Knowing the days of the week or knowing the meaning of the word *flammable* both have obvious practical uses. Finally, well-organized and understood verbal information can be useful in forming analogies during problem solving and meaningful learning. For example, understanding the characteristics of a computer might help students understand the structures of the information-processing model.

Why is the learning of verbal information useful to students?

Intellectual Skills. The learning of an **intellectual skill** involves knowing how to apply acquired understandings to examples or experiences not encountered previously (Dick, Carey, & Carey, 2001; Gagné, 1985). It is what information-processing psychologists refer to as procedural knowledge. The intellectual skills category is subdivided into five subcategories that can be arranged from simplest to most complex. These categories are discriminations, concrete concepts, defined concepts, rules and principles, and higher order rules. Table 9.1 provides definitions and examples for the subcategories of intellectual skills.

Attitudes. **Attitudes** are acquired internal states that guide people's choices of personal action (Gagné & Driscoll, 1988). For example, schools might want to help students develop the attitude that cultural diversity is to be respected and honored. Attitudes can also involve personal preferences such as students enjoying classical music or great literature. Attitudes usually don't develop from a single lesson, but develop over time and multiple exposures.

What are some examples of attitudes that you think are an important part of being an effective teacher?

Psychomotor Skills. **Psychomotor skills** require that students execute muscular actions to accomplish a particular goal, with or without the assistance of equipment

TABLE 9.1 Gagné's Hierarchy of Intellectual Skills

Intellectual Skill Category	Description	Examples
Discrimination	Discriminations involve being able to recognize that two events are different, without necessarily understanding the nature of the difference.	Being able to discriminate between the letters *b* and *d* to read and write
Concrete concept	They represent categories of object features, objects, and events. Concrete concepts can be pointed to in the environment.	*Tree, dog, up,* and *table* are examples of concrete concepts
Defined concepts	Defined concepts tend to be more general and abstract than concrete concepts. Students need to be able to match examples to the definition or list of characteristics. Defined concepts are often hypothetical constructs or agreed upon ideas that are fundamental to the structure of a discipline.	Negative reinforcement, democracy, and negative numbers are examples of defined concepts
Rules and principles	Rules and principles are generalizations that we apply in making sense of the world. Relational rules often take the form of an *if/then* construction. Procedural rules are the steps for executing a procedure. To demonstrate an understanding of a rule, students need to be able to apply the procedure.	Relational rule: If the litmus paper turns red, then the solution must be an acid Procedural rule: Students' ability to apply the steps in balancing a chemical equation
Higher order rule	Higher order rules involve the sequencing and application of acquired rules, principles, and concepts to meet the demands of novel situations. They are the basis for problem-solving.	Students combine various principles and concepts of science to develop a habitat for an endangered species

(Dick, Carey, & Carey, 2001). Learning to do a front somersault or to cut sheet metal are examples of psychomotor skills.

Cognitive Strategies. **Cognitive strategies** are internal processes by which learners select and adapt their ways of attending, remembering, learning, and thinking (Gagné, Briggs, & Wager, 1988). They involve the techniques often discussed by others as learning or problem-solving strategies (Weinstein & Mayer, 1986). Examples include strategies such as mnemonics, concept mapping, or an approach for solving story problems. Cognitive strategies can be viewed as a special subtype of intellectual skills because they involve learning how to learn or think, but because of their special purpose, they can also be treated as a separate type of learning outcome (Gagné, 1985; Gagné, Briggs, & Wager, 1988).

Principle 3.2: Coordinating Mental Processes

Gagné (1985) views instructional design as the process of arranging external events and conditions to influence students' mental processes. Effective instruction helps students engage in the mental processes necessary for the acquisition of the knowledge implied in the learning goal. These ideas form the basis for the final two components of Gagné's theory: the events of instruction and the conditions of learning.

Gagné's Events of Instruction.   The **events of instruction** are nine instructional conditions that need to be considered when planning any lesson (Driscoll, 2002). They are designed to support internal mental processes such as attention, selective perception, encoding, and retrieval. The nine events of instruction include the following.

- Gaining learners' attention
- Informing learners of the instructional objective or intent
- Stimulating the recall of prior learning

Looking in on

Mona Carrie

9.2

I was embarrassed to tell Karen that I didn't know what an idiom was, so I looked it up in the dictionary later. I found that idioms are colorful expressions whose meaning cannot be understood from the actual words spoken. For example, "keeping someone in stitches," is an idiom. It dawned on me that Amelia had trouble understanding idioms, and that's why Karen chose these books for teaching idioms. It also occurred to me that a lesson on idioms would fit nicely with recent lessons on the use of adjectives, metaphors, and analogies. All of these lessons are intended to help students' writing become more descriptive and colorful, which is one of our goals for the year.

I wanted to begin by teaching students to recognize examples of idioms when they saw them, to know how idioms differ from the other language forms we had studied, and to be able to use them in their writing. However, Karen had also asked me to include paragraph writing in my lessons. When

we did metaphors, she had students write paragraphs using metaphors, so I wondered why she wanted them to write paragraphs again. When I asked Karen about this, she told me that the students' metaphor paragraphs didn't flow very well, and they tended to wander off the topic. I could have them use idioms in their writing, but she wanted me to teach them how to follow these three steps for writing a paragraph: (1) Brainstorm ideas and write a topic sentence for these ideas; (2) select and sequence the brainstormed ideas; and (3) write a closing or ending sentence.

● **According to Gropper and Gagné, what types of behaviors or learning outcomes is Mona going to be teaching?**

Decision Point: What factors are involved in Karen's decisions about what she would like Mona to teach in the idiom unit?

- Presenting the instructional stimulus
- Providing learning guidance
- Eliciting performance
- Providing feedback
- Assessing performance
- Enhancing retention and transfer of learning

For each of these events, instructional designers have identified various actions teachers can take when implementing each event (Branch, 1997; Gagné, Briggs, & Wager, 1988; Gagné & Medsker, 1996; Orey Okey, Jones, & Stanley, 1991). Table 9.2 provides examples of these actions for each event.

Although the nine events of instruction can be interpreted as a sequence of events in a teacher-directed lesson, they also can be viewed as components of any approach to instruction. For example, the events of instruction have been observed in cooperative learning and in technology-assisted math instruction (Flynn, 1992; House, 2002). They also have been used to design instruction in virtual classrooms and to demonstrate how culturally appropriate instruction can be designed, and are compatible with important elements of constructivist instructional design (Branch, 1997; Johnston, 2000; Richey, 1996). One way to think about the events of instruction is as a framework that can be applied to different ways of teaching specific knowledge outcomes (Dempsey & Van Eck, 2002).

Additional ideas for implementing these events can be found in the discussion of information processing in Chapter 7.

Gagné's Conditions of Learning. Gagné's theory of instructional design is based to a large extent on the assumption that different learning outcomes require somewhat different instructional experiences (Spector, 2001). Although the events of instruction are important components of any lesson, the conditions of learning describe how these events can be modified or adapted for different types of learning outcomes.

Conditions for Verbal Information. In designing instruction for verbal information, a number of conditions of learning should be considered (Driscoll, 1994;

TABLE 9.2   Implementing the Events of Instruction

Learners' Mental Process or Mental State	Event of Instruction	Examples of Teacher Actions
Attention	Gaining attention	Vary stimulus properties (e.g., intensity, color, format); connect lesson content to students' interests and needs
Expectancy	Informing the learner of the objective	Provide statements of instructional goals; provide inserted or adjunct questions; provide an example of the desired outcome or use of the lesson content
Retrieval of relevant prior knowledge to working memory	Stimulating the recall of prior learning	Review prerequisites skills or concepts; provide advance organizers; engage students in K-W-L
Pattern recognition and selective attention	Presenting the stimulus	Select instructional stimuli that are aligned to the learning outcome
Chunking, rehearsal, encoding	Providing learner guidance	Determine how much independence you want from the learner; provide cues, scaffolding, and coaching
Retrieval, responding	Eliciting performance	Provide opportunities for practice and application
Reinforcement, error correction	Providing feedback	Provide informational feedback; schedule guided practice
Responding, retention	Assessing performance	Select aligned assessments
Retrieval, transfer	Enhancing retention and transfer	Provide a variety of contexts for practice; provide opportunities for students to reflect on their own learning

Marisol Hernandez

9.1

George Fremont, our technology teacher, is using multimedia software to produce some tutorials for math concepts and procedures that our students need during our problem-based learning modules. If and when students need this type of support, they can access the program from the school website. The tutorials basically have the same set of components. They begin by showing a humorous video of a student incorrectly calculating values and what can go wrong. Our students sometimes look at the tutorial just to see these vignettes. The tutorials then list the skills students will be learning and provide students with a list of prerequisites for the math skills being taught. Eventually, George will have each of these prerequisite skills connected to a review screen for that prerequisite skill. The actual lesson on the skill proceeds in a step-by-step fashion with the student from the opening vignette modeling how to do the skill. This student also occasionally asks key procedural questions. These questions are turned into a series of prompts to help students avoid common errors. Finally, our students are provided with some practice problems with feedback. After they do those, they are given additional problems from different science domains.

● **How are Gagné's events of instruction reflected in the components of these tutorials (see Table 9.3, p. 301)?**

Decision Point: What practical issues would need to be considered in implementing these tutorials?

What conditions for helping you focus attention are present in this chapter?

Gagné & Driscoll, 1988). First, because verbal information is often presented in the form of an extended discourse such as a book chapter, a lecture, or a film, teachers should help students differentiate between important and unimportant information. To accomplish this, written material can provide devices such as headings, italics, bold print, margin notes, and repetition (Mayer, 1999). As noted in Chapter 7, teachers can help students select important information by providing objectives or adjunct questions.

Providing a meaningful context for learning is a second important condition of learning verbal information (Smith & Ragan, 1993). This primarily involves helping students connect what they are learning to prior experiences and knowledge, but it may also involve teaching information in terms of its use. Teachers or written materials can provide questions that ask students to elaborate on the information being presented (Mayer, 1980). Teachers can also introduce information in the context of problem-solving activities (Yelon, 1996). For example, students could learn information about how bills become laws as part of a legislative simulation. Additionally, techniques discussed in previous chapters, such as mnemonics, imagery, advance organizers, analogies, and K-W-L, are also useful for this condition of learning.

Designing instruction that provides multiple cues for recall and generalization of learned information is a third condition of learning verbal information. You can create multiple retrieval cues by presenting information in different ways and with varied uses and implications (Driscoll, 1994). Here is how Francis Turner does this in his high school civics class.

➤ When we discuss the first ten amendments to the constitution, I try to connect these basic rights to varied experiences the students might have had. For example, I relate freedom of speech to censorship issues in music and dress codes in high schools. I want them to understand the first amendment in terms of its multiple implications for their lives.

Another way to provide retrieval cues is to design instruction that uses similar organizational structures for related topics. Students can use parallel organizational structures as a way of organizing their learning. For example, you might provide an outline or series of questions for different related topics such as key elements of a world religion.

Conditions for Intellectual Skills.   Because some rules and concepts involve the use of previously learned concepts, and some procedures rely on previously learned skills, it's helpful to have students recall those previously learned component skills. A learning hierarchy analysis can help you identify the relevant prior learning.

A second condition of learning intellectual skills is to focus students' attention on the distinctive features of the intellectual skill being learned. Here are some suggestions for focusing students' attention during intellectual skill learning.

- In the case of concept learning, reduce the likelihood that students will inaccurately encode unessential details as part of a concept definition. For example, in the case of a lesson on triangles, you would want to vary the internal angles while keeping the three-sided shape intact so that students understand how triangles can vary in appearance.
- In the case of a rule, help students understand the reason for the rule, because it makes the rule more meaningful and memorable. For example, in a lesson on dividing fractions, explain to students why they should invert the denominator before multiplying.
- In the case of a procedural rule with multiple steps, focus students on the steps that determine success or failure or that have been difficult for previous students.

A third condition for intellectual skill learning is to provide sufficient retrieval cues. This can be accomplished by presenting verbal cues for the sequencing of component skills. For example, you could provide cue cards that list the steps of a procedure or create an acronym for the steps.

Finally, provide opportunities for effective practice of intellectual skills. Chapter 7 provides the behavioral view of effective practice, and here are additional recommendations to those provided in Chapter 7 (Yelon, 1996).

- Effective practice allows every student to participate and receive feedback. For example, a teacher could give students small white boards for math practice. When students have finished a math problem, they can show their work to the teacher.
- Effective practice suggests how students need to recall or apply the intellectual skill. Teach intellectual skills in terms of their intended use. For example, show how an environmental science procedure is used in the field.
- Effective practice should provide opportunities to apply intellectual skills in varied contexts, and the practice should be distributed over time. The use of varied examples and practice contexts is very important in facilitating transfer (Driscoll, 1994).

Conditions for Attitudes.   The first condition of learning for attitudes is that students need opportunities to practice the behaviors and choices associated with an attitude (Gagné, 1985). If the goal is to encourage love of reading, students should be allowed to participate in free reading and to experience reading as an enjoyable activity.

Second, students need to connect an attitude and associated behaviors with success or positive outcomes. You can connect attitudes with success by reinforcing the behaviors associated with an attitude. This is how Carmen Johnson accomplishes this with her school's character education program

> ➤ We run periodic assemblies during which students who have demonstrated positive character traits are honored in front of the school. Additionally, teachers have little certificates to award in their classrooms for demonstrations of positive character traits.

Students can also learn to associate positive outcomes with an attitude by interacting with models who have achieved positive outcomes through that attitude, especially if these models are similar to the learner or have high levels of prestige (Driscoll, 1994). These models also can communicate to students how particular attitudes have

What are two ways to help students associate positive outcomes with an attitude?

contributed to their success or happiness. This component is also present in Carmen Johnson's character education program.

> ➤ Our students read about people with backgrounds similar to their own whose success can be traced to positive character traits. We also bring in local heroes who can describe their experiences.

Conditions for Psychomotor Skills. When students are first learning a psychomotor skill, it is important to provide them with verbal guidance (Fitts & Posner, 1967). Verbal guidance can take the form of a self-instructional routine that students use to talk themselves through the skill.

What similarities do you see between the conditions for intellectual skill learning and psychomotor skill learning?

Second, teachers should provide opportunities for repeated practice over time, especially if the goal is automaticity. This practice should be accompanied by feedback on the accuracy of performance (Gagné & Driscoll, 1988).

Finally, as students become more proficient, they may profit from mental or covert rehearsal of the skill. Athletes often find that mental imagery can improve their skill performance (Driscoll, 1994). For example, divers might imagine how they will perform a dive successfully.

Conditions for Cognitive Strategies. Because cognitive strategies can be considered a subtype of intellectual skill, the conditions for learning intellectual skills are relevant to cognitive strategy learning with some adaptations.

First, many task-specific strategies such as outlining or mnemonics can be taught well through demonstration and explanation. The explanation of the strategy should include a verbal description of how the strategy is being used and why it's being used in this situation.

Second, students need opportunities to practice the strategy in different contexts and distributed across time. Teachers of different grade levels or content areas can help this by collaborating on the teaching of similar strategies (Derry & Murphy, 1986). Paula Romanowski, principal at Johnson Junior High School, does it this way.

➤ Rather than trying to teach 100 different strategies, our staff has identified five strategies that will be taught in each class, but for different purposes. We want our students to know a few strategies well.

Third, strategy practice should include opportunities for informational feedback. This feedback should include information on the effectiveness, efficiency, and creativity of the strategy used by the student. This is how Donald Perry addresses this in his high school science class.

➤ After I have demonstrated a science learning strategy and students have used it, we hold a class discussion about how they used it and how well it worked. I not only emphasize the successful uses, but we talk about how to improve less successful uses.

A Comparison of Gagné and Gropper.   You may have noticed a number of similarities between Gropper's instructional treatments and Gagné's conditions of learning. This is because both theories describe how instruction can be designed to teach specific types of behavior or knowledge. Combining the ideas from both theories can provide a comprehensive view of how to teach information, concepts, and skills. Table 9.3 combines important ideas from both theories that may help you integrate the two theories.

TABLE 9.3   A Synthesis of Gropper's Routine Treatments and Gagné's Conditions of Learning for Facts, Concepts, and Procedural Rules

Type of Learning Outcome	Gropper's Routine Treatments	Gagné's Conditions of Learning
Facts (Gropper) Verbal information (Gagné)	Students need to be told or shown what the facts are Students need to practice and review the facts either by stating or applying the facts, or both	Draw students' attention to the important information to be learned Provide a meaningful context for learning Provide multiple cues for recall and generalization of learned information
Concepts	A definition of the concept and possibly some guidelines for helping distinguish related concepts Examples and nonexamples of the concept are provided Practice that requires students to state the definition and to categorize or produce examples of the concept correctly	Help students recall relevant previously learned concepts Focus students' attention on the distinctive features of the concept being learned Provide sufficient retrieval cues Allow for effective practice: • Allow every student to participate and to receive feedback • Align practice to how students need to recall or apply the concept Provide practice with varied examples and nonexamples and distributed over time
Procedural rule (intellectual skills)	The steps in a procedure need to be identified The steps need to be demonstrated or modeled Rules or rationales provided for each step Students practice the steps in the procedure with feedback and varied examples requiring the procedure	Help students recall relevant previously learned skills Focus students' attention on the distinctive features of the procedure being learned Provide sufficient retrieval cues • Allow for effective practice • Allow every student to participate and to receive feedback • Align practice to how students need to recall or apply the procedure Provide practice in varied contexts and distributed over time

Looking in on

When I finished my lesson plan for the first *Amelia Bedelia* book, I showed it to Karen to get feedback. I thought the students and I would read the first book together as a class. When we came to the first idiom, I would stop and ask what was funny about what Amelia just did. I would then explain what an idiom is, and ask them to look for additional examples of idioms as we read. When they identified a potential idiom, we would discuss whether or not the example fit with the definition. As a lesson extension, I thought I could connect the idiom lesson in language arts to the discussion we are having in social studies about political slogans such as, "A chicken in every port."

As a writing activity, we would brainstorm other idioms we had heard, students would select one of those idioms to write about, and they would write an Amelia-type incident around that idiom. Before students wrote their own paragraphs, I would model how to use the three-step procedure for writing a paragraph on the overhead projector. Karen told me that when I'm demonstrating it's important to tell them why I'm doing what I'm doing. For example, tell them that the topic sentence helps keep the paragraph on topic. Also, it's important to keep students involved by having them make suggestions. After we did a paragraph together, they would select one of the remaining idioms or another that comes to mind, they would write paragraphs, and I would walk around the room to provide guidance.

I thought the writing lesson would work for most students, but I was concerned about our students who could barely write a single sentence. Karen agreed and made a number of suggestions. She said we could have those students dictate their paragraphs to one of us and then copy what we wrote, or we could have those students read their paragraphs into a speech-to-writing converter on the computer. Another suggestion she had was to have students write in groups with one student identified as the recorder or writer.

● **What treatment tools and conditions of learning has Mona included in her lesson plan?**

Decision Point: What are the strengths and weaknesses of Karen's various suggestions for accommodating students with writing difficulties?

Principle 3.1: Connecting New Knowledge to Existing Knowledge

The importance of considering prior knowledge during instructional design is emphasized throughout Gagné's model. For example, goal analysis involves the identification of prerequisite knowledge and skills. Verbal information is more meaningful if students connect new information to existing information. In the case of an intellectual skill lesson, students need the appropriate prerequisite skills.

Because of the importance of prior knowledge, you may decide to pretest students to determine if they possess the relevant prior knowledge. Pretesting can be done in a number of ways including paper and pencil tests, behavioral samples, questionnaires, and the review of academic records (Kemp, Morrison, & Ross, 1994). If you decide to pretest, however, you need to be aware of both the benefits and cautions involved with pretesting (Kemp, Morrison, & Ross, 1994; Yelon, 1996).

What are potential benefits of pretesting and cautions with the use of pretesting?

An important benefit of pretesting is that you can avoid teaching a lesson for which students are unprepared. Also, boredom can result when students participate in lengthy but unnecessary lessons on content that is already mastered. Be aware, however, that pretesting involves a time commitment. You will need to schedule the necessary time to administer and interpret pretests. Interpretation can be particularly complicated because students may make the same mistakes during pretesting, but for radically different reasons. Finally, pretesting can create negative feelings in students who do not do well.

Because of the concerns with pretesting, you should pretest in informal and non-threatening ways if possible, and you should be clear to students about why you are pretesting and what level of performance you expect. Let students know that they are not expected to know everything on a pretest. Here is how Octavio Morales does some informal pretesting with his kindergartners early in the year.

➤ When children come into my class on the first day of class, I greet them and tell them I have a hook for their jackets and a cubicle with their names under it for their other stuff. I ask them to see if they can find them. This way I know if they can recognize their own name in print.

Principle 3.3: The Limitations of Students' Working Memory

The issue of limited working memory capacity also figures prominently in Gagné's discussions of conditions of learning. For example, Gagné recommends that you present verbal information in short and manageable chunks. Also, pace instruction so that students have time to rehearse and understand information during your lessons. Here is how Susan Moreno addresses this with her seventh grade social studies students.

➤ When I prepare to teach a unit on American history, I look over the list of events and terms at the end of the chapter. I find ways to group topics so that we are focusing on a few events each day with plenty of time for practice activities and review.

An understanding of working memory limitations is also important for intellectual skill learning. Some procedures involve a large number of steps or decisions, some rules have complicated conditions for their use, and some concepts are very broad. Teach complicated procedures in chunks or parts and focus on a limited number of concept examples and nonexamples at one time when teaching a broad concept. Some complex intellectual skill learning requires that the subskills be coordinated and integrated. In that case, it may be better to teach the whole skill, but to use simple applications of that skill at first (van Merrienboer, Clark, & De Croock, 2002). Worked examples that show the sequence of steps for applying a skill can also be useful for managing working memory load (Sweller & Cooper, 1985).

When students are asked to learn higher order rules or to solve problems through their explorations and inventions, these explorations often pose considerable memory load (Land, 2000). As discussed earlier in this text, technology can be useful for off-loading some of that cognitive load.

Refer to Chapter 3 for additional suggestions for how to manage working memory load in instruction.

Constructivist Perspectives on Instructional Design

Behavioral and information-processing approaches to instructional design focus on teaching specific types of knowledge. Constructivists, on the other hand, focus on the design of instructional environments that allow students to construct understandings. Effectively designed constructivist learning environments encourage students to engage in the active process of developing meaning through authentic learning experiences and interactions with others (Tan & Hung, 2002). This discussion of how to design these environments is framed around the principles developed in Chapter 5.

The Cognitive Developmental Basis for Constructivism

As you learned in Chapter 5, educational constructivism has connections to the cognitive developmental theories of Piaget, Vygotsky, and Bruner and the philosophy of John Dewey among others. These influences are reflected in Principle 5.2, learning experiences are more effective if they take into account the cognitive developmental levels of the learners. The implications of this principle for instructional design are reflected in the idea of developmentally appropriate practice.

Developmentally Appropriate Practice. Developmentally **appropriate practice** is an approach to designing classroom learning environments that bases educational decisions on available knowledge about students and how they develop (Gestwicki, 1999). Although DAP can be applied across all grade levels, it has been a particularly influential idea in early childhood education. Figure 9.1 provides an overview of DAP principles abstracted from different sources (Bredekemp et al., 1992; National Association for the Education of Young Children, 1996a, 1996b, 1996c). A number of the DAP principles provided in Figure 9.1 are consistent with a constructivist view of learning.

Piagetian Theory and DAP. Piagetian stage theory has historically been important in determining the types of learning experiences that are developmentally appropriate for students of different ages. For example, Piagetian theory suggests that there are developmental constraints on students' thinking, particularly in earlier stages. As you remember from Chapter 5, preoperational children's logic is characterized by egocentrism, centration, and irreversibility, while Piagetians believe that abstract reasoning is difficult for students in the concrete operational stage. Developmentally appropriate instruction based on Piagetian stage theory would account for these constraints. In the case of concrete operational students, for example, the problematic suggestion has been made by some to postpone science learning that requires inferential reasoning about a series of complex variables until adolescence (Stone, 1996).

However, connecting Piagetian theoretical constructs and instructional design has had problems. First, even developmentalists recognize that it is difficult to make assumptions about an individual student's cognitive development purely on the basis of her or his age (Bredekamp, Knuth, Kunesh, & Shulman, 1992; Kostelnik, 1993; National Association for the Education of Young Children, 1996c). Students in the same age cohort vary widely in terms of their cognitive development, possibly making a lesson designed for students at a particular stage inappropriate for some and appropriate for others.

Second, it is difficult to infer cognitive development directly from students' performances on various tasks designed to assess Piagetian development. Children often have better capabilities than they show on these tasks (Gelman & Baillargeon, 1983; National Association for the Education of Young Children, 1996a; Siegler, 1998; Stone, 1996). Accurate assessment of Piagetian stage development is difficult, making it problematic to use these data to plan instruction.

Finally, some of the implications for designing instruction based on Piaget's stages of development potentially represent a misreading of Piaget's writings, or failure to consider data from neo-Piagetian research (Metz, 1995). Although younger students' rea-

FIGURE 9.1 Principles of Developmentally Appropriate Practice

- There is no one right way to implement developmentally appropriate practice, but instruction and curriculum should be matched to the needs of the learner.
- Learning should stress the development of conceptual understandings and strategies, rather than the acquisition of isolated facts and skills.
- Students benefit from the opportunity to balance self-initiated or self-selected learning activities with teacher-directed or -selected activities.
- Learners need to construct knowledge through active and hands-on exploration of their worlds.
- Learners benefit both socially and cognitively from interactions with peers and other adults.
- Learners benefit from cross-curricular learning experiences that promote connections across content domains.
- Learning needs to be motivated by students' natural interests and desires to know.
- Rich and varied learning experiences are needed to account for differences among learners.

Focus on Learner Diversity

Development and Instructional Design

As discussed in the text, the application of developmental generalizations to individual students can be problematic. Designing developmentally appropriate instruction requires a careful understanding of the nature of development. Some selected characteristics of the nature of development that are pertinent to instructional design at all grade levels follow (Bredekamp & Copple, 1997; Gestwicki, 1999).

- Students' physical, cognitive, and social/personal development all influence each other. For example, adolescents' concerns for peer acceptance can influence the effort they put forth in learning cognitive skills.
- Development occurs at different rates for different children and adolescents. Students in the same age cohort can differ widely from each other in terms of social and physical maturity and cognitive development. Be careful of applying rigid age expectations to individual students.
- A particular student may develop more quickly in some areas than others. For example, a student's verbal abilities may be more developed than that child's social abilities. Be careful about making assumptions in one area of development based on development in another. Students with intellectual gifts may or may not show the same level of development socially or physically.

- Development and learning are affected by the social and cultural contexts in which they occur. For example, students' daily experiences contain a number of opportunities for students to learn as part of their community and family life (Gallimore & Goldenberg, 1993; Rogoff, 1982). You may find it useful to include those day-to-day learning structures in your classroom. For example, if story telling is a commonly used instructional approach, in your students' families, then you might consider ways of incorporating story telling in your instructional design.
- Development is assisted if students are provided tasks that are just beyond their current level of mastery. This characteristic reflects an understanding of the zone of proximal development from Chapter 5.
- Students have different modes of representing knowledge and learning. According to Bruner and Piaget (see Chapter 5), novices and young children can benefit from physical or concrete learning experiences.

● **When implementing developmentally appropriate instruction, why is it important to be a careful observer and evaluator of your students? (For your authors' perspective on this question, go to the text website for this chapter.)**

---

soning may be less sophisticated for a number of reasons, this does not suggest that these students are incapable of profiting from instructional experiences requiring mental activities such as inferential reasoning.

Although broad theories of development such as Piagetian stage theory are difficult to apply to specific instructional design decisions, that does not mean that cognitive development is irrelevant to instructional design. Certainly, characteristics such as attention span, background knowledge, and language development need to be considered when designing instruction. Additionally, if students are going to be asked to self-regulate their own learning, developmental trends in self-regulation are important. For example, five- and six-year-old students are less effective than older students at monitoring and planning behaviors that require self-awareness of their own learning (Schneider, 1998). Once again, however, any developmental trends for self-regulation need to be applied cautiously to a specific student or group of students. Also, students' ability to monitor attention and self-regulate can be improved with instruction (Schneider, 1998).

What are the issues with applying Piagetian stage theory to instructional design?

The Design of Problem-Based Learning

Although constructivist learning environments can vary, problem-based learning is useful for understanding how to apply Principle 5.1, learning is more powerful if learners construct their own understandings, and Principle 5.3, students' knowledge construction is facilitated by the nature of their interactions with people and objects in their environment to designing a constructivist learning environment.

Characteristics and Components of Constructivist Learning Environments.   Several examples of constructivist learning environments exist, including but not limited to Rich Environments for Active Learning (Grabinger & Dunlap, 1995), Open-ended Learning Environments (Hannafin, 1995; Hannafin, Land, & Oliver, 1999; Land & Hannafin, 1996), and Goal Based Scenarios (Schank, Berman, & Macpherson, 1999; Schank, Fano, Bell, & Jona, 1993). These constructivist learning environments have the following characteristics: learning through problem solving in authentic environments; an emphasis on student collaboration; helping students view problems from multiple disciplinary perspectives; an emphasis on self-directed learning and assessment that employs student-generated artifacts or student exhibitions (Arends, 2001; Dahlgren & Dahlgren, 2002; Savoie & Hughes, 1994; Stepien & Gallagher, 1993).

Constructivist learning environments also have the following major components (Jonassen, 1999; Tan & Hung, 2002).

- A problem, case, issue, or project that guides and structures the learning
- Information resources or information banks to provide needed background information
- Supporting tools, often in the form of technology applications, that include cognitive tools to support students' learning and problem solving, and conversation and collaboration tools to facilitate group problem solving and interactions
- Social/contextual support to provide training and environmental support needed by teachers and students

These characteristics and components of a constructivist learning environment are useful for thinking about instructional design issues for problem-based learning.

Selecting the Problem, Question, or Issue.   The key instructional design decision in planning problem-based learning is the identification of the problems. These problems are the focus of problem-based learning, and students use them to acquire important knowledge and skills. An effective problem should have a number of characteristics.

What are the characteristics of ill-defined problems?

First, the problems should typically be ill-defined problems (Arends, 2001; Stepien & Gallagher, 1993). **Ill-defined problems** are like the complex problems that are encountered in everyday life. They should require students to define some aspects of the problem as they solve it, they should cross academic domains, they should not have obvious or clear solutions and solution paths, and their solutions need to be evaluated on multiple criteria (Jonassen, 1999).

Second, the problems should be engaging, meaningful, and appropriate for the age of the students (Arends, 2001; Delisle, 1997). It's important to remember that many children and adolescents do not have the goal of becoming a content expert in an academic domain (Maxwell, Bellisimo, & Mergendoller, 2001). Therefore, meaningful problems need to connect academic disciplines to students' lives. For example, adolescents face some critical health issues such as sexually transmitted diseases. Understanding how to reduce the incidences of sexually transmitted diseases requires application of knowledge from biology, history, political science, and sociology, to name a few disciplines, and this problem has relevance for students' lives.

Effective problems not only need to be ill-defined and relevant, but also realistic in terms of the level of expertise students are expected to show (Jonassen, 1999). If expectations are not matched to a student's level, frustration can result.

Finally, when identifying a problem, consider its potential alignment to important standards or curricular objectives (Delisle, 1997; Torp & Sage, 2002). This is particularly important as schools become places where students are required to pass high-stakes examinations that cover prescribed standards or content.

Communicating the Problem.   Once a problem has been selected, it must be communicated to students in an understandable manner. First, students need to understand the context in which the problem is situated. For example, what advantages and restrictions does the context pose for solving the problem? Students also need to know who the stakeholders and community of practitioners are that they will need to interact with or consider in their problem solving (Jonassen, 1999).

The problem statement should clearly identify the issue or problem and any conditions that signal a successful solution. It can be written in this format, "How can we [state the issue] so that we address [state the conditions]?" (Torp & Sage, 2002, p. 64). For example, "How can we provide timely information about sexually transmitted diseases to students in this high school so that we address the concerns and opinions of schools, parents, churches, and the medical community?"

Social and Contextual Support. To be successful, problem-based learning requires appropriate social and contextual support. To identify needed social and contextual support, consider the resource and logistical issues for implementing problem-based learning. For example, students may go outside of school to research a problem (Arends, 2001). You need to become familiar with district policies on field trips, arrange transportation, coordinate, if necessary, with other professionals, and arrange for additional adults to supervise and scaffold.

You also need to identify the necessary support to implement problem-based learning effectively. The first time you design and implement problem-based learning, you may need considerable social and technical support. Attempts at problem-based learning can fail if these types of support are not available (Jonassen, 1999). You may want to use already developed problem-based learning approaches at first, or work as a member of a team with other professionals who have experience with this type of learning. Also, there are websites to help guide you through some of the components of problem-based learning (Ngeow & Kong, 2001). (See Web Resources at the end of this chapter.)

You also need to consider the characteristics of your learners. For example, your students may be unprepared to be self-regulating and independent learners, inexperienced with some of the required skills involved in inquiry, or inexperienced with managing group work (Ngeow & Kong, 2001; van den Hurk, Dolmans, Wolfhagen, & van der Vleuten, 2001). Assuming that students will naturally learn if you provide them with hands-on experiences is a common misunderstanding (Hausfather, 2001). Make sure to provide students with needed instruction or support for some or all of the issues listed previously (Torp & Sage, 2002). You have to identify the types of supporting tools you need.

Supporting Tools.   In general, but not always, **supporting tools** are applications of technology that guide and scaffold students' problem solving. Here are some examples of supporting tools for problem-based learning.

- Students can be provided with completed analyses of analogous cases to help guide their solution of their case (Jonassen, 1999; Jonassen & Hernandez-Serrano, 2002).
- Students also may need resources for accessing information they lack. For example, they may need self-instructional modules or access to appropriate websites.
- Students are also likely to need tools that scaffold complex performances. For example, they need data analysis tools, graphing or concept mapping tools, and spreadsheets.
- Students are likely to need tools to support collaboration and conversation, such as access to chat rooms and e-mail, and ways of tracking of group decisions.

For additional examples of technology applications to support knowledge construction, refer to Chapter 7.

Evaluation and Problem-Based Learning.   To some extent, the principles of effective assessment are the same for problem-based learning as they are for other forms of learning. One of these principles is that teachers should continuously monitor students'

E-mail is one of several supporting tools for problem-based learning.

learning. When students are constructing knowledge, it's important to make sure that students are constructing accurate or useful knowledge and not developing misconceptions (Brooks & Brooks, 1999; Simpson, 2001; Torp & Sage, 2002). You should provide time for students to reflect, talk, and write about their learning and problem-solving processes (Arends, 2001).

A second important evaluation principle is that assessment needs to align to instructional goals. Given the nature of constructivist learning environment, assessment should target both students' knowledge and learning processes (Swanson & Case, 1997). For example, teachers should assess students' ability to apply the knowledge they have learned, and to integrate that knowledge within and across domains. Assessment might also focus on students' ability to self-evaluate their learning or their abilities to collaborate with others.

Because of the complicated, interdisciplinary nature of the learning, assessment procedures such as artifacts and exhibitions are often recommended (Arends, 2001). An **artifact** can be a videotape, concrete model, portfolio, or any representation that captures the complexity of what students have learned. An **exhibition** is an opportunity for students to present what they have learned to an audience. The exhibitions you may be most familiar with are science fairs and student presentations in classes and seminars. The use of artifacts and exhibitions needs to be planned carefully. For example, rubrics or rating scales need to be developed for the students' artifacts and exhibitions. Other professionals may need to serve as evaluators for the exhibitions. Chapter 13 contains additional details on the use of these approaches.

*M*otivation and Instructional Design

Learners are motivated by lessons that they find reasonably challenging, that appeal to their needs and interests, that help them achieve relevant goals, and that are characterized by some amount of choice and the unexpected. These characteristics of motivating instruction are important regardless of your approach to instructional design, and they are reflected in Keller's ARCS instructional design model.

Keller's ARCS Theory

Keller's ARCS instructional design theory is a framework for embedding motivational strategies into instructional design (Keller, 1983, 1987a, 1987b, 1999a, 1999b; Keller & Kopp, 1987; Keller & Litchfield, 2002). The letters **ARCS** represent four categories of motivational variables (attention, relevance, confidence, and satisfaction) and the research that supports them. Each of the four categories has three subcategories of strategies that are used to guide implementation of ARCS (Keller & Kopp, 1987; Small, 1997, 1999). The categories and subcategories of strategies are based on a number of theories of motivation, but to a large extent ARCS represents an expectancy value view of motivation (Dempsey & Johnson, 1998). As you remember from Chapter 6, expectancy value theory describes levels of motivation in terms of learners' expectations for success and the value they place on that success. Table 9.4

TABLE 9.4 ARCS Categories, Subcategories and Principles of Motivation

ARCS Category	ARCS Subcategories and Strategies	Motivation Principle
Attention	Perceptual arousal (surprise, incongruity, uncertainty) Inquiry arousal (stimulate curiosity) Variability (variety in methods and activities)	Principle 6.4: Learners are more motivated when appropriate levels of variety, choice, and surprise are incorporated into lessons
Relevance	Goal orientation (present the objectives) Motive matching (students' needs and motives) Familiarity (relate to students' experience and values)	Principle 6.2: Learners are more motivated by activities that appeal to their personal needs, desires, and interests Principle 6.3: Learners are more motivated when they have specific near-term goals that they believe are important
Confidence	Learning requirements (inform students of performance requirements) Success opportunities (challenging and meaningful tasks) Personal responsibility (link success to effort and ability)	Principle 6.1: Learners are more motivated when they believe their actions will result in the successful completion of challenging tasks Principle 6.3: Learners are more motivated when they have specific near-term goals that they believe are important
Satisfaction	Intrinsic reinforcement (intrinsic value) Extrinsic rewards (feedback and positive reinforcement) Equity (consistent standards)	Principle 6.1: Learners are more motivated when they believe their actions will result in the successful completion of challenging tasks Principle 6.2: Learners are more motivated by activities that appeal to their personal needs, desires, and interests

Source: Adopted from Keller, J. M., & Litchfield, B. C. (2002). Motivation and performance. In R. A. Reiser & J. V. Dempsey (Eds.). *Instructional design and technology* (p. 92). Upper Saddle River, NJ: Merrill Prentice Hall.

contains the categories and subcategories of ARCS, and how they relate to the principles of motivation developed in Chapter 6.

Using the ARCS model in designing instruction is a four-step process (Keller & Kopp, 1987). First, an audience evaluation is conducted to determine which motivational strategies to include in instruction. An audience evaluation considers the characteristics of the learners and their attitudes toward the content and the lesson delivery modes that have been selected (Keller, 1999b; Song & Keller, 2001). The goal is to identify the motivational strategies that best address the needs of the learners. For example, if your students lack confidence in their mathematics skills, then emphasis would be placed on strategies that enhance learner confidence.

The second event is the preparation of motivational objectives, which specify the behaviors you want to observe as indicators of changes in students' motivation. For example, if your goal is to increase confidence, you might look for an increase in students' persistence on difficult tasks or an increase in positive expectancy statements from students.

The third event is the selection of strategies. Motivational strategies should be time and resource efficient, supportive of the instructional objectives, acceptable to the audience, and compatible with the lesson delivery system and teachers' personal style. The intent is not necessarily to address all categories or subcategories, but only those that are relevant to your audience and objectives. In fact, unnecessary motivational strategies can distract students from the lesson goal, and can significantly increase the length of the lesson (Keller, 1999b; Keller & Kopp, 1987). Also, motivated

Looking in on

We like our choice of problem for our problem-based learning because it has far-reaching implications even outside our community. Pollution levels actually decreased for about five years in our city, but they are gradually increasing again. The students are developing recommendations on how to help curb pollution levels again, while attending to other issues such as economic growth. Some students are taking an historical perspective on the problem and examining what changes over the last few years have resulted in the increase in pollution. Others are engaged in field work to judge the impact of pollution on vegetation and water quality, while still others are looking at changes in rates of certain illnesses.

A number of community and university scientists, business leaders, and even a politician have volunteered to work with our students or to be available for advice. Also, we have a minigrant to buy equipment and to cover field research costs. At the end, students will present their findings in poster sessions, and a panel of students will be selected to present the recommendations in a community forum. The whole class, however, will work to prepare the presentation.

● **What components of problem-based learning are observable in this description? What components are missing?**

Decision Point: What supporting tools would be useful for this problem?

---

students may have decreased motivation levels when exposed to unnecessary motivational strategies (Song & Keller, 2001).

The fourth event is evaluation. Although motivation can be evaluated in a number of ways, Keller sees effort as the student variable that is most directly affected by motivation (Main, 1993). As noted in Chapter 6, effective classroom experiences should help students perceive that their achievement is related to the quantity and quality of their efforts.

What are the events in implementing ARCS?

Motivation Strategies. Keller's categories of motivation provide general guidance on the types of motivation strategies you might embed in your instruction. They also provide a useful context for discussing how the principles of motivation from Chapter 6 (see Table 9.4) and various techniques discussed in other parts of this text can be used to enhance student motivation.

Attention. For students to profit from instruction, they must be interested enough to pay attention to it. Attention is generated and maintained through perceptual arousal, inquiry arousal, and variability (Keller & Kopp, 1987; Keller & Litchfield; 2002). These strategies also represent an application of Principle 6.4, learners are more motivated when appropriate levels of variety, choice, and surprise are incorporated into lessons.

Perceptual arousal involves gaining and maintaining student attention by the use of novel, surprising, uncertain, incongruous, or uncertain events. For example, as noted in Chapter 7, you can begin a lesson with a discrepant event. Students' attention can be maintained by providing instruction that has interest value for them. Keller (1983) observed that students are more interested in those things that are concrete and personalized. Because of this, you might use anecdotes and examples that connect to their life or that are about real human beings. This is how Paul O'Brien does this in his twentieth century American history class.

➤ My students find it interesting that I was alive and experienced what they are studying in the latter half of the twentieth century. They like it when I tell them what it was like when I was their age.

Inquiry arousal stimulates information-seeking behavior in students by posing questions or problems. A number of constructivist strategies such as discovery learning, inquiry training, and problem-based learning employ this process. During a teacher-directed lesson, inquiry arousal can be addressed by asking questions that require students to transfer what they are learning to novel situations.

Why would creating curiosity in students make them more likely to attend to instruction?

Variability refers to the importance of varying instructional experiences for students. To accomplish this, you need to be comfortable with various modes of instruction. Technology can also be helpful because of its ability to rapidly vary visual images and experiences. Remember, however, that too much variability might confuse rather than motivate. You should vary instructional activities at points in the lesson that make sense. For example, switch to group work when that accomplishes your instructional goals.

Relevance. Relevance may be the most important of the four categories for enhancing students' motivation (Means, Jonassen, & Dwyer, 1997). Relevance can be demonstrated through the strategies of familiarity, goal orientation, and motive matching (Keller & Kopp, 1987; Keller & Litchfield, 2002). Relevance strategies provide examples of applications of Principle 6.2, learners are more motivated by activities that appeal to their personal needs, desires, and interests, and Principle 6.3, learners are more motivated when they have specific near-term goals that they believe are important.

Familiarity can be accomplished by connecting learning to students' own experiences (Keller & Kopp, 1987; Small, 1997). As discussed in Chapter 3, learning is more meaningful if it can be related to students' prior knowledge and experience. These connections can be accomplished by using familiar language and concrete experiences, creating analogies between new learning and students' prior experiences, embedding instruction in authentic or familiar situations, and using human interest examples (Means, Jonassen, & Dwyer, 1997). Given how diverse students' backgrounds are, teachers also need to consider the use of multiple examples.

Goal orientation is accomplished by providing students with the purposes of the instruction and some suggestions for how to accomplish those purposes (Keller & Kopp, 1987; Small, 1997). A number of ideas discussed throughout this text are useful here. You can help students identify task value for what they are learning or relate the lesson to possible long-term goals. You can also help students develop the metacognitive skills necessary to identify strategies that match their goals.

Motive matching is a process of identifying student's needs and motives and providing instruction that addresses them (Keller & Kopp, 1987; Keller & Litchfield, 2002). For example, students' belonging need and their affiliation motive can be addressed by letting students work together through strategies such as cooperative learning and problem-based learning. Students' power and self-determination needs can be met by giving students some control over what they experience in the classroom. For example, plan opportunities for students to make decisions about what is learned or how learning will occur. John O'Brien does it this way in his junior high school English classes.

> ➤ I try to let my students write about topics they choose within broad guidelines or categories that I provide.

Confidence. Students may avoid interesting and desired goals if they feel they lack the competence to achieve those goals (Keller & Kopp, 1987). Motivating instruction should help students believe that with effort they can succeed. This is accomplished through the strategies of learning requirements (expectancy for success), success opportunities (challenge setting), and personal responsibility (attribution modeling) (Keller & Kopp, 1987; Small, 1997). These strategies represent an application of Principle 6.1, learners are more motivated when they believe their actions will result in the successful completion of challenging tasks, and Principle 6.3, learners are more motivated when they have specific near-term goals that they believe are important.

Learning requirements are communicated by informing students about performance requirements and how these requirements will be evaluated. Make sure your instructional design includes clear statements of your expectations for success, and the requirements students need to meet. For example, if you have a scoring rubric for a project, allow students to see that rubric as they plan their efforts. Also, make sure that the evaluations you design are logical and well aligned to your objectives so that students can predict how they will be evaluated.

How does well-aligned instruction affect students' expectations?

Success opportunities imply that if students are to build an expectation for success, they must experience success. As discussed in Chapter 6, success should occur in meaningful tasks with an appropriate level of difficulty. Assess students' learning frequently to make sure that tasks are at the appropriate level.

Personal responsibility involves strategies that help students attribute their successes to their ability and effort. When designing instruction, plan how you will provide attributional feedback to help students connect effort to success. Also involve your students in activities such as goal setting and contracting in your instructional design. Here is how Marion Jones does this in her sixth grade classroom.

> ➤ I use a contracting grading system in my teaching. Students need to all take and pass my tests, but they can select from a list of different activities to fulfill the rest of their requirements for a grade.

Satisfaction. Students become unmotivated if the outcomes of their efforts don't match their expectations, and if their efforts don't lead to tangible successes. Satisfaction is enhanced through the strategies of intrinsic reinforcement (natural consequences), extrinsic rewards (positive consequences), and equity (Keller & Kopp, 1987; Small, 1997). These strategies are useful for implementing Principle 6.1, learners are more motivated when they believe their actions will result in the successful completion of challenging tasks, and Principle 6.2, learners are more motivated by activities that appeal to their personal needs, desires, and interests.

What is a task-endogenous incentive?

Keller (1983) recommends that teachers use both task-endogenous (intrinsic reinforcement) and task-exogenous (extrinsic reinforcement) strategies to help develop students' satisfaction with learning. Task-endogenous incentives flow naturally from participating in learning. As discussed in Chapter 2, behaviorists refer to endogenous incentives as natural reinforcers. Examples of task-endogenous incentives include the following (Good & Brophy, 2000):

- Design instruction that includes opportunities for students to engage in fantasy and simulation activities, such as role-playing.
- Provide opportunities for students to interact with each other. Identify parts in your lesson design in which students can collaborate.
- When relevant, provide lessons that are designed with higher order or thought-provoking objectives in mind.
- Design opportunities for students to work on and complete projects based on what they are learning. The problem-based focus of constructivism is an example of this recommendation.

Task-exogenous incentives are external rewards. Keller (1983) recommends the judicious use of exogenous or extrinsic incentives because of the concerns about the potential damaging effects of exogenous or extrinsic rewards on intrinsic motivation (Kohn, 1993a; Lepper & Greene, 1975). However, if the following guidelines are fol-

312 **PART II** Principles into Practice

As we have attempted to design problem-based learning opportunities for our students, we have met periodically to discuss how the process is going. We've generated a number of, "We have learned . . ." statements from our discussion. Here are some of our ideas.

- Problem-based learning must take into account important curricular objectives and state standards, and learning experiences and assessments need to be aligned to those goals.
- Although you can teach important content through problem-based learning, it is helpful if students already have a basic understanding of some key concepts and procedures. These should be identified and planned for early in the curriculum.
- An effective problem should be personally interesting to students, at a reasonable level of complexity, and should provide different ways for students with different interests and capabilities to feel successful.

- Exhibitions and artifacts can be impressive ways to evaluate students, but students' progress should be monitored along the way. Students need continuous guidance and feedback.
- Appropriate technology must be available to help students manage the complexity of what they are doing. The number of variables that must be considered simultaneously during complicated problem solving can be overwhelming to novice learners.

● **How are instructional alignment, learning hierarchy analysis, ARCS, and working memory limitations related to these ideas?**

Decision Point: Why would the types of discussions these teachers are having be important when implementing something as complex as problem-based learning?

---

lowed, exogenous rewards can be useful for increasing students' satisfaction with their learning (Alderman, 1999; Good & Brophy, 2000).

For additional information on the use of feedback, refer to Chapter 7.

- Exogenous incentives should be tied to performance, rather than to participation. For example, incentives can be provided for students' improvement.
- Exogenous rewards are more powerful if the students have a clear sense of their goal and strategies for meeting that goal. Incentives are unlikely to be experienced if students do not know how to earn them.

Students need both intrinsic and extrinsic reinforcement.

- Incentives should be plentiful and available to all learners. All learners in a classroom should feel that they have a chance to earn the incentives offered.
- Feedback should be immediate or timely and should help students identify what they are doing successfully and what needs to be improved.

Equity strategies are concerned with fairness and consistency of evaluation standards. Make sure that your evaluation approaches align to what you have communicated that students need to learn, and that once standards are established that they are applied consistently. Checklists and rating scales that are used consistently can be important in this regard.

Principles into Practice:
Illustrating Key Concepts

The experiences of Mona Carrie and Marisol Hernandez provide examples of how theoretical principles of learning and motivation can be translated into instructional design models. Both teachers found it necessary to use instructional design models from different theoretical perspectives to accomplish their goals. Your authors believe that this will be your experience also. As you read about these teachers' experiences you were asked to reflect on their use of instructional design models through a series of questions. Here are your authors' perspectives on those questions.

Looking back on
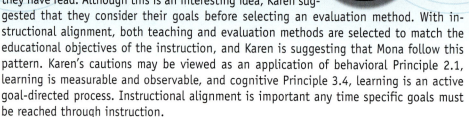

Mona and Karen, her supervising teacher, are beginning to plan lessons around the *Amelia Bedelia* books. Mona had read about a new way to evaluate comprehension that involves having students pantomime the meaning of what they have read. Although this is an interesting idea, Karen suggested that they consider their goals before selecting an evaluation method. With instructional alignment, both teaching and evaluation methods are selected to match the educational objectives of the instruction, and Karen is suggesting that Mona follow this pattern. Karen's cautions may be viewed as an application of behavioral Principle 2.1, learning is measurable and observable, and cognitive Principle 3.4, learning is an active goal-directed process. Instructional alignment is important any time specific goals must be reached through instruction.

Mona decided she wanted her students to know what an idiom is, to identify examples of idioms in their reading, and to distinguish idioms from other language forms such as metaphors. Both Gropper and Gagné would view this as concept learning. Gagné would further see this as an example of a defined concept. Mona also wants her students to know how to write a paragraph using a three-step process. Both Gropper and Gagné would view this as procedural rule learning. The intent of identifying the type of behavior or knowledge in an objective is to guide the selection of treatments or conditions that match that type of behavior or knowledge. This makes instructional design a goal-directed process and applies behavioral Principle 2.1, learning is measurable and observable, and cognitive Principle 3.4, learning is an active goal-directed process.

For the concept lesson on idioms, Mona was planning a deductive approach (see Enriching Your Understanding). She included the routine treatments of providing the definition and examples of the concept. Also, students would demonstrate their understanding of the concept by brainstorming additional examples. Although nonexamples are not mentioned in her design, she probably will want to supply examples of metaphors or analogies as appropriate nonexamples. This helps students distinguish these language forms. In terms of conditions of learning for concepts, her suggestion to tie the language arts lesson to the lesson on political slogans is an attempt to practice in varied contexts.

In terms of learning how to write a paragraph, she has planned routine treatments such as modeling the skill and providing practice with feedback. In terms of conditions of learning, Karen has reminded Mona to explain the reason for each step to make them more meaningful. Mona has combined elements of Gropper's and Gagné's approaches to instructional design and has applied behavioral Principle 2.3, learning results from the effects of stimuli on responses, and cognitive Principle 3.2, effective instruction encourages learners to coordinate their various mental processes. ●

Looking back on

Marisol Hernandez and her colleagues are implementing a problem-based learning approach to science teaching. Although their overall approach to instructional design is from a constructivist perspective, they employ instructional design ideas from a number of theoretical perspectives. For example, George Fremont's technology-assisted math tutorials have incorporated a number of the events of instruction, including the following.

- His opening humorous video segments work well to gain learners' attention.
- Students are told what skills they will be learning in a particular tutorial, which is George's way of informing learners of the instructional objective or event.
- The relevant prerequisite skills are identified for students, and he has even started to create tutorials for each of those skills. This is a good way to use technology to stimulate the recall of prior learning.
- Each lesson proceeds in a step-by-step fashion with a video model of the procedure being taught, which is a reasonable way to present the instructional stimulus for this type of learning.
- Prompts are built into the teaching module so that students are provided with learner guidance.
- The tutorial elicits performance through practice problems, and the tutorial also provides feedback.
- Problems from varying science domains are also provided to enhance retention and transfer of learning.

George Fremont has taken a cognitive information-processing view of instructional design and has implemented cognitive Principle 3.2, effective instruction encourages learners to coordinate their various mental processes.

The problem-based unit on city pollution includes a number of key components of problem-based learning. Students' study of the causes and effects of pollution in their own city represents a relevant and meaningful ill-defined problem. These teachers have identified important sources of social/contextual support in terms of community and university resources, and they have sought funding to cover some of the costs of the problem-based learning. They also have a general idea of an exhibition they want to use as an evaluation tool, but they will need to give this more attention. They still have additional planning to do because information resources, cognitive tools, and conversation and collaboration tools have not been included in their design. Their initial efforts are an attempt to apply constructivist Principle 5.1, learning is more powerful if learners construct their own understandings, and Principle 5.3, students' knowledge construction is facilitated by the nature of their interactions with people and objects in their environment.

Marisol's list of "I learned . . ." statements provides numerous connections to key instructional design ideas. These teachers acknowledge the importance of instructional alignment to curricular standards if their problem-based learning approaches are going to be sensitive to their context. As mentioned previously, these goal-directed activities can be applications of behavioral Principle 2.1, learning is measurable and observable, and cognitive Principle 3.4, learning is an active goal-directed process. Their recognition that it's useful for students to have certain prerequisite skills and knowledge is an application of behavioral Principle 2.2, the learning of complicated behaviors occurs gradually and step by step. Their desire to find personally meaningful problems that are reasonably challenging and that can account for varying student interests are relevance and confidence strategies. Their desire to provide sufficient guidance and feedback is also a confidence strategy, and together these strategies represent an attempt to embed ARCS strategies into their planning. They are applying Principle 6.1, learners are more motivated when they believe their actions will result in the successful completion of challenging tasks, and Principle 6.2, learners are more motivated by activities that appeal to their personal needs, desires, and interests. Finally, their use of technology to reduce cognitive load in learning is an application of cognitive Principle 3.3, the limitations of students' working memory must be accounted for in instruction. ●

Teachers as Decision Makers

At various decision points in this chapter, you were asked to participate in the decision making of Mona Carrie and Marisol Hernandez. Your authors want to share their views of those decision points.

Mona Carrie's Decision Points

As Mona begins her lesson planning, a number of contextual variables are influencing her decision making. Clearly, the state-mandated tests and the pressures they create for accountability are affecting instructional design decisions in this classroom. The state law regarding the teaching of non-English speaking students will also influence her instructional design. The needs of particular students in her class, such as her English language learners, need to be considered.

Mona is excited about a way to assess comprehension by having students pantomime their understanding. In part, her excitement was due to the potential of this activity to assess learners who may have issues with writing or speaking. As Karen suggested, however, evaluation needs to be matched to objective in an aligned lesson. Mona's idea could be a way to check on comprehension or could be used to vary instructional experiences. To fit better with this lesson, however, she needs to think about this assessment approach in relationship to what Karen has asked her to teach.

Mona is beginning to recognize the logic behind Karen's decision making. Karen is making sure that she selects high-interest books that also help her students accomplish important goals. Karen's decision to incorporate writing instruction into the idiom unit is based on her careful analysis of students' performances on previous writing assignments. Overall, she is trying to balance the needs of her students with curricular requirements to design effective instruction.

Each of Karen's suggestions for accommodating differences in students' writing levels has strengths and weaknesses. Having students dictate their paragraph and then copying what they had dictated gives them some low-level practice with writing. Composing while dictating, however, is challenging and they will need help managing the working memory load posed by this approach. Using a computer to convert their speech to print may allow them to complete the project, but it will not provide needed practice on basic writing skills. Group work can be useful for providing students with access to other language models. However, whenever one project comes out of a group, it's hard to know who did what. As is typical for these types of issues, some compromise or hybrid may provide a better answer. For example, in the writing groups, maybe each student can write a sentence to include in the paragraph, and all take a role in revising and editing their paragraph.

Marisol Hernandez' Decision Points

Marisol and her colleagues are trying to resolve a number of issues as they implement problem-based learning in their high school science classrooms. The interdependence among teachers in a district is one interesting contextual variable influencing their decision making. In their case, they needed to cooperate not only with teachers in other grade levels, but also with other departments in their high school. In selecting problems for students to solve, they also had to be aware of community standards. They want to select problems that would be appropriate given the backgrounds of their students. Finally, as with many teachers in this country, their instructional design decisions are influenced by curricular expectations.

The effective use of the technology-assisted math tutorials requires planning. First, they need to provide enough access to the tutorials to make them useful to their classes. This may mean pooling computer resources or dedicating certain computers for certain functions. Procedures may need to be established to make sure that students' access is equitable. Finally, although the tutorials are meant to be self-instructional, students may still need help. Procedures need to be established for how to get help, which might include the use of student tutors or technology aides.

Marisol and her colleagues need to consider the types of supporting tools they need for their problem-based learning. In general, they might put themselves in the place of the students and ask what help they would need to solve the problem successfully. For example, some form of e-mail or chat room might help increase access to community resources. Also, if the students are to conduct research, then they need access to resources such as electronic search capabilities.

Marisol and her colleagues are meeting to discuss how the problem-based learning is progressing. These meetings are a good idea for a number of reasons. First, teachers can use these meetings to resolve issues immediately, to continue their planning, and to provide emotional support for each other. These meetings also provide a forum for presenting data on their decisions and time to reflect on those decisions. So often teachers are asked to implement complicated ideas without sufficient social support. These teachers have been proactive about this issue.

Name _____ Date _____

Chapter 9 Study Guide

Use this Study Guide to review and test your knowledge of key concepts introduced in this chapter and to search out further information on issues and topics raised in this chapter.

 **Key Terms**

Review the following key words from the chapter and then connect to Research Navigator (www.researchnavigator.com) either directly or through this book's Companion Website to explore research on the topics as they relate to education today.

ARCS (p. 308)
Artifact (p. 308)
Attitudes (p. 295)
Cognitive objectives (p. 284)
Cognitive strategies (p. 296)
Concept (p. 292)
Criterion stimulus (p. 291)
Cue (p. 291)
Developmentally appropriate
    practice (p. 304)
Educational objectives (p. 284)
Environment analysis (p. 290)
Events of instruction (p. 296)

Exhibition (p. 308)
Fact (p. 291)
Ill-defined problems (p. 306)
Information-processing analysis
    (p. 289)
Instructional alignment (p. 285)
Intellectual skill (p. 295)
Learner analysis (p. 287)
Learning hierarchy analysis
    (p. 289)
Mager-style instructional objective
    (p. 284)
No Child Left Behind Act (p. 286)

Nonroutine treatments (p. 291)
Performance analysis (p. 290)
Procedural analysis (p. 289)
Procedural rule learning (p. 293)
Psychomotor skills (p. 295)
Routine treatments (p. 291)
Skill analysis (p. 291)
Supporting tools (p. 307)
Task analysis (p. 288)
Universal design for learning (UDL)
    (p. 288)
Verbal information (p. 294)

Alternative Response Items

Multiple Choice

1. Ms. Quiroz wants her students to be able to write a capital letter *Q* in cursive. Which one of the following assessments is most directly aligned to her goal?

   a. She will have her students cut out pictures from magazines of things that begin with a *Q*.
   b. She will have her students try to mold their bodies into the cursive letter *Q* as they lie on the gym floor.
   c. She will have students write a number of capital *Q*s in cursive on a paper.
   d. She will have students identify the capital *Q*s in a sample of cursive handwriting.

2. Mr. Ferris is going to teach his students how to solve a quadratic equation. In planning his lesson, he lists the steps to follow in solving a quadratic equation. What instructional design technique is he using?

   a. Procedural task analysis
   b. Hierarchical skills analysis
   c. Context analysis
   d. Learner analysis

3. Mr. Roybal wants students to be able to use the characteristics of mammals so that they can classify animals correctly as mammal or nonmammal. This type of learning is an example of a(n):

   a. Procedural rule
   b. Fact
   c. Concept
   d. Attitude

4. At the beginning of her lesson, Ms. Gallagher tells students that she wants them to be able to remember four characteristics of a deciduous tree at the end of today's lesson. What event of instruction is she demonstrating?

   a. Gaining learners' attention
   b. Informing learners of the instructional objective
   c. Eliciting performance
   d. Stimulating recall of prior knowledge

5. What similarities are there between Gropper's and Gagné's approaches to instructional design?

   a. Both ask teachers to select lesson elements that align to a type of learning.
   b. Both provide a system for categorizing types of learning.
   c. Both provide suggestions for how to teach concepts.
   d. All of the above.

6. Mr. Lee wants to make sure that his lesson is at a level that his students can succeed at with effort. What component of ARCS is he addressing?

   a. Attention
   b. Relevance
   c. Confidence
   d. Satisfaction

Matching

Match the lesson description with the appropriate Gagné learning outcome. One type of learning outcome is not used.

_____ 7. Students will learn the titles of the members of the president's cabinet.

_____ 8. Students will learn how to use mnemonics to help recall factual information.

_____ 9. Students will learn how to find the area of a rectangle.

_____ 10. Students will learn to value cultural diversity.

a. Verbal information
b. Intellectual skills
c. Psychomotor skills
d. Attitudes
e. Cognitive strategies

Constructed Response Items

Short Answer/Completion Items

1. The form of task analysis that identifies the required prerequisite knowledge and skills for a task is _____.

2. In Gropper's instructional design model, specifying the behaviors to be learned and the conditions under which the behaviors are to be demonstrated is called a(n) _____.

3. Which event of instruction involves helping students retain and apply what they have learned?

4. What is developmentally appropriate practice?

5. What do the letters ARCS stand for in Keller's instructional design model?

Essay Items

1. Why is instructional alignment such an important concept in instructional design?

2. How are Gropper's and Gagné's approaches to instructional design similar and different?

3. How does a constructivist approach to instructional design differ from behavioral and information-processing approaches?

4. Explain the relevance of these terms from Chapter 7 for implementing ARCS.

Attributions	Task value
Needs	Motives

Practicing Your Decision Making

1. Using your understanding of the theories of Gropper and Gagné, design an aligned lesson for the following objectives.

   Students will learn and remember the capitals for the fifty United States.
   Students will be able to differentiate between mammals and reptiles and categorize examples of these animals correctly.
   Students will learn how to solve quadratic equations.

2. Identify any technology skills you have developed so far and describe how they could be useful in providing supporting tools in a constructivist learning environment. What other technology competencies would you need to develop?

INTASC in Action

Use the following activities to think about how concepts and principles from this chapter relate to the INTASC standards.

Standard 2: Student Development. Based on your reading of this chapter, explain the following observation.

The statement, "This is the best way for children to learn," may be an incomplete thought. We would need to know what children are trying to learn before we identify the most effective way to learn.

Standard 3: Diverse Learners. Select a lesson you have designed or one you have observed in this class. Conduct a learner analysis of that lesson to determine learner characteristics that need to be considered for that lesson.

Standard 4: Multiple Instructional Strategies. How are the ideas of Gropper and Gagné relevant to someone who is designing problem-based learning?

Standard 5: Motivation and Management. Review the following ideas from Chapter 6 and describe their relevance for the ARCS model of instructional design.

1. Attributions
2. Performance and learning goals
3. Achievement and affiliation motives
4. Arousal potential

Standard 7: Planning. Identify a relevant state standard for your teaching area or level, conduct a learning hierarchy analysis of that standard, and identify relevant prerequisites. Pick one of those prerequisites and design a lesson based on your understanding of the conditions of learning for the type of knowledge represented by that prerequisite.

Standard 9: Reflective Practice and Professional Growth. Professional educators should be aware of local and state issues that affect their instructional design decisions. Select one such issue in your state or school district and research it carefully. State-mandated testing programs, district policies on academic freedom, and state-mandated character education are two examples of the types of issues you might select.

Web Resources

Instructional Design Models
http://carbon.cudenver.edu/~mryder/itc_data/idmodels.html

Read more information on various instructional techniques and strategies including advance organizers, concept mapping, discovery learning, and problem-based learning. Prepared by Martin Ryder of the University of Colorado at Denver.

For additional information on the components of problem-based learning, go to these websites:

Concept to Classroom: Cooperative Learning
www.thirteen.org/wnetschool/concept2class/month5/index.html

This special site offered by Public Broadcasting Station WNET, New York, offers a series of online workshops to help teachers learn techniques for the classroom, including this workshop on cooperative learning.

From Now On: Inquiry Skills
http://fromnowon.org/nov97/toolkit.html

From Now On, the educational technology journal, offers an online Questioning Toolkit, which provides guidance for developing inquiry skills in the classroom.

Managing the Classroom Environment

To help you with complicated decisions about classroom management, this chapter begins by reviewing key findings from research on effective classroom management. These findings provide general guidelines for classroom management, regardless of your overall approach to teaching. This is followed by a discussion of classroom management approaches that are consistent with the theories of learning and motivation described in Chapters 2 through 6. As in the previous application chapters, the theoretical principles from these theories are used to organize the discussions.

By the time you finish this chapter, you should have an understanding of the following.

● What are key findings from the research on effective classroom management?

● What classroom management applications have developed from behavioral learning theory?

● What classroom management applications have developed from social cognitive theory?

● What classroom management applications are supportive of the goals of a constructivist classroom?

● How can the application of principles of motivation improve classroom management?

Close-ups on the Classroom

Elementary

Although I've taught a couple of years in a local preschool, this is my first year as a second grade teacher at Washington Elementary School. I'm lucky to be at a school with a strong first-year teacher-mentoring program, especially since my mentor, Rosa Fairwell, is so supportive and helpful. She's been in my classroom to observe me twice, and I've been in her classroom two or three times to observe her. Also, we meet a minimum of twice a month to talk about concerns. I have a lot of things to talk to Rosa about, so I hope she can make extra time for me this week.

For example, it bothers me that even after a month in the classroom I still have trouble with simple things such as getting students to line up and walk through the halls quietly. I'm sure that the other teachers think I'm a horrible teacher because I can't keep my students quiet in the hall. I'm also discouraged today because my students were particularly bad during science.

Sometime soon I need to get her advice on Dennis. He's having trouble getting along with other students in the classroom and on the playground, and he is distractible and disorganized in class. Also, when things get hard for him, he gets frustrated and angry with himself. Talking with him hasn't helped, so maybe Rosa will have some ideas.

Rosa has been trying to teach me to be a better data collector on my students, because she says you have to understand a problem before you can solve it. I know she'll ask me to tell her what I've tried with Dennis and how it's worked. I've got some data, but I'll need to collect more.

Decision Point: What types of data can Maria collect on Dennis that could help her and Rosa understand him better?

Classroom management consists of the actions you take as a teacher to establish and maintain a productive learning environment (Brophy, 1999). Research on effective teaching and experienced teachers' self-reports suggest that classroom management is an extremely important component of effective classroom teaching. In fact, it may even be the most important component (Wang, Haertel, & Walberg, 1993). Additionally, beginning teachers have fairly consistently identified classroom management as one of their most difficult challenges (Jones, 1996; Veenman, 1984). Classroom management is challenging because it involves a complicated decision-making process that requires you to consider factors such as your instructional goals, the nature of your learners, the nature of your school and community, and your personality and abilities.

Before proceeding with Chapter 10, be sure you read the Close-ups on the Classroom features about Maria Torres and Oji Samms. At various points in the chapter, you will revisit both teachers in their classrooms and follow their decision-making progress. Their classroom experiences are closely integrated with the key concepts of this chapter and serve as important models of classroom management methods.

Classroom Management Research

Research on effective classroom management conducted primarily in the 1970s and 1980s yielded a number of findings, two of which are focused on in this chapter. First, effective teachers structure their classrooms to prevent discipline problems (Bauer, 2001; Brownell & Walther, 2001; Emmer & Stough, 2001; Evertson & Harris, 1992; Kounin, 1970; Soar & Soar, 1979). Second, successful classroom managers use a number of effective group management strategies (Anguiano, 2001; Kounin, 1983; Kounin, 1970; Kounin & Doyle, 1975; Kounin & Gump, 1974; Kounin & Sherman, 1979). Although this research was conducted primarily in classrooms where teacher-directed instruction was occurring, the findings are adaptable enough to serve as guidelines for a variety of teaching approaches.

Oji Samms and the Middle School Team

I am a math teacher at North Middle School. Our faculty is divided into instructional teams with an English, math, science, and social studies teacher on each team. Students are assigned to a team so that we all teach the same students. We've found a number of benefits in terms of planning and coordinating our teaching, but the team concept has been most helpful in working with students with discipline problems. We share ideas and strategies, and we discuss how to be consistent with each other. I've asked for some time at our next team meeting to discuss Inez.

Inez is hard to understand. Some days she's on-task, willing, and even a little outgoing. Other days she alternates between being sullen, withdrawn, and outwardly belligerent. I just had one of those belligerent days today and had to send her to the office. I don't want to send her to the office because that typically results in in-school suspension. She is definitely a student who needs to be in class because learning is hard for her. In fact, I think some of her discipline issues are related to how hard school is for her.

I know it's not just me because other team members have reported having problems with Inez. Yesterday, she was kicked out of physical education for being mouthy and belligerent. This surprised me because she had a good day in math. Margo, the physical education teacher, said that Inez got very upset with her when she politely asked her to play volleyball. I think it may be a good idea to invite the physical education teacher to the meeting, and I've also invited the school counselor.

Decision Point: How should this team begin trying to help Inez?

Beginning the School Year: Structuring Classroom Interactions

Research on classroom management suggests that the first few weeks of school are important for establishing effective classroom management for the remainder of the school year (Emmer, Evertson, & Anderson, 1980; Evertson & Emmer, 1982a, 1982b). As you get ready for the beginning of the school year, you will need to decide how to arrange your classroom and what types of introductory activities to use to learn about your students. In terms of establishing classroom management, however, probably no decisions are more important than the ones you make concerning the rules and procedures for your classroom.

Classroom Rules.   **Classroom rules** help teachers communicate their standards for classroom behavior and can be thought of as classroom norms or expectations (Campbell, 1999; Jones & Jones, 2001). Research on classroom management suggests that effective teachers take time at the beginning of the year to help students understand these expectations and their purpose (Doyle, 1986; Emmer, Evertson, & Anderson, 1980). This is how Maria Ortega accomplishes this in her third grade classroom.

> ➤ I play a game with my students that requires them to pass a paper from one student to the next until every student touches the paper. Throughout the game, I change or add rules. Eventually the students get frustrated and we have a discussion about why rules are important, and why they need to be established at the beginning.

Additionally, effective teachers attend to a number of important guidelines in establishing classroom rules.

- A small number of rules are preferable to a long list of rules. The recommended number is between four and eight rules (Cangelosi, 2000; Malone & Tietjens, 1998; Susi, 2002).
- Classroom rules should be reasonable, understandable, and enforceable. They should make sense in terms of the age and experience levels of your students, and

students should be able to meet the stated expectations (McQueen, 1992; Naka-mura, 2000).

- Rules should be stated as observable, positive expectations (Bicard, 2000). Rather than saying, "Don't interrupt," say, "Listen quietly while others speak."
- Classroom rules should be stated simply and concisely. Use language that is age appropriate. If you use general ideas such as "show respect" or "be polite," provide specific examples, especially for younger students (Bauer & Shea, 1999; Jones & Jones, 2001; McQueen, 1992).
- Rules should be flexible. As students change during the year, you should revisit and modify rules as necessary (Miller, 2001a; Nakamura, 2000).
- Discuss the rules with students. Help them understand the rationale for the rules and why rules are important. If necessary, teach the students what they need to know to follow the rules. For less experienced students consider providing practice with following the rules (Cangelosi, 2000; Jones & Jones, 2001; McQueen, 1992; Savage, 1999).
- Enforce the rules consistently from the beginning. This communicates to students that you intend to follow the rules (Campbell, 1999). Also, rules are more likely to influence students' behaviors if they are connected with consequences for breaking or following the rules (Bicard, 2000).
- Consider involving your students in setting up the classroom rules. Although this may take additional time, especially with younger students, students may be more likely to accept and follow rules that they had a role in establishing (Keith, Puzerewski, & Raczynski, 1999; Murdick & Petch-Hogan, 1996; Rich, 1984).

What useful classroom rules do you remember from when you were in school?

Keith, Puzerewski, and Raczynski (1999) provide some interesting discussion starters for involving students in establishing classroom rules. Even if you decide not to involve students in setting rules, these sentence starters are also helpful for identifying key areas of classroom life for which rules would be useful. As you consider these sentence starters, think about how you might modify them to fit the classroom environment you want to establish.

- Be prepared: I should have . . .
- Be respectful, which means . . .
- Be on time: I should . . .
- Be positive when I am . . .
- Be polite, which means . . .

A small number of positively stated classroom rules are preferable.

Classroom Procedures.   Considerable amounts of academic time can be wasted on administrative tasks such as taking roll or transitioning students from one activity to another. To prevent this, effective teachers help their students learn classroom procedures during the first few days of class (Moskewitz & Hayman, 1976; Rathvon, 1999). A **classroom procedure** is a routine way of accomplishing administrative and learning tasks. For example, a teacher may save time by taking roll and a lunch count at the same time with a simple procedure. When students' names are called for roll, they respond with either "hot," "cold," or "home." These responses let the teacher know how many students need the "hot" lunch provided by the school cafeteria.

The first step in establishing routines is to identify the areas of classroom life that could benefit from a procedure or

ritual. In general, the following types of classroom activities may benefit from a procedure (Evertson & Emmer, 1982b).

- **Use of classroom facilities and resources:** These procedures would be designed for tasks such as sharpening pencils, accessing classroom supplies, and hanging up coats. For example, Savage (1999) describes a secondary teacher's procedure for *renting* classroom supplies such as pencils and pens to students who have neglected to bring their own to class. Students have to leave their driver's license until the pencil is returned.
- **Students' behavior outside of the classroom:** Some procedures are designed to ensure that activities such as going to the restroom, going to the library, or using playground equipment occur with minimal loss of time and minimal distraction of other learners. For example, Rebecca Lee, a kindergarten teacher, has her students attempt to be quieter than they were the last time they walked to physical education. If they improve, there is a group incentive.
- **Whole group learning:** Engaging in some classroom activities such as volunteering to participate, seeking help, or turning in completed in-class assignments may reduce a learner's time on-task and be distracting to others in the class. A procedure can minimize this potential loss of learning time. For example, Consuela Perez, a middle school math teacher, provides each student with a laminated card with a question mark on it. If they need help during seatwork, they place the card on their desk with the question mark showing.
- **Small group learning:** These include procedures for activities such as how to get into groups and how to access materials for the assignment. For example, Chris Clark, a secondary history teacher, assigns students a number from one to six at the beginning of class. She designates a part of the room for each number. If students have that number, that is their group and assigned work space.
- **Other repetitive classroom events:** Teachers may reduce the negative effects of activities such as fire drills, lock downs, or entering and leaving the classroom by providing students with advanced guidance and information about these types of events. John Miller, a second grade teacher, posts a letter to his students on the door every Monday. It welcomes them back, informs them of any special events that are going to happen that day, and tells them what they should be doing when they enter the classroom.

Why do classroom procedures help you be a more effective classroom manager?

The second step in establishing a routine is to teach it to your students. With secondary students, this may be as simple as modeling the procedure and providing reminders until it becomes familiar to them. The modeling for younger students might involve actually role playing the expected behaviors ("The First Hour," 2002). For preschool or primary students, you might use the say-show-check approach to teaching a procedure (Wolfgang & Wolfgang, 1995). During the say step, describe the procedure. At the show step, demonstrate the procedure or have a student model the procedure. At the check step, show either an incorrect or correct application of the procedure and have students explain why it is correct or incorrect.

When implementing a procedure, you may also find it necessary to have a signal that informs students that it is time for a procedure (Greenberg, 2000; Miller, 2001b). For example, you could flash the lights to let students know it's time to clean up their areas, or a physical education teacher might blow a whistle to let students know it's time to put equipment away.

Effective Group Management Strategies

From the 1950s through the early 1980s, Jacob Kounin conducted a number of classroom observation studies that investigated the effect of teachers' behaviors on student on-task behavior (Kounin, 1970, 1983; Kounin & Doyle, 1975; Kounin & Gump, 1974; Kounin & Sherman, 1979). He found that effective teachers had certain

group management strategies that were effective in reducing or preventing student misbehavior. Foremost among these strategies was **withitness,** defined as the ability of teachers to communicate their awareness of what is happening in the classroom (Anguiano, 2001). In general, teachers achieve *withitness* by learning to engage in these types of monitoring behaviors (Evertson, Emmer, Clements, & Worsham, 1981).

- They scan the room periodically and tend not to focus too long on one student.
- They stand or position themselves so that they can observe the entire classroom.

Overlapping is the ability to monitor more than one classroom activity at a time.

- As students participate in seatwork or group projects, the teacher walks around the room and monitors the activity.
- They limit the number of students at their desk to one or two at a time, so that their vision is not blocked.

Teachers who are with it are accurate in their responses to misbehavior, and they avoid target and timing errors in their reactions to students. A **target error** occurs if a teacher misidentifies the misbehaving students. For example, a teacher who cannot tell who was talking and keeps everyone in at recess has committed a target error. A **timing error** occurs if a teacher waits too long to intervene. Timing errors often result in the escalation of misbehaviors or the spreading of misbehavior to other students. For example, a teacher who fails to intervene quickly with a student who is throwing spit wads may soon have others engaging in this same behavior.

How are timing and a target error different?

The ability to demonstrate *withitness* often requires that teachers monitor more than one activity in the classroom or on a playground (Anguiano, 2001). Kounin (1970) referred to this ability as **overlapping.** This is how Grace Jones demonstrates overlapping in her high school social studies class.

➤ I do a lot of group work. As I circulate around to listen to the different groups, I make sure I kneel or sit in such a way that I can listen to one group, while I look around the room at the others."

*B*ehavioral Learning Theory and Classroom Management

Behavioral learning theory provides classroom management applications for modifying students' behavior. As you read in Chapter 2, these applications have their critics (Kohn, 1993a). However, they also have a long history of effectiveness, especially for special needs learners (Simpson, 1998; Walker, Colvin, & Ramsey, 1995). This discussion of behavioral classroom management applications is organized around the behavioral learning principles introduced in Chapter 2.

Principle 2.1: Learning Is Measurable and Observable

In designing a systematic behavioral approach to classroom management, you need to identify the specific behaviors you want to change, an intervention to change those behaviors, and a way to evaluate whether or not your intervention produced the de-

Although many of the classroom management ideas presented in this chapter have broad application, your successful use of these ideas is going to depend on your ability to select and adapt approaches based on the needs and characteristics of your students. A complete understanding of your students involves an understanding of their cultural and community experiences (Wielkiewicz, 1995).

An understanding of your students' culture and language may prevent you from misinterpreting aspects of culture and language as misbehavior (Nakamura, 2000; Wielkiewicz, 1995). For example, even though your English language learners may be able to converse competently with you in English, they still may lack the academic English skills necessary to understand lesson requirements (Khisty, 1997). If you are unaware of this, you might misinterpret students' failure to understand the requirements of an assignment as resistance or lack of cooperation. Other students in your classroom may have been taught at home that it is disrespectful to have direct eye contact with an adult. If you are

unaware of this, you may misinterpret students' behavior to mean they are sullen or uninterested. The general implication is to become aware of the cultural norms and practices of your students.

Teachers also need to be sensitive to equity and fairness issues in classroom management. Historically, minority students have been affected differentially by discipline strategies, including severe interventions such as suspension or corporal punishment (Nakamura, 2000). In her qualitative study of Chicano students' reactions to disciplinary events, Rosa Henández Sheets (2002) found the students in her study often perceived confrontations with teachers that resulted in disciplinary actions as discriminatory. The implication is that you need to make sure that you are applying rules and consequences in a consistently fair manner.

● **What could teachers do to learn about the cultural norms and practices of their students? (For your authors' perspective on this question, go to the text website for this chapter.)**

---

sired changes. This systematic approach is referred to as **applied behavior analysis,** and it is implemented through a sequence of four steps (Birnbrauer, Burchard, & Burchard, 1970; Porter, 2000; Sulzer-Azaroff & Mayer, 1991).

1. Select and define specific behaviors to modify.
2. Observe the behavior.
3. Apply a behavioral intervention.
4. Monitor the success of that intervention.

Selecting and Defining Behaviors.   Applied behavior analysis begins with a specific definition of the target behavior. Rather than having the vague goal of helping students be better class participants, identify specific, observable classroom participation behaviors. You might target behaviors such as students raising their hands before speaking during class discussions or reducing the number of times they verbally interrupt other students who are speaking.

What are the advantages of identifying specific behaviors you want to change?

Observing the Behaviors.   The second step in applied behavior analysis is to observe students' behaviors carefully to determine the purposes or functions of those behaviors. Behaviorists refer to this process as **functional analysis,** which has as its goal the identification of the antecedents and consequences that set the occasion for a behavior or maintain a behavior (Daly, Witt, Martens, & Dool, 1997; Symons, McDonald, & Wehby, 1998). In analyzing the antecedents for behaviors, you identify "where, when, with whom, and under what conditions target behaviors occur" (Simpson, 1998, p. 220). A clear understanding of antecedents may help you prevent certain behaviors. For example, if you notice that a student becomes frustrated and aggressive when a task is too hard, you could adjust task difficulty, provide additional help, or provide additional time.

Functional analysis also involves the identification of the consequences that are operating on behaviors. Two students may engage in what appears to be the same behavior, but for different reasons. For example, one student may act out to earn the laughter of specific peers, whereas a second student may engage in the same behaviors to avoid difficult academic tasks. Observational data help you plan an intervention that is specific to the needs of a particular student.

When observing students' behavior, you should also try to establish a **baseline,** which is the level of students' behavior before you intervene. Baseline data allow you to judge whether or not your intervention changed the frequency of a behavior. For example, if you are trying to modify the frequency of classroom interruptions, you could compare the rate of classroom interruptions after you have intervened to the baseline frequency of interruptions.

Applying a Behavioral Intervention.   The next step in applied behavior analysis is to select an intervention based on what you observed about your students. As discussed later in this chapter, three general categories of interventions exist: those that modify antecedents, those that increase behaviors, and those that make a behavior less likely to reoccur. The intervention should make sense in terms of the function of the behavior and what you know about your students. For example, you may decide to avoid interventions that use public reinforcements because they can produce embarrassment.

Monitoring Success.   The final step is to assess the effectiveness of the selected intervention. As mentioned previously, this is done primarily by comparing the student's behavior after the intervention to the student's baseline level of behavior. However, maintenance and generalization are two additional considerations in monitoring the success of an intervention. With maintenance, you are checking to see if the behavior change continues once the intervention has stopped. In the case of generalization, you would determine if the behavior change is observable in environments other than the environment in which the intervention occurred. For example, does a behavior change initiated in a math class transfer to other classes?

Why is applied behavior analysis an example of Principle 2.1?

Principle 2.2: Learning Is Gradual and Step by Step

Principle 2.2 implies that complicated behaviors may take time to be learned or changed. Therefore, behavior change programs need to emphasize improvement rather than perfection. This can be accomplished by applying the behavioral idea of shaping, which is the reinforcement of gradual improvement. For example, for a student who never turns in homework, returning the next homework assignment is an improvement for which you give reinforcement. If a student has gotten in trouble five days in a row at recess, one successful recess is a good starting point.

How would you use shaping to modify a student's frequent tardiness?

Principle 2.3: The Effects of Stimuli on Responses

As you learned in Chapter 2, behavioral theories explain learning in terms of the impact of antecedents and consequences on behavior. Behavioral interventions, therefore, either manage antecedents or employ consequences to change behavior.

Managing Antecedents.   Antecedents are stimuli that occur before a response and that cue or signal the response. In classrooms they are the conditions under which behaviors occur (Porter, 2000). By managing antecedents, you may be able to cue desirable behaviors or prevent less desirable behaviors. Consequently, controlling antecedents can be a humane approach to classroom management because you are preventing students from getting in trouble (Bailey & Pyles, 1989). Antecedents can be managed as preventative measures in a number of ways.

First, many of the preventative ideas discussed in the beginning of this chapter such as establishing classroom rules and procedures are approaches for managing antecedents (Schloss & Smith, 1994). They create environmental stimuli that cue appropriate behavior by making expectations clear.

Second, you can identify the immediate antecedents for a particular behavior, and then try to modify or remove those antecedents. For example, if a student is more likely to get into trouble when sitting by another student, then you can change your seating arrangement.

A third way to manage antecedents is to create classroom prompts that signal students how you want them to behave. For example, teachers of young children might use the phrase "all eyes on me" to signal students that they need to observe the teacher. A secondary teacher might turn the lights on and off to signal to students that it is time to stop their small group discussions and reconvene as a larger group. When you first establish classroom prompts, link them to reinforcements or the avoidance of punishments. For example, if students attend to you when you say, "eyes on me," then praise them or reinforce them in some meaningful way. Then periodically reinforce students to remind them of the connection between the prompt and the reinforcement.

> What are some different ways to manage antecedents in your classroom management?

A fourth way to think about antecedents is to manage the effects of setting events on students' classroom behavior. **Setting events** are external or internal stimuli that simultaneously control a wide range of antecedents, behaviors, and consequences (Kantor, 1959; Mahon, Shores, & Buske, 1999; Sulzar-Azaroff & Mayer, 1991). They tend to alter the effects that environmental stimuli have on students' behavior, and they explain the sometimes erratic behavior of students (Dadson & Horner, 1993; Fox, 1990). Time of day, physical layout of a classroom, classroom temperature and lighting, amount of sleep a student had the night before, previous interactions with students and adults, social composition of a classroom, and family risk factors are all examples of setting events (Conroy & Fox, 1994; Gable, Hendrickson, & Shellady, 1992; Kennedy & Itkonen, 1993). Consider Ms. Budolf's experience with a setting event and a student in her junior high science class.

> John has his bad and good days. He really has problems on the Fridays before and the Mondays after he visits his dad. Almost nothing that typically works with John works on those days.

Teachers can manage key setting events in the classroom in a number of ways (Conroy & Fox, 1994). First, the physical setting of the classroom can be modified. If you have students who are easily distracted, you might reduce the number of competing visual stimuli, such as posters or displays in a class. Second, the schedule can be modified. For example, you might alternate high-energy social activities with quiet reflection and personal study time to allow students to calm down from the first activity. Third, curricular modifications can be made, such as making sure that learning activities are at an appropriate level for students. Fourth, social modifications can be made, such as assigning students who encourage each other to misbehave to different classes.

Key setting events that occur or exist outside of the classroom such as family interaction patterns may be difficult for teachers to manage. Sometimes, however, if you communicate with parents, they can let you know when a student's day is getting off to a rough start (Dadson & Horner, 1993). You can use that information to provide additional support to that student. Ms. Budolf used this technique with John.

> When John's parents alert me to a possible bad day, I make extra efforts to meet John as he comes into the classroom and to schedule activities at the beginning of class that are likely to engage him.

Reinforcement Approaches to Classroom Management. A number of strategies are available for using secondary reinforcers in your classroom. When employed correctly, they can help you establish a positive approach to classroom management.

Looking in on

Oji Samms

10.1

It became clear as we talked about Inez that the only consistency we could find is how inconsistent her behavior was. When she misbehaved in one class, she might be on task and cooperative in another class. Her bad days seemed to happen at random, and no day of the week was any worse than another. Our counselor suggested that it might help to look at recent confrontations more specifically to see if there is a pattern. Margo said that Inez's belligerence during physical education surprised her because she just asked her politely to take her turn in volleyball. It was similar to what happened in my class. She wasn't doing her assignment so I asked her privately to get to work. I thought I had been pretty calm also, but Inez got very angry. The counselor asked Margo what kind of volleyball player Inez is. Margo said she had a lot of trouble with this sport and had even been laughed at yesterday when she missed a ball. I added that Inez sometimes struggles in math, but has trouble asking for help, and today's lesson was hard for most students. Our counselor asked us if we thought asking Inez to do things that were hard for her caused her to become angry. That seemed to make sense to us, but we both agreed that we couldn't stop asking her to do things that are hard for her. The counselor also agreed, but he wondered if there was anything we could do to make Inez less likely to get so frustrated with hard things. I told him that on occasion I had given assignments to her a piece at a time. She would get the next piece when she handed in the first piece. That way I could help her sooner, and I could praise her as she got each part done. It seemed to work. The counselor wondered if Inez got belligerent in order to be sent to the office. She could avoid an unpleasant task, at least in the short run.

● **How are the ideas of functional analysis and shaping relevant in this situation?**

Decision Point: What else might these teachers do to reduce the likelihood that Inez will get frustrated with difficult tasks?

Contingency Contracting.   With contingency contracting, you and your students negotiate behavioral goals and the environmental support for meeting those goals. A **contingency contract** is the product of these negotiations that minimally specifies the students' behavioral goals and what they can earn by meeting those goals. Contingency contracting is adaptable for a number of purposes and student populations and can be used effectively in combination with other behavioral interventions (Brooke & Ruthven, 1984; Homme, Csanyi, Gonzales, & Rechs, 1970; Miller & Kelley, 1994; Newstrom, McLaughlin, & Sweeney, 1999).

Table 10.1 contains a list of key components of a contingency contract, and related considerations for the contingency contracting process (Alberto & Troutman,

TABLE 10.1   The Contingency Contracting Process

Components of a Contingency Contract	Considerations for the Contingency Contracting Process
The contract should contain specific descriptions of the target behaviors	Students and teachers should select the target behavior together
The contract should contain a description of the reinforcement that can be earned	Students and teachers should participate together in selecting the reinforcement
Optionally, the contract may include penalties for noncompletion, or added incentives for exceeding the requirements of the contract	Reinforcement should be contingent on completing the contract and should be provided immediately after the contract is completed Reinforcement should be reasonable for the effort required
The contract should include time limits for completion	Set short-term goals and renew the contract (shaping)
The contract should include the signatures of the involved parties	On occasion, less formal methods such as a handshake may be used
The contract should identify any environmental support that will be provided to the student	Involve people, such as parents, if they can help the student succeed

FIGURE 10.1 An Example of a Contingency Contract

I have met with _____ and together we have come up with this goal.

If _____ can _____

by _____, then _____ can earn

_____

_____   _____   _____
Date   Student   Teacher

1999; Becker, 1986; Homme et al., 1970; Jones & Jones, 2001; Schloss & Smith, 1994; Wielkiewicz, 1995). Figure 10.1 provides a sample contingency contract.

Token Reinforcement Systems. A **token reinforcement system** is a systematic approach for using tokens as reinforcers. As you remember from Chapter 2, a token has value because it can be exchanged for other reinforcers called **backup reinforcers**. For example, students could exchange points for extra computer time. As is the case with contingency contracting, token reinforcement systems have been popular in schools and clinics because they also can be used with students of different ages, in different settings, and in combination with other behavioral interventions (Buisson, Murdock, Reynolds, & Cronin, 1995; Cavalier, Ferrretti, & Hodges, 1997; Higgins, Williams, & McLaughlin, 2001; Hupp & Reitman, 1999; Salend & Gordon, 1987; Wolfe, Boyd, & Wolfe, 1983). Another reason for the popularity of token systems is that they can be tailored to students' individual likes and values. Students can work for the same tokens, but the backup reinforcers or even the behaviors that earn or lose tokens can be different for each student (Cruz & Cullinan, 2001; Wielkiewicz, 1995). Token reinforcement systems are implemented through a sequence of six steps (Becker, 1986; Jones & Jones, 2001).

What token reinforcement systems have you observed in classrooms?

- Identify the behaviors that earn or lose tokens.
- Develop a menu of backup reinforcers.
- Set the value for the reinforcers and behaviors.
- Decide on the tokens.
- Establish and teach the operating procedures.
- Establish and explain a record-keeping system.

Teachers' experiences with implementing token reinforcement systems and classroom research on token reinforcement systems have identified the following guidelines for their use:

- When possible, involve your students in the design of the token system. Minimally, make sure your students understand the rules and procedures of the system thoroughly. You may want to model the system or have a practice run before you implement the system.
- When selecting your backup reinforcers, try not to use classroom activities that you want all students to participate in regardless of their behavior (Williams, Williams, & McLaughlin, 1989). For example, it would be inappropriate to use access to the class computer as a reinforcer, but you could use bonus time with the computer as a reinforcer.
- When selecting tokens, it is important to select tokens that are difficult to counterfeit (Alberto & Troutman, 1999). For example, students can buy paper clips or poker chips on their own and it makes them easy to counterfeit. It might be better to use a token that you can mark in a unique way, perhaps with a two letter code that changes.

Group-Oriented Contingency Systems.   A group-oriented contingency system is when management contingencies are applied to more than one person in a group. There are three types of group-oriented contingency systems: dependent, independent, and interdependent contingencies (Alberto & Troutman, 1999; Litow & Pumroy, 1975; Theodore, Bray, Kehle, & Jenson, 2001). A **dependent group-oriented contingency system** is when the same expectations are in effect for all members of a group, but certain students' behavior results in the consequences being applied to the whole group. For example, the whole class gets extra free time if two students finish their assignments. The **independent group-oriented contingency system** is when the same expectations are in effect for the whole group, but consequences are applied on an individual basis. An example of this is a classroom token system in which each student can earn or lose tokens based on her or his own behavior. The **interdependent group-oriented contingency system** is when each student's behavior can affect whether or not the group earns reinforcement. For example, all students need to turn in their homework for the group to receive an incentive.

If you decide to implement interdependent or dependent group-oriented contingencies, be aware of certain cautions (Alberto & Troutman, 1999; Romeo, 1998). First, be sure that the students involved can perform the target behaviors. For example, if a student has a severe math learning disability, then an interdependent or dependent group contingency based on math test performance is unfair to both the individual and the group. Second, be cautious of students who might find it reinforcing to sabotage the group's effort (Barrish, Saunders, & Wolf, 1969). These students may need to be grouped together or allowed to work in an individualized system. Third, some students may turn against or even seek revenge against students who are preventing their group from being successful, which in turn creates a hostile classroom environment (Romeo, 1998). You can manage this directly by instituting a penalty for that type of behavior (Davies & Witte, 2000).

> **What are the three types of group-oriented contingencies and how do they differ from each other?**

Strategies for Reducing Behaviors.   When you intervene with students' misbehaviors, it's a good idea to begin with the least restrictive or punitive alternatives (Cooper, Heron, & Heward, 1987; Wielkiewicz, 1995). In general, try to manage with an-

ENRICHING YOUR UNDERSTANDING
The Good Behavior Game

The Good Behavior Game and its variants are examples of an interdependent group-oriented contingency system to help manage the disruptive behavior of elementary school students (Barrish, Saunders, & Wolf, 1969). In the Good Behavior Game, students are divided into teams. Team names are written on the board, and a point is entered under a team name any time a member of that team exhibits one of the target misbehaviors. The team with the fewest points, or any team that meets a preestablished criterion for points earns a reinforcer. The Good Behavior Game has been shown to be effective in reducing disruptive behaviors during instruction and independent work (Fishbein & Wasik, 1981; Harris & Sherman, 1973; Medland & Stachnik, 1972; Tankersley, 1995).

Two variations of the Good Behavior Game are the Good Behavior Game plus merit (Darveaux, 1984; Wielkiewicz, 1995) and the Good Student Game (Babyak, Luze, & Kamps, 2000; Landrum & Tankersley, 1997). In the Good Behavior Game plus merit, students can also erase points by engaging targeted appropriate behaviors. The Good Student Game differs from the Good Behavior Game in a number of ways, but two key differences are that students self-monitor their behavior during the game, and the game can also be set up as an individual contingency.

> ● **What do you see as the strengths and weaknesses of these approaches? (For your authors' perspective on this question, go to the text website for this chapter.)**

tecedents or reinforcement approaches before trying a punishment approach. In terms of punishments, try milder punishment strategies before using more severe or restrictive punishment approaches.

Extinction.   As you learned in Chapter 2, extinction is when a behavior is eliminated because the reinforcement for that behavior is removed from the environment. Extinction can occur both intentionally and unintentionally (Cangelosi, 2000). Ignoring a student who misbehaves to get your attention is an example of an attempt at intentional extinction. A student who stops working because parents, peers, and teachers do not acknowledge her improvements is an unfortunate example of unintentional extinction.

Although extinction can be an effective intervention, there are some considerations in using it well (Alberto & Troutman, 1999; Lerman & Iwata, 1995; Schloss & Smith, 1994; Wielkiewicz, 1995). First, extinction does not work well for all behaviors. For example, self-reinforcing behaviors such as daydreaming are hard to extinguish.

Second, extinction can be a very slow process, especially if the target behavior was originally maintained by an intermittent reinforcement schedule. Also, remember that behaviors are functional and often have a goal. Try to replace the extinguished behavior with a reasonable alternative. This is how Roberta Jones handles this issue.

> When students are misbehaving for my attention, I have learned that it is not enough to ignore them. I get better and quicker results if I also reinforce them for seeking attention in better ways.

Third, when you try to extinguish a behavior be aware that it may worsen before it improves. This is called the **extinction burst.** Also, some students may become angry and hostile at your attempts to take their reinforcement away, this phenomenon is known as **extinction-induced aggression.**

What is an extinction burst and why is it important to understand?

Finally, it may not be possible to identify or control all the reinforcers for a behavior. You may decide to ignore a behavior, but family members and siblings may continue to reinforce that same behavior. Try to elicit cooperation from others who are reinforcing the behavior. Consider Loretta Gordon's experience with one of her middle school English students.

> I have been trying to extinguish John's swearing. When I had a parent conference, John's mother and father swore at each other as a part of their normal conversation. I knew why my attempts were unsuccessful, and I needed to talk with them about how they could help me.

Presentation Punishment.   As noted in Chapter 2, presentation punishment occurs when the likelihood of a behavior is decreased because that behavior is followed by an aversive stimulus. **Verbal reprimands** or scoldings are a commonly used form of presentation punishment. Reprimands tend to be more effective if teachers establish eye contact with students, reduce physical distance between themselves and the student, deliver them privately, and if reprimands are paired with other punishments such as loss of privileges (Bear, 1998; Kerr & Nelson, 1998). This is how Tom Konstantine administers reprimands to his first graders.

> When I need to talk with a student about his behavior, I go to his desk and kneel so that we are at eye level. I make sure I am firm, but courteous.

Overcorrection is a type of presentation punishment based on the principle of contingent effort (Foxx & Azrin, 1972). Contingent effort is when students must exert themselves as a consequence of their behavior. To be effective, the exertion should be connected logically to the effects of the behavior and should help students understand the effects of their misbehavior. Effective overcorrection, therefore, has similar characteristics to a strategy discussed later called logical consequences (Porter, 2000).

Restitutional overcorrection and positive practice overcorrection are the two major forms of overcorrection (Foxx & Azrin, 1972; Henderson, French, & Fritsch, 2000; Porter, 2000; Schloss & Smith, 1994). **Restitutional overcorrection** requires that students fix or correct any damage caused by their behavior and to repair the environment to a condition better than it was before it was damaged. For example, a student who writes on his desk is asked to clean his desk and others in the room. **Positive practice overcorrection** is when students are asked to practice the correct alternative behavior to their misbehavior repeatedly. For example, students who push while getting on a bus are asked to practice getting on the bus correctly four or five times. A potential benefit is that the misbehavior is interrupted in the short run by the requirement to practice the positive alternative.

How are restitutional overcorrection and positive practice overcorrection different?

Overcorrection is a fairly intrusive and severe intervention. As noted before, these types of interventions should not be used until less severe interventions have failed. Also, there are a number of factors to consider in using overcorrection, including the time and supervision requirements, the possibility that students may find the additional attention reinforcing, and difficulty you may have in identifying a reasonable and potent overcorrection behavior (Henderson, French, & Fritsch, 2000). Finally, because this is an intervention that may not be accepted by parents, you should contact parents before instituting an overcorrection process (Jones et al., 1998).

Removal Punishment. Removal punishment occurs when a student's behavior is made less likely to occur because of the loss of something the student values. Response cost and time-out are two commonly used removal punishment techniques in the classroom.

TABLE 10.2   **Commonly Used Types of Time-Out**

Type of Time-Out	Location for Time-Out	Description	Intended Age Range of Student
Nonseclusionary time-out	In the classroom	Students lose the right to participate in the learning activity, but they can still observe the instructional activity. It can take many forms	Varies depending on the particular technique
• Planned ignoral	In the classroom	A form of nonseclusionary time-out. Teacher and students ignore a student when she or he engages in target behaviors	Elementary and secondary
• Contingent observation (sit and watch)	In the classroom	Both contingent observation (Barton, Brulle, & Repp, 1987) and sit and watch (White & Bailey, 1990) are a form of nonseclusionary time-out that requires a student to sit and watch an activity. They cannot participate nor earn reinforcement	Originally for elementary age students; can be adapted for secondary students
• Time-out ribbon	In the classroom	Originated by Foxx and Shapiro (1978). Students wear a time-out ribbon. If they have the ribbon, they can earn reinforcement. If they lose the ribbon, they lose the right to earn reinforcements for three minutes	Elementary
Exclusionary time-out	In the classroom in a screened area, or in another classroom	Student is removed from the activity and placed in screened-off area or another classroom	Elementary and secondary
Seclusionary time-out	In a time-out room	Most severe form of time-out	Elementary and secondary

Looking in on

When I met with Rosa we talked about helping my students behave better in line. Rosa said that the teachers in the building use a lot of different approaches, and I should find one that works for me. For example, one of the third grade teachers has a classroom management system that involves a marble and jar system. If her students follow classroom rules and work hard, they can earn a marble or marbles to put in the jar. If they misbehave or break a rule, they can lose a marble or marbles. When she walks them in the hall, she gives them two marbles for being quiet in line, and takes away two marbles if they continue to be noisy after they have been warned. A sixth grade teacher in our building tells his students that if anyone is noisy, they will all go back and practice walking quietly. They will do that until they show they can walk quietly. He says peer pressure kicks in when some of the students realize they are going to be late for lunch. Rosa thinks it's important to understand a behavior before you try to intervene. She asked me to consider a number of questions. How often this week did the students misbehave in line? Are there times when they are better at passing in the hall? Is it all the students or just a few that are having trouble being quiet? She thinks it's important to prevent problems if she can. For example, she tries to schedule a quiet activity such as silent reading before lunch. That way her students are already in a quiet mode before she dismisses them. She also reminds them of the rules for walking in the halls before they leave the classroom.

● **What examples of behavioral approaches to classroom management are present in this discussion?**

Decision Point: Of the management strategies described by Rosa, which one would you try first if you were Maria?

Response cost is when students lose earned reinforcers because they have engaged in misbehaviors (Azrin & Holz, 1966; Kazdin, 1994; Reid, 1999). The term *fine* is sometimes used as a synonym for response cost. Response cost procedures work well when combined with token reinforcement systems and clearly stated expectations (Musser, Bray, Kehle, & Jenson, 2001). The fine or response cost in that case involves the loss of earned tokens.

Time-out is short for time-out from reinforcement, because when students are in time out they lose the right to earn reinforcement. Table 10.2 contains descriptions of various forms of time-out in order of severity.

Time-out has been one of the most commonly used interventions in special education settings (Zabel, 1986). It tends to be particularly effective for students' attention-seeking behaviors (Turner & Watson, 1999). However, it is also a strategy that has both educational and legal concerns (Gartrell, 2001, 2002; Lawyer-Tarr, 1999; Porter, 2000; Schreiber, 1999; Yell, 1994). For example, time out has been criticized for its inability to teach positive behaviors and for isolating students from classroom experiences. Because of this, you should consult your district policies regarding the use of the more serious forms of time-out, especially for students with disabilities. Also, consider these guidelines for use of time-out.

Why would a teacher's increased use of time-out be an example of negative reinforcement?

- Time-out should typically be a short-term intervention, lasting about one to five minutes (Burton & Parks, 1998; Ewing, 2000).
- For time-out to be effective, participating in your classroom should be more reinforcing or engaging than being in time-out. Be aware that some students will use time-out to avoid disliked classroom tasks (Ewing, 2000; Reid, 1999).
- With time-out procedures that remove students from the classroom, be careful of a negative reinforcement effect. Teachers may use these procedures to avoid problem students.
- If you have a separate time-out room, it should be well lit, well ventilated, and temperature controlled, and students should be able to exit the room quickly in case of an emergency (Torem, 2000).

Social Cognitive Theory and Classroom Management

Social cognitive theory contributes to an understanding of classroom management by providing techniques to help students self-regulate their behavior. These techniques are sometimes referred to as cognitive behavioral interventions. As done previously, this discussion is organized around the relevant learning theory principle.

Principle 4.3: Learners Have the Potential to Self-Regulate

Self-management involves goal setting, self-monitoring and self-evaluation, self-reinforcement, self-instruction, and coping skills approaches (Bauer & Shea, 1999; Shapiro & Cole, 1994). Teaching students to manage their own behavior is important for a number of reasons. First, external or teacher-provided management systems may actually prevent students from developing their own internal behavior controls (Savage, 1999). Second, classroom management procedures are more likely to be successful if students are involved in their design and application (Jones & Jones, 2001). Finally, self-management is philosophically consistent with student-centered views of learning that require students to exercise control over their own learning. Consequently, the ideas discussed in this section also have relevance for the later discussions of constructivism and classroom management.

Goal Setting. Goal setting is used to involve students in the establishment of criteria for successful management of their own behavior (Belfiore & Hornyak, 1998). Goal setting focuses students on what they need to monitor or evaluate, and it sets the criteria for self-reinforcement. Typically, goal setting is used in conjunction with other self-management strategies such as self-monitoring, self-evaluation, and self-reinforcement (Trammel, Schloss, & Alper, 1994). To be effective, students' goals need to be specific, moderately difficult, acceptable, or valuable to the students and supported by feedback regarding progress toward meeting those goals (Oppenheimer, 2001).

Why is goal-setting an important self-regulation activity?

Students' involvement in goal setting can have a number of benefits. First, when students are oriented toward meeting personally relevant goals, they tend to be more willing to persist in the face of difficulty and to plan and self-monitor their own performance (Meichenbaum & Biemiller, 1998). Goal setting also is a way to involve students in their own learning and give them a sense of personal identity and purpose (Jones & Jones, 2001; Nakamura, 2000).

How might you use contingency contracting and shaping with goal setting?

Morris (1982) has developed the powwow goal-setting meeting as a way of making goal setting a regular part of a classroom management system. In the powwow meetings, students and teachers sit together in a circle and each student sets and commits to behavior goals for the week. Each of these goals is recorded on a classroom chart. During subsequent meetings, students' progress toward meeting their goals is assessed and new goals or better plans for meeting old goals are established. Mr. Gregory, a junior high science teacher handles goal setting in a slightly different way.

> ➤ Each Monday students begin the day by writing in their journals. They tell me what they would like to do better this week, and how they plan to improve. I write back to them about their goals and ask questions about their progress.

Self-Monitoring and Self-Evaluation. In order for students to self-manage their behavior, they first must be aware of that behavior (Bandura, 1986). Self-monitoring and self-evaluation are the processes used to develop this type of self-awareness. With **self-monitoring**, students identify and record

How are self-monitoring and self-evaluation different?

occurrences of target behaviors (O'Reilly et al., 2002; Shapiro & Cole, 1994; Trammel, Schloss, & Alper, 1994). For example, students may make a mark on an index card every time they raise their hands before speaking in a class discussion. **Self-evaluation** is when students judge their behavior in terms of a standard or criterion (Manning, 1991). An example of a self-evaluation technique would be students using a five-point scale to rate their ability to follow directions.

Self-Monitoring. Self-monitoring can be viewed as both an assessment and intervention approach. When self-awareness leads to modification of a behavior, it is called the **reactive effect** (Schloss & Smith, 1994). For example, asking you to count the number of times you daydream while reading this text may cause you to daydream less often. If so, that would be an example of the reactive effect.

Goal setting helps students self-regulate their behavior.

The reactive effect is more likely to occur when students are motivated to change a behavior, when the focus is on positive behaviors rather than undesirable behaviors, when students are trained to self-record accurately, and when self-monitoring is combined with other approaches such as goal setting and the opportunity for reinforcement and feedback (Akande, 1997). Also, the reactive effect typically tends to decrease over time, but you may be able to compensate for this decrease by combining self-monitoring with a self-reinforcement strategy (Alberto & Troutman, 1999).

Implementing self-monitoring programs usually involves a number of steps (McConnell, 1999; Jones & Jones, 2001). First, the target behavior must be selected, defined, and observed for baseline. Students should be involved in this process, and they should commit to changing the behavior. It's important to make sure students can accurately identify the target behavior when it occurs. Mr. O'Reilley, an elementary school counselor, uses this approach with his young students.

> ➤ With my second and third grade clients, we role play both the target behavior and its opposite. Together, we then create a brief description of the behavior I want them to monitor.

Next, a self-monitoring system is selected that is appropriate for the behavior being observed. For discrete behaviors such as raising their hands during class discussions, students probably record each occurrence of a behavior. In the case of behaviors such as time spent on an assignment, students would record the duration of the behavior, which is the actual period of time during which they were performing the behavior. For behaviors such as how long a student takes to get started on an assignment after the directions are given, students would record latency, which is how long it takes them to actually initiate the requested behavior (Mace, Belfiore, & Shea, 1989).

You also need to determine if the recording system will be unprompted or prompted (Shapiro & Cole, 1994). With an unprompted system, students self-monitor when they determine it's time to do so. With a prompted system, students are provided with visual or auditory prompts to remind them to self-monitor. For example, Hallahan, Marshall, and Lloyd (1981) used tape-recorded tones as auditory prompts for students to monitor their on-task behavior. When the tone sounded, students asked themselves whether or not they were paying attention. For older students, it may be more engaging to use musical excerpts from popular songs to prompt self-monitoring (Shapiro & Cole, 1994).

The actual recording mechanism also must be identified. The most common form is a paper and pencil recording form on which students make a mark for every occurrence of a behavior. Besides paper and pencil systems, you can also use mechanical counters, tokens or pegs in a hole, chips in a can, or paper clips removed from an index card (Bauer & Shea, 1999; Shapiro & Cole, 1994; Shapiro, Browder, & D'Huyvetters, 1984).

Finally, the self-monitoring and recording systems need to be taught to the students. You can use role playing to help students get comfortable with the system. Once students understand these systems, the program is implemented and monitored for effect using the ideas presented earlier from applied behavior analysis. The eventual goal is to create an independent, self-monitoring student, so teacher involvement and self-monitoring prompts typically are phased out gradually.

Self-Evaluation. As noted previously, self-evaluation is when students judge the quality of their behavior. Typically, students are asked to complete a simple rating scale or self-report form about their classroom behaviors. For example, Clees (1994/1995) had students use a class schedule with the expectations of the teachers for the different classes printed on it. Students evaluated how well they met their different teachers' expectations. Cami Williams, an elementary school teacher from Illinois, has her students with behavior problems complete a self-report form at the end of each day. Her students identify any good things they did that day, any problems they had, and what they might do differently tomorrow (Scheinman, 2000). Students can use a rating scale to self-evaluate their contributions during cooperative learning, and other students can also evaluate them with the same scale (Strom & Strom, 1999).

It is important for students to self-evaluate their behaviors accurately if they are going to establish meaningful goals or identify the types of self-help strategies they may need (Stone & May, 2002). One way to increase accuracy is to reinforce students for ratings that match the ratings of their classroom teacher for the same behaviors (Shapiro, DuPaul, & Bradley-Klug, 1998).

Self-Reinforcement. Self-reinforcement is when students participate in reinforcing their successes. This participation can include determining the target behaviors and criteria for success, self-monitoring or self-evaluating to determine when they have met those criteria, and selecting the reinforcers (Alberto & Troutman, 1999).

Some important points need to be considered in the use of self-reinforcement approaches. First, students may have a tendency to set relatively lenient criteria for success (Alberto & Troutman, 1999). A contracting or goal-setting process should be used to guide students toward more realistic criteria for success. This is how Bobby Hammond, a middle school special education teacher, handles this when she contracts with her students with learning disabilities.

➤ When I do my weekly behavior contracts with my students, I always include a bonus clause. If they exceed the criteria we have established, then they can earn better or more reinforcers. I want them always to strive to do their best.

Second, self-reinforcement tends to be more effective when used for behaviors that are already under environmental control (Fredericksen & Fredericksen, 1975; Zirpoli & Melloy, 1997). Self-reinforcement, therefore, becomes a way of transferring behavioral control to your students.

Self-Instruction. Self-instruction is when students use verbal self-prompting to guide their behavior (Zirpoli & Melloy, 1997). Self-instruction usually begins by having students talk aloud to themselves, another person, or tape recorder, but eventually the self-instruction becomes covert or internal speech (Swaggert, 1998). Self-instruction approaches have been used for many purposes; including helping students control impulsive behavior and helping students manage academic and social behaviors (Man-

Defining the Problem
- What is my problem to solve?
- What am I supposed to do here?
- What will a successful paper look like?
- Is this like a problem I have seen before?
- What strategies do I know for this?

Self-Monitoring/Self-Evaluation
- Am I following my plan?
- Have I used my strategy?
- Does this word I just spelled look right?
- Do I understand what I just read?
- Does this word make sense in this sentence? (Reading)

Motivation/Self-Reinforcement
- I did a good job of this.
- I am proud of how well I am staying on task.
- I did that without help this time.

Coping Statements
- I need to calm down and count to ten.
- I should probably come back to this later when I am more calm.
- I made a mistake, but I know how to fix it.
- Math is hard for me, but I know how to start.

ning, 1991; Meichenbaum, 1972; Prater, 1994). Figure 10.2 contains some sample self-instruction statements for a variety of academic and behavioral self-management purposes.

Self-instruction approaches need to be taught to your students. Although there are different approaches for teaching self-instruction routines, in general, you should model the self-instruction routine, allow students to practice these routines with feedback, and then provide cues as they try to apply them on their own (Manning, 1991). Here is how Sam Waterson uses a self-instruction cue in his sixth grade classroom.

➤ I have a chart up in my room with the steps we follow when solving any problem. When we discuss a problem, I point to the steps and we work through them. Eventually, students don't need me to guide them.

Coping Skills Approaches. Coping skills approaches attempt to teach students ways of coping with stressful or anger-producing situations. In these approaches, students are typically taught to use positive self-statements (e.g., "I can handle this.") or calming visual images, while they employ some type of relaxation technique (e.g., "Take three deep breathes and count to ten.") (Schneider, 1974; Whitfield, 1999). For example, with the turtle technique, young children with anger or impulse control issues are asked to imagine that they are turtles in their shells (Schneider, 1974). They pull their limbs in and engage in positive self-talk such as counting to ten or saying, "I am in control."

*C*onstructivism and Classroom Management

As we noted in Chapter 5, constructivism is a broad view of knowledge acquisition that emphasizes the need for students to construct their own knowledge, the importance of developmentally appropriate learning experiences, and the usefulness of students collaborating together as they construct their own knowledge. As you remember from Chapter 7, these ideas have resulted in a view of teachers as guides or

Maria Torres

10.2

As Rosa and I were meeting together in my room, Dennis rushed in the room and announced in a loud voice that he had forgotten to take his math book. He had to dig through quite a mess in his desk to find the book, and in the process he dropped things on the floor. He picked them up, shoved them in his desk, and started to run out of the room. When I stopped him and reminded him to walk, he smiled and said he had forgotten again. When he left, Rosa asked me if this was typical behavior for Dennis. I told her that carelessness was a big problem for him. She had a similar experience with a student like Dennis, and she had some luck teaching him to slow down by talking to himself. She taught him to say things such as, "I need to take my time on this. It's not a race," or to ask questions such as, "What am I supposed to do next, and do I need help?" I told her that Dennis also gets frustrated when he can't get something done quickly. I've actually seen him tear up a paper he was working on in class when he got frustrated. Rosa asked me to make sure the work was at an appropriate level. She also suggested that I teach him to recognize the early signs of his frustration, get up from his desk, and walk away from the frustrating task. I could allow him to pace in the back of the room and to think calming thoughts such as, "I can do this, and if not, my teacher would help." If he calms down, I should praise him for his improvement and encourage him to congratulate himself for keeping his cool.

● **How are Rosa's recommendations examples of self-evaluation, self-instruction, self-reinforcement, and coping strategies approaches?**

Decision Point: What are the potential benefits of using these approaches with Dennis? What issues or concerns might there be with this approach?

facilitators of knowledge. Consequently constructivism requires classroom management strategies that are consistent with the view of teachers as facilitators of students' learning and problem solving (Brophy, 1999; McCaslin & Good, 1992).

Historically, those types of classroom management ideas have been associated with humanistic and personal and social responsibility approaches to classroom management (e.g., Dreikurs, 1968; Glasser, 1969). These ideas were developed independently of constructivism, and certainly can be used by nonconstructivist teachers. However, they can support a constructivist view of learning. The discussion of these ideas is organized around the learning principles developed in Chapter 5.

Principle 5.1: Learners Constructing Understanding

Students in a constructivist classroom are active participants in their own learning, and they take considerable responsibility for their own learning. Also, learning occurs through the process of investigating and solving authentic problems. If this principle were extended into the area of classroom management, students would be viewed as active participants in the classroom management processes of their classrooms. Obviously, one way to accomplish this is to involve students in important decisions about how the classroom is structured. As a specific example, students could have an active role in establishing the rules and procedures for the classroom. To be effective participants in the classroom management process, students would also need to learn the necessary problem solving and communication skills.

Student Involvement with Classroom Rules and Procedures. Although terms such as *rules* and *procedures* may seem somewhat antithetical to ideas such as self-directed learning, they play an important role in the constructivist classroom. Constructivist teachers need to prevent problems from occurring, and they need to ensure that necessary classroom structures such as rules and procedures are in place (Evertson & Harris, 1999; Freiburg, 1999; Jones & Jones, 2001). Also, students who are constructing their own understandings need to do so in a safe and supportive environment, and rules and procedures help establish that environment (Jones & Jones, 2001). The rules in a construc-

Why might it help students feel more in control of their own learning if they help establish classroom rules?

tivist classroom would need to reflect a balance between providing students the necessary freedom to explore and learn and providing safe environments where students' behaviors don't interfere with the learning processes.

Learning to Be Self-Responsible through Problem Solving.   From a constructivist perspective, students acquire important understandings through their efforts at solving authentic problems. Classroom management could be viewed as an opportunity to involve students in problem solving about their own classroom behavior. William Glasser's problem-solving approach provides a structure for that type of experience.

Beginning with his book *Schools without Failure* (Glasser, 1969) and continuing with his later work on control theory, choice theory, and quality schools (Glasser, 1986, 1990, 1998), William Glasser has become one of the most recognized names in classroom management. Although his work has evolved over the years, he has consistently recommended that schools need to be places where students want to be, and that students need to be involved in classroom management processes. His desire to include students in classroom management is fundamental to his steps for effective problem-solving conferences with students (Glasser, 1969). This approach is a way for teachers and students to work together to solve management problems in the classroom and consists of the following steps.

- **Be personal:** Students are more likely to become involved with adults whom they care about and who care about them. This step actually occurs both before and during the problem solving steps.
- **Identify the problem:** This is accomplished through the question "What are you doing?" Ask students to talk about what they are currently doing and get them to focus on their behavior in this particular situation.
- **Ask for a value judgment:** Ask students to evaluate the outcomes of their behavior. Ask questions such as, "Is it helping you?" or "Is it against the rules you helped develop?"
- **Make a plan to do better:** If students agree that their behavior is not helping them, collaborate to make a simple, short-term plan to improve. Think about the behavioral idea of shaping here.
- **Get a commitment:** Ask students to demonstrate their commitment to the plan. This can be done through a handshake or with a formal process such as a contract.
- **Don't accept excuses:** If the plan does not succeed, focus on how to make a better plan. Don't dwell on the reasons or excuses for the plan's failure.
- **Don't punish:** Don't interfere with the natural consequences for students' behaviors, but don't punish them for failing to execute the plan.
- **Be persistent:** Glaser describes this as "one more day than the student expects." Evaluate why the process failed and restart the process. Sometimes the process fails because your level of involvement is not high enough with the student. Sometimes environmental factors exist that need to be modified.

To use a process such as this with individual students, you need classroom procedures that provide time to work individually with students. This is how Robin Quiroz does this in her junior high civics class.

> ➤ I have a time set aside for students to catch up on projects and to spend time discussing current events. It's a time when they function on their own, and I use that time for individual conferences. Every student knows that we will have at least one or two of these a month.

What types of classroom procedures could you establish in your classroom to allow you to have time for individual conferences?

Communication Skills.   Effective communication skills are important for any successful classroom interaction and particularly for problem-solving approaches to classroom management. Thomas Gordon (1974) in his book *T.E.T: Teacher Effectiveness Training* provides a number of recommendations for effective communication skills in

Looking in on

Maria Torres

10.3

When I went into Rosa's room, the students were getting ready for a class meeting. Emiliano, the class leader for the day, was telling the students to place their chairs in a circle to begin the meeting. Once they were in a circle, Emiliano asked students to review the rules for working in a group, and then he asked the students to raise their hands if they agreed to the rules. While this was happening, Rosa was sitting in the circle, and although she didn't say anything yet, she did raise her hand to support the rules. Today's class meeting was to select a field trip destination from the list that had been brainstormed previously. Emiliano asked students to list the good things about each destination and the bad things, and he asked each student to only talk about one idea at a time.

Later that day I talked with Rosa and told her how impressed I was with her class meeting. She told me it had taken time to get to this point, and she had learned a lot by doing them. First, it helps keep the students involved if they fo-

cused their discussions on one issue they could resolve such as the field trip destination. She also found that her students worked together better if the topics were of importance to most students, and if they didn't always use the meeting for the same purpose. Finally, she thought it was extremely important for the students to feel that they had some control and responsibility. That's why she tried to let them structure these meetings and to resolve any conflicts if they could. That was hard at first because the students kept looking to her to answer questions or resolve conflicts.

● **What characteristics of an effective classroom meeting are observable in this example? What principles of motivation are being applied through these classroom meetings?**

Decision Point: What could a teacher do in a class meeting to help students take responsibility for managing the group?

---

the classroom, but active listening and the I-message are two basic communication skills from T.E.T.

Why is the active listening paraphrase offered in a tentative fashion?

Active Listening. According to Gordon (1974) **active listening** involves conveying understanding and acceptance of another person's communication by reflecting the meaning of that communication back to the speaker. Active listening involves trying to understand what another person is thinking and feeling by listening and watching that person carefully. The listener then paraphrases that understanding so that the speaker can verify its accuracy. This paraphrase is often made tentatively to allow the speaker to accept or reject the understanding being offered by the listener. Active listening is important in mutual problem solving because mutual problem solving is more likely to occur if people listen to each other (Warnemuende, 2000). Also, active listening helps create a warm, friendly environment (Harris, 2000).

I-Message. An **I-message** is a three-part communication that can be used to confront another person in a potentially less threatening manner (Gordon, 1974). The I-message begins with a nonjudgmental description of the other person's behavior. For example, you might begin by saying, "When you are late to class . . ." or "When you criticize Sally. . . ." The next part of the I-message is a statement of the tangible effect of that behavior for other people. For example, you might say, "When you are late to class, *it interrupts our lesson*. . . ." or "When you criticize Sally, *it hurts her feelings*. . . ." The final part is a statement about the feelings associated with the behavior and its effects. For example, the complete I-messages in our examples are, "When you are late to class, it interrupts my lesson, and *I feel frustrated*." When you criticize Sally, it hurts her feelings, and *she and I feel angry with you*." The I-message is less threatening because you are focusing on what you have observed, rather than on making value judgments about the person. The I-message also allows the speaker to accept responsibility for her or his feelings (Warnemuende, 2000).

Principle 5.2: Cognitive Developmental Levels of the Learners

A constructivist teacher strives to provide a developmentally appropriate educational experience. In terms of classroom management, teachers consider how developmental research and theory inform classroom management practices.

Learners' Developmental Characteristics and Classroom Management. An understanding of the typical developmental characteristics of your students can help you make better classroom management decisions, particularly in terms of preventing some discipline problems. For example, knowing that very young children tend to have limited attention spans and restricted vocabularies, you can frequently vary your instructional activities and make sure that directions are appropriately worded. Young adolescents are going through a period of rapid physical, cognitive, and social and personal changes (Manning, 2002). Knowing that some middle school students may be experiencing *growing pains* as they enter puberty helps you understand the importance of allowing these students to get up and move around from time to time. Also, knowing that young adolescents are preoccupied with their sense of self and peer relationships may cause you to discipline in private to avoid embarrassment. Mr. Greyson applies his understanding of development in the following way in his high school speech classes.

> ➤ Many of my students are very sensitive to the opinions of their peers. We spend the first few days talking about their fears of speaking in front of their peers. It seems to help them to know others feel as they do.

Authoritative Leadership. McClasin and Good (1992) credit Baumrind's (1971, 1980) developmental research as the basis for their view of classroom management as "authoritative leadership" (p. 11). According to Baumrind, parents with an authoritative style set firm and clear limits, express warmth and concern for their children, are more consistent with their discipline, are more likely to provide explanations for their discipline actions, and are more likely to listen to their children during discipline. Teachers who use the **authoritative leadership style** are similar to authoritative parents in that they establish clear expectations and enforce them, involve students in decision making, demonstrate warmth and acceptance, and discipline in a consistent manner. The authoritative parenting style is generally associated with positive outcomes for children (Feldman, 2000). Similarly, the ability of teachers to hold high expectations and to limit negative feedback or lack of nurturance is correlated with positive social and academic outcomes for early adolescents (Wentzel, 1992).

Principle 5.3: Knowledge Construction and Interactions with People

From a social constructivist perspective, students construct knowledge through their interactions with other people. Classrooms are viewed as communities in which students collaborate to build understanding, and classroom management is the process of helping students socialize into the learning community (Brophy, 1999). This involves teaching students how to work together to resolve classroom management issues.

The Classroom Meeting. A classroom meeting provides an opportunity for students to talk with each other and share in the governance of the classroom. According to Nakamura (2000) classroom meetings provide an opportunity for students to participate in democratic procedures, cooperate, and develop mutual respect and responsible honesty. Classroom meetings are a part of several classroom management approaches including the work of William Glasser (1969) and programs such as judicious discipline (Landau & Gathercoal, 2000).

In a classroom meeting, students and teachers are equal participants.

Glasser (1969) identified three types of classroom meetings. Open-ended meetings provide an opportunity for students to explore issues of personal interest or to engage in role playing and fantasy. The educational/diagnostic meeting allows students to discuss academic content they are learning. For example, this type of meeting can be used at the beginning of a lesson to assess students' existing knowledge. The problem-solving meeting is designed to help clarify problems, add information about the problem, and commit to proposed solutions. Generally, effective classroom meetings have the following characteristics.

- Classroom meetings are held regularly, perhaps as often as once a week (Dreikurs & Cassel, 1990; Glasser, 1969; Nakamura, 2000).
- Participants, including the teacher, should be seated in a circle to demonstrate equal rights and responsibility to participate (Glasser, 1969; Jones & Jones, 2001).
- A specific plan or agenda should be set for the classroom meeting. It broadens participation if students can have input into the agenda (Jones & Jones, 2001; Nakamura, 2000).
- Rules should be established for participation, and participants should be committed to them. Rules might include the following: "Only one person talks at a time; the rest listen." "Stick to the point." "There are no wrong answers." (Glasser, 1969; Jones & Jones, 2001).
- Students should be afforded the right to chair meetings (Nakamura, 2000).

This is how Elaine Kubota uses classroom meetings at the beginning of the year in her fifth grade class.

> ➤ I do the typical classroom rules meeting, but I also schedule some meetings where we discuss topics of interest to students. I use them so that we can get to know each other's likes and dislikes. Also, I use these less serious meetings to teach my classroom meeting rules and procedures.

Conflict Resolution Approaches. Conflict resolution or negotiation involves a step-by-step process for guiding individuals toward a mutually agreeable solution to a problem (Girard & Koch, 1996). Conflict resolution skills can be important in learning environments that require students to work together to succeed. Jones and Jones

Oji Samms

10.2

As we continued our discussion about Inez, Paula Marsten, the history teacher, said she had different problems with Inez. She likes to involve students in collaborative research projects that require that each student develop expertise on some aspect of a research topic to share with their group. Inez seems to get excited initially about this process, but then her enthusiasm decreases and she becomes difficult in these groups. She puts down the other students, and she interferes with the progress of the group. Paula doesn't want to kick her out of class, and she prefers that her students learn how to solve their own problems. She asked the counselor if he had any ideas. He recommended that the students need to let Inez know in a nonthreatening way how she is affecting the group. When they confront her, they should identify what she is doing, how her behavior is affecting others, and how they feel about her behavior. Also, he is aware of a program in another school that trains a group of students to serve as me-

diators in these types of situations. Once students agree to mediation, they all work together to find a mutually satisfying conclusion. He thought this approach might fit nicely with Paula's approach to teaching. Paula said that as odd as it may seem, Inez could be very good as one of those mediators. She has a well-defined sense of fairness, and she likes it when she asks her to help other students. The counselor said he had approached Inez about this type of opportunity, and she was excited. I suggested, however, that it might not be fair to give her an opportunity to be a mediator if she is in trouble a lot. These students should be models for other students.

● **How are the ideas of an I-message and peer mediation relevant to this discussion?**

Decision Point: Should Inez's participation in the peer mediation program depend on her behavior?

(2001) describe a prototypical conflict resolution process that can be used by teachers in the classroom.

- Teachers and students hold class discussions about how problems can be solved. This might involve a discussion of peer-relationship problems or for older students a discussion of how countries solve their problems. This helps activate students' current understandings of conflict resolution.
- Students are taught communication skills such as I-messages to help them resolve their conflicts effectively.
- An area of the classroom is designated as a conflict resolution area. Teachers might also assign a time when this space is available, and a time limit for how long students may use this space.

Other conflict resolution approaches employ peer mediators to guide and facilitate conflict resolution sessions (Chittooran, 2000; Peterson & Skiba, 2001: Schrumpf, Crawford, & Bodine, 1997). Peer mediation approaches to conflict resolution can be especially effective for peer relationship issues that arise from misunderstandings, jealousies, or the ending of friendships (Wolfgang, 1999). In the peer mediation program described by Schrumpf, Crawford, and Bodine (1997), a cadre of peer mediators is trained to act as third parties in a negotiation between other peers. The goal is to find a solution to a problem that meets the needs of all parties involved, and the negotiation occurs through the following steps.

- First, the involved parties commit to mediation and to following the ground rules established by the mediator. The ground rules usually stress the importance of mutual respect.
- Next, by focusing on the participants' interests and needs, an attempt is made to find common interests in the situation being negotiated.
- Next, an attempt is made to brainstorm win-win options to resolve the conflict. What solutions will help each party meet their needs?
- The various options are weighed and evaluated.
- An agreement is reached and committed to by the involved parties.

Motivation Theory and Classroom Management

Students' motivation is connected to their classroom behavior in many complicated ways. In general, however, providing a motivating classroom environment is one more way to prevent discipline problems. The principles of motivation theory that were developed in Chapter 6 provide a basis for understanding how motivation theory can be connected to important classroom management concerns.

Principle 6.1: The Successful Completion of Challenging Tasks

Principle 6.1 addresses the importance of providing students with moderately challenging tasks at which they can succeed. When teachers fail to provide appropriately challenging tasks, they usually provide tasks that are too challenging (Jones & Jones, 2001). Students who feel incapable of meeting the academic demands of a classroom may find more intrinsic rewards in misbehaving than in doing their school assignments (Campbell, 1999). The implication is that you need to monitor students' learning to make sure that the challenge level is optimal. Millie Grayson, a high school math teacher, does it this way.

How is level of academic challenge in a classroom related to classroom management?

➤ I always have students try the first problem I give them, and then we discuss it. That way, I know if they need additional help or not.

Principle 6.2: Learners' Personal Needs, Desires, and Interests

Adapting instruction to students' interests is an important way to help prevent misbehavior (Savage, 1999). Also, classrooms that help students meet their basic psychological needs are classrooms in which students are less likely to misbehave (Glasser, 1969; Gordon, 2001). In Chapter 6, you read about Maslow's hierarchy of needs. This hierarchy is useful for reminding teachers that students have needs other than a need to succeed at school. If they do not have their basic physiological and safety needs met, it's hard for them to concentrate on academics.

Glasser (1986) also identified five basic needs. The first need is the need to survive or reproduce, which is similar to Maslow's physiological and safety needs. A second basic need suggested by Glasser is the need to belong and give and receive love.

How might you help students meet their belonging needs, and their needs for power and freedom in your classroom?

Students want to feel that their teachers care about them, and they have a need to care about others. A third need is the need for fun. A fourth need is the need for power. Students need to feel that they have control over at least some of what happens to them. You may find that this need is particularly strong in young adolescents. Finally, students have a freedom need, or a need to be free of the control of others. All of these needs are important to consider, but you may want to pay special attention to the need to belong and the need for power.

Principle 6.3: Specific Near-Term Goals

Earlier in the chapter, a number of ideas were discussed that are relevant to goal setting and classroom management. The process of goal setting clearly relates to activities such as shaping, contingency contracting, and self-management. With contingency contracting, students are encouraged to set proximal or short-term goals and to meet them (shaping). Self-evaluation involves establishing standards or goals and assessing progress toward meeting those goals. In this case, the literature in classroom management and the literature in motivation tend to emphasize the same idea. Students perform better when they are working successfully toward personally important goals.

Understanding Misbehavior.   In addition to helping students set productive and personally helpful goals, you may need to help students modify or change maladaptive goals. One approach for identifying maladaptive goals and modifying them is Rudolf Dreikurs' social discipline model (Dreikurs, 1968; Dreikurs & Cassel, 1990; Dreikurs & Soltz, 1964; Wolfgang, 1999).

Dreikurs' social discipline model is based on theoretical ideas from Alfred Adler. Adler believed that people want to feel that they are important and that they belong. Dreikurs suggests that when children and adolescents find they cannot belong or feel important through socially acceptable means, they misbehave. However, their misbehavior is not random; it is goal directed. The goal, whether students are aware of it or not, is to find a way to feel important. The nature of students' misbehavior informs teachers of the type of importance students are seeking.

Dreikurs identifies four goals for misbehavior. They are summarized in Table 10.3. For some students, the goal is *attention*. The faulty belief is that they can only be important if people pay attention to them. Seeking attention is positive, but these students demand it. A *power* goal is based on students' faulty belief that they can only feel good about themselves if they are in charge or keeping adults from being in charge. Students with a power goal want to engage adults in a power struggle for control. Extremely discouraged and hurt students may seek revenge as the goal for their misbehavior. Students with a *revenge* goal want people to feel as hurt as they do. They tend to engage in behavior that they know will hurt the adults around them. Consider Constance Molina's experience with a student with a revenge goal.

> ➤ One of my very angry and discouraged first grade students would get very sullen when I disciplined him. Then he would catch my eye, walk over to a young girl, and hit her in the face with his fist. I felt angry, but also hurt that he would do that to another person.

The final goal, *display of inadequacy*, represents the highest level of discouragement. These students believe that there is no hope of success, so they give up on trying. Their hopelessness is contagious, and adults who work with them soon feel helpless too.

One of the more reliable ways to determine a student's goal for misbehavior is how their behavior makes you feel as a teacher (Dreikurs, 1968; Wolfgang, 1999). As you can see from Table 10.3, each goal is connected to a different emotional reaction.

TABLE 10.3   Adlerian Goals of Misbehavior

Student's Goal	Student's Faulty Belief	Teacher's Reaction	Possible Interventions
Attention	"I need people's attention to feel good about myself."	Teacher feels irritated or annoyed	Ignore misbehavior; use logical consequence; provide attention when student is behaving appropriately
Power	"I need to be in control to feel good about myself."	Teacher feels angry or threatened	Choose fights carefully; provide limited choices; remain calm; use logical consequences
Revenge	"I want others to be hurt the way I've been hurt."	Hurt	Provide logical consequences; refrain from hurting back; form a relationship
Display of inadequacy	"I will never be able to succeed."	Hopeless Desire to pity student	Refrain from showing pity; encourage and support student

Source: Adapted from Dinkemeyer, D. & McKay, G. D. (1976). *Systematic training for effective parenting: Parents handbook.* Circle Pines, MN: American Guidance Service, p. 14.

The value of identifying a student's goal for their misbehavior is that you are better prepared to know how to respond. For example, if you know the student has a power goal, then you realize that the student is going to try to engage you in a struggle for power. You can minimize these attempts by staying calm in the face of provocative behavior, providing the student with choices, and helping the student find constructive ways to be in control. This is how Arturo Romero works with power students in his junior high music class.

> ➤ When a student tells me he won't do what I have asked, I like to give the student clear choices, but in a courteous manner. For example, "You may do this now with me, or later in detention." When students tell me they don't want to do either, I remind them that that is not one of their choices. I calmly repeat the choice, and tell them that if they cannot decide, I will have to decide. It doesn't always work, but it does sometimes.

Although, there are specific interventions for each of the goals, there are also general interventions for all goals. A **logical consequence** is a consequence that is related to the misbehavior, is administered respectfully, and is reasonable (Nelson, 1985; Pryor & Tollerud, 1999). For example, if a student trashed a bathroom, a related consequence is to have the student clean up the mess. It would be unreasonable to have the student clean it with a toothbrush. Logical consequences are an attempt to discipline students in a way that does not further discourage them.

Principle 6.4: Variety, Complexity, and Surprise

Variety, complexity, and surprise all help promote curiosity and interest in students (Burden & Byrd, 1999). Interesting and engaging instruction is one of your primary tools for preventing misbehavior. When students are disinterested in instruction, they find other ways to entertain themselves. You may find it useful to review Chapters 6 and 7 for some particular recommendations for providing intellectually engaging instruction.

Looking in on

Oji Samms

10.3

As I was sitting listening to our discussion about Inez, it occurred to me how little I really knew about Inez. I spend so much time focusing on her behavior, that I don't have time to get to know her. For example, I know Inez struggles with math, but I don't always know why. I'm going to make it a point to sit down with Inez and assess her math skills so I know what she needs. She may even be in the wrong math class. I also don't know what she does well or what her interests are. I've heard that she is a very good skateboarder, but I've never talked to her about that. As I was thinking about this, it occurred to me that I don't know what she wants to do with her life. Are there ways I could help connect what I'm doing to her goals in life? Finally, I thought it was important to realize that even with all her special behavioral issues, she is still a teenager with all the typical teenage issues. It must hurt to have the other students reject you the way they reject Inez. Maybe she needs to get involved in the peer mediation program so that she can belong somewhere.

● **How are principles of motivation relevant to Oji's thinking about Inez?**

Decision Point: What could Oji do to get to know Inez better?

Principles into Practice:
Illustrating Key Concepts

The experiences of Maria Torres and Oji Samms provide examples of how theoretical principles can be translated into classroom management approaches. Both teachers found it necessary to use techniques and strategies from different theoretical perspectives to accomplish their goals. This is likely to be your experience also. As you read about these teachers' experiences you were asked to reflect on their use of teaching techniques and strategies through a series of questions. Here are your authors' perspectives on those questions.

Looking back on  *Maria Torres*

Rosa provided Maria with a number of options for helping her students behave more appropriately in the hallway. For example, she described a third grade teacher who uses a token reinforcement system with marbles as tokens. Students can earn two tokens for appropriate hallway behavior, and they can lose earned tokens for misbehaving in the hall, a form of response cost. A sixth grade teacher uses positive practice overcorrection. Both teachers are applying Principle 2.3, learning results from the effects of stimuli on responses. Rosa, however, believes that Maria needs to understand a behavior before she tries to intervene. She has asked her to determine baseline, or how often the behavior is currently occurring. She has also asked her to understand when and under what circumstances the behavior is occurring. In general, she is asking Maria to be a careful observer of her students and to apply Principle 2.1, learning is measurable and observable. Rosa's preference for preventing problems by alternating quiet and high-energy activities is an attempt to control antecedents by managing setting events and is an application of Principle 2.3, learning results from the effects of stimuli on responses.

Maria met Dennis, and she had some ideas about how to work with Dennis. Rosa first wanted Maria to make sure the work was at an appropriate level. If the work is too difficult for Dennis, it can serve as a setting event for his anger and frustration, Once again, Rosa is looking for a way to prevent misbehavior, and she is applying Principle 2.3, learning results from the effects of stimuli on responses. Most of her recommendations to Maria, however, are applications of social cognitive Principle 4.3, learners have the potential to self-regulate their own learning processes. Rosa recommended teaching Dennis self-instruction statements such as, "I need to take my time on this." Rosa also described a self-management approach that began with self-evaluation as students are taught to recognize early signs of their frustration. They then are taught the coping strategy of getting up, walking around, and using self-talk to manage frustration. Finally, students are taught to use self-reinforcement by congratulating themselves if they managed their anger successfully.

Maria had an opportunity to observe a number of key components of an effective classroom meeting in Rosa's classroom. First, Rosa used classroom meetings throughout the year for different purposes. Second, a student chaired the meeting, and Rosa participated in the meeting but on an equal footing with the other students. The student who chaired the meeting did an excellent job of reminding students of the rules for classroom meetings and kept the meeting focused on the single agenda idea for discussion. The way Rosa structured these meetings allowed her students some control over events in their classroom and helped involve them in topics that were personally relevant and interesting. Her classroom meeting allowed her to implement constructivist Principle 5.3, students' knowledge construction is assisted by the nature of their interactions with people and objects in their environment, and Principle 6.2, learners are more motivated by activities that appeal to their personal needs, desires, and interests. ●

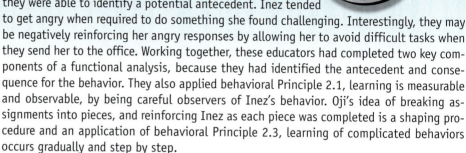

Looking back on *Oji Samms*

Oji Samms and his colleagues are trying to understand Inez's angry behavior. They began to look for an overall pattern to her behavior, but were unable to detect one. When they looked at specific incidences of angry behavior, they were able to identify a potential antecedent. Inez tended to get angry when required to do something she found challenging. Interestingly, they may be negatively reinforcing her angry responses by allowing her to avoid difficult tasks when they send her to the office. Working together, these educators had completed two key components of a functional analysis, because they had identified the antecedent and consequence for the behavior. They also applied behavioral Principle 2.1, learning is measurable and observable, by being careful observers of Inez's behavior. Oji's idea of breaking assignments into pieces, and reinforcing Inez as each piece was completed is a shaping procedure and an application of behavioral Principle 2.3, learning of complicated behaviors occurs gradually and step by step.

Paula Marsten, the team's history teacher, asked for ideas to help Inez in her classroom. Based on her brief description of her classroom, Paula seems to be trying to implement constructivist Principle 5.3, students' knowledge construction is assisted by the nature of their interactions with people and objects in their environment, through her jigsaw approach to student research. She wanted some management suggestions that would be consistent with her view of classroom learning. The counselor suggested teaching students to use I-messages to confront other students appropriately. The counselor also described a peer mediation approach to conflict resolution. He seemed to think that this approach would be consistent with Paula's content and her overall approach to teaching.

As the meeting continued, Oji was reflecting on how little he knows about Inez. The types of things he wondered about might help him create a more motivating environment for Inez and reduce the need for her to misbehave. For example, a more careful assessment of Inez's math skills may help him provide instruction at an appropriate level of challenge and help him implement Principle 6.1, learners are more motivated when they believe their actions will result in the successful completion of challenging tasks. His desire to learn about Inez's strengths and interests may allow him to personalize the learning environment. Also, his understanding that Inez probably is motivated by wanting to belong may help guide his decision about her participation in the peer mediation program. Together these ideas may help him implement Principle 6.2, learners are more motivated by activities that appeal to their personal needs, desires, and interests. Finally, his desire to learn about her goals may allow him to help her find connections between school and those goals. He may even find he can help her establish goals if she does not have any. By doing so, he can implement Principle 6.3, learners are more motivated when they have specific near-term goals that they believe are important. ●

Teachers as Decision Makers

At various decision points in this chapter you were asked to participate in the decision making of Maria Torres and Oji Samms. Your authors want to share their views of those decision points.

Maria Torres' Decision Points

Rosa has asked Maria to consider the types of data she might collect to understand Dennis's behavior better. Identifying consequences that have been effective in the past allows her to continue doing things that have worked. In addition, she could collect data to help her understand when Dennis is more likely to get in trouble or when he is more likely to get frustrated and angry about his school work. Rosa's suggestion that it's important to understand a problem before trying to solve it is good advice.

Rosa has given Maria a number of ideas for how to manage her students' hallway behavior. We think it makes sense to start with Rosa's recommendation to prevent problems. If this is unsuccessful, then she should intervene with reinforcement approaches followed by mild punishment techniques. This sequence allows her to use the least punitive approach necessary and helps her maintain a positive classroom environment.

To help Dennis, Rosa recommended the use of self-management strategies. One of the potential benefits of involving Dennis in the management of his own behavior is that he will learn strategies he can use when Maria is not around. For this to work, Maria needs to elicit Dennis's cooperation. Also, the coping strategy Rosa is recommending makes Dennis's attempts to manage anger and frustration observable to other students. Maria may want to ask other students to help by not bothering Dennis at these times and by congratulating him for his success. This may provide an opportunity to build a sense of community and could reduce inappropriate attention from other students.

To help her students take responsibility for class meetings, Maria could let the students plan the meetings, chair the meetings, or evaluate the meetings. She can also provide rules and structures that encourage each student to participate.

Oji Samms' Decision Points

The educators who work with Inez are meeting to discuss how to help her. It seems clear from Oji's statements that there are things he does not know or understand about Inez. To plan effective interventions, you need to understand the student and her behavior. Your authors would recommend using their first meeting to pool information and identify data that still needs to be collected.

To help reduce Inez's anger outbursts when she is given something challenging, they could begin by making sure that the academic tasks are not too challenging. They could also remind her that they are there to help. It might also be helpful to teach Inez to self-manage her anger using some of the techniques discussed in this chapter.

Later you were asked if Inez's behavior should be used as a criterion for her participation in the peer mediation program. Obviously, teachers want to avoid reinforcing students for misbehaving. It is possible that if she participates in this program, it is reinforcing her for misbehaving. However, if she is not allowed to participate, they may be taking away an important incentive for her to improve her behavior. Your authors tend to support an approach that uses her behavior as a criterion for staying in the program, but past behavior should not be used to disqualify her. Interestingly, she may bring a somewhat unique perspective to the mediation process.

Oji Samms has decided that it's important to get to know Inez better, based on what Inez will value or even allow. He should start slowly so that he does not overwhelm Inez. He has come to this important decision, and he probably will be anxious to put it into action. Perhaps as he sits down to assess her skills, he can talk to her about out of school interests and topics not related to the classroom.

Chapter 10 Study Guide

Use this Study Guide to review and test your knowledge of key concepts introduced in this chapter and to search out further information on issues and topics raised in this chapter.

 **Key Terms**

Review the following key words from the chapter and then connect to Research Navigator (www.researchnavigator.com) either directly or through this book's Companion Website to explore research on the topics as they relate to education today.

Active listening (p. 342)
Applied behavior analysis (p. 327)
Authoritative leadership style (p. 343)
Backup reinforcers (p. 331)
Baseline (p. 328)
Classroom management (p. 322)
Classroom procedure (p. 324)
Classroom rules (p. 323)
Contingency contract (p. 330)
Coping skills approaches (p. 339)
Dependent group-oriented
   contingency system (p. 332)
Extinction burst (p. 333)

Extinction-induced aggression
   (p. 333)
Functional analysis (p. 327)
Group-oriented contingency system
   (p. 332)
I-Message (p. 342)
Independent group-oriented
   contingency system (p. 332)
Interdependent group-oriented
   contingency system (p. 332)
Logical consequence (p. 348)
Overcorrection (p. 333)
Overlapping (p. 326)

Positive practice overcorrection (p. 334)
Reactive effect (p. 337)
Response cost (p. 335)
Restitutional overcorrection (p. 334)
Self-evaluation (p. 337)
Self-monitoring (p. 336)
Setting event (p. 329)
Target error (p. 326)
Time-out (p. 335)
Timing error (p. 326)
Token reinforcement system (p. 331)
Verbal reprimands (p. 333)
Withitness (p. 326)

Alternative Response Items

Multiple Choice Items

1. Mr. Redman has waited too long to intervene with two students who are talking. Now he has more students talking rather than listening. This is an example of Kounin's idea of:

   a. Withitness
   b. A timing error
   c. A target error
   d. A baseline error

2. Mr. Batista has students complete a form each week that sets the goal for the week in math, and what they would like to earn if they meet that goal. If Mr. Batista agrees with the student, they both sign the form. This is an example of:

   a. Contingency contracting
   b. Negative reinforcement
   c. Concurrent praise
   d. A token system

3. When Mrs. Bakken uses cooperative learning, her students can earn or lose group incentive points that can eventually be exchanged for an incentive the group has selected. Because each student can earn or lose points for the whole group, she is using a(n):

   a. Independent group-oriented contingency
   b. Dependent group-oriented contingency
   c. Interdependent group-oriented contingency

4. Mr. Roberts is just starting to intervene with Kelly's disruptive behavior. According to guidelines suggested in this chapter, which one of these interventions would be his best staring point?

   a. He should use positive overcorrection with Kelly first.

   b. He should use verbal reprimands paired with loss of privileges first.
   c. He should use exclusionary time-out first with Kelly.
   d. He should find ways to reinforce Kelly for appropriate behavior.

5. Sarah has been caught writing graffiti on the wall again. This time the principal has her repaint the wall she wrote on and the two connecting walls. The principal seems to be using:

   a. Extinction
   b. Restitutional overcorrection
   c. Positive practice overcorrection
   d. Response cost

6. Sally notices that just keeping track of how many times she interrupts when someone is talking has caused her to interrupt less. This is an example of the:

   a. Reactive effect
   b. Extinction burst
   c. Self-evaluation effect
   d. Spontaneous recovery effect

7. Which of the following are characteristics of effective classroom meetings?

   a. Students and teachers sit in a circle during classroom meetings.
   b. The classroom meeting has a clear purpose or agenda.
   c. Classroom meetings should be held regularly for various purposes.
   d. All of the above.

Matching

Match the appropriate goal of misbehavior to the behavioral description. One goal is not used.

Behavioral Description

_____ 8. Mr. Gallegos feels angry and threatened when Sam refuses to work.

_____ 9. Ms. Dunbar feels annoyed when Sally keeps interrupting her.

_____ 10. Mrs. Noyes feels hurt when Brad gets caught shoplifting.

Goal of Misbehavior

a. Attention
b. Power
c. Revenge
d. Display of inadequacy

Constructed Response Items

Short Answer/Completion Items

1. Ms. Gregson is unsure who was making noise so she keeps everyone in for recess. Because some students are punished who didn't misbehave, she has committed a _____.

2. Ms. Perez positions herself so she can scan the classroom while she helps students with seatwork. Her ability to monitor more than one activity at a time is_____.

3. Mr. Allen's students earn points for their appropriate behaviors that they can exchange for free time on the computer. What is the back-up reinforcer in his classroom?

4. Each week Mr. Quiroz schedules an improvement conference in which students identify what they hope to improve at this next week. What self-management technique is he using?

5. Setting clear limits while being supportive and accepting of students describes what classroom management style based in developmental theory?

Essay Items

1. Why would you want to try to manage antecedents or a reinforcement approach before using something such as a time-out?

2. How might the social cognitive ideas about self-management be used in a constructivist classroom.

3. How might Glasser's problem-solving steps be turned into a self-instruction approach?

Practicing Your Decision Making

The first column contains some common classroom management issues, and the second column has some classroom management approaches. Determine which of the management approaches you could use for each problem, and how you would use them.

1. Tardiness
2. Failing to complete homework
3. Rudeness to other students
4. Rudeness to the teacher
5. Pushing in the lunch line
6. Cheating
7. Fighting

a. Contingency contract
b. Token economy
c. Time-out
d. Self-monitoring
e. Self-instruction
f. Glasser's problem-solving steps
g. Goals of misbehavior

INTASC in Action

Use the following activities to think about how classroom management ideas in this chapter relate to the INTASC Standards.

Standard 2: Student Development. How might the following classroom management processes be different at the elementary and secondary level?

1. Establishing classroom rules and procedures
2. Maintaining behavior through positive reinforcement
3. Asking students to self-evaluate their behavior

Standard 3: Diverse Learners. Consistency is often discussed as an important characteristic of classroom management. However, students have different needs and backgrounds. What are the challenges in trying to be both consistent and fair to students at the same time? What does it mean to be consistent?

Standard 5: Motivation and Management. Classroom management issues can vary somewhat for different

teaching strategies. What are some of the unique challenges involved in these teaching strategies?

1. Direct instruction
2. Cooperative learning
3. Problem-based learning

Standard 9: Reflective Practice and Professional Growth. Your students' families are influenced by your classroom management decisions and also influence those decisions. Develop a strategy to keep your parents informed and involved in your classroom management. How will you communicate your classroom management expectations and seek support? How might technology help with parent involvement?

 ## Web Resources

The following websites have practical suggestions for effective classroom management. You can use the search words *classroom management* to access other sites such as these.

Best Practices Portfolio, Office of School Readiness
www.osr.state.ga.us/bestprac/intro.htm
Created by the Department of Early Childhood at Georgia State University, this site provides a collection of activities useful in the classroom. Visit the Classroom Management page for practical tips.

I Love Teaching.com
www.iloveteaching.com
Connect with a classroom teacher who shares suggestions for survival in the classroom, including tips on classroom management.

Education World
http://db.educationworld.com/perl/browse
Visit the online version of this leading teacher resource to explore the great many articles addressing the latest topics in education. Visit the Professional Development Center button and click on the button for Classroom Management to read what various scholars and practitioners advise.

Teachers Helping Teachers
www.pacificnet.net/~mandel/
ClassroomManagement.html
This page provides practical ideas for teachers in the area of classroom management and learning.

Intelligence and Exceptionality

Standards in This Chapter

The concepts presented in this chapter will contribute to your mastery of all of the INTASC standards, however, the material presented in Chapter 11 relates most strongly to the following standards:

● **Standard 3:** Diverse Learners

● **Standard 7:** Planning

● **Standard 9:** Reflective Practice and Professional Growth

● **Standard 10:** School and Community Involvement

Chapter 11 begins an exploration of academic diversity by exploring two important topics. The chapter begins with a discussion of intelligence, a psychological construct that has received considerable attention in the educational and psychological literature. Next, learner exceptionality is examined as a source of academic diversity that poses important challenges for classroom teachers.

By the time you are finished with this chapter you should be able to do the following:

● Understand these three views of intelligence: the psychometric view of intelligence, Sternberg's triarchic theory, and Gardner's multiple intelligences theory.

● Understand the provisions of the Individuals with Disabilities Act (IDEA) for the education of students with disabilities.

● Understand primary and secondary characteristics of students with disabilities.

● Understand the classroom teachers' role in the education of students with disabilities.

● Understand characteristics of students with gifts and talents and educational options for these students.

Close-ups on the Classroom

Elementary

Margaret Lew and Academic Diversity

This is my first year teaching third grade, and one of the most surprising things is the range of academic abilities in my classroom. For example, I have some students who still are not reading. On the other hand, another one of my students, Brenda, became bored one day during reading and pulled *Time* magazine out of her desk and started reading it to herself. Also, it's not just that some students do better than others, but each student has her or his own strengths and weaknesses. One of my goals this year is to improve my ability to design lessons that address the different capabilities of my students. I plan to accomplish this by using what I learned in an in-service presented by Maggie Baker on Gardner's multiple intelligences.

Calista is a good example of what I am talking about because she presents so many contradictions. When we have class discussions her vocabulary and general knowledge blow me away. She is just so bright and articulate. However, al-

though she is not my lowest reader, she does struggle with reading. I'm always surprised how slowly she is progressing in reading, especially because she is a super math student. She seems to be more frustrated about her progress in reading than she used to be, and I'm afraid she's going to quit trying. Because of these concerns, I got parent permission to discuss Calista with our special education prereferral team. I'm not sure that I want to refer Calista for testing, but I could use some help. I am on the agenda for next Friday's meeting, and I need to prepare for the meeting. The members of the prereferral team want to see data on Calista's performance, and they also want me to discuss what I have already tried to do to help Calista.

As if I don't have enough to worry about, Mrs. Portello wants to talk with me because she is concerned that her son Robbie is not being challenged enough. One thing is for sure. I'm being challenged enough.

> **Decision Point:** What types of routines or procedures could Margaret use to make it easier to respond to requests for performance data on a student?

As you can see from the opening vignettes, one of the more challenging issues you face as a teacher is how to meet the educational needs of an academically diverse student population. **Academic diversity** refers to the individual differences among students that influence your decision making. You have already encountered information on academic diversity in previous chapters. For example, in Chapters 3 and 7 you considered the nature of learners' prior knowledge, an extremely important source of academic diversity. In this chapter, the focus is on two sources of academic diversity—intelligence and learner exceptionality.

Before proceeding with Chapter 11, be sure you read the Close-ups on the Classroom features about Margaret Lew and Li-Sheng Ma. At various points in the chapter, you will revisit both teachers in their classrooms and follow their decision-making progress. Their experiences are closely integrated with the key concepts of this chapter and serve as important models of addressing issues of intelligence and exceptionality in the classroom.

*I*ntelligence as an Individual Difference Construct

Intelligence is one of the most studied and written about psychological constructs. Over time, these varied considerations of intelligence have produced both consensus and controversy. At a general level, professionals tend to agree about the nature of intelligence (Eysenck, 1998). For example, when professional educators, psychologists, and sociologists were surveyed about the general nature of intelligence, well over 90 percent of the respondents indicated that abstract reasoning, problem-solving ability, and the capacity to acquire knowledge are important elements of intelligence (Snyderman & Rothman, 1987). Additionally, these general understandings have

Li-Sheng Ma
and High School Special Education

I've been a special education teacher at Fillmore High School for a number of years. In the past I used to teach in a cross-categorical resource room setting. However, for the last three years I am the inclusion specialist for our school. The inclusion specialist position is something new we are trying, and we're still trying to work all the bugs out. Our goal is to educate students with disabilities as much as possible in the regular classroom. So far my role as an inclusion specialist has mainly involved helping teachers modify instruction and curricula. Occasionally, however, I get to team teach or model certain inclusion lesson strategies for my teachers.

As an additional part of my job description, I have been assigned the responsibility of following up with parents af-ter we meet with them as part of our special education process. I'm always surprised how many questions parents have. We give them written notification of their rights, but the special education process is confusing to them.

One of the least favorite parts of my job is my involvement with decisions about suspensions and expulsions for our students with disabilities. Federal law prohibits the expulsion of students with disabilities if their misbehavior is due to the nature of their disability. That's a tough call, and in my position I can find myself on the opposite side of this issue from teachers and administrators. We have a tough one of these meetings this afternoon.

Decision Point: What is Li-Sheng doing that might increase the likelihood of successful inclusion of their students with disabilities?

---

been relatively stable over time. For example, there is a moderately strong correlation between expert opinions about the general nature of intelligence solicited in the 1920s, and the opinions of different experts who were surveyed sixty years later (Sternberg, 1990).

Although there is a reasonably high level of consensus about the general nature of intelligence, specific issues concerning intelligence continue to be debated. For example, what types of intelligence are there? How is one form of intelligence related to another? How might intelligence best be assessed? This chapter focuses on three views of intelligence that attempt to answer these types of questions: the psychometric view of intelligence, Sternberg's triarchic theory, and Gardner's theory of multiple intelligences.

Psychometric View of Intelligence

The major contribution of the psychometric approach has been the development of tests to assess different types of intellectual capabilities such as spatial reasoning, memory, and verbal reasoning. Psychometric theories of intelligence are attempts to explain the pattern of performance that emerges when tests of different intellectual capabilities are administered to large numbers of people.

Positive Manifold.   **Positive manifold** is the observation that scores on different types of intelligence tests tend to correlate positively with each other (Sternberg, 1990). If you were to administer a number of tests of different intellectual capabilities to a large number of people and compute correlations between each possible pair of tests, you would find correlations that would range from very low to very high. Tests that seem to measure similar or related skills tend to be the ones that correlate more highly with each other. For example, a test of word knowledge would correlate highly with a test of general information. This relationship is assumed to exist because both tests are measures of the same underlying ability or factor. Psychometric theories identify those underlying abilities or factors.

Early Psychometric Theories of Intelligence.   Using the statistical approach of factor analysis, early psychometric theorists attempted to identify the underlying abilities or factors that explained positive manifold. The debate became whether performance on tests of intellectual capabilities is best explained by one general intellectual factor, or if it was best explained by the existence of a number of separate intellectual factors.

What are g and s in Spearman's model of intelligence?

Spearman and g.   As a result of his statistical analyses of people's performances on a number of different intelligence tests, Spearman (1904, 1927) proposed a two-factor theory of intelligence. He believed that positive manifold is due to the existence of a general intellectual factor (g). This overall or general intellectual factor is present in all intelligent behavior, but it tends to be more predictive of performance on complex mental tasks (Jensen, 1998b). His second factor (s) refers to the specific abilities required by particular tasks. Consequently, a person's performance on a measure of intelligence is due to the combination of g and the specific abilities (s) tapped by that task. Although he identified specific factors in intelligence, Spearman tended to emphasize the role of g in intelligent behavior.

How are Thurstone's and Guilford's models of intelligence different from Spearman's model?

Thurstone and Guilford.   Louis Thurstone and Joy Guilford rejected the idea of a single general factor (g). Instead, they argued that positive manifold is better explained in terms of a number of underlying factors. Thurstone (1931, 1938) suggested that there are seven primary mental abilities, and Guilford suggested that there may be as many as 150 underlying factors or capabilities (Guilford, 1967, 1981, 1985).

Current Psychometric Views of the Structure of Intelligence.   Currently, hierarchical factor models of intelligence seem to fit the accumulated data from various statistical analyses best (Gustafsson & Undheim, 1996). Hierarchical factor theories propose different levels of factors in terms of their generality. For example, Carroll (1993, 1997) proposed a three-level hierarchy for the structure of intelligence. At the top level is the conceptual equivalent of g. At the second level are eight second-order or broad factors. Under the eight second-order factors are sixty-five numerous specific or narrow abilities that tend to correlate at different levels with the eight second-order factors. Carroll's hierarchical model maintains the concept of g, while also identifying numerous specific abilities.

Educational Applications of Psychometric Views of Ability.   The major educational application of the psychometric view of intelligence has been the design of intelligence tests to assist with educational decision making. However, the psychometric view also has some general implications for instruction.

Intelligence Tests.   Historically, intelligence tests were developed for practical and clinical purposes, rather than as applications of theories of intelligence (Kaufman, 2000). For example, Binet's 1905 intelligence test was designed to help distinguish between children with mental retardation and intellectually normal students in Parisian classrooms. Although some recently developed intelligence tests are applications of theories of intelligence (Ittenbach, Esters, & Wainer, 1997), the primary purpose of intelligence testing in schools is still to identify students with special learning needs.

A number of different intelligence tests are available for assessing the intelligence of children and adolescents including the Wechsler Intelligence Scale for Children, Fourth Edition (Wechsler, 2003), the Stanford-Binet Intelligence Scales, Fifth Edition (Roid, 2003), and the Das-Naglieri Cognitive Assessment System (Naglieri & Das,

1997). Although these tests may differ in structure and theoretical rationale, they share these characteristics in common.

- Special training and credentials are required to administer intelligence tests. Typically, school psychologists administer them in schools.
- These tests are individually administered, and administration time usually is an hour or more.
- These tests are typically only administered if teachers or parents refer students for special education or programs for students with intellectual or academic gifts.
- These tests are standardized, which means they are administered and scored uniformly according to a strict set of guidelines.
- These tests are interpreted in a norm-referenced fashion, which means that students' scores tells how they compared with people their age who took the test as part of a nationally selected norm group.
- These tests include a number of different subtests that assess different specific abilities.
- These yield both an overall estimate of ability in terms of a global score and estimates of specific abilities as reflected in factor scores or subtest scores. Historically, this global score has been the IQ, but more recently developed tests use terminology other than IQ, such as the General Conceptual Ability score (GCA) for example (Elliott, 1997).

What does it mean to say that an intelligence test is standardized, norm-referenced, and individually administered?

The Psychometric View and Classroom Instruction. Intelligence tests were not designed with the goal of helping teachers plan instruction. Consequently, the implications for instruction tend to be very broad and generally are related to the amount of structure teachers provide for students of different ability levels.

Relatively consistent interactions have been found between students' general ability to learn (g) and the level of structure present during instruction. In general, less structured methods such as discovery or inquiry learning tend to be less effective with students with lower ability levels than with students with higher ability levels (Gustafsson & Undheim, 1996). However, this interaction may be influenced by students' metacognitive skills. In one study, the problem-solving performance of students with low ability and low levels of metacognitive skill was enhanced by the provision of a more structured environment. However, the performance of students with low ability but who had better metacognitive skills was actually adversely affected by the provision of additional structure (Veenman & Elshout, 1995). An important implication for teachers is that they need to be aware of both students' ability and metacognitive skills when determining how and when to provide additional structure during methods such as discovery or inquiry learning. This is how Brenda Wong addresses this with her special needs learners in her fifth grade classroom.

Individual intelligence tests are administered by trained psychologists.

> I have a very good working relationship with our special education teachers. They work with me to teach my students with mild disabilities important background knowledge and any strategies these students may need to be more effective problem solvers.

Evaluation of the Psychometric Perspective. Eighty years ago, Terman (1921), a pioneer in intelligence testing, warned against limiting an understanding of intelligence to how people performed on

What are two major criticisms of the use of test performances to define intelligence?

intelligence tests. In general, the use of test performances to define intelligence has been criticized for two reasons. First, the use of different tests, different statistical methods, and different interpretations of the data can all lead to different models of intelligence (Davidson & Downing, 2000). Also, the focus on test performance restricts the range of abilities that are defined as intelligence only to those abilities that are important to test performance (Gardner, 1999a).

The value of g as an individual differences construct also continues to be debated (Pyryt, 1999; Stuart-Hamilton & McDonald, 2001). For example, Howard Gardner has expressed serious doubt about the usefulness of g for understanding students' abilities and for planning educational experiences (Gardner, 1985, 1999a). Arthur Jensen (1998a, 1998b), on the other hand, has noted that students' general ability to learn has consistently been found to be a strong predictor of students' academic achievement.

Although commonly used intelligence tests are developed according to fairly rigorous technical standards, their use in schools has been criticized for a number of reasons (Bracken & Walker, 1997; Flanagan, Andrews, & Genshaft, 1997; Gould, 1981; Reschly, 1997; Samuda, 1998). Among the many criticisms, two seem to be repeated frequently in different critiques. First, intelligence tests have been criticized for failing to provide useful information for planning instruction. Second, intelligence tests have been criticized for being biased against certain cultural groups and for helping perpetuate social inequalities. Test bias arguments have been made on a number of bases including the concern that intelligence tests may be less reliable for minority students, and that they may assess minority students using language and experiences that are unfamiliar to them (Samuda, 1998).

Sternberg's Triarchic Theory of Intelligence

Sternberg's triarchic theory of intelligence is based on information-processing theory and is comprised of the componential, experiential, and contextual subtheories (Sternberg, 1985, 1990, 1997). These three subtheories are used to explain the internal mental world of the learner, and how learners use intelligence to interact with their environments.

Componential Subtheory.   The componential subtheory identifies the information-processing components that operate on internal representations of experience (Sternberg & Gardner, 1982). Consequently, the componential subtheory is used to describe the internal mental functioning of learners. Sternberg has identified three types of information-processing components that differ in terms of their function.

What are the three types of performance components?

Performance components are the three categories of lower order mental processes used in the execution of a particular intellectual task (Sternberg, 1985). Encoding components are involved in perceiving the elements of a task or problem. Combination and comparison components are used to connect information in a problem together, while response components are involved in executing a solution to a problem.

How do the knowledge acquisition components relate to the discussion of encoding in Chapter 3?

Knowledge acquisition components are the three processes used to acquire the knowledge necessary to solve problems (Sternberg, 1990). Selective encoding is the process of identifying what is important to learn from an experience. Selective combination is the process of organizing incoming information into a coherent whole, and selective comparison involves relating new information to existing knowledge in memory.

The **metacomponents** serve executive control or self-regulatory functions during intelligent behavior. Sternberg (1981) identified seven self-regulatory functions that metacomponents serve. As you can see, they are the types of functions that are discussed by information-processing theorists as metacognitive regulation.

- Decisions about what the problem is that needs to be solved
- Selection of ways to represent and organize information

- Selection of lower order components
- Selection of strategies for combining lower order components
- Decisions regarding attentional resources
- Monitoring of solutions
- Sensitivity to external feedback

Experiential Subtheory. According to Sternberg (1997) the environmental tasks that information-processing components are applied to vary in terms of familiarity to the learner. He believes that intelligence is best measured with tasks that involve intellectual skills that are in the process of being automatized or with tasks that are somewhat novel to the learner. Learners' ability to automatize certain skills and their ability to deal with novelty are both effective ways of measuring people's ability to apply their intelligence.

Contextual Subtheory. The contextual subtheory reflects Sternberg's belief that a major purpose of intelligent behavior is to accomplish practical goals (Sternberg, 1985, 1997). In doing this, people use their information-processing components to adapt to the demands of their environments, to modify or shape the environment, or to select environments that are better matched to their intellectual capabilities (Sternberg, 1997).

> What are some similarities between Sternberg's contextual subtheory and Piaget's view of the purpose of intelligence (see Chapter 5)?

Educational Applications of the Triarchic Theory. Sternberg and his colleagues have provided numerous examples of how triarchic theory can be applied to education (Kolligian & Sternberg, 1987; Sternberg, 1984, 1990, 1994, 1995, 1998a, 1999a, 1999b). Some of his more recent work has been conducted under the heading of teaching for wisdom and teaching for successful intelligence (Sternberg, 1996, 2001a, 2002a; Sternberg & Grigorenko, 2000).

Teaching for Wisdom. Sternberg's view of teaching for wisdom is based on the idea that intellectual abilities are not enough; students need to be able to use their intellect wisely. According to Sternberg, wisdom is reflected in people's ability to balance their self-interests with the interest of greater entities such as society (Sternberg, 2002a, 2002b). He further believes that smart, educated people are susceptible to four fallacies. The egocentrism fallacy is when intelligent people act in ways that benefit themselves, regardless of the effect on others. The omniscience fallacy is when intelligent people believe they know all they need to know and do not need to listen to others. The omnipotent fallacy is when intelligent people believe that their intellect and education make them all powerful. Finally, the invulnerability myth is that others will not be clever enough to catch them in wrongdoing. Teaching for wisdom involves helping students avoid those fallacies by providing learning experiences that help them realize that learning is a lifelong process that help them develop prosocial values, help them consider diverse perspectives, and encourage them to share credit with collaborators (Sternberg, 2002a). For example, a course in history might help students view the same historical event from multiple perspectives and help them realize how complex and incomplete knowledge of an event can be.

Teaching for Successful Intelligence. Sternberg suggests that there are three kinds of abilities that are based generally on the triarchic theory (Sternberg, 1998b). Analytical ability involves mental activities such as being able to analyze, judge, evaluate, compare, and contrast. Creative ability involves mental activities such as being able to create, invent, discover, imagine, and suppose. Practical ability involves mental activities such as being able to put ideas to use, to connect ideas to practice, and to see the practical implications of ideas.

Although he has done some research in terms of matching instruction and assessment to a person's strongest ability (Sternberg, Ferrari, Clinkenbeard, & Grigorenko, 1996), teaching for successful intelligence is primarily a model to infuse intelligence into the curriculum. In addition to teaching for memorization of facts and ideas, which Sternberg believes has an important purpose, teachers are asked to have students think about ideas using the performance components of all three forms of intelligence. By approaching topics in different ways, students' intellectual strengths are nurtured, and their intellectual weaknesses are strengthened (Sternberg, 1998c). Consider how Mr. Peterson applies the ideas of teaching for successful intelligence during a biology unit.

➤ I make sure my students learn key terminology and procedures. They will need these basic skills and ideas to problem solve. Beyond that, I have my students engage in these types of activities. I provide my students with computer-generated data on animal survival in a particular area of the state over a number of years. I ask them to predict the impact of increasing and decreasing numbers of predators on survivability of certain animals (analytical ability). I also ask my students to invent a new system for tracking animal survivability and migration (creative ability). In inventing these new systems, I have my students consider how the principles of systematic sampling can be used in the design of their animal tracking system (practical ability).

Evaluation of the Triarchic Theory.   Sternberg's theory clearly expands thinking about intelligence beyond the limits established by the psychometric view. For example, he includes creativity and wisdom in his discussions of intelligence. Although a broadening of the definition of intelligence can be interpreted as a strength, a tendency toward overinclusiveness can also pose problems (Eysenck, 1998). For example, intelligence may become so inclusive of other constructs that it will lack meaning as a separate construct. Also, even if Sternberg's broadening of intelligence is a welcome change, some of his expansions may be lacking in clarity and defensibility (Martinez, 2000). For example, creativity often tends to be domain specific, and it is hard to conceptualize it as a general ability.

Sternberg has made considerable contributions to an understanding of the role of information-processing theory in the assessment of intelligence through his use of componential analysis (Sternberg, 1977, 1980). In a componential analysis, performance on an intelligence test item is broken down into the information-processing components for that item type (Goetz & Hall, 1984; Goldman & Pellegrino, 1984; Martinez, 2000). Sternberg (1980) applied componential analysis to verbal analogies in the form of Doctor: Patient :: Lawyer: _____. This work provided important insights into how people solve these types of problems, and demonstrated how information-processing theory and psychometric theory can be connected.

What is a componential analysis?

Gardner's Multiple Intelligences Theory

Beginning in the late 1970s and early 1980s, Howard Gardner became concerned about the nature of the field of intelligence (Gardner & Hatch, 1989). For example, he observed that the psychometric approach really failed to capture the full range of human problem-solving capabilities (Gardner, 1983). He believed that any ability that is valued in a culture merited consideration as a potential form of intelligence, not just those abilities assessed on intelligence tests (Gardner, 1994). He began to investigate the nature of intelligence using methods and data sources other than statistical analyses of test data (Chen & Gardner, 1997). For example, he studied the literature on atypical populations (e.g., individuals with special gifts and talents), the literature on the effects of cerebral trauma on human performance, and the cross-cultural literature on different forms of abilities. His **multiple intelligences (MI) theory** emerged from these studies.

Gardner's Defining Criteria for Intelligence.   Gardner (1999a, pp. 33–34) defines intelligence as "a biopsychological potential to process information that can be activated in a cultural setting to solve problems or create products that are of value in a particular culture." In addition, Gardner identified eight criteria to determine if a human faculty qualifies as an intelligence (Gardner, 1983, 1999a; Krechevsky & Seidel, 1998; Sternberg, 1990).

- **Potential isolation by brain damage:** Gardner believes that each intelligence resides primarily in particular areas of the brain. Damage to those areas of the brain should affect that intelligence.
- **The existence of atypical populations for that intelligence:** Savants, prodigies, and other exceptional people should be identifiable for the intelligence.
- **An identifiable core set of mental operations:** Each type of intelligence should have its own characteristic mental processes for manipulating the symbol system associated with that intelligence.
- **A distinctive developmental history with specifiable end points or expertise:** Each intelligence should show a clear developmental pattern that leads to some form of expertise associated with that intelligence. For example, students with well-developed logico-mathematical intelligence might become philosophers or mathematicians.
- **The ability to identify an evolutionary history for the ability that goes back millions of year:** Earlier evolutionary forms of the intelligence should exist, such as forms of language-based communication in nonhuman animals.
- **Support from experimental work in individual differences for the existence of the ability:** Studies should show a lack of interference or overlap between abilities.
- **Support from psychometric findings on the nature of intelligence:** Patterns of correlation among assessments can be used to support or refute the existence of an independent form of intelligence, as long as multiple forms of assessment are used.
- **Susceptibility to encoding of a particular symbol system:** Each intelligence should have an associated symbol system such as musical notes, mathematics, and pictorial representations.

The Eight Intelligences.   Based on his definition and criteria, Gardner originally identified seven intelligences (Gardner, 1983). These seven intelligences are linguistic, logico-mathematical, musical, spatial, bodily-kinesthetic, intrapersonal and interpersonal intelligence. Later, Gardner (1999a, 1999b) added naturalist intelligence as the eighth intelligence. Descriptions of these eight intelligences are provided in Table 11.1. It should be noted that the number of Gardner's intelligences can increase if additional abilities are identified that meet Gardner's criteria. For example, one potential candidate for a

TABLE 11.1   Gardner's Eight Intelligences

Intelligence	Description
Linguistic	Allows individuals to communicate and make sense of the world through language
Logico-mathematical	Allows individuals to understand and appreciate abstract relationships
Musical	Allows people to understand and create meaning out of sounds
Spatial	Allows people to perceive spatial information, to transform visual information, and to represent knowledge visually
Bodily-kinesthetic	Allows individuals to use their bodies to solve problems
Intrapersonal	Allows individuals to distinguish between their own feelings to build mental models of who they are and to make decisions about their lives
Interpersonal	Allows people to recognize and interpret the feelings and intentions of others
Naturalist	Allows people to understand, classify, and use aspects of their environment

ninth intelligence is existential intelligence. However, at the time this was written, Gardner did not believe there was sufficient evidence to qualify it completely as a form of intelligence (Scherer, 1999; Solomon & Hunter, 2002).

Educational Implications of Multiple Intelligences Theory.   MI theory has probably produced more educational applications than any other current theory of intelligence. In fact, Gardner himself was surprised by how well his theory was accepted by educators (Krechevsky, Hoerr, & Gardner, 1995). MI theory has been viewed as a way of individualizing instruction, a way of teaching for understanding, and as a way of expanding the types of assessments used in intelligence testing.

What are the three major types of applications of MI theory for education?

Individualizing Instruction with Multiple Intelligences Theory.   Gardner's theory has been viewed as a way of individualizing students' education by accommodating for the full range of students' intellectual capabilities (Krechevsky & Seidel, 1998). For some, MI theory is a powerful model for understanding learning differences and individual potential (Strong, Silver, & Perini, 2001). This is how Josie Manolito, a third grade teacher thinks about this.

> ➤ MI theory reminded me that students have different strengths and weaknesses. I need to try to help them find their strengths.

The work of Gardner and his colleagues on Project Spectrum provides another example of this approach. Project Spectrum is a collaboration between Howard Gardner and David Henry Feldman. The goal has been to develop assessments and curricular materials that allow teachers to identify and foster the different intellectual strengths of young children and to use those strengths to help at-risk students succeed (Chen, Krechevsky, Viens, & Isberg, 1998; Krechevsky, 1998).

Teaching for Understanding with Multiple Intelligences Theory.   Gardner also views MI theory as a structure for helping students develop meaningful understandings of key topics (Gardner, 1999a, 1999b). First, he suggests that teachers should select rich and meaningful topics that can be experienced in multiple ways. He provides Darwin's theory of evolution, Mozart's life, and the Holocaust as examples of topics that have this potential (Gardner, 1999b). Once an engaging and complicated topic has been selected, MI theory can help students develop meaningful understanding of rich topics in three ways.

First, Gardner (1999b) has suggested that MI can provide varied entry points into material. An entry point is how the material is introduced to students. According to Gardner, the way in which content is introduced to students is important for generating their engagement in learning, and the same content can be introduced in different ways to account for students' different intellectual strengths. For example, in introducing Darwin's theory of evolution, students could read narratives that personalize Darwin, or they could trace Darwin's thinking as he attempted to figure out the distribution of finches on the Galapagos Islands. Other students could be introduced to evolution through documentaries or art that depicts the power of nature.

Second, MI theory can also provide a structure for presenting useful analogies. Gardner views analogies as examples drawn from other areas of expertise that are more familiar to students (Gardner, 1999b). For example, an analogy can be made between evolution in genres of modern music and Darwin's naturalistic use of the term *evolution*.

What are the three ways that Gardner describes for using MI theory to teach rich topics in meaningful ways?

Finally, an MI framework allows teachers to represent key content in different ways. For example, evolution could be examined through linguistic, mathematical, and naturalistic experiences.

Assessment and Multiple Intelligences Theory.   MI theory can also be viewed as a way of broadening the view of how intelligence is assessed (Fasko, 2001; Krechevsky & Seidel, 1998). From an MI perspective, assessments need to be intelli-

I was very impressed with the in-service Maggie Baker presented on Gardner's MI theory. I think this approach will allow me to design lessons that will better meet the needs of many different types of learners. I plan to incorporate MI into the centers I am planning for next week's lesson on counting change. For example, at the spatial intelligence center, students will see if they can identify by touch the quarters, nickels, dimes, and pennies I've placed in paper bags. At the musical intelligence center, they will listen to the old rock and roll song, "Money." For the kinesthetic center, I am going to have them cut out coins from a worksheet. For interpersonal intelligence, the students at that center will play customers and sales clerks in a mock store. Of course, we will practice counting change for logico-mathematical intelligence. I'm still working to get the other intelligences into my lesson, because I think it's im-

Margaret Lew

11.1

portant to address every intelligence in every lesson. When I described my lesson to Maggie Baker, she congratulated me on my desire to teach in different ways, but she did have some concerns. She said it sounded like it would take a long time to do this unit, and she wasn't sure all the centers connected to my goal of teaching students to count change. Also, she said I might want to review the handout on misconceptions concerning the use of MI theory.

● **According to Gardner, what misuses of his MI theory are observable in this lesson?**

Decision Point: Why might an understanding of instructional alignment (see Chapter 9) be important for Margaret in deciding how to teach a lesson in different ways?

gence fair and go beyond paper and pencil measures. For example, young children's logico-mathematical and spatial abilities could be assessed by having them take apart and put together again a common household appliance such as a meat grinder (Chen et al., 1998). Assessments should also allow for multiple ways of understanding and responding, help track growth over time, and should be a fundamental part of learning.

Evaluation of Gardner's Theory. Gardner's MI theory has had a fairly significant impact on schools (Collins, 1998). However, the theory also has had its share of criticism (Delisle, 2001; Gustafsson & Undheim, 1996; Messick, 1992; Morgan, 1996; Sternberg, 1990; White & Breen, 1998). A number of criticisms have been leveled against Gardner's theory in terms of his definition and identification of intelligences, and they include the following key concerns.

- Gardner has not identified intelligences, but in many cases has identified talents and cognitive styles, or in some cases domain-specific expertise.
- The assumption that intelligences are independent of each other does not fit a considerable amount of available data.
- Gardner has really only supplied a taxonomy or list of abilities and not a theory of intelligence.
- The number of intelligences seems to grow with no logical upper limit to the potential number of intelligences.
- The inclusion of an ability as an intelligence seems to be a subjective judgment made by Gardner.

Gardner has responded to these criticisms and others (Gardner, 1995, 1999a; Walters & Gardner, 1986). In general, his reaction has been to address these criticisms as myths and misunderstandings. However, he does take some responsibility for these misunderstandings of his theory. For example, his definition of intelligence presented in this chapter is an attempt to be more specific about what he means when he uses the term intelligence.

The number and types of educational interventions connected to Gardner's theory make it hard to render overall judgments about their effectiveness. However, teaching in various ways to increase understanding seems defensible from the perspectives of both cognitive learning theory and constructivism. In general, the jury is still out on approaches such as adjusting for intellectual strengths. It is also worthwhile to consider the educational applications of MI theory that concern Gardner himself (Gardner, 1995, 1999a).

- **Attempting to teach all concepts or lessons using all of the intelligences:** He supports teaching content in different ways, but sees limited value in trying to approach all topics in eight ways.
- **Believing that going through certain motions activates or exercises specific intelligences:** For example, he would suggest having students exercise by running around a room will not enhance bodily-kinesthetic intelligence.
- **Using intelligences as mnemonic devices:** It may help to remember facts by singing them, but this type of activity is not designed to enhance intelligence.

How would Gardner react to the idea that every lesson should address all eight intelligences?

- **Conflating intelligence with other desired outcomes:** He would ask people not to equate interpersonal intelligence with learning group process strategies as part of cooperative learning, or intrapersonal intelligence with elevating student self-esteem.
- **Labeling people in terms of their intelligences:** As with any labels, they may have unintended consequences. Calling students linguistic learners, for example, may restrict their confidence in learning other ways.

Exceptional Learners

The term **exceptional learners** refers to students who differ from the norm to the extent that they need specialized educational services to meet their needs (Heward, 2000). This definition includes both students with disabilities and students with special gifts and talents (Vaughn, Bos, & Schumm, 2000). **Special education** is specially designed instruction to meet the needs of exceptional learners (Hallahan & Kauffman, 2000).

The Individuals with Disabilities Act

Special education services for students with disabilities as we know them today were mandated and outlined in P. L. 94-142 *The Education for All Handicapped Children Act,* which was passed in 1975, and Section 504 of the Rehabilitation Act of 1973. Later P. L. 94-142 was reauthorized and amended as the IDEA in 1990, once again in 1997, and is currently undergoing reauthorization as this is being written. (Please note that if the current reauthorization is not completed before this text goes to print, any significant amendments will be posted on the authors' website if and when they occur.)

Because of the significant overlap between IDEA and Section 504, your authors will concentrate on IDEA, which is the key piece of education law on special education.

IDEA was established with four purposes in mind (Armstrong, 2001).

- To ensure that students with disabilities have access to a free and appropriate public education that provides services to meet their unique needs
- To guarantee that the rights of students with disabilities and their parents are protected
- To assist states and local educational entities in providing services for students with disabilities
- To help ensure the effectiveness of services provided to students with disabilities

IDEA contains the following key provisions that schools need to attend to in meeting the needs of students with disabilities (Turnbull & Cilley, 1999; Turnbull & Turnbull, 1998).

Individuals with Disabilities Act Definitions of Disabilities. IDEA identifies thirteen specific categories of disabilities and the criteria to determine whether a student qualifies as having a particular disability (Knoblauch & Sorenson, 1998). According to IDEA, students with a disability are students with a specific learning disability, mental retardation, hearing impairments, deafness, speech or language impairments, visual impairments (including blindness), emotional disturbance, orthopedic impairment, autism, deaf-blindness, traumatic brain injury, other health impairments, or multiple disabilities that require special education and related services. Additionally, the 1997 authorization of IDEA allows states to use the term *developmental delay* for students aged 3 to 9 who show developmental delays in physical development, cognitive development, communication development, social or emotional development, and adaptive development. According to the Office of Special Education Programs' *Twenty-Third Annual Report to Congress on the Implementation of the Individuals with Disabilities Education Act* (OSEP, 2001), over five and one-half million students are provided services under IDEA. Table 11.2 contains the **IDEA definitions of disabilities.**

> According to IDEA, what is a developmental delay?

Free Appropriate Public Education. According to IDEA, all children with disabilities are entitled to a free appropriate public education (FAPE), regardless of the severity of the disability. This is sometimes referred to as the **zero reject principle.** P. L. 94-142 guaranteed this right for students between the ages of six and seventeen, and also extended this right to students between the ages of three to five and eighteen to twenty-one if states provided educational services to students without disabilities in those age ranges (Heward, 2000). In the mid-1980s, P. L. 99-457 extended this right to all students between the ages of three and five.

To ensure that young children with disabilities are identified, the **child find** provision of IDEA mandates that states locate, assess, and identify students with disabilities between the ages of three and twenty-one (Smith, 2001). This requirement extends to students living in a district but who do not attend public schools, as in the case of private school students (DeBettencourt, 2002). This is how John Jacoby, a kindergarten teacher, participates in child find.

> ➤ Every summer, in cooperation with local preschools, we offer a free kindergarten screening. Psychologists, speech pathologists, physical therapists, nurses, and teachers work together in an attempt to identify any young children with special needs.

What constitutes an *appropriate* education for students with disabilities has been controversial and has been addressed through court decisions (Bauer & Shea, 1999; Katsiyannis & Maag, 1997; Maag & Katsiyannis, 2000; Pittman & Huefner, 2001). A commonly used legal criteria for FAPE was established in *Rowley v. Hendrick Hudson School District* in 1982. According to the Rowley decision, schools have met the FAPE requirement if they follow the procedural requirements of IDEA, and if they provide individualized instructional programs that help students progress reasonably (Bauer & Shea, 1999; Yell & Dragow, 2000). More recently, the courts have interpreted reasonable progress as programs that produce meaningful educational benefit (Yell & Dragow, 2000).

Least Restrictive Environment. Beginning with P. L. 94-142 and continuing with IDEA, students with disabilities are to be educated in the **least restrictive environment.** This means that students with disabilities are to be educated with students without disabilities to the maximum extent possible (Yell, 1995). For the last twenty-five years, integration of students with disabilities into the regular classroom has been the norm (Kavale & Forness, 2000). The P. L. 94-142 term for educating students in the regular education classroom was *mainstreaming.* Today this approach is often referred to as **inclusion** (Scruggs & Mastropieri, 1996).

> How would you summarize the research on the effectiveness of inclusion?

TABLE 11.2 Individuals with Disabilities Act Categories of Disabilities

Disability Category	Definition
Specific learning disability	A disorder in one or more of the basic psychological processes involved in understanding or in using language, spoken or written, that may manifest in an imperfect ability to listen, think, speak, read, write, spell, or do mathematical calculations. This term includes such conditions as perceptual disabilities, brain injury, minimal brain dysfunction, dyslexia, and developmental aphasia. This term does not include children who have learning problems that are primarily the result of visual, hearing, or motor disabilities; mental retardation; or environmental, cultural, or economic disadvantage
Mental retardation	Significantly subaverage general intellectual functioning existing concurrently with deficits in adaptive behavior and manifested during the developmental period that adversely affects a child's educational performance
Emotional disturbance	A condition exhibiting one or more of the following characteristics, displayed over a long period of time and to a marked degree that adversely affects a child's educational performance: • An inability to learn that cannot be explained by intellectual, sensory, or health factors • An inability to build or maintain satisfactory interpersonal relationships with peers or teachers • Inappropriate types of behavior or feelings under normal circumstances • A general pervasive mood of unhappiness or depression • A tendency to develop physical symptoms or fears associated with personal or school problems
Autism	A developmental disability significantly affecting verbal and nonverbal communication and social interactions, generally evident before age three and that adversely affects educational performance. Other characteristics often associated with autism are engagement in repetitive activities and stereotyped movements, resistance to environmental change or changes in daily routines, and unusual responses to sensory experiences
Deafness	A hearing impairment so severe that the child cannot understand what is being said even with a hearing aid
Deaf-blindness	A combination of hearing and visual impairments causing such severe communications, developmental, and educational problems that the child cannot be accommodated in either a program specifically for the deaf or a program specifically for the blind
Hearing impairment	An impairment in hearing, whether permanent or fluctuating, that adversely affects a child's educational performance but that is not included under the definition of deafness as listed previously
Multiple disabilities	A combination of impairments (such as mental retardation, blindness, or mental retardation-physical disabilities) that cause such severe educational problems that the child cannot be accommodated in a special education program solely for one of the impairments. The term does not include deaf-blindness
Orthopedic impairment	A severe orthopedic impairment that adversely affects educational performance. The term includes impairments such as amputation, absence of a limb, cerebral palsy, poliomyelitis, and bone tuberculosis
Other health impairment	Having limited strength, vitality, or alertness due to chronic or acute health problems such as a heart condition, rheumatic fever, asthma, hemophilia, and leukemia that adversely affects educational performance
Speech or language impairment	A communication disorder such as stuttering, impaired articulation, language impairment, or a voice impairment that adversely affects a child's educational performance
Traumatic brain injury	An acquired injury to the brain caused by external physical force, resulting in total or partial functioning disability or psychosocial impairment, or both that adversely affects a child's educational performance
Visual impairment including blindness	An impairment in vision that, even with correction, adversely affects a child's educational performance. The term includes both partial sight and blindness

As with FAPE, a seminal court case has provided a legal test to determine if schools are meeting the least restrictive environment requirement. In *Daniel R. R. v. State Board of Education, 1989*, it was determined that schools need to determine first if education in the regular classroom is feasible with supplementary aids and services. If the answer to the first question is no, then schools must endeavor to mainstream students with disabilities to the maximum extent possible (Yell, 1995).

Although IDEA operates under the assumption that it is preferable to educate students with disabilities with their peers without disabilities, the data on the effectiveness of full inclusion is inconclusive (Farrell, 1997; Hegarty, 1993; Salend & Duhaney, 1999). A number of variables can affect the success of inclusion. First, teachers may not specifically design instruction for the special needs students included in their classrooms (Baker & Zigmond, 1995). Second, the severity or nature of the student's disability may affect the success of full inclusion or inclusion activities (Mills, Cole, Jenkins, & Dale, 1998; Pomplun, 1997). Finally, teachers need appropriate resources and organizational support for inclusion to work. According to one survey of teachers, this support includes the need for additional training, appropriate materials, personnel assistance, additional time, and smaller class sizes to make inclusion work (Scruggs & Mastropieri, 1996). Also, as the severity of the disability increases, teachers reported that the need for these supports also increased.

Successful inclusion also depends on the ability of school professionals to collaborate effectively. Special education and regular education teachers should work together to meet the needs of special learners in regular classrooms. Special and regular education teachers could team teach or teach cooperatively, or special education teachers could be available to help special needs learners with the lessons being provided by the regular education teacher (Smith, Polloway, Patton, & Dowdy, 2001). This is how Callie Ohlson, a special education teacher, supports her teachers.

> When I am in the classroom, I do a variety of jobs. Sometimes I take a small group of students, including my special learner, and I teach or reteach a lesson. Other times I might team teach, which is when we plan and present a lesson together.

In some schools, inclusion support is provided to teachers through the use of instructional assistants or inclusion aides. These instructional assistants are typically paraprofessionals who are placed in a classroom to help support a special education student. Based on an observation and interview study, Giangreco, Edelman, Luiselli, and MacFarland (1997) made the following observations about these types of instructional assistants.

Inclusion means educating students with disabilities as much as possible with students without disabilities.

- Instructional assistants remained in close proximity to their students on an ongoing basis. This proximity adversely affected students' peer interactions.
- The presence of instructional assistants tended to reduce teachers' sense of responsibility for the student's learning.
- The instructional assistants often operated with complete autonomy, making changes to activities without consulting with the teacher and often providing less effective instruction.
- The presence of instructional assistants tended to reduce students' sense of personal control.

To reduce the likelihood of these negative consequences, you need to communicate effectively with inclusion aides about your goals and the types of support you would like them to provide.

Individuals with Disabilities Act and the Assessment of Learners with Disabilities. Beginning with P. L. 94-142 and continuing with IDEA, federal legislation concerning special education has stressed a team approach to decision making. The team approach has the benefits of involving individuals with different perspectives and expertise indecision making about students with disabilities. The assessment team approach is referred to as a multidisciplinary assessment team (Pierangelo & Giuliani, 2002). A **multidisciplinary assessment team** is a group of professionals with different expertise related to the students' special needs who work together to determine students' eligibility for special education. The actual members of a multidisciplinary team can vary based on the characteristics and needs of a child, because at least one member of the team should have expertise in the area of suspected disability for a student. The multidisciplinary assessment approach means that the teacher collaborates with a number of different educational professionals. Table 11.3 contains a list of school professionals and their potential roles in the assessment of students.

An extremely important IDEA provision in the area of assessment is that schools need to employ nondiscriminatory identification and evaluation procedures. Evaluation procedures must be nonbiased, administered in the child's preferred language, and no eligibility decision can be based on a single measure (Heward, 2000). Students who are deaf are allowed to have an interpreter, and students with a visual impairment have the right to be tested in Braille, with large print materials, or to have the tests read to them (Knoblauch & McLane, 1999).

Due Process Safeguards. Essentially IDEA is civil rights legislation that extends equal access to a free public education to students with disabilities. Consequently, IDEA provides several procedural safeguards to protect students' rights to that education (Knoblauch & McLane, 1999).

- Parents or legal guardians have a right to request an evaluation to determine if their child has a disability. They also have the right to request, at no cost to them, an independent evaluation if they are dissatisfied with the results of the school's evaluation.
- Parents or legal guardians must be notified in writing of any intent to evaluate, reevaluate, or change their student's educational placement. Parents must also give

TABLE 11.3   **Potential Members of the Multidisciplinary Assessment Team**

Educational Professional	Role
School psychologist	A person with graduate training in psychology, who typically would administer intelligence tests, personality assessments, and provide classroom observations if necessary. School psychologists often make themselves available to consult with teachers about students' academic and social adjustment issues
School nurse	The school nurse would review relevant medical records and is often the person who administers initial hearing and vision screenings
Educational diagnostician	This professional helps administer educational assessments and can do classroom observations. In some situations, special education teachers or school psychologists assume this role
Physical therapist	This professional provides assessments, consultations, and interventions for students with gross motor difficulties
Speech/language therapist	This professional provides assessments and therapy for students with speech and language disabilities
Audiologist	This professional provides assessment in the areas of hearing impairment and may refer the student for medical evaluation if necessary
Occupational therapist	Evaluates students in the areas of fine-motor skill and living and self-help skills. Provides therapy and helps identify assistive technology as necessary

their informed consent for any of the processes mentioned previously, and this permission is voluntary and can be withdrawn at any time.

What rights do parents have regarding the evaluation of their children for special education services?

- Parents or legal guardians may request a reevaluation of the student at any time. In addition, the law states that a reevaluation must be done minimally every three years.
- Parents or legal guardians have access to their students' public school records. A school must comply within forty-five days to a request by parents or guardians to review files. Parents also must provide permission for their students' records to be released to other schools or agencies.
- Parents or legal guardians have the right to participate fully in the evaluation, development of educational plans, and placement decisions for the student.
- Parents or legal guardians have the right to request voluntary mediation or a due process hearing to resolve differences with the school that cannot be resolved in less formal ways.

The Individualized Educational Program. The **Individualized Educational Program** (**IEP**) is a written document that results from the process of considering the special educational needs of a student with a disability. It describes the educational needs of a student, the goals and objectives that guide instruction, required educational programming and placements, and measurement and evaluation criteria for assessing progress (Drasgow, Yell, & Robinson, 2001). It is a blueprint rather than a contract, and it should be created before placement decisions are made (Hallahan & Kauffman, 2000). This means that the IEP should guide placement decisions, and it is to a large extent what makes special education special. The Individualized Family Services Program mandated by P. L. 99-457 for infants, toddlers, and preschoolers has the same intent as the IEP. Here is how Jonathan Brown, a school psychologist, views the IEP process.

➤ The purpose of the assessment data we gather is to determine what a student needs to learn. These data help us write objectives for the IEP. We then ask, "Where can we best meet these objectives for this student?"

The process of developing an IEP can best be understood in terms of the required content and components of the IEP, the factors that need to be considered in developing an IEP, and who is required by law to participate in developing the IEP (Huefner, 2000).

An IEP is a written document that must contain the following content or components (Huefner, 2000; United States Department of Education, 2000).

- A description of the student's current level of educational performance including descriptions of how the student's particular disability will affect her or his participation in regular education classrooms
- Measurable annual goals with benchmarks and short-term objectives to assess progress toward those goals
- Any special education and related services such as aides or program modifications required by the students

Parents have an important role in any decision made about the education of their student with a disability.

- The extent of participation with students without disabilities, and an explanation for the time that the student will not participate in a regular education classroom
- Dates for beginning services, duration of services, and location of services
- An explanation of how progress will be evaluated and communicated to parents
- A description of any modifications necessary to state or district mandated testing, or, if the student will need alternative assessments, what those alternatives will be

Looking in on

- Beginning at age fourteen or younger, a description of transition services the student needs to reach postschool goals
- Beginning at least at age sixteen, a statement of transition services to help the student prepare for leaving school
- At least one year before the child reaches the age of maturity, a statement that the child has been informed of any rights that transfer to her or him at the age of maturity

The appropriateness of the decisions contained in the IEP must be reviewed at least annually, and goals should be modified as necessary (Smith, 2000).

What are the required components of an IEP?

The factors that should be considered in developing an IEP are the students' strengths, the views and ideas of the parents, evaluation data, strategies to support students with behavioral problems, any second language learning needs, communications needs, and necessary **assistive technology** or support services. The IEP must demonstrate clear connections between the goals and the classroom activities that support those goals.

IDEA also mandates the participation of certain key individuals in the development of the IEP (Smith, 2000). An IEP team should include a local education representative who understands available programs and services, the regular education teacher, a special education teacher or related services provider, the parent or legal guardian, the student, if appropriate, and a person qualified to interpret assessment data, who is typically a school psychologist or educational diagnostician.

For high school students, the individualized education plan should address the transition from school to work or post-secondary education.

Characteristics of Students with Disabilities

Students with disabilities are a diverse group. Not only are there differences between the various types of disabilities, but students within a particular disability category also differ from one another. For example, students with learning disabilities may differ in terms of the nature of their learning disability and also their social and personal characteristics. Consequently, you want to be careful in applying any list of general characteristics

It has long been recognized by special educators that technology provides some important tools for helping students with disabilities succeed in school. The 1997 reauthorization of the IDEA defines assistive technology as a piece of equipment or product that increases, maintains, or improves the functional capabilities of learners with disabilities. Assistive technology is defined in such broad terms that it could range from a large pencil grip to a voice recognition computer system (Merbler, Hadadian, & Azar, 1999). Some examples of assistive technology for students with milder disabilities such as a learning disability would include the following (Bryant & Bryant, 1998; Edyburn, 2000; Hart, 2000; MacArthur, 2000; Mondak, 2000):

- Tape recorders to help students with fine motor difficulties present or summarize their ideas
- Weekly or daily planners for students with organizational problems
- Visual enhancers such as the zoom function on some word processing programs for students with partial vision

- Books on tape or written in Braille for students with visual impairments
- Word processors with spell checkers or Word Prediction that provide students with options for spelling a word based on the first few letters they enter.
- Alternative keyboards or touch screens on computers for students with visual tracking or motor difficulties
- Speech-to-text or text-to-speech programs for students with writing and reading difficulties

The identification of assistive technology for a particular student occurs during the meeting to write the IEP for the student (see Chapter 12). Your role as a classroom teacher is to learn how to use the necessary assistive technology for your students.

> ● How many of the examples of assistive technology listed previously might be effective for students without disabilities? (For your authors' perspective on this question, go to the text website for this chapter.)

to a particular student with a disability. Your authors have tried to include characteristics that are typically associated with a particular disability and that are useful when planning for exceptional students.

Students with Learning Disabilities. Students with learning disabilities are by far the largest category of students with disabilities, accounting for 51 percent of students with disabilities (OSEP, 2001). As a primary characteristic, students with learning disabilities demonstrate a significant discrepancy between their cognitive ability and their achievement level as a result of a disorder in a basic psychological process. Although this discrepancy can show up in different curricular areas, the most common type of learning disability is in reading (Sorrell, 2000). In addition to the learning difficulties, the following secondary characteristics can be associated with students with learning disabilities. They may be the result of the learning disabilities or they may be additional factors that contribute to learning problems (Gilbert, 2000; Hallahan & Kauffman, 2000; Heward, 2000; Sorrell, 2000).

- Depending on the particular school district, 25 to 50 percent of students diagnosed with attention deficit/hyperactivity disorder also have a learning disability (Shelton & Barkley, 1994). In general, difficulties managing attention are quite common as a secondary characteristic of a learning disability.
- Although some students with learning disabilities do quite well socially, students with learning disabilities are more likely to demonstrate social skills deficits that lead to lower levels of social acceptance than their peers without learning disabilities (Kavale & Forness, 1996).
- Higher rates of behavior problems in the classroom have been observed for students with learning disabilities when compared with students without learning disabilities (Heward, 2000).

- Students with learning disabilities often show memory deficiencies and difficulty selecting the important components of a task to attend to during learning (Gettinger & Koscik, 2001). In part, these difficulties are due to a failure to use appropriate strategies.

Students with Mental Retardation.   Students with mental retardation make up about 11 percent of students being served under IDEA (OSEP, 2001). The primary characteristics of students with mental retardation are significantly subaverage intellectual functioning with associated deficits in adaptive behavior that manifest during the developmental period. Significantly subaverage intellectual functioning is typically defined in terms on IQ, and students with retardation are categorized into ranges based on the severity of intellectual impairment (Utley & Obiakor, 2000). Mild retardation is defined as an IQ in the range of 50 to 55 and 70, moderate retardation is defined as an IQ in the range of 35 to 40 and 50 to 55, severe retardation is defined as an IQ in the range of 20 to 25 and 35 to 40, and profound retardation is defined as an IQ below 20 to 25.

Adaptive behavior refers to people's ability to cope with their day-to-day environment and involves communication skills, self-care, home living, social skills, community use, self-direction, health and safety, functional academics, and leisure and work-coping skills (American Association on Mental Retardation, 1992). The provision that the subaverage intellectual functioning and impaired adaptive behavior manifest during the developmental period (before age 18) is to separate mental retardation from cognitive impairments caused by brain injury or illness (Vaughn, Bos, & Schumm, 2000).

In addition to these primary characteristics of students with mental retardation, the following secondary characteristics have been identified (Hallahan & Kauffman, 2000; Handen, 1998; Utley & Obiakor, 2000).

- Students with mental retardation have difficulty regulating their attention. In particular, they may have difficulty separating key elements from unessential elements in a problem situation.
  - Students with mental retardation may exhibit a range of difficulties with memory. Students with mental retardation may have difficulty transferring new learning to other appropriate settings.
  - Students with mental retardation often fail to develop appropriate cognitive and metacognitive strategies for learning. For example, they are less likely than their same-age peers without mental retardation to use memory strategies such as rote rehearsal.
  - Students with mental retardation are more likely than their peers without retardation to demonstrate social and behavioral problems.

What similarities are there between the secondary characteristics for learning disabilities and mental retardation?

Students with Emotional Disturbances.   Students with emotional disturbances make up approximately 8 percent of students being served under IDEA (OSEP, 2001). The primary characteristic of students with an emotional disturbance is an emotional or behavioral problem that has existed over a prolonged period of time and to a marked degree. These requirements are meant to separate emotional disturbances from behavioral problems that occur as a reaction to transient stressors, such as family breakup, and from milder conduct problems in the classroom.

A common way to classify emotional disturbances is to describe them as externalizing or internalizing behavior patterns (Quay, 1986). Students with **externalizing behaviors** engage in aggressive behaviors such as yelling, talking out, cursing, hitting, arguing, stealing, and lying (Walker, 1997). Externalizing behaviors are the most commonly identified behaviors for students with an emotional disturbance (Vaughn, Bos, & Schumm, 2000). **Internalizing behaviors** include anxiety, depression, and withdrawal. Both externalizing and internalizing behaviors tend to be associated with school learning problems and social relationship issues.

In addition to the primary behavioral and emotional characteristics, the following secondary characteristics have been identified for students with emotional disturbances (Frankin, Prince, & Yu, 2000; Hallahan & Kauffman, 2000; Heward, 2000; Obiakor, 1999; Platt, 1992).

Why might students with externalizing behaviors be the most common type of student identified as having an emotional disturbance?

- Students with emotional disturbances tend to display inadequate academic achievement.
- Students with emotional disturbances tend to demonstrate difficulty with attending behaviors.
- Students with emotional disturbances tend to demonstrate a difficulty with remembering information from week to week.
- Students with emotional disturbances tend to have poor self-concepts and low self-esteem.

Characteristics of Students with Autism.   The 1990 reauthorization of IDEA made autism a separate disability category for the first time (Knoblauch & Sorenson, 1998). Students with autism make up approximately 1.2 percent of students being served under IDEA (OSEP, 2001). As with any diagnostic category, autism reflects a group of students who can differ from each other in significant ways. Not all autistic children, for example, have difficulties forming loving and caring relationships with adults (Greenspan & Weider, 1997). Although 75 percent of autistic children have mental retardation (Volkmar & Lord, 1998), high-functioning autistic students also exist. With these cautions, however, here are some characteristics typically associated with autism (Hallahan & Kauffman, 2000; Trevarthen, Aitken, Papoudi, & Robarts, 1998).

- Primary inability to perceive others as people and a tendency to build distant, suspicious, or bizarre relationships.
- Extreme or peculiar communication problems: For example, they may engage in **echolalia** or the repetition of what has just been said to them.
- Self-stimulation: Students with autism may engage in bizarre, repetitive behavior such as rocking, patting their cheeks, or flapping hands that seem to have no intent except to produce sensory stimulation.
- Self-injurious behavior: Students with autism may engage in behaviors such as biting, head banging, or scratching themselves to the point of drawing blood or causing injury.
- Perceptual anomalies: Students with autism may stare in a fixated way or fail to switch attention appropriately.
- Apparent cognitive deficits: Students with autism may demonstrate cognitive and achievement deficits as reflected on intelligence and achievement tests.
- Aggression toward others: Students with autism may throw tantrums and may attack others.
- Difficulty with daily living skills: Students with autism may have difficulty with skills such as washing and dressing themselves.

Students with Communicative Disorders.   Speech disorders and language disorders are the two major categories of a communicative disorder. Students with a speech or language disorder make up approximately 19 percent of students being served by IDEA (OSEP, 2001). A speech disorder exists when a student's speech pattern deviates from the speech patterns of others sufficiently to call attention to itself, to interfere with communication, or to make the speaker or listener uncomfortable (Van Riper & Erickson, 1996). Students with a speech disorder would typically receive services through a trained speech pathologist. Three major types of speech disorders exist (Heward, 2000).

An **articulation disorder** occurs when there is an atypical production of speech sounds. The word *atypical* is used to differentiate articulation disorders from normal developmental errors or errors due to regional dialect. Four common types of articulation errors occur (Smith et al., 2001).

- **Substitution errors:** One sound is substituted for another as when a student says *woom* for *room*.
- **Distortion errors:** A sound is produced in an atypical manner as in the example of a student with a lisp.

- **Omission errors:** Sounds are left off as when a student says *cool* for *school*.
- **Addition errors:** Sounds are added as when a student says *berreak* for *break*.

Why is stuttering an example of a fluency disorder?

In a **fluency disorder** disruptions occur in the rate or flow of speech. Dysfluencies in speech are common and developmentally appropriate for preschool-aged children. They often start a sentence and then get stuck on a word or phrase such as "and uh." For older students, stuttering is an example of a fluency disorder. Stuttering is a rapid repetition of certain sounds that often increases under stress (Smith, 2001).

A **voice disorder** is fairly uncommon in young children (Smith, 2001). It involves an absence of vocal quality such as when the voice is hoarse or raspy or when the pitch or volume of speech is atypical. Voice disorders would not include the developmentally normal changes that occur in young men's voices as they enter puberty. Voice disorders can be the result of accidents, misuse, or congenital problems with the formation of voice mechanisms, and they are hard to differentiate from voice qualities that may be within normal range but somewhat unpleasant to the listener.

A **language disorder** exists when students have significant receptive or expressive language delays. Difficulties in understanding language are receptive language disorders, whereas expressive language disorders are when students have trouble expressing themselves in language. Typically, students with language impairments show an atypical or delayed pattern in the milestones for acquiring language. Table 11.4 presents typical language acquisition milestones for comparison purposes.

Students with Sensory Impairments. Students with sensory impairments would qualify for special education under the categories of visual impairment, hearing impairment, and the combination deaf-blind category.

Visual Impairments. A visual impairment is defined as vision that even after correction still adversely affects students' educational performance and includes both partial sightedness and blindness. The legal definition of **blindness** is when the better eye has vision no better than 20/200, even with best correction, or when a significant reduction in visual field or peripheral vision exists (Vaughn, Bos, & Schumm, 2000). Students with visual impairments make up about 0.5 percent of students being served under IDEA (OSEP, 2001).

What is the legal definition for blindness?

Students with visual impairments are a heterogeneous group, and tend to be more like their sighted peers than different from them (Vaughn, Bos, & Schumm, 2000). Because of their visual impairment, students may have difficulty developing social skills and awareness that are heavily dependent on vision (Smith, 2001). Also, sighted students and students with visual impairments may need to be taught how to interact with each other to avoid conflict and misunderstanding (Hallahan & Kauffman, 2000).

Hearing Impairments. A **hearing impairment** is a general term used to describe any level of hearing loss from mild to profound (Smith et al., 2001). Students with hearing impairments make up approximately 1.3 percent of students being served under IDEA (OSEP, 2001). Impaired hearing can mean that a student will have special communication needs. Depending on the degree of hearing loss, students may communicate through oral/aural language, manual means such as sign language, or some combination of oral/aural methods and sign language (Salend, 1998).

In addition to impaired hearing that may or may not be correctable, students with hearing losses may also demonstrate the following secondary characteristics (Smith et al., 2001).

- Articulation disorders
- Voice quality problems
- Social issues that may include difficulty forming peer relationships, withdrawal, and resistance to wearing hearing aids
- Achievement problems in the areas of reading and spelling in particular

TABLE 11.4	Speech and Language Developmental Milestones
Age	**Developmental Milestones**
Birth to 6 months	Infant first communicates through crying. Different types of crying develop (hungry cry, and so forth)
	Comfort sounds or cooing usually happen next
	This is followed by babbling (e.g., "pa ma") for pleasure
	Does not attach meaning to spoken words, but may react differently to loud or soft voices
6 to 12 months	Babbling develops inflection such as raising voice at end of a string of babbles (expressive jargon)
	May respond to own name or may clap hands, and so forth, when asked to by others
12 to 18 months	At 12 months start using one-word speech
	Pronunciation is imperfect, such as "bankie" for blanket
	Responds to simple commands by end of this period
18 to 24 months	Many children go through an echolalia stage where they mimic what is said to them
	Children start using two-word sentences that omit key words (telegraphic speech)
	By age two may have a receptive vocabulary as large as 1,000 words
2 to 3 years	Starts sequencing words in questions correctly (e.g., "Where is daddy?" versus "Where daddy is?")
	May have an expressive vocabulary of as many as 900 words
	Can follow compound commands such as, "Pick up the toy and put it on the dresser"
3 to 4 years	Tend to speak rapidly, but with dysfluencies
	Can use speech to make requests, protest, and make jokes
	Still may have articulation errors such as sound substitutions
4 to 5 years	Mean length of sentences is five words
	Begins to modify speech for the listener
	Can recite poems and songs from memory
	Still may have trouble with sounds such as *tr, sk, gl,* and *str*
After 5 years	Language develops steadily but in a less dramatic fashion
	Six year olds can use most forms of language used by adults
	Some consonant sounds such as *th* not mastered until age eight

Source: W. L. Heward (2000). *Exceptional children: An introduction to special education* (6th Ed.). pp. 332–333.
Upper Saddle River, NJ: Merrill.

Students with Physical Disabilities and Health Impairments. IDEA identifies three categories of disabilities for students with physical and health-related needs: students with orthopedic impairments, students with other health impairments, and students with traumatic brain injury.

Orthopedic Impairments. Students with orthopedic impairments are students with a severe physical impairment that adversely affects their educational performance. Students with orthopedic impairments make up about 1.3 percent of students being served under IDEA (OSEP, 2001). Included in this category are students with amputated or missing limbs, students with cerebral palsy, poliomyelitis, and bone tuberculosis.

Other Health Impairments. The category of students with other health impairments consists of ailments that affect strength, vitality, or alertness and that affect educational performance. It can include ailments such as AIDS, heart conditions, rheumatic fever, asthma, hemophilia, leukemia, asthma, and epilepsy if they affect educational performance (Vaughn, Bos, & Schumm, 2000). Students with other health impairments make up approximately 4.5 percent of students being served under IDEA (OSEP, 2001).

Traumatic Brain Injury.   Students with traumatic brain injury have neurological damage caused by an external force that results in a partial or total functional disability or psychosocial disability that affects educational performance. Students with traumatic brain injuries make up about 0.2 percent of students being served under IDEA (OSEP, 2001). The nature of learning and social problems experienced by students with traumatic brain injury varies depending on the type and severity of the injury.

Attention Deficit/Hyperactivity Disorder.   IDEA does not provide a separate category for **attention deficit/hyperactivity disorder** (ADHD). In some cases, however, a student with ADHD can qualify for special education as a student with a health impairment (Davila, Williams, & MacDonald, 1991). Also, ADHD frequently coexists with learning disabilities and emotional disturbances (Raymond, 2000; Ward & Guyer, 2000; Weyandt, 2001). Consequently, it seems appropriate to discuss ADHD within the discussion of students with disabilities.

The primary characteristics of students with ADHD can be summarized by the acronym HIDE, which stands for hyperactivity, inattentiveness, disorganization of behavior, and easy distractibility (Greenhill, 1995). Students with ADHD tend to have

What types of behavioral issues are typically associated with students with ADHD?

great difficulty paying sustained attention to a task (Barkley, 1998). In addition, students with ADHD get out of their seats frequently, tend to blurt out answers in class, are easily distracted, and are prone to be disorganized (Franklin & Warshawsky, 2000). It should be noted that these behaviors vary by situation (Anastopoulos, Kinger, & Temple, 2001). For example, these behaviors tend to be more noticeable with tasks that are repetitive, familiar, and boring.

The diagnosis of ADHD should involve multiple forms of assessment including adult and student interviews, direct observations of the student, behavior rating scales and self-report instruments, testing data, and review of educational records (Barkley, 1998; Weyandt, 2001). Students are usually also referred for a medical examination to determine if there are other physical reasons for the attention issues or hyperactivity. The medical examination can also be used to determine if medication should be prescribed.

Typically, a treatment approach that involves some combination of psychological, educational, and pharmacological interventions is preferable for many students with ADHD (Anastopoulis, Kinger, & Temple, 2001). Self-instructional training, social skills training, and behavioral contingences are psychological treatments with demonstrated short-term effectiveness for students with ADHD (Nolan & Carr, 2000). Pharmacological interventions involve the use of a number of psychoactive drugs such as methylphenidate (Ritalin) and pemoline (Cylert) that have been found helpful in alleviating some of the behavioral symptoms of ADHD. Educational interventions involve accommodations teachers provide for students with ADHD that help those students be more successful in the classroom. These accommodations may include some combination of the following (Franklin & Warshawsky, 2000; Guyer, 2000; Stevens, 2000; Weyandt, 2001).

- Provide action-oriented instruction that includes movement and hands-on activities
- Vary the nature of the instructional activity frequently
- Reduce the length of assignments or provide assignments in parts
- Allow students to manipulate objects such as clay with their hands
- Allow students to stand or pace in the back of the classroom
- Provide clear directions and classroom structures that help students stay organized, such as schedules and work folders
- Allow students to talk out loud while doing independent work
- Sit students closer to the teacher
- Provide devices such as highlighting to help students identify important elements of text

Classroom Teachers and Special Education

With the increased emphasis on inclusion, the teacher plays an important role in the education of students with disabilities. The teacher's involvement often begins with the important decision of referring students for special education assessment and continues as the teacher helps students with disabilities succeed in the classroom.

Teacher Referrals. Although parents or guardians can request an assessment to determine if their child is eligible for special education, referrals more typically originate with classroom teachers. The decision to refer is important because 90 percent of students who are referred are tested, and 73 percent of students tested are declared eligible for special education (Ysseldyke, 2001). When you are considering referring a student for special education assessment, the following recommendations can help you make a more thoughtful and effective referral (Hallahan & Kauffman, 2000).

- Keep parents informed and involved. Establish and maintain contact with parents so they know the types of problems the student is having.
- Check existing school records to see if previous problems have been reported. Is this a long-term problem or one that has developed recently?
- Talk to other professionals and teachers. They may be able to shed some light on the student's problem or suggest some interventions that have worked. Also, the problems you are seeing may or may not exist when the student is in other classrooms or with other teachers.
- Document your concerns about a student and what you have done to help that student. With behavior problems, be specific about when, where, and with whom the problems are occurring.
- When you make a referral, be prepared to describe the student's performance in terms of both the student's strengths and weaknesses, any interventions that have been tried, and any pertinent data you have collected (Olson & Platt, 2000).

You may find that your school district has a system to help you work with students before you decide to make a referral. These systems are sometimes called teacher-assistance teams, prereferral teams, or school-based intervention teams (Bahr, Whitten, Dieker, Kocarek, & Manson, 1999; Chalfant & Pysh, 1989; Graden, 1989; Heward, 2000; Olson & Platt, 2000). The purposes of these teams are to help reduce the number of students assessed, to help teachers develop their skills for working with students with learning or behavior problems, and to provide timely support to teachers. These teams usually consist of classroom teachers and counselors, psychologists, and speech pathologists who have expertise in helping students who are not succeeding. Although the effectiveness of these teams in accomplishing their goals can vary (Burns & Symington, 2002), teachers who use them generally feel they are helpful (Bahr et al., 1999). Here is Mary Olson's experience with her teacher-assistance team in the junior high.

> ➤ I asked our team for assistance with a student who was having serious discipline problems. First, it was reassuring to hear that other teachers had problems with this student in the past. The counselor was also able to give me some ideas that had worked last year.

Classroom Accommodations, Modifications, and Interventions. Given the current emphasis on inclusion, you will be involved in the design and delivery of supported education, which means providing the necessary supports to help students with disabilities succeed in the classroom (Snell & Drake, 1994). Specifically, you help provide accommodations, modifications, and interventions to assist your students with disabilities.

Accommodations and Modifications. Part of your instructional role with students with disabilities is to implement accommodations and modifications for these students (Smith et al., 2001). **Accommodations** are changes made in the ways students

TABLE 11.5 Sample Classroom Accommodations for Learners with Disabilities

Type of Accommodation	Examples
Instruction	Preteach important new vocabulary
	Allow students to record lectures
	Seat students closer to the blackboard
	Provide partial outlines or study guides
	Use multimodal presentation styles
Assignments/homework	Provide students with alternative ways of responding (e.g., oral versus written response)
	Allow parents to write down dictated responses
	Write or find informational text at a lower level
	Pair students with more competent readers
Evaluation	Read tests to students
	Provide additional time
	Allow alternative responses such as taking tests orally
	Provide large-print test materials
	Allow the use of dictionaries or spell checkers
Classroom arrangement	Provide increased work spaces for students
	Arrange room to facilitate your movement to students and students' movement
	Reduce distracting stimuli

are taught and disciplined, the types of assignments and homework provided, the way the classroom is arranged and organized, and the ways in which students are evaluated and graded. Table 11.5 provides examples of accommodations in these various areas that focus on the needs of what have been termed mild or high-prevalence disabilities, such as learning disabilities, mild retardation, and emotional disturbances (Raymond, 2000). **Modifications** generally refer to changes in policies that affect the participation of students with special needs in the classroom. An example of a classroom modification would be when an attendance policy is modified to account for the physical and health needs of a student. Modifications should be identified as part of the IEP, and your role is primarily to help implement modifications. Classroom discipline and evaluation of learning are two areas that may require you to make modifications and/or accommodations.

Because students with emotional and behavioral problems tend to engage in behaviors that require severe interventions such as suspension and expulsion, it is important to understand what IDEA says about these types of discipline approaches (Katsiyannis & Maag, 2001; Reilly, 1999; Skiba & Peterson, 2000; Walther-Thomas & Brownell, 1998; Zurkowski, Kelly, & Griswold, 1998). Currently IDEA says that students with disabilities can be removed from their classrooms for periods of less than ten days under the same considerations that apply to students without disabilities. Suspensions that exceed the ten-day limit constitute a change in placement, and the IEP team and other qualified personnel must meet to determine manifestation determination. **Manifestation determination** is whether the behavior is due to the nature of the student's disability. In making this determination, the IEP team considers whether current IEP and placements are appropriate and if services and interventions are consistent with the IEP and placement, whether the student's disability impaired the student's ability to control the behavior, and whether the disability impaired the student's ability to understand the impact and consequences of the behavior. If the behavior is not due to the nature of the student's disability, then the same disciplinary

I'm preparing to present Calista to the prereferral team, which means that I have to answer certain questions on a referral form. For example, I need to describe how I have communicated my concerns to Calista's parents. Luckily, I keep a parent contact log of any meetings or phone calls with all my parents and what was discussed. I also need to list any test score information that I currently have for Calista. It was interesting to go to her cumulative file and to look at her last two years' standardized achievement scores. She consistently scored extremely high in mathematics, but somewhat below grade level in reading, which is what I had noticed. In our process, it's also recommended that I contact Calista's previous teachers to see what they observed about Calista. Her first and second grade teachers both described Calista as very bright. Although they noticed that her reading wasn't

progressing as quickly as they expected, they both thought she would eventually catch on to reading. Also, neither teacher saw any frustration about reading, which differs from my experience. Finally, I must list what I have already tried to do to help Calista. Oddly enough, the form doesn't ask me to identify any strong areas for Calista, which I think is a mistake.

● **Although a process such as this could be viewed as time consuming, how might it help the prereferral team to assist Margaret? Why might a teacher decide to keep a parent contact log as Margaret has done?**

Decision Point: Why would it be important to discuss students' areas of strength as part of a process such as this?

procedures that are applicable to students without disabilities can be applied to students with disabilities. However, appropriate special education services need to continue. If the reviewing team decides that the behavior is due to the nature of the disability, then long-term suspension and expulsion are not options. In this case, the student's program needs to be reevaluated (Taylor & Baker, 2001/2002).

IDEA also stipulates that for weapons and drug offenses students with disabilities may be moved unilaterally to an interim alternative educational setting for forty-five days. Students who are determined to be a substantial risk to themselves or others may be removed to an interim alternative educational setting for forty-five days if this intervention is supported by a hearing officer.

IDEA currently provides that students with disabilities should be included in district and state assessment programs with appropriate accommodations if possible (Kleinert, Haig, Kerns, & Kennedy, 2000). If accommodations are not feasible, then schools can assess using parallel alternative assessments. Either way, these accommodations should be specified in the IEP. The law does not mandate, however, how test scores will be reported or used.

To a large extent, few data exist on the effects of various testing accommodations for K–12 students (Tindall, Heath, Hollenbek, Almond, & Harniss, 1998). In general, the test accommodation is intended to provide a valid measure of the construct, rather than optimizing student performance (Fuchs et al., 2000). In other words, the accommodations should not change the intent of the assessment. Also, the accommodation should provide what Phillips (1994) refers to as an **optimal boost.** If the accommodation addresses the disability, then it should increase the performance of students with a disability more than for students without the disability. It should not be an accommodation that all students would benefit from equally.

Interventions. An intervention is a classroom technique or strategy designed to help students learn or perform more successfully. While accommodations and modifications help students with disabilities participate in regular classroom activities, interventions help them develop the skills and knowledge necessary to learn and to demonstrate that learning.

Selecting interventions is a matter of identifying appropriate classroom management and instructional techniques and strategies. Fortunately, many of these approaches are well suited to the needs of all learners. For example, Mastropieri and

Looking in on

11.2

Today I am meeting with the school psychologist, classroom teachers, parents, and vice principal to determine what to do about George, a student with moderate mental retardation, who brought a hunting knife to school yesterday. Our school has a zero-tolerance policy, which means that you are expelled if you bring a weapon to school. The principal sent George home yesterday, but now we are meeting to determine if he should be expelled. All of us believe that we should treat weapons on campus seriously, but we disagree about the appropriate way to respond to this situation. None of us believe that George meant to do any harm with the knife, and some of us doubt that he knew he was doing anything wrong. He brought the knife in for show and tell, and when his teacher confiscated it, George was very concerned and confused. I am suggesting a two-day suspension to help George know that the offense is serious. However, I want to modify the life skills part of his IEP to add an objective on knowing school and community rules and laws. Our vice principal Robert, however, is concerned that we are being unfair to other students and that we are teaching George a bad lesson. Other students have been expelled for similar offenses during the year, and as hard as it is to think about doing this with George, Robert believes that it is in George's best interest to learn that the laws apply to him also. During the meeting, his mother stated that she could see both sides of the issue, but she really thinks expulsion is too severe for George.

● **What are the relevant IDEA issues related to this discipline decision?**

Decision Point: What factors would you consider in making the decision to expel or not to expel this student?

Scruggs (2000) have developed the acronym PASS to describe the characteristics of effective instruction for students with disabilities. Each letter in the PASS acronym represents an important consideration in designing effective instruction for almost all students.

- **P**rioritize objectives: Teachers should identify the critical objectives that students need to master. For students with disabilities, less essential objectives may be omitted or reduced in importance. The idea is to provide more time and focus on key objectives.
- **A**dapt instruction, materials, and environment: Teachers should identify any accommodations and modifications that are important for students with disabilities in their classrooms.
- **S**ystematic instruction: According to Mastropieri and Scruggs (2000), systematic instruction is delivered using the components of SCREAM. Effective instruction is structured and well organized, clear, redundant, enthusiastic, appropriately paced, and provides maximized engagement through activities, discussion, and meaningful feedback.
- **S**ystematic evaluation: Teachers provide ongoing and frequent assessment aligned to the objectives on the IEP.

A number of techniques and strategies discussed in this text have been identified as effective interventions for students with mild disabilities. Here are some of those techniques and strategies and where they can be found in this text.

- Direct instruction (Chapter 7)
- Applied behavior analysis (Chapter 10)
- Cognitive behavioral interventions (Chapter 10)
- Cooperative learning/peer-mediated instruction (Chapter 7)
- Strategy training (Chapter 8)

It is also important to remember that modifications, accommodations, and interventions can be supported through technology (see Enriching Your Understanding p. 373).

When I work with teachers on inclusion, we collaborate in a number of ways. First, we have worked as teams to identify core objectives and standards at each grade level that we want all students to learn, including our students with disabilities. These key standards get added emphasis on IEPs. I also help teachers find areas of overlap in their curricula so they can work together better.

I'm also available to help teachers collect data on their students. For academic goals, I help provide accommodations during testing, and for behavioral and social goals I help observe and interview students. We find that we need to monitor students' learning carefully, or we often fail to make progress.

I also try to help teachers find materials and activities that can help students with disabilities participate more fully in the classroom learning. For example, I help identify textbooks written at lower reading levels or any assistive technology teachers might find helpful.

My favorite part of my job is that I get to team teach and model instructional strategies for students with disabilities. For example, I show teachers how to build review or distributed practice into their lessons to make sure there is enough redundancy. I show them how to provide outlines and spatial organizers and how to manage group work with students at different levels. Oddly enough, we often find that the strategies that help students with disabilities also help students without disabilities.

Li-Sheng Ma

11.3

● **What elements of PASS are present in these activities to support including those students with disabilities?**

Decision Point: Which of Li-Sheng's inclusion activities might be beneficial for most if not all students?

Students with Special Gifts and Talents

Unlike students with disabilities who are guaranteed special education under IDEA, no parallel federal legislation exists guaranteeing special education for students with special gifts or talents (Karnes & Marquardt, 1997). However, most states have mandated programs for students with special gifts and talents (Hallahan & Kauffman, 2000). Also, the federal government has enacted and reauthorized the Jacob K. Javits Gifted and Talented Students Education Act to provide funding for research, demonstration, and personnel preparation in gifted and talented education (Smith, 2000).

Definition of Students with Special Gifts and Talents. Although each state has adopted its own definition, the majority of the states are using some form of the definition provided in federal law (P. L. 95-561, Title IX, sec. 902) (Stephens & Karnes, 2000). Students with special gifts and talents are typically defined as students of preschool, elementary, or secondary age who have demonstrated or potential capabilities for levels of high performance in the following areas: intellectual, creative, specific academic, leadership, and performing and visual arts. Because of their potential or demonstrated excellence, these students may require special educational services from schools.

In many state laws, what types of special gifts and talents are recognized?

Joseph Renzulli has proposed an alternative definition of giftedness that is both controversial and influential (Ford, 1999; Johnson, 1999; Kitano, 1999; Olszewski-Kubilius, 1999; Renzulli, 1977, 2002). Renzulli's triad model defines giftedness in terms of these three overlapping clusters of behavior: above average but not necessarily superior intelligence, task commitment, and creativity. The triad model attempts to shift emphasis away from IQ as a single determinant of giftedness and provides a more inclusive definition of giftedness. The intent to be more inclusive has been perceived as both a strength and weakness of this model.

Characteristics of Students with Special Gifts and Talents. As you can see from the discussion of definitions, students with special gifts and talents are a diverse group.

Consequently, any list of characteristics will apply to some students with gifts and talents, but not others. However, here are ten core characteristics that have been associated with giftedness (Davis & Rimm, 1998; Piirto, 1999).

- Evidence of a desire to learn and an enthusiasm for learning
- Highly developed communication skills such as effective use of words, numbers, symbols, and so forth
- Intense interests that are sometimes unusual for other children of the same age and background
- Problem-solving ability that often involves inventive strategies
- Imagination and creativity
- An extensive memory for facts and information
- A tendency to want to question, explore, and experiment
- The ability to quickly grasp new ideas and to make connections between ideas
- A well-developed ability to reason logically
- The ability to convey and pick up on humor

What might this heightened sensitivity of children with intellectual gifts mean for how you provide feedback?

Although generalizations are difficult to make about the social and personal characteristics of students with special gifts and talents, the stereotype of the maladjusted loner does not seem to hold true for many students with special gifts and talents (Freeman, 1994). However, these students commonly display characteristics of heightened sensitivity, perfectionism, and intensity (Piechowski, 1997). Consequently, they may have trouble accepting constructive criticism, and they may tend to dwell on errors or unpleasant social interactions.

Educational Approaches for Students with Special Gifts and Talents. Although there are a range of options for educating students with special gifts and talents, including mentorships, magnet schools, residential schools, and after school programs, the two most commonly used general approaches have been acceleration and enrichment. A third option, cluster grouping, provides some flexibility when grouping students for instruction.

Acceleration. Approaches that provide early entry into educational programs or that involve delivering curriculum at a more rapid pace than is typical are referred to as **acceleration** (Schiever & Maker, 1997; Piirto, 1999). Rapid movement of students through grades and early admission are called student acceleration, while rapid movement through curriculum is called content acceleration (Gallagher & Gallagher, 1994). Examples of acceleration are early admission to kindergarten and colleges, grade skipping, and self-paced, individualized curricula.

What are the two forms of acceleration?

In selecting acceleration as an educational option, both potential academic and social effects need to be considered. One of the key studies in this regard is the Study of Mathematically Precocious Youth (Stanley & Benbow, 1983; Stanley & McGill, 1986). Students who attended accelerated math programs and students who entered college early tended to do very well academically and in terms of college completion. Although the Study of Mathematically Precocious Youth found no real harm to social and emotional development, the evidence in these areas is less clear (Southern & Jones, 1991). Consequently, acceleration needs to be decided on a case-by-case basis, and the emotional adjustment of accelerated students should be monitored.

Enrichment. Attempts to educate students with special gifts and talents by modifying or adding to the curriculum in some way are referred to as **enrichment** approaches (Schiever & Maker, 1997). The additions are intended to increase the depth or breadth of the curriculum, and there are three general approaches to enrichment (Howley, Howley, & Pendarvis, 1986). Process enrichments focus on enhancing students' thinking or problem-solving processes. Typically, students are taught problem-solving approaches. The content-oriented approach refers to the presentation of content in greater depth or breadth, such as often occurs in college placement courses for high school students. Product-oriented enrichment involves having students apply their gifts and talents to the creation of a product such as a painting, exhibition, or software application.

These three types of enrichment are reflected more or less in Renzulli's enrichment triad model (Reis & Renzulli, 1985). Type I enrichment allows students to broaden their understanding of areas of interest. Type II enrichment is designed to help students develop higher-order reasoning skills, and type III enrichment is designed to engage learners in the actual investigation of a problem or topic through inquiry methods that can result in a product or exhibition. To make time for enrichment, Renzulli recommends curriculum compacting, which involves reducing the emphasis on or eliminating curricular objectives that students in the talent pool have accomplished (Reis & Renzulli, 1985).

Cluster Grouping. Cluster grouping is an approach that can be used to provide both enrichment and acceleration to students with intellectual or academic gifts (Winnebrenner & Devlin, 1991). In **cluster grouping,** a cohort of five to eight gifted students would be placed in one classroom. The remaining students in the class would be heterogeneous in terms of ability. The gifted students could work together when the goal is enrichment or acceleration, but at other times they could work with other students in the class when heterogeneous learning groups are more appropriate.

What are the different forms of enrichment?

Focus on Learner Diversity
Minority Student Representation in Special Programs

One of the key issues in academic diversity is the representation of minority students in special education and programs for students with special gifts and talents. Historically, minority students have been underrepresented in programs for students with special gifts and talents and overrepresented in special education programs, particularly for students with mild retardation (Dunn, 1968; Ford & Harmon, 2001; Zhang & Katsiyannis, 2002). For example, African American students are three times more likely to be categorized as qualifying for special education than white students (Black Issues in Higher Education, 2001). African American students make up 16 percent of school enrollment, but only 8 percent of the enrollment in programs for students with special gifts and talents (Patton & Baytops, 1995).

A number of possible reasons may exist for the numbers of minority students in special programs. First, it may be the case that educators confuse differences with deficits (Ford & Harmon, 2001). For example, minority students who speak a nonstandard English could still be intellectually or verbally gifted. Second, the assessments that are used to qualify students may be culturally or linguistically inappropriate (Heward, 2000). Third, the referral process may work against some students. Teachers may confuse underachievement with lack of ability or

perceive culturally based behavior as defiant or provocative (Ford & Harmon, 2001; Kornhaber, 1999). In the latter case, this may make teachers more likely to refer minority students for special education, and less likely to refer them for programs for students with special gifts and talents.

A number of recommendations have been made to help teachers address the representation issue. First, it is important to broaden the definition of giftedness beyond IQ and to use more varied and culturally and linguistically appropriate measures in decision making (Ford, 2000; Ford & Harmon, 2001). Also, systemic changes have been suggested such as early identification and prevention of school learning problems, providing a more culturally relevant curriculum, increasing home-school partnerships, and better training for teachers in the identification and education of minority students with special needs (Ford & Harmon, 2001; Serna & Forness, 1998; Warger & Burnette, 2000).

● Although it is generally important for teachers to develop awareness of their students' cultures, why is it particularly important for this issue? (For your authors' perspective on this question, go to the text website for this chapter.)

Looking in on

Mrs. Portello dropped by today to talk about what I was doing for Robbie in the area of math, which is Robbie's strongest area. I told her that I typically assign more challenging problems to Robbie as homework. Although I don't do this often, he also has an opportunity to tutor other students. I think the tutoring helps solidify his understanding. Mrs. Portello told me that she doesn't mind if Robbie tutors occasionally and she does appreciate the more difficult homework problems, but she is concerned that Robbie isn't progressing as quickly as he could. I had to admit that she has a point. It's hard to plan an entirely different lesson for one or two students. Our gifted program emphasizes creativity and critical thinking, but is not geared to helping students move more quickly through a specific curricular area. As we talked it over, it occurred to me that maybe Robbie could be placed in fifth grade for math. That way we could keep him with his friends for most of the day, but still challenge him in math. I've done this successfully in the past with other students. We both agreed that it might work, but we wanted to talk it over with Robbie and think about it.

● **What types of educational approaches for students with special gifts are described in this situation? Why might cluster grouping be an option here?**

> **Decision Point:** What factors might Margaret and this mother consider in deciding about the fifth grade placement? Why would it be good to talk to Robbie about this?

Principles into Practice:
Illustrating Key Concepts

Throughout this chapter you looked in on Margaret Lew and Li-Sheng Ma as they described their experiences with academic diversity, and you considered questions about their application of ideas. We now share our views of those decision points.

Looking back on

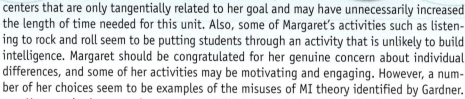

Margaret Lew is planning a unit on money for her third graders that involves Gardner's MI theory as an organizing structure. As you recall from reading the text, Gardner sees limited value in including all eight intelligences in every lesson. Margaret's attempt to do this is resulting in some centers that are only tangentially related to her goal and may have unnecessarily increased the length of time needed for this unit. Also, some of Margaret's activities such as listening to rock and roll seem to be putting students through an activity that is unlikely to build intelligence. Margaret should be congratulated for her genuine concern about individual differences, and some of her activities may be motivating and engaging. However, a number of her choices seem to be examples of the misuses of MI theory identified by Gardner.

Margaret is also preparing to present Calista to the building prereferral team. Although completing the required forms is time consuming, it is likely to improve the quality of her referral. For example, by talking with previous teachers, Margaret will know if the problems she is observing with Calista are recent or long-term problems. Also, these teachers can talk about what they found to be effective with Calista. Collecting performance data such as test results can help Margaret understand the specific nature of Calista's learning problems. Finally, if she documents what she has tried with Calista, the prereferral team may able to make more useful recommendations.

Margaret's parent contact log seems like a useful idea. Margaret does not have to rely on memory to identify what has been discussed with parents and when those contacts occurred. Sometimes teachers use a log such as this to help them make sure they are contacting all their parents.

Margaret also spent time conferencing with Mrs. Portello about Robbie's progress in math. Margaret primarily provides content enrichment in the form of more thought-provoking homework problems. Her use of peer tutoring could also have an enrichment effect if it results in a deeper understanding for the tutor. Margaret and Mrs. Portello are discussing placing Robbie in sixth grade math as an example of acceleration. Cluster grouping might be useful in this case by providing enough students with similar math needs to work together as a group. The acceleration may not be necessary if cluster grouping is feasible. ●

Looking back on

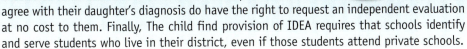

Li-Sheng Ma

In her role as inclusion specialist, Li-Sheng Ma has to answer parents' questions about the school's special education process and their rights under IDEA. The parent who is moving needs to provide the current school with written permission to send records to the next school. The parents who disagree with their daughter's diagnosis do have the right to request an independent evaluation at no cost to them. Finally, The child find provision of IDEA requires that schools identify and serve students who live in their district, even if those students attend private schools.

Li-Sheng Ma is a member of a team that is determining whether to expel a student with moderate mental retardation for bringing a knife to school. Given both the nature of the offense and the proposed expulsion, a manifestation determination is necessary. According to IDEA, this group must decide whether the offense is due to the nature of the student's disability or not. Because this is a weapon offense the school can move this student to an interim alternative educational setting for up to forty-five days. However, they seem to be considering expulsion instead, which would qualify as a change of placement. If the offense is due to the nature of this student's disability, then expulsion is not an option. If the offense is not due to the nature of the disability, then the student can be expelled, but special services need to continue.

A number of Li-Sheng's inclusion activities fit well with PASS. She is helping teachers prioritize objectives and adapt materials for instruction. She also helps teachers provide systematic instruction by showing them how to provide redundancy and by modeling how to use strategies such as spatial organizers with their students. She also helps her teachers collect data so that they can be systematic evaluators of students' learning. ●

Teachers as Decision Makers

At various decision points in this chapter you participated in the decision making of Margaret Lew and Li-Sheng Ma. Here we share our views of those decision points.

Margaret Lew's Decision Points

Margaret Lew is preparing to refer Calista to the prereferral team. The prereferral team requires that teachers provide performance data on students. Because this is not an uncommon request, you should consider the types of routines or procedures Margaret could use to be better prepared to respond to this type of request in the future. One way to collect data of this sort is to establish a procedure for collecting and maintaining work samples. Although a portfolio assessment approach can help, you may also want to keep an additional work folder into which you place work samples that highlight a particular difficulty for a student. As simple as it may seem, having students use a routine way of heading a paper can help you keep track of who did what and when. It is also recommended that you develop a procedure for maintaining anecdotal records on students. It may be as simple as a loose-leaf notebook with a divided section for each student in which you record any noteworthy observations about a student. These observations can provide a rich source of data.

Margaret is using Gardner's MI theory as a framework for planning lessons. Her main goal is to create lesson experiences that meet the needs of her many different learners. Certainly she should be congratulated for her desire to do this. However, by failing to consider instructional alignment, she created some lesson experiences that had little if anything to do with her main goal. Lesson designing is a complicated decision-making process that requires you to consider both students' characteristics and your goals. The idea is to select varied lesson experiences that meet both the needs of your learners and your goals.

Calista provides an example of why it's important to present information both on students' strengths and weaknesses. It appears that Calista could be a student with academic gifts and a specific learning disability, and both would need to be addressed. Even if this is not the case, Margaret might be able to use identified strengths to help students compensate for areas of weakness.

Margaret and Robbie's mother need to decide if they should place Robbie in sixth grade for math or leave him in his current placement. This decision is motivated by the desire to meet Robbie's academic needs, but there are other considerations. The impulse to talk with Robbie seems like a good one. How would he feel about this change? Does he have sufficient personal and social development to fit in well in this new environment, or would he prefer another option that does not require him to move to another grade? If this option is selected, what is the long-term plan? If the school only goes up to sixth grade, what will they do the next year? Is it better to move him up to the sixth grade for all his academics? There is a lot to consider here.

Li-Sheng Ma's Decision Points

A number of Li-Sheng's activities are designed to help make inclusion more successful. She meets with faculty to discuss options and to plan, and she is available to provide assistance and advice to her teachers. Her willingness to team teach sounds like a good way to provide training to teachers and to build rapport. Note that Li-Sheng is also available to help parents, another important resource in students' lives. She might want to consider using her parent contacts to provide training to the parents on how they can help their students at school.

Part of Li-Sheng's job is to follow-up with parents after special education placement meetings. The school's decision to do this seems to emphasize the informed part of informed consent, because they want to make sure that parents understand what is happening in these meetings. We need to be sure that when parents are asked to sign consent forms, they've had a chance to consider carefully what is being asked of them. This option gives parents a chance to think about any questions or issues and underlines that their consent is voluntary and can be rescinded at any time. It is also a good way to establish a cooperative working environment between home and school.

Li-Sheng and her colleagues are involved in a difficult discipline decision about a student with moderate mental retardation who brought a weapon to school. Please note that it is possible for reasonable people to disagree about the appropriate decision in these situations. As noted in the text, this team is asked to consider if the placement and services were appropriate for the student, if the student knows the consequences of his actions, and if the student could control the behavior at issue. Some of the information provided could be interpreted to mean that this student did not understood the consequences of his behavior. Also, the IEP apparently did not address a relevant adaptive behavior issue. The vice principal's issues with fairness and the unintended message they may be giving to this student are legitimate concerns. The school does have the right to remove this student to an interim alternative educational setting for forty-five days. That might satisfy the concern that the student is getting off too lightly, but the ultimate question would be whether or not this is in the best interest of the student. This decision involves a host of both legal and practical issues.

One way to help make inclusion more effective is to identify modifications or strategies that would benefit most students, not just students with disabilities. The focus on systematic instruction seems like it would be useful for most if not all students. Also, certain assistive technology applications and curriculum modifications could be helpful to a number of students in a classroom. Finally, good decision making requires appropriate data. Having more than one person in a classroom provides opportunities for data collection that may not be practical for one teacher.

Name _____ Date _____

Chapter 11 Study Guide

Use this Study Guide to review and test your knowledge of key concepts introduced in this chapter and to search out further information on issues and topics raised in this chapter.

Key Terms

Review the following key words from the chapter and then connect to Research Navigator (www.researchnavigator.com) either directly or through this book's Companion Website to explore research on the topics as they relate to education today.

Academic diversity (p. 356)
Acceleration (p. 384)
Accommodations (p. 379)
Articulation disorder (p. 375)
Assistive technology (p. 372)
Attention deficit hyperactivity disorder (p. 378)
Blindness (p. 376)
Child find (p. 367)
Cluster grouping (p. 385)
Echolalia (p. 375)
Enrichment (p. 384)
Exceptional learners (p. 366)
Externalizing behaviors (p. 374)

Fluency disorder (p. 376)
g (p. 358)
Hearing impairment (p. 376)
IDEA (p. 366)
IDEA definitions of disabilities (p. 367)
IEP (p. 371)
Inclusion (p. 367)
Internalizing behaviors (p. 374)
Knowledge acquisition component (p. 360)
Language disorder (p. 376)
Least restrictive environment (p. 367)

Manifestation determination (p. 380)
Metacomponent (p. 360)
Modifications (p. 380)
Multidisciplinary assessment team (p. 370)
Multiple intelligences (MI) theory (p. 362)
Optimal boost (p. 381)
Performance component (p. 360)
Positive manifold (p. 357)
Special education (p. 366)
Voice disorder (p. 376)
Zero reject principle (p. 367)

Alternative Response Items

1. The overall or general ability that affects our intellectual performance in all areas is referred to as _____.

   a. g
   b. s
   c. Positive manifold
   d. Analytic intelligence

2. Which one of the following is a common characteristic of the most widely used intelligence tests?

   a. They are intended to be administered to large groups of students at a time.
   b. They are intended to be administered and interpreted by classroom teachers.

   c. They are standardized and norm-referenced tests.
   d. They usually only yield one overall intelligence score.

3. Which one of the following would be an example of a metacomponent?

   a. During problem solving, Sarah identifies the goal for her problem solving.
   b. Sam identifies the strategies that are necessary to solve a problem.
   c. John realizes that he needs to attend closely to certain variables during problem solving.
   d. All of the above.

4. A politician who believes that he is too clever to be caught when he violates campaign laws is demonstrating which of Sternberg's fallacies?

    a. Omniscience fallacy
    b. Egocentrism fallacy
    c. Invulnerability myth
    d. Omnipotent fallacy

5. Which one of the following is a criticism of Gardner's MI theory discussed in this text?

    a. He is not broad enough and inclusive enough in his identification of intelligences.
    b. He fails to appreciate that the different forms of intelligence are independent of each other.
    c. His list of intelligences fails to include examples of artistic abilities that are important in society.
    d. It could be argued that his list of intelligences contains characteristics that are not intelligence.

6. Which one of the following is *not* a separate disability category under IDEA 1997?

    a. Specific learning disability
    b. Attention deficit disorder
    c. Mental retardation
    d. Autism

7. The key principle of IDEA that entitles students with disabilities to a free and appropriate public education is referred to by the initials _____.

    a. LD/GT
    b. IEP
    c. MI
    d. FAPE

8. The current term for the idea that students with disabilities should be educated to the maximum extent possible in regular education settings is_____.

    a. Mainstreaming
    b. Inclusion
    c. MI
    d. IEP

9. According to IDEA, what can parents do if they disagree with the results of an evaluation conducted by a school district to determine their students' eligibility for special education services?

    a. They have the right to request an independent evaluation at no expense to themselves.
    b. They can obtain an independent evaluation if they pay for that evaluation.
    c. This situation is not addressed by IDEA.
    d. Parents' rights to disagree with school district decisions apply only to decisions about where a student will be educated.

10. Mr. Johnson has a self-paced math learning program that allows his students with mathematical gifts to progress through the math curriculum more quickly. What type of educational strategy is this?

    a. Content acceleration
    b. Student acceleration
    c. Cluster grouping
    d. Content enrichment

Constructed Response Items

Short Answer/Completion Items

1. A psychologist administers a vocabulary test and a verbal analogies test to a large number of students and finds that students' performances correlate on the two tests. This observation is an example of _____.

2. The need to use intelligence to adapt to the demands of an environment is reflected in which of Sternberg's subtheories?

3. The IDEA requirement that schools institute procedures to identify all students with disabilities in their service area is referred to as _____.

4. Changes in policies or regulations that affect the participation of students with disabilities in the classroom are referred to as _____.

5. Renzulli refers to enrichment activities intended to improve students' problem-solving or reasoning skills as _____ enrichment activities.

Essay Items

1. What connections are there between Sternberg's triarchic theory and information-processing theory?

2. What similarities are there between Gardner's and Sternberg's views of how to infuse intelligence into the curriculum?

3. What are the key parental rights under IDEA?

4. What similarities are there between the secondary characteristics of learning disabilities and mental retardation?

5. Briefly describe the characteristics of autism.

6. Define the major types of speech and language disorders.

7. How might a student with ADHD qualify for services under IDEA?

Practicing Your Decision Making

1. You are considering referring a student for special education services. Describe the types of data you would collect to help make your decision.

2. Assume you have a student with special needs included in your classroom. How would you decide what types of data to collect to monitor the effectiveness of inclusion for that student?

INTASC in Action

Use the following activities to think about how concepts and principles from this chapter relate to the INTASC standards.

Standard 3: Diverse Learners. Your students are likely to demonstrate a wide range of academic skills. Describe how the following ideas from this text can help you identify students' learning needs, and respond to them effectively.

1. Shaping (Chapters 2 and 7)
2. Mastery learning (Chapter 7)
3. Instructional prompts (Chapters 7 and 9)
4. Pretesting (Chapter 9)
5. Self-monitoring (Chapters 4 and 10)

Standard 7: Planning. Why is it important for teachers to meet with their students' teachers from previous years in planning educational programs for learners with special needs? Create a list of questions you generally would want to ask those teachers.

Standard 10: School and Community Involvement. Table 11.3 provides a list of school professionals with whom you may work. You may also want to consider entering one of these professions. Research the training requirements and typical job responsibilities for at least one of these professionals.

Web Resources

IDEA Practices
www.ideapractices.org

Visit the primary source of the latest information regarding IDEA. Explore the entire site, but be sure to review the complete laws and associated regulations for IDEA.

ERIC Clearinghouse: Including Students with Disabilities
http://ericec.org/minibibs/eb14.html

Read brief biographies of publications on inclusion found in the ERIC database.

National Center for Learning Disabilities
www.ncld.org/info/index.cfm

The National Center for Learning Disabilities provides a compendium of information on students with learning disabilities. Find out the facts about living with a learning disability and about the various programs for people living with learning disabilities.

University of Northern Iowa College of Education
www.uni.edu/coe/inclusion

Visit this special section from UNI's College of Education containing helpful information on inclusion. Check out the Teaching Strategies section for helpful tips for the classroom.

Wisconsin Special Education Services: Inclusion Strategies for Teachers
www.cesa7.k12.wi.us/sped

Explore the Special Education pages of Service Agency 7 of Wisconsin's Cooperative Education program. The site offers a great many tips and strategies for the special education and mainstream classroom teacher. See if you can find inclusion strategies.

Council for Exceptional Children (CEC)
www.cec.sped.org/

Check out the resources available from the major professional organization for teachers of students with disabilities.

National Research Center on the Gifted and Talented
www.ucc.uconn.edu/~wwwgt/nrcgt.html

Check out the resources available from a major professional organization for teachers working with students with gifts and talents.

Personal, Social, and Cultural Diversity

With Urie Bronfenbrenner's ecological theory in mind, Chapter 12 examines personal, social, and cultural factors that contribute to the student diversity in classrooms. The chapter begins with a discussion of psychological characteristics that have important implications for understanding students. Next, the nature of families and peer groups are examined as examples of two important microsystems. This discussion also explores the points of contact between peers, family, and school as examples of important mesosystems in students' lives. Finally, the chapter ends with a discussion of the literature on gender differences and the role of culture in students' lives as examples of macrosystem influences.

By the end of this chapter, you should be able to do the following:

● Describe the components of Bronfenbrenner's ecological theory of development

● Describe and contrast Erikson's psychosocial theory of personality, the five-factor view of personality, and person/environmental fit explanations of personality

● Understand the concepts of cognitive and learning style and the issues with style constructs

● Understand the role of self-concept and self-esteem in learning

● Understand Kohlberg's theory of moral reasoning and its criticisms

● Understand the role of peer groups and family in students' socialization and learning

● Understand the role of gender and culture in student learning and performance

● Understand instructional delivery models and approaches for linguistically diverse students

Close-ups on the Classroom

Octavio Fuentes and the Bilingual School

I am a teacher in a grant-funded K–3 bilingual magnet school. Half of my first grade students are Spanish speaking, while the other half are English speaking. My students are economically, culturally, and linguistically diverse. For example, some of my Spanish-speaking students are recent immigrants to this country from northern Mexico. The ultimate goal is to have all students fluent and literate in both languages by the end of third grade.

A major organizing theme for our school is the classroom as an extended family. For example, our teachers stay with the same group of students for all four years, because we believe that our students do better if they form close relationships with their teachers and other students. I admit that this approach poses some interesting challenges that I think we need to discuss.

We also value parent and family involvement in our school. All teachers are expected to contact their parents as often as possible by phone, mail, home visit, or parent conference. We also schedule periodic open houses and parent meetings. For example, we have our informational meeting for parents who are considering sending their children to our school in a week or so. Because of our outreach efforts, our parents are generally willing to volunteer in our classrooms or to just stop by and talk.

Because this is only our second year of operation, we release students early on Friday afternoon so we can meet as a faculty. We use that time to think about how things are working and to brainstorm alternatives. Sometimes these meetings can get heated, but I think they are necessary.

Decision Point: What do you see as the strengths and weaknesses of having students stay with the same teacher and students throughout their time in school?

As you can tell from the opening vignettes, personal, social, and cultural factors have a major impact on life in classrooms. Urie Bronfenbrenner's (1979, 1993) ecological theory of development provides a useful way to organize thinking about the complex relationships between personal, social, and cultural factors and classroom attitudes and behavior.

Before proceeding with Chapter 12, be sure you read the Close-ups on the Classroom features about Octavio Fuentes and Rhonda Greyson. At various points in the chapter, you will revisit both teachers in their classrooms and follow their decision-making progress. Their experiences are closely integrated with the key concepts of this chapter and serve as important models of how to adapt to personal, social, and cultural diversity needs in the classroom.

Bronfenbrenner's Ecological Theory

Bronfenbrenner provides a conceptualization of the environment from the perspective of the developing individual. Environments are conceived as a set of nested structures, not unlike the Russian nesting dolls (Bronfenbrenner, 1994). Understanding human development requires knowledge of the interactions between a person and those layers of environmental structures.

According to Bronfenbrenner (1993), an individual's personal characteristics, interest in and exploration of their environment, disposition to pursue increasingly complicated activities, and ability to conceptually organize experiences all can influence environmental reactions to that individual. For example, a depressed person may elicit different reactions from other people in that environment than a nondepressed person. To understand students and their social environments, it is helpful to learn about the personal characteristics of those students.

Teachers also need to understand the nature of the environmental layers that affect students, because these environments determine the types of social interactions and

Secondary

Today was one of those days that poses a lot of different challenges. Last night we heard on the news that the local tire factory is closing and it's going to put a number of our students' parents out of work. This is not an affluent community to begin with, and this will make things worse. A number of my students wanted to talk about the factory closing because they were obviously upset. I decided to postpone today's lesson to allow them to get some things off their chests. I predict from this discussion that a number of these students will drop out so they can get full-time jobs to help support their families.

In my second period algebra class, two girls got into a shouting match. This was unexpected because they have been good friends all year. When I pulled them aside and talked to them, neither one would tell me why they were yelling at each other during class. I decided not to push the issue at this time, but instead I made them promise to keep their personal arguments out of our class. I also warned them if they did it again I would have to send them to the discipline office.

When I went to pick up my mail at lunchtime, I had a note from Mrs. Thompson requesting an immediate conference about Bradley. The note said that she wanted to talk about homework. I was going to call her because Bradley has not been turning in homework. I asked the secretary to call her and to set up a meeting at 3:30 today.

Decision Point: What do you see as the strengths and weaknesses of how Rhonda Greyson chose to respond to the two girls who were yelling at each other?

---

activities available to them. The first level of environmental influence is the microsystem. The **microsystem** consists of the activities, roles, and interpersonal relationships of the social settings with which the student has direct contact (Bronfenbrenner, 1979). A student's classroom, family, and peer group are all examples of microsystems.

A **mesosystem** represents the interaction between two microsystems. An example of a mesosystem is when a student's home life affects schoolwork and vice versa (Bronfenbrenner, 1979). Another example is when students try to meet conflicting peer and parental expectations.

An **exosystem** has an influence on a student even though the student does not interact directly with the exosystem (Bronfenbrenner, 1979). The closing of the tire plant in the opening vignette is an example of an exosystem. Students do not work in the plant, but its closure can affect them.

The **macrosystem** is used to explain some of the consistencies observed at the microsystem and mesosystem levels such as families from a cultural group showing similar interaction patterns (Bronfenbrenner, 1979). Generally, it is the influence of culture, subculture, society, or social class on a person's microsystems, mesosystems, and exosystems.

How would macrosystems influence microsystems?

In later discussions of his theory, Bronfenbrenner (1994, 1995) added the notion of a **chronosystem** to encompass developmental change or consistency over time in the individual and that individual's environments. For example, historical changes such as the Great Depression impact all levels of Bronfenbrenner's model.

Personality, Style, Self-Concept, and Moral Reasoning

Your students will differ in their typical moods, preferences, self-perceptions, and the feelings they have about themselves and others. You may also notice that students of about the same age share some common issues as they try to develop a sense of who they are. In this section a number of theoretical constructs are presented that are useful for describing and understanding these observations.

Looking in on

The topic of conversation at lunch today was the closing of the tire factory. A number of our students had mentioned increased stress at home in anticipation of the closing. One of the teachers who had worked at the factory noted that the people who work there have a *blue-collar* view of life and take great pride in their work and being able to support their families. He said it will be tough on them being out of work. Another teacher said she remembered a few years ago when the factory had large numbers of layoffs, and how a number of students dropped out to help support their families. I mentioned some of the conversations that I had with my students that day. It struck me that some of the students seemed more upset than others. I think in part that was due to their personalities, but also I think the amount of support that they get from their families also matters. For example, one student told me that his parents had already forbidden him to drop out of school. As we were leaving, Karen Seal reminded us that a number of teachers in this district had spouses who worked at that plant. I had forgotten about that until she mentioned it.

● **What components of Bronfenbrenner's ecological theory are visible in this example?**

Decision Point: How can teachers' decision making be improved by knowing what's going on in their community?

Personality

Personality consists of the enduring personal characteristics that distinguish one person from another in terms of beliefs, attitudes, and ways of behaving. A variety of theoretical perspectives on personality exist, including developmental views, trait perspectives, and person/environment fit models.

Erikson's Developmental Theory of Personality.   Erikson (1963, 1972) theorized that personality develops across the life span through eight psychosocial stages. The order of these stages is fixed and they are universal, but people's personal and social experiences affect their development during each stage. Each stage is also defined by a developmental crisis that can be resolved positively or negatively. How a crisis is resolved influences later development. If these crises are resolved positively, the eight virtues of hope, will, purpose, competence, fidelity, love, care, and wisdom are developed (Cross, 2001). The eight stages or crises are summarized for you in Table 12.1.

Erikson's theory is to a large extent descriptive rather than prescriptive. Consequently, the implications for classroom practice are mainly in terms of understanding key developmental issues for your students. For example, the industry and inferiority stage highlights the importance of elementary school children developing a personal sense of competence, which is their belief that they can master challenges. You have encountered related ideas in earlier chapters such as self-efficacy, ability and effort attributions, and the value of strategic learning. Together these ideas emphasize the value of helping students develop the beliefs and strategies necessary to succeed at meaningful tasks.

What does it mean to develop a sense of industry?

During adolescence identity versus role diffusion is the key developmental crisis. Students during this period may experiment with a number of different roles and physical appearances before settling on those that are comfortable to them. Also, according to Erikson, adolescents may overly identify with a peer group or clique to provide protection from role confusion (Erikson, 1972). Erikson's idea of identity formation has been extended in a number of ways including Marcia's identity statuses and the notion of an oppositional identity.

What two factors are used to define an identity status?

Marcia's Identity Statuses.   James Marcia (1966, 1980, 1993) has proposed four identity statuses that older adolescents may assume as they attempt to establish their identities. An identity status is defined by the presence or absence of students' exploration of possible identities, and the

TABLE 12.1 Erikson's Psychosocial Stages

Stage	Age (years)	Developmental Crisis
Trust vs. mistrust	0–1	To develop a sense that the world is predictable and trustworthy Failure to do so leads to fear and distrust of others
Autonomy vs. shame and doubt	1–3	To develop a sense of self-sufficiency Failure to do so leads to self-doubt and dependence
Initiative vs. guilt	3–5	To develop a sense of self-direction and self-assertion Failure leads to guilt about not meeting potential
Industry vs. inferiority	6–12	To develop a sense of personal competence Failure to do so leads to feelings of inferiority
Identity vs. role diffusion	12–18	To select a personal identity Failure to do so leads to confusion over the roles a person will select
Intimacy vs. isolation	19–25	To develop loving relationships with others Failure leads to a fear of intimacy and isolation
Generativity vs. stagnation	25–50	To develop a sense of productivity and of making a contribution Failure to do so leads to a lack of productivity
Integrity vs. despair	50+	To develop a sense of contentment when looking back Failure to do so leads to feelings of regret

presence or absence of commitment to certain occupational and ideological identities. **Identity achievement** status is when adolescents have carefully explored their options and committed to certain roles or identities. For example, you may have weighed the pros and cons of becoming a teacher and gradually decided it was the right career for you. **Identity foreclosure** occurs when adolescents commit to an identity without exploration or crisis. Identity foreclosure occurs when others such as parents make identity decisions for an adolescent. For example, consider an adolescent who understood early in life that he would be a pharmacist because his father and mother were pharmacists and owned several pharmacies. **Identity moratorium** occurs when the exploration of options is ongoing. These adolescents are in the middle of their identity crisis, and identity moratorium usually comes before identity achievement (Schwartz & Dunham, 2000). **Identity diffusion** is when adolescents have no clear direction in terms of ideological and occupational identity, and there may or may not have been exploration. These adolescents often appear to be disinterested and apathetic to others (Marcia, 1980).

Certain personality characteristics have been found to be associated with different identity statuses (Kidwell, Dunham,

Adolescence is a time of experimentation with identity.

Bacho, Pastorino, & Portes, 1995; Marcia, 1980; Schwartz & Dunham, 2000). In general, identity achievement is associated with the highest levels of maturity and self-esteem. Moratorium status adolescents tend to be the most anxious, while the foreclosure status is associated with the least amount of anxiety. The identity foreclosure status also can be associated with smugness or authoritarianism. Identity diffusion is associated with apathy and academic difficulties.

Teachers are likely to have students in their secondary classrooms who demonstrate anxiety over identity decisions. These teachers can help by providing emotional support and timely information about occupational possibilities and personal issues. This is how Mary Thompson, a high school counselor, thinks about this issue.

> ➤ I like to inform my students about occupations they may not have considered that match their interests and aptitudes. I also like to remind them that deciding on an occupation takes time for many people.

The Oppositional Identity Status. The term **oppositional identity** has been applied to some adolescents' physical and symbolic resistance to what they perceive to be prescribed societal roles and standards. For example, the resistance of some working-class boys to middle class values, the resistance of some adolescent girls to gender prescriptions, and the rejection of white values by some African American adolescents can be viewed as examples of oppositional identities (Fordham & Ogbu, 1986; Hemmings, 2000; Ogbu, 1978, 1994, 1995; Valli, 1986; Willis, 1977). Students also may develop anti-achievement attitudes because of negative peer pressures about achievement (Alderman, 1999; Gorman, Kim, & Schimmelbusch, 2002; Hersch, 1998; Ishiyama & Chabassol, 1985). For example, students who achieve can run the risks of being perceived as geeks or as raising teachers' expectations for everyone (Brown, 1993).

What is an oppositional identity?

The oppositional identity construct has implications for classroom practice. Teachers should create environments in which students learn to value each other's accomplishments. Perhaps students can nominate others for awards or recognition, or students could produce parental newsletters that focus on students' achievements. Teachers can also administer encouragement to students privately and in subtle ways to prevent negative peer reactions to those students.

The oppositional identity needs to be applied carefully as a cultural generalization. Two recent analyses of the attitudes of minority students toward school have failed to provide support for the oppositional identity as a typical response pattern among minority students (Ainsworth-Darnell & Downey, 1998; Cook & Ludwig, 1997). However, as a preventative measure, teachers should still provide classroom environments that are congruent with students' cultural experiences (St. Charles & Costantino, 2000).

A Trait Perspective on Personality: The Big Five. The **big five** are general personality factors that capture the major dimensions of personality that appear both in research and in daily conversations about personality. These five personality factors are agreeableness, extroversion, openness to new experiences, conscientiousness, and emotional stability (Caspi, 1998; Goldberg, 1990, 1993; McCrae & Costa, 1996; Snow, Corno, & Jackson, 1996). Each of these five general characteristics provides a category into which large numbers of more specific personality traits or characteristics can be grouped. You may recognize this structure as being similar to the hierarchical factor structure discussed in Chapter 11 for psychometric views of intelligence. Individuals differ in terms of how well a personality characteristic describes them. The five factors and their descriptions are provided in Table 12.2.

What are the big five personality factors?

The five-factor model has been useful for classifying personality traits and provides a common vocabulary for describing personality. These characteristics are also

TABLE 12.2 The Five Factors of Personality

Personality Dimensions	Descriptions/Related Characteristics
Agreeableness	Selfless concern, generous and trusting impulses, friendliness and likeability; agreeableness contrasts with hostility
Extroversion	Preference for social interactions and lively activities, assertiveness, and ambition; extroversion contrasts with introversion
Conscientiousness	Purposeful, strong-willed, determined, future-oriented, and motivated to succeed
Emotional stability	Tendency for balanced and positive emotions, socially adjusted; emotional stability contrasts with neuroticism and anxiety
Openness to experience	Flexible, receptive to new ideas and experiences, creative, open-minded

observable in students' behavior and correlate with important academic and social variables in the classroom. Here are some examples of these relationships.

- Reward tends to enhance the performance of extroverts more than introverts, but punishment is more debilitating to introverts (Eysenck, 1981).
- Introverts tend to perform better in structured learning situations than in less structured situations, and extroverts tend to have more trouble maintaining attention in independent learning situations (Snow, Corno, & Jackson, 1996).
- Low levels of conscientiousness are associated with procrastination in students (Scher & Osterman, 2002).
- Students' levels of agreeableness tend to correlate with other important social characteristics such as empathy and trust (Sneed, 2002).
- Low levels of conscientiousness and agreeableness are associated with behavioral and social problems in children, while openness to new experiences is associated with higher levels of moral reasoning (Dollinger & LaMartina, 1998; Ehrler, Evans, & McGhee, 1999).

Performance Anxiety.   Anxiety is a correlate of neuroticism (the opposite of emotional stability) that has clear implications for students' classroom performance. For example, some students may demonstrate debilitating levels of test or math anxiety. Performance anxiety is thought to have both a worry and an emotionality component (Cassady & Johnson, 2002; Hembree, 1988; Liebert & Morris, 1967). The worry component centers on the consequences of failure and often involves a set of anxiety-increasing self-statements that can interfere with information processing (Cassady & Johnson, 2002; Tobias, 1985; Wine, 1980). For example, dwelling on statements such as, "I am no good at math," can interfere with a problem-solving focus. The emotionality or physiological component has to do with bodily reactions that signal anxiety such as increased heart rate.

Interventions for performance anxiety have focused on both the emotionality and worry component (Eccles, Wigfield, & Schiefele, 1998). For example, relaxation techniques have been used to try to help students control autonomic responses such as breathing and heart rate. The interventions for the worry component have used self-instruction routines to help replace maladaptive thoughts with more productive thoughts. (Review Chapters 4 and 10 for examples of self-instructional programs.) As a classroom teacher, you can also reduce performance anxiety by providing different ways for students to show their learning, providing opportunities to improve unsuccessful performances, and helping students develop better learning and study strategies.

What is self-instruction (see Chapter 4)?

Personality and Small-Group Work.   The study of personality factors can influence the use of small-group learning in classrooms. For example, extroverts can be influential on group decision making when the decision to be made is moderately ambiguous, when no group consensus exists, and when information is plentiful (Bonner, 2000). This decision-making context seems somewhat descriptive of problem-based learning structures as discussed earlier in this text. Also, extroverts may employ more confrontational or conflictual strategies when arguing for a position than do introverts (Nussbaum, 2002). Consequently, one or two outgoing students could significantly influence the nature of small-group discourse, and teachers may need to help highly extroverted students learn how to share the time in a group and how to give others' ideas fair consideration.

Students' conscientiousness may influence group work also. Students high in conscientiousness may tend to focus more on quality of ideas than quantity of ideas when caucusing or brainstorming with other students. (Waung & Brice, 1998). This may help teachers understand one possible source of discord in a learning group.

Person/Environment Fit Views of Personality.   Person/environment fit or **goodness of fit** models of personality propose that the quality of a person's adjustment depends on how well matched environmental demands are to the personality or temperament of a person. The better the match between the person and the environment, the better the adjustment (Caplan & Harrison, 1993; Chess & Thomas, 1986, 1996; Eccles, Midgley, et al., 1993; Lerner, 1993; Thomas & Chess, 1980).

What does goodness of fit mean?

In trying to establish goodness of fit in classrooms and families, a number of factors should be considered. First, some difficult temperaments or personalities are harder to establish a fit for than others (Carey, 1998). Also, middle and late adolescence can be particularly challenging times of life for establishing goodness of fit (Nunn & Miller, 2000) (see the Enriching Your Understanding). It may take systematic planning and collaboration to accomplish an effective match for these students. Maria Gonzales, a kindergarten teacher, has this approach.

> ➤ Jonathan is very volatile and once he gets upset he tends to stay that way for the whole day. I like to have his mother tell me if he is off to a rough start. That way, I know I need to be a little more involved with him that day.

Second, we should understand that goodness of fit does not imply the absence of stress (Chess & Thomas, 1996). A certain amount of stress or discord is natural in a family or in a classroom. It's how stress is handled that matters. Disagreements and stressful situations should be discussed and reasonable compromises sought.

Third, demands that are seriously mismatched to a person's characteristics can escalate problems (Chess & Thomas, 1986). For example, mutually coercive interactions between violent or impulsive boys and adults, and the tendency of adults to detach emotionally from these boys or to reject them, can increase the odds of acting out behavior (Garbarino, 1999; Lengua, Wolchik, Sandler, & West, 2000). Often the students who most need positive interactions with adults make it hardest for adults to be positive with them.

Fourth, different contexts such as the student's home and classroom can place different demands on a student (Lerner, 1993). Behavioral patterns that are accommodated in one environment may produce a mismatch in another. The parent who says that her child didn't have the same problems with another teacher may be expressing this concept to you. It might be helpful to talk about why the goodness of fit appears to be better in some places.

Finally, establishing goodness of fit is accomplished generally in two ways (Chess & Thomas, 1986). First, the environment can be modified. These modifications may involve physical characteristics of the environment such as noise level, or they may involve the social and personal demands made on students (Lerner, 1993). For example, teachers may allow extremely active students opportunities to stand and walk in the back of the room while watching a film. Public and enthusiastic praise may backfire for students who become overly stimulated by those types of interactions (Manassis, 2001). Consequently, teachers can administer praise in a low-key and private manner to those students.

The second approach to obtaining a goodness of fit is to encourage students to adapt to the demands of their environments by developing behavioral patterns and understandings that increase the likelihood of a match. For example, you might teach impulsive students to slow down and think before acting.

Both environmental accommodations and accommodations by students are important, and they need to be done in balance. If the environment is always modified for the child or adolescent, then parents or teachers run the risk of creating a child tyrant (Chess & Thomas, 1986). On the other hand, an environment that never accommodates a student's temperament can be discouraging for that student.

What are the considerations in establishing a goodness of fit?

Self-Concept and Self-Esteem

Self-concept and self-esteem are characteristics of students that have had a storied history in education. At times self-concept and self-esteem have been used interchangeably (Elbaum & Vaughn, 2001). For this discussion, however, your authors accept the distinction made by some that **self-concept** is how students define or perceive themselves as a person, while **self-esteem** is how students feel about who they are (Houck & Spegman, 1999). This is not meant to imply that these concepts are unrelated because they clearly are. For example, students' self-competence beliefs are an important component of self-concept that affects the development of self-esteem (Cole et al., 2001). Also, as discussed next, there are similar developmental patterns.

How does self-concept differ from self-esteem?

Self-Concept in Preschool and Elementary School.   When asked to describe who they are, preschoolers and primary grade students usually define themselves in terms of their possessions, physical attributes, and social relationships (Damon & Hart, 1982). For example, a preschooler might describe herself as the person who has a puppy and who can run fast.

ENRICHING YOUR UNDERSTANDING
The Developmental Stage/Environment Fit

Another variant of the person/environment fit explanation for adjustment is the idea of the developmental stage/environment fit. This idea has been proposed as a possible explanation for the general observation that students' motivation for school and their academic performance often drop as they leave elementary school for junior high school (Eccles & Midgley, 1989; Eccles, Midgeley, et al., 1993). The developmental stage/person fit explanation proposes that when adolescents make this transition, they often encounter a school structure that is not matched to many of their developmental characteristics. The result is a decrease in motivation and academic performance. For example, Eccles and her colleagues noted that junior high schools often place a greater emphasis on teacher control and discipline and provide reduced opportunities for student decision making at a time when students have a high

need for self-determination. There may also be a decrease in personal and close relationships between teachers and students at a time when students need personal guidance. By creating schools that are more responsive to students' developmental characteristics, tensions caused by a mismatch between person and environment could be reduced. This discussion may seem familiar to you because it is similar to the discussion of developmentally appropriate education earlier in this text.

● **Based on your understanding of development, how would the developmental stage/environment fit concept be extended to apply to the design of early childhood classrooms? (For your authors' perspective on this question, go to the text website for this chapter.)**

In our meeting I brought up my concern about our policy that students stay with the same teacher throughout their time in our school. Although I understand the purpose of establishing a family atmosphere, I don't think this approach is always in the best interest of our students. For example, one of my students, Marissa, and I have not hit it off from the beginning. I think we've both tried, but I believe it's just one of those personality conflicts that can occur. We set each other off over the littlest things almost every day. On the other hand, I've watched her do quite well with both the music and the physical education teachers. I've started wondering if Marissa and I just aren't a good match, and also if there are other teachers who are experiencing the same thing with their students. A number of teachers spoke up immediately and said they have at least one student who poses the same kind of challenges. Our director, Michael, however, expressed the point of view that all families have problems getting along at times, but they try to work these problems out. Also, he asked if students such as Marissa might think they are being punished if they were removed from their friends in their classrooms. I agreed he had valid points, but Marissa and I had tried to work things out for two years. My concern is that it might be more damaging for Marissa to spend a number of years in an environment that was mismatched to her needs as a learner. As the meeting broke up, Michael asked us to send him suggestions about the criteria we might use to determine if a move is needed because of a personality conflict.

● **How does the concept of goodness of fit apply in this situation?**

Decision Point: What criteria do you think would make sense for determining whether or not to move a student to another classroom?

During the middle and later elementary school period, students' understanding of self changes. First, older elementary school students are more likely to include psychological traits in their self-descriptions (Aboud & Skerry, 1983; Livesley & Bromley, 1973). For example, "I am a worrier," or "I am a person who gets angry easily." However, their self-descriptions still tend to be more concrete than those of adolescents (Montemayor & Eisen, 1977). Self-concept also tends to become more differentiated during this period, which means that global self-concepts begin to be divided into domains such as academic and personal self-concepts (Burnett, 1996; Marsh, 1990; Marsh & Holmes, 1990). Also, when making judgments about their competence, older elementary school students are likely to compare themselves with their peers, especially when no clear criteria for success exist (Suls & Wills, 1991). Finally, self-concepts tend to become more realistic during the middle and later elementary school period. Students' competence beliefs decline during elementary school and into adolescence (Dweck & Elliott, 1983; Eccles & Midgley, 1989).

Self-Concept in Adolescence. As discussed, students' academic self-concept becomes less positive as they enter the junior high and middle school period (Eccles, Wigfield, et al., 1993). The emphasis on social comparison data in forming self-concept also continues (Pintrich & Schunk, 2002).

In addition, young adolescents tend to become overly self-conscious. Elkind (1967, 1985) refers to this phenomenon as **adolescent egocentrism,** which involves a number of ideation patterns. First, young adolescents may develop a sense of the **imaginary audience,** which is the idea that everyone is as interested in me as I am. Second, they may develop the belief that they are interesting to others because they are so unique. Elkind referred to this as the **personal fable.** Examples of personal fables include the beliefs that no one has parents who are as strict as mine or no one has ever loved as deeply as I do. One personal fable of particular concern to parents and educators is the myth of invulnerability. Adolescents may believe that they are invulnerable to harm, which may increase the likelihood of risky behavior such as unsafe driving or unprotected sex. A final component of adolescent egocentrism is the willingness of adolescents to be critical of authority figures and their peers.

Elkind's concept of adolescent egocentrism has intuitive appeal and provides a simple explanation for some commonly observed adolescent behaviors. However, both the theoretical foundation for adolescent egocentrism and its relationship to certain adolescent behaviors have been debated (Lerner, 1988; Vartanian, 2000, 2001). For example, evidence for the supposed relationship between adolescent egocentrism and the development of formal operational thought has been inconsistent, as have the data for a casual relationship between egocentrism and risk taking by adolescents. Adolescents' decisions to engage in risky behavior are complex, probably vary somewhat for each adolescent, and, therefore, are unlikely to be understood in terms of one factor. However, it's useful to remember that adolescents may be somewhat self-conscious while simultaneously critical of others, and that they may fail to realize that some of their feelings are fairly common for people their age. Teachers might need to help adolescents distinguish between friendly and hurtful teasing, and they may want to provide opportunities for students to feel less isolated or unique in a negative sense. Literature, films, and class discussions can be used to help adolescents see that they are not the only ones who feel a certain way.

How might a myth of invulnerability affect adolescents' reactions to information on drug abuse?

Self-Esteem. Self-esteem shows many of the same developmental trends as those observed for self-concept. For example, self-esteem tends to become more differentiated with age, social comparison data are important to children and adolescents in developing self-esteem, and a decline in self-esteem typically occurs around the end of elementary school (Eccles, Wigfield, et al., 1993; Harter, 1998).

Self-esteem has educational importance because self-esteem both influences achievement and is influenced by achievement. However, the relationship between self-esteem and achievement is complicated. For example, some students may do well in school, but feel badly about themselves, while others do poorly in school and feel fine about themselves. To understand these possibilities, think about earlier discussions about attributions and task value in Chapter 6.

The perceived importance of self-esteem as a moderator of achievement has led to a number of different self-esteem programs (Elbaum & Vaughn, 2001; Harter, 1998). Self-enhancement programs are designed to intervene directly with self-esteem through classroom activities. For example, students might be asked to identify their personal strengths and strengths they see in others. The skills or academic approach focuses on developing necessary knowledge and skills to succeed academically. Counseling approaches are affectively oriented and involve techniques such as relaxation training, coping skills training, communications skills training, and bibliotherapy. Mediated interventions target adults in a student's life typically to help them develop ways of interacting with children and adolescents that are thought to enhance self-esteem.

In general, skills approaches are better supported by available research than self-enhancement programs (Harter, 1998). However, a recent metaanalysis of self-esteem interventions for students with learning disabilities indicates that interventions of any type only had a small impact on self-concept (esteem) (Elbaum & Vaughn, 2001). Also, the effectiveness of interventions may be different for different age groups. The most effective interventions for elementary school students were intensive skill-based approaches, but counseling approaches were found to be more effective for middle and high school students. An effective program should focus both on academic skills and students' affect and beliefs. For example, one program for students with learning disabilities focuses on fostering success behaviors and characteristics including perseverance, proactivity, self-awareness, goal-setting, effective support systems, and emotional stability (Raskind, Goldberg, Higgins, & Herman, 2002).

How might a teacher's knowledge about learning strategies be helpful when intervening with academic self-esteem?

Cognitive and Learning Styles

Style, in general, refers to how students process information or prefer to learn. These differences have been categorized as cognitive styles or learning styles.

TABLE 12.3 Cognitive Style Dimensions

Cognitive Style	Description
Field dependence	Are very reliant on the visual field or background; have trouble separating object from background stimuli.
Field independence (Witkin, 1950; Witkin & Goodenough, 1978)	Are not reliant on the visual field; can separate objects from the background stimuli
Conceptual tempo (Kagan, 1966)	Impulsivity: Impulsives tend to emphasize speed over accuracy in problem solving
	Reflectivity: In problem solving reflectives tend to emphasize accuracy over speed
Equivalence range (Bruner, Goodnow, & Austin, 1956)	Some people tend to perceive things more in terms of their similarities than differences (leveling); other people tend to emphasize the differences between perceptions (sharpening)
Category width (Pettigrew, 1958)	When people are asked to estimate ranges, some give broad estimates of ranges, while others restrict the range of possibilities
Conceptual style (Kagan, Moss, & Sigel, 1963)	Analytic-descriptive style: These people tend to group pictures together on the basis of shared elements (e.g., birds and planes have wings)
	Relational style: These people group objects together on the basis of function (e.g., a spoon and fork are both for eating)
	Inferential categorical style: These people group objects on some inferred but not observable abstraction (e.g., dolphins and people are both mammals)
Wholist/analytic (Riding, 2001)	The tendency to perceive wholes versus the tendency to perceive parts; includes the field dependence/field independence style
Verbal/imagery (Riding, 2001)	The tendency to represent information in a verbal or pictorial form

Cognitive Styles.   Although the distinctions between learning style and cognitive style are not completely agreed on, **cognitive styles** are usually thought of as an individual's way of processing information as revealed through information-processing tasks developed in the laboratory (Yates, 2000). Table 12.3 contains a sampling of the numerous cognitive style dimensions that have been identified.

Learning Styles.   In contrast to cognitive styles, **learning styles** are learners' expressed preferences for how they like to learn, usually identified through learners' self-report about their learning preferences. For example, students may be asked to choose which one of a set of statements best describes their learning preferences. These self-reported preferences are then used to suggest optimal learning situations for learners (Callan, 1997/1998; Dunn, 1998; McNeal & Dwyer, 1999). Here are some examples of learning styles models.

How are cognitive and learning styles different?

- **Kolb's learning style model:** Kolb's (1984) learning style model identifies four learning styles. Divergers prefer to learn by concrete experiences and reflective observation. Assimilators prefer to learn by reflective observation and abstract conceptualization. Convergers prefer to learn by active, physical experimentation and abstract conceptualization. Finally, accommodators prefer active experimentation and concrete learning experiences.
- **The Dunn and Dunn model:** Rita Dunn and her colleagues (Carbo, Dunn, & Dunn, 1986; Dunn & Dunn, 1978) have developed a model that identifies more

than twenty style dimensions or variables. Through a paper and pencil inventory, students identify their preferences for types of learning experiences including physical factors (e.g., temperature and noise level, and so forth), emotional factors (e.g., amount of structure, responsibility), sociological factors (e.g., preferences for working alone or in groups), perceptual factors (preference for kinesthetic, visual, or auditory inputs, and so forth), psychological factors (e.g., cerebral preference, analytic or global methods).

- **Gregoric's learning style model:** Gregoric (1985) use the variables of time and space to identify four learning styles. In terms of space, people are concrete or abstract. With regard to time, people are sequential or random. For example, concrete sequential learners prefer step-by-step learning experiences with opportunities for physical experiences. In contrast, concrete random learners also like physical learning experiences, but prefer a more holistic or haphazard approach.

Evaluation of the Style Construct. The observation has been made that the major area of consensus in the style literature is that conceptual and empirical problems exist with using style as an individual difference construct (Sternberg & Grigorenko, 2001). First, the constructs of cognitive and learning style developed without the benefit of an overarching theory of individual differences or a common conceptual framework and language (Riding, 2000; Sternberg, 2001c; Yates, 2000). Consequently, multiple style models exist, but they may represent variations of the same underlying dimensions. For example, it has been suggested that cognitive style dimensions can be categorized using the wholist-analytic style dimension and verbal-imagery style dimension (Rayner & Riding, 1997; Riding & Cheema, 1991). The wholist-analytic dimension refers to the tendency to organize information either in wholes or in parts. The verbal-imagery style dimension is the tendency of individuals to represent information either verbally or with mental pictures. It remains to be seen whether attempts to organize style constructs into finite categories will succeed.

In addition, the style construct is complicated to apply. Is a person's style the same in all learning contexts, or does cross-situational inconsistency occur? If situational inconsistency occurs, then students would have learning styles rather than a single learning style. There are reasons to believe that people do not fit neatly into categories, and that behavior is influenced heavily by context (Yates, 2000). It is also unclear if learning style is an innate trait or if a style develops as a result of how students experience different learning situations. If a style can change with age and experience, then once again a student could have multiple styles. Some evidence suggests that style does change as a result of exposure to innovative instruction (Yates & Higgs, 1999, cited in Yates, 2000).

Style is difficult to measure as well. Both self-report methods and the use of experimental tasks have difficulties. Self-reports are often gathered with a paper and pencil inventory that requires learners to pick the statement that best describes them. These self-report inventories can suffer from reliability and validity issues, leading to inconsistent scores and concerns about what these instruments are measuring (Curry, 1990). It's also not always clear what complex experimental tasks are measuring because they can be influenced by a number of learner characteristics besides style (Riding, 2001).

In terms of the educational implications, the picture is equally unclear. Research has failed to lend consistent support for the value of adjusting instruction for style (Curry, 1990; Graham & Kershner, 1996; Kavale & Forness, 1987). Students may need to modify their style based on task characteristics, and they need to be prepared to be flexible because the world will not always adjust for them (Renzulli & Dai, 2001).

Given the construct, measurement, and intervention issues identified previously, your authors offer the following recommendations for the use of the style construct. Teachers should use multiple sources of data taken over time to determine how students learn most effectively. Teachers should also consider when it is appropriate to modify instruction based on style, and when it is more appropriate to help learners develop the skills necessary to learn in different environments.

What are the major issues with the style construct?

Finally, thoughtfully aligned lessons that provide multiple ways of learning seem to make sense for a number of reasons. For example, they provide multiple opportunities for elaboration and they may enhance students' interest in those lessons.

Moral Reasoning

An important contact point between individuals, their microsystems, and their macrosystems is their ability to reason about moral issues. A number of theories have been developed to explain how our ability to engage in moral reasoning develops with age, but probably the most influential of these theories is the work of Lawrence Kohlberg (Kohlberg, 1963, 1984; Kohlberg, Levine, & Hewer, 1983).

Kohlberg's Theory of Moral Reasoning. Kohlberg based his theoretical ideas on concepts from Piaget's work. For example, Kohlberg (1963) believed that more mature levels of moral reasoning required learners not to be egocentric and to factor multiple perspectives into moral reasoning. He also suggested that moral development required two processes (Kohlberg & Diessner, 1991). First children and adolescents needed to experience moral conflict or disagreements between people (a form of disequilibrium). Second, they needed to identify with the moral reasoning of significant people in their lives (a form of assimilation).

Kohlberg's Moral Dilemmas. Kohlberg developed and tested his theory by interviewing children and adolescents using a series of moral dilemmas. These moral dilemmas required children and adolescents to make judgments about conflicts or dilemmas in hypothetical social situations that concerned life issues, social obligations, law and authority, and retribution. For example, one of his more well-known dilemmas involves a woman who is dying from a rare form of cancer. A treatment exists, but the husband can only come up with a fraction of its cost, and the scientist who developed the treatment will not take time payments or sell it more cheaply. Students are asked if they would break into the laboratory and steal the drug (Kohlberg, 1984). Kohlberg believed that people's responses to these types of dilemmas would be based on the level of moral reasoning they had reached.

Kohlberg's Levels of Moral Reasoning. Kohlberg's theory of moral reasoning consists of three levels with two stages per level. Table 12.4 presents Kohlberg's descriptions of his stages (Colby & Kohlberg, 1987). Because the stages are intended primarily to provide different examples of moral reasoning within a level, this discussion focuses on the three levels.

The **preconventional level** of moral reasoning is based on subjective feelings of self (Shweder, Mahapatra, & Miller, 1987). A morally right action avoids punishment, earns reward, or meets some instrumental need of the person. A preconventional response to the moral dilemma presented previously might sound like this: "I wouldn't steal because I would go to jail," or "I would steal because I would feel bad if she dies."

At the **conventional level,** moral reasoning takes into account the collective feelings of others. Morality is based on stereotypical views of good and bad people, and the morally correct action is one that obeys rules and authority or that other members of a society would like. A conventional response might be, "If I didn't try to save her life, people wouldn't respect me."

Postconventional level moral reasoning is based on a set of objective moral principles. By objective, Kohlberg meant the ability to see situations from a decentered or detached perspective (Shweder et al., 1987). Postconventional reasoning is the ability to rise above personal and social concerns, to reason from a set of universal moral principles, and to create social contracts based on those principles. A postconventional response might be, "Respect for human life should be a primary concern in economic systems." Interestingly, postconventional reasoning can be at odds with conventional reasoning. For

How are conventional and postconventional moral reasoning different?

TABLE 12.4   Kohlberg's Theory of Moral Reasoning

Stage	Characteristics of Moral Reasoning
I. Preconventional level	
Stage 1: heteronomous morality	Right is avoiding breaking rules that have associated punishments, obeying authority and avoiding physical damage. Child has trouble considering two separate points of view and acts defined in terms of physical consequences. Child confuses self-perspective with the perspective of authorities
Stage 2: individualism, instrumental purpose, and exchange	It is right to follow rules that support self-interests and to let others do the same, and it is right to do what is fair in an exchange. Everyone has own interests that may come in conflict. Right is relative to the person's self-interests
II. Conventional level	
Stage 3: mutual interpersonal expectations, relationships, interpersonal conformity	It's right to live up to what people expect of you, have good motives, and to keep mutual trusting relationships A person needs to be a good person in own eyes and eyes of others, and a person should maintain rules and authority
Stage 4: social system and conscience	A person must fulfill duties to which they have agreed Laws are upheld except in extreme cases. Person seeks to maintain institutions and keep them running
III. Postconventional level	
Stage 5: social construct or utility and individual rights	There is a sense of obligation to the law and social contracts Laws based on what will do the most good for the most people Values and rights exist before societal laws; rules are a social contract and should be upheld impartially
Stage 6: universal ethical principles	Particular laws are only valid if they are based on moral principles. Doing right may involve violating laws and social norms. Moral reasoning based on universal moral principles

Source: Adapted from Colby, A., & Kohlberg, L. (1987). *The measurement of moral judgment.* New York: Cambridge University Press.

example, think about people in history who put themselves at risk because of their adherence to general moral principles.

Evaluation of Kohlberg's Theory.   Kohlberg's work has been influential, but various critiques have been offered (Arnold, 2000). He responded to some of these critiques by modifying his stage definitions and scoring procedures for dilemmas (Rest, Narvaez, Bebeau, & Thomas, 1999). Here are a few of the key criticisms.

- Moral reasoning can vary by the type of task used to assess moral reasoning, and the same person can demonstrate moral reasoning at more than one stage (Eisenberg, 1989a, 1989b; Gilligan, Kohlberg, Lerner, & Belenky, 1971).
- Kohlberg's theory is a theory of moral reasoning, not moral behavior (Eisenberg & Fabes, 1998). Just because someone reasons at a certain moral level does not mean that they will behave at that level (Blasi, 1980; Kutnick, 1986; Malinowski & Smith, 1985; Snarey, 1985). However, moral reasoning may be reflected in behavior when the moral values expressed are more central to the person's sense of self (Coie & Dodge, 1998).
- Kohlberg's emphasis on a justice perspective may not reflect moral reasoning in other cultures or for women in this society (Arnold, 2000; Garrod & Beal, 1993; Gilligan, 1993). This criticism led to the development of Gilligan's ideas of the morality of caring.

What issues have been identified with Kohlberg's theory?

The Morality of Caring.   Gilligan (1982, 1993) has proposed that Kohlberg's theory does not reflect how girls and women are raised to think about moral issues. She further noted that Kohlberg based his stages on interviews with boys using dilemmas that she thought had a masculine flavor. She concluded that the failure to attend to gender differences put girls and women at risk for scoring lower on assessments of moral reasoning.

In contrast to Kohlberg, Gilligan identifies two voices or types of moral reasoning (Gilligan, 1993; Brown, Tappen, Gilligan, Miller, & Argyris, 1989). One of these voices is an approach to moral reasoning that stresses the morality of justice. This is similar to Kohlberg's view of morality. The second voice is the **morality of caring**, which takes a more collectivist view and stresses compassion and the needs of others. For example, we shouldn't treat others unfairly and we shouldn't turn away from people in need (Brown et al., 1989). According to Gilligan, both views of morality are present in men and women; however, the morality of caring predominates in women (Gilligan & Attanucci, 1988; Lyons, 1983).

What is a morality of caring?

In general, Gilligan's claim of a gender bias in the Kohlberg dilemmas has not been supported (Ford & Lowery, 1986; Walker, 1984, 1991). Additionally, the data on the gender relationship to the morality of caring is inconsistent (Pratt, Golding, Hunter, & Sampson, 1988; Rothbart, Hanley, & Alpert, 1986; Walker, 1989; Walker, DeVries, & Trevethan, 1987). Both views of morality are present to different degrees in men and women, and the type of moral reasoning that is used may vary based on the nature of the moral dilemma to be resolved. From a teacher's perspective, however, both the morality of caring and the morality of justice are important, because both a sense of justice and a sense of compassion have value (Cassidy, Chu, & Dahlsgaard, 1997). For example, during classroom discussions of moral issues, teachers can ask students to discuss if an action is just and also if it is compassionate.

Moral Education.   Historically, American schools either intentionally or unintentionally have played a role in the development of the morals, values, and the character of their students. For example, four different approaches to moral education have been tried in schools (DeRoche & Williams, 2001; Edgington, 2002). Values inculcation approaches have attempted to transmit a core set of values or beliefs to students. A number of character education programs in use currently are values inculcation approaches. Values clarification approaches were popular in the 1970s and attempted to help students develop an awareness of their personal value systems and how those systems affect their choices (Raths, Harmin, & Simon, 1978). Values analysis approaches focus on having students examine alternatives as they reason about moral decisions. Finally, moral reasoning approaches are typically based on Piaget's or Kohlberg's stage theories of moral reasoning and engage students in moral discussions so they can be exposed to levels of moral reasoning that are higher than their own (Blatt, 1969; Kohlberg, 1980; Leming, 1986).

Character Education.   Beginning in the 1990s and continuing today, the **character education** movement has become one of the fastest growing school reform movements in the country (Williams, 2000). It developed out of a sense that as a nation this is a confusing and dangerous time in terms of students' understanding of morality (Tappan, 1998). Character education is an attempt to teach explicitly a set of core values such as honesty, perseverance, and responsibility (Hoge, 2002). The materials for character education programs are often books, tapes, and posters that highlight these character traits in real or imagined people. As an educational approach, character education is a broad concept that includes direct instruction, cooperative learning, inductive learning approaches, service learning projects, literary analysis, conflict resolution strategies, and mentorships (Anderson, 2000; Pearson & Nicholson, 2000; Williams, 2000).

Character education has also raised controversy, and the appropriate role of schools in moral education continues to be debated (Schaps & Williams, 1999;

Williams, 2000). The long-term effectiveness of character education programs is un-clear. Few well-controlled experimental studies exist for character education, and the implementation of these programs is occurring more quickly than research efforts on the effectiveness of character education (DeRoche & Williams, 2001). Some studies have found positive impacts on suspension rates and achievement test scores (Coyne & Coyne, 2001). However, these studies can be criticized for investigating variables that may or may not reflect a change in students' character. Character education pro-grams also have been criticized for failing to incorporate educational psychology theory and research. For example, research on reading comprehension and the de-velopment of moral reasoning suggests that readers may often get a different message than was intended by a text, and that the ability of readers to comprehend a moral theme in a text depends both on their reading skills and their levels of moral reason-ing. Also, the level of moral message derived from the reading tends to be consistent with the student's level of moral reasoning, rather than the intended level of the mes-sage (Narvaez, 2002). Please note that components of character education programs such as increased parental involvement and schoolwide focus on students' attitude and deportment can yield important changes in school climate. The long-term effect on students' character is unclear, however.

The Family

"A family is characterized by two or more persons related by birth, marriage, adoption, or choice" (Allen, Fine, & Demo, 2000, p. 1). As you can tell from this de-finition, the family represents a diverse social structure. For example, children and adolescents grow up in two-parent homes, single-parent homes, step-families, and families with same sex parents. Each of these structures poses its own set of chal-lenges, and the family is generally the most influential microsystem that children and adolescents experience in their daily life.

The family also can be conceived of as a complicated social system in which mem-bers interact so that what happens to one person in the family affects others in the fam-ily (Olson & DeFrain, 1994; Peterson & Hann, 1999). Parents exert influence on their children, while children in a family are exerting influence on each other and their par-ents. An effective family system avoids both enmeshment, in which individuality is dis-couraged in the name of family harmony, and disengagement, in which family members act as separate noninteracting members (Cooper, Grotevant, & Condon, 1983). This balance between family involvement and independence becomes particu-larly tricky during adolescence when these students are trying to establish their own identities.

Family Risk Variables

The concept of risk was borrowed from the commerce and insurance fields and includes both demographic and psychological variables that are associated with higher proba-bilities of academic, personal, and social problems for children and adolescents (Cowan, Cowan, & Schulz, 1996; Keogh, 2000). The presence of a risk factor does not auto-matically cause adjustment problems, but it increases the likelihood of those problems. Socioeconomic status, divorce, and child abuse are three examples of risk factors.

Socioeconomic Status. Socioeconomic status (SES) is a catchall variable that typi-cally reflects some combination of parent income, education, and occupation (Jeynes, 2002). SES is used to represent a person's economic and social level in a society, and it has been generally observed that children who come from lower SES families tend to perform less well as a group on measures of academic performance than do chil-dren who come from middle or high SES families (Bryk & Thum, 1989; Coleman et al., 1966; Jimerson, Egeland, & Teo, 1999; Keogh, 2000; Lam, 1997). Given this potential relationship between poverty and achievement and the estimate by the National Children's Defense Fund that 12.1 million American children under the age 18 lived below the poverty line in 2002, poverty is an important risk factor (www.childrensdefense.org/family/income/childpoverty/default/). In fact, poverty may be the greatest risk factor (Schorr, 1988).

The relationship between SES and school achievement, however, is complicated. First, not all children and adolescents who live in poverty are equally at risk. Parental and community levels of support can influence the impact of family income on developmental outcomes (Duncan, Brooks-Gunn, Yeung, & Smith, 1998). These support systems can operate as buffers against the effects of poverty. Second, income has large but selective effects. The largest correlations, for example, between income and school performance are for ability and achievement measures (Duncan et al., 1998).

What factors can mediate the effects of low SES?

A number of explanations have been offered for the relationship between family income and achievement. The quality of the home environment in terms of opportunities for learning, warmth, and support between mother and child, and the physical condition of the living environment are significantly related to how well children do cognitively (Smith, Brooks-Gunn, & Klebanov, 1997). Additionally, low income living situations can increase the levels of stress and conflict over money and can also diminish the capacity of parents to offer support to children (Conger, Conger, & Elder, 1997; McLoyd, 1990).

The quality of education that some low SES students receive in urban schools can also be a factor in the observed lower levels of achievement (Darling-Hammond, 1995). In poor urban schools, teachers may be inadequately prepared for their teaching environment, and it is also harder to retain qualified teachers in these environments. Additionally, students in these schools can also have less access to important curricular materials and equipment than students in more advantaged schools (Oakes, 1990).

Divorce.   Divorce is a difficult crisis for the majority of children who experience divorce, but two years after the divorce most children are functioning well (DeFrain & Olson, 1999; Hetherington & Kelly, 2002). It is also important to remember that a lot of variation occurs in children's responses to divorce (Hetherington, Bridges, & Insabella, 1998). Some of the commonly noted reactions of children to divorce are presented here (Amato, 1993; DeFrain & Olson, 1999; Hetherington, Bridges, & Insabella, 1998; Hetherington & Kelly, 2002; Wallerstein & Blakslee, 1989; White, 1991).

- Early elementary school students tend to blame themselves for the divorce and are typically angry at their parents.
- The effects of divorce are painful, but living long-term with marital hostilities is even more negative. Some behavioral issues observed in children actually begin before the divorce because of marital discord.
- Children of divorce have increased odds of significant marital problems as adults (Amato & DeBoer, 2001).
- Girls are more likely to benefit from contact with the noncustodial mother, while boys are more likely to benefit from contact with the noncustodial father.

What are some typical reactions of children to divorce?

- Girls are more likely than boys to be strengthened by learning to cope with the stresses of divorces.
- Preadolescent boys have more trouble adjusting to life in a single-parent family with a mother, but girls have more trouble adjusting to stepfamilies.

According to Hetherington and Kelly (2002) parents can help children adjust to divorce by setting firm limits, demonstrating concern, and helping children understand what is happening. As a teacher, you can help by keeping parents informed about their child's progress in school and providing a stable and caring classroom environment.

Child Abuse and Neglect.   In 2000 5 million children were referred to child protection service for suspected child maltreatment. Nearly two-thirds of those reports were determined to need investigation and assessment by child protective services. Almost one-third of these cases were determined to be cases of child maltreatment (National Clearinghouse on Child Abuse and Neglect Information, 2002). Unfortunately, these statistics suggest that you are likely to encounter a case of abuse or neglect at some time.

There are three major categories of abuse. **Child abuse** is the infliction of intentional physical or psychological injuries on children. It contrasts with **neglect,** which can be intentional or unintentional and involves the failure of a caregiver to care for their children and to meet their physical, medical, and psychological needs (Craig, 1999; Lipsitt, 1988). **Sexual abuse** involves sexually stimulating behavior or sexual interaction with a child or adolescent, or using the child or adolescent as an object to be exploited for sexual gratification of others (Lipsitt, 1988).

By law, a teacher's major role in cases of abuse is to report it to the appropriate agency. A recent survey of teachers, however, found that nearly half the teachers in the sample had not received training to recognize signs of abuse, that many teachers were misinformed about the reporting process and their legal obligations, and that teachers may fail to report abuse for a number of reasons (Hinson & Fossey, 2000). There are a number of things you can do to avoid these issues.

First, familiarize yourself with your school's reporting procedures by talking to school nurses and counselors. Also, ask questions about legal responsibilities if you are uncertain, because they can vary somewhat by state. In looking for signs of abuse, be attentive to indicators such as serious and not easily explained injuries; fear of adult contact; reluctance to go home; untreated medical problems; pain or itching in genital area; sexual acting out; inappropriate clothing in warm weather such as sweaters and high-necked shirts; signs of malnutrition and depression; and extremely aggressive or withdrawn behavior (Hinson & Fossey, 2000; Robbins, 1990). Finally, it may help to remember that the record of prior complaints is an important factor in decisions made by child welfare systems about abuse (Rossi, Schuerman, & Budde, 1999). Your report can be important in establishing a pattern.

Resilient Children.   **Resilient children** live in environments associated with high levels of risk, and somehow not only survive but manage to thrive (Dole, 2000; Gallagher et al., 2002; Henry, 1999; Keogh, 2000; Masten & Garmezy, 1985; Werner, 1989, 1993). Resilience in children and adolescents is associated with a complex array of personal factors, family cohesion variables, and external support systems (Garmezy, 1985). When these children have been studied, they tend to have   **What is a resilient child?** easy temperaments and effective interpersonal and problem-solving skills. Also, these children and adolescents tend to have a relationship with at least one competent and nurturing person. A teacher can be an additional support person and can provide one more competent and caring person for children and adolescents.

Parent Involvement in Schools

The importance of having parents involved in their students' education has been recognized both in federal legislation and in school reform documents (Baker & Soden, 1998). The research on the effects of parent involvement on students' school achievement, however, can be characterized as providing mixed results (Baker & Soden, 1998; Fan & Chen, 2001; McNeal, 2001). In part, this is due to disagreements about how parental involvement should be implemented and how the effects should be measured. For example, parent involvement may affect some measures of achievement more readily than others. Teachers' grades seem to be correlated more strongly with parental involvement than are standardized test scores (Desimone, 1999). This may be because the relationships formed between parents and teachers are more influential on teachers' judgments and perceptions of students than on test scores. Regardless of these types of issues, you will want to consider how to involve parents effectively in your school because of the potential positive effects.

How Do Parents Decide to Become Involved?   In general, parents' decisions about becoming involved in their students' education are based on a consideration of three factors (Hoover-Dempsey & Sandler, 1997). The first factor is their beliefs about the level and types of involvement that are important in their children's education. This factor is influenced by their implicit theories about achievement, development, and learning. The second factor is their sense of self-efficacy for being able to help their students. As you remember from Chapter 4, self-efficacy is a person's beliefs about the likelihood

What factors influence parents' decisions to become involved in school?

of success with effort. Parents' implicit theories about the nature of ability and their attributions for success and failure are relevant here. For example, if parents believe that some people are just born smart, then their desire to become involved can be affected. The third factor includes the availability for opportunities, how welcome they feel in the school, and the demands they have on their time. Schools can affect all three factors by teaching parents how to help, by making sure there are meaningful ways for parents to become involved, and by eliminating barriers to participation.

Barriers to Participation.   A number of barriers have been identified for parental involvement and may be particularly important for low SES parents and minority parents (Moles, 1993; Pena, 2000). Some parents may feel that they lack the background and authority to help, or they may feel threatened by contacts with people in authority such teachers or principals, or they may be made to feel uncomfortable by the use of technical educational jargon. Teachers may believe that nonparticipation by parents equals disinterest, but this is an unsafe assumption. For example, some Mexican American families may see it as respectful to keep their distance and let teachers do their jobs (Pena, 2000). Also, lack of communication can be a major factor in parental involvement. Schools need to make sure that opportunities for involvement are clearly communicated.

What can we do as teachers to eliminate barriers to parent participation?

Types of Parental Involvement.   Parents can be involved in their children's schools in a number of ways (Epstein, 1992, 1994). Schools can offer parent education to help parents develop child-rearing skills. Parents can be recipients of school communication, an important source of volunteers, and they can become involved in school decision making through the parent-teacher organization or building management councils. Parents can also supervise and support home-based learning such as school projects or homework assignments. Finally, schools can work with parents to gain access to community resources. All of these ideas are important, but your use of homework and your communications with parents are almost daily points of contact between your classroom and home.

Homework.   Homework activities provide an important but controversial contact point between schools and families. Homework is fairly commonly used, particularly at the secondary school level, where it can account for as much as 20 percent or more of time students spend on academic tasks, and for as much as 32 percent of course grades in junior and senior high schools (Cooper & Nye, 1994; Putnam, Deshler, & Schumaker, 1993).

A number of potential benefits have been identified for homework (Cooper & Valentine, 2001; Corno, 2000). It can be used to bridge home and school, encourage parents to spend time with their children, provide reinforcement and practice, teach self-regulation skills and attitudes such as time management and perseverance, and help prepare elementary school students for high school.

Critics of homework suggest that homework increases stress in families, takes away from time for other family activities and community involvement, and that students themselves often have difficulty understanding the value of the assignments they have been given (Bryan, Nelson, & Mather, 1995; Buell, 2000; Ratnesar, 1999; Rowell & Hong, 2002).

The research on the effects of homework on achievement is complicated to interpret, and presents a mixed picture on the effects of homework (Cooper & Valentine, 2001; Trautwein & Köller, 2003). The positive effects on achievement tend to be significantly less for elementary students than for secondary students (Cooper, 1989; Cooper, 2001). However, there may be other reasons to assign homework to younger students such as helping them develop responsibility (Cooper, 2001). Also, the positive effects of homework for achievement are for the assigned homework that is completed (Cooper, Lindsey, Nye, & Greathouse, 1998). This may partially explain the mixed research results because 28 percent of average students and 56 percent of students with learning disabilities have trouble completing homework assignments (Polloway, Epstein, & Foley, 1992). The effectiveness of homework, therefore, depends on how well teachers think through their homework assignments. Figure 12.1 contains some suggestions for improving homework assignments.

What are the potential benefits and issues with homework?

Parent-Home Communications. The ability of teachers to maintain open communications with parents is important for students' progress. However, communication between home and school is often infrequent, and both parents and teachers blame each other for a lack of communication (Munk et al., 2001). Schools can

FIGURE 12.1 Suggestions for Improving Homework

- Directions for homework should include the purpose of the homework, clear directions for completing the assignment, time estimates, due date, examples formats, materials needed, and evaluation criteria.
- The assignments should be made in small units (Warger, 2001). For example, rather than assigning fifty math problems, assign them in sets of ten over a period of time.
- Coordinate with other teachers so that major homework assignments are not due at the same time.
- Periodic reminders should be provided about upcoming due dates.
- Assignments need to be at the appropriate developmental level, and there should be positive outcomes for completing homework (Hughes et al., 2002). This may mean different assignments for different students. Some accommodations that can be made include providing additional help, allowing alternative responses, adjusting length, using peer tutors to help with homework, allowing learning tools such as calculators, and giving fewer assignments.
- Teachers can use homework contracts with students (Storemont-Spurgin, 1997). For example, students can earn incentives for turning in a number of successfully completed assignments. The criteria for success can be gradually increased.
- Teachers need to increase the relevance and available rewards for homework (Bryan & Sullivan-Burstein, 1998). You can increase relevance and interest by varying assignments, by connecting to home culture, by using community service projects, or through interactive homework projects that allow family members and students to discuss what is being learned (Corno, 2000; Moll, Amanti, Neff, & Gonzales, 1992).
- Support may need to be provided through homework websites or homework hotlines (Blesh, 2000; Glazer & Williams, 2001).
- Students with disabilities can be taught important self-regulation skills such as listening skills, accurately recording assignments, time planning, self-monitoring, and self-rewarding (Hughes et al., 2002; Polloway, Bursuck, & Epstein, 2001).
- Cooperative homework teams can be used (O'Melia & Rosenberg, 1994). Students work within teams to remind and support each other. Teams can earn incentives for improving homework turn-in rate (Stormont-Spurgin, 1997).

communicate and collaborate with parents in a number of ways (Hiatt-Michael, 2001; Patton, Jayanthi, & Polloway, 2001).

- Teachers can write letters, notes, and newsletters. With this approach, teachers need to consider issues such as parental literacy rates and home language. For example, written materials may need to be translated into different languages.
- Teachers can use telephone or e-mail systems. The use of the telephone historically has been restricted to crisis situations. However, phones are now placed in some classrooms and can be used to receive voice mail and to record messages such as homework information ("Montana School").
- Teachers can use parent groups to disseminate information. These groups also can be used to educate parents about topics such as child rearing and developing literacy at home (Dicamillo, 2001).
- Parent-teacher conferences can be used for administrative purposes such as when teachers explain their classrooms during open houses. They can also be used in crisis situations that require parental support and for routine reporting of progress.
- Teachers can conduct home visits. This can be a good way to get to know families, but it needs to be coordinated with parents. For example, some traditional Asian American families may perceive this as an intrusion (Hiatt-Michael, 2001).

Of these suggestions, the parent conference is one that often concerns new teachers. Effective parent conferencing requires attention to scheduling and timing and basic communication and interpersonal skills. Figure 12.2 contains a number of suggestions for conducting parent conferences that have been taken from these sources and your authors' own experience (Hiatt-Michael, 2001; Jones, 2001; Nicolau & Ramos, 1993; "Nine tips," 2000; Potter & Bulach, 2000; Swiderek, 1997).

Peers

The peer group is another important microsystem for children and adolescents. Elementary school children spend approximately 40 percent of their time with peers, and having a peer group to belong to in adolescence is very important for adolescent

---

FIGURE 12.2 Parent Conferencing Tips

Setting and Scheduling

- Try to schedule around parents' work schedules. Consider having an open-door policy in the morning so parents can drop by.
- Make sure the conferencing area is comfortable and friendly and affords an appropriate level of privacy. With elementary school classrooms, have adult furniture for conferences.
- If multiple school personnel need to meet with parents, make sure everyone is introduced. If appropriate, consider having some people come in as needed to avoid intimidating parents.

Communication and Interpersonal Skills

- Be honest and tactful when talking with parents.
- Begin the conference with a positive comment about the student and end with a positive comment.
- Do not become defensive. Anger can escalate in a conference.
- Have interpreters available if needed. Consider having an interpreter meet parents as they enter. Plan the conference with the interpreter so that technical ideas are explained well.
- Avoid educational jargon.
- Have examples of student work to support comments. Consider having anonymous comparison papers so parents can see how the student compares with peers.

adjustment (Brown, Eicher, & Petrie, 1986; Cole & Cole, 1993). For example, peer relationship problems are one of many variables associated with substance abuse among adolescents, and access to positive peer support is one important protective factor against drug involvement (Coker, 2001; Hawkins, Catalano, & Miller, 1997). The relationships between students' families and their peer groups also form an important mesosystem. For example, the ability of young children to form close, positive relationships with peers depends to some extent on skills and knowledge acquired through family interactions (Parke & Buriel, 1998; Updegraff, Madden-Derdich, Estrada, Sales, & Leonard, 2002).

Work samples help parents understand what their children are doing in class.

Friendship Purposes and Patterns

Friends serve a variety of purposes for children and adolescents (Geisthardt, Brotherson, & Cook, 2002; Hartup, 1989a, 1989b; Zarbatany, Hartmann, & Rankin, 1990). Friends provide cognitive resources to help each other acquire knowledge and problem-solving skills and develop communication skills, cooperation behaviors, and methods for accessing and entering groups. They also provide relationship models on which to base future relationships. In addition, friends provide emotional resources for stressful situations, and they can even serve as buffers against negative life experiences (Brown University Child and Adolescent Behavior Letter, 1995). During adolescence, friends provide emotional and social support in areas such as identity exploration and confirmation of values and goals (Savin-Williams & Berndt, 1990). It tends to be the case, however, that different types of peer activities produce different benefits, and these benefits tend to occur only when the friendships are of high quality. For example, two somewhat troubled children who find each other may not participate in the types of experiences that lead to positive growth (Hartup, 1996).

What purposes do friendships serve?

Friendship Patterns. Young children and adolescents use somewhat different criteria for selecting friends (Doll, 1996; Hartup, 1989a, 1989b; McDevitt & Ormrod, 2002). During the preschool and kindergarten period, friends are children who are accessible to play within schools and at home and who like the same play activities. Because of this focus on shared play interests, friends change as interests change.

During the early elementary school period, students have a contractual understanding of friendship (Doll, 1996). They have a sense of their responsibilities as a friend and what they expect from their own friends. Friends exchange favors such as sleeping over at each other's houses or saving a place in line at a movie. Friendships, however, are still likely to be transitory.

The contractual understanding of friendship continues into later elementary school, but the exchanged favors are more adult-like (Doll, 1996). For example, friends can tell each other things and keep secrets. Also, the friendships tend to become more stable and enduring.

During adolescence a need for shared support, commitment, a sense of loyalty, and intimacy are important (Douvan & Adelson, 1966; Marcus, 1996; Youniss & Smollar, 1985). In addition, adolescents tend to choose friends who are similar to them in terms of experience and world view (Urberg, Degirmencioglu, Tolson, & Halliday-Scher, 2000).

What are the developmental trends in friendship selection criteria?

Looking in on

Mrs. Thompson and Bradley showed up for our parent conference thirty minutes late. Unfortunately, I had a math department meeting scheduled in thirty minutes. However, I decided to tell the head of the department that I would be late to the meeting, rather than cutting this parent meeting short or canceling it. Mrs. Thompson began the meeting by saying that my homework assignments were confusing and way too complicated. She was tired of fighting with Bradley over homework, and she did not have the time and knowledge in math to teach Bradley what he needed to know to do the homework. My initial impulse was to get a little defensive. Her statements seemed quite unfair because I work hard to provide learning support for my students. Rather than reacting out of that anger, however, I decided to ask Bradley some questions. I asked him if he knew what he could do if he didn't know what the assignment was. He said he could ask me or someone else, or he could call the school's homework hotline. I asked what he could do if he needed help. He said he could come to one of my after-school help sessions also. When he was asked if he had done any of these things, he said no. Mrs. Thompson said that this was typical for Bradley, and that he needs someone looking over his shoulder. She asked me to call and leave the homework assignments on her phone answering machine so we could make sure he does the homework. I suggested that maybe we try some things to help Bradley take responsibility for his homework before I start calling home. Mrs. Thompson asked me to make some suggestions.

● **What suggestions for parent conferences from this text are present in this example?**

Decision Point: What do you think of the following decisions Rhonda made: telling her chair she would be late; asking Bradley specific questions about her homework policies and practices; and not wanting to call with the homework right now. What might they do in place of calling home with the assignments?

Peer Acceptance

Peer acceptance relates to how students' peer groups like them and respond to them. Historically, peer acceptance statuses are identified for students based on interviews, questionnaires, and sociometric techniques. Sociometric techniques typically ask students about levels of desired association with peers (Asher & Dodge, 1986; Greener, 2000). For example, students might be asked to nominate the three people they would like to have in their study group, or three people they do not want to work with in groups. These methods have identified some important peer acceptance patterns.

Popular students receive a lot of positive nominations or ratings from their peers. They tend to be seen by teachers, peers, and other observers as being friendly, cooperative, emotionally predictable, helpful, and as having positive temperaments (Rubin, Bukowski, & Parker, 1998; Walker, Berthelsen, & Irving, 2001). The term *popular student* should not be confused with other ideas such as being popular or belonging to the popular group (Parkhurst & Hopmeyer, 1998). Also, students who are high in popularity are not always the students who are preferred by teachers (Gorman, Kim, & Schimmelbusch, 2002).

Neglected students receive neither positive nor negative nominations or ratings from their peers. They are not disliked, but instead are ignored by their peers. This can be due to their shyness, anxiety, or lack of social skills for initiating contact with others (Margolin, 2001). However, some students isolate themselves by choice because they prefer that status. The long-term adjustment pattern for neglected children is unclear, but it is possible for students who are identified as neglected students in elementary school to end up doing fine when they are older (Doll, 1996).

Rejected students receive large numbers of negative nominations or ratings from their peers. Peers can reject individuals for aggressive behavior (rejected-aggressive students), but individuals can also be rejected because they withdraw from their peers (rejected-withdrawn students) (Broderick & Blewitt, 2003).

Rejected-aggressive students tend to offer fewer positive solutions to problems and instead offer more aggressive solutions (Buzzelli, 1992). They tend to misread so-

Looking in on

Marcy, one of my students in my second period algebra class, stopped by to talk about the two girls who got in a fight today in class. Specifically, she wanted to talk about Sarah who is her very good friend. Marcy began by telling me that Sarah told her something in confidence that she thought she needed to tell a teacher. She wanted me to promise that I would not tell anyone else because she didn't want to lose Sarah's friendship by breaking a confidence. I told her I couldn't make that promise because I am required by law to report some things, but I did want to help if I could. She told me that Sarah has been getting in a lot of trouble lately, but there is a reason. Sarah told her that her father was beating her, and two weeks ago she had a terrible bruise on her back that Marcy had seen. She wanted Sarah to trust her, but she thought this was important to tell. I told her that this is one of the things that

I was legally required to report, but that I would try to do it in a way that would not harm her friendship. I also thanked her for being such a good friend, and told her if she needed to talk, I would be here. I also made a mental note to talk to the counselors about a presentation on when it is important to tell.

● **Based on your understanding of friendship patterns in adolescence, why would Marcy be so concerned about violating a confidence? Based on your understanding of laws regarding the reporting of abuse, did Rhonda Greyson follow the law?**

Decision Point: Why do you think Rhonda Greyson decided to inform Marcy up front that she cannot keep some things confidential?

---

cial situations and attribute aggressive intent to others in accidental or ambiguous situations (Crick & Dodge, 1994; Dodge & Feldman, 1990; Dodge, Murphy, & Buchsbaum, 1984). For example, if someone accidentally brushes against them in line, they may interpret this as an aggressive act and react immediately with aggression. Rejected-aggressive students are also less likely than more popular students to consider the effects of their behavior on others (Buzzelli, 1992). Some data also suggest that girls' aggression may be more subtle such as personal criticisms and the withdrawal of friendship (Doll, 1996).

In the early school years, withdrawn behaviors tend not to be correlated with rejection. However, withdrawn behaviors become more strongly associated with rejection during middle childhood and adolescence (Deater-Deckard, 2001; Rubin, Bukowski, & Parker, 1998). Rejected-withdrawn students are characterized as having extreme social nonassertiveness and low levels of social interactions. They also tend to be easy targets for peer ridicule and derision and tend to perceive themselves as less worthy and competent than more popular students (Evans & Eder, 1993; Verschueren & Marcoen, 2002). Although not always the case, they may have low athletic competence, physical weaknesses, or are viewed as unattractive by others (Margolin, 2001).

Cliques are relatively small and tightly knit groups of friends who spend a lot of time if not all their time together and serve as important reference groups for social behavior (Bagwell, Coie, & Terry, 2000; Brown, 1989, 1990). Cliques tend to be prevalent during adolescence; homogenous in terms of gender, race, or mothers' educational level; and stable (Ennett & Bauman, 1996). One interesting peer status relative to cliques is the liaison. Liaisons have no particular allegiance to a clique but can interact successfully with a number of different cliques (Shrum & Cheek, 1987).

Students' peer relationships clearly can affect school performance. As a teacher, you will have to identify if and when to become involved in peer relationship problems. If you

Loyalty and intimacy are important to friendships during adolescence.

FIGURE 12.3 Possible Interventions for Friendship and Peer Relationship Issues

(*Source:* Adapted from Doll, B. (1996). Children without friends: Implications for practice and policy. *School of Psychology Review, 25*(2), 165–181.)

- Teachers can use questionnaires and sociometric techniques to identify students who may need help.
- Where relevant, provide opportunities for students to discuss peer relationship issues in classes. For example, some literature highlights peer relationships as themes.
- Shape reluctant students' social behavior. Get them involved in pairs and then gradually increase the size of the group.
- Use role playing and discussion to explore peer issues.
- Teach younger students social skills, such as how to ask to play.
- Use flexible grouping patterns in classes to allow students to work with different students.
- Include a morality of caring in classrooms. Encourage students to help each other and to understand the impact of their words.
- Allow time for social interaction during the day. Be careful about no-talking rules in lunchrooms or the removal of free play and recess.
- Vary games and activities in physical education to allow more and less skilled athletes to participate successfully.

decide to intervene, the recommendations presented in Figure 12.3, which are based on Doll (1996) and your authors' experiences, may be useful.

Gender

Gender refers to the behaviors and attitudes that are connected to being a male or female (Seifert & Hoffnung, 1994). Gender is the result of sociocultural experiences and is contrasted with sex, which refers to the biologically determined anatomical and physiological characteristics of men and women (Richardson, 1997). For example, the process of deciding what it means in this society to be a man or woman is a gender issue, while the types of primary and secondary sexual characteristics that develop during puberty are examples sex characteristics.

The Development of Gender Knowledge

Children develop their knowledge about gender in three areas (Shepherd-Look, 1982). First, children develop a sense of their own **gender identity**. The majority of one-year-olds can discriminate between boys and girls and men and women on the basis of physical cues such as hair length (Leinbach & Fagot, 1993). By age two, most children can accurately identify themselves as male or female (Seifert & Hoffnung, 1994).

Knowledge of **gender stereotypes** or the roles, activities, and preferences of a particular gender also develop early. By age three, children understand the types of activities and toys that are associated with a particular gender (Lawson, 1989; Maccoby & Jacklin, 1974; Thompson, 1975). For example, by the preschool period, boys are more likely to engage in rough and tumble play, while girls are more likely to engage in organized games and role playing (Etaugh, 1983; Huston, 1983). Children's knowledge of gender stereotypes for personality traits usually develops later during the preschool or early elementary school period (Huston, 1983).

What are some examples of gender stereotypes?

Gender constancy is the idea that gender does not change as people grow older or if they change their physical appearance (Bem, 1989). Generally, by the ages of five to seven, they develop this understanding (Kohlberg, 1966; Stangor & Ruble, 1987).

Explanations for the Development of Gender Knowledge. A number of explanations have been suggested for the development of gender knowledge, including biological, psychoanalytical, and learning theory explanations (Eisenberg, Martin, & Fabes, 1996; Ruble & Martin, 1998). Social cognitive, cognitive, and cognitive developmental explanations have been offered as learning theory explanations for the development of gender role knowledge.

From a social cognitive perspective, gender knowledge could be acquired through direct or vicarious learning experiences (Mischel, 1966). Children could be directly reinforced or punished for behavior judged as gender appropriate or gender inappropriate by important socialization agents in their environment. For example, if a boy earns praise and attention from his peers for being physically active, then those behaviors could be more likely to reoccur in the future. From a vicarious perspective, children could acquire gender information by observing important gender models in their environment. As parents and teachers will attest, one important source of modeling for gender-appropriate behavior is the media, particularly television. Media portrayals of gender-appropriate behavior are often problematic because they fail to portray this information accurately or completely (Gollnick & Chinn, 1998).

> **What role does modeling play in establishing gender stereotypes?**

A Piagetian-based cognitive developmental explanation suggests that the development of gender constancy is a key component in the development of gender knowledge (Kohlberg, 1966; Kohlberg & Ullian, 1974). Once children learn that gender is irreversible (gender constancy), then they are motivated to accumulate more information about gender.

From a cognitive perspective, students may develop a **gender schema** that contains their general knowledge about the nature of gender (Bem, 1981). As is the case with any schema, these gender schemata can influence what children attend to, how they interpret experiences, and how they organize and store gender-related experiences.

Gender Differences in Academic Abilities

Gender difference research is both controversial and important because it has social and political implications (Hollway, 1994). For example, gender difference research has the potential both to eliminate stereotypes or to create or maintain stereotypes about genders (Crawford & Chaffin, 1997; Hare-Mustin & Marecek, 1994). In interpreting the gender difference literature, it is important to keep the following observations in mind.

- While significant gender differences may not be found at a global or general level, differences can be found for certain tasks or more specific abilities (Jannsen, De Corte, Verschaffel, Knoors, & Colément, 2002; Leahey & Guo, 2001). For example, significant gender differences are found for specific verbal abilities such as speech production, but not for verbal ability overall (Hyde & McKinley, 1997).
- Gender differences can be mediated by other variables such as age, life experiences, students' attitudes, and ethnicity (Ai, 2002; Coley, 2001; Quaiser-Pohl & Lehmann, 2002). For example, Maccoby and Jacklin (1974) reported that the reliable differences in quantitative and spatial reasoning abilities were not observed until around ages twelve to thirteen.
- Although the magnitude of observed gender differences for some abilities has decreased over the last twenty-five years, other differences have remained stable or even increased (Halpern, 1997).
- Men and boys have demonstrated a greater degree of variability for some cognitive skills (Hyde & McKinley, 1997).
- Gender differences tend to be larger for selected populations such as applicants to college than for the general population (Becker & Hedges, 1984; Halpern, 1997; Janssen et al., 2002; Stanley, Benbow, Brady, Daube, & Lupkowski, 1991).

> **What cautions should be applied in interpreting gender differences in achievement?**

Gender Differences in Math Ability.   Maccoby and Jacklin (1974) concluded from their review of research on gender differences in math ability that there were reliable differences favoring boys beginning in adolescence. More recent analyses, however, have found that there are no reliable differences between boys and girls in terms of general math ability (Hyde, Fennema, & Lamon, 1990; Hyde & McKinley, 1997). Whatever differences do exist are for more specific math processes, content, or selected groups of students (Eisenberg, Martin, and Fabes, 1996; Hyde et al., 1990). For example, girls tend to do better than boys on math tests that require the careful and precise application of standard procedures (Hyde et al., 1990; Jannsen et al., 2002; Willingham, Cole, Lewis, & Leung, 1997).

However, women tend to be underrepresented in both higher level math courses and math-related professions (Maple & Stage, 1991). A number of studies both in this country and internationally have demonstrated a tendency of both men and women to see math as a male domain (Hyde et al., 1990; Iben, 1991; Keller, 2001; Tartre & Fennema, 1995). In addition, men tend to be more extreme in their view of math as a male domain (Hyde et al., 1990).

The reasons for these differences in attitudes are complex, but probably include interactions among factors such as parent and teacher attitudes toward math as a male domain, the ways in which teachers interact with girls in math classrooms, and girl's confidence levels about math (Ai, 2002; Crawford & Chaffin, 1997; Keller, 2001; Sherman, 1983). For example, girls have a greater tendency to attribute difficulty in math to a lack of ability (Fennema, 1981).

Gender Differences in Verbal Ability.   As was the case for math, no consistent gender differences exist in general verbal ability. However, women tend to perform better on tests of speech production (Hyde & McKinley, 1997). Additionally, some data suggest that girls outperform boys on some writing and reading tasks and do somewhat better on tests of verbal fluency that require learners to generate words that begin or end with a certain letter ("Gender differences," 2001; Hyde & Linn, 1988; Kimura, 1999; United States Department of Education, 1997).

Gender Differences in Spatial Ability.   Spatial reasoning consists of a series of reasoning tasks that require students to manipulate objects in space or to predict the effects of certain manipulations. For example, students may be asked to predict what happens when an object is folded or put together with other objects, to hit a target or intercept a projectile, or to remember objects' location in space. Generally, there are differences in favor of men on spatial reasoning tasks (Halpern & LaMay, 2000). The nature of these differences, however, differs depending on how spatial reasoning is measured. For example, on average, men perform better on targeting tasks than women, but not as well as women on a test of object location memory (Kimura, 1999). Also, these differences are somewhat mediated by educational experiences (Pohl & Lehmann, 2002).

Gender Differences on the Scholastic Assessment Test.   The Scholastic Assessment Test (SAT), formally known as the Scholastic Aptitude Test, has historically been taken by entering freshmen as part of the college admissions process. Previous analyses of students' performance on the SAT have found that men achieve higher mean scores on both the math and verbal portions of the SAT, with a greater discrepancy for math (Arbeiter, 1985; Ramist & Arbeiter, 1986; Stumpf & Jackson, 1994; Wainer & Steinberg, 1992). More recently, an analysis of test scores of 12,500 graduates from the Baccalaureate and Beyond Study have supported these earlier findings (Mau, 2001). These data are particularly interesting given other data suggesting that women and girls achieve higher average grade point averages than men and boys (Kimura, 1999; Linn, 1990; Mau, 2001; Stricker, Rock, & Burton, 1993; Young, 1991, 1994).

It should be noted, however, that the difference in grade point averages in favor of women should not automatically be viewed as evidence of test bias. A number of possible reasons exist for this observed difference including differences in course-taking patterns and differences in grading patterns across courses and majors (Hoover, 2003; Willingham & Cole, 1997; Young, 1994).

Gender Equity in Special Education

One place where gender equity emerges as an issue is in the referral and placement of students in special education. For example, the majority of students identified for special education services are boys. They are 71 percent of the students identified with learning disabilities and 80 percent of students identified with emotional and behavioral disabilities (Sadker & Sadker, 1994). The reasons for these apparent overrepresentations for boys are complicated. They could be the result of both a tendency to underrefer girls and to overrefer boys (Wehmeyer & Rousso, 2001). Boys may be overreferred because they are more likely to act out than are girls, with the opposite being the case for girls. The underreferral of girls could also be due to societal standards that lead to lowered expectations for girls in terms of academic performance (Kratovil & Bailey, 1986).

In addition to the referral issue, gender equity is also an issue in terms of the life outcomes for young women with disabilities. They may face double the discrimination of other women, and their occupational outcomes tend to be less positive (Asch, Rousso, & Jeffries, 2001; Wehmeyer & Rousso, 2001). The latter may be due to differences in job training received by men and women, with women receiving training for less monetarily lucrative positions.

These data raise some interesting questions for you about your own classroom practice. Are you more likely to refer and place students who pose discipline problems than those who do not? Are you less likely to refer students who have acting-in problems such as depression and withdrawal? As one of your authors' colleagues used to note, teachers may be focused on emotionally disturbing students rather than students with emotional disturbances. Are your academic and behavioral expectations different for boys and girls in your class? Do you portray those different expectations through your behavior? Are other factors such as gender, race, or language problems affecting your judgment to refer or not?

Probably the best way to seek answers to these questions is to self-monitor. When deciding whether to refer students, you might ask certain questions. Does the student have a significantly lower performance than other students or not?

● **Why might it be helpful to formulate a strategy that causes you to consider gender fairness explicitly? (For your authors' perspective on this question, go to the text website for this chapter.)**

Implications of Gender Difference Research.   Halpern (1997, pp. 1097 ff.) has identified a number of implications from the literature on gender differences. The following recommendations from that list seem most applicable for classroom teachers.

- The differences between boys and girls should not be interpreted as meaning one gender is better than the other.
- Observed differences between the genders can vary by tasks, methods of assessment, and population.
- Be careful about applying group averages to a particular student. Enormous variability exists within a gender group.
- Be aware that the literature on gender differences can produce stereotypes that can influence perceptions and behavior in subtle ways (e.g., girls aren't good at math).
- Boys tend to mature later than girls in many areas. Be aware of that when making decisions about grade retention and referrals to special education.
- Be reasonably skeptical about generalizations provided about gender differences. Remember how complicated the issues are.

Cultural and Linguistic Diversity

America is a diverse society, and its classrooms reflect that diversity. For example, approximately one-third of students enrolled in United States public schools speak a language other than English at home (Lustig & Koester, 1999). In two American states, Texas and California, less than 50 percent of the student population is white, a demographic trend repeated in twenty-five of America's largest cities (Gollnick & Chinn, 1998).

A major challenge you will face as a teacher is helping students from diverse backgrounds succeed. Unfortunately, an achievement gap exists between economically disadvantaged and minority students and other American students on measures of academic achievement (Haycock, 2001; Hoff, 2003; McCombs, 2000). Your ability to work effectively with students from varying cultures, consequently, is likely to be a critical variable in improving the quality of education offered by American schools.

Culture Defined

Culture has been defined in different ways, and certainly disagreement exists in terms of what qualifies as a cultural group. For our purposes, we use the definition proposed by Nieto (2002, p. 53). **Culture** consists of the "ever-changing values, traditions, social and political relationships, and world view created and shared by a group of people bound together by a combination of factors (which can include a common history, geographic location, language, social class, and/or religion)." Banks (2001) further identifies these six major components of culture.

- **Values and behavioral styles:** The principles of behavior that are valued by a particular culture
- **Language and dialects:** The language and speech patterns used by a particular cultural or subcultural group
- **Nonverbal communication:** Gestures, postures, cultural guidelines for eye contact, and so on
- **Cultural cognitiveness:** The awareness and thoughts people have about their own culture
- **Perspectives, world views, frames of reference:** Ways of viewing and interpreting experiences, social and physical worlds, and so forth
- **Identification:** The extent to which individuals identify with the norms and expectations of their cultural group

How might these components of culture affect students' success in classrooms?

Members of a particular cultural group can differ from each other in terms of these components of culture. For example, some members of a cultural group may be more traditional in their world view, whereas others may have a world view that melds aspects of two different cultures. Even a quick examination of these components of culture, however, reveals a number of factors that could influence classroom success. As a teacher, you need to be prepared to understand a variety of perspectives, ways of communicating, and learning.

Culturally Responsive Teaching

Culturally responsive teaching and management validates and affirms the cultures of the students, and culturally responsive teachers help students understand and praise their own culture and cultures of others (Brown, 2000; Gay, 2000; Weinstein, Tomlinson-Clarke, & Curran, 2004). Creating a classroom environment that affirms diversity involves a number of understandings about diversity.

What is culturally responsive teaching?

Teachers' Attitudes toward Diversity. Teachers need to examine their own attitudes about diversity, because they are powerful models of those attitudes toward diversity. Unfortunately, teachers are subject to the same messages and teachings about cultural stereotypes as anyone else. For example, teachers may have internalized the stereotype that parents of minority children do not care about their children's achievement (Aaronsohn, Carter, & Howell, 1995). Teachers may also expect less of students of color and economically disadvantaged students because of a learned generalization that these students do not do well in school (Baron, Tom, & Cooper, 1985).

These beliefs may result in teachers unknowingly transmitting culturally biased attitudes to their students (Manning & Baruth, 2000). Because teachers are not always aware of these attitudes, it is important to monitor their classroom behavior.

You may find it useful to keep track of the nature and amounts of interactions you have with students, or even to periodically videotape your lessons to look for subtle behaviors that communicate negative messages to culturally different students (Goll-nick & Chinn, 1998).

Teachers' Knowledge about Cultural Diversity. To teach in a culturally responsive way, teachers need to understand the cultural and family backgrounds of their students. This knowledge can be accumulated in a number of ways (Ogbu, 1995). First, you can observe your students carefully and talk with them about their life experiences. Let them help you learn about their backgrounds. You can also use parents and family members as resources. Finally, you can look to research and published resources such as those referenced in this chapter. Getting to understand culture and the experiences of your students is a complicated and long-term process. Here are a few key areas in which you should try to develop a knowledge base.

Cultural Beliefs, Rituals, and Taboos of Your Students. It is important to familiarize yourself as much as possible with important cultural norms, rituals, and taboos. For example, some Native American students may have clear beliefs and taboos about issues such as keeping animals in cages, and stories concerning certain animal characters. Understanding these beliefs can help you avoid culturally insensitive activities.

Cross-Cultural Communication. Teachers also need to understand how cultural backgrounds can influence cross-cultural communication. For example, when studying the idea of the "silent Native American," Phillips (1983, 1985) noted that the choice to be silent depended on the types of participation structure in classrooms. Native American students in his sample were reluctant to participate when asked to respond as an individual or as a group in front of an audience. They tended to be more willing to participate when teachers interacted with them privately or when they interacted with others in a group.

The rules of social etiquette when interacting with other students and teachers can differ across cultural groups (Gay, 2000). The informal give and take between teachers and students in American classrooms may make some immigrants to this country uncomfortable. Attempts to draw these students out may fail because of this, eventually causing teachers to give up. African American students can show a participation style called the *call-response style* (Asante, 1998; Smitherman, 1977). Listeners speak over the talker, offering support, encouragement, and even criticism. This may conflict with a turn-taking conversational style some teachers may value and cause them to perceive the call-response style as rude.

Members of different cultural groups may also have different expectations about how attention is demonstrated nonverbally. Eye contact, posture, and gaze are indicators of attention in some cultures, while other students' cultural backgrounds may define those behaviors as disrespectful (Gay, 2000; Gollnick & Chinn, 1998).

> How might differences in communication style be incorrectly interpreted as lack of motivation?

Integrating a Cultural Perspective into Teaching. In general, teachers who care about their students and demonstrate warmth and acceptance tend to be more effective than teachers who do not (Brophy, 1983). The attitudes of warmth and caring have also been found to be important for teachers of culturally diverse students (Foster, 1995; Gay, 2000; Howard, 1998; Ladson-Billings, 1994). Caring teachers nourish, protect, support, and encourage, but they also hold students accountable by having reasonable but high expectations for culturally diverse learners (Gay, 2000). These teachers can be described as *warm demanders* (Kleinfeld, 1973, 1974, 1975). Additionally, caring teachers show respect for the cultural heritages of their students.

You can demonstrate respect for cultural diversity by integrating multicultural materials and learning experiences into your classroom and by monitoring classroom texts, materials, and curricula for absent, biased, or stereotypic portrayals of cultural groups. Bias can be present in textbooks and curricular materials in a number of ways (Gollnick & Chinn, 1998).

- **Invisibility:** Cultural models are missing or underrepresented in a textbook or classroom material.
- **Stereotyping:** Women and cultural minorities are presented in traditional, rigid roles.
- **Selectivity:** Issues or information are only presented from the side of the majority culture.
- **Unreality:** Contemporary and unpleasant topics are avoided.
- **Fragmentation:** Information on diversity is presented in isolated pieces rather than integrated through a textbook or material.
- **Linguistic bias:** For example, male pronouns are used to represent all people, or offensive terminology and labels are used.

You need to examine your classroom materials and textbooks for these types of biases, and select materials that do not contain them. As an alternative, detected forms of bias can be used for discussion about bias, or students can be encouraged to research the effects of bias through media (Gay, 2000).

Another way to show respect for diversity is to make use of the cultural capital diverse students bring to the learning situation. **Cultural capital** develops from the life experiences students have had and is reflected in their values, language, tastes, behaviors, and cultural identities (Bourdieu, 1986; Nieto, 2002). One hypothesized reason for the higher levels of school failure for diverse learners is that the culture of the school is mismatched to the culture of the home, and the cultural capital that is accumulated before school is undervalued (Manning & Baruth, 2000; Thomas, 2000).

The goal, therefore, is to increase **cultural congruence,** or the match between school and home culture (Au & Kawakami, 1994; Cajete, 1999). Cultural congruence is also referred to as culturally compatible and culturally responsive teaching (Erickson, 1987; Gay, 2000). Creating cultural congruence in a classroom entails more than fragmented celebrations of diversity as reflected in the *holidays and heroes* approach (Banks, 1991; Nieto, 2002), but should reflect an ongoing attempt to integrate diverse perspectives into the core elements of the classroom. The Hawaiian Kamehameha Elementary Education Program (KEEP) (Au & Kawakami, 1994; Vogt, Jordan, & Tharp, 1993) provides an example of culturally congruent instruction. This program integrated Hawaiian children's cultural capital by emphasizing cooperative learning experiences that build on the collectivist nature of the children's culture. In addition, a cultural form of story telling called the talk story was integrated into literacy instruction.

Similar arguments in favor of culturally congruent teaching have been made for the teaching of science to Native American students. Indigenous views of science often differ from western views of science. For example, in a western view, science is seen as objective, impartial inquiry, while indigenous views of science incorporate spirituality into understanding science phenomena (Garroutte, 1999). Culturally responsive science teaching for Native American students would respect and incorporate the Native American view of science rather that treating it as an interesting footnote or aside.

What is culturally congruent teaching?

Linguistic Diversity

As noted earlier, a significant number of students speak a language other than English at home. School districts are faced with the challenge of educating a linguistically diverse student population and also preparing all students for a linguistically diverse world (Christian, Howard, & Loeb, 2000; Genesee & Cloud, 1998). Considerable interest and controversy surround the issue of how best to meet those challenges.

I've given a lot of thought about how to help my students value their own culture and the cultures of others. Because there are so many different cultural backgrounds in my class, I've had to do a lot of reading and talking with my students and their parents.

One of my early social studies activities is a family tree activity that allows the students to get to know each other's background. Another of my favorite language arts units for second grade is a myths and legends unit. We look at myths and legends from different cultures and students compare these myths and legends to the myths and legends of their own cultures. Both my students and I are surprised to find out the number of similarities across different groups. I also think it's key to have the families of

my students at our school. Because of this, I've started a parent-teaching day on Friday. Different parents come in and teach skills, music, or stories from their cultural heritages. The students really look forward to this, as do the parents. For example, many parents tell me that their families come from a mixed cultural heritage, and they like having their children learn about their varied backgrounds.

● **How is the idea of culturally responsive teaching reflected in Octavio's classroom?**

Decision Point: Why might Octavio's parent involvement activities help him when he needs to contact parents about a problem their child is having in school?

Programs for Second Language Learning. A number of program delivery models exist for meeting the needs of second language learners. Newcomer programs or schools are designed typically to meet the needs of recent arrivals to this country who have limited English proficiency (Genessee, 2000). The goal is to provide intensive short-term instruction to help students develop the necessary skills to succeed in mainstream American schools.

Transitional bilingual programs are designed to help students with limited English proficiency to develop proficiency quickly (Baker, 1997; Ovando & Collier, 1998; Lessow-Hurley, 2000). These programs are usually designed to make the transition between the home language and English in two or three years. Instruction is initially provided in the home language with an emphasis on rapid transition to the use of English in instruction.

Developmental or maintenance bilingual programs use both English and the student's home language to introduce academic content (Genesee, 2000; Ovando & Collier, 1998). There is no emphasis on reducing the use of students' home language in instruction, and content is introduced in both languages throughout the program. The goal is to develop bilingualism.

How do transitional and maintenance bilingual education programs differ?

Two-way immersion bilingual programs integrate majority language learners and minority language learners into the same classroom (Christian, Howard, & Loeb, 2000; Howard & Sugarman, 2001). The goal is to develop bilingualism, academic proficiency, and cultural awareness in both groups. For example, content is taught in both languages so that English speaking students learn Spanish, while Spanish speaking students learn English.

English as a Second Language (ESL) programs provide access to the standard curriculum to English language learners by providing instructional techniques and supports to those learners (Ovando & Collier, 1998). Although ESL can be conceptualized as a program, these strategies are also important components of bilingual education approaches (Samway & McKeon, 1999).

The available literature does not clearly identify a program delivery model that is most effective (Samway & McKeon, 1999). To a certain extent, this is because widely differing variants of each type of program delivery model exist. In general, however, data suggest that second language learners benefit from instruction that builds on their understanding of their native language (Collier, 1992; Cziko, 1992;

Looking in on

I have been selected to speak at our spring informational meeting for new parents. This is when we try to answer any questions that parents of prospective students might have. We hold one meeting in Spanish and one in English so that all interested parents can attend the meeting that works best for them. During the meeting I will tell parents that our kindergartens are taught mainly in Spanish, with a gradual increase in the amount of English offered until the instruction in fourth grade is 50 percent in English and 50 percent in Spanish. The goal is to help our students become bilingual and biliterate. When we make the switch to English instruction in the content areas, we also provide instructional supports for our Spanish-speaking students. We do this because although these students develop English conversational competencies quickly, they often need support in processing the academic language involved in content instruction.

Octavio Fuentes

12.3

Throughout this process, we allow students to use their native language whenever it helps them to learn content more effectively. I also tell parents that everyone in our school is bilingual, and both staff and faculty work together to provide rich language experiences for the students. We continually work as a staff to improve our language skills and our teaching skills through a series of periodic training sessions. After the meeting we provide coffee, punch, and cookies so that parents can talk informally with teachers and each other.

● **What type of second language learning program is this school offering? What characteristics of effective programs for second language learners are present in this program?**

Decision Point: Why might the informal get-together after the meeting be important for involving parents in this school?

Willig, 1985). The literature on the education of second language learners has identified a number of indicators of program effectiveness (Samway & McKeon, 1999).

- Effective programs hold high expectations for their second language learners.
- Effective programs allow for long-term use of students' native language for concept development. Even if the instruction is in English, teachers encourage the use of students' native language to assist their understanding.
- Effective programs provide meaningful learning contexts that require students to interact with each other. Students can be powerful language models for each other.
- Effective programs provide comprehensive training for teachers and staff.
- Effective programs have the active support of school leaders.
- Effective programs tend to have supportive whole-school contexts. The education of second language learners is seen as a shared responsibility.

English as a Second Language Strategies for Classroom Teachers. At some point in their learning, second language learners need ESL support as they develop their competencies in English. This need would arise fairly quickly for students whose native language is fairly rare in a district, and consequently for whom bilingual teachers and materials may not be available. However, ESL instruction is also an important component of bilingual education programs (Samway & McKeon, 1999). It seems useful, therefore, for teachers to have some familiarity with ESL strategies.

In thinking about second language instruction, it is useful to consider that different forms of language proficiency exist. Cummins (1984a, 1984b) distinguishes between **basic interpersonal communication skills (BICS)** and **cognitive/academic language proficiency (CALP)**. BICS involves the language proficiencies required for face-to-face communication in commonly occurring contexts. For example, the language skills necessary to order a hamburger at a restaurant would be an example of BICS. CALP involves the language proficiencies required for academic learning and typically involves language that is

How are BICS and CALP different?

more abstract and may be more domain specific. For example, science learning involves the acquisition of terminology that has been created by scientists to communicate scientific understanding. BICS is often acquired quickly from peer interactions, the media, and other day-to-day experiences. CALP, on the other hand, typically does not develop from everyday experiences and takes longer to develop. Although limitations have been identified for the BICS/CALP distinction, it is useful to remember that even if English language learners can converse comfortably in English, they may lack the CALP necessary to learn academic content in English (Baker, 1997).

A number of different ESL strategies have been developed for helping second language learners in the classroom (Watts-Taffe & Truscott, 2000; Williams, 2001). Here are a few examples.

Labeling classroom objects in different languages can help second language learners.

- Help students identify cognates between the two languages. Cognates are words in one language that have a similar or identical word in another. For example, *history* and *historia* are cognates.
- Provide learning environments that are rich in visual cues such as models, diagrams, and demonstrations.
- Relate instruction to students' background experiences.
- Provide reading materials that are at the appropriate level for the student or reading materials in their language.
- Avoid the use of idioms in English.
- Speak clearly and provide appropriate wait time for students.
- Provide opportunities for students to interact with each other on complicated tasks that require communication.
- Plan lessons with both a content and language goal in mind.
- Teach important survival words early such as *bathroom, stop,* and *look at me.*
- Initially, teach language through the use of simple commands to the whole class that students can respond to through physical action. English language learners can learn to connect the language to the action, and this is referred to as *total physical response* (Asher, 1982).
- Label objects in the room in different languages.

Principles into Practice:
Illustrating Key Concepts

Throughout this chapter you looked in on Octavio Fuentes and Rhonda Greyson as they described their experiences with personal, social, and cultural diversity. Each time you looked in on these two teachers, you were asked to consider questions about their application of ideas from this chapter. Here is your authors' perspective on those questions.

Looking back on *Octavio Fuentes*

In Octavio's school, students remain with the same teacher every year because teachers move up to the next grade with their students. Octavio and Marissa seem to have a personality conflict that is not getting better. However, Marissa gets along better with other teachers, which has caused him to wonder if she might do better with another teacher. He is wondering if goodness of fit for Marissa might be better accomplished with another teacher.

Octavio described a number of things he does to help his students value their culture and the cultures of others. First, he tries to understand the cultural backgrounds of his students. He has also integrated culture into his classroom naturally through activities such as his family tree activity. Finally, he strives to involve his students' families in his classroom. These few ideas he shared seem consistent with the idea of culturally responsive teaching.

Octavio is preparing for a parent meeting during which he will describe the structure of their bilingual school. The overall approach seems to be an example of a two-way immersion bilingual program, because all the children in the school, regardless of home language, are learning to be bilingual. In his school, students are encouraged to think with their native language as they acquire a second language, the whole school supports the learning of two languages, and the administration supports faculty professional development. Their program seems to have a number of the characteristics of effective programs for second language learners. ●

Looking back on *Rhonda Greyson*

Rhonda is concerned about the impact of the closing of a tire factory on her students. Bronfenbrenner's ecological theory provides a useful organizer for thinking about these issues. The impact of the factory closing on family life is an example of an exosystem. What students experience within their particular family represents an interaction with one of their more important microsystems. The impact of their family experiences on school performance provides an example of a mesosystem. The *blue-collar* values of factory workers are an example of a macrosystem influence. Finally, consistent with Bronfenbrenner's theory, the effects of the factory closure will be moderated by students' personalities and beliefs.

Rhonda is dealing with the serious issue of child abuse. In this case, her knowledge of the abuse came from another student, Marcy, who wanted to help her friend. Marcy's concern for the importance of keeping her friend's secret is consistent with the nature of friendships during adolescence when trust and intimacy are extremely important for friendships. However, Rhonda will need to follow through on her legal responsibility and report this suspected abuse.

A number of suggestions made in this text for parent conferencing are observable in Rhonda's short parent conference. She arranged to meet in a place that offered both privacy and freedom from interruption, which seems like a good choice given the topic of this conference. Rhonda did an excellent job of remaining calm in this somewhat confrontational conference. She remained assertive, but demonstrated that she was willing to listen. Although Rhonda did not invite Bradley to the conference, it turns out that this was a time when it was helpful to have the student in attendance. ●

Teachers as Decision Makers

At various points in this chapter, you were asked to participate in the decision making of Octavio Fuentes and Rhonda Greyson. We would like to share our views of those decision points.

Octavio Fuentes' Decision Points

At various times this text has emphasized the importance of examining decisions in terms of what you gain and lose as a teacher with a particular decision. In the case of teachers remaining with their students, the teachers will be able to spend more time with students, which could help them know their students' needs better. Also, students will be able to form close relationships with each other. However, this structure may limit students' opportunities to form relationships outside of class. Also, some teachers and students may not be well matched to each other, an issue that Octavio faces later.

Octavio and his colleagues are establishing a policy for determining when it is appropriate to change a student's classroom placement. The literature on goodness of fit would suggest that a policy that allows no changes, or a policy that allows changes to occur too quickly, may both have problems. If no changes are allowed, a student and a teacher may end up having a terrible year that could have been avoided. However, if changes are made too quickly, both the teacher and the student lose the opportunity to try to work things out. It is suggested that both for parent and teacher requests, the policy should indicate that changes will be made on the basis of personality conflict only after reasonable attempts to work things out have been tried and documented.

Octavio's efforts to keep parents informed and involved throughout the year can help him when he needs to work with parents to resolve an issue. First, they will already know each other, and the parents will have had a chance to interact with Octavio under more positive circumstances. Also, his students will know that he knows their parents. Although this may not be a deterrent to some students, it might for others.

Octavio's informal get-togethers with parents after meetings could also increase parent involvement. Similar to the last decision point, familiarity can break down boundaries. The parents might get to know Octavio as a person, which might make it easier to want to interact with him. Also, the social event allows parents to interact with each other, and it can help make school a little less frightening.

Rhonda Greyson's Decision Points

Deciding when and how to get involved in students' personal problems is a complicated process. In this case, the two girls are good friends, and Rhonda had no reason to expect that this confrontation would become violent. Her decision not to press the girls, but to ask them to keep the problem out of class, is a reasonable request. She might want to follow up with other teachers who have the two girls to see if she is missing anything, and if the problem continues she will need to take stronger actions.

Teachers' knowledge of their community can improve their ability to teach in that community. For example, knowing community standards may prevent you from doing something that unnecessarily antagonizes your students' parents or that is insensitive to their needs. In this case, Rhonda knew that the closing of the factory was important to many of her students, so she gave them a chance to discuss it.

Rhonda's decision to tell Marcy up front that she couldn't guarantee total confidentiality was a difficult one. It is possible that this might have prevented Marcy from talking to her, but it did not do so in this case. It possibly let Marcy know that Rhonda would be honest with her, and wouldn't tell her one thing and do the opposite. Most counselors inform students of the limits of confidentiality before beginning counseling with them, and Rhonda seems to be doing the same thing.

Rhonda decided to meet with a parent even though the parent was late and to tell her chair she would be late to a scheduled meeting. This is an appropriate decision because the parent had a concern that needed to be addressed. Although it may be frustrating when parents are late, it might help you to remember that there can be many reasons for this, including that the parent could not leave work. Rhonda's decision to involve Bradley seemed appropriate given his age and the nature of the problem.

Rhonda was able to tell the parent how much help was available to Bradley without doing so in a confrontational manner. Rhonda's desire to postpone calling about the homework also seems appropriate given Bradley's age. Rhonda could suggest a number of alternatives to the parent, such as assignment sheets and homework contracts, to help Bradley take personal responsibility.

Name _____   Date _____

Chapter 12 Study Guide

Use this Study Guide to review and test your knowledge of key concepts introduced in this chapter and to search out further information on issues and topics raised in this chapter.

💻 Key Terms

Review the following key words from the chapter and then connect to Research Navigator (www.researchnavigator.com) either directly or through this book's Companion Website to explore research on the topics as they relate to education today.

Adolescent egocentrism (p. 402)
BICS (p. 426)
Big five (p. 398)
CALP (p. 426)
Character education (p. 408)
Child abuse (p. 411)
Chronosystem (p. 395)
Cliques (p. 417)
Cognitive styles (p. 404)
Conventional level (p. 406)
Cultural capital (p. 424)
Cultural congruence (p. 424)
Culturally responsive teaching (p. 422)
Culture (p. 422)

Exosystem (p. 395)
Gender (p. 418)
Gender constancy (p. 418)
Gender identity (p. 418)
Gender schema (p. 419)
Gender stereotypes (p. 418)
Goodness of fit (p. 400)
Identity achievement (p. 397)
Identity diffusion (p. 397)
Identity foreclosure (p. 397)
Identity moratorium (p. 397)
Imaginary audience (p. 402)
Learning styles (p. 404)
Macrosystem (p. 395)
Mesosystem (p. 395)

Microsystem (p. 395)
Morality of caring (p. 408)
Neglect (p. 411)
Neglected students (p. 416)
Oppositional identity (p. 398)
Personal fable (p. 402)
Personality (p. 396)
Popular students (p. 416)
Postconventional level (p. 406)
Preconventional level (p. 406)
Rejected students (p. 416)
Resilient children (p. 411)
Self-concept (p. 401)
Self-esteem (p. 401)
Sexual abuse (p. 411)

Alternative Response Items

1. Which one of the following is an example of a microsystem for a five-year-old boy named Bobby?

   a. Bobby's kindergarten class
   b. Bobby's mother's real estate office where she works
   c. Bobby's cultural group
   d. None of the above

2. Which of Erikson's psychosocial stages occurs during the elementary school period?

   a. Trust versus mistrust
   b. Initiative versus guilt
   c. Industry versus inferiority
   d. Identity versus role diffusion

3. Gregorio is extremely outgoing, strong-willed, and future-oriented. Which combination of personality traits fit this description?

   a. Highly introverted and conscientious
   b. High agreeableness and extroversion
   c. Highly extroverted and conscientious
   d. Highly extroverted and open to new experience

4. Which one of these cognitive styles is associated with emphasizing speed over accuracy in problem solving?

   a. Impulsivity
   b. Reflectivity
   c. Field dependence
   d. Field independence

5. When asked why it is wrong to steal, Sarah says that if you steal you will get in trouble. Which level of Kohlberg's theory is reflected in her answer?

   a. Preconventional
   b. Conventional
   c. Postconventional

6. Which one of the following statements regarding children's reactions to divorce is most accurate?

   a. Divorce is less problematic for mothers and their sons than for fathers and their sons.
   b. Very few children recover from the stress of divorce within five years of the divorce.
   c. Young children tend to blame themselves for their parents' divorce.
   d. Boys typically have more trouble than girls coping with the issues involved in a step-family.

7. The student who receives no positive or negative nominations from peers on a sociometric devices is referred to as a(n)

   a. Isolated student
   b. Rejected student
   c. Neglected student
   d. Liaison

8. Which one of the following statements concerning gender differences in ability is most accurate?

   a. The observed gender differences in ability tend to be larger for measures of general ability than measures of specific abilities.
   b. Gender differences tend to be fairly similar across groups and are not affected by variables such as culture or SES.
   c. Boys significantly outperform girls at most age levels in general mathematical ability.
   d. Gender differences tend to be larger for selected populations such as applicants to college.

9. The concept that schools should try to build on students' cultural experiences from home is:

   a. Immersion
   b. Cultural congruence
   c. Identity formation
   d. Bilingual education

10. What type of second language delivery model emphasizes language development in both the student's language and English?

   a. Transitional   c. Maintenance
   b. ESL   d. Submersion

Constructed Response Items

Short Answer/Completion Items

1. The personality term for an effective match between environments and people's characteristics is_____.

2. Elkind's terms for the observation that young adolescents are particularly concerned with their self-perceptions is_____.

3. A view of moral reasoning that stresses collectivism and compassion is the_____.

4. A child's understanding that gender does not change if someone cuts her or his hair or dresses differently is referred to as_____.

5. Classroom teaching that helps students value their culture and the culture of others has been referred to as _____.

Essay Items

1. What are the differences between a microsystem, mesosystem, exosystem, and macrosystem?

2. How could the concept of goodness of fit be used to explain why children from the same family may do better or worse in terms of personality adjustment?

3. What are the major issues with the style construct?

4. As a child grows older, why might it be accurate to say that the child has self-concepts rather than a self-concept?

5. Provide a preconventional, conventional, and post-conventional response to this question, "Why is it wrong to lie?"

6. How are the neglected and rejected peer acceptance statuses different?

7. What is a resilient child?

8. What is a culturally congruent education?

Practicing Your Decision Making

1. Discuss how knowledge of personal, social, and cultural diversity helps inform your use of the following techniques:

   Positive reinforcement
   Cooperative learning
   Classroom meetings

2. Develop a plan to help self-monitor your classroom behaviors for gender and cultural bias.

INTASC in Action

Use the following activities to think about how social cognitive concepts and principles relate to the INTASC standards.

Standard 3: Diverse Learners. Adapting to the needs of learners is a complicated decision making process. Clearly in many situations it is important to adjust to the needs of diverse learners, but it may be equally important in other situations to help learners adjust to the demands of their environment (Review the goodness of fit concept). What criteria would you use to determine when is more effective to adjust to the learner or to ask the learner to adjust?

Standard 10: School and Community Involvement. Interview three or four parents of school-aged children about their experiences with parent conferences. What did they like and dislike about the experience? Compare their experiences to the discussion in this chapter of barriers to parent participation, and the suggestions provided for parent conferencing.

 ## Web Resources

A number of serious personal and social adjustment issues exist for children and adolescents. Comprehensive coverage of these issues goes beyond the scope of this text. The following are some websites you might find helpful.

National Eating Disorders Association
www.nationaleatingdisorders.org

For information about eating disorders go to the following website. Check out the Parents and Family Network section of the site, which provides information for educators and coaches as well as a connection to a Students Assistance Program called ReconnectingU. This special site is specifically for college-age students.

American Academy of Pediatrics
www.aap.org/visit/suicideinfo.htm

For information about precursors of adolescent suicide, visit the AAP online. You'll find a list of articles discussing the AAP's views on suicide and social causes and what can be done to help young people.

American Association of Suicidology
www.suicidology.org/index.cfm

For additional information about child and adolescent suicide, visit this website and explore the prevention section to review the Guidelines for School-Based Suicide Prevention Programs.

American Psychological Association
www.apa.org/ppo/issues/pbviolence.html
http://helping.apa.org/index.html

Visit these websites for information on youth violence. The second site links you to a Help Center that offers advice and assistance with various issues. Check out the special connections for young people on violence, as well as other resources.

Assessment and Decision Making in the Classroom

Chapter 13 is intended to provide you with a basic understanding of the nature of assessment, specific assessment techniques and strategies, and how information from both standardized and classroom assessments can help you make decisions in your future classrooms.

When you have completed this chapter you should be able to:

- Identify and discuss the purposes of assessment in educational practice
- Explain the relationship between assessment and decision making
- Define reliability and list and discuss factors that affect the reliability of data
- Define validity and discuss the factors that affect the validity of educational decisions
- List and discuss the advantages and disadvantages of different types of assessment methods
- Discuss the nature and purpose of grades and grading

Standards in This Chapter

The concepts presented in this chapter will contribute to your mastery of all of the INTASC standards; however, the material presented in Chapter 13 relates most strongly to the following standards:

- **Standard 8:** Assessment
- **Standard 9:** Reflective Practice and Professional Growth
- **Standard 10:** School and Community Involvement

Close-ups on the Classroom

Hana Saad's Third Graders' Standardized Tests

It is near the end of my first year of teaching, we only have six weeks to go, and I feel like I'm just getting the hang of teaching. Teaching third grade has been harder than I thought; the kids have so much energy and so many questions. It has been a lot of fun too, and I am proud to say I think all of my students have worked hard and learned a lot. I've learned a lot also.

Despite what I think has been a good year, I'm concerned about the standardized test that was administered to all of the third, sixth, and ninth graders in the district. From what I've read, the test is meant to check the progress of students and to identify students who may need any special help. I have to admit that I don't have much confidence in these kinds of multiple-choice tests. It just seems that humans are too complex to be measured in such a simplistic way.

The tests didn't seem to bother the kids too much. Most of them seemed to appreciate the change in routine and thought it was fun. I wasn't too concerned about the tests until the results came back. I felt overwhelmed by the information. I still wasn't too worried until I heard some of the other teachers talking in the break room. They were saying that the test is used by the district's administration to determine how well we are doing our jobs. I didn't do anything special for the test, but some of the other teachers said they had been preparing their students for the test since the first of the year. This worries me, because it is my first year teaching, and I want them to renew my contract.

I've asked to talk with Ms. Grambling after school today. She is my mentor teacher and maybe she can give me some advice about what I should be doing, if it's not too late.

Decision Point: Many school districts are required to administer standardized tests. What, if anything, should teachers do to prepare their students for standardized tests?

Assessment is an important part of what teachers do. While students tend to focus on what assessment means to them personally, for educators, assessment is an important tool that can assist them in making more effective decisions. Teachers, administrators, and educational policy makers all rely on some form of assessment to gather information to improve their ability to make decisions. In spite of this, however, many educators lack a basic understanding of the nature of assessment and its role in improving learning (Stiggins, 2002). Stiggins suggests that we need to think in a balanced way about assessment of learning and assessment for learning.

The standardized test used in Ms. Saad's school is an example of assessment of learning. Many standardized tests are designed to be assessments of learning. The data from these instruments allow comparisons of students' performance on a broad scale and provide a snapshot of students' learning to date. This information is of value to teachers and other educational professionals in making decisions about individual students and school programs. Because standardized tests allow large-scale comparisons, they are especially useful to educational policy makers.

Standardized tests, however, are not suitable for gathering the kind of information teachers need to make day-to-day classroom decisions. Therefore, teachers must have the knowledge and skills necessary to design their own assessment tools. Teacher-designed assessments are examples of assessments for education. The information from these assessments help teachers make decisions about the effectiveness of individual instructional techniques and to provide feedback to students, and their parents, about how well students are learning. This is the concern expressed by Susan Decatur in the opening vignette.

Before proceeding with Chapter 13, be sure you read the Close-ups on the Classroom features about Hana Saad and Susan Decatur. At various points in the chapter, you will revisit both teachers in their classrooms and follow their decision-making progress. Their experiences are closely integrated with the key concepts of this chapter and serve as important models of how various forms of assessment can serve as valuable tools in the classroom.

The New York Times
nytimes.com
expect the world®

THEMES OF THE TIMES
Expand your knowledge of the concepts discussed in this chapter by reading current and historical articles from the New York Times by visiting the "Themes of the Times" section of the Companion Website.

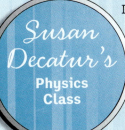

Susan Decatur's Physics Class

I am in the process of planning for my second year teaching physics at Essex High School. It seemed like I just barely made it through my first year. The kids who take my classes are mostly seniors with a few juniors; all of them are planning to go to college and are pretty darn smart. Last year I had to work really hard just learning school procedures and planning lessons. Throughout the whole year it seemed I was always just one step ahead of the students. This year I want to use what I learned last year and be more proactive and organized.

One of the things I am concerned about is whether my lessons are really effective in helping my students learn what I want them to learn. I am not confident that my classroom assessments are giving me the information I need to improve my teaching. Last year I had the students do labs and lab reports, complete a group project, and take a series of unit tests. But I was so busy with all of the other things I was trying to do that I'm afraid I didn't do a very good job planning these activities. Now looking over the results of these different activities it is hard to figure out exactly what the students did learn.

Mr. Ralph Isaacs is the chemistry teacher who teaches in the classroom next to mine. He has been teaching for about ten years and is the head of the science department. He has agreed to help me with my assessment plan this year. Next week the department is having a meeting to discuss the upcoming year. Ralph has agreed to meet with me before the meeting to look over what I did last year and give me some pointers.

Decision Point: What is the role of classroom assessment in effective instruction?

The Nature and Purposes of Assessment

As a teacher you will be asked to make many decisions each day. If you are to make good decisions, you will need to combine your general knowledge of learners and learning with knowledge about the specific situation in your classroom. Assessment is the general term that describes all the actions you will take to gather information and make decisions about your students' learning (Linn & Gronlund, 2000). As a teacher many of your assessments will be made informally. You will be faced with a situation and you will make a decision quickly, based on your instincts and the information that you recall at that time. However, you are likely to use more formal approaches to assessment when the stakes are high; that is when the decision is likely to have far-reaching consequences for you or your students.

For what types of decisions will you want to use information from more formal assessments?

While it may appear that the assessment process is simple and straightforward, it is actually quite complex. To help study and understand the assessment process, it is useful to break the process into a series of three steps: (a) information gathering, (b) analysis, and (c) evaluation. These three steps are represented in the steps shown in Figure 13.1.

The assessment begins with the gathering of information. Teachers gather information about their students in a variety of ways, including reviews of school records, talking to other teachers, tests, and direct observations of students' performances (McMillan, Myran, & Workman, 2002; Stiggins & Bridgeford, 1984). Analysis is the process of finding patterns in the data. The analysis may occur in an informal way or formally through the use of statistics. Evaluation is the process of using prior knowledge to explain and make judgments about the observed patterns. Depending on the nature of a decision to be made, different types of knowledge may be relevant, including knowledge of learning theories, instructional design, and the characteristics of specific learners in your class, school policy, and ethics. In this section, the importance of each of the steps in the assessment process is discussed.

FIGURE 13.1 The Assessment Process

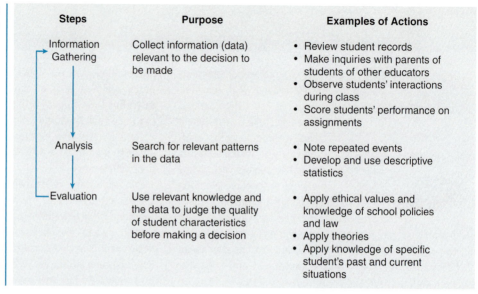

Steps	Purpose	Examples of Actions
Information Gathering	Collect information (data) relevant to the decision to be made	• Review student records • Make inquiries with parents of students of other educators • Observe students' interactions during class • Score students' performance on assignments
Analysis	Search for relevant patterns in the data	• Note repeated events • Develop and use descriptive statistics
Evaluation	Use relevant knowledge and the data to judge the quality of student characteristics before making a decision	• Apply ethical values and knowledge of school policies and law • Apply theories • Apply knowledge of specific student's past and current situations

Gathering Information for Formal Assessments

As previously stated, assessment begins with gathering information that you think will be useful in making a particular decision. Formal assessments are made to address a specific type of decision and are planned in advance. The decisions made when planning such an assessment will affect the quality of the information gathered, and ultimately the quality of the decision made. Planning an assessment begins by selecting an observational technique. Formal observation techniques involve gathering information through the observation of students' performance on a tasks intended to elicit a specific type of performance. An **observation technique** is composed of an assessment task and a scoring method.

Assessment Tasks. An **assessment task** is an activity or assignment designed to elicit a performance from the learner or learners who will be affected by the decision to be made. Examples of assessment tasks include tests, papers, projects, and formal presentations. Observing the students' performance on the assessment task allows teachers to make some inferences about students' characteristics, such as level of knowledge, skill, or aptitude.

Assessment tasks may vary in terms of the amount of structure planned into the task. In this context, structure refers to the amount of freedom that students have in making a response. Some assessment tasks are divergent in that they allow for a great deal of variation and freedom in the students' responses. Other assessment tasks are convergent because there is a single correct response to the task. The degree of structure associated with the observation affects the way the data are analyzed later.

Scoring Methods. Scoring is the process of categorizing or rating students' perfor-

Teachers gather information in a variety of ways to help them make decisions in their classrooms.

mances. Most often this is done by applying some type of scale. A **scale** is a system for interpreting or organizing students' performances or responses. The data points or categories on a scale refer to observable differences in a particular characteristic. For instance, if researchers wanted to make observations about the characteristic of sex, they would use a scale that has two categories, male and female. If they wanted to observe learners' ability in some area, they might administer a test and use a scale that had scores from zero to one hundred. Scales are useful for organizing data for analysis in the next step of the assessment process. Scales may be characterized by considering the characteristics of:

- **Exclusivity:** The categories of the scale are mutually exclusive.
- **Order:** The presence of a logical sequence to the categories of the scale.
- **Constant interval:** The difference between one unit and the next is constant.
- **Meaningful zero:** A score of zero represents the absence of the characteristic being observed.

Considering these characteristics, scales are classified as, nominal, ordinal, interval, or ratio. Table 13.1 summarizes the characteristics of each type of scale.

Nominal scales organize data into mutually exclusive and qualitatively different categories. Data are organized by recording the number of observations in each category. Observations about a student's gender, ethnicity, or grade level are examples of data that may be organized using a nominal scale. That the categories of a nominal scale are mutually exclusive means that membership in one category of the scale excludes membership in the other categories. A student who is a girl cannot also be a boy. There is no logical way to order nominal data as the differences between the categories are purely qualitative.

Ordinal scales organize data into mutually exclusive categories that occur along a continuum. Ordinal scales are common on surveys and inventories. Consider these examples of instructions for survey items.

- Indicate your level of agreement with the following statements by marking strongly disagree, disagree, agree, or strongly agree.
- Indicate how often you participate in the following activities by marking never, seldom, sometimes, often, or always.
- Rate your level of preference for each of the activities on the list, using a scale from one to ten, with one being the lowest rating and ten being the highest.

In each case, the responses represent points on a continuum, which can be ordered in a logical way; however, the difference or interval between different responses is undetermined. In other words, the difference in the level of agreement between a response of disagree and agree may not be the same as the difference between agree and strongly agree. The lack of a constant interval between the points of an ordinal scale means that mathematical operations such as addition, subtraction, multiplication, and division may be inappropriate. Consequently the results of these operations cannot be interpreted in a meaningful way.

What are the four characteristics used to describe different types of scales?

TABLE 13.1 Characteristics of Types of Scales

Type of Data	Exclusivity	Logical Order	Constant Interval	Meaningful Zero
Nominal	Yes	No	No	No
Ordinal	Yes	Yes	No	No
Interval	Yes	Yes	Yes	No
Ratio	Yes	Yes	Yes	Yes

Interval scales possess the qualities of exclusivity and logical order. In addition, the different categories or scores represent constant intervals of difference. The Fahrenheit temperature scale is an example of an interval scale. Observations of temperature are organized as degrees along the scale. The difference in temperature between 35 degrees and 45 degree is the same as the difference between 65 degrees and 75 degrees. Because the intervals between points on the scale are constant, mathematical operations such as addition, subtraction, multiplication, and division are appropriate because the results of these operations can be interpreted in a consistently meaningful way.

Ratio scales possess all of the qualities of interval scales, exclusivity, logical order, and constant intervals, with the added characteristic that the zero point means that the quality that is being observed is missing. For instance, if a basketball coach is keeping track of how many baskets each player makes each game, an observation of zero for a player means that that player did not make any baskets that game.

In addition to the scale used, scoring methods also differ in terms of the objectivity of the scoring procedure. **Objectivity** refers to the degree to which an observation or score is free from the bias of the scorer (Phillips, 2000). Objectivity is related to the amount of judgment exercised during the scoring process. In general, as the amount of judgment required by the scorer increases, the objectivity decreases. Objective scores result when there are precise rules for scoring a particular observation. For example, the rules governing the scoring of multiple choice tests are clearly determined in advance; if the correct response is selected, the student receives credit, otherwise he or she doesn't. Subjective scores result when the rules are less precise and require the scorer to exercise judgment. Scoring student projects, papers, or portfolios often requires a great deal of judgment and so the results are less objective.

> **What actions can you take to increase the objectivity of your classroom assessment?**

Reliability of Scores.   **Reliability** is a characteristic of data and refers to its consistency. If the same observation and scoring techniques were used to gather data from the same group of students twice, the scores from the second observation should be similar to the first. The greater the degree of similarity between the two sets of scores, the more reliable the data. The reliability of scores affects the confidence with which teachers can interpret the scores. The more reliable the scores, the more confident they can be that a second measurement would lead to the same interpretation.

It is important to note that the reliability of scores is a matter of degree. Almost any observation results in data with some degree of reliability. Typically the reliability of scores derived from a test is expressed in terms of a number between zero and one, and may be low (less than 0.80), moderate (between 0.80 and 0.90), or high (0.90 or higher) (Murphy & Davidshofer, 2001). It is also important to note that reliability is not the same as accuracy (Rogosa, 2001). Suppose a person who actually weighs 200 pounds steps on a bathroom scale and the scale reads 150 pounds. The person then steps off and on the scale, and it reads 150 pounds a second time. The data from the scale is very reliable, i.e., consistent, but it is not accurate.

You may ask, what good is reliable data if it is not accurate? Expanding on the previous example, another person steps on the scale and it reads 100 pounds. If the data from the scale is reliable, then you could confidently say that the second person weighs less than the first person. The same idea can be applied to assessments of academic achievement. If the data from a mathematics test are reliable, then teachers can make some decisions about which students have more mathematics knowledge and skills than others, even if they cannot say exactly how much knowledge or skill any particular student has.

Sources of Error and Reliability.   Unintended variations in the way observations are made or scored are referred to as **error** and negatively affect the reliability of data. In general, the more sources of error, the less reliable the data. Variations in the way tests are administered is one source of error. Such variations include the actions of the teacher while the students are taking the test or something as simple as the time of day that the test is given. Variations in the scoring process represent another threat to the reliability of data. Personal characteristics of the scorer, such as bias or even fatigue, can be sources of error affecting reliability.

What is the relationship between the objectivity of scoring procedures and reliability?

Improving Reliability. As noted previously, variations in the way observations are made or scored can have a negative effect on the reliability of data. One way to address this potential source of error is standardization. **Standardization** is the process of developing careful guidelines for administering and scoring assessment tasks and may include the provision of special training in how to make and score observations objectively. **Standardized tests** are tests that have been standardized; they have strict rules that are followed when the test is administered and scored, and frequently the persons who administer and score these tests have had special training.

Another way to increase the reliability of data is to increase the number of data points making up an observation. In other words, a test composed of twenty well-written questions is likely to be more reliable that one composed of ten well-written questions. Likewise a score based on two essays, presentations, or projects is more reliable than a score based on a single essay, presentation, or project.

Analyzing Observations and Finding Patterns in the Data

Previously, analysis was defined as looking for patterns. In this section, several statistical concepts and techniques are discussed that are useful in analyzing the data you collect in your classrooms.

Frequency Distributions. The concept of the frequency distribution is key to finding patterns in data. A **frequency distribution** is a display of how many observations were made in each category or for each score. Creating a frequency distribution shows how many individuals share a particular characteristic. Frequency distributions may be presented as a table or in a graphic form. Graphic representations of frequency distributions include bar graphs and distribution curves. Figure 13.2 provides examples of frequency distributions represented as tables, bar graphs, and frequency curves.

The tables shown in Figure 13.2 show the score or characteristic in the left-hand column and the number of observations in the right-hand column. If appropriate, the scores or categories may be arranged in either ascending or descending order. Sometimes it is convenient to arrange the observations into groups called *intervals,* as shown in the right-hand table in Figure 13.2. The selection of the most appropriate interval is something of an art. If the interval selected is too small or too large, the patterns in the data will be obscured.

When creating graphic representations of frequency distributions, the horizontal axis denotes the category or score and the vertical axis represents the number of individuals who fall into each category. Graphs *a* and *b* shown in Figure 13.2 are examples of bar graphs. The chief advantage of bar graphs is that they are easy to construct and can accommodate any type of data. Graph *c* is an example of a frequency curve. Frequency curves represent the continuous nature of the observations and are usually only used with large data sets.

Frequency distributions allow teachers to inspect and detect important patterns in data. For instance, inspecting graph *a* of Figure 13.2 shows that there are more children in first grade than in ninth grade, and that there may be a trend of increased enrollment in lower grades. This may cause a school administrator to do a more thorough analysis to determine if there will be a need for more junior high classroom space in the future.

Describing Frequency Distributions. A complete description of a frequency distribution requires consideration of three characteristics: (a) central tendency, (b) variability,

FIGURE 13.2
Representations of
Frequency Distributions

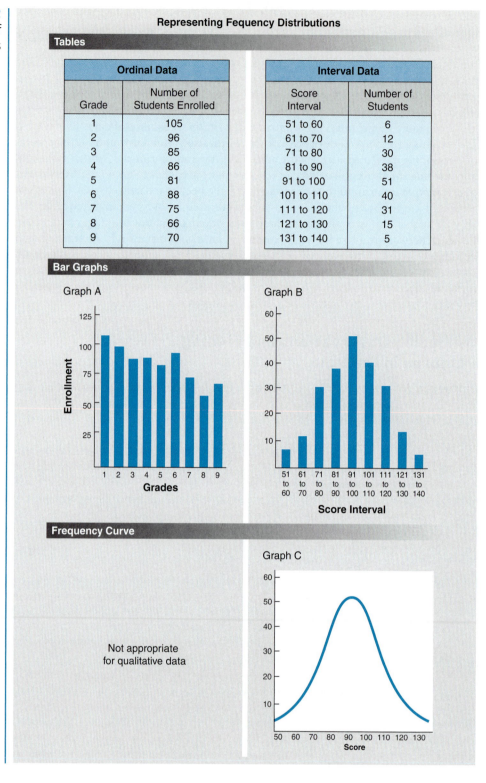

Representing Fequency Distributions

Tables

Ordinal Data		Interval Data	
Grade	Number of Students Enrolled	Score Interval	Number of Students
1	105	51 to 60	6
2	96	61 to 70	12
3	85	71 to 80	30
4	86	81 to 90	38
5	81	91 to 100	51
6	88	101 to 110	40
7	75	111 to 120	31
8	66	121 to 130	15
9	70	131 to 140	5

Bar Graphs

Graph A

Graph B

Frequency Curve

Not appropriate
for qualitative data

Graph C

and (c) shape. These descriptive statistics are briefly described in this section. These statistics are important for communicating observations and for making comparisons among different data sets.

Central Tendency. Description of central tendency is useful when describing data organized along ordinal, interval, or ratio scales. Three statistics are commonly used to describe central tendency: mode, median, and mean. The **mode** of a distribution is the most frequently occurring observation in the distributions. The mode is easy to find and can be used for all types of scales. The disadvantage is that sometimes the mode isn't really in the center of the distribution. For instance in graph *a* of Figure 13.2, there are more children in first grade than any other, and so that is the mode. Although this may be a useful observation, it doesn't really describe the center of the distribution.

The **median** of a distribution is the score that divides the distribution in half. If there are one hundred observations in the frequency distribution, then fifty of the observations will be less than the median and fifty will be greater than the median. The median for graph *a* of Figure 13.2 is between fourth and fifth grade. Half of the students are in first through fourth grade and half of the students are in fifth grade or above. In graphs *b* and *c*, the median is a score of 95.6. As you can see, the median is closer to the center of the distribution. The median also has the advantage of not being influenced by a few high or low scores. The disadvantage of the median is that because it is difficult to manipulate in a mathematically meaningful way, it is difficult to use in more advanced analyses.

The **mean** is basically the average of score for a set of observations and is the most frequently used statistic for describing central tendency. In part, this is because the mean is frequently the basis for more complex statistical analysis. The main disadvantage of the mean is that it may be strongly influenced by a few very high or very low scores.

Variability. The variability of a distribution refers to the amount of variation among the data points of a set of observations. The simplest statistic describing this variation is the range. The **range** of a distribution is simply the difference between the highest and lowest scores. In the distributions shown in Figure 13.2, the range of grades shown in the left-hand table and graph *a* is eight. The range of scores for the right-hand table and graphs *b* and *c* is eighty-nine. The range of a distribution has the advantage of being easy to calculate and easily understood. However, the range has limited utility for later analyses.

The **variance** is another statistic used to describe the variability of a distribution. The variance is calculated using the mean and is equal to the sum of the squared differences between each observed score (X_i) and the mean, divided by the number of observations (N).

$$\text{Variance} = \Sigma(X_i - \text{mean})^2 \div N$$

This statistic is useful for many advanced forms of analysis; however, because it is in the form of squared values it may be difficult to interpret relative to the actual student scores.

The most common statistic used to describe the variation of a set of scores is the standard deviation. The **standard deviation** indicates how much scores within a set of observations vary from the mean and is found by taking the square root of the variance. By taking the square root of the variance we are left with a number that can be more easily related to the original students' scores.

The Shape of Distributions. Two factors should be considered when describing the shape of a distribution: modality and skew. **Modality** refers to how many peaks (modes) occur in a distribution. When only one peak occurs, the distribution is referred to as unimodal. If there are two peaks, the distribution is referred to as bimodal. If there are more than two peaks, the distribution may be described as multimodal. Figure 13.3 shows how both a unimodal and bimodal frequency distribution with the same mean and standard deviation. The modality of a distribution is easily determined by just looking at a graph of a frequency distribution. The observation of a bimodal or multimodal distribution may signal that there are important differences among the persons being assessed.

FIGURE 13.3 The Shape of Frequency Distributions

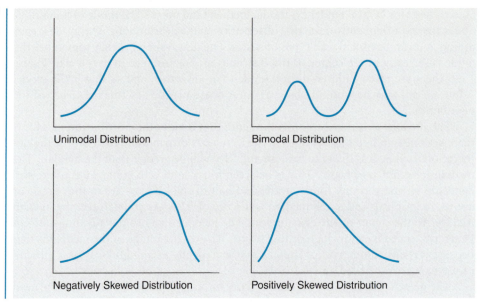

Skew refers to the symmetry of the distribution. Symmetry is the degree to which the portion of the distribution on one side of the mean is similar to the portion of the distribution on the other side. If the distribution appears to be stretched to the low end of the scale of scores, it is said to have a negative skew. If it is stretched to the high end of the scale, the distribution is said to have a positive skew. Figure 13.3 shows examples of distributions with a negative and a positive skew. Please note that a negative skew means there were more scores at the high end of the scale, whereas a positive skew means there are more scores at the low end of the scale. The skew of a distribution can provide useful information about the match between an assessment task and the characteristic being assessed. For instance, skew may indicate that a test was too hard (positive skew) or too easy (negative skew) relative to the ability being assessed. Or it may indicate a change in some characteristic. For instance, in a pretest–posttest situation, you might expect a positive skew on the pretest and a negative skew on the posttest.

What are the three characteristics of a frequency distribution?

The Normal Distribution. Now that the characteristics of frequency distributions have been described, you are ready to learn about a special family of frequency distributions called normal distributions. Frequency distributions from this family are what are referred to when people are discussing the famous (or in the opinion of some, the infamous) bell curve. This section describes the characteristics of normal distributions and the importance of these special distributions to assessment.

You may have noticed in the preceding paragraph that a reference was made to a family of distributions, not a single distribution. This is because the normality of a distribution has to do with its possession of several family characteristics. The family characteristics of normal distributions are as follows:

- The mean, median, and mode are all equal to one another.
- The distribution is symmetrical.
- The inflection point, i.e., the point at which the slope of the curve begins to flatten out, occurs at one standard deviation on either side of the center of the distribution.

Figure 13.4 shows frequency curves for three normal distributions. Notice that each curve satisfies the three characteristics for family membership. Also notice what happens to the shape of the curves as the standard deviation changes. When the stan-

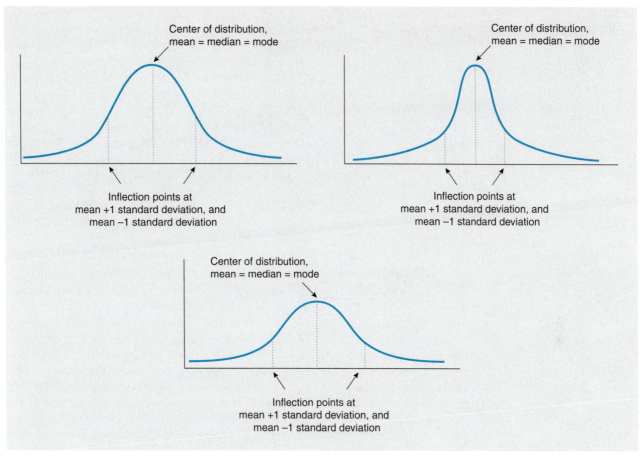

Center of distribution,
mean = median = mode

Inflection points at
mean +1 standard deviation, and
mean −1 standard deviation

Center of distribution,
mean = median = mode

Inflection points at
mean +1 standard deviation, and
mean −1 standard deviation

Center of distribution,
mean = median = mode

Inflection points at
mean +1 standard deviation, and
mean −1 standard deviation

FIGURE 13.4 The Family of Normal Curves

dard deviation is relatively small, the curve becomes tall and peaked. A relatively large standard deviation causes the curve to flatten out.

In assessment, normal curves are important for two reasons. First, when data are collected from naturally occurring populations, the resulting frequency distribution is often a normal curve. In other words, if you were to measure the various heights of a large population of trees, the resulting frequency distribution would be a normal curve. The same can be said for many human characteristics, including measures of mental ability, academic achievement, preference for instructional activities, and any number of other psychological characteristics.

The second reason for the importance of the normal curve is that the proportion of observations that occurs between any two scores is represented by the proportion of the area under the curve between those two points. This proportion is constant for all normal curves and therefore predictable. For instance, for a normal distribution, the proportion of observations that occurs between the mean and a point on the scale one standard deviation from the mean is always 0.3413, or approximately 34 percent. The proportion of observations that occurs between one and two standard deviations from the mean is 0.1359, or approximately 13.5 percent. Figure 13.5 provides a graphic representation of this property. These two properties of normal frequency distributions are important for evaluating data and making decisions.

What three characteristics define a normal distribution?

Describing Relationships. Sometimes educators want to know if different types of observations are related. For instance, a teacher might want to know if a relationship exists between a student's vocabulary and reading comprehension. To check this, the teacher would collect data on students' vocabulary knowledge and their ability to read and comprehend text. The teacher would then try to determine if a pattern existed in the way these two sets of data were related.

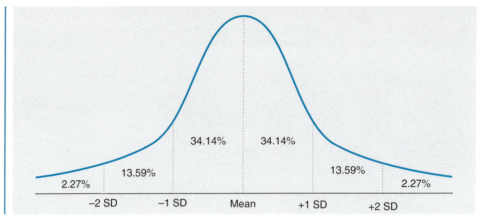

One approach to finding a pattern would be to create a graph called a scatter plot. The **scatter plot** is a Cartesian graph with the scores of one measure on the x axis and the scores for the other measure on the y axis. Figure 13.6 shows a two hypothetical scatter plots. Scatter plot *a* shows a hypothetical relationship between the number of books in a group of students' homes and their grade point average (GPA). Scatter plot *b* shows a relationship between the GPA and television viewing habits for a group of students. Each point on the scatter plot represents one person, and the person's scores can be found by drawing a perpendicular line from each axis through the point. The point where lines cross each axis represents the person's score on that measure.

A **correlation coefficient** is a numerical expression of the strength and direction of a relationship between two measures. The value of a correlation coefficient can vary from −1 to +1. The strength of the relationship is indicated by the absolute value of the correlation coefficient. The closer the value is to either +1 or −1, the stronger the relationship is. The closer the correlation to is to zero, the weaker the relationship.

The value of the correlation coefficient is related to the patterns shown in the scatter plots. A perfect relationship between two sets of observations, indicated by a correlation coefficient of either +1 or −1, would have a scatter plot with all of the data points falling on a straight line. As the correlation coefficient for a relationship approaches zero, the points of the scatter plot become more dispersed. Referring to Figure 13.6, the data points of graph *b* are more closely packed than are the points on graph *a*, indicating that the relationship represented by plot *b* is stronger.

What is the range of possible values for a correlation coefficient?

The sign of the correlation coefficient indicates the direction of the relationship between two variables. Refer again to the scatter plots shown in Figure 13.6. A verbal description of plot *a* would be "In general, as the number of books in the home increases, the GPA also increases." The two variables, books in the home and GPA are positively related. This is indicated by a positive sign on the corresponding correlation coefficient. A verbal description of plot *b* of Figure 13.6 would be, "in general as the hours of TV viewing increase, the GPA decreases." In this case, the two variables, hours of TV viewing and GPA, are negatively related, and the corresponding correlation coefficient has a negative sign.

A correlation coefficient is a valuable measure of a relationship; but it does not mean that the relationship is one of cause and effect. Consider the hypothetical relationship shown in scatter plot *a* of Figure 13.6. If the number of books in a home causes a child to do better in school, then all teachers would need to do to solve the problem of low academic achievement is to place a few cases of books in the homes of students who are not doing well.

A correlation coefficient can also be used to construct a regression line. Plots *c* and *d* of Figure 13.6 are examples of regression lines constructed from the correla-

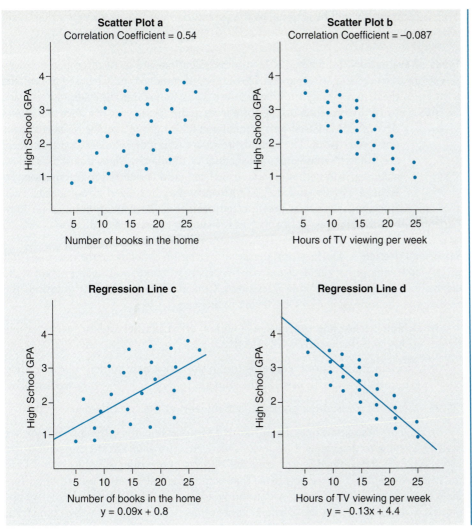

FIGURE 13.6 Scatter Plots and Regression Lines

Scatter Plot a
Correlation Coefficient = 0.54

High School GPA
Number of books in the home

Scatter Plot b
Correlation Coefficient = −0.087

High School GPA
Hours of TV viewing per week

Regression Line c

High School GPA
Number of books in the home
y = 0.09x + 0.8

Regression Line d

High School GPA
Hours of TV viewing per week
y = −0.13x + 4.4

tion coefficients for plots *a* and *b*, respectively. Simple regression lines are defined by a linear equation of the form:

$$Y = bX + c$$

Where Y is the value on the vertical axis, X is a value on the horizontal axis, b is the slope of the regression line, and c is where the regression line crosses the vertical axis. Regression lines allow predictions to be made about the Y variable from an observation of the X variable. For instance, referring to plot *d* in Figure 13.6, if a child watches twenty hours of television per week, it might be predicted that his GPA would be about 2.0. Please note there is no guarantee that predictions such as these are perfect, only that the prediction made using the information about television viewing is likely to be better than a prediction made without that information.

Evaluation and Decision Making

Evaluation is defined as making a judgment based on a rational interpretation of data and other relevant pieces of information. This is the final step in the assessment process. Judgment requires that you select and apply some criterion or standard to the available data. Your selection of a standard affects your interpretation of the data.

Your interpretation will be rational to the extent that it is consistent with other available information.

Types of Evaluation Standards. Classroom evaluations are most often based on observations of students' performances. Three types of standards may be used to evaluate the data resulting from these observations. Sometimes the evaluation is made by comparing students' performances to the average performance of a group. An evaluation based on a comparison with a group average is referred to as **norm referenced.** The second alternative is to judge students' performances according to some preestablished set of standards. An evaluation based on a comparison with a preestablished standard is referred to as **criterion referenced.** Finally students' performances may be judged by comparing each student's performance with their previous performances. An evaluation based on comparison with individual past performances is a **success-referenced** evaluation.

What is the difference between norm-referenced and criterion-referenced tests?

Selecting Criterion. The appropriateness of a criterion depends on the questions you are trying to answer or the decision you are trying to make. So it is important to be clear about the purpose of your assessment. Consider the decisions or questions the teachers in the following cases are trying to answer:

➤ A biology class has just finished a unit on cell structures and the teacher wants to know if the lessons were effective.

➤ An elementary school teacher is trying to place a new student in the reading group that would be best for the student.

➤ A teacher is assigning grades to her students at the end of a marking period.

In each of these situations, the purpose of the assessment is different. The science teacher is trying to determine if his lessons were effective. The effectiveness of the lesson is typically determined by the students' success in reaching the objectives set for the instructional unit. These objectives represent a preestablished standard of performance so a criterion-referenced evaluation would be appropriate. An alternative approach would be to assess the learners' improvement. This would involve comparing students' performance on a pretest to their performance on the unit examination. This approach suggests a success criterion.

Deciding about a new student's placement in a reading group is more complex. To make this decision, the teacher may consider how students with similar reading levels are succeeding with the reading materials she has at hand. The evaluation suggests a norm-referenced criterion.

Under what situations is a criterion-referenced evaluation most appropriate?

The decision involved in the assignment of grades is also complex and requires that the teacher understands what information the grades are intended to communicate to whom. Are the grades meant to communicate a relative standing of the students within the class, or are the grades to communicate a level of mastery of the content? It is also possible that the grades are to communicate some combination of the two alternatives. The first alternative suggests a norm-referenced evaluation, while the second alternative suggests a criterion-referenced evaluation.

Validity of Classroom Decisions

The traditional definition of validity is the degree to which the test measures what it is designed to measure. However, this definition may lead a person to believe that validity resides in the nature and arrangement of the materials comprising assessment tasks such as tests, interviews, or surveys. In Chapter 1 your authors defined *validity* as the quality or the correctness of an explanation or a decision. Messick (1988) defines validity as ". . . an overall evaluative judgment, founded on empirical evidence and theoretical rationales . . ." (p. 33). This definition focuses on the decision-making processes and highlights the importance of a theoretical understanding of learners and classrooms to the assessment process. For teachers, this means that they must consider the nature of learning and learners in their assessments. In other words, when planning assessment tasks or evaluating students' performances, you should start by considering (a) your instructional objectives, (b) how the nature of your instruction is expected to affect students' ability to reach those objectives, and (c) how mastery of the objectives might be reflected in observable performances. The concepts and principles developed in Chapters 2 through 5 should help you in this regard.

Summary of Educational Assessment

The assessment process begins with observation. The choice of observational technique is critical because it determines the characteristics of information you gather and the reliability of the data. The characteristics of the data affect your analysis of the data, the way you evaluate the situation, and ultimately the validity of your decision.

Many different observational techniques are used by educators. In the next sections some observational techniques frequently used in educational assessments are discussed. These observational techniques may be classified into two broad categories: standardized and teacher-made assessment tasks. Standardized assessments are designed by assessment professionals to measure some specific student characteristic. Teacher-made assessments are designed by teachers to make observations more closely related to day-to-day classroom decisions.

Standardized Assessments

To many people, the concept of standardized assessment bring to mind pencil-and-paper exercises where small *bubbles* are filled in with a number two pencil to indicate responses to series of multiple-choice items. However, many other types of standardized assessment tools exist, including interviews, surveys, and personality inventories. Even the famous inkblot tests used in psychoanalytic settings have, to a degree, been standardized by specifying the way these tests are administered, scored, and interpreted (Exner, 1986, 1995; Holtzman, 1968). Remember, standardization is a way to reduce errors associated with the administration and scoring of different types of tests and thereby improve the reliability of the resulting data.

> Standardized tests provide reliable information about student characteristics, which can be used to make decisions about the effectiveness of instructional methods of programs.

Standardized Assessments of Achievement and Aptitude

Achievement and aptitude tests are two types of standardized assessments commonly used by educators. The real difference between an achievement test and an aptitude test has to do more with the decision you are trying to make than with the nature of the items on the test. **Achievement tests** are designed to measure the amount of knowledge or skill a learner has acquired. So an achievement test is looking back to assess the results of past experience. **Aptitude tests** are designed to measure a person's potential. In other words, aptitude tests are looking forward to predict a learner's future performance.

The focus of both achievement and aptitude tests may be general or specific.

Some tests attempt to measure a broad area, such as general academic knowledge or skills, while other tests focus on a narrower domain, such as reading comprehension or mathematics proficiency.

Both achievement and aptitude tests are carefully designed and prepared with specific types of decisions in mind. Test designers consider the age of the potential test takers as well as other demographic variables that might affect the utility of the tests.

What is the difference between an achievement test and an aptitude test?

The reliability of the data derived from these types of tests can be relatively high, in the neighborhood of 0.80 to 0.90 or higher (Impara & Plake, 1998; Cohen & Swerdlick, 1999). When these tests are used appropriately, they generally make a positive contribution to the validity of decisions made.

Reports of Standardized Test Scores

Many standardized tests are designed to be evaluated using norm-referenced criterion. Consequently, students' performances are often reported by converting a student's raw score to some type of norm-referenced standardized score. Several types of scores are commonly reported. Each of these scores provides information as to how well a test taker did with reference to the performance of others who have taken the test.

Percentile Scores. A **percentile score** indicates the percentage of test takers who scored lower than a specific raw score. For instance, suppose a learner completed a test of mathematics achievement and had a raw score of sixty-five. To find the percentile you need to know how many people took the tests, and how many of those scored below sixty-five. If half of the people scored lower than sixty-five, then we would report the learner as scoring in the fiftieth percentile. It is important to stress that the percentile score doesn't say anything about the percentage of items an individual answered correctly; it does report the persons standing in the comparison group.

Grade Equivalents. A **grade-equivalent score** is another type of norm-referenced score, computed by comparing test-takers' raw scores to the average score of children in the same grade level. These scores are intended to allow comparison of a test taker's performance with that of children with similar educational experiences. For instance, a learner who receives a grade-equivalent score of 5.5 is performing as well as an average child who is halfway through the fifth grade. Grade equivalent scores are easily misinterpreted and teachers must use caution when using grade equivalents to make decisions. An example would be if a third grader who has a grade-equivalent score of 4.3 on a test of reading comprehension is not reading at the same level as a fourth grader who has completed three months of fourth grade. What it means is that the student did as well as an imaginary fourth grader who took the third grade reading test.

Z-Scores. A *z*-score reports an individual's score in terms of standard deviations above or below the mean score for some comparison group. For instance, a person receiving a *z*-score of 1.2 on a norm-referenced test has a score that is 1.2 standard deviations above the mean for the comparison group, while a person who has a *z*-score of –1.1 has a score that is 1.1 standard deviations below the group mean. A *z*-score of zero means that the person's score was exactly the same as the mean for the group. Students' *z*-scores are fairly simple to interpret once you have information about the comparison group.

T-Scores. While *z*-scores are relatively easy to interpret, scores that are negative or zero can be disconcerting and difficult to explain to the layman. Some standardized test scores are reported as T-scores. The **T-scores** are derived by converting the scores to a scale that has a mean of fifty and a standard deviation of ten. So a person with a *z*-score of 1.1 would have T-score of 61, while a person with a *z*-score of –1.1 would have a T-score of 49.

Assessment and Group Differences

Psychologists and teachers are concerned with understanding and helping individuals. As teachers we are concerned with providing the best educational experience possible for each individual student in our charge. However, much of the public controversy associated with assessment has been related to the measurement of group differences. These controversies are usually associated with the results of some standardized test. Whenever a test seems to indicate that one group scores higher than another, there are concerns that the test is biased and that the test gives one group an unfair advantage over another. So what do the controversies about group differences mean for teachers?

To answer this question we must first discuss how group differences and individual differences are evaluated. Group differences are typically reported as differences between the means of two groups. It is important to remember that a mean is just a measure of the central tendency of a distribution. To get a clearer idea of what this means, take a look at Figure 13.7.

Figure 13.7 shows the frequency distributions of two hypothetical groups on a standardized achievement test. The figure shows a difference between the means of approximately one standard deviation. One conclusion that someone might draw is that, on average, students in group B score higher on the test than the students in group A. But notice how much overlap exists between the two distributions. Notice that a significant number of individuals in group A scored better than half of the students in group B. This overlap leads to a potential source of error if decisions are made based on group membership. If we assume that a person in group A is less likely to succeed than a person in group B, there is good chance we will underestimate the potential of

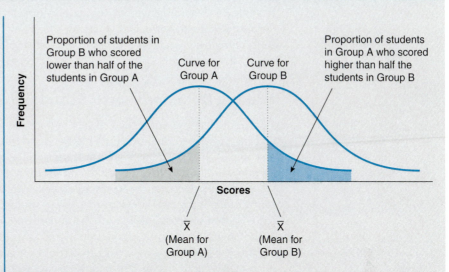

FIGURE 13.7 Frequency Curves with Overlap

one student and overestimate the potential of another. This might result in denying the person from group A an enriched learning experience, or in denying the person in group B the extra help the person may need.

This is frequently the case when groups are compared. Because the variability of scores among members of a group is greater that the difference between the means of groups, usually a great deal of overlap occurs in the distributions. It should also be noted that a full standard deviation difference, between group means represents a large group difference, and smaller differences are more likely. As the difference between the groups' means shrinks, the amount of overlap between the groups increases. This means that decisions made based on group memberships run a serious risk of errors when applied to individuals. As teachers we must be careful not to make assumptions about students based on their race, ethnicity, or gender. We must keep our focus on what each individual student knows and is able to do.

● Why should teachers not use their students' memberships in racial or ethnic groups when making instructional decisions? (For your authors' perspective on this question, go to the text website for this chapter.)

Normal-Curve Equivalents. A **normal-curve equivalent** or NCE score is another type of standardized score that is derived by converting scores to an arbitrary scale. Like T-scores, the NCE scale has a mean of fifty; however, the standard deviation has been set at 21.06. Increasing the standard deviation from 10 to 21.06 ensures that all scores fall between one and ninety-nine. Using the previous example a student with a z-score of 1.1 would have a NCE score of 73.17; and the student with a z-score of −1.1 would have a NCE of 26.83.

Stanine Scores. A Standard nine or **stanine score** is a type of standardized score frequently used to report the results of aptitude and achievement tests. The scores are derived by converting a raw score into single-digit scores ranging from one to nine. Students whose scores fall in the middle of the normal distribution, i.e., between the fortieth and sixtieth percentile, receive a stanine score of five. The remaining scores are evenly distributed every one-half standard deviation above and below the score of five.

Figure 13.8 provides a graphic relationship of each of the standard scores discussed in this section.

Making Decisions with Standardized Tests

While standardized tests can provide valuable information for educational decision making, educators need to understand the nature and limitations of this form of assessment. In particular, it is important to understand how the concepts of reliability and validity apply to the use of standardized tests in schools.

As noted earlier, reliability refers to consistency. Standardized test manufacturers are typically interested in three types of consistency. **Stability** is consistency over time. Consider the issues involved with a standardized intelligence test that yields an IQ of 130 one week and an IQ of 110 the next. This type of inconsistency would make it inappropriate to use that test for important decisions such as which students qualify for a school's gifted program. Standardized test manufacturers typically assess stability by administering a test twice to the same group of students over a period of weeks, and correlating the two scores. This process is referred to as determining **test-retest reliability.**

Equivalence is the second form of consistency that is of interest to manufacturers of standardized tests. **Equivalence** is consistency over forms of a test. In many cases it is useful to have two or more equivalent forms of a test. For example, if a single form of a standardized test is used to determine professional licensure or certification, it is likely that the test questions could get out eventually. Having more than one form of a test would make this less of a concern. To determine equivalence, test manufactur-

FIGURE 13.8 Comparison of Standardized Scores
(*Source:* Adapted from Anastusi, A., & Urbina, S. (1997). *Psychological testing* (7th ed.). Upper Saddle River, NJ: Prentice Hall.)

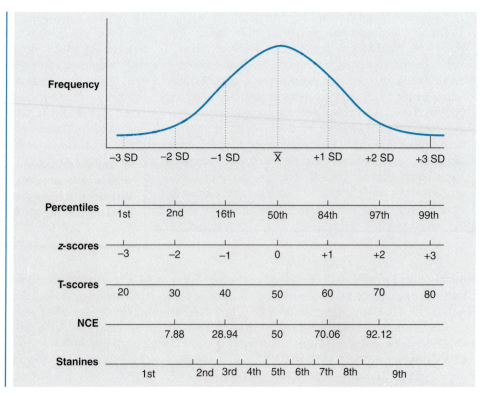

ers administer two different forms of the test to the same students, and then correlate the two scores. This process is referred to as determining **alternate-forms reliability.**

Internal consistency is the final form of reliability. **Internal consistency** is consistency over items on a single test. The question is to what degree do the items on a test measure the same thing? There are multiple ways to compute internal consistency reliability, but one approach is to correlate students' performance on the even items with their performance on the odd items. This approach is referred to as determining **split-half reliability.**

Validity data can be collected for different purposes. In some cases, test manufacturers want evidence that their test assesses the intended psychological or educational construct. For example, does an intelligence test actually measure intelligence as defined by the test manufacturer? This is referred to as **construct validity.** In the case of achievement tests, manufacturers will collect evidence that the test content completely and accurately reflects the academic domain being assessed. For example, does a science achievement test cover key scientific ideas and terms. This process is conducted to provide evidence of **content validity.** Finally, validity evidence can be provided for a standardized test by demonstrating that the test correlates with other measures of the same content or construct, or that the test predicts important nontest criteria. For example, does a college placement examination accurately predict college grade point averages? This is referred to as collecting evidence for **concurrent** or **predictive validity.**

For standardized, norm-referenced tests, it is important to consider the norms provided by the test manufacturer. **Norms** are test performance data that are collected from a group of test takers during the development of a norm-referenced test. This group of test taker is referred to as the **norm group.** The performances of future test-takers are compared to the performance of the norm group. This allows teachers to determine how their students' performances compare to the average performance of the students in the norm group. When selecting individuals for the norm group, test manufacturers try to create a group that is representative of the types of people who will take the test. Consequently, they consider age, sex, ethnicity, SES, and other relevant variables in selecting people for the norm group.

The development and interpretation of standardized tests is a complicated process, and national standards exist that can guide these processes (American Educational Research Association, American Psychological Association, National Council on Measurement in Education, 1999). To safeguard against misuse of standardized, norm-referenced tests, your authors would make the following suggestions:

- Remember that no test is perfectly reliable, and that students' scores could change somewhat if they were retested. Test manufacturers communicate this sometimes by placing **confidence intervals** or score bands around a student's score. A confidence interval provides an estimate of how much people's scores could vary because of error of measurement.
- The validity evidence for a test should support the use of this test for the decision that needs to be made? Tests should not be used for purposes for which they have not been validated.
- The norm group should be representative of the types of people being tested. For example, evidence of appropriateness would need to be provided before a test normed in this country is used with students who have immigrated from other countries.
- Be aware of and consider evidence of test bias. Test bias is a characteristic of some tests that results in systematic errors in the assessment of a particular group. Test bias is a measurable characteristic and information on the bias of specific test may be available from test publishers and independent researchers.
- Fair use of a test has to do with the application of moral and ethical standards. Issues of fairness typically the consequences resulting from the use of tests. These issues are usually resolved through legislative or judicial process, therefore, teachers should be aware of and conform to the laws and legal precedence governing the fair use of tests.

Classroom Assessment

While standardized tests are useful in many situations, for the most part they are unsuitable for the day-to-day assessment needs of classroom teachers (Stiggins, 1985, 2002; Stiggins & Bridgeford, 1985). Consider each of the situations presented below:

➤ Mr. Johnson begins his prealgebra class by giving his students a pretest of math facts.

➤ Mrs. Albright requires her chemistry students to write a report after each completed lab activity.

➤ Ms. Greenway gives her students a test after completing a unit on long division.

In each case, the teacher's goal is to improve learning in the classroom. By gathering information about the concepts and skills that his students have already mastered, Mr. Johnson may be more able to design challenging and effective instruction for his prealgebra students. The lab reports of Mrs. Albright's students allow her to monitor her students' learning and to modify her instruction to correct misconceptions or to take advantage of opportunities to help her students make meaningful connections between the events that occurred in specific labs and important chemistry concepts. Ms. Greenway's unit test also allows her to assess the effectiveness of her instruction so that she may make decisions for improving future lessons and units.

Notice that in each of the situations described, the teacher's decision is based on an assessment of students' specific levels of achievement with regard to a specific content. For the most part, the information from standardized tests would be too general to help the teacher make such instructional decisions.

Classroom assessment is also a valuable source of information that students may use to monitor and regulate the effectiveness of their learning efforts (Brookhart, 1997; Guskey, 2003; Stiggins, 2002). Consider the students in the following situations:

➤ Matt is using the results of Mr. Johnson's pretest to decide what he needs to concentrate on during his study time.

➤ Ellie uses the comments Mrs. Albright has written on her previous lab reports as she prepares a report of the latest lab activity.

➤ As Jill looks over her results on Ms. Greenway's long division test she decides she needs to look over the section on converting fractions to decimals again.

Classroom assessments provide valuable information to the teacher and students that then can be used to improve learning.

Each of these students is using the results of classroom assessment activities to make decisions about and guide their own learning. Matt is using the result of a pretest to assess his own level of understanding and set his own learning goals. Ellie is using feedback on previous lab reports to improve her performance on her next report. Jill is using the results of a test to identify a weakness that she needs to remediate. These examples highlight the importance of effective assessment to the process of metacognition, introduced in Chapter 3, and to learners' ability to self-regulate, discussed in Chapter 4. In other words, effective learners use the results of classroom assessment to improve their learning (Brookhart, 2001), but this is only possible if teachers design and administer effective classroom assessments.

Learning how to conduct effective classroom assessments will provide you with valuable information to improve your decision making in the classroom. There are three steps in the process of creating classroom assess-

Looking in on

When I arrived in Lisa Grambling's classroom, she had just finishing entering grades. She has been my mentor teacher and we have spoken frequently this past year. She must have noticed the concerned look on my face, because she immediately asked me what was wrong. I told her I had heard the other teachers talking about how the standardized test might be used to evaluate teachers' performances. She said that while that happens in some districts, our administration is more sophisticated than that. She pointed out that this test was designed to assess students' achievements and are used to make decisions about individual students. She said that our administrators understand that using this test to assess teacher effectiveness will likely lead to invalid decisions.

I told Lisa that I didn't think that multiple choice tests such as these provided any information that was reliable or meaningful. She smiled and said that actually the data from the test used by the district were very reliable. When I mentioned my concern that I hadn't done anything to prepare my students for the test, Lisa laughed. Since the test items are changed from year to year, nobody really knows what's on the test. She also showed me a copy of a study conducted by a group of researchers from the local university. The report found strong relationships between students' performance on the test and their grades in most of the subjects we taught. She assured me that by teaching my students to be better readers and math problem solvers that I had prepared my students for the test.

I was beginning to feel a little better, but when Lisa told me I would have to explain the test results to parents at the parent teacher conference, I began to panic again. However, Lisa agreed to show me what the scores meant and to give me tips on how to explain them to parents. The percentile scores and T-scores didn't mean what I thought they did. A T-score of fifty really wasn't a bad score; it actually indicates that the student's ability is about average. Lisa explained that the test we used was a norm-referenced test, and that the scores really represented how a student compared with the group, not an absolute level of ability.

Even more interesting was her explanation of something called confidence intervals. Lisa explained that many things may affect a student's test scores and that if we were to give the test again we might get a different score. The **confidence interval** shows the range of possible scores we might expect if we gave the test several times. I'll have to do a little studying before the parent-teacher conference, but I am starting to understand what these scores mean and how they are used.

● **What accounts for the generally high reliability associated with standardized tests of student achievement?**

Decision Point: If you were asked to select a standardized test to assess the achievement of your students, what characteristics would you consider?

---

ments: (a) conceptualization, (b) creation of assessment tasks, and (c) evaluation of the effectiveness of the assessment. Careful attention to each of these steps will help you improve the effectiveness of your own classroom tests.

Conceptualization of Classroom Assessment

The concepts of reliability and validity are not limited to the use of standardized tests, but apply to the design and use of teacher-made assessments as well. The effort you invest in conceptualizing an assessment will have an important impact on the reliability of the data you collect, and on the validity of the decisions you make based on the assessment. In the conceptualization phase of assessment, you must consider the answers to four critical questions:

- Who is being assessed?
- Why conduct the assessment?
- What is the object of assessment?
- How can the object of assessment be observed?

Who Is Being Assessed?   When planning an assessment, you should think about various characteristics of your students and how those characteristics might affect their performance on the assessment task. For instance, you may wish to consider your students' level of maturity, familiarity with assessment procedures, and any special characteristics or circumstances that might affect the assessment process. An assessment of very young students would not work if it required them to sit for fifty minutes. Nor would it make sense to assess your students' understanding of a topic by having them construct a concept map if they had no experience in creating concept maps. And it probably wouldn't make sense to conduct an assessment after some unusually exciting or traumatic event. Failure to consider such factors could result in your students' performance being affected by extraneous factors, resulting in a threat to the construct validity of your decision.

Why Assess?   You may conduct an assessment for a number of reasons:

- You may wish to gather information that will help you plan a lesson.
- You may want to evaluate the effectiveness of a new instructional strategy.
- You may need to assign final grades.

Focus on Learner Diversity
Assessing Special Needs Learners

The education of learners with disabilities is regulated by several federal laws, including the Rehabilitation Act (P.L. 93-112), the Education of All Handicapped Children Act (P.L. 101-476), the Individuals with Disabilities Education Act Amendments (P.L. 105-17), and the Americans with Disabilities Act (P.L. 101-336). These regulations are intended to prevent discrimination that would prevent disabled individuals from reaching their potentials. This regulation extends to the assessment of disabled learners. A test is discriminatory if the test measures the learner's disability instead of ability (Burns, 1998). The exception to this is when the disability is the object of measure. Measurement of disabilities is necessary to diagnose the disability and to track the effectiveness of treatment programs. The guiding idea is that the assessment is conducted in such a way as to result in a valid decision.

Burns (1998) proposes a hierarchy of actions, arranged from least restrictive to most restrictive, to be considered when planning assessment for a learner with special needs. The least restrictive response would be to use the same assessment used for other students, without any accommodations or modifications. This option should always be considered first. There may be many situations in which the validity of the assessment process is unaffected by the disability of a particular student.

If the normal assessment techniques do not allow for a valid decision, then adaptation should be considered. Adaptation involves changing the way the test is administered or interpreted, while maintaining the content and format of the test (Burns, 1998). For example, a learner who has a reading disability may be given more time to complete a test or be allowed to take the test in a quiet location.

The next level of the hierarchy is modification, defined as changes in the format of the test (Burns, 1998). Examples of

modifications might include reading items to the learner taking the test, providing the learner with a large print version of the test, or allowing the learner to use a calculator or dictionary. With modification and accommodation, the changes to the test may affect the validity of the assessment process. The purpose is not to ensure that the learner gets a higher score, but that a more accurate assessment is achieved.

The fourth level of the hierarchy is to find an alternative form of assessment. Burns (1998) describes three situations in which the use of an alternative form of assessment should be used, including (a) when the difficulty of the test is too high, (b) the test's norms are not appropriate for the learner, and (c) the test cannot be modified. For example, assessing the ability of a student who has a developmental delay may require the use of a test designed for younger students, rather then a test matched to the student's chronological age.

The final level in the hierarchy is to exempt the learner from taking the test altogether (Burns, 1998). While there may be some situations that warrant this response, this should be the last resort. Not assessing the learner may be also result in discrimination by denying the learner access to a normal education.

The validity of assessment is the primary concern whenever planning assessments for the special needs learner. Remember, assessments are intended to aid in decision making, which requires the most accurate information possible. The purpose of the decisions should always be to do what is best for the learner.

> ● **How might adapting and modifying a standardized test affect the validity of decisions made based on that test? (For your authors' perspective on this question, go to the text website for this chapter.)**

You may even have multiple purposes for conducting an assessment. In any case, you should always consider whether the data gathered will be helpful to your decision-making process. Failure to keep the purpose of the assessment in mind as you gather, analyze, and evaluate data, represents another threat to the construct validity of your decision.

What Is Being Assessed?   The object of assessment is what you are trying to assess. Typically, this is some mental or physical characteristic of the learners, such as level of conceptual understanding, the mastery of a mental or physical skill, the learners' degree of physical strength or coordination, or perhaps even the learners' attitudes toward some topic or activity. In answering the question of what is being assessed, you are trying to ensure the content validity of your assessment. Bloom's taxonomy is a useful way to understand different types of instructional objectives and objects of assessment.

Bloom's Taxonomy of Cognitive Objectives.   Bloom and his colleagues (1956) developed a classification system for instructional objectives in the cognitive domain. Subsequently, similar work was done for the affective and psychomotor domains (Harrow, 1972; Krathwohl, Bloom, & Masia, 1964). The work of Bloom and his colleagues with objectives within the cognitive domain has come to be known as Bloom's taxonomy. The original purpose of Bloom's taxonomy was to facilitate communication among educators in terms of the nature of their objectives, test items, and assessment procedures (Seels & Glasgow, 1998). The taxonomy consists of a hierarchy of levels of understanding from most simple, the knowledge level, to the most complex, the evaluation level. The five levels of Bloom's taxonomy are listed in Table 13.2, along with examples of student cognitive processes associated with each level.

What are the five levels within Bloom's taxonomy?

Although Bloom's taxonomy is well known and often used, it has not been without its critics (Martin & Briggs, 1986; Postlewaite, 1994). Critics have noted that the levels in the taxonomy are not mutually exclusive. This makes categorizing objectives and test items consistently a problem. The same objective or item often is placed at different levels within the taxonomy by different raters. Your authors encountered a possible explanation for this issue when constructing Table 13.2. The same process descriptions and terminology seemed appropriate at different levels in various descriptions of the taxonomy. Finally, the assumption of a hierarchy has also been questioned. A hierarchy implies a progression, with lower levels forming a foundation or prerequisite for higher levels. This may not always hold true, and the taxonomy may be more of a set of categories than a hierarchy.

Although these criticisms have merit, Bloom's taxonomy still can be useful to teachers. Its primary usefulness is in reminding teachers to plan for levels of understanding beyond simple recall (Smith & Ragan, 1993). This is possible to do without worrying about placing objectives or test items in one of the five categories.

TABLE 13.2   Bloom's Taxonomy of the Cognitive Domain

Level of Understanding	Typical Activities
Evaluation	Judges, appraises, contrasts, criticizes, justifies, supports, discriminates
Synthesis	Puts together, combines, categorizes, rearranges, relates, summarizes, organizes
Analysis	Breaks down, subdivides, infers, illustrates
Application	Performs, solves
Comprehension	Understands, paraphrases, gives examples
Knowledge	Defines, lists, recalls, matches, labels

Assessment Plans. An **assessment plan** defines how each instructional objective will be assessed. Different levels and types of objectives may be assessed using different types of assessment tasks. For instance, a science teacher might assess students' knowledge of science facts and principles by giving the students a test, while students' ability to apply facts and principles would be assessed by having the students plan and execute a lab activity. The creation of an assessment plan will help you coordinate different types of assessment activities over time.

What is a table of specification and what is its purpose?

Careful planning should also be applied to the construction of teacher-made tests. One way to plan tests is to create a table of specifications before the test is written. A **table of specifications** is a two-way chart that details the combination of content and level of the instructional objectives that are being assessed and how many test items will address each such combination (Linn & Gronlund, 2000). Figure 13.9 provides two examples of tables of specifications.

Using Bloom's taxonomy to create an assessment plan and tables of specifications is a useful technique for ensuring alignment between instructional objectives, and the way students' mastery of those objectives is assessed. These techniques will help ensure that you measure what you've taught, thereby enhancing the content validity of your assessment and therefore the quality of decisions based on the assessment (Nimmer, 1984).

What questions should a teacher answer when planning a classroom assessment?

How to Assess? Finally, you must decide the best way to observe the object of assessment. All assessments consist of requiring the students to complete an assessment task and then observing and evaluating their performance. Your choice of assessment task will influence the construct validity of your subsequent decisions. Different types of assessment tasks will generate different types of information, which in turn will be more or less useful, depending on the decision you are going to make. In addition, assessment tasks may vary in terms of their potential to contribute error to

FIGURE 13.9 Examples of Two Tables of Specifications

Table of Specifications for a Unit on World War I

Content	Objectives		
	Knows Names, Dates, and Terms	Understands Causes of World War I	Number of Items
Politics	12	10	22
Culture	5	5	10
Technology	8	10	18
Number of items	25	25	50

Table of Specifications for Unit on Basic Punctuation

Content	Objectives		
	Knows Rules	Applies Rules	Number of Items
Periods	1	5	6
Question marks	1	5	6
Commas	2	8	10
Colons	1	4	5
Semicolon	2	6	8
Number of items	7	28	35

Looking in on

Susan Decatur

13.1

I met with Ralph today to discuss how to assess the learning of my students. Ralph suggested that a good first step was to think about exactly what types of knowledge I want my students to have, and what kinds of student performances would give me evidence about that knowledge. For instance, a test score may provide good evidence of my students' knowledge of certain facts about physics, such as laws, formula, and constants, but other types of evidence may be required if I want to know about their ability to use these concepts to design experiments, analyze data, and solve problems.

Ralph and I looked over my objectives and the kind of assessment activities I had used and decided that in general a combination of tests, lab reports, and projects was appropriate for assessing what I wanted my students to learn. However, these activities needed to be improved to better assess my objectives.

Ralph noted that the objectives for my units and for individual lessons were pretty clear. However, there wasn't always a real clear connection between the lesson objectives and the tests or other assessment activities. Ralph referred to this as alignment and after looking at last year's grade book, he noted that when the tests were closely aligned with my lesson objectives the class averages on the tests were also higher.

As we began to examine my tests and unit plans more closely, we realized that some lesson objectives were not tested at all. Also, there were objectives implied by the items that I really hadn't considered when I was planning my instructional activities. I found that these items were generally the ones that were most likely to give the students trouble. We also noted that the extent to which a concept was covered in class was not reflected in my tests. I might have spent two days working on a single topic and then on the test asked few questions that related to that topic. At other times, concepts that were given only brief coverage in class were covered extensively on the test.

I decided to look at how well my other class assignments aligned with my unit objectives. Ralph suggested that I create a table of specifications for each of my instructional units. He suggested that I should include all of my objectives and assessment tasks in the table of specifications. He loaned me a textbook on assessment that showed how a test blueprint might be constructed. It seemed like a good tool that would help me organize my thinking about more than just the way I assessed my students' learning.

● **What is the relationship between the kind of knowledge that students are acquiring and the way that knowledge may be assessed?**

Decision Point: Why is alignment an important consideration when planning instruction and assessment?

---

the assessment process. This means that the choice of assessment task also has implication for the reliability of the resulting data.

Collecting Information in Classrooms

The purpose of an assessment task is to elicit some type of performance from a learner to evaluate the learner's understanding, skill, or mental state. Teachers use a variety of tasks for this purpose. Pencil-and-paper tests, writing assignments, projects, and performances (in and out of the classroom) are all examples of tasks that teachers have used to assess their students' levels of achievement. Each of these techniques has advantages and disadvantages depending on the nature of the learners and what aspect and type of learner characteristic the teacher wishes to assess.

Tests. Pencil-and-paper tests are the most common types of assessment tasks used by classroom teachers. Pencil-and-paper tests may be composed of a variety of different test items, including multiple choice, true or false, matching, short-answer items, or essays.

Pencil-and-paper tests have the important advantages of flexibility and efficiency. Pencil-and-paper tests may be tailored to assess a variety of educational outcomes. Tests are flexible in that the tests can be constructed to provide useful information about learners' ability to recall facts, their understanding of concepts, and their ability to apply-knowledge to the analysis and solution of problems. The efficiency of

What are the advantages and disadvantages of tests as a means of gathering information on student achievement in the classroom?

pencil-and-paper tests results from their ability to collect information simultaneously from all the students in a class.

Pencil-and-paper tests also have two disadvantages. First, while tests are time efficient, classroom time constraints may limit the variety and complexity of tasks that a student might reasonably be expected to complete. The second disadvantage is the emotional response of some students to the test situation. Many students feel some anxiety in a test situation. For most students this anxiety is not a problem, but for a few students, high levels of anxiety may interfere with their performance on the test.

Tests may be characterized by the types of test items that make up the test. Two broad categories of items are: (a) alternative response and (b) constructed response. Each type has advantages and disadvantages. Table 13.3 provides a summary of the characteristics of various types of test items.

Alternative Responses.　**Alternative response items** include multiple choice, true or false, and matching items. With these items the learner is presented with two or more possible responses and must select the response that is correct.

Alternative response items have a number of advantages for classroom teachers, including the following:

- The students' responses are objectively scored.
- The item format is adaptable to a wide range of educational outcomes and can efficiently assess breadth and depth of understanding or skill.
- The responses require few special skills unrelated to the object of measure.

As was previously discussed, objectivity refers to the degree to which the procedures for scoring or classifying responses are free from observer bias. The rules for scoring alternative response items are pretty straightforward; if the specified response was selected, then it is classified as correct, otherwise the item is classified as incorrect. Because scorer judgments are more or less eliminated as a source of error, the relative objectivity of these types of items contributes to the overall reliability of the data collected.

The criticism is often made that alternative response items can only be used to measure trivial types of learning outcomes associated with the lower levels of Bloom's taxonomy, such as learners' ability to recognize isolated facts. However, Lukhele, Thissen, and Wainer (1994) concluded, after comparing alternative response items

TABLE 13.3　Characteristics of Test Item Formats

Alternative Response			
Form	**Uses**	**Advantages**	**Disadvantages**
Multiple choice Matching True or false	May be used to assess knowledge of and the ability to apply facts, concepts, and rules	Objective scoring leads to improved reliability Allows assessment of breadth and depth of students' knowledge	Construction of good items is difficult and time consuming Security Guessing

Constructed Response			
Form	**Uses**	**Advantages**	**Disadvantages**
Short answer Fill in the blank Computations Essays	May be used to assess knowledge of and the ability to apply facts, concepts, rules, or skills	Flexibility in student responses provides an opportunity to assess students misconceptions Allows assessment of breadth and depth students' knowledge	Because of potential flexibility of student responses, scoring these items may be more subjective than alternative response items

with other types of test items, that alternative response items assessed the same characteristics as other types of test items and did it more efficiently.

Alternative response items can be adapted to measure a wide variety of educational outcomes and can even be written to help teachers detect some common misconceptions. The most common example of this would be a multiple choice mathematics question, with alternatives presented that correspond to the answers a student would find if specific mistakes were made during the solution process. The same idea can be applied to other educational domains. The primary limitation to the adaptability of alternative response items is the experience and creativity of the person writing the test items.

The final advantage of these items is that the students require few special skills to respond to the items. In other words, the learners' responses don't depend on an unrelated skill such as writing. This means that the item provides a cleaner indication of the students' understanding of the concept or skill that is the object of measure.

While alternative response items provide a useful tool for gathering information about what students know or can do, several disadvantages exist:

- Effort and skill are required to write good alternative response items.
- The security of the test items must be maintained.
- Guessing on items can cloud the assessment of learning outcomes.

The primary disadvantage of alternative response items is related to the difficulty of writing good test items. In general, this difficulty increases as more complex forms of performance and higher cognitive functions are measured. Matching and true or false items are relatively easy to write, but tend to measure fairly low levels of learning. Multiple choice items can be used to measure effectively higher levels of cognitive function, but providing plausible alternatives can be difficult, requiring high levels of domain knowledge and creativity on the part of the teacher.

Because of the effort required to create good alternative response items, they are typically used repeatedly. This means that the teacher must be concerned with the security of the items. The value of these items as an assessment tool is voided if students have access to the items and can just memorize specific responses to specific items. Taking steps to prevent students from obtaining advanced access to test items, such as not allowing students to keep and study from old examinations, may be offensive to some students and may have a negative effect on the psychological climate of the class and student motivation. One partial solution is the creation of a test bank. Alternative forms of tests can then be constructed using items from the bank. However, this requires a test bank with many more items than will appear on a single test, adding to the amount of work involved.

Guessing is another problem with alternative response items, especially with true or false items. Cunningham (1998) suggests three partial solutions to the guessing problem. The first is to ensure that students have a reasonable amount of time to respond to each item. Students are more likely to guess if they feel rushed. The second solution is to increase the number of items on the test. As the number of items on the test increases, the effect of a correct guess on the overall test score decreases. The third suggestion is to ensure that the items that make up the test are written at an appropriate level of difficulty. If a student finds a test too difficult, he or she is more likely to guess.

What are the advantages and disadvantages of alternative response tests?

Constructed Response. **Constructed response items** include short answer, computation, and essay items. Short answer items vary in terms of the length of the response from a single word to a few phrases or sentences to an entire essay.

Constructed response items have two main advantages:

- Item format is adaptable to the assessment of a wide range of educational outcomes.
- These items provide definite information about what students know or can do.

As with alternative response items, constructed response items may be used to assess a variety of educational outcomes. Short answer items can effectively measure students' knowledge of facts and terminology. Computation items can assess students' ability to appropriately apply a skill or problem-solving technique. Essay items may be used to assess higher levels of Bloom's cognitive hierarchy such as students' ability to synthesize and evaluate ideas.

Since a student is not cued by the available alternatives, the student's response is a direct indication of what the student knows or can do. In addition, since the students are not constrained by the available responses, incorrect answers may give valuable diagnostic information about their misconceptions.

The primary disadvantage of constructed response items is the degree of subjectivity associated with the scoring of students' responses. **Subjectivity** is the opposite of objectivity and is the degree to which a score, classification, or rating is dependent on the judgment of individual scorers. The judgment of different scorers is an additional potential source of error and may lead to a decrease in the reliability of the resulting data.

Even short answer items, unless they are carefully written, may be difficult to score objectively. Consider the question, "When did the Japanese attack Pearl Harbor?" A student might correctly answer, 1941, December, on a Sunday, or in the morning. Which answer would you accept as correct, and how would you defend your decisions to the students who gave one of the other answers? With computation problems the difficulty comes in deciding if or how to award partial credit for imperfect responses.

The problem of subjectivity is especially acute with essay items. Scores of essay items may be affected by biases related to:

- The scorer's expectations for specific students
- The degree of correspondence between the opinions expressed in the essay with those of the scorer
- Penmanship, grammar, or organization style of the respondent
- The mood of the scorer as it is affected by fatigue or emotional responses to the essays of other students

The subjectivity associated with scoring essay items reduces the reliability of your data; however, careful construction of test items and prior planning of how the items will be scored can reduce scoring error.

Three steps can be taken when scoring constructed response items to control or reduce the error associated with scoring. The first is to develop and use a scoring rubric. A **scoring rubric** is a plan for scoring a response. It should include the elements of an ideal response and the relative importance or point value of each element. Second, you should arrange the responses in such a way as to hide the names of the student whose paper you are grading. This helps reduce the possibility that your personal opinions of individual students might influence your scoring. Finally, you should grade by item and not by student. That is to say you should grade all of the responses to a particular item, before you grade responses to any others. This reduces the influence of fatigue and helps you maintain a uniform standard for scoring each item.

In addition to subjectivity, essay items have two other disadvantages. The first is that student responses are heavily dependent on their ability to write. This means that student responses are a combination of what they know and how they write. A student

What are the advantages and disadvantages of constructed response tests?

may know the information you are trying to assess, but be unable to produce a good answer because of poor writing skills. This problem is made worse by the time constraints of testing situations. The second disadvantage of essay items is the limited breadth of coverage possible in the available test time. While the depth of students' knowledge of a specific topic may be assessed with an essay, you cannot assume that the depth is uniform across a subject area. Variation in students' previous knowledge and motivations are likely to result in students knowing and understanding more about some aspects of an instructional unit than others. Students who do well on one essay may not have done as well on a different essay question, while those who did poorly may have done better.

Writing Test Items and Preparing Tests. A good test can provide you with reliable information that will help you make decisions in your classroom. Preparing a good test depends on your knowledge of the content and of your students and your skill as a test writer. The skills required to write a good test, like all skills, are only acquired slowly with practice. In this section, some guidelines are presented that will help you get started.

Guidelines for Writing Alternative Response Items. Alternative response items consist of a stem, or in the case of matching items, a premise, and several choices of responses. The stem may be a statement, definition, or description of a problem. The responses consist of a correct response and one or more distracters listed after the stem. In the case of true or false items, the responses may or may not be listed. For matching items the premises and responses may appear in separate columns.

To ensure that students' responses provide useful information, you should be careful to relate each item to a meaningful learning objective. Test blueprints are useful for this purpose. You should also avoid writing items that simply require the students to recall trivial or rotely learned information. In addition to failing to provide useful information, the inclusion of trivial items may have a detrimental effect on your students' motivation toward your tests and the content you are teaching.

You should also do your best to ensure the items are clearly and unambiguously written. This means you should avoid double negatives, broad generalizations, or sentence structures that are overly complex. Do not include extraneous information in the stem or premises of the item. Avoid ambiguity in the responses by keeping them as short as possible. This may be accomplished by including as much information as possible in the stem or premise. Responses such as none of the above or all of the above should be avoided.

Finally, you should be careful not to give hints or clues that aid in guessing. For instance, sophisticated test takers can often eliminate responses because of a grammatical mismatch with the stem or differences in response length. Don't include implausible responses among the choices. Be careful that hints or clues for an item do not occur in other items. For matching items make sure there are more responses than there are premises.

Guidelines for Writing Constructed Response Items. Although the format of constructed response items differs significantly from alternative response items, some of the same guidelines apply. It is still important that items be matched to meaningful learning objectives and to avoid writing items that test the rote recall of trivial information.

Ambiguity should also be avoided when writing constructed response items. For short answer items make sure each item is a clearly stated question or problem statement. For completion, avoid leaving too many blanks, and if possible the blank should be situated at the end of the statement. When preparing essay items use words, such as *compare, contrast, predict*, and so forth, that clearly indicate the type of response that is required.

While you will not have to write responses and distracters for constructed response items, it is still important to consider what types of answers you would accept. In cases in which the response is clearly divisible into distinct parts, you might also consider if or how you will award partial credit. You may find that considering the ideal response will indicate how an item might be rewritten so as to be clearer.

Guidelines for Preparing Tests. When composing the test, you should arrange the items in a logical way. The test may include a number of different item types. Since you will need to include separate instructions for each type of item format, you should group all items of similar format in sections together. Within a section you should group items covering similar content together. Finally, you should arrange items by difficulty, with the easier items occurring first.

Projects and Performance in Assessments. In addition to classroom tests, teachers may assess their students' learning by assigning projects or having the students engage in some type of classroom performance. Properly planned projects and classroom performance can provide the teachers with unique information about their students' capabilities. We define a **project** as a complex assessment task, of which part or all of the activity occurs outside of the classroom. The result of a project may be a poster, science project, report, or some other artifact. The quality and content of the artifact provide an indication of each student's knowledge or skill.

Performance-based assessments also involve the performance of a complex task, but they are different from a project in that the basis for assessment is the observation of the student's actions during the performance. Examples of performance-based assessment tasks might include classroom presentations, athletic performances, role-playing activities, or any activity that can be observed and rated by the teacher. This means that performance-based assessment must occur where it can be observed by the teacher.

Using projects and performances as a basis for the assessment of learning is sometimes called alternative or authentic assessment. **Authentic assessment** involves the creation of assessment tasks that are as similar as possible to the situations outside of the classroom, for which the students would need to use the knowledge and skills they have learned.

Projects and performance assessment tasks share many of the characteristics, advantages, and disadvantages of constructed response test items. Project and performance assessment tasks are adaptable to the assessment of different educational outcomes and provide direct information about what students know or can do. In addition, performance assessment tasks are especially useful for assessing students' skills.

Projects and performance assessment tasks also have some disadvantages. As with constructed response items, projects and performance assessments also have the problem of subjectivity. The methods for dealing with the subjectivity of constructed response items may be adapted for use with projects and performance assessments. In addition to subjectivity, projects and performance assessments have some unique disadvantages. Because much of a project may be performed outside of the classroom, there is the potential that the artifact produced does not solely represent the knowledge and skills of the student. Parents, siblings, and other students may assist the student in the completion of the project. This is especially true if the project requires resources or skills that are beyond those available to the average student. A performance may be influenced by individual differences in students that are not the object of measure. For instance, a student's performance when making a speech or presentation to the class may be affected by a personality characteristic such as extroversion.

When selecting an assessment task you need to consider many factors: the nature of your students, why you are conducting the assessment, what your are trying to measure, and the time and resources available. You must keep an open mind when making your selection. Use your judgment and select an assessment task that is most suited to your situation.

> **What are the advantages and disadvantages of projects and performances as assessment tasks?**

> **Performance assessments are especially useful for gathering information about students' skills.**

Evaluating the Effectiveness of Assessment

The final step in the creation and use of classroom assessments is the evaluation of the assessment technique. For this evaluation you are trying to determine whether the assessment technique resulted in information that was reliable and made a positive contribution to the validity of your decision.

For tests the evaluation usually begins with an item analysis. A basic item analysis looks at the difficulty of the items, the ability of items to discriminate the knowledge or skill being assessed, and unusual patterns of responses.

Susan Decatur

13.2

It has taken me a while, but I now have table of specifications for each of my instructional units. It has been a good exercise; I had to consider what things I wanted my students to learn, and what evidence I needed to prove to myself, and others, that they had actually learned it. Now I need to actually design the assessment tasks. I had decided to keep the unit tests and lab reports, and I have decided to have the students complete two class projects instead of one.

One of the problems I had with the lab reports and projects was consistency in grading. I wasn't always clear about what a good lab report or project looked like. The test blueprint helps a little, but it is not nearly specific enough. I've decided that I need to create some scoring rubrics for these activities. This is easier for the lab reports because I am looking for similar things for each lab, and the students are basically all reporting on the same thing. Coming up with a rubric for the project is a little more difficult, because the students each pick their own projects.

In the past, I have used short-answer items on my unit tests. These items work really well for assessing the students'

ability to apply laws, principles, and formulae to solve problems. However, responding to these short answer items can take a long time, which really limits the amount of concepts I can cover in a single test. To increase the coverage, I will try to incorporate some multiple-choice items into my tests. I know that writing good items can be a challenge, but if I can develop a test bank, I can save some time in the long run. Having a test bank of items will also allow me to check my performance from year to year and the effectiveness of changes to my lessons.

Preparing my assessment plan and assessments has been a lot of work, but I think that it has really improved my lessons, and I think it will improve my effectiveness as a teacher.

● **What is the relationship between the types of assessment tasks and the reliability of the data obtained?**

Decision Point: What should you consider when you are deciding what types of assessment tasks to include in your assessment plan?

Item difficulty is assessed by looking at the proportion of students who responded correctly or incorrectly on an item. Items that seem too easy or too hard may not be measuring what you intended and are candidates for further analysis.

The discrimination is a little more difficult to determine. One simple method is to compare the performance of students with overall high scores with the performance of students with overall low scores. To accomplish this, the students' tests or papers are placed in rank order from highest to lowest. Then two groups are formed one of high performing and the other of low performing students. If the number of students in the low performing group correctly responded to an item, as often or more often than the students in the high performing group, the item may not be assessing what you think it is and should be looked at more carefully.

Unusual difficulty and discrimination may indicate that an item is in need of improvement. To see what is actually going on, you need to inspect the item itself and look for patterns in the way students are responding. Sometimes such an inspection will reveal ambiguous wording that you missed when preparing the item. You may even find that the students developed a common misconception because of the way the information was presented.

What useful information can be gathered by an item analysis?

Making Decisions in the Classroom

As noted in the previous sections of this chapter, teachers make many decisions. Many of these decisions are made after a quick and informal assessment of the situation. However, when the stakes are high, it is wise to use a more deliberate and formal assessment. The stakes are considered high, when the decision is likely to have a far-reaching or profound impact on the students affected. While teachers may make a variety of decisions that qualify as high stakes, there are four types of decisions that routinely qualify and include (a) decisions about student placements, (b) diagnostic decisions, (c) decisions about instructional effectiveness, and (d) reports of student progress and achievement.

Placement Decisions

Decisions that attempt to match a student with the most beneficial program of study are called **placement decisions.** Typically, information is gathered about a student's knowledge, skills, or aptitudes to match them to a specific program. The decisions to place a child in a special education or gifted and talented program are examples of placement decisions. Data for these decisions may be gathered using standardized tests, interviews, or assessment tasks designed for a specific class or school. These decisions are typically not the sole responsibility of classroom teachers, but are made by school administrators on the recommendation of counselors or school psychologists.

Diagnostic Decisions

Diagnostic decisions are decisions about the existence and extent of learner disabilities that might affect the student's learning. This type of decision is related to placement decisions in that the ultimate goal is to provide an optimal learning experience for the child. However, unlike placement decisions, a diagnosis is typically made using data from multiple types of observations. For instance, when diagnosing a learning disability, information from several different psychological assessments as well as a physical examination may be used. Although diagnostic decisions are not made by classroom teachers, they often occur because a classroom teacher has referred a student for evaluation based on observations made in class. In these cases, the teacher's observations are a valuable source of information for the school psychologist or doctors making the assessment.

What is a diagnostic decision?

Assessing Instructional Effectiveness

Teachers also use formal assessments to evaluate and improve their instruction. Assessments made for this purpose are often referred to as **formative assessments.** The object of assessment is the students' current level of understanding or skill on a specific instructional topic. This information is then used to modify or plan instruction to optimize the learners' academic achievement, or by students to monitor and regulate the effectiveness of their study strategies. Student progress is typically evaluated relative to the instructional objectives established by the teacher. For this reason, formative assessments typically depend on information gathered using assessment activities designed by the teacher for the specific class. In class tests and quizzes, homework assignments, papers, student projects, and presentation may all provide data that can be used for a formative assessment.

What is the purpose of formative assessments?

Reports of Student Progress and Achievement

Finally, teachers make decisions about how and what to report about students' performance. Often this decision is made based on the students' performance over an extended period of time on many different assessment tasks (McMillan, Myran, & Workman, 2002). It is also common to collect data using an assessment designed to measure the learner's final mastery of concepts or skills taught. Assessments made for this purpose are called **summative assessments** and are typically made at the end of an instructional sequence.

The primary purpose of these reports is to communicate information about students' performance briefly and concisely. The information in your reports may be used to help a variety of people make different decisions. Consider how the information

Today I met with Larry Coble, the school psychologists, to discuss two of my students. The first student we discussed was Edward. Larry and I had had some problems with Ed earlier in the year. He seemed to become easily frustrated in class and was falling behind the other students. Larry said that it was possible that Ed had a learning disability and suggested that we conduct a formal assessment. After discussing the matter with Ed's parents, it was decided to go ahead with the evaluation. In addition to tests of mental ability, Ed also had a medical examination that revealed that he had a vision problem. Ed's parents scheduled an appointment with an optometrist and he now wears glasses. When Larry asked me how Ed was doing in class, I was happy to report that Ed was doing much better. Larry said that Ed's test result confirmed my observation, and that Ed's problem seemed to be solved.

The second student Larry wanted to discuss was Linda. Linda is bright and friendly but in the beginning of the year was always getting into trouble. Part of the problem was that she always finished the assignments ahead of her peers, so I always try to have extra work to keep her busy. This strategy seems to be working because Linda now rarely gets into trouble. Larry noted that Linda's test scores put her in the ninety-ninth percentile of all students who took this achievement test. Larry suggested that perhaps Linda should be in a class for gifted children. He suggested that we should contact Linda's parents to get permission to conduct some additional testing.

Hana Saad
13.2

● **What information, in addition to that provided by standardized tests, would you want if you were making a placement decision?**

Decision Point: What other types of decisions might be aided by information from norm-referenced testing?

about students' performance and achievement might influence the decision making in the following situations.

> ➤ Mrs. Cohen, the assistant principal, must decide which students should receive special recognition for their academic performance.

> ➤ Ms. Franklin, an advisor at a community college, must decide if a student is ready for college level work, or should instead be advised to take remedial mathematics and literacy courses.

> ➤ Mr. and Mrs. Drukker are trying to decide whether their son Eddie needs a tutor to help him through his seventh grade science class.

> ➤ Carl must decide if his current learning strategies are sufficient for him to succeed in his high school French class or if he should join a study group.

In each of these situations, grades are being used to aid specific decision-making processes. Mrs. Cohen is comparing students' performance to decide who has shown the highest level of academic achievement. Ms. Franklin is trying to place a student in course work that will maximize the student's success in college. Mr. and Mrs. Drukker are trying to determine what type of support they should give their son to improve his chances for success. Carl is trying to determine the best way to study.

Reporting Formats.   The primary purpose of these reports is to communicate information about students' performances briefly and concisely; but however reports are made, it is important to remember the purpose of the report is to improve student learning by assisting others' decision making (Linn & Grondlund, 1995). Traditionally, reports have been made in the form of a letter grade; however, other reporting formats are available, each with its own advantages and disadvantages.

The letter grade system has the advantage of being familiar to anyone who has had any significant contact with the public schools in the United States. In addition, because letter grades are readily converted to numeric equivalents, it is relatively easy to represent a student's overall performance by calculating an average.

Portfolios are an effective way to communicate students' progress over time.

Familiarity with this reporting system does not guarantee consistent interpretation. Part of the confusion results because the system does not separately identify the contribution of motivation, development, or learning to students' performance. For instance, in the case of Mr. and Mrs. Drukker, from the preceding section, does a D grade indicate that their son was not motivated to do his best, or does it mean that he is developmentally unready to deal with the concepts presented in the seventh grade science class?

Inconsistencies in the application of a criterion for assigning letter grades is another factor contributing to confusion about the meaning of grades. Are letter grades a norm-referenced indicator of performance or do they indicate a level of mastery to some fixed criterion? Some schools define a C as indicative of an average level of performance. In other words, the grades are norm referenced. Since statistically we are all average, it would be expected that most students would receive a C. Letter grades of B or A are reserved for those students whose performance indicates an exceptional mastery of the content. A D indicates performance that was below average and an F indicates a more or less complete failure to master the content. In other schools, the letter grade may have a criterion-referenced connotation. In these schools an A indicates complete mastery of a topic. Lower grades indicate successively less complete mastery of academic content.

Pass-fail is another reporting option that has been used in some schools. This system has a clear criterion-referenced interpretation, either the content was mastered or it was not. However, this system suffers from of the same disadvantage as traditional letter grades in that the effects of learning motivation and development cannot be separated. In addition, there may be uncertainty about what level of mastery is required for a pass. For those students receiving a fail, the system does not convey any information about how much effort or additional instruction would be required for achieve a pass.

Checklists of objectives provide a third option for reporting students' performance. The checklist report consists of lists of objectives with an indication of how the student is doing with respect to each objective. This system is flexible and informative and provides teachers and school administrators with information useful for their decision-making needs. However, the complexity makes record keeping something of an administrative chore. Communication of information to persons outside of the school may also be a problem. Parents, college admission officers, or even educators in other school systems may not have clear understandings of the meanings of the objective statements.

Any reporting system represents a compromise with different advantages and disadvantages. As a teacher, you must become familiar with the system used in your school and do your best to be consistent in its application.

Communicating Reports. Students' performances may be communicated in a number of ways. These include the traditional report cards, letters to parents, portfolios, and parent-teacher conferences. Report cards typically employ one of the systems previously discussed: letter, pass-fail grades, or checklists of objectives.

Letters to parents and others outside of the school system provide another means of reporting on students' performance. Reports presented in letters are not required to follow a set of rules associated with more formalized reporting systems. The teacher is free to comment on the students' level of skills in various areas, motivation, and developmental progress. However, letters are time consuming. Preparing a letter requires time to reflect and plan what you want to say.

Portfolios provide a third option for reporting on students' performance and progress. A **portfolio** is a collection of artifacts produced by the student intended to communicate the student's level of accomplishment in some area (Stiggins, 1997). A portfolio need not include every piece of work produced by the student, and the student should participate in the selection of the contents for the portfolio. The contents should provide a record of the student's development or progressive mastery in a particular domain. Portfolios provide an effective way to communicate the student's strengths and weaknesses to parents and others making educational decisions.

While portfolios may be an effective way to communicate some kinds of information, several disadvantages exist. The primary disadvantage is that reviewing a portfolio may be time consuming (Wolfe & Miller, 1997). Consider the case of Mrs. Cohen trying to decide which students should receive special recognition. Looking through fifty or one hundred portfolios is a time-consuming process.

In addition, since great variation may exist across portfolios, the final decision is likely to be highly subjective and influenced by the biases of the reader. This characteristic brings into question the fairness of basing educational decisions on portfolios and, in the case of high-stakes decisions, the legal defensibility of decisions made using portfolios (Mauck & Veichnicki, 1994).

Parent-teacher conferences are the fourth means of communicating students' performances. These conferences allow teachers to elaborate on the information presented in traditional report cards (Linn & Gronlund, 1995). Teachers can explain the specific factors that contributed to a particular grade and parents are able to ask questions to clarify their understanding of formal and limited grading systems. See Chapter 12 for suggestions about parent conferences.

As you can see from this discussion, you will be making many decisions as part of your day-to-day professional life. To make these decisions you will use information gathered by both informal and formal observations of your students' performances. When the stakes are high, you will want to take steps to ensure that you make the right decision for each student by using a more formalized approach to assessment. Careful planning, collection, and analysis of information will help ensure the reliability of your observations and the validity of your decisions.

What is a portfolio?

Principles into **Practice:**
Illustrating Key Concepts

In this chapter you looked in on Hana Saad and Susan Decatur as they dealt with issues related to assessment. Each time you returned to look in on these two teachers, you were asked to answer questions about their application of ideas from this chapter. Here are your authors' answers to these questions.

Looking back on

Hana Saad

When you first met Hana Saad she had several concerns about the standardized tests that had been administered to her third graders and how they would be used. She expressed a lack of confidence in standardized multiple choice tests. In addition, she was worried about how her students' performance on the test might affect her teaching career. Her concerns have to do with the concepts of reliability and validity. Reliability had to do with the consistency of the data derived from a measure. The more reliable the data from a test, the more confidence you can have in the data. In the case of commercially produced standardized tests, there is strong evidence for the reliability of data if the test is administered and scored correctly.

Validity is a characteristic of a decision. Again, when standardized tests are constructed, considerable effort is made to determine the expected validity of a specific decision made based on data from the test. Any changes in the type of decision being made may result in a decision that is less valid. In Hana's situation, the test was designed to aid educators to make decisions about the overall achievement of individual students. Using the data from such a test to make decisions about teacher effectiveness is clearly a different type of decision and should not be done.

Hana is also concerned about how to interpret the data she receives on her students' performance. When Hana meets with her mentor teacher, her mentor explains that the test is a norm-referenced test. This means that the scores are based on a comparison with a group average. Hana's mentor explains how to interpret the various scores that are provided with the test results and about the confidence interval for these scores. The confidence interval is a range of scores that reflects the learner's true ability on the measure. The confidence interval is derived from the reliability of the test data. When the reliability is high, the range of possible scores is narrower.

When next you look in on Hana Saad she had met with the school psychologist, this time to discuss placement and diagnostic decisions of two students. Norm-referenced tests are appropriate for both of these situations. A diagnosis, even a medical diagnosis, is based on detecting patterns of abnormalities. A common definition of *normal* is how much the characteristics of an individual differ from a group average. Norm-referenced measures are able to detect how far an individual's characteristics vary from the group average. The same logic applies to placement decisions. These decisions are based on detecting students who are achieving significantly above or below the average of their peers. Again norm-referenced tests are well suited to these decisions. ●

Looking back on

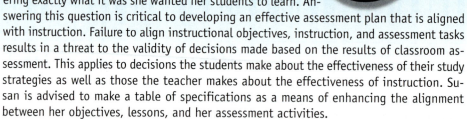

Susan Decatur

Susan Decatur is a physics teacher who is preparing for the coming school year by revising and improving her assessment plan. When you first looked in on Susan she had just met with a more experienced teacher and was considering exactly what it was she wanted her students to learn. Answering this question is critical to developing an effective assessment plan that is aligned with instruction. Failure to align instructional objectives, instruction, and assessment tasks results in a threat to the validity of decisions made based on the results of classroom assessment. This applies to decisions the students make about the effectiveness of their study strategies as well as those the teacher makes about the effectiveness of instruction. Susan is advised to make a table of specifications as a means of enhancing the alignment between her objectives, lessons, and her assessment activities.

When next you looked in on Susan she was considering the nature of specific assessment tasks such as labs and lab reports. These activities can be classified as constructed response or performance assessment activities. A common problem with these assessment tasks is the reliability of the data they produce. Susan decides to address this problem by developing detailed scoring rubrics. Scoring rubrics reduce unintended differences in the way a teacher scores from one student to the next. Reducing error in the scoring process enhances the reliability of the data. When Susan considers the items on her test, she observes that although constructed response items allow a more natural assessment of students' problem-solving and reasoning skills, they take a lot of time. This means that the number of concepts or skills covered by a single test is limited. This may be a problem, because she may not be able to assess all of the objectives listed on a test blueprint, resulting in another threat to the validity of her and the students' decisions. To strike a balance between depth and breadth of coverage, she decides to incorporate multiple choice item tests into her assessment plan. ●

Teachers as Decision Makers

As the cases of Hana Saad and Susan Decatur were presented, you were asked to participate in the decision-making processes. At this point your authors present their views on these decisions.

Hana Saad's Decision Points

The case of Hana Saad deals with the nature and use of standardized tests. One of the questions that teachers frequently face is what if anything they should do to prepare their students for standardized tests. A criticism of standardized tests is that some teachers teach to the test. If teaching to the test means providing students with the answers to specific items on the test, then that will likely reduce the validity of any decisions made using data from the test. Given the nature of most commercially available standardized tests, it seems unlikely that teachers would have access to the kind of information that would allow them to provide answers. An alternative definition of teaching to the test is having students practice the kind of test items they are likely to encounter on the test. This may actually be effective instruction for certain kinds of content. For instance, practicing syllogisms and analogies may actually help students develop the mental skills these types of test items measure. To the extent that such mental skills transfer to other tasks in a useful way, this may actually be a good instruction.

After reading about Hana's meeting with her mentor teacher, you were asked to consider what you would look for if you were selecting a standardized test for your school. When selecting a test, you should consider the expected reliability of the data the test is likely to provide and whether the data will enhance the validity of the decision you are trying to make. The manufacturers of standardized tests typically provide information on the reliability of their tests and recommendations and evidence that the data from these tests enhance the validity of certain types of decisions. The information on validity should tell you who the test was designed to assess. When selecting a test, it is important that the sample of people, called the norm group, that was used to develop the test **norms** be as similar as possible to the people who are to be tested. Significant differences between the norm group and the population of people who are to take the test, in terms of characteristics such as ethnicity, age, or gender, may affect the reliability of the data and the validity of decisions based on the test results.

At Hana's meeting with the school psychologist, she found out how the information from the tests was used in making decisions about placing students in special programs. You were asked to consider what other types of decisions might be made using norm-referenced tests. Norm-referenced tests can provide information that can enhance the validity of both placement and diagnostic decisions. The utility of the test in the situations depends on how well the test matches the decision you are trying to make. Once again you need to consider the norm group that was used during the construction of the test and how well it matches the students you are assessing. You must also consider the psychological characteristic the test is designed to measure, and whether this characteristic is relevant to your decision.

Susan Decatur's Decision Points

After introducing Susan Decatur, you were asked to consider what role assessment plays in effective classroom instruction. The improvement of any performance is dependent on accurate information about the contributions that specific techniques and strategies make toward reaching specific goals. The effectiveness of these techniques and strategies is determined by how close they get us to our goals. This same sort of reasoning applies to teaching. Teachers make choices about what and how to teach. To assess the effectiveness of these decisions, they must assess the consequences as they relate to their instructional objectives.

After Susan met with Ralph, the chemistry teacher, she began to consider the alignment between her instructional objectives and her assessment activities. You were asked to consider why alignment was important. Classroom assessment serves several purposes. First, it provides the teacher with specific information about the effectiveness of the lessons. Classroom assessment also provides information to the students about the effectiveness of their efforts toward learning in the class. Finally, classroom assessment provides the information that allows the teacher to assign grades. In each case the decisions made, whether by the teacher, students, or school administrators, are based on the students' achievement of the classes' instructional objectives. If tests and other assessment tasks are not aligned with these objectives, the information they provide is of no help in making these decisions.

As Susan prepared her table of specifications she began to consider what types of assessment tasks would provide her with the most useful information. You were asked to consider the types of assessments that you might use in you own future classroom. The answer to this depends most heavily on what you are trying to teach. If your objective is that your students acquire conceptual knowledge, then pencil-and-paper assessment tasks are probably a good choice. If your objectives include the application of mental or physical skills, then you should design assessment tasks that use the target skills.

Name _____ Date _____

Chapter 13 Study Guide

Use this Study Guide to review and test your knowledge of key concepts introduced in this chapter and to search out further information on issues and topics raised in this chapter.

 Key Terms

Review the following key words from the chapter and then connect to Research Navigator (www.researchnavigator.com) either directly or through this book's Companion Website to explore research on the topics as they relate to education today.

Achievement tests (p. 447)
Alternate-forms reliability (p. 451)
Alternative response items (p. 458)
Aptitude tests (p. 447)
Assessment plan (p. 456)
Assessment task (p. 436)
Authentic assessment (p. 462)
Concurrent validity (p. 451)
Confidence intervals (p. 451)
Constructed response items (p. 459)
Construct validity (p. 451)
Content validity (p. 451)
Correlation coefficient (p. 444)
Criterion-referenced evaluation (p. 446)
Diagnostic decisions (p. 464)
Equivalence (p. 450)
Error (p. 438)
Formative assessments (p. 464)
Frequency distribution (p. 439)
Grade-equivalent score (p. 448)

Internal consistency (p. 451)
Interval scales (p. 438)
Mean (p. 441)
Median (p. 441)
Modality (p. 441)
Mode (p. 441)
Nominal scales (p. 437)
Normal-curve equivalent (p. 449)
Norm group (p. 451)
Norm-referenced evaluation (p. 446)
Norms (p. 451)
Objectivity (p. 438)
Observation technique (p. 436)
Ordinal scales (p. 437)
Percentile score (p. 448)
Performance-based assessments (p. 462)
Placement decisions (p. 464)
Portfolio (p. 467)
Predictive validity (p. 451)
Project (p. 462)
Range (p. 441)

Ratio scales (p. 438)
Reliability (p. 438)
Scales (p. 437)
Scatter plot (p. 444)
Scoring (p. 436)
Scoring rubric (p. 460)
Skew (p. 442)
Split-half reliability (p. 451)
Stability (p. 450)
Standard deviation (p. 441)
Standardization (p. 439)
Standardized tests (p. 439)
Stanine score (p. 450)
Subjectivity (p. 460)
Success-referenced evaluation (p. 446)
Summative assessments (p. 464)
T-score (p. 448)
Table of specifications (p. 456)
Test-retest reliability (p. 450)
Variance (p. 441)
z-score (p. 448)

Alternative Response Items

Multiple Choice

1. Ms. Palacio is concerned because a test of learning styles yields different scores when it is administered repeatedly to the same students. What concept is most closely related to Ms. Palacio's concern?

    a. Reliability
    b. Validity
    c. Standardization
    d. Test bias

2. A set of scores is normally distributed, and they range from 2 to 22. The mean of the distribution is 16. What is the mode of this distribution?

    a. 20
    b. 22
    c. 16
    d. It cannot be determined from the information provided.

3. Which one of the following correlation coefficients represents the strongest level of relationship between two variables?

    a. 0.67
    b. −0.10
    c. 0.82
    d. −0.98

4. What type of evaluation compares a student's performance with the average performance of a group?

    a. Group-referenced
    b. Norm-referenced
    c. Criterion-referenced
    d. Success-referenced

5. Tests designed to measure a person's potential are referred to as _____ tests.

    a. Achievement
    b. Personality
    c. Aptitude
    d. Projective

6. Joann scored at the fiftieth percentile on a standardized achievement test. What is the best interpretation of Joann's score?

    a. Scored at a level better than or equal to 50 percent of the norm group.
    b. Answered 50 percent of the test items correctly.
    c. Is below average when compared with other students.
    d. Is well above average compared with other students.

7. Which level in Bloom's taxonomy represents students' ability to break down a problem into its component parts?

    a. Knowledge
    b. Comprehension
    c. Analysis
    d. Synthesis

8. What is the major goal of authentic assessments?

    a. To create assessment tasks that are similar to real-world situations
    b. To create assessment tasks that are as objective as possible
    c. To reduce the need for the use of scoring rubrics
    d. To standardize performance-based assessments

9. What term refers to the ability of a test item to differentiate between students who know material well and students who know the material less?

    a. Item difficulty
    b. Item discrimination
    c. Item objectivity
    d. Item clarity

10. Ms. Gill uses in-class assignments, class discussions, and quizzes to determine if she needs to modify her instruction. What term best describes this assessment situation?

    a. Diagnostic
    b. Placement
    c. Formative
    d. Summative

Constructed Response Items

Short Answer/Completion Items

1. An activity or assignment designed to elicit a performance from learners is called a(n) _____.

2. When there are two peaks in a frequency distribution, that distribution is described as being _____.

3. Tests that measure the amount of knowledge or skill that a student possesses are referred to as _____ tests.

4. Which stanine would a student be in who scored at the fiftieth percentile?

5. In Bloom's taxonomy, factual recall is at the _____ level.

Essay Items

1. Consider the following instructional objectives. For each, what type of assessment activity would you recommend? Explain your rationale.

   a. The learner will identify the chemical symbol for commonly occurring elements.
   b. The learner will identify the similarities and differences between the American and French revolutions.
   c. The learner will read and comprehend texts written at a third grade level.
   d. The learner will compose complete sentences.
   e. The learner will correctly bunt.

2. Describe the students in your first class, identify the objectives you will have for your students for the first marking period and design an assessment plan for your the objectives you will have for your students.

INTASC in Action

Use the following activities to think about how motivational concepts relate to INTASC Standards.

Standard 8 Assessment. Identify a relevant state standard for your teaching area or level and write an instructional objective that would be associated with that standard. You may wish to refer to the section on instructional objectives presented in Chapter 9. Then:

a. Describe an assessment task that you would use to determine if, or to what degree, your students had mastered the objective.
b. Discuss threats to the reliability of the data this assessment task would generate.
c. Discuss potential threats to the validity of your assessment of your students' level of master, associated with this assessment task.

Standard 9: Reflective Practice and Professional Growth. Select three principles presented in Chapters 2 through 6. Discuss how assessment can help you apply these principles more effectively.

Standard 10: School and Community Involvement. Describe a grading system that you are familiar with. Discuss how the advantages and disadvantages of this system might impact the decisions of students, parents, other educators, and people outside of the school system.

Web Resources

No Child Left Behind Testing Requirements (U.S.D.O.E.)
http://www.nclb.org/
Obtain all the latest information on this landmark educational program, including a Toolkit for Educators and much more.

Gender Bias and Fairness in Testing from ERIC Digest
http://www.ericfacility.net/ericdigests/ed328610.html
Read an article on ERIC discussing gender bias in education and its potential impact on opportunities for men and women.

Constructing Tests
http://www.ericfacility.net/ericdigests/ed398236.html
This ERIC article provides valuable suggestions for writing multiple choice items.

Eisenhower National Clearinghouse Classroom Assessments
www.enc.org/topics/assessment/classroom/
This education topics page provides articles in which teachers share their ideas on classroom assessment.

Center for the Support of Teaching and Learning
http://cstl.syr.edu/cstl/t%2Dl/assess2.htm
The Center for the Support of Teaching and Learning at Syracuse University provides information and links to practical information about classroom assessment.

Center for the Excellence in Learning and Teaching
www.psu.edu/celt/Lowe.html
This page provided by the Center for Excellence in Learning and Teaching at Penn State University presents suggestions for the use of assessment to enhance learning.

$\mathcal{A}$ppendix: Study Guide Answers

CHAPTER 1

Answers to Alternative Response Items

1. b	5. c	9. a
2. b	6. a	10. c
3. d	7. b	
4. d	8. a	

Answers to Short Answer/Completion Items

1. Implicit
2. Psychological constructs
3. Predictive accuracy, internal consistency, external consistency, unifying power, fertility
4. Problem identification, data gathering, decision making, and action

CHAPTER 2

Answers to Alternative Response Items

1. b	5. b	9. a
2. a	6. c	10. d
3. d	7. d	
4. a	8. a	

Answers to Short Answer/Completion Items

1. Natural reinforcer
2. Discrimination
3. Activity reinforcer; Premack principle
4. The teacher's yelling is serving as a positive reinforcer for the misbehavior.

CHAPTER 3

Answers to Alternative Response Items

1. a	5. b	9. a
2. c	6. a	10. a
3. b	7. c	
4. a	8. c	

Answers to Short Answer/Completion Items

1. Knowledge in working memory is represented by chunks of declarative knowledge.
2. Elaine has the information stored as a temporal string, and it is difficult to retrieve in any other order.
3. The review may aid learning in three ways: (a) activating previously learned information may aid the selective perception of new information, (b) activating previously learned information makes it available for elaborating the new information, and (c) activating the new information provides an opportunity for rehearsal.
4. All of them, selective perception, retrieval of relevant prior knowledge, encoding, and compilation.
5. Working memory because of its limited capacity and duration.

CHAPTER 4

Answers to Alternative Response Items

1. c	5. d	9. a
2. b	6. a	10. b
3. a	7. d	
4. c	8. c	

Answers to Short Answer/Completion Items

1. Reciprocal determinism
2. Forethought
3. Outcome expectations
4. Specific, proximal, and challenging at an appropriate level

CHAPTER 5

Answers to Alternative Response Items

1. a	5. a	9. c
2. b	6. b	10. d
3. a	7. a	
4. b	8. b	

Answers to Short Answer/Completion Items

1. Object permanence
2. Identity
3. Scaffolding
4. Social constructivism

CHAPTER 6

Answers to Multiple Choice

1. b	5. b	9. a
2. c	6. c	10. c
3. a	7. a	
4. b	8. a	

Answers to Short Answer/Completion Items

1. Mastery goal orientation and performance approach goal orientation
2. Self-actualization, aesthetic and intellectual needs
3. Affiliation motive
4. Variety, novelty, complexity, and surprise
5. Mastery goal orientation

CHAPTER 7

Answers to Alternative Response Items

1. a	5. c	9. d
2. c	6. a	10. a
3. a	7. c	
4. b	8. a	

Answers to Short Answer/Completion Items

1. Instructional technique
2. Time

3. Students are asked what they already know about a topic
4. Cognitive modeling
5. Discrepant event

CHAPTER 8

Answers to Alternative Response Items

1. c	**5.** c	**9.** d
2. a	**6.** d	**10.** a
3. b	**7.** a	
4. d	**8.** b	

Answers to Short Answer/ Completion Items

1. This is an example of deductive teaching.
2. Spanish and Latin share many identical elements.
3. This is an example of a derived structural schema.
4. Inductive learning
5. Negative transfer

CHAPTER 9

Answers to Alternative Response Items

1. c	**5.** d	**9.** b
2. a	**6.** c	**10.** d
3. c	**7.** a	
4. b	**8.** e	

Answers to Short Answer/ Completion Items

1. Learning hierarchy analysis
2. Performance analysis

3. Enhancing retention and transfer of learning
4. The use of knowledge of development and learner characteristics to inform instructional design decisions
5. Attention, relevance, confidence, and satisfaction

CHAPTER 10

Answers to Alternative Response Items

1. b	**5.** b	**9.** a
2. a	**6.** a	**10.** c
3. c	**7.** d	
4. d	**8.** b	

Answers to Short Answer/ Completion Items

1. Target error
2. Overlapping
3. Computer time
4. Goal setting
5. Authoritative leadership model

CHAPTER 11

Answers to Alternative Response Items

1. a	**5.** d	**9.** a
2. c	**6.** b	**10.** a
3. d	**7.** d	
4. c	**8.** b	

Answers to Short Answer/ Completion Items

1. Positive manifold
2. Contextual subtheory

3. Child find
4. Modifications
5. Type II

CHAPTER 12

Answers to Selected Response Items

1. a	**5.** a	**9.** b
2. c	**6.** c	**10.** c
3. c	**7.** c	
4. a	**8.** d	

Answers to Short Answer/ Completion Items

1. Goodness of fit
2. Adolescent egocentrism
3. Morality of care
4. Gender constancy
5. Culturally responsive teaching

CHAPTER 13

Answers to Selected Response Items

1. a	**5.** c	**9.** b
2. c	**6.** a	**10.** c
3. d	**7.** c	
4. b	**8.** a	

Answers to Short Answer/ Completion Items

1. Assessment task
2. Bimodal
3. Achievement
4. Fifth
5. Knowledge

Glossary

Abstract modeling When people create a principle or generalization from the combined information from several modeling experiences

Academic diversity Refers to the differences in learning skills and approaches that result from individual differences among students

Acceleration Educational approaches that provide early entry for students into educational programs or approaches that involve delivering curriculum at a faster pace than is typical

Accommodation According to Piagetian theory, the act of altering existing schemes based on experience

Accommodations for students with disabilities Changes made in the way students with disabilities are assessed, taught, and disciplined

Achievement motive A desire to complete challenging tasks successfully

Achievement tests Tests designed to measure the amount of skills or knowledge that students have acquired

Action research Teacher initiated, school based research

Active listening A communication skill that involves conveying understanding and acceptance of another person's communication

Activity reinforcer A privilege or behavior that has a reinforcing effect for the learner and that is administered according to the Premack principle

Adaptation From a Piagetian perspective, adaptation consists of the processes (assimilation and accommodation) learners use to develop and refine their schemes

Adjunct questions Questions that are inserted in text or a presentation to help learners focus attention

Adolescent egocentrism According to Elkind, the tendency of some adolescents to become overly self-conscious

Advance organizer Material that is presented before new learning that helps students link new learning with more general and inclusive prior knowledge

Aesthetic needs According to Maslow, the desire to experience beauty and to find or create symmetry or completeness

Affiliation motive The desire to establish, maintain, or restore effective relationships with other people

Algorithm A rule or procedure for solving a problem that when properly applied yields a correct problem solution

Alternative response test items Test items such as multiple choice, matching, and true or false that require learners to select a correct response

Alternative-forms reliability Evidence of the equivalence obtained using alternate-form techniques. Two forms of the same test are given to the same group of people and the scores are correlated

Analogical problem construction Learners are provided with worked examples of problems and asked to create their own examples of these problems

Antecedent A stimulus that precedes a response and that cues learners to behave in certain ways to earn reinforcement or to avoid punishment

Anxiety Cognitive-based emotion that causes students to withdraw from or avoid a person or situation

Applied behavior analysis A systematic approach to planning, implementing, and evaluating a behavior intervention

Aptitude tests Tests designed to measure students' potential

ARCS Keller's four categories of motivational variables (attention, relevance, confidence, and satisfaction)

Arousal potential How stimulating or exciting students find the learning environment

Articulation disorder The atypical production of speech sounds

Artifact A concrete representation of what students have learned during problem-based learning

Assessment plan A document that defines the types of observation techniques that will be used to assess a set of related instructional objectives

Assessment task An activity or assignment designed to elicit a performance from the learner or learners. Part of an observation technique

Assimilation According to Piagetian theory, the act of interpreting experiences in terms of existing schemes

Assistive technology A piece of equipment or product that increases, maintains, or improves the functional capabilities of learners with disabilities

Associative stage The second stage in the skill learning process during which the learner has proceduralized portions of a skill

Attainment value Value attached to a task because learners believe that it is important to do well

Attention (1) In information-processing theory, cognitive process of selecting information from the sensory register for further processing. (2) In social cognitive theory, the component of observational learning concerned with attending to the key elements of modeled behavior

Attention Deficit/Hyperactivity Disorder (AD/HD) A disorder with the primary characteristics of hyperactivity, inattentiveness, disorganization, and easy distractibility

Attitudes Acquired internal states that guide our choices of personal action

Attribution An explanation for the cause of an event that can be described in terms of locus of causality, controllability, and stability

Attributional feedback Feedback that links students' successes and failures to causes of those successes and failures

Authentic assessment Assessment tasks that are as similar as possible to application situations outside the classroom

Authentic learning activities Learning activities that involve a focus on higher level thinking, collaboration among learners, social support for learners, depth of knowledge, and connections to the world outside the classroom

Authoritative leadership style An approach to classroom management that conveys warmth and concern for students while setting clear and firm limits

Autism A developmental disability that can be characterized by impairments in social relationships, peculiar communication patterns, self-injurious behavior, perceptual anomalies, self-stimulation, apparent cognitive deficiencies, aggression, and difficulty with daily living skills (not all of these characteristics apply to all children with autism)

Automaticity The degree to which a skill can be performed without consciously thinking and deciding the step of the performance

Autonomous stage The third stage in the skill learning process in which the compilation of the skill is complete and the skill may be performed automatically

Back-up reinforcers The reinforcers that tokens can be exchanged for in a token reinforcement system

Backward chaining Teaching a behavioral chain by beginning at the last step and ending with the first step

Baseline The preintervention level of a target behavior

Basic Interpersonal Communication Skills (BICS) According to Cummins, the language competencies required for daily living and face-to-face communications

Behavioral fluency The ability to perform a skill quickly and with minimal or no errors

Belonging needs The need for supportive or cooperative relationships with other people

Between-group differences How much members of one group differ on average from members of another group

Big Five General personality traits that encompass the full range of personality descriptors and characteristics

Big Five personality traits General personality traits that can be used to capture a number of commonly observed personality characteristics

Blindness When the vision in a person's better eye is no better than 20/200 even with best correction or if there is a significant reduction in the visual field or peripheral vision

Bottom-up processing Perceptual processes that occur when context does not activate prior knowledge

Branching program Programmed learning during which students progress through the program differently based on their correct and incorrect responses

Centration According to Piagetian theory, the tendency of preoperational children to limit their perception or attention to one aspect of a complicated situation

Chaining The idea that stimuli and responses can connect together to form a sequence of events. It has both teaching and management implications

Character education Educational programs that attempt to develop certain character traits in students

Child abuse The infliction of intentional physical or psychological injuries on children

Child find The IDEA provision that states must locate, assess, and identify students with disabilities between the ages of three and twenty-one

Chronosystem In Bronfenbrenner's ecological theory, the developmental changes or consistency over time in an individual and that individual's social systems

Chunk A packet of declarative knowledge that represents learned information

Chunking Grouping information into larger meaningful pieces to reduce memory load

Circular reactions In Piagetian theory, an infant's behavior creates an environmental effect that motivates the infant to repeat the behavior

Classical conditioning Two eliciting stimuli become connected and now elicit a similar response

Classification In Piagetian theory, the operation involved in grouping objects that share a common characteristic

Classroom management The actions teachers take to establish and maintain a productive learning environment

Classroom procedure A routine way of accomplishing administrative and learning tasks

Cliques Relatively small and tight knit groups of friends who almost exclusively spend time with each other

Cluster grouping A way of organizing classrooms to provide for the enrichment or acceleration of students with academic gifts

Cognitive apprenticeship A cognitive apprenticeship occurs when students' authentic learning experiences are scaffolded by more experienced learners

Cognitive context In skill learning, cognitive context is learners' beliefs about why they are learning a skill

Cognitive modeling The process of a model thinking aloud as the model demonstrates a skill or strategy

Cognitive objective A generally worded objective that is supported by specific behavioral indicators of the desired learning

Cognitive stage The first stage of skill learning when learners form a declarative knowledge representation of a skill

Cognitive strategy A plan of action that is relevant for solving problems Cognitive strategies can also be thought of as internal processes by which learners adapt their ways of attending, remembering, learning, and thinking

Cognitive styles A person's approach to processing information as assessed typically by their performance on laboratory tasks

Cognitive/Academic Language Proficiency (CALP) According to Cummins, the language proficiencies required for academic learning

Comparative advance organizers Advance organizers that present similar or related ideas to new ideas in a lesson to help students compare and contrast the new ideas with other similar ideas in their existing knowledge

Compensation According to Piagetian theory, children's understanding that a change in one dimension can explain the change in another dimension

Compilation Using declarative knowledge in working memory to create new procedural knowledge naturally through practice

Composition The process of combining two or more productions into a single more efficient production representing a more complex skill

Concept A categorical idea that is used to represent a group of items, ideas, or relationships

Concurrent validity Evidence that data from an assessment task correlates with data from other assessment tasks completed at the same time

Conditioned response A response that is elicited by a conditioned stimulus because of the connection between the conditioned stimulus and unconditioned stimulus

Conditioned stimulus A stimulus that through its connection to the unconditioned stimulus now elicits the conditioned response

Conditions of learning Gagné's guidance on how to modify or adapt events of instruction for different types of learning outcomes

Confidence intervals A range of scores constructed around a student's score that provides an estimate of how much the student's scores could be expected to vary given the reliability (error) of observation technique

Consequence A stimulus that occurs immediately after a response and modifies the likelihood of that response

Conservation According to Piagetian theory, children's understanding that quantity is unrelated to the arrangement and/or physical appearance of objects

Construct validity Evidence that the test measures the psychological construct the test was designed to measure

Constructed response test items Test items that require the learner to construct a response such as essay and short answer items

Constructionists Individuals who support technology-based applications that engage students in explorations that produce an external product that can be exhibited, examined, and evaluated by others

Content validity Evidence that the items composing a test provide adequate coverage of the psychological construct or academic domain being assessed

Contiguity learning An eliciting stimulus connects with a response through contiguity, and now the eliciting stimulus automatically elicits that response

Contingency contract A product of negotiations between students and teachers that specifies students' behavioral goals and the consequences for achieving those goals

Continuous reinforcement Reinforcement is provided for every occurrence of a behavior

Controllability The dimension of an attribution relating to whether a perceived cause is contingent (controllable), or not contingent (uncontrollable) on a person's actions

Conventional level of moral reasoning Kohlberg's second level of moral reasoning during which morality is judged in terms of the collective feelings of others

Cooperative learning A small group learning structure that stresses the interdependence of learners in accomplishing a goal

Coping model A model who demonstrates what learners encounter when they are first learning and how they handle the challenges they encounter as they learn

Coping skills approaches Self-management approaches for teaching students to cope with stressful or anger-producing situations

Correlation coefficients A statistic that represents both the direction and magnitude of a relationship between two measures

Criterial tasks The component of the tetrahedral model that describes how learning is assessed

Criterion stimuli The stimuli that must gain control over a response by the time instruction is completed

Criterion-referenced evaluation An evaluation that compares students' performances with a preestablished standard

Cue An instructional stimulus that helps establish stimulus control for the criterion stimulus

Cultural capital The knowledge and experiences students bring to the classroom based on their life experiences within their culture

Culturally responsive teaching An approach to classroom teaching that values the cultural backgrounds of students and helps students value the cultures of others

Culture The dynamic worldview, values, traditions, and political relationships created and shared by a group of people who are connected together by various factors

Curiosity A cognitively based emotion that causes people to engage in exploratory behaviors

Declarative knowledge How our mind represents facts, ideas, and concepts

Declarative knowledge network A model of declarative knowledge storage that represents knowledge organization through a series of nodes connected by lines

Deferred imitation The ability to imitate a model that is no longer present

Deficiency needs Needs that operate on the principle of homeostasis or the maintenance of an optimal state

Dependent group contingency The same expectations are in effect for all members of the group, but certain students' behavior will result in the consequences being applied to the whole group

Derived structural schema A structural schema that is consciously derived or produced by an expert as a learning aid for students

Developmentally appropriate practice An approach for designing classroom learning based on the knowledge of how students learn and develop

Diagnostic decisions Decisions about the types of conditions a student might possess that affect learning

Direct instruction A highly structured and interactive form of teacher-directed instruction that originated out of behavioral learning theory

Direct observation Techniques that require observers to record behaviors as they occur

Discovery learning An inductive learning process that allows learners to invent important principles, relationships, or concepts through their own experiences

Discrimination When learners identify two similar stimuli as different and respond to them differently

Disinhibitory effect Learners engage in previously inhibited behavior because an observed model engages in that behavior without anticipated aversive consequences

Distributed cognition The idea that people think in conjunction with other people or cultural tools

Distributed practice Spacing learning or practice over time to make new knowledge more permanent

Diversive exploration Exploratory behaviors to relieve boredom by increasing the arousal potential of the situation

Drill and practice programs Computer software that provides students with questions to answer or problems to solve to help them practice already learned information and skills

Echolalia A speech pattern of repeating what was just said

Educational objective The intended learning outcomes or objectives for instruction

Educational objective The intended learning outcomes or objectives for instruction

Educational psychology The branch of psychology that is concerned with the study of mental processes and behaviors associated with human learning and instruction

Educational technology Teaching tools and the processes necessary to apply those tools

Egocentric speech When young children talk aloud, but are talking to themselves

Egocentrism The tendency of preoperational children to judge experiences from their points of view

Elaboration The association of newly learned information to existing knowledge

Eliciting stimulus Observable environmental events that automatically elicit a response

Emotional disturbance Students with an emotional disturbance demonstrate behavioral and emotional problems to a marked degree and over a long period of time

Emotions Automatic physical and mental responses to a perceived situation

Enactive knowledge representation The representation of knowledge through motor responses

Enactive learning Bandura's term for learning through direct experience

Encoding Process of preparing information to be stored in declarative long-term memory

Enrichment Attempts to educate students with special gifts or talents by modifying or adding to the curriculum

Entity view of ability A view of ability as a fixed amount or entity

Environment analysis A form of task analysis that allows instructional designers to consider the impact of learning contexts on the success of instruction

Epistemic value The power of a theory to contribute to our understanding of a specific situation or the world in general

Equilibration A Piagetian term for the self-regulating activities learners engage in to achieve cognitive balance

Equivalence An aspect of reliability that refers to the degree to which different forms of the same test produce similar results

Error Unintended variations in the way observations are made or scored that negatively affect the reliability of the resulting data

Esteem needs According to Maslow, a need for status within a group as well as a positive self-concept

Events of instruction According to Gagné, the events of instruction are nine instructional conditions that need to be considered in planning a lesson

Exceptional learners A category that includes both students with disabilities and students with academic gifts

Exhibition An opportunity for students to present what they have learned to an audience

Exosystem In Bronfenbrenner's ecological theory, a social system that affects a student, even though the students do not directly interact with that social system

Explicit strategy instruction An approach to teaching strategies through direct explanation and modeling of cognitive strategies

Exploratory behavior A category of behaviors directed toward the investigation of the environment

Expository advance organizers Advance organizers that present a relevant general idea, principle, or category for the specific information contained in a lesson or lessons

Externalizing behaviors Aggressive and acting out behaviors such as yelling, talking out, cursing, hitting, arguing, stealing, and lying

Extinction burst The observation that behavior may worsen before it extinguishes

Extinction-induced aggression The observation that some students may become angry or hostile if reinforcement is taken away from them

Extraneous cognitive load Cognitive load that results from inadequately designed instruction

Extrinsic motivation Motivation that arises from an external reward

Fact A statement of association between two things

Far transfer Transfer that occurs when the learning and transfer situation are dissimilar

Feedback Information provided to students about their performances

First letter strategy A mnemonic strategy that involves making a word or acronym from the first letters of a list of facts or concepts

Fluency disorder Disruptions in the rate or flow of speech

Forethought Bandura's term for learners' ability to take a future orientation by setting goals and making plans to achieve those goals

Formal (mental) discipline The view that the mind is like a muscle that can be strengthened through mental exercise to improve performance across a number of situations

Formative assessment Assessments conducted to provide information about how to improve instruction

Forward chaining Teaching a chain by beginning with the first step and teaching the remaining steps in sequence until the last step has been taught

Frames The individual units of programmed learning

Frequency distributions A set of scores organized to show the number of observations occurring for each category or score. May be displayed as table or graph

Functional analysis An analysis of student behavior with the goal of identifying the antecedents and consequences that set the occasion for that behavior

Functional value When a modeled behavior is clearly linked to positive outcomes for the model

g General intellectual capability that is present in any intellectual task

Gender The behavior patterns and beliefs that are usually associated with being a male or female human being

Gender constancy The understanding that gender remains constant even if appearance changes

Gender identity Children's sense of their own gender

Gender schema The general knowledge about the nature of gender that people have acquired

Gender stereotypes Students' understanding of the typical roles, activities, and preferences of a particular gender

General transfer The application of general skills and knowledge to apparently dissimilar situations

Generalizability The generalizability of a theoretical conclusion refers to the number of different situations to which the conclusion may be applied

Generalization Occurs when learners respond to similar stimuli with the same behavior

Generalized expectancies A person's expectation for success in general categories of skills

Germane cognitive load Cognitive load that results from the additional cognitive effort needed to create deeper constructions of information or automatize schemata

Goal content A characteristic of a goal that defines the result or object being sought

Goal intensity A characteristic of a goal that refers to the effort that the person setting the goal is willing to expend in pursuit of the goal

Goal orientation The habitual way in which a person perceives and sets goals for achievement tasks

Goal-free problem statements Statements that allow learners to focus on relationships within a problem rather than working toward a particular solution

Goals Objectives that people consciously intend to pursue

Goodness of fit When used in discussions of temperament, goodness of fit refers to the match that exists between the characteristics of the person and the characteristics and demands of the environment

Grade equivalents A norm-referenced score that reports test performance in relationship to the performance of average students for a grade level

Group investigation Cooperative learning designed to help students acquire complex academic information and inquiry skills

Group-oriented contingency system Management contingencies are applied to more than one person in a group

Growth needs According to Maslow, needs that exhibit a stronger influence on motivation when they are gratified

Guided discovery Discovery learning that is structured or led by the teacher

Guided practice Teachers provide feedback, prompts, and encouragement as students practice what they have just been taught

Hearing impairment Any level of hearing loss from mild to profound

Heuristic A flexible problem solving approach that must be adapted to the demands of a problem solving situation

High road transfer The thoughtful transfer of learning based on the recognition of abstract principles that govern the learning and transfer situations

Higher mental functions According to Vygotsky, mental functions that are under the control of the person, are social in nature, and are assisted by psychological tools

Homeostasis A state of equilibrium or the tendency of an organism or system to strive toward such a state

Horizontal décalage The tendency of related cognitive abilities to develop at different times

Hypothetico-deductive reasoning The ability of students in Piaget's formal operational stage to reason from hypotheses

Iconic knowledge representation According to Bruner, the use of visual images to represent knowledge

IDEA Federal legislation that governs the education of students with disabilities

Identical elements Thorndike's idea that transfer is most likely to occur when the learning and transfer situations are similar

Identity From a Piagetian perspective, children's understanding that if nothing is added or removed, the existing quantity or amount does not change

Identity achievement Marcia's identity status that results from carefully considering identity options and then making a commitment to an identity

Identity diffusion According to Marcia, adolescents who lack clear direction in terms of ideological and occupational identity

Identity foreclosure Marcia's identity status that results from committing to identities without exploration or crisis

Identity moratorium Marcia's identity status that is associated with currently being in the exploration of identity options

Ill-defined problems Complex problems that are similar to those encountered in everyday life that require students to define aspects of the problem, and to apply knowledge from different domains and for which there are no clear solutions and solution paths

Image A chunk of declarative knowledge that represents information about the way things are arranged in space

Imaginary audience According to Elkind, adolescents' belief that others are as interested in them as they are

I-message A three-part communication that can be used to confront another person in a less threatening manner

Implicit theories Informal beliefs or intuitions developed from encounters with similar problems

Inclusion The education of students with disabilities with their peers without disabilities

Incremental view of ability A view of ability as a characteristic that can be improved through experience and effort

Independent group-oriented contingency The same expectations are in effect for the entire group, but consequences are administered independently

Independent practice Students practice what they have learned on their own, as in the case of homework or a test

Individual interest Interest derived from the specific knowledge, beliefs, and values of the learner

Individualized Educational Program (IEP) A written document that results from considering the needs of a student with a disability

Information Patterns of energy present in the environment

Information-processing analysis A procedural task analysis of the series of mental processes involved in a learning task

Inhibitory effect Bandura's term for when a modeling experience has the effect of strengthening inhibitions on a performance

Inquiry training Suchman's inductive learning approach that begins with the presentation of a discrepant event that intrigues the students

Instructional alignment A match between learning objectives, teaching methods, and methods of assessment, so that teaching methods and assessments are supportive of the objective

Instructional analogy An instructional technique that relates new ideas to structurally similar ideas in learners' memory

Instructional prompt An antecedent stimulus that encourages correct responses from students

Instructional strategy An instructional approach that combines instructional principles and techniques

Instructional technique A specific action taken by a teacher during the instructional process

Integration Actions taken by learners to find connections between new learning and existing knowledge

Intellectual needs The need to understand and explain the world

Intellectual skill Gagné's type of learning outcome that requires learners to apply acquired understandings to previously unencountered examples or experiences

Intelligent tutors Computer tutorials designed to be more responsive to students' learning needs

Intention Bandura's term for mentally representing a future course of action

Interdependent group-oriented contingency Each student's behavior can affect whether or not the group earns reinforcement

Interest value The value learners assign to a task because it has inherent interest associated with it

Intermittent schedule A reinforcement schedule in which only some occurrences of a behavior are reinforced

Internal consistency An aspect of reliability that refers to the degree to which all of the items of a test measure the same thing

Internalization The gradual development of higher mental processes from social interactions

Internalizing behaviors Behavior patterns that include anxiety, depression, and withdrawal

Interval scales A measurement scale characterized by equal intervals between all pairs of score points

Intrinsic cognitive load Cognitive load that derives from the material to be learned and is determined by the complexity of the material to be learned and learners' prior knowledge about that material

Intrinsic motivation Motivation directed toward achieving and maintaining a pleasant psychological state

Irreversibility The inability of young children during Piaget's preoperational stage to demonstrate reversible operations

Jigsaw A cooperative learning strategy that requires each student in the group to become expert on a part of a learning task so that the student can help the other members of the group learn that portion of the task

Keyword strategy A mnemonic strategy that involves associating a list of facts or concepts with a list of key words

Knowledge A meaningful representation of information in the mind of the learner

Knowledge acquisition components In Sternberg's triarchic theory of intelligence, knowledge acquisition components are the mental processes used to acquire required knowledge for problem solving

K-W-L A sequence of three questions that help students manage prior knowledge during learning

Language disorder Exists when students have significant expressive or receptive language delays

Law of effect An early conception of how reinforcement and punishment work that was provided by Thorndike

Learned helplessness When students internalize the causes of failure and externalize the causes of success

Learner analysis An analysis of relevant learner characteristics that need to be accounted for in instruction

Learning disability Students with a learning disability demonstrate a significant discrepancy between their cognitive ability and achievement as a result of a disorder in basic psychological processes

Learning hierarchy analysis A task analysis that results in the identification of prerequisite skills and knowledge for a particular learning task

Learning styles Learners' preferences for how they like to learn

Least restrictive environment The idea that students with disabilities are to be educated to the maximum extent possible with their peers without disabilities. Today this is referred to as inclusion

Levels of processing A model of memory that suggests that the permanence of a memory trace depends on how deeply that trace is processed

Linear program Programmed learning during which all students work through the frames of the program in the same order

Link systems A mnemonic that connects information together to make it more meaningful

Live model A model who has direct contact with the learner

Locus The dimension of an attribution defining the source of a perceived cause as either internal (intrinsic) or external (extrinsic) to the person

Logical consequences Consequences that are reasonable, rational, and related to the nature of the misbehavior

Long-term memory Where relatively permanent knowledge is stored in the information-processing model

Low-road transfer The automatic and direct transfer of previously learned knowledge to a new situation

Macrosystem In Bronfenbrenner's ecological theory, the influence of culture, subculture, or social class on a person's microsystems

Mager-style objective A specific and measurable objective that includes the behavior, conditions, and criterion for the learning

Maintenance rehearsal The process of repeating information over and over to maintain it in working memory

Manifestation determination A formal process to determine if a student's misbehavior is the result of that student's disability

Mastery goal A goal to achieve some level of mastery or competence

Mastery goal orientation A habitual preference for setting goals to master knowledge or skills

Mastery learning A strategy for organizing instruction based on the assumption that students can learn if given the time and help they need

Mastery model A model who performs a behavior flawlessly and with great confidence

Materials The component of the tetrahedral model that describes the way in which the learning task is presented

Mean The arithmetic average of a set of scores

Median The midpoint of a score distribution

Memory strategies Techniques that can be used to improve memory performance

Mental retardation Students with mental retardation exhibit significantly subaverage intellectual functioning with associated deficits in adaptive behavior

Mesosystem In Bronfenbrenner's ecological theory, an interaction between two microsystems

Metacognition Knowledge students have about learning, and their ability to use that knowledge to self-regulate their learning and problem solving

Metacomponents In Sternberg's triarchic theory of intelligence, metacomponents serve executive control or self-regulatory functions

Method of loci A mnemonic strategy that involves associating a list of facts or concepts with well known physical locations

Microsystems In Bronfenbrenner's ecological theory, the activities, roles, and interpersonal interactions of the social settings that students have face to face contact with in their lives

Mnemonics Any of a group of memory strategies for enhancing recall of facts or ideas

Modality When applied to shapes of score distributions, modality refers to the number of peaks in a distribution

Mode The most frequently occurring observation in a score distribution

Model In social cognitive theory, a model is any stimulus array that an observer can extract information from so the observer does not need to have direct learning experience with that information

Modeling A transmission process that involves interactions between learners and models that results in changes for the learner

Modifications for students with disabilities Changes in policies that affect the participation of students with special needs in the classroom

Morality of caring Gilligan's view of moral reasoning that factors in a collectivist view of morality and stresses compassion and the needs of others

Motivation (1) A mental process that activates, directs, and maintains behavior. (2) A key component in Bandura's observational learning

Motive to avoid failure A disposition to avoid the shame or humiliation associated with failure

Motives Habits or tendencies to seek out and enjoy certain activities or accomplishments

Multidisciplinary assessment team A group of professionals with different expertise who collaborate in determining a student's eligibility for special education

Multiple intelligences theory Howard Gardner's view of the nature of intelligence

Natural categories Schemata that contain our experiences with naturally occurring objects

Natural reinforcers Reinforcers that occur naturally in the environment as a result of engaging in a behavior

Natural structural schema A structural schema that is derived through learners' inductive reasoning about a large number of experiences

Near transfer Transfer that occurs when the learning and transfer situations are similar

Need A physical or psychological condition that a person must maintain to stay healthy

Negation In Piagetian theory, children's understanding that for a particular operation or action, there is another action or operation that will reverse it

Negative example An example for which a specific response would be inappropriate

Negative reinforcement A behavior is made more likely to occur because that behavior allows a learner to escape or avoid an unpleasant situation

Negative transfer The application of previously learned knowledge actually interferes with performance in a new situation

Neglect In the area of child mistreatment, neglect is the intentional or unintentional failure of a caregiver to provide for the physical, medical, or psychological needs of the children

Neglected students In terms of peer acceptance, students who are neither accepted nor rejected by their peers

Neo Piagetian theories Modern cognitive developmental theories that extend and modify Piagetian developmental constructs

No Child Left Behind Federal legislation that among several things establishes accountability standards for schools

Nominal scales A scale that allows for categorization of observations based only on the judgment that one performance or characteristic is different from another

Nonroutine treatments Gropper's modifications and extensions to routine treatments for teaching facts, concepts, and procedural rules

Norm group The group of test takers used to develop norms during the development of a norm-reference test

Normal curve equivalents A standard score with a distribution mean of 100 and a standard deviation of 21.06 that is often used in reporting standardized achievement test results

Norm-referenced evaluation An evaluation based on comparing students' performance to the average performance of a relevant comparison group (norm group)

Norms Data collected from a group of test takers during the development of a norm-referenced test

Numbered heads together A small group structure to encourage participation of all students in a group

Object permanence According to Piagetian theory, an infant's understanding that objects continue to exist when they are out of sight

Objectivity The extent to which a score is free of the bias of the scorer

Observational learning According to social cognitive theory, when a learner acquires or learns new understandings, behaviors, or standards from observing a model. The observational learning process includes attention, retention, productions, and motivation

Observational technique A technique for gathering data, composed of an assessment task and a scoring method

Open/free discovery A discovery learning approach with minimal teacher guidance and supervision

Operant conditioning A behavioral learning model that explains learning in terms of the effects of antecedents and consequences on behavior

Operation In Piagetian theory, an operation is a reversible mental process

Operational definitions Defining a characteristic in terms of a score or some other type of numerical observation

Oppositional identity The physical or symbolic resistance of some adolescents to what they perceive to be prescribed societal roles and standards

Ordinal scales A scale that allows performances to be grouped into mutually exclusive categories that can be ranked along a continuum. There is no assumption of equal score intervals

Orienting response When external events produce an automatic shift in attention

Organization The learners' creation of logical connections among ideas and concepts in a learning situation

Orienting stimulus A stimulus that produces an orienting response or shift in attention

Orienting tasks The component of the tetrahedral model that consists of the types of instruction and learning activities being used by the teacher

Orthopedic impairment A severe physical impairment that adversely affects student's educational performance

Other health impairment Ailments that affect strength, vitality, or alertness and that affect educational performance

Outcome expectations According to Bandura, learners' beliefs about the possible outcomes or consequences for engaging in a behavior

Overcorrection A form of presentation punishment based on the principle of contingent effort

Overlapping According to Kounin, teachers' ability to monitor more than one activity at a time

Pens in the middle A strategy for encouraging students to participate during small-group learning

Perceived task difficulty Students' beliefs about the amount of effort needed to perform a task successfully and the standards by which success will be judged

Percentile score A norm-referenced score that indicates the percentage of test takers who scored lower than a specific score

Perception The process of identifying meaningful patterns of information in sensations

Performance analysis An analysis of what students need to learn and under what conditions they must demonstrate that learning

Performance approach goals Approach goals that focus on demonstrating a level of competence relative to other people

Performance avoidance goals Avoidance goals that focus on not appearing incompetent relative to other people

Performance components In Sternberg's triarchic theory of intelligence, performance components are the mental processes used in the execution of a particular intellectual task

Performance goals An achievement goal that focuses on how other people will judge a learner's performance

Performance-based assessments Techniques that evaluate students' learning by having them complete a predetermined task

Personal fable According to Elkind, the belief among some adolescents that they are interesting to others because they are so unique

Personality The enduring personal characteristics that help distinguish one individual from another in terms of beliefs, attitudes, and ways of behaving

Physiological needs In Maslow's hierarchy, needs that are essential to survival

Placement decisions Decisions that attempt to match students to educational approaches or programs

Popular students A peer acceptance status defined by wide acceptance and positive regard of a person by that person's peers

Portfolio(s) A collection of artifacts produced by students that are intended to communicate students' accomplishments and progress in some area

Positive example An example to which a response can be appropriately applied

Positive manifold The observation that scores on different types of intelligence tests tend to correlate positively with each other

Positive practice overcorrection Students are asked to practice the correct alternative behavior to their misbehavior repeatedly

Positive reinforcement A behavior is more likely to occur because when it does occur a valued or satisfying consequence is provided to the learner

Positive transfer The application of previously learned knowledge improves performance in a new situation

Postconventional level of moral reasoning Kohlberg's third level of moral reasoning during which morality is judged in terms of a set of objective moral principles

Power motive The desire to control the means for influencing others

Preconventional moral reasoning Kohlberg's first level of moral reasoning during which morality is judged on the basis of subjective feelings of self

Predictive validity Evidence that the data from an assessment instrument can predict future performance on other forms of assessment

Premack principle Learners will engage in a less favored behavior if it allows them to engage in a more favored behavior

Preoperational stage The second Piagetian stage that typically occurs between ages two and seven, and during which children's reasoning tends to be intuitive

Presentation punishment A behavior is less likely to occur because it is followed by the presentation of an aversive stimulus

Principle A consistent relationship between specific situations, actions, and outcomes

Problem solving The physical or mental actions necessary to solve a problem

Problem space Learners' mental representations of a problem situation

Problem-based learning An instructional strategy that incorporates a number of constructivist learning principles

Procedural analysis A task analysis that results in a series of steps for performing a particular learning task

Procedural knowledge "How-to" knowledge that guides the performance of physical and mental skills

Procedural rule learning According to Gropper, learning how to perform a task according to rules or a set of procedural steps

Proceduralization The cognitive process that creates new productions from declarative knowledge in working memory

Process-outcome research A series of studies that attempted to link teacher behavior to students' learning

Production The basic unit of procedural knowledge with two parts: the conditions and the action

Production systems Units of procedural knowledge combined into complex sequences of actions

Programmed learning A self-teaching approach based on behavioral principles that allows students to learn at different rates

Project(s) A complex assessment task, for which part or all of the activity occurs outside of the classroom and some form of artifact is evaluated

Proposition A language-based representation that stores information about the semantic relationship between at least two elements of a chunk

Propositional logic The ability of children and adolescents during Piaget's formal operational stage to determine the truth of propositions that may not have a basis in experience

Psychological construct A hypothetical human characteristic that explains patterns of behavior

Psychological constructivism A form of constructivism with strong connections to Piagetian theory

Psychological processes Actions that create or modify psychological constructs

Psychological tools/signs According to Vygotsky, cultural tools that guide or mediate thoughts and behaviors

Psychology of a subject matter According to Bruner, the key organizing principles or ideas of a discipline and the typical methods of inquiry for that discipline

Psychomotor skill Gagné's learning outcome that requires that students learn to execute muscular actions to accomplish a particular goal, with or without the assistance of equipment

Punishments Consequences that have the effect of making behaviors less likely to occur again

Qualitative data Observations of essential characteristics or differences that are of-ten in the form of verbal descriptions of a person, group, or situation

Quantitative data Measures of the quantity or amount of something that are expressed in numbers in the form of scores or counts

Range The difference between the highest and lowest score in a distribution

Ratio scales A scale with both equal score intervals and a meaningful zero point

Reactive effect Occurs when self-monitoring by itself leads to modification of the target behavior

Reciprocal determinism Bandura's idea that behavior is determined by mutual influences of the behavior, the person, and the environment

Reciprocal teaching An approach for teaching strategies that relies on collaborative and interactive learning

Reinforcement potency The value of a potential reinforcer for a learner

Reinforcements Consequences that increase or maintain the likelihood that a behavior will occur again

Rejected students In terms of peer acceptance, students who are rejected by their peers either for aggressive behavior or withdrawn behaviors

Reliability The extent to which measurement yields consistent results

Removal punishment A behavior is likely to occur because it is followed by the removal of a valued stimulus

Resilient children Children who live in high-risk environments and who somehow manage not only to survive but to thrive

Response An overt behavior by a learner

Response cost A form of removal punishment that involves the loss of earned reinforcers when the person misbehaves

Response facilitation According to Bandura, when a model's behavior acts as a social cue or reminder for observers to engage in the modeled behavior

Restitutional overcorrection Students are required to fix or correct any damage they have caused and to repair the environment to a state better than its original state

Retrieval The process of activating or recalling knowledge from long-term memory

Routine treatments Gropper's generic teaching formats for facts, procedural rules, and concepts

Safety needs In Maslow's hierarchy, the need for stable and predictable environments

Satiation When an appetite for a reinforcer is satisfied completely. If students satiate on a reinforcer, it loses its value

Scaffolding The guidance and support teachers provide to learners during the learning process

Scales In assessment, a scale is a system for interpreting or organizing students' performances

Scatter plot A graph that shows the relationship between one variable graphed on the X axis and the other variable graphed on the Y axis

Schedule of reinforcement A determination of how often reinforcement will be available during learning

Schema (pl. Schemata) In information-processing theory, a memory structure that contains organized and interconnected declarative knowledge in a particular area

Schemes In Piagetian theory, organized patterns of thought or action that people use to understand and interact with the world

Scientific theories A set of formal statements that describes variables and relationships that are important for understanding some part of the world

Scope of a theory The type of phenomena that a theory attempts to explain

Scoring rubric A plan for scoring student productions such as essays, projects, and exhibitions

Scoring The process of rating or categorizing a student performance

Scripts Schemata that learners form for events with which they have had repeated experiences

Selection The process of focusing attention on important information

Selective perception processes Cognitive processes that accomplish initial screening of information in the sensory register

Self-actualization According to Maslow, people's need to develop their own unique abilities and talents

Self-concept How individuals define or perceive themselves as a person

Self-concept of ability A person's assessment of her or his own competence to perform a specific task or to carry out role-appropriate behaviors

Self-efficacy According to Bandura, people's beliefs about their capabilities to control their own lives that tend to be situation or task specific

Self-esteem How individuals feel about who they are as people

Self-evaluation A self-management intervention that involves students making judgments about the quality of their performance

Self-instructional programs An approach to self-regulation that provides students with written or verbal prompts to guide their thinking and problem solving

Self-modeling An intervention that uses visual images of a student engaged in adaptive behavior to strengthen or teach that behavior

Self-monitoring Procedures that require learners to observe and record their behaviors systematically

Self-reactiveness Bandura's term for the processes of setting personal standards for success, self-evaluating progress toward those standards, and the use of self-administered consequences to self-regulate

Self-reflectiveness Bandura's term for the ability to think about our own thought processes and to self-analyze experiences

Self-reinforcement An approach to self-regulation that require learners to set standards for success, select possible reinforcers, evaluate performance, or self-administer reinforcement

Self-report techniques Students are asked to report or discuss their perceptions, beliefs, and thought processes

Self-serving bias A bias toward creating attributions that are self-protective

Semiotic function In Piagetian theory, the ability to think symbolically that increases during the preoperational stage

Sensation A signal from the senses to the brain when a particular type of energy is present in the environment

Sensorimotor stage The first Piagetian stage that typically occurs between the ages of birth to two, and during which students reason through physical actions

Sensorimotor stage The first Piagetian stage that typically occurs between the ages of birth to two, and during which students reason through physical actions

Sensory register A component of the information-processing model where sensations are held briefly

Seriation The Piagetian operation involved in sequencing objects in terms of a size dimension

Setting events External or internal stimuli that simultaneously control a wide range of antecedents, behaviors, and consequences

Sexual abuse Sexually stimulating behavior or sexual interactions with children or using children or adolescents as objects to be sexually exploited

Shaping Reinforcing learners for making gradual improvement toward a terminal goal

Signals Text devices that highlight important ideas or the structural organization of ideas in text without conveying additional content

Situated cognition An approach to learning based on the idea learning cannot be separated from the contexts for that learning

Situational interest Interest generated by challenging and enjoyable tasks

Skew A term used to describe the degree of asymmetry of a score distribution

Skill analysis A task analysis that identifies the discriminations, generalizations, associations, or chains that are present in a learning task

Social constructivism A form of constructivism with strong connections to Vygotsky's theory

Social reinforcers Reinforcers that provide attention, affection, or approval to students

Software-realized scaffolding Scaffolding that is supported or provided by computer software

Spatial/semantic organizers Instructional tools that represent the organizational structure of information in a visual/spatial manner

Special education Educational programs and services provided for exceptional learners

Specific expectations A person's expectation for completing a specific task successfully

Specific exploration Actions directed toward an understanding of a specific situation

Specific transfer The application of specific behaviors learned in one situation to another situation

Spiral curriculum Bruner's view of a curriculum organization that periodically reintroduces key principles or ideas at increasing levels of sophistication

Split-half reliability Evidence of the internal consistency of a test obtained using a split half technique. For a group of people, scores for half of the test items are correlated with the scores for the other half

Spread of activation When declarative knowledge in working memory cues the retrieval of related knowledge in memory

Stability (1) An aspect of reliability that refers to the degree to which data is consistent over time. Estimated by test-retest techniques. (2) The dimension of an attribution relating to the expectation that a perceived cause will change (unstable) or remain constant (stable)

Stage of concrete operations The third Piagetian stage that typically occurs between the ages of seven to eleven, and during which operations for understanding the physical world develop

Stage of formal operations The fourth Piagetian stage during which people develop the abilities to reason hypothetically and to reason about abstractions

Standard deviation A mathematical representation of how much scores vary from the mean on average

Standardization Providing specific instructions for administering and scoring an assessment task

Standardized tests Tests that have standard and strict rules for administration and scoring

Stanine scores A standard score distribution with a mean of 5

State A mental characteristic that arises from a specific situation and goes away when the situation changes

Stimulus An observable environmental event that has the potential to exert influence over a behavioral response

Structural schema Schemata that preserve the structural relationships of a category of events or objects

Student Teams Achievement Divisions (STAD) A cooperative learning strategy that begins with a teacher presentation of a skill or informational lesson. Students then work in teacher-selected groups to master the information or skill that has been presented

Subjectivity The degree to which a score, classification, or rating is dependent upon the judgment of individual scorer. It is the opposite of objectivity

Subjects The component of the tetrahedral model that describes the learners' characteristics that might influence learning

Successive approximations In a shaping procedure, successive approximations are the intermediate improvement steps that lead to the final goal

Success-referenced evaluation An evaluation based on comparing students' performances with their previous performances

Summative assessments Assessments made at the end of instruction to determine learners' final mastery level

Supporting tools Applications of technology that guide and scaffold students' problem solving during problem-based learning

Symbolic knowledge representation According to Bruner, representing knowledge through arbitrary symbols systems such as language

Symbolic models Pictorial models such as characters in a story

Symbolic play A type of play that occurs when children use themselves or objects in the environment to represent other experiences or objects

Symbolic representation Bandura's idea that experiences can be transformed into mental models that guide behavior

T-Scores A standard score distribution with a mean of 50 and a standard deviation of 10

Table of specifications A table that is used in designing a test that specifies how objectives or content will be assessed

Tangible reinforcer A valued object that when earned has a reinforcing effect on behavior

Target error According to Kounin, when a teacher misidentifies misbehaving students

Task analysis The process of specifically identifying the subtasks, information flow, inputs, or decisions that are required by a particular learning task

Task value The anticipated reward associated with the successful completion of a task

Temporal string A chunk of declarative knowledge that preserves a perception of timing or order in which things occur

Test-retest reliability Evidence of the stability data, obtained by test-retest techniques The techniques involve re-testing the same group of subjects after a delay and correlating the two sets of scores

Tetrahedral model A model of four key instructional variables and how they affect each other

Text schema Schemata for knowledge about the organizing structures that appear in text

Theory A set of beliefs about how the world works, or at least some part of it

Think-Pair-Share A three-step strategy to encourage students to discuss questions before answering them

Time-out A behavioral intervention that removes students from the opportunity to earn reinforcement

Timing error According to Kounin, an error in the timing of an intervention such as when a teacher waits too long to intervene with misbehavior

Token A reinforcer that has no value itself but can be exchanged for other reinforcers

Token reinforcement system A systematic approach for using tokens as reinforcers

Top-down processing When perception is guided by the prior knowledge activated by context

Total task presentation Teaching all the steps in a chain at one time

Trait A psychological construct that represents a relatively permanent and consistent mental characteristic

Transfer The process whereby previous learning influences performance in a new situation

Transfer appropriate processing When the processes of retrieval are aligned to the processes involved in the learning situation

Traumatic brain injury Neurological damage caused by external force that results in a partial or total functional disability or psychosocial disability that affects educational performance

Unconditioned response The response that is automatically elicited by the unconditioned stimulus

Unconditioned stimulus A stimulus that elicits the unconditioned response

Universal design for learning An approach to instructional design that emphasizes flexible instruction with options for students that provide broad access to learning

Utility value The value learners associate with a task because the task will help them obtain a future goal

Validity Refers to the quality or the correctness of an explanation or decision

Variance A statistic that represents the variability of scores from the mean

Verbal directions A type of model that provides guidance on how to perform a behavior

Verbal information Gagné's learning outcome that consists of facts, lists, names, and organized information that students are expected to learn

Verbal reprimands Scoldings that are intended to serve as presentation punishments

Vicarious consequences A consequence that occurs to models, but that has an impact on the behavior of the observer

Vicarious learning In social cognitive theory, learning by observing the experiences of others

Visual impairments Vision that even with correction still adversely affects students' educational performance

Voice disorder An absence of voice quality such as when the voice sounds raspy or hoarse

Wait time An intentional pause during questioning to allow time to think or reflect

Within-group differences How much members of the same group differ from each other

Withitness According to Kounin, the ability of teachers to communicate their awareness of what is happening in the classroom

Working memory load The amount of information that must be maintained and processed to accomplish a task

Working memory The component of the information-processing model responsible for temporary storage of information and thinking and problem solving

Zero reject principle The component of IDEA that all students with disabilities are entitled to free and appropriate education

Zone of Proximal Development According to Vygotsy, the difference between what a learner can accomplish independently and what that same learner can accomplish when working with a more competent learner

z-Scores A standard score with a mean of zero and a standard deviation of one that reports students' performance in terms of how many standard deviation units they are above or below the mean of a comparison group

References

Aaronsohn, E., Carter, C. J., & Howell, M. (1995). Preparing monocultural teachers for a multicultural world: Attitudes toward inner-city schools. *Equity and Excellence in Education, 28*(1), 5–9.

Aboud, F. E., & Skerry, S. A. (1983). Self and ethnic concepts in relations to ethnic constancy. *Canadian Journal of Behavioral Sciences, 15,* 14–26.

Abrami, P. C. (2001). Understanding and promoting complex learning using technology. *Educational Research and Evaluation, 7*(2–3), 113–136.

Adams, D., & Hamm, M. (1996). *Cooperative learning: Critical thinking and collaboration across the curriculum.* Springfield, IL: Charles C. Thomas.

Adams, G. L., & Englemann, S. (1996). *Research on Direct Instruction: 25 years beyond DISTAR.* Seattle, WA: Educational Achievement Systems.

Ai, X. (2002). Gender differences in growth in mathematics achievement: Three-level longitudinal and multilevel analysis of individual, home, and school influences. *Mathematical Thinking & Learning, 4*(1), 1–22.

Ainsworth-Darnell, J. W., & Downey, D. B. (1998). Assessing the oppositional culture explanation for racial/ethnic differences in school performance. *American Sociological Review, 63,* 536–553.

Airasian, P. W., & Walsh, M. E. (1997). Constructivist cautions. *Phi Delta Kappan, 78*(6), 444–449.

Akande, A. (1997). The role of reinforcement of self-monitoring. *Education, 118,* 275–281.

Albanese, M. A., & Jacobs, R. M. (1990). Reliability and validity of a procedure to measure diagnostic reasoning and problem-solving skills taught in predoctoral orthodontic education. *Evaluation and the Health Professions, 13*(4), 412–424.

Alberto, P. A., & Troutman, A. C. (1999). *Applied behavior analysis for teachers* (5th ed.). Upper Saddle River, NJ: Prentice Hall.

Alden, L. (1986). Self-efficacy and causal attributions for social feedback. *Journal of Research in Personality, 20*(4), 460–473.

Alderman, M. K. (1990). Motivation for at-risk students. *Educational Leadership, 48,* 27–30.

Alderman, M. K. (1999). *Motivation for achievement: Possibilities for teaching and learning.* Mahwah, NJ: Erlbaum.

Alexander, P. A., & Murphy, P. K. (1999). Nurturing the seeds of transfer: A domain-specific perspective. *International Journal of Educational Research, 31*(7), 561–576.

Allal, L., & Ducrey, G. P. (2000). Assessment of or in the zone of proximal development. *Learning and Instruction, 10*(2), 137–152.

Allen, K. R., Fine, M. A., & Demo, D. H. (2000). An overview of family diversity: Controversies, questions, and values. In D. H. Demo, K. R. Allen, & M. A. Fine (Eds.), *Handbook of family diversity* (pp. 1–14). New York: Oxford University Press.

Allsopp, D. H., Santos, K. E., & Linn, R. (2000). Collaborating to teach prosocial skills. *Intervention in School and Clinic, 35*(3), 141–146.

Allwright, D., & Bailey, K. M. (1991). *Focus on the language classroom: An introduction to classroom research for language teachers.* New York: Cambridge University Press.

Amato, P. R. (1993). Children's adjustment to divorce: Theories, hypothesis, and empirical support. *Journal of Marriage and the Family, 55,* 23–38.

Amato, P. R., & DeBoer, D. D. (2001). The transmission of marital instability across generations: Relationship skills or commitment to marriage? *Journal of Marriage and Family, 63*(4), 1038–1051.

American Association on Mental Retardation. (1992). *Mental retardation: Definition, classification, and systems of support* (9th ed.). Washington D.C.

Ames, C. (1992). Classrooms: Goals, structures and student motivation. *Journal of Educational Psychology, 84*(3), 261–271.

Anastopoulos, A. D., Klinger, E. E., & Temple, E. P. (2001). Treating children and adolescents with attention-deficit/hyperactivity disorder. In J. N. Hughes, A. M. La Greca, & J. C. Conoley (Eds.), *Handbook of psychological services for children and adolescents* (pp. 245–266). Oxford: Oxford University Press.

Anderson, C. A., & Bushman, B. J. (2001). Effects of video games on aggressive behavior, aggressive cognition, aggressive affect, physiological arousal, and prosocial behavior: A meta-analytic review of the scientific literature. *Psychological Science, 12*(5), 353–359.

Anderson, D. R. (2000). Character education: Who is responsible? *Journal of Instructional Psychology, 27*(3), 139–142.

Anderson, J. R. (1983). *The architecture of cognition.* Mahwah, NJ: Lawrence Earlbaum.

Anderson, J. R. (1987). Skill acquisition: Compilation of weak-method problem solutions. *Psychological Review, 94,* 192–210.

Anderson, J. R. (1993). *The Rules of the mind.* Hillsdale, NJ: Erlbaum.

Anderson, J. R. (1996). A simple theory of complex cognition. *American Psychologist, 51*(4), 355–365.

Anderson, J. R., Reder, L. M., & Simon, H. A. (1996). Situated versus cognitive perspectives: Form versus substance. *Educational Researcher, 26*(1), 18–21.

Anderson, J. R., Reder, L. M., & Simon, H. A. (1997). Situated learning and education. *Educational Researcher 25*(4), 5–11.

Anderson, R. C., & Biddle, B. (1975). On asking people questions about what they are reading. In G. H. Bower (Ed.), *Psychology of learning and motivation* (Vol. 9, pp. 90–132). New York: Academic Press.

Anderson, R. C., & Pearson, P. D. (1984). A schema-theoretic view of basic processes in reading comprehension. (Rep. No. 306). National Institute of Education.

Andre, T. (1986). Problem solving and education. In G. D. Phye & T. Andre (Eds.), *Cognitive classroom learning: Understanding thinking and problem solving* (pp. 169–204). Orlando, FL: Academic Press.

Anguiano, P. (2001). A first-year teacher's plan to reduce misbehavior in the classroom. *Teaching Exceptional Children, 22*(3), 52–55.

Anolli, L., Antonietti, L. C., & Cantoia, M. (2001). Accessing scource information in analogical problem-solving. *The Quarterly Journal of Experimental Psychology, 54*(A), 237–261.

Arbeiter, S. (1985). *Profiles, college bound seniors.* New York: College Entrance Examination Board.

Arends, R. I. (1997). *Classroom instruction and management.* New York: McGraw-Hill.

Arends, R. I. (2001). *Learning to teach* (5th ed.). Boston: McGraw-Hill.

Arfaniarromo, A. (2001). Towards a psychosocial and sociocultural understanding of achievement motivation among Latino gang members in U.S. schools. *Journal of Instructional Psychology, 28*(3), 123–136.

Armstrong, R. (2001). Is the new IDEA a good idea? *Techniques, 76*(3), 29.

Arnold, M. L. (2000). Stage, sequence, and sequels: Changing conceptions of morality, post-Kohlberg. *Educational Psychology Review, 12*(4), 365–383.

Aronson, E., Blaney, N., Stephan, C., Sikes, J., & Snapp, M. (1978). *The jigsaw classroom.* Beverly Hills, CA: Sage.

Asante, M. K. (1998). *The Afriocentric idea* (rev. and exp. ed.). Philadelphia: Temple University Press.

Asch, A., Rousso, H., & Jeffries, T. (2001). Beyond pedestals: The lives of girls and women with disabilities. In H. Rousso & M. L. Wehmeyer (Eds.), *Double jeopardy: Addressing equity in special education* (pp. 13–48). New York: State University of New York Press.

Asher, J. (1982). *Learning another language through actions: The complete teacher's guide book* (2nd ed.). Los Gatos, CA: Sky Oaks Publications.

Asher, S. R. (1980). Topic interest and children's reading comprehension. In R. J. Spiro, B. C. Bruce, & W. F. Brewer (Eds.), *Theoretical issues in reading comprehension* (pp. 525–534). Hillsdale, NJ: Erlbaum.

Asher, S. R., & Dodge, K. A. (1986). Identifying children who are rejected by their peers. *Developmental Psychology, 22,* 444–449.

Atkinson, J. W. (1957). Motivational determinants of risk-taking behavior. *Psychological Review, 64*(6) 359–372.

Atkinson, R. C., & Shiffrin, R. M. (1968). Human memory model: A proposed system and its control processes. In K. W. Spence & J. T. Spence (Eds.), *The Psychology of learning and motivation: Advances in research and theory* (Vol. 2, pp. 90–197). New York: Academic Press.

Atkinson, R. C. (1975). Mnemotechnics in second language learning. *American Psychologist, 30,* 821–818.

Au, K. H., & Kawakami, A. J. (1994). Cultural congruence in instruction. In E. R. Hollins, J. E. King, & W. C. Hayman (Eds.), *Teaching diverse populations: Formulating a knowledge base* (pp. 5–23). Albany, NY: State University of New York Press.

Ausubel, D. P. (1963). *The psychology of meaningful verbal learning.* New York: Grune & Stratton.

Ausubel, D. P. (1968). *Educational psychology: A cognitive view.* New York: Holt, Rinehart & Winston.

Ausubel, D. P., & Youssef, M. (1963). The role of discriminability in meaningful parallel learning. *Journal of Educational Psychology, 54,* 331–336.

Avramidis, E., Bayliss, P., & Burden, R. (2000). A survey into mainstream teachers' attitudes towards the inclusion of children with special education needs in the ordinary school in one local education authority. *Educational Psychology, 20*(2), 191–211.

Azrin, N. H., & Holz, W. C. (1966). Punishment. In W. A. Honig (Ed.), *Operant behavior: Areas of research and application* (pp. 380–447). New York: Appleton.

Babkie, A. M., & Provost, M. C. (2002). 20 ways to select, write, and use metacognitive strategies in the classroom. *Intervention in the School and Clinic, 37*(3), 173–177.

Babyak, A. E., Luze, G. J., & Kamps, D. M. (2000). The good student game: Behavior management for diverse classrooms. *Intervention in the School and Clinic, 35*(4), 216–223.

Baddeley, A. (1990). *Human Memory: Theory and Practice.* Boston, MA: Allyn & Bacon.

Baguley, T., & Payne, S. J. (2000). Long-term memory for spatial and temporal mental models includes construction processes and model structure. *The Quarterly Journal of Experimental Psychology, 53A*(2), 479–512.

Bagwell, C. L., Coie, J. D., & Terry, R. A. (2000). Peer clique participation and social status in preadolescence. *Merrill Palmer Quarterly, 46*(2), 280–305.

Bahn, D. (2001). Social learning theory: Its application in the context of nurse education. *Nurse Education Today, 21,* 110–117.

Bahr, G. S., & Dansereau, D. F. (2001). Bilingual knowledge maps (BiK-Maps) in second language vocabulary learning. *Journal of Experimental Education, 70*(1), 8–24.

Bahr, M. W., Whitten, E., Dieker, L., Kocarek, C. E., & Manson, D. (1999). A comparison of school-based intervention teams: Implications for educational and legal reform. *Exceptional Children, 66*(1), 67–83.

Bailey, J. S., & Pyles, D. A. M. (1989). Behavioral diagnostics. In E. Cipani (Ed.), *The treatment of severe behavior disorders: Behavior analysis approaches* (pp. 85–107). Washington, D.C.: AAMR.

Baines, L. A., & Stanley, G. (2000). 'We want to see the teacher.' Constructivism and the rage against expertise. *Phi Delta Kappan, 82*(4), 27–330.

Baker, A. J. L., & Soden, L. M. (1998). The challenges of parental involvement research. (ERIC Document Reproduction Services No. ED407127).

Baker, C. (1997). *Foundations of bilingual education and bilingualism* (2nd ed.). Clevedon, England: Multilingual Matters Ltd.

Baker, J. M., & Zigmond, N. (1995). The meaning and practice of inclusion for students with learning disabilities: Themes and implications from the five cases. *Journal of Special Education, 29,* 163–180.

Baloche, L. A. (1998). *The cooperative classroom: Empowering learning.* Upper Saddle River, NJ: Prentice Hall.

Bambara, L. M., & Gomez, O. N. (2001). Using a self-instructional training package to teach complex problem-solving skills to adults with moderate and severe disabilities. *Education and Training in Mental Retardation and Developmental Disabilities, 36*(4), 386–400.

Bandura, A. (1965). Influence of models' reinforcement contingencies on the acquisition of imitative responses. *Journal of Personality and Social Psychology, 1,* 589–595.

Bandura, A. (1971). *Psychological modeling: Conflicting theories.* Chicago: Aldine-Atherton.

Bandura, A. (1973). *Aggression: A social learning theory analysis.* Englewood Cliffs, NJ: Prentice Hall.

Bandura, A. (1974). Behavior theory and the models of man. *American Psychologist, 29,* 859–869.

Bandura, A. (1977). *Social learning theory.* Upper Saddle River, NJ: Prentice Hall.

Bandura, A. (1982). Self-efficacy mechanisms in human agency. *American Psychologist, 37,* 122–147.

Bandura, A. (1986). *Social foundations of thought and action: A social cognitive theory.* Upper Saddle River, NJ: Prentice Hall.

Bandura, A. (1989). Human agency in social cognitive theory. *American Psychologist, 44*(9), 1175–1184.

Bandura, A. (1991). Self-regulation of motivation through anticipatory and self-reactive mechanisms. In R. A. Dienstbier (Ed.), *Nebraska symposium on motivation, 1990* (Vol. 38, pp. 69–164). Lincoln, NE: University of Nebraska Press.

Bandura, A. (1993). Perceived self-efficacy in cognitive development and functioning. *Educational Psychologist, 28*(2), 117–148.

Bandura, A. (1995). *Self-efficacy in changing societies.* New York: Cambridge University Press.

Bandura, A. (1997). *Self-efficacy: The exercise of control.* New York: Freeman.

Bandura, A. (1998). Exploration of fortuitous determinants of life paths. *Psychological Inquiry, 9,* 95–99.

Bandura, A. (1999). Social cognitive theory of personality. In L. A. Pervin & O. P. John (Eds.), *Handbook of personality theory and research* (2nd ed., pp. 154–196). New York: Guilford.

Bandura, A. (2001). Social cognitive theory: An agentic perspective. *Annual Review of Psychology, 52*(1), 1–26.

Bandura, A., & Cervone, S. (1983). Self-evaluative and self-efficacy mechanisms governing the motivational effects of goal systems. *Journal of Personality and Social Psychology, 45,* 1017–1028.

Bandura, A., Adams, N. E., & Beyer, J. (1977). Cognitive processes mediating behavioral change. *Journal of Personality and Social Psychology, 33,* 125–139.

Bandura, A., Barbaranelli, C., Caprara, G. V., & Pastorelli, C. (2001). Self-efficacy as shapers of children's aspirations and career trajectories. *Child Development, 72*(1), 187–206.

Bandura, A., Ross, D., & Ross, S. A. (1961). Transmission of aggression through imitation of aggressive models. *Journal of Abnormal and Social Psychology, 63*(3), 575–582.

Bandura, A., Ross, D., & Ross, S. A. (1963). Imitation of film-mediated aggressive models. *Journal of Abnormal and Social Psychology, 66*(1), 3–11.

Bandura, A., & Schunk, D. H. (1981). Cultivating competence, self-efficacy, and intrinsic interest through proximal self-motivation. *Journal of Personality and Social Psychology, 41,* 586–598.

Bangert, R. J., Kulik, J. A., & Kulik, C.-L. C. (1983). Individualized systems of instruction in secondary schools. *Review of Educational Research, 53*(2), 143–158.

Bangert-Downs, R. L., Kulik, C. C., Kulik, J. A., & Morgan, M. (1991). The instructional effect of feedback in test-like events. *Review of Educational Research, 61,* 213–238.

Banks, J. A. (1991). *Teaching strategies for ethnic studies* (6th ed.). Boston: Allyn & Bacon.

Banks, J. A. (2001). *Cultural diversity and education: Foundations, curriculum, and teaching.* Boston: Allyn & Bacon.

Bannert, M. (2002). Managing cognitive load—recent trends in cognitive load theory. *Learning and Instruction, 12*(1), 139–146.

Bargh, J. A., Chartrand, T. L., (1999). The unbearable automaticity of being: Automatic action. *American Psychologist, 54*(7), 462–479.

Barker, G. P., & Graham, S. (1987). Developmental study of praise and blame as attributional cues. *Journal of Educational Psychology, 79*(1), 62–66.

Barkley, R. A. (1998). Attention-deficit/hyperactivity disorder. In E. J. Mash & R. A. Barkley (Eds.), *Treatment of childhood disorders* (pp. 55–110). New York: Guilford.

Baron, R. M., Tom, D. Y. H., & Cooper, H. M. (1985). Social class, race, and teacher expectations. In J. B. Dusek, V. C. Hall, & M. J. Meyer (Eds.), *Teacher expectancies* (pp. 251–270). Hillsdale, NJ: Erlbaum.

Baroody, A. J., & Bartels, B. H. (2000). Using concept maps to link mathematical ideas. *Mathematics Teaching in the Middle School, 5*(9), 604–609.

Barrish, M. M., Saunders, M., & Wolf, M. M. (1969). Good behavior game: Effects of individual contingencies for group consequences on disruptive behavior in the classroom. *Journal of Applied Behavior Analysis, 2,* 119–124.

Barron, R. F. (1969). The use of vocabulary as an advance organizer. In H. L. Herber & R. T. Vacca (Eds.), *Research in reading in the content areas: The third report* (pp. 29–39). Syracuse, NY: Syracuse University Reading and Language Arts Center.

Barrows, H. S. (1996). Problem-based learning in medicine and beyond: A brief overview. In L. Wilkerson & W. H. Gijselaers (Eds.), *Bringing problem-based learning to higher education: Theory and practice.* San Francisco: Jossey-Bass.

Bartlett, F. (1958). *Thinking: An experimental and social study.* New York: Basic Books.

Bartlett, F. (1967). *Remembering.* Cambridge: Cambridge University Press.

Basden, J. C. (2001). Authentic tasks as the basis for multimedia design curriculum. *T.H.E. Journal, 29*(4), 16–18, 20–21.

Bassoppo-Moyo, T. C. (1997). The effects of pre-instructional activities and mental maps in enhancing learner recall. *International Journal of Instructional Media, 24*(3), 239–252.

Bauer, A. M., & Shea, T. M. (1999). *Inclusion 101: How to teach all learners.* Baltimore: Paul H. Brooks.

Bauer, W. I. (2001). Classroom management for ensembles. *Music Educators Journal, 87*(6), 27–32.

Baumrind, D. (1971). Current patterns of parental authority. *Developmental Psychology Monographs, 1,* 1–103.

Baumrind, D. (1980). New directions in socialization research, *American Psychologist, 35,* 639–652.

Baylor, A. L. (2000). Cognitive strategies for training with technology. *TechTrends, 44*(5), 13–15.

Bear, G. G. (1998). School discipline in the United States: Prevention, correction, and long-term social development. *Educational & Child Psychology, 15*(1), 15–39.

Beard, R. M. (1969). *An outline of Piaget's developmental psychology for students and teachers.* New York: Basic Books.

Becker, B. J., & Hedges, L. V. (1984). Meta-analysis of cognitive gender differences: A comment on an analysis by Rosenthal and Rubin. *Journal of Educational Psychology, 76*(4), 583–587.

Becker, W. C. (1986). *Applied psychology for teachers.* Chicago: Science Research Associates.

Becker, W. C., Englemann, S., & Thomas, D. R. (1975). *Teaching 2: Cognitive learning and instruction.* Chicago: SRA.

Belfiore, P. J., & Hornyak, R. S. (1998). Operant theory and self-monitoring in adolescents. In D. H. Schunk & B. J. Zimmerman (Eds.), *Self-regulated learning: From teaching to self-reflective practice* (pp. 184–202). New York: Guilford.

Belmont, J. M., Ferretti, R. P., & Mitchell, D. W. (1982). Memorizing: A test of untrained mildly mentally retarded children's problem-solving. *American Journal of Mental Deficiency, 87*(2), 197–210.

Bem, S. L. (1981). Gender schema theory: A cognitive account of sex typing. *Psychological Review, 88,* 354–364.

Bem, S. L. (1989). Genital knowledge and gender constancy in preschool children. *Child Development, 60,* 649–662.

Benson, J. S. (1998). Using an inquiry approach with preservice teachers to explain the process of facts, concept, generalization. *Social Studies, 89*(5), 227–231.

Berg, C. A., & Clough, M. (1991). Generic lesson design: The case against. *Science Teacher, 58*(7), 26–27, 29–31.

Berk, L. E. (1985). Research in review: Why children talk to themselves. *Young Children, 40*(5), 46–52.

Berk, L. E. (1996). *Infants, children, and adolescents* (2nd ed.). Boston: Allyn & Bacon.

Berlyne, D. E. (1967). Arousal and reinforcement. In David Levine (Ed.). *Nebraska symposium on motivation* (pp. 1–110). Lincoln, NE: University of Nebraska Press.

Bernardo, A. B. (1998). Language format and analogical transfer among bilingual problem solvers in the Philippines. *International Journal of Psychology, 33*(1), 33–44.

Bernardo, A. B. I. (2001). Analogical problem construction and transfer in mathematical problem solving. *Educational Psychology, 21*(2), 137–150.

Betz, N. E., & Hackett, G. (1997). Applications of self-efficacy theory to the career assessment of women. *Journal of Career Assessment, 5*(4), 383–402.

Bevevino, M. M., Dengel, J., & Adams, K. (1999). Constructivist theory in the classroom: Internalizing concepts through inquiry learning. *The Clearing House, 72*(5), 275–278.

Beyer, B. K. (1998). Improving student thinking. *The Clearing House, 71*(5), 262–267.

Bicard, D. F. (2000). Using classroom rules to construct behavior. *Middle School Journal, 31*(5), 37–45.

Biemiller, A., & Meichenbaum, D. (1992). The nature and nurture of student expertise. *Educational Leadership, 50*(2), 75–80.

Biemiller, A., Meichenbaum, D. (1998). The consequences of negative scaffolding for students who learn slowly: A commentary on C. Addison Stone's "The metaphor of scaffolding: Its Utility for the Field of Learning Disabilities." *Journal of Learning Disabilities, 31*(4), 365–369.

Bigge, M. L., & Shermis, S. (1999). *Learning theories for teachers* (6th ed.). New York: Longman.

Binder, C. (1993). Behavioral fluency: A new paradigm. *Educational Technology, 33*(10), 8–14.

Bjorklund, D. F. (1987). How age changes in knowledge base contribute to the development of children's memory: An interpretative review. *Developmental Review, 7,* 93–130.

Bjorklund, D. F., & Coyle, T. R. (1995). Utilization deficiencies in the development of memory strategies. In F. E. Weinert & W. Schneider (Eds.), *Memory performance and competencies: Issues in growth and development* (pp. 161–180). Hillsdale, NJ: Erlbaum.

Black Issues in Higher Education (2001). Report: Blacks more likely to be placed in special education. *18*(3), 22.

Blasi, A. (1980). Bridging moral cognition and moral action: A critical review of the literature. *Psychological Bulletin, 88*(1), 1–45.

Blatt, M. (1969). *The effects of classroom discussion on the development of moral judgment.* Unpublished PhD dissertation, University of Chicago, Chicago.

Blesh, T. E. (2000). Homework central. *Book Report, 19*(2), 84.

Block, J. H., & Burns, R. B. (1976). Mastery learning. In L. S. Shulman (Ed.), *Review of research in education* (Vol. 4, pp. 3–49). Itasca, IL: Peacock.

Bloom, B. S. (1968). Learning for mastery. *Evaluation Comment (UCLA-CSIEP), 1*(2), 1–12.

Bloom, B. S., & Broder, L. J. (1950). *Problem-solving processes of college students.* Chicago: University of Chicago Press.

Bloom, B. S., Englehart, M. B., Furst, E. J., Hill, W. H., & Krathwohl, O. R. (1956). *Taxonomy of educational objectives: The classification of educational goals. Handbook I: The cognitive domain.* New York: Longman.

Bloome, D., & Kinzer, C. K. (1998). Hard times and cosmetics: Changes in literacy instruction. *Peabody Journal of Education, 73*(3 & 4), 341–375.

Boaler, J., William, D., & Brown, M. (2000). Students' experiences of ability grouping—disaffection, polarization and the construction of failure. *British Educational Research Journal, 26*(5), 631–648.

Bodner, G., Klobuchar, M., & Geelan, D. (2001). Online symposium: Piaget, constructivism, and beyond the many forms of constructivism. *Journal of Chemical Education, 78,* 1107.

Boker, J. (1974). Immediate and delayed retention effects of interspersing questions in written instructional passages. *Journal of Educational Psychology, 66,* 96–98.

Bong, M., & Clark, R. E. (1999). Comparison between self-concept and self-efficacy in academic motivation research. *Educational Psychologist, 34*(3), 139–153.

Bong, M., & Skaalvik, E. M. (2003). Academic self-concept and self-efficacy: How different are they really? *Educational Psychology Review, 15*(1), 1–40.

Bonner, B. L. (2000). The effects of extroversion on influence in ambiguous group tasks. *Small Group Research, 31,* 225–244.

Borko, H., & Putnam, R. T. (1996). Learning to teach. In D. C. Berliner & R. C. Calfee (Eds.), *Handbook of educational psychology* (pp. 673–708). New York: Simon and Schuster Macmillan.

Borkowski, J. G. (1992). Metacognitive theory: A framework for teaching literacy, writing, and math skills. *Journal of Learning Disabilities, 25*(4), 253–257.

Bornstein, M. H., & Bruner, J. S. (Eds.). (1989). *Interaction in human development.* Hillsdale, NJ: Erlbaum.

Bos, C. S., & Vaughn, S. (2002). *Strategies for teaching students with learning and behavioral Problem* (5th ed.). Boston: Allyn & Bacon.

Bourdieu, P. (1986). The forms of capital. In J. G. Richardson (Ed.), *Handbook of theory and research for the sociology of education* (pp. 241–248). Westport, CT: Greenwood Press.

Bower, G. H., & Hilgard, E. R. (1981). *Theories of learning.* Englewood Cliffs, NJ: Prentice Hall.

Boyajian, A. E., DuPaul, G. J., Handler, M. W., Eckert, T. L., & McGoey, K. E. (2001). The use of classroom-based brief functional analysis with preschoolers at-risk for attention deficit hyperactivity disorder. *School Psychology Review, 30*(2), 278–293.

Braaksma, M. A., Rijlaarsdam, G., & van den Bergh, H. (2002). Observational learning and the effects of model-observer similarity. *Journal of Educational Psychology, 94*(2), 405–415.

Brackbill, Y., Bravos, A., & Starr, R. H. (1962). Delay-improved retention of a difficult task. *Journal of Comparative and Physiological Psychology, 55,* 947–952.

Bracken, B. A., & Walker, K. C. (1997). The utility of intelligence tests for preschool children. In D. P. Flanagan, J. L. Genshaft, & P. L. Harrison (Eds.), *Contemporary intellectual assessment theories, tests, and issues* (pp. 484–502). New York: Guilford.

Branch, R. M. (1997). Educational technology frameworks that facilitate culturally pluralistic instruction. *Educational Technology, 37,* 38–41.

Brandt, D. S., Uden, L. (2002). A simplified method of eliciting information from novices. *Educational Technology, 42*(1), 52–55.

Bransford, J. D., Brown, A. L., & Cocking, R. R. (2000). *How people learn: Brain, mind, experience, and school.* Washington D.C.: National Academy Press.

Bredekamp, S., & Copple, C. (Eds.). (1997). *Developmentally appropriate practice in early childhood programs* (rev. ed.). Washington, D.C.: National Association for the Education of Young Children (ED 403 023).

Bredekamp, S., Knuth, R. A., Kunesh, L. G., & Shulman, D. D. (1992). *What does research say about early childhood education?* Oak Brook: North Central Regional Educational Laboratory.

Brehm, J. W. (1999). The intensity of emotions. *Personality and Social Psychology Review, 3*(1), 2–22.

Broderick, P. C., & Blewitt, P. (2003). *The life span human development for helping professionals.* Upper Saddle River, NJ: Pearson Education.

Bronfenbrenner, U. (1979). *The ecology of human development: Experiments by nature and design.* Cambridge: Harvard University Press.

Bronfenbrenner, U. (1993). The ecology of cognitive development: Research models and fugitive findings. In R. H. Wozniak & K. Fischer (Eds.), *Scientific environments* (pp. 3–44). Hillsdale, NJ: Erlbaum.

Bronfenbrenner, U. (1994). Ecological models of human development. In T. Husen & T. N. Postlethwaite (Eds.), *International encyclopedia of education* (2nd ed., pp. 1643–1647). Oxford, England: Pergamon Press/Elsevier Science.

Bronfenbrenner, U. (1995). Developmental ecology through space and time: A future perspective. In P. Moen, G. H. Elder, & K. Luscher (Eds.), *Examining lives in context: Perspectives on the ecology of human development* (pp. 619–647). Washington, D.C.: American Psychological Association.

Brooke, R. R., & Ruthven, A. J. (1984). The effects of contingency contracting on student performance in a PSI class. *Teaching of Psychology, 11*(2), 87–89.

Brookhart, S. M. (1997). A theoretical framework for the role of classroom assessment in motivating student effort and achievement. *Applied Measurement in Education, 10*(2), 161–179.

Brookhart, S. M. (2001). Successful students' formative and summative uses of assessment information. *Assessment in Education, 8*(2), 153–169.

Brookhart, S. M., & DeVoge, J. G. (1999). Testing a theory about the role of classroom assessment in student motivation and achievement. *Applied Measurement in Education, 12*(4), 409–425.

Brooks, G. J., & Brooks, M. G. (1999). *In search of understanding: The case for constructivist classrooms.* Alexandria, VA: Association for Supervision and Curriculum Development.

Brooks, L. W., & Dansereau, D. F. (1987). Transfer of information: An instructional perspective. In S. M. Cormier & J. Hagman (Eds.), *Transfer of learning* (pp. 121–151). San Diego: Academic Press.

Brophy, J. (1981). Teacher praise: A functional analysis. *Review of Educational Research, 51,* 5–32.

Brophy, J. (1999). Perspectives of classroom management: Yesterday, today, and tomorrow. In H. J. Freiburg (Ed.), *Beyond behaviorism: Changing the classroom management paradigm* (pp. 43–56). Boston: Allyn & Bacon.

Brophy, J. E. (1983). Classroom organization and management. In D. C. Smith (Ed.), *Essential knowledge for beginning educators* (pp. 23–37). Washington, D.C.: American Association of Colleges of Teacher Education.

Brophy, J., & Good, T. (1986). Teacher behavior and student achievement. In M. C. Wittrock (Ed.), *Handbook of research on teaching* (2nd ed., pp. 328–375). New York: Macmillan.

Brothen, T., Wambach, C. A., & Hansen, G. C. (2002). Accommodating students with disabilities: PSI as an example of universal instructional design. *Teaching of Psychology, 29*(3), 239–240.

Brown University Child & Adolescent Behavior Letter. (1995, July). Your child's friendships provide an important and lasting lesson. *11*(7), 5–6.

Brown, A. L. (1994). The advancement of learning. *Educational Researcher, 23*(8), 4–12.

Brown, A. L. and Campione, J. C. (1990). Communities of learning and thinking, or a context by any other name. *Human Development, 21,* 108–125.

Brown, A. L., & Campione, J. C. (1990). Communities of learning and thinking, or a context by any other name. In D. Kuhn (Ed.), *Developmental perspectives on teaching and learning* (Vol. 21, pp. 108–126). Basel, Switzerland: Karger.

Brown, A. L., & Campione, J. C. (1994). Guided discovery in a community of learners. In K. McGilly (Ed.), *Classroom Lessons: Integrating cognitive theory and classroom practice* (pp. 229–270). Cambridge MA : MIT Press/Bradford Books.

Brown, B. B. (1989). The role of peer groups in adolescents' adjustment to secondary school. In T. J. Berndt & G. W. Ladd (Eds.), *Peer relationships in child development* (pp. 188–215). New York: John Wiley.

Brown, B. B. (1990). Peer groups and peer cultures. In S. S. Feldman & G. R. Elliott (Eds.), *At the threshold: The developing adolescent* (pp. 171–196). Cambridge, MA: Harvard University Press.

Brown, B. B. (1993). School culture, social politics, and the academic motivation of U.S. students. In T. M. Tomlinson (Ed.), *Motivating students to learn* (pp. 63–98). Berkley, CA: McCutchan.

Brown, B. B., Eicher, S. A., & Petrie, S. (1986). The importance of peer group ("crowd") affiliation in adolescence. *Journal of Adolescence, 9,* 73–96.

Brown, D. F. (2003). Urban teachers' use of culturally responsive management strategies. *Theory into Practice, 42*(4), 277–282.

Brown, I., Jr., & Inouye, D. K. (1978). Learned helplessness through modeling: The role of perceived similarity in competence. *Journal of Personality and Social Psychology, 36,* 900–908.

Brown, J. S., Collins, A., & Duguid, P. (1989). Situated cognition and the culture of learning. *Educational Researcher, 18*(1), 32–42.

Brown, L. M., Tappan, M. B., Gilligan, C., Miller, B. A., & Argyris, D. E. (1989). Reading for self and moral voice: A method of interpreting narratives of real-life moral conflict and choice. In M. J. Packer & R. B. Addison (Eds.), *Entering the circle: Hermeneutic investigation in psychology* (pp. 1111–1164). Albany, NY: State University of New York Press.

Brown, R., El-Dinary, P. B., Pressley, M., & Coy-Ogan, L. (1995). A transactional strategies approach to reading instruction. *The Reading Teacher, 49*(3), 256–258.

Brownell, M. T., & Walther, T. C. (2001). An interview with Stephen W. Smith: Strategies for building a positive classroom environment by preventing behavior problems. *Intervention in School and Clinic, 37*(1), 31–35.

Bruner, J. S. (1960). *The process of education.* Cambridge, MA: Harvard University Press.

Bruner, J. S. (1961). The act of discovery. *Harvard Educational Review,* 31:21–32.

Bruner, J. S. (1964). The course of cognitive growth. *American Psychologist, 19,* 1–15.

Bruner, J. S. (1965). The growth of mind. *American Psychologist, 20,* 1007–1017.

Bruner, J. S. (1978). *Toward a theory of instruction.* Cambridge, MA: Belknap Press of Harvard University Press.

Bruner, J. S. (1995). On learning mathematics. *Mathematics Teacher, 88*(4), 330–335.

Bruner, J. S. (1996). *The culture of education.* Cambridge, MA: Harvard University Press.

Bruner, J. S., Goodnow, J., & Austin, (1956), *A study of thinking.* New York: Wiley.

Bruning, R. H., Schraw, G. J., & Ronning, R. R. (1999). *Cognitive psychology and instruction* (3rd ed.). Englewood Cliffs, NJ: Merrill.

Bryan, T., & Sullivan-Burstein, K. (1998). Teacher-selected strategies for improving homework completion. *Remedial and Special Education, 19*(5), 263–275.

Bryan, T., Nelson, C., & Mathur, S. (1995). Homework: A survey of primary students in regular, resource, and self-contained special education classrooms. *Learning Disabilities Research and Practice, 10*(2), 85–90.

Bryant, D. P., & Bryant, B. R. (1998). Using assistive technology adaptations to include students with learning disabilities in cooperative learning activities. *Journal of Learning Disabilities, 31*(1), 41–54.

Bryk, A., & Thum, Y. (1989). The effects of high school organization on dropping out: An exploratory investigation. *American Educational Research Journal, 26,* 353–383.

Buell, J. (2000). The politics of homework. *Humanist, 60*(6), 39–40.

Buggey, T. (1999). "Look! I'm on TV!": Using videotaped self-modeling to change behavior. *Teaching Exceptional Children, 31*(4), 27–30.

Buisson, G., Murdock, J., Reynolds, K., & Cronin, M. (1995). Effects of tokens on response latency of students with hearing impairments in a resource room. *Education and Treatment of Children, 18*(4), 408–421.

Bulgren, J. A., Deshler, D. D., Schumaker, J. B., & Lenz, B. K. (2000). The use and effectiveness of analogical instruction in diverse secondary content classrooms. *Journal of Educational Psychology, 92*(3), 416–441.

Bunce, D. M. (2001). Does Piaget still have anything to say to chemists? *Journal of Chemical Education, 78*(8), 1107.

Burden, P. R., & Byrd, D. M. (1999). *Methods for effective teaching* (2nd ed.). Boston: Allyn & Bacon.

Burnett, P. C. (1996). Gender and grade differences in elementary school children's descriptive and evaluative self-statements and self-esteem. *School Psychology International, 17,* 159–170.

Burns, E. (1998). *Test accommodations for students with disabilities.* Springfield, IL: Charles C. Thomas.

Burns, H. L., & Capps, C. G. (1988). Foundations of intelligent tutoring systems: An introduction. In M. C. Polson & J. J. Richardson (Eds.), *Foundations of intelligent tutoring systems* (pp. 1–20). Hillsdale, NJ: Erlbaum.

Burns, M. K., & Symington, T. (2002). A meta-analysis of preferral intervention teams: Student and systemic outcomes. *Journal of School Psychology, 40*(5), 437–447.

Burns, U. D. (1980). The perfectionist's script for defeat. *Psychology Today,* (November) 34–51.

Burton, M., & Parks, S. (1998). *Intensive time out program evaluation.* New Brunswick, Canada: University of New Brunswick (ED 424 289).

Butterfield, E. C., Slocum, T. A., & Nelson, G. D. (1993). Cognitive and behavioral analyses of teaching and transfer: are they different? In D. K. Detterman & R. J. Sternberg (Eds.), *Transfer on trial: Intelligence, cognition, and instruction* (pp. 192–257). Norwood, NJ: Ablex.

Buzzelli, C. A. (1992). Popular and rejected children's social reasoning: Linking social status and social knowledge. *Journal of Genetic Psychology, 153*(3), 331–342.

Cajete, G. A. (1999). The Native American learner and bicultural science education. In *Next steps: Research and practice to advance Indian education.* (ERIC Document Reproduction Services, No. ED427908).

Calderhead, J. (1996). Teachers: Beliefs and knowledge. In D. C. Berliner & R. C. Calfee (Eds.), *Handbook of educational psychology* (pp. 709–725). New York: Simon and Schuster Macmillan.

Callan, R. J. (1997/1998). Giving students the (right) time of day. *Educational Leadership, 55*(4), 84–87.

Cameron, J. (2001). Negative effects of reward on intrinsic motivation—a limited phenomenon: Comment on Deci, Koestner, and Ryan (2001). *Review of Educational Research, 71*(1), 29–42.

Cameron, J., & Pierce, W. D. (1994). Reinforcement, reward, and intrinsic motivation. *Review of Educational Research, 64,* 363–423.

Camp, B. W. (1977). Verbal mediation in young aggressive boys. *Journal of Abnormal Psychology, 86,* 145–153.

Camp, B. W., & Bash, M. A. (1978). *The classroom "Think Aloud" program.* Paper presented at the Annual Convention of the American Psychological Association, Toronto, Canada.

Camp, B. W., Blom, G. E., Herbert, F., & van Doorninck, W. J. (1977). "Think aloud": A program for developing self-control in young aggressive boys. *Journal of Abnormal Child Psychology, 5,* 157–169.

Camp, D. (2000). It takes two: Teaching with twin texts of fact and fiction. *Reading Teacher, 53*(5), 400–408.

Campbell, D. S. (1985). Television feedback in self-instruction training for an impulsive student. *Journal of Special Education, 9,* 163–168.

Campbell, J. (1999). *Student discipline and classroom management; Preventing and managing discipline problems in the classroom.* Springfield, IL: Charles C. Thomas.

Campione, J. C. (1996). Assisted assessment: a taxonomy of approaches and an outline of strengths and weaknesses. In H. Daniels (Ed.), *An introduction to Vygotsky* (pp. 219–250). London: Routledge.

Campione, J. C., Brown, A. L., Ferrara, R. A., & Bryant, N. R. (1984). The zone of proximal development: Implications for individual differences and learning. In B. Rogoff & J. V. Wertsch (Eds.), *Children's learning in the zone of proximal development* (pp. 77–91). San Francisco: Jossey-Bass.

Campione, J. C., Shapiro, A. M., & Brown, A. L. (1995). Forms of transfer in a community of learners: Flexible learning and understanding. In A. McKeough, J. Lupart, & A. Marini (Eds.), *Teaching for transfer: Fostering generalization in learning* (pp. 35–68). Mahwah, NJ: Erlbaum.

Cangelosi, J. S. (2000). *Classroom management strategies: Gaining and maintaining students' cooperation* (4th ed.). New York: John Wiley.

Caplan, R. D., & Van Harrison, R. (1993). Person-environment fit theory: Some history, re-

cent developments, and future directions. *Journal of Social Issues, 49*(4), 253–275.

Carbo, M., Dunn, R., & Dunn, K. (1986). *Teaching students to read through their individual learning styles.* Englewood Cliffs, NJ: Prentice Hall.

Carey, S., & Xu, F. (2001). Infants' knowledge of objects: Beyond object files and object tracking. *Cognition, 80*(1–2), 179–213.

Carey, W. (1998). Temperament and behavior problems in the classroom. *School Psychology Review, 27,* 522–533.

Carlson, C. D., & Francis, D. J. (2002). Increasing the reading achievement of at-risk children through direct instruction: Evaluation of the Rodeo Institute for Teacher Excellence (RITE). *Journal of Education for Students Placed at Risk, 7*(2), 141–166.

Carlson, R. A., Khoo, H., & Elliot, I. (1990). Component practice and exposure to a problem-solving context. *Human Factors, 32*(3), 267–286.

Carnine, D. W. (1993). Effective teaching for higher cognitive functioning. *Educational Technology, 33*(10), 29–33.

Carnine, D., & Silbert, J. (1979). *Direct instruction reading.* Columbus, OH: Charles E. Merrill.

Caroff, X. (2002). What conservation anticipation reveals about cognitive change. *Cognitive Development, 17,* 1015–1035.

Carr, E., & Newsom, C. (1985). Demand related tantrums: Conceptualization and treatment. *Behavior Modification, 9,* 403–426.

Carr, E., & Ogle, D. (1987). K-W-L plus: A strategy for comprehension and summarization. *Journal of Reading, 30*(7), 626–631.

Carr, S. C., & Punzo, R. B. (1993). The effects of self-monitoring of academic accuracy and productivity on the performance of students with behavioral disorders. *Behavioral Disorders, 18*(4), 241–250.

Carroll, J. B. (1963). A model for school learning. *Teachers College Record, 64,* 723–733.

Carroll, J. B. (1993). *Human cognitive abilities. A survey of factor-analytic studies.* Cambridge: Cambridge University Press.

Carroll, J. B. (1997). The three-stratum theory of cognitive abilities. In D. P. Flanagan, J. L. Genshaft, & P. L. Harrison (Eds.), *Contemporary intellectual assessment theories, tests, and issues* (pp. 122–130). New York: Guilford.

Case, R. (1987). Neo-Piagetian theory: Retrospect and prospect. *International Journal of Psychology, 22,* 773–791.

Case, R. (1992). *The mind's staircase: Exploring the conceptual underpinnings of children's thought and knowledge.* Hillsdale, NJ: Erlbaum.

Caspi, A. (1998). Personality development across the life course. In W. Damon (Editor-in-Chief) & N. Eisenberg (Vol. Ed.), *Handbook of child psychology: Vol. 3, Social, emotional, and personality development* (5th ed., pp. 311–388). New York: John Wiley & Sons.

Cassady, J. C., & Johnson, R. E. (2002). Cognitive test anxiety and academic performance. *Contemporary Educational Psychology, 27,* 270–295.

Cassidy, K. W., Chu, J. Y., & Dahlsgaard, K. K. (1997). Preschoolers' ability to adopt justice and care orientations to moral dilemmas. *Early Education & Development, 8*(4), 419–439.

Casteel, C. P., Isom, B. A., & Jordan, K. F. (2000). Creating competent and confident readers: Transactional strategies instruction.

Intervention in School and Clinic, 36(2), 67–74.

Catania, A. C. (2000). Ten points every behavior analyst needs to remember about reinforcement. In J. C. Leslie & D. Blackman (Eds.), *Experimental and applied analysis of human behavior* (pp. 23–37). Reno, NY: Context Press.

Catania, A. C. (2001). Positive psychology and positive reinforcement. *American Psychologist, 56*(1), 86–87.

Cavalier, A., Ferretti, R., & Hodges, A. (1997). Self-management within a classroom token economy for students with learning disabilities. *Research in Developmental Disabilities, 18*(3), 167–178.

Chalfant, J. C., & Pysh, M. V. (1989). Teacher assistance teams: Five descriptive studies on 96 teams. *Remedial and Special Education, 10*(6), 49–58.

Chance, P. (1992). The rewards of learning. *Phi Delta Kappan, 74*(3), 200–207.

Chance, P. (1993). Sticking up for rewards. *Phi Delta Kappan, 74*(10), 787–790.

Chandler, M., & Chapman, M. (Eds.). (1991). *Criteria for competence: Controversies in the conceptualization and assessment of children's abilities.* Hillsdale, NJ: Erlbaum.

Chang, K. E., Sung, Y. T., & Chen, S. F. (2001). Learning through computer-based concept mapping with scaffolding aid. *Journal of Computer Assisted Learning, 17,* 21–33.

Chen, J.-Q., & Gardner, H. (1997). Alternative assessment from a multiple intelligences theoretical perspective. In D. Flanagan, J. Genschaft, & P. Harrison (Eds.), *Contemporary intellectual assessment: Theories, tests, and issues* (pp. 105–121). New York: Guilford.

Chen, J.-Q., Krechevsky, M., Viens, J., & Isberg, E. (1998). *Building on children's strengths: The experience of project spectrum.* New York: Teachers College Press.

Chess, S., & Thomas, A. (1986). *Temperament in clinical practice.* New York: Guilford.

Chess, S., & Thomas, A. (1996). *Temperament: Theory and practice.* New York: Brunner/Mazel.

Chi, M. T. H., Bassok, M., Lewis, M. W. Reiman, P., & Glaser, R. (1989). Self-explanations: How students study and use worked examples in learning to solve problems. *Cognitive Science, 13,* 145–182.

Chi, M. T. H., Fletovich, P. J., & Glaser, R. (1981). Categorization and representation of physics problems by experts and novices. *Cognitive Science, 5,* 121–152.

Chinn, C. A., & Brewer, W. F. (1993). The role of anomalous data in knowledge acquisition: A theoretical framework and implications for science instruction. *Review of Educational Research, 63*(1), 1–49.

Chittooran, M. M. (2000). Conflict resolution and peer mediation: A guide for educators. In *Behavioral interventions: Creating a safe environment in our schools.* Bethesda, MD: National Association of School Psychologists (ED 437 600).

Chmielewski, T. L., & Dansereau, D. F. (1998). Enhancing the recall of text: Knowledge mapping training promotes implicit transfer. *Journal of Educational Psychology, 90*(3), 407–413.

Choi, I., & Jonassen, D. H. (2000). Learning objectives from the perspective of the experienced cognition framework. *Educational Technology, 40*(6), 36–40.

Choi, J., & Hannafin, M. J. (1997). The effects of instructional context and reasoning complexity on mathematics problem-solving. *Educational Technology, Research and Development, 45*(3), 43–55.

Christian, D., Howard, E. R., & Loeb, M. I. (2000). Bilingualism for all: Two-way immersion education in the United States. *Theory into Practice, 39*(4), 258–266.

Clark, C. M., & Peterson, P. L. (1990). Teachers' thought processes. In M. C. Wittrock, C. M. Clark, & P. L. Peterson (Eds.), *Student thought processes-teacher thought processes: A project of the American Educational Research Association.* New York: Macmillan.

Clark, C. M., & Peterson, P. L. (1986). Teachers' thought processes. In M. C. Wittrock (Ed.), *Handbook of research on teaching* (3rd ed., pp. 255–296). New York: Macmillan.

Clark, R. E. (1983). Reconsidering research on learning from media. *Review of Educational Research, 53*(4), 445–459.

Clark, R. E. (1994). Media will never influence learning. *Educational Technology, Research and Development, 42*(2), 21–29.

Clark, R. E., & Sugrue, B. M. (1995). Research on instructional media, 1978–1988. In G. J. Anglin (Ed.), *Instructional technology: Past present, and future* (2nd ed., pp. 348–364). Englewood, CO: Libraries Unlimited, Inc.

Clees, T. J. (1994–95). Reflections on "self-recording of students' daily schedules of teachers' expectancies: Perspectives on reactivity, stimulus control, and generalization." *Exceptionality, 5*(3), 183–187.

Clements, D. H., & Sarama, J. (1998). Using computers for algebraic thinking. *Teaching Children Mathematics, 5*(3), 186–190.

Cobb, P., & Bowers, J. (1999). Cognitive and situated learning perspectives in theory and practice. *Educational Researcher, 28*(2), 4–15.

Cobb, P., Wood, T., & Yackel, E. (1993). Discourse, mathematical thinking, and classroom practice. In E. A. Forman, N. Minick, & C. A. Stone (Eds.), *Contexts for learning sociocultural dynamics in children's development* (pp. 91–119). New York: Oxford University Press.

Cobb, T. (1999). Breadth and depth of lexical acquisition with hands-on concordancing. *Computer Assisted Language Learning, 12*(4), 345–360.

Cognition and Technology Group at Vanderbilt. (1992). The Jasper experiment: An exploration of issues in learning and instructional design. *Educational Technology Research & Development, 40*(1), 65–80.

Cohen, E. G. (1994). Restructuring the classroom: Conditions for productive small groups. *Review of Educational Research, 64*(1), 1–35.

Cohen, E. G., Lotan, R. A., & Holthuis, N. (1995). Talking and working together: Conditions for learning in complex instruction. In M. T. Hallinan (Ed.), *Restructuring schools: Promising practices and policies* (pp. 157–174). New York: Plenum Press.

Cohen, E. G., Lotan, R., & Catanzarite, L (1990). Treating status problems in the cooperative classroom. In S. Sharan (Ed.), *Cooperative learning: Theory and research.* New York: Praeger.

Cohen, L. M., & Younghee, M. (1999). Piaget's equilibration theory and the young gifted child: A balancing act. *Roeper Review, 21*(3), 201–206.

Cohen, L., & Manion, L. (1977). *A guide to teaching practice.* London: Routledge.

Cohen, R. J., & Swerdlick, M. E. (1999). *Psychological testing and assessment: An introduction to tests and measurement* (4th ed.). Mountain View, CA: Mayfield Publishing.

Cohen, S. A. (1987). Instructional alignment: Searching for a magic bullet. *Educational Researcher, 16*(8), 16–20.

Cohen, S. A. (1995). Instructional alignment. In J. H. Block, S. Everson, & T. R. Guskey (Eds.), *School improvement programs: A handbook for educational leaders* (pp. 153–180). New York: Scholastic.

Coie, J. D., & Dodge, K. A. (1998). Aggression and antisocial behavior. In N. Eisenberg (Ed.), *Handbook of child psychology* (5th ed., Vol. 3, pp. 780–862). New York: John Wiley & Sons.

Coker, J. K. (2001). Four-fold prevention strategies to prevent substance abuse among elementary school-aged children. *Professional School Counseling, 5*(1), 70–74.

Colby, A., & Kohlberg, L. (1987). *The measurement of moral judgment.* New York: Cambridge University Press.

Cole, D. A., Maxwell, S. E., Martin, J. M., Peeke, L. G., Serocrynski, A. D., Tram, J. M., et al. (2001). The development of multiple domains of child and adolescent self-concept: A cohort sequential longitudinal design. *Child Development, 72*(6), 1723–1746.

Cole, M. (1985). The zone of proximal development: Where culture and cognition create each other. In J. V. Wertsch (Ed.), *Culture, communication, and cognition: Vygotskian perspectives* (pp. 146–161). New York: Cambridge University Press.

Cole, M. (1990). Cognitive development and formal schooling: The evidence from cross-cultural research. In L. C. Moll (Ed.), *Vygotsky and education instructional implications and applications of sociohistorical psychology* (pp. 89–110). Cambridge: Cambridge University Press.

Cole, M., & Cole, S. R. (1993). *The development of children.* New York: Scientific American Books.

Cole, M., & Engeström, Y. (1993). A cultural-historical approach to distributed cognition. In G. Salomon (Ed.), *Distributed cognitions psychological and educational considerations* (pp. 1–46). New York: Cambridge University Press.

Coleman, J., Campbell, E., Hobson, C., McPartland, J., Mood, A., Weinfield, F., et al. (1966). *Equality of educational opportunity.* Washington, D.C.: U.S. Government Printing Office.

Coleman, P., Thiessen, R., Wilson, D., Arey, B., & Barrow, L. H. (1999). Studying land snails. *Science Activities, 36*(2), 28–30.

Coley, R. (2001). *Difference in the gender gap: Comparisons across racial-ethnic groups in education and work,* from http://www.ets.org/research/pic

Coley, R. J., Cradler, J., & Engel, P. K. (2000). *Computers and classrooms: The status of technology in U.S. schools.* Princeton, NJ: Policy Information Center, Educational Testing Services.

Coley, R. J., Cradler, J., & Engel, P. K. (2000). *Computers and the classroom: The status of technology in U.S. schools.* Princeton, NJ: Information Center, Educational Testing Service.

Collier, V. P. (1992). A synthesis of studies examining long-term language minority student data on academic achievement. *Bilingual Research Journal, 16*(1–2), 187–212.

Collins, A., Brown, J. S., & Newman, S. E. (1989). Cognitive apprenticeship: Teaching the crafts of reading, writing, and mathematics. In B. Resnick (Ed.), *Knowing, learning, and instruction: Essays in honor of Robert Glaser* (pp. 453–494). Hillsdale, NJ: Erlbaum.

Collins, J. (1998). Seven kinds of smart. *Time, 152,* 94–97.

Collins, J. L. (1982). *Self-efficacy and ability in achievement behavior.* Paper presented at the American Educational Research Association, New York.

Conger, R., Conger, K., & Elder, G. H. (1997). Family economic hardship and adolescent adjustment: Mediating and moderating processes. In G. Duncan & J. Brooks-Gunn (Eds.), *Consequences of growing up poor* (pp. 288–310). New York: Russell Sage.

Conroy, M. A., & Fox, J. J. (1994). Setting events and challenging behaviors in the classroom. *Preventing School Failure, 38*(3), 29–34.

Cook, L. K., & Mayer, R. E. (1988). Teaching readers about the structure of scientific text. *Journal of Educational Psychology, 80*(4), 448–456.

Cook, P. J., & Ludwig, J. (1997). Weighing the burden of 'acting white': Are there race differences in attitudes toward education? *Journal of Policy Analysis and Management, 16*(2), 656–678.

Cooke, A. (1999). *Authoritative guide to evaluating information on the internet.* New York: Neal-Schuman.

Coon, D. J. (1982). Eponymy, obscurity, Twitmyer, and Pavlov. *Journal of the History of the Behavioral Sciences, 18,* 255–262.

Cooper, C. R., Grotevant, H. D., & Condon, S. M. (1983). Individuality and connectedness both foster adolescent identity formation and role taking skills. In H. D. Grotevant & C. R. Cooper (Eds.), *Adolescent development in the family: New directions for child development* (pp. 43–59). San Francisco: Jossey-Bass.

Cooper, H. M. (1989). Synthesis of research on homework. *Educational Leadership, 47,* 85–91.

Cooper, H. M. (2001). Homework for all—in moderation. *Educational Leadership, 58*(7), 34–38.

Cooper, H., & Nye, B. (1994). Homework for students with learning disabilities: The implications of research for policy and practice. *Journal of Learning Disabilities, 27*(8), 70–79.

Cooper, H., & Valentine, J. C. (2001). Using research to answer practical questions about homework. *Educational Psychologist, 36*(3), 143–153.

Cooper, H., Lindsay, J. J., Nye, B., & Greathouse, S. (1998). Relationships among attitudes about homework, amount of homework assigned and completed, ands student achievement. *Journal of Educational Psychology, 90,* 70–83.

Cooper, J., Heron, T., & Heward, W. (1987). *Applied behavior analysis.* Columbus, OH: Merrill.

Cooper, P. A. (1993). Paradigm shifts in designed instruction: From behaviorism to cognitivism to constructivism. *Educational Technology, 33*(5), 12–19.

Corkill, A. J. (1992). Advance organizers: Facilitators of recall. *Educational Psychology Review, 4,* 33–67.

Corkill, A. J., Bruning, R. H., & Glover, J. A. (1988). Advance organizers: Concrete versus abstract. *Journal of Educational Research, 82*(2), 76–81.

Cornfold, I. R. (2002). Two models for promoting transfer: A comparison and critical analysis. *Journal of Vocational Education and Training, 54*(1), 85–102.

Corno, L. (2000). Looking at homework differently. *The Elementary School Journal, 100*(5), 529–545.

Cornoldi, C., Carretti, B., & De Beni, R. (2001). How the pattern of deficits in groups of learning disbled individuals help to understand the organization of working memory. *Issues in Education, 7*(1), 71–78.

Covington, M. V. (2000). Intrinsic versus extrinsic motivation in schools: A reconciliation. *Current Directions in Psychological Science, 9*(1), 22–25

Covington, M. V., Crutchfield, R. S., & Davies, L. B. (1966). *The productive thinking program.* Berkeley, CA: Brazelton.

Cowan, P. A., Cowan, C. P., & Schulz, M. S. (1996). Thinking about risk and resilience in families. In M. Hetherington & E. A. Blechman (Eds.), *Stress, coping, and resiliency in children and families* (pp. 1–38). Mahwah, NJ: Erlbaum.

Cox, R., McKendree, J., Tobin, R., Lee, J., & Mayes, T. (1999). Vicarious learning from dialogue and discourse. *Instructional Science, 27*(6), 431–458.

Coyne, K., & Coyne, R. (2001). Dispelling the myths of character education. *Principal Leadership (High School Ed.), 2*(3), 58–60.

Craig, G. J. (1999). *Human development.* Upper Saddle River, NJ: Prentice Hall.

Craik, F. I. M., & Lockhart, R. S. (1972). Levels of processing: A framework for memory research. *Journal of Verbal Learning and Verbal Behavior, 11,* 671–684.

Crawford, M., & Chaffin, R. (1997). The meanings of difference: Cognition in social and cultural context. In P. J. Caplan, M. Crawford, J. S. Hyde, & J. T. E. Richardson (Eds.), *Gender differences in human cognition* (pp. 81–132). New York: Oxford University Press.

Creer, T. L., & Miklich, D. R. (1970). The application of a self-modeling procedure to modify inappropriate behavior: A preliminary report. *Behavior Research and Therapy, 8,* 91–92.

Crick, N. R., & Dodge, K. A. (1994). A review and reformulation of social information-processing mechanisms in children's social adjustment. *Psychological Bulletin, 115*(1), 74–101.

Cross, T. L. (2001). Gifted children and Erikson's theory of psychosocial development. *Gifted Child Today, 24*(1), 54–55, 61.

Cruthirds, J., & Hanna, M. S. (1997). *Programmed instruction and interactive multimedia: A third consideration.* Annandale, VA: National Communication Association.

Cruz, L., & Cullinan, D. (2001). Awarding points, using levels to help children improve behavior. *Teaching Exceptional Children, 33*(3), 16–23.

Cummins, J. (1984a). *Bilingualism and special education: Issues in assessment and pedagogy.* Clevedon, England: Multilingual Matters.

Cummins, J. (1984b). Wanted: A theoretical framework for relating language proficiency to academic achievement among bilingual students. In C. Rivera (Ed.), *Language proficiency and academic achievement* (pp. 2–19). Clevedon, England: Multilingual Matters.

Cunningham, G. K. (1998). *Assessment in the classroom.* London: The Falmer Press.

Curry, L. (1990). A critique of the research on learning styles. *Educational Leadership, 48*(2), 50–52, 54–56.

Cziko, G. A. (1992). The evaluation of bilingual education: From necessity and probability to possibility. *Educational Researcher, 21*(2), 10–15.

Dadson, S., & Horner, R. (1993). Manipulating setting events to decrease problem behaviors. *Teaching Exceptional Children, 25*(3), 53–55.

Dagher, Z. R. (1995). Review of studies on the effectiveness of instructional analogies in science education. *Science Education, 79*(3), 295–312.

Dahlgren, M. A., & Dahlgren, L. O. (2002). Portraits of PBL: Students' experiences of the characteristics of problem-based learning in physiotherapy, computer engineering, and psychology. *Instructional Science, 30,* 111–127.

Dallenbach, K. M. (1959). Twitmyer and the conditioned response. *American Journal of Psychology, 72,* 633–638.

Daly, E. J., Witt, J. C., Martens, B. K., & Dool, E. J. (1997). A model for conducting a functional analysis of academic performance problems. *School Psychology Review, 26*(4), 554–574.

Damon, W., & Hart, D. (1982). The development of self-understanding from infancy through adolescence. *Child Development, 53*(4), 841–864.

Daneman, M. (2001). Learning disabled individuals show deficits on working memory tasks: The question is why. *Issues in Education, 7*(1), 79–85.

Daniels, H. (1996). Introduction: Psychology in a social world. In H. Daniels (Ed.), *An introduction to Vygotsky* (pp. 1–27). London: Routledge.

Dansereau, D. F. (1995). Derived structural schemas and the transfer of knowledge. In A. McKeough, J. Lupart & A. Marini (Eds.), *Teaching for transfer: Fostering generalization in learning* (pp. 93–122). Mahwah, NJ: Erlbaum.

Darling-Hammond, L., & Wise, A. E. (1983). Teaching standards or standardized teaching? *Educational Leadership, 41*(1), 66–69.

Darling-Hammond, L. (1995). Inequality and access to knowledge. In J. A. Banks & C. A. M. Banks (Eds.), *Handbook of research on multicultural education* (pp. 465–483). New York: Macmillan.

Darveaux, D. (1984). The good behavior game plus merit: Controlling disruptive behavior and improving student motivation. *School Psychology Review, 13,* 510–514.

Davidson, J. E., & Downing, C. L. (2000). Contemporary models of intelligence. In R. J. Sternberg (Ed.), *Handbook of intelligence* (pp. 34–52). Cambridge: Cambridge University Press.

Davies, S., & Witte, R. (2000). Self-management and peer monitoring within a group contingency to decrease uncontrolled verbalization of children with attention deficit/hyperactivity disorder. *Psychology in the Schools, 37*(2), 135–147.

Davila, R., Williams, M. & MacDonald, J. (1991). *Certification of policy to address the needs of children with attention deficit disorders within general and special education.* Washington, D.C.: U.S. Department of Education.

Davis, G. A., & Rimm, S. B. (1998). *Education of the gifted and talented* (4th ed.). Boston: Allyn & Bacon.

de Groot, A. D. (1965). *Thought and choice in chess.* The Hague, The Netherlands: Mouton.

de Guerrero, M. C. M., & Villamil, O. S. (2000). Activating the ZPD: Mutual scaffolding in L2 peer revision. *Modern Language Journal, 84*(1), 51–68.

de Jong, T., & van Jollingen, W. R. (1998). Scientific discovery learning with computer simulations of conceptual domains. *Review of Educational Research, 68,* 179–201.

Deater-Deckard, K. (2001). Annotation: Recent research examining the role of peer relationships in the development of psychopathology. *Journal of Child Psychology & Psychiatry & Allied Disciplines, 42*(5), 565–579.

DeBacker, T. K., & Nelson, R M. (2001). Motivation to learn science: Differences related to gender, classtype, and ability. *The Journal of Educational Research, 93*(4), 245–254.

DeBettencourt, L. U. (2002). Understanding the differences between IDEA and Section 504. *Teaching Exceptional Children, 34*(3), 16–23.

Deci, E. L. (1992). The relation of interest to the motivation of behavior: A self-determination theory perspective. In K. A. Renninger, S. Hidi, & A. Krapp (Eds.), *The role of interest in learning and development* (pp. 43–70). Hillsdale, NJ: Erlbaum.

Deci, E. L., Koestner, R., & Ryan, R. M. (2001a). Extrinsic rewards and intrinsic motivation in education: Reconsidered once again. *Review of Educational Research, 71*(1), 1–27.

Deci, E. L., & Ryan, R. M. (1987). The support of autonomy and the control of behavior. *Journal of Personality and Social Psychology, 53,* 1024–1037.

Deci, E. L., Ryan, R. M., & Koestner, R. (2001b). The pervasive negative effects of rewards on intrinsic motivation: Response to Cameron (2001). *Review of Educational Research, 71*(1), 43–52.

DeCorte, E. (1999). On the road to transfer: An introduction. *International Journal of Educational Research, 31*(7), 555–559.

DeFrain, J., & Olson, D. H. L. (1999). Contemporary family patterns and relationships. In M. B. Sussman, S. K. Steinmetz, & G. W. Peterson (Eds.), *Handbook of marriage and the family* (2nd ed., pp. 309–326). New York: Plenum Press.

DeLeon, I. G., Fisher, W. W., Rodriquez-Catter, V., Maglieri, K., Herman, K., & Marhefka, J.-M. (2001). Examination of relative reinforcement effects of stimuli identified through pretreatment and daily brief assessments. *Journal of Applied Behavior Analysis, 34,* 463–473.

Delisle, J. (2001). In praise of elitism. *Gifted Child Today, 24*(1), 14–15.

Dempsey, J. V., & Johnson, R. B. (1998). The development of an ARCS gaming scale. *Journal of Instructional Psychology, 25*(4), 215–221.

Dempsey, J. V., & Van Eck, R. N. (2002). Instructional design on-line: Evolving expectations. In R. A. Reiser & J. V. Dempsey (Eds.), *Trends and issues in instructional design and technology.* Upper Saddle River, NJ: Merrill Prentice Hall.

Dempster, F. (1987). Effects of variable encoding and spaced presentations n vocabulary learning. *Journal of Educational Psychology, 79*(2), 162–170.

Dempster, F. N. (1991). Synthesis of research on reviews and tests. *Educational Leadership, 48*(7), 71–77.

Dempster, F. N. (1993). Exposing our students to less should help them learn more. *Phi Delta Kappan, 74*(6), 71–76.

Dempster, F. N., & Perkins, P. G. (1993). Revitalizing classroom assessments: Using tests to promote learning. *Journal of Instructional Psychology, 20*(3), 197–203.

Denning, R., & Smith, P. J. (1997). Cooperative learning and technology. *Journal of Computers in Mathematics and Science Teaching, 16*(2/3), 177–200.

DeRoche, E. F., & Williams, M., M. (2001). *Educating hearts and minds: A comprehensive character education framework* (2nd ed.). Thousand Oaks, CA: Corwin Press, Inc.

Derry, S., & Murphy, D. A. (1986). Designing systems that train learning ability: From theory to practice. *Review of Educational Research, 56*, 1–39.

Deshler, D. D., & Lenz, B. K. (1989). Strategies instructional approach. *International Journal of Disability, Development, & Education, 36*(3), 203–224.

Deshler, D., Ellis, E. S., & Lenz, B. K. (1996). *Teaching adolescents with learning disabilities: Strategies and methods*. Denver: Love Publishing.

Desimone, L. (1999). Linking parental involvement with student achievement: Do race and income matter? *Journal of Educational Research, 93*(1), 11–30.

Deslisle, R. (1997). *How to use problem-based learning in the classroom*. Alexandria, VA: ASCD.

Detterman, D. K. (1993). The case for the prosecution: Transfer as an epiphenomenon. In D. K. Detterman & R. J. Sternberg (Eds.), *Transfer on trial: Intelligence, cognition, and instruction*. Norwood, NJ: Ablex..

Dewey, J, (1916). *Democracy and education: An introduction to the philosophy of education*. New York: Macmillan.

Dicamillo, M. P. (2001). Parent education as an essential component of parent involvement programs. In D. B. Hiatt-Michael (Ed.), *Promising practices for family involvement in schools* (pp. 153–180). Greenwich, CT: Information Age Publishing.

Dick, W., Carey, L., & Carey, J. O. (2001). *The systematic design of instruction* (5th ed.). New York: Longman.

Dihoff, R. E., Brosvic, G. M., & Epstein, M. L. (2003). The role of feedback during academic testing: The delay retention effect revisited. *The Psychological Record, 53*, 533–548.

Dihoff, R. E., Brosvic, G. M., Epstein, M. L., & Cook, M. J. (2004). Provision of feedback during preparation for academic testing: Learning enhanced by immediate but not delayed feedback. *The Psychological Record, 54*, 207–231.

Dimaraki, E. V., Black, J. B., & Brown, M. K. (1998). What pedagogy for the age of abundant information? Lessons from "archaeotype." *Educational Media International, 35*(3), 181–185.

Dochy, F. J. R. C., Segers, M. S., & Buehl, M. M. (1999). The relation between assessment practices and outcomes of studies: The case of research on prior knowledge. *Review of Educational Research, 69*(2), 145–186.

Dockterman, D. (1998). Cooperative learning and technology: Using interactive group software. *Library Talk, 11*(4), 26–29.

Dodge, K. A., & Feldman, E. (1990). Issues in social cognition and sociometric status. In S. R. Asher & J. D. Cole (Eds.), *Peer rejection in childhood* (pp. 119–155). New York: Cambridge University Press.

Dodge, K. A., Murphy, R. R., & Buchsbaum, K. (1984). The assessment of intention-cue detection skills in children: Implications for developmental psychopathology. *Child Development, 55*, 163–173.

Dole, S. (2000). The implications of the risk and resilience literature for gifted students with learning disabilities. *Roeper Review, 23*(2), 91–96.

Doll, B. (1996). Children without friends: Implications for practice and policy. *School Psychology Review, 25*(2), 165–181.

Dollinger, S. J., & LaMartina, A. K. (1998). A note on moral reasoning and the five-factor model. *Journal of Social Behavior & Personality, 13*(2), 349–358.

Dolmans, D. H. J. M., Gijselaers, W. H., Moust, J. H. C., de Grave, W. S., Wolfhagen, I. H. A. P., & van der Vleuten, C. P. M. (2002). Trends in research on the tutor in problem-based learning: Conclusions and implications for educational practice and research. *Medical Teacher, 24*(2), 173–180.

Domjan, M., Cusato, B., & Villarreal, R. (2000). Pavlovian feed-forward mechanisms in the control of social behavior. *Behavioral and Brain Sciences, 23*, 235–282.

Donato, R. (1994). Collective scaffolding in second language learning. In J. P. Lantolf & G. Appel (Eds.), *Vygotskian approaches to second language research* (pp. 33–56). Norwood, NJ: Ablex.

Douvan, E., & Adelson, J. (1966). *The adolescent experience*. New York: Wiley.

Downey, C. J. (2001). Special delivery: Elements of instruction. *Leadership, 31*(2), 35–36.

Dowrick, P. W. (1999). A review of self-modeling and related interventions. *Applied & Preventive Psychology, 8*(1), 23–39.

Doyle, W. (1986). Classroom organization and management. In M. C. Wittrock (Ed.), *Handbook of Research on Teaching* (3rd ed.). New York: Macmillan.

Drasgow, E., Yell, M. L., & Robinson, T. R. (2001). Developing legally correct and educationally appropriate IEPs. *Remedial and Special Education, 22*(6), 359–373.

Dreikurs, R. (1968). *Psychology in the classroom: A manual for teachers* (2nd ed.). New York: Harper and Row.

Dreikurs, R., & Cassel, P. (1990). *Discipline without tears* (2nd ed.). New York: Dutton.

Dreikurs, R., & Soltz, V. (1987). *Children: The challenge*. New York: Dutton.

Driscoll, M. P. (1994). *Psychology of learning for instruction*. Boston: Allyn & Bacon.

Driscoll, M. P. (2001). Computers for what? Examining the roles of technology in teaching and learning. *Educational Research and Evaluation, 7*(2–3), 335–349.

Driscoll, M. P. (2002). Psychological foundations of instructional design. In R. A. Reiser & D. J. V. (Eds.), *Trends and issues in instructional design and technology* (pp. 57–69). Upper Saddle River, NJ: Merrill.

Druckman, D., & Bjork, R. A. (Eds.). (1991). *In the mind's eye: Enhancing human performance*. Washington D.C.: National Academy Press.

Duell, O. K. (1974). Effect of type of objective, level of test questions, and the judged importance of tested materials upon posttest performance. *Journal of Educational Psychology, 66*(2), 225–232.

Duell, O. K. (1986). Metacognitive skills. In G. D. Phye & T. Andre (Eds.). *Cognitive classroom learning: Understanding, thinking, and problem solving* (pp. 205–242). London: Academic Press.

Duffy, G. G., & Roehler, L. R. (1989). Why strategy instruction is so difficult and what we need to do about it. In C. B. McCormick, G. E. Miller & M. Pressley (Eds.). *Cognitive strategy research: From basic research to educational applications* (pp. 133–154). Berlin, NY: Springer-Verlag.

Duffy, G., Roehler, L., & Rackliffe, G. (1986). How teachers' instructional talk influences students' understandings of lesson content. *Elementary School Journal, 87*(1), 357–366.

Duncan, G. J., Brooks-Gunn, J., Yeung, W. J., & Smith, J. R. (1998). How much does childhood poverty affect the life chances of children? *American Sociological Review, 63*(3), 406–423.

Duncan, R. M. (1991, April). *An examination of Vygotsky's theory of children's private speech*. Paper presented at the biennial meeting of the Society for Research in Child Development, Seattle, WA.

Duncan, T. K., Kemple, K. M., & Smith, T. M. (2000). Reinforcement in developmentally appropriate early childhood classrooms. *Childhood Education, 76*(4), 194–203.

Dunn, L. M. (1968). Special education for the mildly retarded: Is much of it justifiable? *Exceptional Children, 23*, 5–21.

Dunn, R. S. (1998). Timing is everything. *Momentum, 29*(4), 23–25.

Dunn, R., & Dunn, K. (1978). *Teaching students through their individual learning styles*. Englewood Cliffs, NJ: Prentice Hall.

DuPaul, G. J., Eckert, T. L., & McGoey, K. E. (1997). Interventions for students with attention-deficit/hyperactivity disorder: One size does not fit all. *School Psychology Review, 26*(3), 369–381.

Duveen, G. (1997). Psychological development of a social process. In L. Smith, J. Dockrell, & P. Tomlinson (Eds.), *Piaget, Vygotsky, and beyond future issues for developmental psychology and education* (pp. 67–90). London: Routledge.

Dweck, C. S. (1992). The study of goals in psychology. *Psychological Science, 3*, 165–167.

Dweck, C. S. (1998). Development of early self-conceptions. In J. Heckhausen & C. S. Dweck (Eds.), *Motivation and self-regulation across the life span* (pp. 257–280). Cambridge: Cambridge University Press.

Dweck, C. S. (1999). Caution—Praise can be dangerous. *American Educator, 23*(1), 4–9.

Dweck, C. S., & Elliott, E. S. (1983). Achievement motivation. In P. H. Mussen (Ed.), *Handbook of child psychology* (3rd ed.) (Vol. 4, pp. 643–691). New York: Wiley.

Eacott, M. J. (1999). Memory for the events of early childhood. *Current Directions in Psychological Science, 8*, 46–49.

Earl, F. A. (1982). The use of backward chaining in demonstration films. *Performance and Instruction, 21*(7), 23–26.

Eccles (Parsons), J., Adler, T. F., Futterman, R., Goff, S. B., Klaczala, C. M., Meece, J. L., & Midgley, C. (1983). Expectancies, values and academic behaviors. In J. T. Spence (Ed.), *Achievement and schievement motives*. San Francisco: W. H. Freeman and Company.

Eccles, J. S., & Midgley, C. (1989). Stage/environment fit: Developmentally appropriate classrooms for early adolescents. In R. E. Ames & C. Ames (Eds.), *Research on motivation in education* (pp. 139–186). San Diego: Academic Press.

Eccles, J. S., & Wigfield, A. (1995). In the mind of the actor: The structure of adolescents' achievement task-values and expectancy-related beliefs. *Personality and Social Psychology Bulletin, 21*(3), 215–225.

Eccles, J. S., Midgley, C., Wigfield, A., Buchanan, C. M., Reuman, D., Flanagan, C., et al. (1993). Development during adolescence: The impact of stage-environment fit on young adolescents' experiences in schools and in families. *American Psychologist, 48*(2), 90–101.

Eccles, J. S., Wigfield, A., Midgley, C., Reuman, D., Mac Iver, D., & Feldlaufer, H. (1993). Negative effects of traditional middle schools on students' motivation. *Elementary School Journal, 93*(5), 553–574.

Eccles, J., Wigfield, A., & Schiefele, U. (1998). Motivation to succeed. In W. Damon (Ed.), *Handbook of child psychology* (5th ed., Vol 3, pp. 1017–1096). New York: Wiley.

Echevarria, J., Vogt, M., & Short, D. J. (2000). *Making content comprehensible for English language learners: The SIOP model.* Boston: Allyn & Bacon.

Edens, K. M. (2000). Preparing problem solvers for the 21st century through problem-based learning. *College Teaching, 48*(2), 55–60.

Edgington, W. D. (2002). To promote character education, use literature for children and adolescents. *The Social Studies, 93*(3), 113–116.

Edmondson, K. M. (1995). Concept mapping for the development of medical curricula. *Journal of Research in Science Teaching, 32* (7), 777–793.

Edyburn, D. L. (2000). Assistive technology and students with mild disabilities. *Focus on Exceptional Children, 32*(9), 1–23.

Ehrler, D. J., Evans, J. G., & McGhee, R. L. (1999). Extending big-five theory into childhood: A preliminary investigation into the relationship between big-five personality traits and behavior problems in children. *Psychology in the Schools, 36*(6), 451–458.

Eisenberg, N. (1989a). *The development of prosocial moral reasoning in childhood and mid-adolescence.* Paper presented at the Society for Research in Child Development, Kansas City.

Eisenberg, N. (1989b). The development of prosocial values. In N. Eisenberg, J. Reykowski, & E. Staub (Eds.), *Social and moral values: Individual and social perspectives* (pp. 87–104). Hillsdale, NJ: Erlbaum.

Eisenberg, N., & Fabes, R. A. (1998). Prosocial development. In W. Damon (Editor-in-Chief) & N. Eisenberg (Vol. Ed.), *Handbook of child psychology: Vol. 3, Social, emotional, and personality development)* (Fifth ed., pp. 701–778). New York: John Wiley & Sons.

Eisenberg, N., Martin, C. L., & Fabes, R. A. (1996). Gender development and gender effects. In D. C. Berliner & R. C. Calfee (Eds.), *Handbook of educational psychology* (pp. 358–398). New York: Macmillan.

Elbaum, B., & Vaughn, S. (2001). School-based interventions to enhance the self-concepts of students with learning disabilities: A meta-analysis. *The Elementary School Journal, 101*(3), 303–329.

Elkind, D. (1967). Egocentrism in adolescence. *Child Development, 38,* 1025–1034.

Elkind, D. (1976). Elkind updates Piaget. *Day Care and Early Education, 4*(1), 9–10.

Elkind, D. (1985). Egocentrism redux. *Developmental Review, 5,* 218–226.

Elliot, A. J. (1999). Approach and avoidance motivation and achievement goals. *Educational Psychologist, 34*(3), 169–189.

Elliot, A. J., & Covington, M. V. (2001). Approach and avoidance motivation. *Educational Psychology Review, 13*(2), 73–88.

Elliott, C. D. (1997). The differential ability scales. In D. P. Flanagan, J. L. Genshaft, & P. L. Harrison (Eds.), *Contemporary intellectual assessment theories, tests, and issues* (pp. 183–208). New York: Guilford.

Ellis, A. K., & Fouts, J. (1993). *Research on educational innovations.* Princeton Junction, NJ: Eye on Education.

Emerson, C. (1997). The outer word and inner speech Bakhtin, Vygotsky, and the internalization of language. In H. Daniels (Ed.), *An introduction to Vygotsky* (pp. 123–142). London: Routledge.

Emmer, E. T., & Stough, L. M. (2001). Classroom management: A critical part of educational psychology, with implications for teacher education. *Educational Psychologist, 36*(2), 103–112.

Emmer, E. T., Evertson, C., & Anderson, L. (1980). Effective classroom management at the beginning of the school year. *Elementary School Journal, 80*(5), 219–231.

Engelmann, S., & Carnine, D. (1991). *Theory of instruction: Principles and applications.* Eugene, OR: ADI Press.

Engeström, C. (1996). Bob scolae se vitae discimus: Toward overcoming the encapsulation of school learning. In H. Daniels (Ed.), *An introduction to Vygotsky.* London: Routledge.

Englemann, S., & Bruner, E. (1974). *DISTAR reading level I.* Chicago, IL: Science Research Associates.

Englemann, S., & Bruner, E. C. (1995). *The SRA reading mastery rainbow.* New York: McGraw Hill.

Ennett, S. T., & Bauman, K. E. (1996). Adolescent social networks: School, demographic, and longitudinal considerations. *Journal of Adolescent Research, 11*(2), 194–215.

Eppler, M., Carsen-Plentl, C., & Hrju, B. L. (2000). Achievement goals, failure attributions and academic performance in nontraditional and traditional college students. *Journal of Social Behavior and Personality, 15*(3) 353–372.

Epstein, J. L. (1992). School and family partnerships. In M. Aiken (Ed.), *Encyclopedia of educational research* (6th ed., pp. 1139–1151). New York: Macmillan.

Epstein, J. L. (1994). *Perspectives and previews on research and policy for school, family, and community partnerships.* Paper presented at the National Symposium, Family-Schools Links: How do They affect Educational Outcomes? Pennsylvania State University.

Ericcson, K. N. & Charness, N. (1997). Expert performance: Its structure and acquisition. *American Psychologist, 49*(8), 725–747.

Erickson, F. (1987). Transformation and school success: The politics and culture of educational achievement. *Anthropological and Educational Quarterly, 18,* 335–356.

Ericsson, K. A., & Simon, H. A. (1993). *Protocol analysis: Verbal reports as data.* Cambridge, MA: MIT Press.

Ericsson, K. A., & Charness, N. (1997). Expert performance: Its structure and acquisition. *American Psychologist, 49*(8), 725–747.

Erikson, E. H. (1963). *Childhood and society* (2nd ed.). New York: Norton.

Erikson, E. H. (1972). Eight ages of man. In C. S. Lavatelli & F. Stendler (Eds.), *Readings in child behavior and child development.* San Diego: Harcourt Brace Jovanovich.

Etaugh, C. (1983). The influence of environmental factors on sex differences in children's play. In M. B. Liss (Ed.), *Social and cognitive skills: Sex roles and children's play* (pp. 1–21). New York: Academic Press.

Evans, C., & Eder, D. (1993). "No exit": Processes of social isolation in middle school. *Journal of Contemporary Ethnography, 22,* 139–170.

Evertson, C. M., & Emmer, E. T. (1982a). Effective management at the beginning of the year in junior high classes. *Journal of Educational Psychology, 74*(4), 485–498.

Evertson, C. M., & Emmer, E. T. (1982b). Preventative classroom management. In D. Duke (Ed.), *Helping teachers manage classrooms* (pp. 28–29). Alexandria, VA: Association for Supervision and Curriculum Development.

Evertson, C. M., & Harris, A. H. (1992). What we know about managing classrooms. *Educational Leadership, 50,* 74–78.

Evertson, C. M., & Harris, A. H. (1999). Support for managing learning-centered classrooms: The classroom organization and management program. In H. J. Freiberg (Ed.), *Beyond behaviorism: Changing the classroom management paradigm* (pp. 59–74). Boston: Allyn & Bacon.

Evertson, C. M., Emmer, E. T., Clements, B. S., & Worsham, M. E. (2000). *Classroom management for elementary teachers* (5th Ed.). Boston: Allyn & Bacon.

Evertson, C., Emmer, E. T., & Worsham, M. E. (2000). *Classroom management for elementary teachers* (5th ed.). Boston: Allyn & Bacon.

Ewing, T. S. (2000). Time-out: Guidelines for teachers. In *Behavioral interventions: Creating a safe environment in our schools* (pp. 28–29). Bethesda, MD: National Association of School Psychologists (ED437600).

Exner, J. E. (1986). *The Rorschach: A comprehensive system: Volume 1: Basic foundations* (2nd ed.). Cambridge, MA: John Wiley.

Exner, J. E. (1995). The Rorschach: *A comprehensive system: Volume 3: Assessment of children and adolescents* (2nd ed.). New York: John Wiley.

Eysenck, H. J. (1998). *A new look intelligence.* New Brunswick, NJ: Transaction Publishers.

Eysenck, M. W. (1981). Learning, memory, and personality. In H. J. Eysenck (Ed.), *A model for personality* (pp. 169–203). Berlin: Springer.

Fall, M., & McLeod, E. H. (2001). Identifying and assisting children with low self-efficacy. *Professional School Counseling, 4*(5), 334–341.

Fan, X., & Chen, M. (2001). Parental involvement and students' academic achievement: A meta-analysis. *Educational Psychology Review, 13*(1), 1–22.

Farmer, H. S., Wardrop, J. L., & Rotella, S. C. (1999). Antecedent factors differentiating women and men in science/nonscience careers. *Psychology of Women Quarterly, 23,* 763–780.

Farrell, P. (1997). The integration of children with severe learning difficulties: A review of the recent literature. *Journal of Applied Research in Intellectual Disabilities, 10,* 1–14.

Farrow, S., Tymms, P., & Henderson, B. (1999). Homework and attainment in primary schools. *British Educational Research Journal, 25*(3), 323–341.

Farver, J. A. M., & Frosch, D. L. (1996). L. A. stories: Aggression in preschoolers; spontaneous narratives after the riots of 1992. *Child Development, 67*(1), 19–32.

Fasko, D. (2001). An analysis of multiple intelligences theory and its use with the gifted and talented. *Roeper Review, 23*(3), 126–130.

Faw, H. W., & Waller, T. G. (1976). Mathemagenic behaviours and efficiency in learning from prose materials: review, critique and recommendations. *Review of Educational Research, 46*(4), 691–720.

Feigenbaum, R. (2000). Algebra for students with learning disabilities. *Mathematics Teacher, 93*(4), 270–274.

Feldman, R. S. (2000). *Development across the life span* (2nd ed.). Upper Saddle River, NJ: Prentice Hall.

Felixbrod, J. J., & O'Leary, K. D. (1974). Self-determination of academic standards by children: Toward freedom from external control. *Journal of Educational Psychology, 66*, 845–850.

Fennema, E. (1981). The sex factor. In E. Fennema (Ed.), *Mathematics education research: Implications for the 80s* (pp. 92–110). Reston, VA: NCTM.

Fenwick, T. J. (2000). Expanding conceptions of experiential learning: A review of the five contemporary perspectives on cognition. *Adult Education Quarterly, 50*(4), 243–272.

Ferguson, E. D. (2000). *Motivation: A biosocial and cognitive integration of motivation and emotions.* New York: Oxford University Press.

Fernberger, S. W. (1943). Edwin Burket Twitmyer 1873–1943. *The Psychological Review, 50*(3), 345–349.

Ferrari, M. (1996). Observing the observer: Self-regulation in the observational learning of motor skills. *Developmental Review, 16*, 203–240.

Ferster, C. B. (2002). Schedules of reinforcement with Skinner. *Journal of Experimental Analysis of Behavior, 77*(3), 303–311.

Ferster, C. B., & Skinner, B. F. (1957). *Schedules of reinforcement.* Englewood Cliffs, NJ: Prentice Hall.

Fiedler, E. D., Lange, R. E., & Winebrenner, S. (2002). In search of reality: Unraveling the myths about tracking, ability grouping, and the gifted. *Roeper Review, 24*(3), 108–111.

Fischbein, E. (1999). Psychology and mathematics education. *Mathematical thinking & Learning, 1*(1), 47–58.

Fishbein, J., & Wasik, B. (1981). Effect of the Good Behavior Game on disruptive library behavior. *Journal of Applied Behavior Analysis, 14*, 89–93.

Fisher, W. W., & Thompson, R. H. (2000). Facilitating tolerance of delayed reinforcement during functional communication training. *Behavior Modification, 24*(1), 3–29.

Fitts, P. M., & Posner, M. I. (1967). *Human performance.* Belmont, CA: Brooks/Cole Publishers.

Flanagan, D. P., Andrews, T. J., & Genshaft, J. L. (1997). The functional utility of intelligence tests with special education populations. In D. P. Flanagan, J. L. Genshaft, & P. L. Harrison (Eds.), *Contemporary intellectual assessment theories, tests, and issues* (pp. 457–483). New York: Guilford.

Flavell, J. R. (1979). Metacognition and cognitive monitoring A new area of cognitive-developmental inquiry. *Educational Psychologist, 34*(10), 906–911.

Flower, L., & Hayes, J. R. (1981). Plans that guide the composing process. In C. H. Frederiksen & J. F. Dominic (Eds.), *Writing: Volume 2.* Hillsdale, NJ: Erlbaum.

Flynn, J. L. (1992). Cooperative learning and Gagne's events of instruction: A syncretic view. *Educational Technology, 32*, 53–60.

Ford, D. Y. (1999). Renzulli's philosophy and program: Opening doors and nurturing potential. *Journal for the Education of the Gifted, 23*(1), 117–124.

Ford, D. Y. (2000). The Office for Civil Rights and non-discriminatory testing, policies, and procedures. *Roeper Review, 23*(2), 109.

Ford, D. Y., Harmon, D. A. (2001). Equity and excellence: Providing access to gifted education for culturally diverse students. *Journal of Secondary Gifted Education, 12*(3), 141–147.

Ford, M. R., & Lowery, C. R. (1986). Gender differences in moral reasoning: A comparison of the use of justice and care orientations. *Journal of Personality and Social Psychology, 30*, 777–783.

Fordham, S., & Ogbu, J. U. (1986). Black students' school success: Coping with the "burden of acting white." *Urban Review, 18*(3), 176–206.

Foshee, V. A., Bauman, K. E., & Linder, G. F. (1999). Family violence and the perpetration of adolescent dating violence: Examining social learning and control processes. *Journal of Marriage & Family, 61*(2), 331–342.

Foster, M. (1995). African American teachers and culturally relevant pedagogy. In J. A. Banks & C. A. M. Banks (Eds.), *Handbook of research on multicultural education* (pp. 570–581). New York: Macmillan.

Fox, J. (1990). Ecology, environmental arrangement, and setting events: An interbehavioral perspective on organizing settings for behavioral development. *Education and Treatment of Children, 13*(4), 364–372.

Foxx, R. M., & Azrin, N. H. (1972). Restitution: A method of eliminating aggressive-disruptive behavior of retarded and brain damaged patients. *Behaviour Research and Therapy, 10*, 15–27.

Foxx, R. M., & Shapiro, S. T. (1978). The time-out ribbon: A nonseclusionary timeout procedure. *Journal of Applied Behavior Analysis, 11*, 125–136.

Fraisse, P., & Piaget, J. (Eds.). (1963). *Experimental psychology: Its scope and method.* New York: Basic Books.

Franklin, M. E., Prince, V. F., & Yu, T. (2000). Reflective practice: Approaches for teaching learners with behavior disorders. In F. E. Obiakor, S. A. Burkhardt, A. F. Rotatori, & T. Wahlberg (Eds.), *Intervention techniques for individuals with exceptionalities in inclusive settings* (pp. 79–94). Stamford, CT: JAI Press.

Franklin, S. C., & Warshawsky, J. D. (2000). Inclusive classroom interventions for children displaying ADHD-type behaviors. In F. E. Obiakor, S. A. Burkhardt, A. F. Rotatori, & T. Wahlberg (Eds.), *Intervention techniques for individuals with exceptionalities in inclusive settings* (pp. 173–198). Stamford, CT: JAI Press.

Fredericksen, L. W., & Fredericksen, C. B. (1975). Teacher determined and self-determined token reinforcement in a special education classroom. *Behavioral Therapy, 6*, 310–314.

Freeman, J. (1994). Some emotional aspects of being gifted. *Journal for the Education of the Gifted, 17*(2), 180–197.

Freeman, J. (1999). Teaching gifted pupils. *Journal of Biological Education, 33*(4), 185–190.

Freiberg, H. J. (1999). Beyond behaviorism. In H. J. Freiberg (Ed.), *Beyond behaviorism: Changing the classroom management paradigm* (pp. 3–20). Boston: Allyn & Bacon.

Freiberg, H. J., & Driscoll, A. (2000). *Universal teaching strategies.* Boston: Allyn & Bacon.

Fuchs, L. S., Fuchs, D., Eaton, S. B., Hamlett, C., Binkley, E., & Crouch, R. (2000). Using objective data sources to enhance teacher judgments about test accommodations. *Exceptional Children, 67*(1), 67–81.

Fuchs, L. S., Fuchs, D., Hamlett, C. L., & Appleton, A. C. (2002). Explicitly teaching for transfer: Effects on the mathematical problem-solving performance of students with mathematics disabilities. *Learning Disabilities Research and Practice, 17*(2), 90–106.

Fulk, B. M., & Starmont-Spurgin, M. (1999). Fourteen spelling strategies for students with learning disabilities. *Intervention in School and Clinic, 95*(1), 16–21.

Furth, H. (1970). *Piaget for teachers.* Englewood Cliffs, NJ: Prentice Hall.

Furth, H. G., & Wachs, W. (1974). *Thinking goes to school.* New York: Oxford University Press.

Gable, R. A., Hendrickson, J. M., & Shellady, S. (1992). Strategies for improving maintenance and generalization of academic skills—so students "don't leave class without it." *Preventing School Failure, 37*(1), 35–40.

Gagné, E. D., Yekovich C. W., & Yekovich, F. R. (1993). *The Cognitive psychology of school learning* (2nd ed.), New York: Harper Collins College Publishers.

Gagné, R. M. (1985). *Conditions of learning* (4th ed.). New York: Holt, Rinehart, & Winston.

Gagné, R. M., & Driscoll, M. P. (1988). *Essentials of learning for instruction* (2nd ed.). Englewood Cliffs, NJ: Prentice Hall.

Gagné, R. M., & Medsker, K. L. (1996). *The conditions of learning: Training applications.* Fort Worth, TX: Harcourt Brace College Publishers.

Gagné, R. M., & Merrill, M. D. (1990). Integrative goals for instructional design. *Educational Technology, Research and Development, 38*(1), 23–30.

Gagné, R. M., Briggs, L. J., & Wager, W. W. (1988). *Principles of instructional design* (3rd ed.). New York: Holt, Rinehart, and Winston.

Gallagher, J. J., & Gallagher, S. A. (1994). *Teaching the gifted child.* Boston: Allyn & Bacon.

Gallagher, L. A., Alvarez-Salvat, R., Silsbee, J., & Kenny, M. E. (2002). Sources of support and psychological distress among academically successful inner-city youth. *Adolescence, 37*(145), 161–182.

Gallimore, R., & Goldenberg, C. (1993). In E. A. Forman, N. Minick, & C. A. Stone (Eds.), *Contexts for learning: Sociocultural dynamics in children's development* (pp. 315–335). New York: Oxford University Press.

Gallimore, R., & Tharp, R. (1990). Teaching mind in society: Teaching, schooling, and literate discourse. In L. C. Moll (Ed.), *Vygotsky and education* (pp. 175–205). New York: Cambridge University Press.

Garbarino, J. (1999). How we can save violent boys. *Education Digest, 65*(4), 28–32.

Gardner, H. (1983). *Frames of mind: The theory of multiple intelligences.* New York: Basic Books.

Gardner, H. (1994). Are intelligence tests intelligent? In R. H. Ettinger, R. L. Crooks, & J. Stein (Eds.), *Psychology: Science, behavior, and life* (pp. 214–221). Forth Worth, TX: Harcourt Brace College Publishers.

Gardner, H. (1995). Reflections on multiple intelligences: Myths and messages. *Phi Delta Kappan, 77*(3), 206–209.

Gardner, H. (1999a). *Intelligence reframed multiple intelligences for the 21st century.* New York: Basic Books.

Gardner, H. (1999b). *The disciplined mind.* New York: Simon & Schuster.

Gardner, H., & Hatch, T. (1989). Multiple intelligences go to school. *Educational Researcher, 18,* 4–10.

Garmezy, N, (1985). Stress resilient children: The search for protective factors. In J. E. Stevenson (Ed.), *Recent research in developmental psychopathology* (pp. 213–233). Oxford: Pergamon.

Garner, R., Brown, R., Sanders, S., & Menke, D. J. (1992). "Seductive details" and learning from text. In K. A. Renninger, S. Hidi, & A. Krapp (Eds.), *The role of interest in learning and development* (pp. 239–254). Hillsdale, NJ: Erlbaum.

Garrod, A., & Beall, C. R. (1993). Voice of care and justice in children's responses to fable dilemmas. In A. Garrod (Ed.). *Approaches to moral development: New research and emerging themes* (pp. 59–71). New York: Teachers College Press.

Garroutte, E. M. (1999). American Indian science education: The second step. *Indian Culture and Research Journal, 23,* 91–114.

Gartrell, D. (2002). Replacing time-out: Part two-using guidance to maintain an encouraging classroom. *Young Children, 57*(2), 36–43.

Gartrell, D. J. (2001). Replacing time-out: Part one—using guidance to build and encouraging classroom. *Young Children, 56*(6), 8–16.

Gaskill, P. J., & Woolfolk Hoy, A. (2002). Self-efficacy and self-regulated learning: The dynamic duo in school performance. In J. Aronson (Ed.), *Improving academic achievement impact of psychological factors on education* (pp. 185–207). Amsterdam: Academic Press.

Gaskins, I. W., Anderson, R. C., Pressley, M., Cunicelli, E. A., & Satlow, E. (1993). Six teachers' dialogue during cognitive process instruction. *Elementary School Journal, 93*(3), 277–304.

Gay, G. (2000). *Culturally responsive teaching: Theory, research, and practice.* New York: Teachers College Press.

Gay, L. R., & Airasian, P. (2000). *Educational research: Competencies for analysis and applications* (6th ed.). Upper Saddle River, NJ: Prentice Hall.

Geisthardt, C. L., Brotherson, M. J., & Cook, C. C. (2002). Friendships of children with disabilities in the home environment. *Education and Training in Mental Retardation and Developmental Disabilities, 37*(3), 235–252.

Gelman, R., & Baillargeon, R. (1983). A review of some Piagetian concepts. In J. H. Flavell & E. M. Markman (Eds.), *Handbook of child psychology: Vol. 3. Cognitive development* (4th ed., pp. 167–230). New York: Wiley.

"Gender differences in educational achievement within racial and ethnic groups." (2001). In *ERIC Digest Number 164* (ERIC Document Reproduction Services No. ED455341).

Genesee, F. (2000). Teaching linguistically diverse students. *Principal, 79*(5), 24–27.

Genesee, F., & Cloud, N. (1998). Multilingualism is basic. *Educational Leadership, 55,* 62–65.

Gentner, D. (1989). The mechanisms of analogic learning. In S. Vosniadou & A. Ortony (Eds.), *Similarity and analogical reasoning* (pp. 197–241). Cambridge, MA: Cambridge University Press.

Gerst, M. S. (1971). Symbolic coding processes in observational learning. *Journal of Personality and Social Psychology, 19,* 7–17.

Gersten, R., & Baker, S. (1998). Real world use of scientific concepts: Integrating situated cognition and explicit instruction. *Exceptional Children, 65*(1), 23–35.

Gesi, A. T., & Massaro, D. W. (1992). Discovery and expository methods in teaching visual consonant and word identification. *Journal of Speech and Hearing Research, 35*(5), 1180–1188.

Gestwicki, C. (1999). *Developmentally appropriate practice: Curriculum and development in early education* (2nd ed.). Albany, NY: Delmar.

Gettinger, M., & Koscik, R. (2001). Psychological services for children with learning disabilities. In J. N. Hughes, A. M. La Greca, & J. C. Conoley (Eds.), *Handbook of psychological services for children and adolescents* (pp. 421–438). Oxford: Oxford University Press.

Giangreco, M. F., Edelman, S. W., Luiselli, T. E., & MacFarland, S. Z. C. (1997). Helping or hovering? Effects of instructional assistant proximity of students with disabilities. *The Council for Exceptional Children, 64*(1), 7–18.

Gick, M. L., & Holyoak, K. J. (1987). The cognitive basis of knowledge transfer. In S. M. Cormier & J. D. Hagman (Eds.), *Transfer of learning: Contemporary research and applications* (pp. 9–46). San Diego: Academic Press.

Gilbert, C. L. (2000). The comorbidity of learning disabilities and social skills deficits: Implications for school intervention. In F. E. Obiakor, S. A. Burkhardt, A. F. Rotatori, A. F., & T. Wahlberg (Eds.). *Intervention techniques for individuals with exceptionalities in inclusive settings* (pp. 327–346). Stamford, CT: JAI Press.

Gilligan, C. (1982). *In a different voice.* Cambridge, MA: Harvard University Press.

Gilligan, C. (1993). Adolescent development reconsidered. In A. Garrod (Ed.), *Approaches to moral development: New research and emerging themes* (pp. 103–131). New York: Teachers College Press.

Gilligan, C. L., Kohlberg, L., Lerner, J., & Belenky, M. (1971). Moral reasoning about sexual dilemmas: The development of an interview and scoring system. In *Technical report of the U.S. committee on pornography and obscenity* (Vol. I).

Gilligan, C., & Attanucci, J. (1988). Two moral orientations: Gender differences and similarities. *Merrill-Palmer Quarterly, 34,* 223–237.

Ginsburg, H. P., & Opper, S. (1988). *Piaget's theory of intellectual development* (3rd ed.). Upper Saddle River, NJ: Prentice Hall.

Girard, K., & Koch, S. J. (1996). *Conflict resolution in the schools: A manual for educators.* San Francisco: Jossey-Bass.

Glaser, R. E. (1984). Education and thinking: The role of knowledge. *American Psychologist, 39*(2), 93–104.

Glasser, W. (1969). *Schools without failure.* New York: Harper & Row.

Glasser, W. (1986). *Control theory in the classroom.* New York: Harper & Row.

Glasser, W. (1990). *The quality school: Managing students without coercion* (1st ed.). New York: Perennial Library.

Glasser, W. (1998). *Building a quality school: A matter of responsibility.* Port Chester, NY: National Professional Resources.

Glazer, N. T., & Williams, S. (2001). Averting the homework crisis. *Educational Leadership, 58*(7), 43–45.

Glick, J. (1975). Cognitive development in cross-cultural perspective. In F. Horowitz (Ed.), *Review of child development research* (Vol. 4, pp. 595–654). Chicago: University of Chicago Press.

Goetz, E. T., & Hall, R. J. (1984). Evaluation of the Kaufman Assessment Battery for Children from an information-processing analysis and critique. *Journal of Special Education, 18*(3), 281–296.

Goldberg, L. R. (1990). An alternative "description of personality": The Big-Five factor structure. *Journal of Personality and Social Psychology, 59,* 1216–1229.

Goldberg, L. R. (1993). The structure of phenotypic personality traits. *American Psychologist, 48,* 26–34.

Goldman, S. R., & Pelligrino, J. W. (1984). Deductions about deduction: Analyses of developmental and individual differences. In R. J. Sternberg (Ed.), *Advances in the psychology of human intelligence* (Vol. 2, pp. 147–197). Hillsdale, NJ: Erlbaum.

Gollnick, D. M., & Chinn, P. C. *Multicultural education in a pluralistic society* (5th ed.).

Good, T. L., & Brophy, J. E. (2000). *Looking in classrooms* (8th ed.). Boston: Allyn & Bacon.

Good, T. L., & Brophy, J. E. (2003). *Looking in classrooms* (9th ed.). Boston: Allyn & Bacon.

Gordon, D. G. (2001). Classroom management: Problems and solutions. *Music Educators Journal, 88*(2), 17–23.

Gordon, T. (1974). *T. E. T. Teacher Effectiveness Training.* New York: Peter. H. Wyden.

Gorman, A. H., Kim, J., & Schimmelbusch, A. (2002). The attributes adolescents associate with peer popularity and teacher preference. *Journal of School Psychology, 40*(2), 143–165.

Gould, S. J. (1981). *The mismeasure of man.* New York: Norton.

Grabinger, R. S., & Dunlap, J. C. (1995). Rich environments for active learning: A definition. *Association for Learning Technology Journal, 5*(2), 3–17.

Graden, J. L. (1989). Redefining prereferral intervention as instructional assistance: Collaboration between general and special education. *Exceptional Children, 56*(3), 227–231.

Graham, N. A., & Kershner, J. R. (1996). Reading styles in children with dyslexia: A neuropsychological evaluation of modality preference on the "Reading style inventory." *Learning Disability Quarterly, 19*(4), 233–240.

Graham, S. (1984). Communicating sympathy and anger to black and white children: The cognitive (attributional) consequences of affective cues. *Journal of Personality and Social Psychology, 47,* 40–54.

Graham, S. (1994). Classroom motivation from an attributional perspective. In H. F. O'Neil & M. Drillings (Eds.), *Motivation: Theory and research* (pp. 31–48). Hillsdale, NJ: Erlbaum.

Graham, S., & Weiner, B. (1996). Theories and principles of motivation. In D. C. Berliner & R. C. Calfee (Eds.), *Handbook of educational psychology* (pp. 63–84). New York: Simon & Schuster Macmillan.

Graham, S., Harris, K. R., & Reid, R. (1992). Developing self-regulated learners. *Focus on Exceptional Children, 24*(6), 1–16.

Gray, J. A. (1979). *Ivan Pavlov.* New York: Viking Press.

Green, G. (2001). Behavior analytic instruction for learners with autism: Advances in stimulus control. *Focus on Autism and Other Developmental Disabilities, 16*(2), 72–85.

Greenberg, P. (2000). The value of classroom rituals and routines. *Scholastic Early Childhood Today, 15*(1), 52–59.

Greener, S. H. (2000). Peer assessment of children's prosocial behaviour. *Journal of Moral Education, 29*(1), 47–60.

Greenfield, P. M. (1999). Cultural change and human development. *New Directions for Child and Adolescent Development, 83,* 37–59.

Greenhill, L. (1995). Attention-deficit hyperactivity disorder: The stimulants. *Child and Adolescent Psychiatric Clinics of North America, 4*(1), 123–168.

Greening, T. (1998). Building the constructivist toolbox: An exploration of cognitive technologies. *Educational Technology, 38*(2), 23–35.

Greeno, J. G. (1991). Number sense as situated knowing in a conceptual domain. *Journal of Research in Mathematics Education, 22*(3), 170–218.

Greeno, J. G. (1997). On claims that answer the wrong questions. *Educational Researcher, 26*(1), 5–17.

Greeno, J. G., Moore, J. L., & Smith, D. R. (1993). Transfer of situated learning. In D. K. Detterman & R. J. Sternberg (Eds.), *Transfer on trial: Intelligence, cognition, and instruction* (pp. 99–167). Norwood, NJ: Ablex.

Greenspan, S. L., & Weider, S. W. (1997). Developmental patterns and outcomes in infants and children with disorders in relating and communicating: A chart review of 200 cases of children with autistic spectrum diagnoses. *Journal of Developmental and Learning Disorders, 1,* 87–141.

Gregoric, A. F. (1985). *Inside styles: Beyond the basics.* Maynard, MA: Gabriel Systems.

Griffin, M. M. (1995). You can't get there from here: Situated learning, transfer, and map skills. *Contemporary Educational Psychology, 20,* 65–87.

Griffin, P., & Cole, M. (1984). Current activity for the future: The Zoped. In B. Rogoff & J. V. Wertsch (Eds.), *Children's learning in the zone of proximal development* (pp. 45–63). San Francisco: Jossey-Bass.

Gronlund, N. E. (2000). *How to write and use instructional objectives* (6th ed.). Upper Saddle River, NJ: Merrill.

Gropper, G. L. (1974). *Instructional strategies.* Englewood Cliffs, NJ: Educational Technology Publications.

Gropper, G. L. (1975). *Diagnosis and revision in the development of instructional materials.* Englewood Cliffs, NJ: Educational Technology Publications.

Gropper, G. L. (1983). A behavioral approach to instructional prescription. In C. M. Reigeluth (Ed.), *Instructional theories and models: An overview of their current status.* Hillsdale, NJ: Erlbaum.

Gropper, G. L. (1987). A lesson based on a behavioral approach to instructional design. In C. M. Reigeluth (Ed.), *Instructional theories in action lessons illustrating selected theories and models* (pp. 45–112). Hillsdale, NJ: Erlbaum.

Gross, J., & Kientz, S. (1999). Collaborating for authentic learning. *Teacher Librarian, 27*(1), 21–25.

Grossman, H. (1995). *Teaching, in a diverse society.* Boston: Allyn & Bacon.

Gruber, H. E., & Vonèche, J. J. (Eds.). (1977). *The essential Piaget an interpretive reference and guide.* New York: Basic Books.

Grusec, J. (1992). Social learning theory and developmental psychology: The legacies of Robert Sears and Albert Bandura. *Developmental Psychology, 28*(5), 776–786.

Guilford, J. P. (1967). *The nature of human intelligence.* New York: McGraw-Hill.

Guilford, J. P. (1981). Higher-order structure-of-intellect abilities. *Multi-variate Behavioral Research, 16,* 411–435.

Guilford, J. P. (1985). The structure-of-intellect model. In B. B. Wolman (Ed.), *Handbook of intelligence: Theories, measurements, and applications* (pp. 225–266). New York: Wiley.

Guskey, T. R. (1997). *Implementing mastery learning* (2nd ed.). Belmont, CA: Wadsworth.

Guskey, T. R. (2001). *Benjamin B. Bloom's contributions to curriculum, instruction, and school learning.* Paper presented at the Annual Meeting of the American Educational Research Association, Seattle, WA.

Guskey, T. R. (2003). How classroom assessments improve learning. *Educational Leadership, 60*(5), 6–11.

Guskey, T. R., & Pigott, T. D. (1988). Research on group-based mastery learning programs: A meta-analysis. *Journal of Educational Research, 60*(2), 265–299.

Gustafsson, J. E. (1996). Individual differences in cognitive functions. In D. C. Berliner & R. C. Calfee (Eds.), *Handbook of educational psychology* (pp. 186–242). New York: Prentice Hall International.

Gustafsson, J. E., & Undheim, J. O. (1996). Individual differences in cognitive functions. In D. C. Berliner & R. C. Calfee (Eds.), *Handbook of educational psychology* (pp. 186–242). New York: MacMillan Library Reference.

Guthrie, E. R. (1935). *The psychology of learning.* New York: Harper & Row.

Guyer, B. P. (2000). Reaching and teaching the adolescent with ADHD. In B. P. Guyer (Ed.), *ADHD: Achieving success in school and in life* (pp. 81–98). Boston: Allyn & Bacon.

Guzdial, M. (1998). Technological support for project-based learning. In C. Dede (Ed.), *ASCD yearbook: Learning with technology* (pp. 47–72). Alexandria, VA: Association for Supervision and Curriculum Development.

Hackett, G. (1995). Self-efficacy in career choice and development. In A. Bandura (Ed.), *Self-efficacy in changing societies* (pp. 232–258). New York: Cambridge University Press.

Hagen, J. W., & Stanovich, K. G. (1977). Memory strategies of acquisition. In J. R. V. Kail & J. W. Hagen (Eds.), *Perspectives on the development of memory and cognition* (pp. 89–112). Hillsdale, NJ: Erlbaum.

Hagopian, L. P., Farrell, D. A., & Amari, A. (1996). Treating total liquid refusal with backward chaining and fading. *Journal of Applied Behavior Analysis, 29,* 573–575.

Hagopian, L. P., Wilson, D. M., & Wilder, D. A. (2001). Assessment and treatment of problem behavior maintained by escape from attention and access to tangible items. *Journal of Applied Behavior Analysis, 34*(2), 229–232.

Hall, R. V., Lund, D., & Jackson, D. (1968). Effects of teacher attention on study behavior. *Applied Behavior Analysis, 1,* 1–12.

Hall, R. W., Butler, L. G., McGuire, S. Y., McGlynn, S. P., Lyon, G. L., Reese, R. L., et al. (2001). Automated web-based second-chance homework. *Journal of Chemical Education, 78*(12), 1704–1708.

Hallahan, D. P., & Bryan, T. H. (1981). Learning disabilities. In J. M. Kaufmann & D. P. Hallahan (Eds.), *Handbook of special education.* Englewood Cliffs, NJ: Prentice Hall.

Hallahan, D. P., & Kauffman, J. M. (2000). *Exceptional learners: Introduction to special education* (8th ed.). Boston: Allyn & Bacon.

Hallahan, D. P., Lloyd, J. W., Kosiewicz, M. M., Kauffman, J. M., & Graves, A. W. (1979). Self-monitoring of attention as a treatment for a learning disabled boy's off-task behavior. *Learning Disability Quarterly, 2,* 24–32.

Hallahan, D. P., Marshall, K. J., & Lloyd, J. W. (1981). Self-recording during group instruction: Effects on attention to task. *Learning Disabilities Quarterly, 4,* 407–413.

Halpern, D. F. (1997). Sex differences in intelligence. *American Psychologist, 52*(10), 1091–1102.

Halpern, D. F., & LaMay, M. L. (2000). The smarter sex: A critical review of sex differences in intelligence. *Educational Psychology Review, 12*(2), 229–246.

Hamaker, C. (1986). The effects of adjunct questions on prose learning. *Review of Educational Research, 56,* 212–242.

Hambrick, D. Z., Wilhelm, O., & Engle R. W. (2001). The role of working memory in learning disabilities. *Issues in Education, 7*(1), 87–92.

Hamilton, R. J. (1985). A framework for the evaluation of adjunct questions and objectives. *Review of Educational Research, 55,* 47–85.

Hamm, J. V., & Perry, M. (2002). Learning in mathematics in first-grade classrooms: On whose authority? *Journal of Educational Psychology, 94*(1), 126–137.

Hampden-Turner, C. (1981). *Maps of the mind.* New York: Macmillan.

Handen, B. L. (1998). Mental retardation. In E. J. Mash & R. A. Barkley (Eds.), *Treatment of childhood disorders* (pp. 369–415). New York: Guilford.

Hannafin, M. J. (1995). Open-ended learning environments: Foundations, assumptions, and implications for automated design. In R. Tennyson (Ed.), *Perspectives on automating instructional design* (pp. 101–129). New York: Springer-Verlag.

Hannafin, M., Land, S., & Oliver, K. (1999). Open learning environments: Foundations, methods, and models. In C. M. Reigeluth (Ed.), *Instructional-design theories and models: Volume II: A new paradigm of instructional theory* (pp. 115–140). Mahwah, NJ: Erlbaum.

Harden, R. M., & Stamper, N. (1999). What is a spiral curriculum? *Medical Teacher, 21*(2), 141–143.

Hareli, S., & Weiner, B. (2002). Social emotions and personality inferences: A scaffold for a new diection in the study of achievement motivation. *Educational Psychologist, 37*(3), 183–193.

Hare-Mustin, R. T., & Marecek, J. (1994). Asking the right questions: Feminist psychology and sex differences. *Feminism & Psychology, 4*(4), 531–537.

Harlan, J. C. (1996). *Behavior management strategies for teachers.* Springfield, IL: Charles C. Thomas.

Harp, S. F., & Mayer, R. E. (1997). The role of interest in learning from scientific text and illustrations: On the distinction between emotional interest and cognitive interest. *Journal of Educational Psychology, 89,* 92–102.

Harp, S., & Mayer, R. E. (1998). How seductive details do their damage: A theory of cognitive interest in science learning. *Journal of Educational Psychology, 90*(3), 414–434.

Harris, K. R., & Graham, S. (1996). Memo to constructivists: Skills count too. *Educational Leadership, 53,* 26–29.

Harris, S. L. (2000). Behave yourself. *Principal Leadership, 1*(3), 36–39.

Harris, V., & Sherman, J. (1973). Use and analysis of the "Good Behavior Game" to reduce disruptive classroom behavior. *Journal of Applied Behavior Analysis, 6,* 405–417.

Harrow, A. J. (1972). *A taxonomy of the psychomotor domain.* New York: David McKay.

Harter, S. (1998). The development of self-representations. In N. Eisenberg (Ed.), *Handbook of child psychology* (Vol. 3, pp. 553–618). New York: John Wiley.

Hartley, E. T., Bray, M. A., & Kehle, T. J. (1998). Self-modeling as an intervention to increase class participation. *Psychology in the Schools, 35*(4), 363–372.

Hartup, W. W. (1989a). Social relationships and their developmental significance. *American Psychologist, 44,* 120–126.

Hartup, W. W. (1989b). Behavioral manifestations of children's friendships. In T. J. Berndt & G. W. Ladd (Eds.), *Peer relationships in child development* (pp. 46–70). New York: John Wiley.

Hartup, W. W. (1996). The company they keep: Friendships and their developmental significance. *Child Development, 67,* 1–13.

Hatch, C. A., & Dwyer, F. (1999). Effect of varied advance organizer strategies in complementing visualized prose instruction. *International Journal of Instructional Media, 26*(3), 311–328.

Haughton, E. C. (1972). Aims: Growing and sharing. In J. B. Jordan & L. S. Robbins (Eds.), *Let's try doing something else kind of thing* (pp. 20–39). Arlington, VA: Council on Exceptional Children.

Hausfather, S. (2001). Where's the content? The role of content in constructivist teacher education. *Educational Horizons, 80*(1), 15–19.

Hawkins, J. D., Catalano, R. F., & Miller, J. Y. (1992). Risk and protective factors for alcohol and other drug problems in adolescence and early adulthood. *Psychological Bulletin, 112,* 64–105.

Haycock, K. (2001). Closing the achievement gap. *Educational Leadership, 58*(6), 6–11.

Hayes, J. R. (1996). A new framework for understanding cognition and affect in writing. In C. M. Levy & S. Ransdell (Eds.), *The science of writing: Theories, methods, individual differences, and applications* (pp. 1–27). Mahwah, NJ: Erlbaum.

Hayes, J. R., & Flower, L. S. (1980). Identifying the organization of writing processes. In L. W. Gregg & E. R. Steinberg (Eds.), *Cognitive processes in writing.* Hillsdale, NJ: Erlbaum.

Hébert, T. P., & Reis, S. M. (1999). Culturally diverse high-achieving students in an urban school. *Urban Education, 34*(4), 428–457.

Hedegaard, M. (1990). The zone of proximal development as a basis for instruction. In L. C. Moll (Ed.), *Vygotsky and education instructional implications of sociohistorical psychology* (pp. 349–371). Cambridge: Cambridge University Press.

Hefzallah, I. M. (1999). *The new educational technologies and learning: Empowering teachers to teach and students to learn in the information age.* Springfield, IL: Charles C. Thomas.

Hegarty, S. (1993). Reviewing the literature on integration. *European Journal of Special Needs Education, 8,* 194–200.

Heider, F. (1958). *The psychology of interpersonal relations.* Hillsdale, NJ: Erlbaum.

Hembree, R. (1988). Correlates, causes, effects and treatment of test anxiety. *Review of Educational Research, 58*(1), 47–77.

Hemmings, A. (2000). Lona's links: Postoppositional identity work of urban youths. *Anthropology and Education Quarterly, 31*(2), 152–172.

Henderson, E., & Beers, J. (1980). *Developmental and cognitive aspects of learning to spell: A reflection of word knowledge.* Newark, DE: International Reading Association.

Henderson, H., French, R. W., & Fritsch, R. E. (2000). Time-out and overcorrection: A comparison of their application in physical education. *Physical Education, Recreation and Dance, 71*(3), 31–35.

Hendricks, C. C. (2001). Teaching causal reasoning through cognitive apprenticeship: What are the results from situated learning? *The Journal of Educational Research, 94,* 302–311.

Henry, D. L. (1999). Resilience in maltreated children: Implications for special needs adoption. *Child Welfare, 78*(5), 519–540.

Herron, J. D. (1975). Piaget for chemists: Explaining what "good" students cannot understand. *Journal of Chemical Education, 52*(2), 146–150.

Hersch, P. (1998). *A tribe apart: A journey into the heart of American adolescence.* Westminister, MD: Random House.

Hetherington, E. M., Bridges, M., & Insabella, G. M. (1998). What matters? What does not? Five perspectives on the association between marital transitions and children's adjustment. *American Psychologist, 53*(2), 167–184.

Hetherington, E. M., & Kelly, J. (2002). *For better or for worse: Divorce reconsidered.* New York: W. W. Norton.

Heward, W. H. (2000). *Exceptional children an introduction to special education* (6th ed.). Upper Saddle River, NJ: Merrill.

Hiatt-Michael, D. B. (2001). Home-school communication. In D. B. Hiatt-Michael (Ed.), *Promising practices for family involvement in schools* (pp. 39–57). Greenwich, CT: Information Age Publishing.

Hidi, S., & Anderson, V. (1992). Situational interest and its impact on reading and expository writing. In K. A. Renninger, S. Hidi, & A. Krapp (Eds.), *The role of interest in learning and development* (pp. 215–238). Hillsdale, NJ: Erlbaum.

Hidi, S., & Harackiewiez, J. M. (2000). Motivating the academically unmotivated: A critical issue for the 21st century. *Review of Educational Research, 70*(2), 151–179.

Hidi, S., Renninger, K. A., & Krapp, A. (1992). The present state of interest research. In K. A. Renninger, S. Hidi, & A. Krapp (Eds.), *The role of interest in learning and development* (pp. 433–446). Hillsdale, NJ: Erlbaum.

Higgins, J. W., Williams, R., & McLaughlin, T. F. (2001). The effects of a token economy employing instructional consequences for a third-grade student with learning disabilities: A data-based case study. *Education and Treatment of Children, 24*(1), 99–106.

Hinson, J., & Fossey, R. (2000). Child abuse: What teachers in the '90s know, think, and do. *Journal of Education for Students Placed at Risk, 5*(3), 251–266.

Hmelo, C. E., & Evensen, D. H. (2000). Introduction. In D. H. Evensen & C. E. Hmelo (Eds.), *Problem-based learning: A research perspective on learning interactions* (pp. 1–18). Mahwah, NJ: Erlbaum.

Hock, M. F., & Desler, D. D. (1993). Learning strategy instruction for at-risk and learning disabled adults. *Preventing School Failure, 38*(1), 43–49.

Hoff, D. J, (2003). Achievement gap in Kentucky demands action. Report says. *Education Week, 23*(6), 19.

Hoge, J. D. (2002). Character education, citizenship education, and social studies. *The Social Studies, 93*(3), 103–109.

Hollender, M. H. (1978). Perfectionism: A neglected personality trait. *Journal of Clinical Psychiatry, 39,* 384.

Hollway, W. (1994). Beyond sex differences: A project for feminist psychology. *Feminism & Psychology, 4*(4), 538–546.

Holtzman, W. H. (1968). Holtzman inkblot technique. In A. I. Rabin (Ed.), *Projective techniques in personality assessment* (pp. 136–170). New York: Springer.

Homme, L., Csanyi, A., Gonzales, M. A., & Rechs, J. R. (1970). *How to use contingency contracting in the classroom.* Champaign, IL: Research Press.

Hooper, F. H., & DeFrain, J. D. (1980). On delineating distinctly Piagetian contributions to education. *Genetic Psychology Monographs, 4*(1), 23–29.

Hoover-Dempsey, K. V., & Sandler, H. M. (1997). Why do parents become involved in their children's education? *Review of Educational Research, 67*(1), 3–42.

Horner, S. L. (2001). The effects of observational learning in preschoolers' book-related behaviors and alphabet knowledge. *Child Study Journal, 31*(1), 1–11.

Houck, G. M., & Spegman, A. M. (1999). The development of self: Theoretical understandings and conceptual underpinnings. *Infants and Young Children, 12*(1), 1–16.

House, J. D. (2002). The use of computers in a mathematical lesson in Japan: A case analysis from the TIMSS videotape classroom study. *International Journal of Instructional Media, 29*(1), 113–124.

Houwer, J. D., Thomas, S., & Baeyens, F. (2001). Associative learning of likes and dislikes: A review of 25 years of research on human evaluative. *Psychological Bulletin, 127*(6), 853–869.

Howard, E. R., & Sugarman, J. (2001). Two way immersion programs: Features and statistics. In *ERIC Clearinghouse on Language and Linguistics.* Washington, D.C. (ED 452739).

Howard, G. S. (1985). The role of values in the science of psychology. *American Psychologist, 40*(3), 255–265.

Howard, T. C. (1998). *Pedagogical practices and ideological constructions of effective teachers of African American students.* Unpublished doctoral dissertation. University of Washington, Seattle.

Howes, M. B. (1990). *The psychology of human cognition: Mainstream and genevan traditions.* New York: Pergamon Press.

Howley, A., Howley, C. B., & Pendarvis, E. D. (1986). *Teaching gifted children: Principles and strategies.* Boston: Little, Brown.

Huefner, D. S. (2000). The risks and opportunities of the IEP requirements under IDEA '97. *Journal of Special Education, 33*(4), 195–104.

Huffman, L. E. (1998). Spotlighting specifics by combining focus questions with K-W-L. *Journal of Adolescent & Adult Literacy, 41*(6), 470–472.

Hughes, C. A., Ruhl, K. L., Schumaker, J. B., & Deshler, D. D. (2002). Effects of instruction in an assignment completion strategy on the homework performance of students with learning disabilities in general education classes. *Learning Disabilities Rresearch and Practice, 17*(1), 1–18.

Hunter, M. (1982). *Mastery teaching.* El Segundo, CA: TIP Publications.

Hunter, M. (1982). *Mastery teaching: Increasing instructional effectiveness in elementary, secondary schools, colleges and universities.* El Segundo, CA: TIP Publications.

Hunter, M. (1984). Knowing, teaching and supervising. In P. L. Hosford (Ed.), *Using what we know about teaching.* Alexandria, VA: ASCD.

Hupp, S. D., & Reitman, D. (1999). Improving sports skills and sportsmanship in children diagnosed with attention deficit/hyperactivity disorder. *Child & Family Behavior Therapy, 21*(3), 35–51.

Huston, A. C. (1983). Sex-typing. In E. M. Hetherington (Ed.), *Handbook of child psychology: Socialization, personality, and social development* (Vol. 4, pp. 388–467). New York: Wiley.

Hyde, J. S. (1994). Gender differences in mathematics ability, anxiety and attitudes: What do meta-analyses tell us? In L. A. Penner, G. M. Batsche, H. M. Knoff, & D. L. Nelson (Eds.), *The challenge in mathematics and science education: Psychology's response* (pp. 237–250). Washington, D.C.: American Psychological Association.

Hyde, J. S., & Linn, M. C. (1988). *Gender differences in verbal ability: A meta-analysis.* Washington, D.C.: National Science Foundation.

Hyde, J. S., & McKinley, N. M. (1997). Gender differences in cognition: results from meta-analyses. In P. J. Caplan, M. Crawford, J. S. Hyde, & J. T. E. Richardson (Eds.), *Gender differences in human cognition* (pp. 30–51). New York: Oxford University Press.

Hyde, J. S., Fennema, E., Ryan, M., Frost, L. A., & Hopp, C. (1990). Gender comparisons of mathematics attitudes and affect: A meta-analysis. *Psychology of Women Quarterly, 14,* 299–324.

Hyde, J. S., Fennena, E., & Lamon, S. J. (1990). Gender differences in mathematics performance: A meta-analysis. *Psychological Bulletin, 107,* 139–155.

Iben, M. F. (1991). Attitudes and mathematics. *Comparative Education, 27*(2), 135–151.

Ignatovich, F. R., Cusick, P. A., & Ray, J. E. (1979). Value/belief patterns of teachers and those administrators engaged in attempts to influence teaching. (Research Series No. 3). East Lansing, MI: Michigan State University, Institute for Research on Teaching.

Igo, S. (2002). Increasing parent involvement. *Principal Leadership (High School Ed.), 3*(3), 10–12.

Impara, J. C., & Plake, B. S. (Eds.). (1998). *The Thirteenth Mental Measurements Yearbook.* Lincoln, NE: The Buros Institute of Mental Measurement, University of Nebraska.

Inglehart, M., Brown, D. R., & Vida, M. (1994). Competition, achievement and gender: A stress theoretical analysis. In P. R. Pintrich, D. R. Brown, & C. E. Weinstein (Eds.), *Student motivation, cognition and learning* (pp. 311–332). Hillsdale, NJ: Erlbaum.

Ishiyama, F. I., & Chabassol, D. J. (1985). Adolescents' fear of social consequences of academic success as a function of age and sex. *Journal of Youth and Adolescence, 14*(1), 37–46.

Ittenbach, R. F., Esters, I. G., & Wainer, H. (1997). The history of test development. In D. P. Flanagan, J. L. Genshaft, & P. L. Harrison (Eds.), *Contemporary intellectual assessment theories, tests, and issues* (pp. 17–31). New York: Guilford.

Jackson, A., Kutnick, A. J., & Kington, A. (2001). Principles and practical grouping for the use of drill and practice programs. *Journal of Computer Assisted Learning, 17,* 130–141.

Jackson, P. (1990). *Life in classrooms.* New York: Teachers College Press.

James, W. (1918). *The principles of psychology Volume II.* New York: Dover Publications.

Jannsen, R., De Corte, E., Verschaffel, L., Knoors, E., & Colémont, A. (2002). National assessment of new standards for mathematics in elementary education in Flanders. *Educational Research and Evaluation, 8*(2), 197–225.

Jenkins, J. J. (1978). Four points to remember: A tetrahedral model of memory experiments. In L. S. Cermak & F. I. M. Craik (Eds.), *Levels of processing and human memory* (pp. 429–446). Hillsdale, NJ: Erlbaum.

Jensen, A. R. (1998a). The g factor and the design of education. In R. J. Sternberg & W. M. Williams (Eds.), *Intelligence, instruction, and assessment* (pp. 111–132). Mahwah, NJ: Erlbaum.

Jensen, A. R. (1998b). *The g factor: The science of mental ability.* Westport, CT: Praeger.

Jeynes, W. H. (2002). The challenge of controlling for SES in social science and education research. *Educational Psychology Review, 14*(2), 205–221.

Jimerson, S., Egeland, B., & Teo, A. (1999). A longitudinal study of achievement trajectories: Factors associated with change. *Journal of Educational Psychology, 91*(1), 116–126.

Jinks, J. L., & Morgan, V. L. (1999). Children's perceived self-efficacy: An inventory scale. *The Clearing House, 72,* 224–230.

Jitendra, A. K., Hoppes, M. K., & Xin, Y. P. (2000). Enhancing main idea comprehension for students with learning problems: The role of a summarization strategy and self-monitoring instruction. *Journal of Special Education, 34*(3), 127–139.

Jitendra, A., Diipi, C. M., & Perron-Jones, N. (2002). An exploratory study of schema-based word-problem-solving instruction for middle school students with learning disabilities. *The Journal of Special Education, 36*(1), 23–38.

Johnson, D. W., & Johnson, R. T. (1994). *Learning together and alone: Cooperative, competitive, and individualistic learning.* Englewood Cliffs, NJ: Prentice Hall.

Johnson, D. W., Johnson, R. T., & Holubec, E. J. (1994). *Cooperative learning in the classroom.* Alexandria, VA: ASCD.

Johnson, J., & Carlson, S. (1992). Developing conceptual thinking: The concept attainment. *The Clearing House, 66*(2), 117–121.

Johnson, S. D. (1995). Transfer of learning. *The Technology Teacher, 54,* 33–34.

Johnson, S. L. (1999). Discovering the potential of gifted girls: The biological and physical science interests of gifted kindergarten girls. *School Science and Mathematics, 99*(6), 302–312.

Johnston, S. (2000). Teaching the FHS way. *Multimedia Schools, 7*(4), 52.

Jonassen, D. (1999). Designing constructivist learning environments. In C. M. Reigeluth (Ed.), *Instructional-design theories and models. Volume II: A new paradigm of instructional theory* (pp. 215–240). Mahwah, NJ: Erlbaum.

Jonassen, D. H., & Hernandez-Serrano, J. (2002). Case-based reasoning and instructional design: Using stories to support problem solving. *Educational Technology, Research and Development, 50*(2), 65–77.

Jonassen, D. H., Tessmer, M., & Hannum, W. H. (1999). *Task analysis methods for instructional design.* Mahwah, NJ: Erlbaum.

Jonassen, D. J., Peck, K. L., & Wilson, B. G. (1999). *Learning with technology: A constructivist perspective.* Upper Saddle River, NJ: Merrill.

Jonckheere, A., Mandelbrot, B., & Piaget, J. (1958). *Studies of genetic epistemology: V. The interpretation of experience/Etudes d'epistemologie genetique: V. La lecture de l'experience.* Paris, France: Presses Universitaires de France.

Jones, M. L., Eyberg, S. M., Adams, C. D., & Boggs, S. R. (1998). Treatment acceptability of behavioral interventions for children: An assessment by mothers of children with disruptive behavior disorders. *Child & Family Behavior Therapy, 20*(4), 15–26.

Jones, R. (2001). Involving parents is a whole new game: Be sure to win. *Education Digest, 67*(3), 36–43.

Jones, V. (1996). Classroom management. In J. Sikula (Ed.), *Handbook of research on teacher education* (pp. 503–524). New York: Macmillan.

Jones, V. F., & Jones, S. (2001). *Comprehensive classroom management: Creating communities of support and solving problems* (6th ed.). Boston: Allyn & Bacon.

Joyce, B. R., & Weil, M. (1996). *Models of teaching* (5th ed.). Boston: Allyn & Bacon.

Judd, C. H. (1908). The relation of special training to general intelligence. *Educational Review, 36,* 28–42.

Kagan, J. (1966). Reflection-impulsivity: The generality and dynamics of conceptual tempo. *Journal of Abnormal Psychology, 71,* 17–27.

Kagan, J., Moss, A., & Sigel, I. E. (1963). Psychological significance of styles of conceptualization. *Monographs of the Society for Research in Child Development.*

Kagan, S. (1992). *Cooperative learning resources for teachers.* San Juan Capistrano, CA: Resources for Teachers.

Kail, R. (1990). *The development of memory in children* (3rd ed.). New York: Freeman.

Kail, R., & Bisanz, J. (1995). The information-processing perspective on cognitive development in children and adolescence. In R. J. Sternberg & C. A. Berg (Eds). *Intellectual development* (pp. 229–260). New York: Cambridge University Press.

Kamii, C. (1985). *Young children reinvent arithmetic.* New York: Teachers College Press.

Kanfer, F. H., & Goldstein, A. P. (Eds.). (1986). *Helping people change: A textbook of methods* (3rd ed.). Tarrytown, NY: Pergamon.

Kantor, J. R. (1959). *Interbehavioral psychology.* Granville, OH: Principia Press.

Karabenick, S. A., & Knapp, J. R. (1991). Relationship of academic help seeking to the use of learning strategies and other instrumental achievement behavior of college students. *Journal of Educational Psychology, 83*(2), 221–230.

Karnes, F. A., & Marquardt, R. (1997). Know your legal rights in gifted education. Washington, D.C. (Office of Educational Research and Improvement No. EDO-EC-95-4).

Katayama, A. D., & Robinson, D. H. (2000). Getting students 'partially' involved in note-taking using graphic organizers. *Journal of Experimental Education, 68*(2), 119–133.

Katsiyannis, A., & Maag, J. W. (1997). Ensuring appropriate education: Emerging remedies, litigation, compensation, and other legal considerations. *Exceptional Children, 63*(4), 451–462.

Katsiyannis, A., & Maag, J. W. (2001). Manifestation determination as a golden fleece. *Exceptional Children, 68*(1), 85–96.

Kauchak, D. P., & Eggen, P. D. (1998). *Learning and teaching: Research-based methods* (3rd ed.). Boston: Allyn & Bacon.

Kaufman, A. S. (2000). Tests of intelligence. In R. J. Sternberg (Ed.), *Handbook of intelligence* (pp. 445–476). Cambridge: Cambridge University Press.

Kavale, K. A., & Forness, S. R. (1987). Substance over style: Assessing the efficacy of modality testing and teaching. *Exceptional Children, 54*(3), 228–239.

Kavale, K. A., & Forness, S. R. (1996). Treating social skills deficits in children with learning disabilities: A meta-analysis of the research. *Learning Disability Quarterly, 19*(1), 2–13.

Kavale, K. A., & Forness, S. R. (2000). History, rhetoric, and reality: Analysis of the Inclusion Debate. *Remedial and Special Education, 21*(5), 279–296.

Kazdin, A. E. (1977). Artifact, bias, and complexity of assessment: The ABC's of reliability. *Journal of Applied Behavior Analysis, 10,* 141–150.

Kazdin, A. E. (1982). Applying behavioral principles in the schools. In C. R. Reynolds & T. B. Gutkin (Eds.), *The handbook of school psychology* (pp. 501–529). New York: John Wiley.

Kazdin, A. E. (1994). *Behavior modification in applied settings.* Pacific Grove, CA: Brooks/Cole.

Kehle, T. J., Bray, M. A., Margiano, S. G., Theodore, L. A., & Zhou, Z. (2002). Self-modeling as an effective intervention for students with serious emotional disturbance: Are we modifying children's memories? *Psychology in the Schools, 39*(2), 203–207.

Keirns, J. L. (1999). *Designs for self-instruction: Principles, processes and issues in developing self-directed learning.* Boston: Allyn & Bacon.

Keith, M., Puzerewski, B., & Raczynski, P. (1999). *Improving student responsibility for learning through ownership development.* Unpublished Action Research Project, Chicago, IL: Saint Xavier University.

Keller, C. (2001). Effect of teachers' stereotyping on students' stereotyping of mathematics as a male domain. *Journal of Social Psychology, 1141*(2), 165–173.

Keller, J. M. (1983). Motivational design of instruction. In C. M. Reigeluth (Ed.), *Instructional design theories and models: An overview of their current status.* Hillsdale, NJ: Erlbaum.

Keller, J. M. (1987a). Strategies for stimulating the motivation to learn. *Performance and Instruction, 28*(8), 1–7.

Keller, J. M. (1987b). The systematic process of motivational design. *Performance & Instruction, 26*(9), 1–8.

Keller, J. M. (1999a). Motivational systems. In H. D. Stolovitch & E. J. Keeps (Eds.), *Handbook of human performance technology* (2nd ed.). San Francisco: Jossey-Bass.

Keller, J. M. (1999b). Using the ARCS motivational process in computer-based instruction and distance education. *New Directions for Teaching and Learning, 78,* 39–47.

Keller, J. M., & Kopp, T. W. (1987). Application of the ARCS model to motivational design. In C. M. Reigeluth (Ed.), *Instructional theories in action: Lessons illustrating selected theories* (pp. 289–320). Hillsdale, NJ: Erlbaum.

Keller, J. M., & Litchfield, B. C. (2002). Motivation and performance. In R. A. Reiser & J. V. Dempsey (Eds.), *Trends and issues in instructional design and technology* (pp. 83–98). Upper Saddle River, NJ: Merrill.

Kemp, J. E., Morrison, G. R., & Ross, S. M. (1994). *Designing effective instruction.* New York: Macmillan College.

Kemps, E. (2001). Complexity effects in visuo-spatial working memory: Implictions for the role of long-term memory. *Memory, 9*(1), 13–27.

Kennedy, C. H., & Itkonen, T. (1993). Effects of setting events on the problem behavior of students with disabilities. *Journal of Applied Behavior Analysis, 26,* 321–327.

Kent, T. W., & McNergney, R. F. (1999). *Will technology really change education? From blackboard to web.* Washington, D.C.: American Association of Colleges for Teacher Education.

Keogh, B. K. (2000). Poor children: Child development deviations. *Focus on Exceptional Children, 33*(4), 1–10.

Kerr, M. M., & Nelson, C. M. (1998). *Strategies for managing behavior problems in the classroom.* Upper Saddle River, NJ: Merrill.

Khisty, L. L. (1997). Making mathematics accessible to Latino students: Rethinking instructional practices. *Yearbook, 1997, 92*–101.

Kidwell, J. S., Dunham, R. M., Bacho, R. A., Pastorino, E., & Portes, P. R. (1995). Adolescent identity exploration: A test of Erikson's theory of transitional crisis. *Adolescence, 30,* 785–793.

Killian, K. J. (1988). Teaching swimming using a backward chain sequence. *Journal of Physical Education, Recreation and Dance, 59*(5), 82–86.

Kimura, D. (1999). *Sex and cognition.* Cambridge, MA: MIT Press.

King, A. (1991). Effects of training in strategic questioning on children's problem-solving success. *Journal of Educational Psychology, 83*(3), 307–317.

King-Sears, M. E., & Cummings, C. S. (1996). Inclusive practices of classroom teachers. *Remedial and Special Education, 17,* 217–225.

Kintsch, W. (1977). *Memory and cognition.* New York: John Wiley.

Kirshner, D. I., & Whitson, J. A. (Eds.). (1997). *Situated cognition: Social, semiotic, and psychological perspectives.* Mahwah, NJ: Erlbaum.

Kirylo, J. D., & Millet, C. P. (2000). Graphic organizers: An integral component to facilitate comprehension during basal reading instruction. *Reading Improvement, 37*(4), 179–186.

Kitano, M. (1999). Bringing clarity to "this thing called giftedness": A response to Dr. Renzulli. *Journal for the Education of the Gifted, 23*(1), 87–101.

Kitfield, E. B., & Masalsky, C. J. (2000). Negative reinforcement-based treatment to increase food intake. *Behavior Modification, 24*(4), 600–608.

Kittel, J. E. (1957). An experimental study of the effect of external direciton during learning on transfer and retention of principles. *Journal of Educational Psychology, 48,* 391–408.

Klauer, K. J. (1984). Intentional and incidental learning with instructional texts: A meta-analysis for 1970–1980. *American Educational Research Journal, 21*(2), 323–339.

Klausmeier, H. J. (1992). Concept learning and concept teaching. *Educational Psychologist, 27,* 267–286.

Kleinert, H. L., Haig, J., Kearns, J. F., & Kennedy, S. (2000). Alternate assessments: Lessons learned and roads to be taken. *Exceptional Children, 67*(1), 51–66.

Kleinfield, J. (1973). Effects of nonverbally communicated personal warmth on the intelligence test performance of Indian and Eskimo adolescents. *Journal of Social Psychology, 91*(1), 149–150.

Kleinfield, J. (1974). Effects of nonverbal warmth on the learning of Eskimo and white students. *Journal of Social Psychology, 92*(1), 3–9.

Kleinfield, J. (1975). Effective teachers of Eskimo and Indian students. *School Review, 83*(2), 301–344.

Knoblauch, B., & McLane, K. (1999). An overview of the Individuals with Disabilities Education Act amendments of 1997 (P.L. 105–17): Update 1999. *ERIC Digest E576.*

Knoblauch, B., & Sorenson, B. (1998). IDEA's definition of disabilities. *ERIC Digest E560.*

Kohlberg, L. (1963). Moral development and identification. In H. W. Stevenson (Ed.), *Child psychology: 62nd yearbook of the national society for the study of education* (pp. 277–332). Chicago: University of Chicago Press.

Kohlberg, L. A. (1966). A cognitive-developmental analysis of children's sex role concepts and attitudes. In E. E. Maccoby (Ed.), *The development of sex differences* (pp. 82–173). Stanford, CA: Stanford University Press.

Kohlberg, L. (1980). Stages of moral development as a basis for moral education. In B. Munsey (Ed.), *Moral development, moral education, and Kohlberg: Basic issues in philosophy, psychology, religion, and education* (15–100). Birmingham, AL: Religious Education Press.

Kohlberg, L. (1984). *The psychology of moral development: The nature and validity of moral stages.* San Francisco: Harper & Row.

Kohlberg, L. A., & Ullian, D. Z. (1974). Stages in the development of psychosexual concepts and attitudes. In R. C. Friedman, R. M. Richart, & R. L. V. Wiete (Eds.), *Sex differences in behavior.* New York: Wiley.

Kohlberg, L., & Diessner, R. (1991). A cognitive developmental approach to moral attachment. In J. L. Gewirtz & W. M. Kurtines (Eds.), *Intersections with attachment.* Hillsdale, NJ: Erlbaum.

Kohlberg, L., Levine, C., & Hewer, A. (1983). A current formulation and a response to critics. In J. A. Meacham (Ed.), *Contributions to human development* (Vol. 10). New York: Karger.

Kohn, A. (1993a). *Punished by rewards: The trouble with gold stars, incentive plans, A's, praise and other bribes*. New York: Houghton Mifflin.

Kohn, A. (1993b). Rewards versus learning: A response to Paul Chance. *Phi Delta Kappan, 74*(10), 783–787.

Kohn, A. (1995). The risk of rewards. *Brown University Child & Adolescent Behavior Letter, 11*(2), 8.

Kolb, D. A. (1984). *Experiential learning: Experience as a source of learning and development*. Englewood Cliffs, NJ: Prentice Hall.

Kolesnik, W. B. (1958). *Mental discipline in modern education*. Madison, WI: University of Wisconsin Press.

Konukman, F., & Petrakis, E. (2001). Verbal and visual teaching cues for tennis. *Journal of Physical Education, Recreation and Dance, 72*(3), 38–43.

Kornhaber, M. (1999). Enhancing equity in gifted education: A framework for examining assessments drawing on the theory of multiple intelligences. *High Ability Studies, 10*(2), 143–161.

Kostelnik, M. J. (1993). *Developmentally appropriate programs*. Syracuse, NY: ERIC-EECE Clearinghouse of Elementary and Early Childhood Education (EDO PS 93 7).

Kottler, E. (1994). *Children with limited English: Teaching strategies for the regular classroom. Survival skills for teacher series*. Thousand Oaks, CA: Corwin Press.

Kounin, J. (1977). *Discipline and group management in classrooms*. New York: Kriegar.

Kounin, J. S. (1970). Observing and delineating technique of managing behavior in classrooms. *Journal of Research and Development in Education, 1*, 62–72.

Kounin, J. S. (1983). Classrooms: Individuals or behavior settings? In *Monographs in teaching and learning. General series, Number 1*. Bloomington, IN: Indiana University.

Kounin, J. S., & Doyle, P. H. (1975). Degree of continuity of a lesson's signal system and the task involvement of children. *Journal of Educational Psychology, 67*, 159–164.

Kounin, J. S., & Gump, P. V. (1974). Signal systems of lesson settings and the task related behavior of preschool children. *Journal of Educational Psychology, 66*, 554–562.

Kounin, J., & Sherman, L. (1979). School environments as behavior settings. *Theory into Practice, 18*, 145–151.

Kozma, R. (2000). Reflections of the state of educational technology research and development. *Educational Technology: Research and Development, 48*(1), 5–15.

Kozma, R., & Shank, P. (1998). Connecting with the 21st century: Technology in support of educational reform. In C. Dede (Ed.), *ASCD yearbook: Learning with technology* (pp. 3–30). Alexandria, VA: Association for Supervision and Curriculum Development.

Krajcik, J., Soloway, E., Blumenfeld, P., & Marx, R. (1998). Scaffolding technology tools to promote teaching and learning in science. In C. Dede (Ed.), *ASCD yearbook: Learning with technology* (pp. 31–46). Alexandria, VA: ASCD.

Krashen, S. (1982). *Principles and practice in second language acquisition*. New York: Prentice Hall.

Krathwohl, D. R., Bloom, B. S., & Masia, B. B. (1964). *Taxonomy of educational objectives, classification of educational goals, handbook II: affective domain*. New York: David McKay.

Kratovil, J., & Bailey, S. M. (1986). Sex equity and disabled students. *Theory into Practice, 25*(4), 250–256.

Krechevsky, M. (1998). *Project spectrum preschool assessment handbook*. New York: Teachers College Press.

Krechevsky, M., & Seidel, S. (1998). Minds at work: Applying multiple intelligences in the classroom. In R. J. Sternberg & W. M. Williams (Eds.), *Intelligence, instruction, and assessment* (pp. 17–42). Mahwah, NJ: Erlbaum.

Krechevsky, M., Hoerr, T., & Gardner, H. (1995). Complementary energies: Implementing MI theory from the laboratory and from the field. In J. Oakes & K. H. Quartz (Eds.), *Creating new educational communities* (pp. 166–186). Chicago: University of Chicago Press.

Kuhn, D. (1979). The application of Piaget's theory of cognitive development to education. *Harvard Educational Review, 49*(3), 340–360.

Kuhn, D., Black, J., Keselman, A., & Kaplan, D. (2000). The development of cognitive skills to support inquiry learning. *Cognition and Instruction, 18*(4), 495–523.

Kuhn, T. S. (1970). *The Structure of Scientific Revolutions* (2nd Ed.). Chicago: The University of Chicago Press.

Kulhavey, R. W., & Anderson, R. C. (1972). Delay-retention effects with multiple-choice tests. *Journal of Educational Psychology, 63*, 505–512.

Kulik, J. A., & Kulik, C. C. (1988). Timing of feedback and verbal learning. *Review of Educational Research, 58*, 82–97.

Kulik, C. C., Kulik, J. A., & Bangert-Downs, R. L. (1990a). Effectiveness of mastery learning programs: A meta-analysis. *Review of Educational Research, 60*, 265–299.

Kulik, J. A., Kulik, C. C., & Bangert-Downs, R. L. (1990b). Is there better evidence on mastery learning? A response to Slavin. *Review of Educational Research, 60*, 303–307.

Kumar, D. D., Smith, P. J., Helgeson, S. L., & White, A. L. (1994). *Advanced technologies as educational tools in science: Concepts, applications, and issues*. Columbus, OH: National Center for Science Teaching and Learning (ED 376 077).

Kumar, D., & Wilson, C. L. (1997). Computer technology: Science education and students with learning disabilities. *Journal of Science Education and Technology, 6*(2), 155–160.

Kun, A. (1977). Development of the magnitude-covariation and compensations schemata in ability and effort attributions and performance. *Child Development, 48*, 862–873.

Kutnik, P. (1986). The relationship of moral judgment and moral action: Kohlberg's theory, criticism and revision. In S. Modgil & C. Modgil (Eds.), *Lawrence Kohlberg: Consensus and controversy* (pp. 125–146). Philadelphia, PA: Falmer Press.

Laberge, D., & Samuels, S. J. (1974). Toward a theory of automatic information processing in reading. *Cognitive Psychology, 6*(2), 293–323.

Laboratory of Comparative Human Cognition (1983). Culture and cognitive development. In W. Kessen (Ed.), *Handbook of child psychology, Vol I, History, theory, and methods* (4th ed., pp. 295–356). New York: Wiley.

Lackey, J. R., Miller, R. B., & Flanigan, M. C. (1997). *The effects of written feedback on motivation and changes in performance*. Paper presented at the American Educational Research Association, Chicago, IL.

Lader, M. (1975). The nature of clinical anxiety in modern society. In C. D. Spielberger & I. G. Sarason (Eds.), *Stress and anxiety* (pp. 3–26). New York: John Wiley.

Ladson-Billings, G. (1994). *The dreamkeepers: Successful teachers for African-American children*. San Francisco: Jossey-Bass.

Lam, S. F. (1997). *How the family influences children's academic achievement*. New York: Garland Publishing.

Lambert, M. A. (2000). Using cognitive and metacognitive learning strategies in classrooms. *Preventing School Failure, 44*(2), 81–82.

Land, S. M. (2000). Cognitive requirements for learning with open-ended learning environments. *Educational Technology Research and Development, 48*(3), 61–78.

Land, S. M., & Hannafin, M. J. (1996). *The process of developing theories-in-action with OELEs: A qualitative study*. Paper presented at the Association for Educational Communications and Technology, Indianapolis, IN (ED 397 809).

Landau, B. M., & Gathercoal, P. (2000). Creating peaceful classrooms: Judicious discipline and class meetings. *Phi Delta Kappan, 81*(6), 450–452.

Landrum, T., & Tankersley, M. (1997). *Implementing effective self management for students with behavioral disorders*. Paper presented at the Midwest Symposium for Leadership in Behavior Disorders, Kansas City, MO.

Laney, J. D. (1999). A sample lesson in economics for primary students. *Social Studies, 90*(4), 152–158.

Langdon, D. (1999). Objectives? Get over them. *Training and Development, 53*(2), 54–58.

Lapan, R. T., Kardach, C., and Turner, S. (2002). Empowering students to become self-regulated learners. *Professional School Counseling, 5*(4), 257–265.

Lapp, D., Flood, J., & Tinajero, V. (1994). Are we communicating? Effective instruction for students who are acquiring English as a second language. *The Reading Teacher, 48*, 260–264.

Lauzon, A. C. (1999). Situating cognition and crossing borders: Resisting the hegemony of mediated education. *British Journal of Educational Technology, 30*(3), 261–276.

Lave, J. (1988). *Cognition in practice*. Boston: Cambridge University Press.

Lave, J. (1993). Word problems: A microcosm of theories of learning. In P. Light & G. Butterworth (Eds.), *Context and cognition: Ways of learning and knowing*. Hillsdale, NJ: Erlbaum.

Lave, J., & Wenger, E. (1991). *Situated learning: Legitimate peripheral participation*. New York: Cambridge University Press.

Lawson, C., (1989, June 15). Toys: Girls still apply makeup, boys fight wars. *New York Times, 138* (47902), C1–C2.

Lawyer-Tarr, S. (1999). Time for "time out" to retire: Let "Balance Center" take its place. *School-Age Notes, 19*(8), 1, 3.

Leahy, E., & Guo, G. (2001). Gender differences in mathematical trajectories. *Social Forces, 80*(2), 713–732.

Lee, J., Dineen, F., McKendree, J., & Mayes, T. (1999). *Vicarious learning: Cognitive and linguistic effects of observing peer discussion*. Paper presented at the American Educational Research Association, Montreal, Quebec.

Leinbach, M. D., & Fagot, B. I. (1993). Categorical habituation to male and female faces:

Gender schematic processing in infancy. *Infant Behavior and Development, 16,* 317–332.

Leming, J. S. (1986). Kohlbergian programmes in moral education: A practical review and assessment. In *Lawrence Kohlberg consensus and controversy.* Philadelphia, PA: The Falmer Press.

Lemire, D. (2002). Math problem solving and mental discipline—The myth of transferability. *Journal of College Reading and Learning, 32*(2), 229–238.

Lengua, L. J., Wolchik, S. A., Sandler, I. N., & West, S. G. (2000). The additive and interactive effects of parenting and temperament in predicting adjustment problems of children of divorce. *Journal of Clinical Child Psychology, 29*(2), 232–243.

Lenz, B. K., Ellis, E. S., & Scanlon, D. (1996). *Teaching learning strategies to adolescents and adults with learning disabilities.* Austin, TX: Pro-Ed.

Lepper, M. R. (1983). Extrinsic reward and intrinsic motivation: Implications for the classroom. In J. M. Levine & M. C. Wang (Eds.), *Teacher and student perceptions: Implications for learning* (pp. 281–317). Hillsdale, NJ: Erlbaum.

Lepper, M. R., & Greene, D. (1975). Turning play into work: Effects of adult surveillance and extrinsic rewards on children's intrinsic motivation. *Journal of Personality and Social Psychology, 31,* 479–486.

Lepper, M. R., & Greene, D. E. (Eds.). (1978). *The hidden costs of reward.* Hillsdale, NJ: Erlbaum.

Lepper, M. R., & Hodell, M. (1989). Intrinsic motivation in the classroom. In C. Ames & R. Ames (Eds.), *Research on motivation in education: Vol 3* (pp. 73–105). San Diego, CA: Academic Press.

Lerman, D., & Iwata, B. (1996). Developing a technology for the use of operant extinction in clinical settings: An examination of basic and applied research. *Journal of Applied Behavior Analysis, 29,* 345–382.

Lerner, J. V. (1993). The influence of child temperamental characteristics on parent behaviors. In T. Lister & L. Okagaki (Eds.), *Parenting: An ecological perspective* (pp. 101–120). Hillsdale, NJ: Erlbaum.

Lerner, R. M. (1988). Early adolescent transitions: The lore and laws of early adolescence. In M. D. Levine & E. R. McAnarney (Eds.), *Early adolescent transitions* (pp. 1–21). Lexington, MA: Lexington Books.

Lessow-Hurley, J. (2000). *The foundations of dual language instruction.* New York: Longman.

Leung, K. (1989). Cross-cultural differences: Individual-level vs. cultural level analysis. *International Journal of Psychology, 24,* 703–719.

Lewis, A. C. (2002). Where is the NCLBA taking us? *Phi Delta Kappan, 84*(1), 4–5.

Lewis, R. B., & Doorlag, D. H. (1987). *Teaching students in the mainstream* (2nd ed.). Columbus, OH: Merrill.

Licht, B. G. (1991). Modifying school attendance of special education high school students. *Journal of Educational Research, 84*(6), 368–373.

Liebert, R. M., & Sprafkin, J. (1988). *The early window effects of television on children and youth.* New York: Pergamon Press.

Liebert, R., & Morris, L. (1967). Cognitive and emotional components of test anxiety: A distinction and some initial data. *Psychological Reports, 20,* 975, 978.

Linn, R. L. (1990). Admissions testing: Recommended uses, validity, differential prediction and coaching. *Applied Measurement in Education, 3,* 297–318.

Linn, R. L., & Gronlund, N. E. (2000). *Measurement and assessment in teaching* (8th ed.). Upper Saddle River, NJ: Merrill.

Linn, R. L., Baker, E. L., & Betebenner, D. W. (2002). Accountability systems: Implications of requirements of the No Child Left Behind Act of 2001. *Educational Researcher, 31*(6), 3–16.

Linnenbrink, E. A. & Pintrinch, P. R. (2002). Achievement goal theory and affect: An asymetrical bidirectional model. *Educational Psychologist, 37*(2), 69–78.

Linnenbrink, E. A., & Pintrich, P. R. (2003). The role of self-efficacy beliefs in student engagement and learning in the classroom. *Reading & Writing Quarterly: Overcoming Learning Difficulties, 19,* 119–137.

Lipsitt, L. P. (Ed.). (1988). *Helping children through crisis: A special report from the editors of the Brown University Child Behavior and Development Letter.* Providence, RI: Manisses Communications Group.

Litow, L., & Pumroy, D. K. (1975). A brief review of classroom group-oriented contingencies. *Journal of Applied Behavior Analysis, 8,* 341–347.

Livesley, W. J., & Bromley, D. B. (1973). *Person perception in childhood and adolescence.* New York: John Wiley.

Lloyd, J. W., Forness, S. R., & Kavale, K. A. (1998). Some methods are more effective than others. *Intervention in School and Clinic, 33,* 195–200.

Locke, E. A., & Latham, G. P. (1990). *A theory of goal setting and task performance.* Englewood Cliffs, NJ: Prentice Hall.

Locke, E. A., & Latham, G. P. (1994). Goal setting theory. In H. F. O'Neil Jr. & M. Drillings (Eds.), *Motivation: Theory and research* (pp. 13–29). Hillsdale, NJ: Erlbaum.

Loewenstein, J., & Gentner, D. (2001). Spatial mapping in preschoolers: Close comparisons facilitate far mapping. *Journal of Cognition and Development, 2*(2), 189–219.

Lohman, D. F. (1994). Component scores as residual variation (or why intercept correlates best). *Intelligence, 19*(1), 1–11.

Lonnecker, C., Brady, M. P., McPherson, R., & Hawkins, J. (1994). Video self-modeling and cooperative classroom behavior in children with learning and behavior problems: Training and generalization effects. *Behavioral Disorders, 20*(1), 24–34.

Looi, C.-K., & Tan, B. T. (1998). A cognitive-apprenticeship-based environment for learning word problem solving. *Journal of Computers in Mathematics and Science Teaching, 17*(4), 339–354.

Lorch, R. F., & Lorch, E. P. (1996). Effects of headings on text recall and summarization. *Contemporary Educational Psychology, 21,* 261–278.

Lue, M. S. (2001). *A survey of communication disorders for the classroom teacher.* Boston: Allyn & Bacon.

Lukhele, R., Thissen, D., & Wainer, H. (1994). On the relative value of multiple-choice, constructed response, and examinee-selected items on two achievement tests. *Journal of Educational Measurement, 31*(3), 234–250.

Lupart, J. L (1995). Exceptional learners and teaching for transfer. In A. McKeough, J. Lupart, & A. Marini (Eds.), *Teaching for trans-*

fer: Fostering generalization in learning (pp. 215–228). Mahwah, NJ: Erlbaum.

Luria, A. R. (1961). Study of the abnormal child. *American Journal of Orthopsychiatry, 31,* 1–16.

Luria, A. R. (1979). *The making of mind.* Cambridge, MA: Harvard University Press.

Lustig, M. W., & Koester, J. (1999). *Intercultural competence: Interpersonal communication across cultures.* New York: Longman.

Lyman, F. (1992). Think-pair-share, thinktrix, thinklinks, and weird facts: an interactive system for cooperative learning. In N. Davidson & T. Worsham (Eds.), *Enhancing thinking through cooperative learning* (pp. 169–181). New York: Teachers College Press.

Lyons, N. (1983). Two perspectives: On self, relationships, and morality. *Harvard Educational Review, 53,* 125–145.

Lyytinen, P., Poikkeus, A.-M., Laasko, M.-L., Eklund, K., & Lyytinen, H. (2001). Language development and symbolic play in children with and without familial risk for dyslexia. *Journal of Speech, Language, & Hearing Research, 44*(4), 873–885.

Maag, J. W. (1999). *Behavior management.* San Diego: Singular Publishing Group.

Maag, J. W. (2001). Rewarded by punishment: Reflections on the disuse of positive reinforcement in schools. *Exceptional Children, 67*(2), 173–186.

Maag, J. W., & Katsiyannis, A. (2000). Recent legal and policy developments in special education. *NASSP Bulletin, 84*(6), 1–8.

Mac Iver, M. A., & Kemper, E. (2002). The impact of direct instruction on elementary students' reading achievement in an urban school district. *Journal of Education for Students Placed At Risk, 7*(2), 197–220.

MacArthur, C. A. (2000). New tools for writing: Assistive technology for students with writing difficulties. *Topics in Language Disorders, 20*(4), i85–100.

Maccoby, E. E., & Hagen, J. W. (1965). Effects of distraction upon central versus incidental recall: Developmental trends. *Journal of Experimental Child Psychology, 2,* 280–289.

Maccoby, E. E., & Jacklin, C. N. (1974). *The psychology of sex differences.* Stanford, CA: Stanford University Press.

Mace, F. C., Belfiore, P. J., & Shea, M. C. (1989). Operant theory and research on self-regulation. In B. J. Zimmerman & D. S. H. Schunk (Eds.), *Self-regulated learning and academic achievement: Theory, research, and practice* (pp. 27–50). New York: Springer-Verlag.

Mace, F. C., Belfiore, P. J., & Hutchinson, J. M. (2001). Operant theory and research on self-regulation. In B. J. Zimmerman & D. H. Schunk (Eds.), *Self-regulated learning and academic achievement theoretical perspectives* (2nd ed., pp. 39–65). Mahwah, NJ: Erlbaum.

Mager, R. F. (1975). *Preparing instructional objectives.* Belmont, CA: Fearon.

Maheady, L., Harper, G. E., & Mallette, B. (2001). Peer-mediated instruction and interventions with students with mild disabilities. *Remedial and Special Education, 22*(1), 4–14.

Mahn, H. (1999). Vygotsky's methodological contribution to sociocultural theory. *Remedial & Special Education, 20*(6), 341–350.

Mahon, K. L., Shores, R. E., & Buske, C. J. (1999). Issues of conducting research on setting events: Measurement and control of dependent and independent variables. *Education and Treatment of Children, 22*(3), 317–332.

Main, R. G. (1993). Integrating motivation into the instructional design process. *Educational Technology, 33*(12), 37–41.

Malinowski, C. I., & Smith, C. P. (1985). Moral reasoning and moral conduct: An investigation prompted by Kohlberg's theory. *Journal of Personality and Social Psychology, 49,* 1016–1027.

Malone, B. G., & Tietjens, C. (1998). *A re-examination of classroom rules.* Paper presented at the Mid-Western Educational Research Association, Chicago, IL (ED 425 129).

Malone, T. W., & Lepper, M. R. (1987). Making learning fun: A taxonomy of intrinsic motivation for learning. In R. E. Snow & M. J. Farr (Eds.), *Aptitude, learning, and instruction: Vol. 3. Cognitive and affective process analysis* (pp. 223–253). Hillsdale, NJ: Erlbaum.

Manassis, J. (2001). Adapting positive reinforcement systems to suit child temperament. *Journal of the American Academy of Child & Adolescent Psychiatry, 40*(5), 603–605.

Mandeville, G. E. (1992). Does achievement increase over time? Another look at the South Carolina PET program. *The Elementary School Journal, 93*(2), 117–129.

Mandeville, G. K., & Rivers, J. L. (1991). The South Carolina PET study: Teachers' perceptions and student achievement. *The Elementary School Journal, 91*(4), 377–407.

Mandeville, T. F. (1994). KWLA: Linking the affective and cognitive domains. *Reading Teacher, 47*(8), 79–80.

Manning, B. (1991). *Cognitive self instruction for classroom processes.* Albany, NY: SUNY Press.

Manning, B. H., & Glasner, S. E. (1996). The self-regulated learning aspect of metacognition: A component of gifted education. *Roeper Review, 18*(3), 217–229.

Manning, M. L. (2002). *Developmentally appropriate middle level schools* (2nd ed.). Olney, MD: Association for Childhood Education International.

Manning, M. L., & Baruth, L. G. (2000). *Multicultural education of children and adolescents.* Boston: Allyn & Bacon.

Maple, S. A., & Stage, F. K. (1991). Influences on the choice of math/science major by gender and ethnicity. *American Educational Research Journal, 28*(1), 37–60.

Marcia, J. E. (1966). Development and validation of ego identity status. *Journal of Personality and Social Psychology, 5,* 551–558.

Marcia, J. E. (1980). Identity in adolescence. In J. Adelson (Ed.), *Handbook of adolescent psychology* (pp. 159–187). New York: John Wiley.

Marcia, J. E. (1993). The relational roots of identity. In J. Kroger (Ed.), *Discussions on ego identity* (pp. 101–120). Hillsdale, NJ: Erlbaum.

Marcus, R. F. (1996). The friendships of delinquents. *Adolescence, 31*(121), 145–158.

Margolin, S. (2001). Interventions for nonaggressive peer-rejected children and adolescents: A review of the literature. *Children & Schools, 23*(3), 143–159.

Marks, S. B. (1998). Understanding and preventing learned helplessness in children who are congenitally deaf-blind. *Journal of Visual Impairment and Blindness, 92,* 200–211.

Marlowe, B. A., & Page, M. L. (1998). *Creating and sustaining the constructivist classroom.* Thousand Oaks, CA: Corwin Press.

Marsh, H. W. (1984). Relationship among dimensions of self-attribution, dimensions of self-concept, and academic achievements. *Journal of Educational Psychology, 76*(6), 1291–1308.

Marsh, H. W. (1990). Influences of internal and external frames of reference on the formation of math and English self-concepts. *Journal of Educational Psychology, 82,* 107–116.

Marsh, H. W., & Holmes, I. W. M. (1990). Multidimensional self-concepts: Construct validation of responses by children. *American Educational Research Journal, 27,* 89–119.

Marsh, H. W., Cairns, L., Relich, J., Barnes, J., & Debus, R. L. (1984). The relationship between dimensions of self-attributions and dimensions of self-concept. *Journal of Educational Psychology, 76*(1), 3–32.

Marshall, S. P. (1995). *Schemas in problem solving.* Cambridge: Cambridge University Press.

Martin, B. L., & Briggs, L. J. (1986). *The affective and cognitive domains: Integration for instruction and research.* Englewood Cliffs, NJ: Education Technology Publications.

Martin, G., & Pear, J. (1996). *Behavior modification: What it is and how to do it.* Upper Saddle River, NJ: Prentice Hall.

Martin, J. (1981). *Models of classroom management.* Calgary, Canada: Detselig Enterprises.

Martinez, M. E. (2000). *Education as the cultivation of intelligence.* Mahwah, NJ: Erlbaum.

Maslow, A. (1955). Deficiency motivation and growth motivation. In M. R. Jones (Ed.), *Nebraska symposium on motivation* (pp. 1–30). Lincoln, NE: University of Nebraska Press.

Maslow, A. H. (1987). *Motivation and personality* (3rd ed.). New York: Harper & Row.

Masten, A. S., & Garmezy, N. (1985). Risk, vulnerability, and protective factors in developmental psychopathology. In B. B. Lahey & A. E. Kazdin (Eds.), *Advances in clinical child psychology* (Vol. 8, pp. 1–52). New York: Plenum.

Mastropieri, M. A., & Scruggs, T. E. (1998). Constructing more meaningful relationships in the classroom: Mnemonic research into practice. *Learning Disabilities Research & Practice, 13,* 138–145.

Mastropieri, M. A., & Scruggs, T. E. (2000). *The inclusive classroom: Strategies for effective instruction.* Upper Saddle River, NJ: Merrill.

Mastropieri, M. A., Scruggs, T. E., Boon, R., & Carter, K. B. (2001). Correlates of inquiry learning in science: Constructing concepts of density and buoyancy. *Remedial and Special Education, 22*(3), 130–137.

Mastropieri, M., & Scruggs, T. E. (1997). How effective is inquiry learning for students with mild disabilities? *Journal of Special Education, 31*(2), 199–211.

Mastropieri, M. A. (1991). *Teaching students ways to remember: Strategies for learning mnemonically.* Cambridge, MA: Brookline.

Matthews, M. R. (2000). Appraising constructivism in science and mathematics education. In D. C. Phillips (Ed.), *Constructivism in education: Opinions and second opinions on controversial issues* (pp. 161–192). Chicago: University of Chicago Press.

Mau, W.-C. (2001). Gender differences on the Scholastic Aptitude Test, the American College Test and college grades. *Educational Psychology, 21*(2), 133–136.

Mauck, K., & Viechnicki, K. J. (1994). Assessing mathematics skills through portfolios: Validating the claims from existing literature. *Educational Assessment, 2*(2), 167–178.

Maxwell, N. L., Bellisimo, Y., & Mergendoller, J. (2001). Problem-based learning: Modifying the medical school model for teaching high school economics. *Social Studies, 92*(2), 73–78.

Mayer, R. E. (1975). Different problem solving competencies established in learning computer programming with and without meaningful models. *Journal of Educational Psychology, 68,* 143–150.

Mayer, R. E. (1979). Twenty years of research on advance organizers: Assimilation theory is still the best predictor of results. *Instructional Science, 8,* 133–167.

Mayer, R. E. (1980). Elaboration techniques that increase the meaningfulness of technical text: An experimental test of the learning strategy hypothesis. *Journal of Educational Psychology, 72,* 770–784.

Mayer, R. E. (1984). Aids to text comprehension. *Educational Psychologist, 19,* 30–42.

Mayer, R. E. (1987). *Educational psychology: A cognitive approach.* Boston: Little, Brown and Company.

Mayer, R. E. (1989). Models for understanding. *Review of Educational Research, 59*(1), 43–64.

Mayer, R. E. (1992). *Thinking, problem solving, and cognition* (2nd ed.). New York: W. H. Freeman and Company.

Mayer, R. E. (1993). Problem-solving principles. In M. Fleming & W. H. Levie (Eds.), *Instructional message design: Principles from the behavioral and cognitive sciences* (2nd ed., pp. 253–282). Englewood Cliffs, NJ: Educational Technology Publications.

Mayer, R. E. (1999). Designing instruction for constructivist learning. In C. M. Reigeluth (Ed.), *Instructional-design theories and models: Volume II. A new paradigm of instructional theory* (pp. 141–160). Mahwah, NJ: Erlbaum.

Mayer, R. E., Hieser, J., & Lonn, S. (2001). Cognitive constraints on multimedia learning: When presenting more material results in less understanding. *Journal of Educational Psychology, 93*(1), 187–198.

Mayer, R. E,. & Wittrock, M. C. (1996). Problem-solving transfer. In D. C. Berliner & R. C. Calfee (Eds.), *Handbook of educational psychology* (pp. 47–62). New York: Simon & Schuster Macmillan.

Mayfield, K. H., & Chase, P. N. (2002). The effects of cumulative practice on mathematics problem solving. *Journal of Applied Behavior Analysis, 35,* 105–123.

McCarthy Gallagher, J., & Reid, D. K. (1981). *The learning theory of Piaget & Inhelder.* Monterey, CA: Brooks/Cole.

McCaslin, M., & Good, T. L. (1992). Compliant cognition: The misalliance of management and instructional goals in current school reform. *Educational Researcher, 21*(3), 4–17.

McClelland, D. C. (1967). *The achieving society.* New York: The Free Press.

McClelland, D., Atkinson, J. W., Clark, R. A., & Lowell, E. L. (1953). *The achievement motive.* New York: Appleton-Century-Crofts.

McComas, J. J., Goddard, C., & Hoch, H. (2002). The effects of preferred activities during academic work breaks on task engagement and negatively reinforced destructive behavior. *Education and Treatment of Children, 25*(1), 103–112.

McCombs, B. L. (2000). Reducing the achievement gap. *Society, 37*(5), 29–36.

McConnell, M. E. (1999). Self-monitoring, cueing, recording, and managing: Teaching students to manage their own behavior. *Teaching Exceptional Children, 32*(2), 14–21.

McCrae, R. R., & Costa, P. T. (1996). Toward a new generation of personality theories: Theoretical contexts for the five-factor model. In J. S. Wiggins (Ed.), *The five-factor model of personality* (pp. 51–87). New York: Guilford.

McCurdy, B. L., & Shapiro, E. S. (1988). Self-observation and the reduction of inappropriate classroom behavior. *Journal of School Psychology, 26*, 371–378.

McDevitt, T. M., & Ormrod, J. E. (2002). *Child development and education.* Upper Saddle River, NJ: Pearson Education.

McDonald, L., & Stuart-Hamilton. (2002). Egocentrism in older adults—Piaget's three mountains task revisited. *Educational Gerontology, 28*, 35–43.

McEwan, E. K., & Damer, M. (2000). *Managing unmanageable students: Practical solutions for administrators.* Thousand Oaks, CA: Corwin Press.

McInerney, D. M. (1995). Achievement motivation and indigenous minorites: Can research be psychometric? *Cross-Cultural Research, 29*(3), 211–239.

McInerney, D. M., Roche, L. A., McInerney, V., Marsh, H. W. (1997). Culural perspectives on school motivation: The relevance and application of goal theory. *American Educational Research Journal, 34*(1), 207–236.

McKeachie, W. J. (1961). Arousal and reinforcement. In M. R. Jones (Ed.), *Nebraska symposium on motivation* (pp. 111–141). Lincoln, NE: University of Nebraska Press.

McLaughlin, T. F., & Skinner, C. H. (1996). Improving academic performance through self-management: Cover, copy, and compare. *Intervention in School and Clinic, 32*(2), 113–118.

McLester, S. (2003). Reading first: An administrator's debrief. *Technology and Learning, 23*(11), 30, 32.

McLoyd, V. C. (1990). The impact of economic hardship on Black families and children: Psychological distress, parenting, and socioeconomic development. *Child Development, 61*, 311–346.

McMillan, J, H., Myran, S., & Workman, D. (2002). Elementary teachers' classroom assessment and grading practices. *The Journal of Educational Research, 95*(4), 203–213.

McNeal, G., & Dwyer, F. (1999). Effect of learning style on consistent and inconsistently designed instruction. *International Journal of Instructional Media, 26*(3), 337–345.

McNeal, R. B. (2001). Differential effects of parental involvement on cognitive and behavioral outcomes by socioeconomic status. *Journal of Socio-Economics, 30*(2), 171–178.

McNeil, J. D. (1987). *Reading comprehension: New directions for classroom practice.* Glenview, IL: Scott, Foresman and Company.

McQueen, T. (1992). *Essentials of classroom management and discipline.* New York: HarperCollins.

McVey, M. D. (2001). Teacher praise: Maximizing the motivational impact. *Teaching strategies. Journal of Early Education and Family Review, 8*(4), 29–34.

Means, T. B., Jonassen, D. H., & Dwyer, F. M. (1997). Enhancing relevance: Embedded ARCS strategies vs. purpose. *Educational Technology: Research and Development, 45*(1), 5–17.

Medland, M., & Stachnik, T. (1972). Good behavior game: A replication and systematic analysis. *Journal of Applied Behavior Analysis, 5*, 45–51.

Meece, J. L. & Miller, S. D. (1999). Changes in elementary school children's achievement goals for reading and writing: Results of a longitudinal and an intervention study. *Scientific Studies of Reading, 3*(3), 207–229.

Meichenbaum, D. H. (1972). Cognition modification of test anxious college students. *Journal of Consulting and Clinical Psychology, 39*, 370–380.

Meichenbaum, D., & Bielmiller, A. (1998). *Nurturing independent learners: Helping students take charge of their learning.* Newton, MA: Brookline Books.

Meichenbaum, D., & Goodman, J. (1971). Training impulsive children to talk to themselves: A means of developing self-control. *Journal of Abnormal Psychology, 77*, 115–126.

Merbler, J. B., Hadadian, A., & Ulman, J. (1999). Using assistive technology in the inclusive classroom. *Preventing School Failure, 43*(3), 113–117.

Merkley, D. M., & Jefferies, D. (2000/2001). Guidelines for implementing a graphic organizer. *Reading Teacher, 54*(4), 350–357.

Merrill, M. D. (1983). Component display theory. In C. M. Reigeluth (Ed.), *Instructional-design theories and models: An overview of their current status* (pp. 279–333). Hillsdale, NJ: Erlbaum.

Merrill, M. D. (2001). Components of instruction toward a theoretical tool for instructional design. *Instructional Science, 29*, 291–310.

Messick, S. (1988). The once and future issues of validity: Assessing the meaning and consequences of measurement. In H. Wainer & H. I. Braum (Eds.), *Test validity* (pp. 33–46). Hillsdale, NJ: Erlbaum.

Messick, S. (1992). Multiple intelligences or multilevel intelligences? Selective emphasis on distinctive properties of hierarchy: On Gardner's *Frames of Mind* and Sternberg's *Beyond IQ* in the context of theory and research on the structure of human abilities. *Psychological Inquiry, 3*(4), 365–384.

Metz, K. E. (1995). Reassessment of developmental constraints on children's science instruction. *Review of Educational Research, 65*, 93–127.

Meyer, B. J. F. (1975). *The organization of prose and its effects on memory.* New York: American Elsevier.

Meyer, B. J. F. (1985). Signaling the structure of text. In D. H. Jonassen (Ed.), *The technology of text: Principles of structuring, designing, and displaying text* (pp. 64–89). Englewood Cliffs, NJ: Educational Technology Publications.

Meyer, B. J. F., Talbot, A., Stubblefield, R. A., & Poon, L. W. (1998). Interests and strategies of young and old readers differentially interact with characteristics of texts. *Educational Gerontology, 24*(9), 747–771.

Meyer, W.-U. (1982). Indirect communications about perceived ability estimates. *Journal of Educational Psychology, 74*(6), 888–897.

Middleton, J. A., & Spanias, P. A. (1999). Motivation for achievement in mathematics: Findings, generalizations, and criticisms of the research. *Journal for Research in Mathematics Education, 30*(1), 65–88.

Miller, D. L., & Kelley, M. L. (1994). The use of goal setting and contingency contracting for improving children's homework performance. *Journal of Applied Behavior Analysis, 27*, 73–87.

Miller, G. A. (1956). The magical number seven, plus or minus two: Some limits on our capacity for processing information. *Psychological Review, 63*, 81–97.

Miller, P. H. (2002). *Theories of developmental psychology* (4th ed.). New York: Worth Publishers.

Miller, S. (2001a). Tips for creating classroom rules. *Scholastic Early Childhood Today, 15*(6), 6.

Miller, S. (2001b). Tips for transitions. *Scholastic Early Childhood Today, 15*(5), 3.

Miller-Jones, D. (1989). Culture and testing. *American Psychologist, 44*(2), 360–366.

Mills, P. E., Cole, K. N., Jenkins, J. R., & Dale, P. S. (1998). Effects of differing levels of inclusion of preschoolers with disabilities. *Exceptional Children, 65*(1), 79–90.

Minick, N. (1987). Implications of Vygotsky's theories for dynamic assessment. In C. S. Lidz (Ed.), *Dynamic assessment: An interactional approach to evaluating learning potential* (pp. 116–140). New York: Guilford.

Minsky, M. (1975). A framework for representing knowledge. In P. H. Winston (Ed.), *The Psychology of computer vision* (pp. 211–277). New York: McGraw-Hill.

Mischel, W. (1966). A social-learning view of sex differences in behavior. In E. E. Maccoby (Ed.), *The development of sex differences* (pp. 57–81). Stanford, CA: Stanford University Press.

Mischel, W., & Mischel, H. N. (1994). A cognitive social-learning approach to morality and self-regulation. In B. Puka (Ed.), *Defining perspectives in moral development. Moral development: A compendium* (Vol. 1, pp. 186–210). New York: Garland Publishing.

Moles, O. C. (1993). Collaboration between schools and disadvantaged parents: Obstacles and openings. In N. F. Chavkin (Ed.), *Families and schools in a pluralistic society* (pp. 21–49). Albany: State University of New York.

Moll, L. C. (1990). Introduction. In L. C. Moll (Ed.), *Vygotsky and education instructional implications of sociohistorical psychology* (pp. 1–27). Cambridge: Cambridge University Press.

Moll, L. C., & Whitmore, K. F. (1993). Vygotsky in classroom practice: Moving from individual transmission to social transmission. In E. A. Forman, N. Minick, & C. A. Stone (Eds.), *Contexts for learning sociocultural dynamics in children's development* (pp. 19–42). New York: Oxford University Press.

Moll, L. C., Amanti, C., Neff, D. & Gonzales, N. (1992). Funds of knowledge for teaching: Using a qualitative approach to connect homes and classrooms. *Theory into Practice, 31.* 132–141.

Mondak, P. (2000). The Americans with Disabilities Act and information technology access. *Focus on Autism and Other Developmental Disabilities, 15*(1), 43–51.

Montague, M. (1993). Student-centered or strategy centered instruction: What is our purpose. *Journal of Learning Disabilities, 26*(7), 443–449.

"Montana school finds classroom telephones indispensable." (1993). *T.H.E., 21*(2), 87–89.

Montemayor, R., & Eisen, M. (1977). The development of self-conceptions from childhood to adolescence. *Developmental Psychology, 13*(4), 314–319.

Moore, B. J. (1998). Situated cognition versus traditional cognitive theories of learning. *Education, 119*(1), 161–171.

Morgan, H. (1996). An analysis of Gardner's theory of multiple intelligence. *Roeper Review, 18,* 263–270.

Moroz, K. B., & Jones, K. M. (2002). The effects of positive peer reporting on children's social involvement. *School Psychology Review, 31*(2), 235–245.

Morris, C. D., Bransford, J. D., & Franks, J. J. (1977). Levels of processing versus tranfer appropriate processing. *Journal of Verbal Learning and Verbal Behavor, 16,* 519–533.

Morris, S. M. (1982). A classroom group process for behavior change. *Pointer, 28,* 3.

Morse, W. H., & Dews, P. B. (2002). Foreword to schedules of reinforcement. *Journal of the Experimental Analysis of Behavior, 77*(3), 313–317.

Moskowitz, G., & Hayman, J. L. (1976). Success strategies of inner-city teachers: A yearlong study. *Journal of Educational Research, 69,* 283–289.

Moyers, S. (1994). Making elementary-schoolers a part of parent conferences. *Education Digest, 60*(4), 57–60.

Mukhopadhyay, M., & Parhar, M. (2001). Instructional design in multi-channel learning system. *British Journal of Educational Technology, 32*(5), 543–556.

Munby, H. (1983, April). A qualitative study of teachers' beliefs and principles. Paper presented at the annual meeting of the American Educational Research Association, Montreal, Canada.

Munk, D. D., Bursuck, W. D., Epstein, M. H., Jayanthi, M., Nelson, J., & Polloway, E. A. (2001). Homework communication problems: Perspectives of special and general education parents. *Reading and Writing Quarterly, 17,* 189–203.

Murdick, N. L., & Petch-Hogan, B. (1996). Inclusive classroom management: Using preintervention strategies. *Intervention in School and Clinic, 31*(3), 72–76.

Murphy, K. R., & Davidshofer, C. O. (2001). *Psychological testing: Principles and applications* (5th ed.). Upper Saddle River, NJ: Prentice Hall.

Murphy, J., Weil, M., & McGreal, T. L. (1986). The basic practice model of instruction. *The Elementary School Journal, 87*(1), 83–96.

Murry, H. A. (1955). Types of human needs. In D. C. McClelland (Ed.), *Studies in motivation* (pp. 63–70). New York: Appleton-Century-Crofts.

Naglieri, J. A., & Das, J. P. (1997). *Cognitive assessment system interpretative handbook.* Chicago: Riverside.

Nakamura, R. M. (2000). *Healthy classroom management: Motivation, communication, and discipline.* Stamford, CT: Wadsworth/Thomson Learning.

Narvaez, D. (2002). Does reading moral stories build character? *Educational Psychology Review, 14*(2), 155–170.

National Association for the Education of Young Children. (1996a). NAEYC position statement: Guidelines for decisions about developmentally appropriate practice.

National Association for the Education of Young Children. (1996b). NAEYC position statement: Moving from either/or to both/and thinking in early childhood practice.

National Association for the Education of Young Children. (1996c). NAEYC position statement: Principles of child development and learning that inform developmentally appropriate practice.

National Clearinghouse on Child Abuse and Neglect Information. (2002). National child abuse and neglect data system (NCANDS). Summary of key findings from calendar year 2000.

Neef, N. A., Shade, D., & Miller, M. S. (1994). Assessing influential dimensions of reinforcers on choice in students with serious emotional disturbance. *Journal of Applied Behavior Analysis, 27,* 575–583.

Nelson, J. (1985). The three R's of logical consequences, the three R's of punishment, and six steps for winning children over. *Individual Psychology, (42),* 161–165.

Nelson, J. D., & White, J. (2001). Impact of peer networks on achievement of high school algebra students. *The Journal of Educational Research, 94*(5), 267–273.

Nelson, T. O., & Narens, L. (1994). Why investigate metacognition? In J. Metcalfe & A. P. Shimamura (Eds.), *Metacognition: Knowing about knowing* (pp. 1–25). Cambridge, MA: The MIT Press.

Newby, T. J., Stepich, D. R., Lehman, J. D., & Russell, J. D. (2000). *Instructional technology for teaching and learning: Designing instruction, integrating computers, and using media.* Upper Saddle River, NJ: Prentice Hall.

Newell, A., & Simon, H. A. (1972). *Human problem solving.* Englewood Cliffs, NJ: Prentice Hall.

Newman, R. S. (1990). Children's help-seeking in the classroom: The role of motivation factors and attributions. *Journal of Educational Psychology, 82,* 71–80.

Newman, R. S. (1991). Goals and self-regulated learning: What motivates children to seek academic help? In M. L. Maehr & P. R. Pintrich (Eds.), *Advances in motivation and achievement* (Vol. 7, pp. 151–183). Greenwich, CT: JAI Press.

Newmann, F. M., & Wehlage, G. G. (1993). Five standards of authentic instruction. *Educational Leadership, 50*(7), 8–12.

Newstrom, J., McLaughlin, T. F., & Sweeney, W. J. (1999). The effects of contingency contracting to improve the mechanics of written language with a middle school student with behavior disorders. *Child & Family Behavior Therapy, 21*(1), 39–48.

Ngeow, K., & Kong, Y. S. (2001). Learning to learn: Preparing teachers and students for problem-based learning. *ERIC Digest* (ED457524).

Nicaise, M. (1997). Computer-supported apprenticeships in math and science. *Journal of Computers in Mathematics and Science Teaching, 16*(4), 443–465.

Nicholls, J. G. (1978). The development of concepts of effort and ability perceptions of academic achievement, and the understanding tha difficult tasks require more ability. *Child Development, 49,* 800–814.

Nichols, J. D. (2000, April). *Schema theory: A new twist using duplo models.* Paper presented at the annual meeting of the American Educational Research Association, New Orleans, LA.

Nichols, J. D., & White, J. (2001). Impact of peer networks on achievement of high school algebra students. *The Journal of Educational Research, 94*(5), 267–273.

Nicolau, S., & Ramos, C. L. (1993). *Together is better: Building strong relationships between schools and Hispanic parents.* New York: Hispanic Policy Development Project, Inc. (ERIC Document Reproduction Services No. ED325543).

Nieto, S. (2002). *Language, culture, and teaching: Critical perspectives for a new century.* Mahwah, NJ: Erlbaum.

Nimmer, D. N. (1984). Measures of validity, reliability and item analysis for classroom tests. *The Clearing House, 58,* 138–140.

"Nine tips for planning successful parent conferences." (2000). *Curriculum Review, 40*(2), 7.

Nolan, M., & Carr, A. (2000). Attention deficit hyperactivity disorder. In A. Carr (Ed.), *What works for children and adolescents: A critical review of psychological interventions with children, adolescents, and their families* (pp. 65–101). London: Routledge.

Norton, P., & Wiburg, K. M. (1998). *Teaching with technology.* Forth Worth, TX: Harcourt Brace.

Novak, J. D. (1990). Concept maps and Vee diagrams: Two metacognitive tools to facilitate meaningful learning. *Instructional Science, 19,* 1–25.

Nunn, G. D., & Miller, M. (2000). At-risk adolescents perceptions of learning temperaments: Implications for educational intervention. *Journal of Instructional Psychology, 27*(4), 266–272.

Nurmi, J.-E., Onatsu, T., & Haavisto, T. (1995). Underachievers' cognitive and behavioral strategies—Self-handicapping at school. *Contemporary Educational Psychology, 20,* 188–200.

Nurrenbern, S. C. (2001). Piaget's theory of intellectual development revisited. *Journal of Chemical Education, 78*(8), 1107–1110.

Nussbaum, E. M. (2002). How introverts approach small-group argumentative discussions. *The Elementary School Journal, 102*(3), 183–197.

Nuzzolo-Gomez, R., Leonard, M. A., Ortiz, E., Rivera, C. M., & Greer, R. D. (2002). Teaching children with autism to prefer books or toys over stereotypy or passivity. *Journal of Positive Behavior Interventions, 4*(2), 80–87.

O'Shea, L. J., O'Shea, D. J., & Algozzine, R. (1998). *Learning disabilities: From theory towards practice.* Upper Saddle River, NJ: Merrill.

Oakes, J. (1990). *Multiplying inequalities: The effects of race, social class, and tracking on opportunities to learn mathematics and science.* Santa Monica, CA: The RAND Corporation.

O'Donnell, J., Crosbie, J., Williams, D. C., & Saunders, K. J. (2000). Stimulus control and generalization of point-loss punishment with humans. *Journal of the Experimental Analysis of Behavior, 73*(3), 261–274.

Office of Special Education Programs (OSEP). (2001). *23rd annual report to congress on the implementation of IDEA.* Washington, D.C.: U.S. Department of Education.

Ogbu, J. U. (1978). *Minority education and caste: The American system in cross-cultural perspective.* New York: Academic Press.

Ogbu, J. U. (1994). Understanding cultural diversity and learning. *Journal for the Education of the Gifted, 17*(4), 355–383.

Ogbu, J. U. (1995). Understanding cultural diversity and learning. In J. A. Banks &. C. A. Banks (Eds.), *Handbook of research on multicultural education* (pp. 582–593). New York: Macmillan.

Ogle, D. M. (1986). KWL: A teaching model that develops active reading of expository text. *The Reading Teacher, 39,* 564–570.

Olson, D. H. L., & DeFrain, J. D. (1994). *Marriage and family: Diversity and strengths.* Mountain View, CA: Mayfield.

Olson, J. K. (1981). Teacher influence in the classroom. *Instructional Science, 10,* 259–275.

Olson, J. L., & Platt, J. M. (2000). *Teaching children and adolescents with special needs* (3rd ed.). Upper Saddle River, NJ: Prentice Hall.

Olson, M. A., & Fazio, R. H. (2002). Implicit acquisition and manifestation of classically conditioned attitudes. *Social Cognition, 20*(2), 89–104.

Olszewski-Kubilius, P. (1999). A critique of Renzulli's theory into practice models for gifted learners. *Journal for the Education of the Gifted, 23*(1), 55–66.

O'Melia, M. C., & Rosenberg, M. S. (1994). Effects of cooperative homework teams on the acquisition of mathematics skills by secondary students with mild disabilities. *Exceptional Children, 60*(6), 538–548.

O'Neill, D. K., & Gomez, L. M. (1994). *The collaborative notebook: A networked knowledge-building environment for project learning.* Paper presented at the ED-MEDIA 94-World Conference on Educational Multimedia, Vancouver, British Columbia, Canada (ED 388 279).

Oppenheimer, R. J. (2001). Increasing student motivation and facilitating learning. *College Teaching, 49*(3), 96–98.

O'Reilly, M., Tieman, R., Lancioni, G., Lacey, C., Hillery, J., & Gardiner, M. (2002). Use of self-monitoring and delayed feedback to increase on-task behavior in a post-institutionalized child within regular classroom settings. *Education and Treatment of Children, 25*(1), 91–102.

Orey, M. A., Okey, J. R., Jones, M. G., & Stanley, L. S. (1991). Integrating cognitive theory into Gagné's instructional events. (ERIC Document Reproduction Services No. ED335004).

Osborne, S. S., Kiburz, C. S., & Miller, S. R. (1986). Treatment of self-injurious behavior using self-control techniques with a severe behaviorally disordered adolescent. *Behavioral Disorders, 12,* 60–67.

Osgood, C. E. (1949). The similarity paradox in human learning: a resolution. *Psychological Review, 56,* 132–143.

Oster, L. (2001). Using the think-aloud for reading instruction. *The Reading Teacher, 55*(1), 64–69.

Ovando, C. J., & Collier, V. P. (1998). *Bilingual and ESL classrooms teaching in multicultural settings* (2nd ed.). Boston: McGraw Hill.

Padilla, A. M., & Lindholm, K. J. (1995). Quantitative educational research with ethnic minorities, In J. A. Banks & C. A. McGee-Banks (Eds.), *Handbook of research on multicultural education* (pp. 97–103). New York: Macmillan.

Paige, R. (2002). An overview of America's education agenda. *Phi Delta Kappan, 83*(9), 708–713.

Pajares, F. (1997). Current directions in self-efficacy research. In M. L. Maehr & P. R. Pintrich (Eds.), *Advances in motivation and achievement* (Vol. 10, pp. 1–49). Greenwich, CT: JAI Press.

Pajares, F. (2003). Self-efficacy beliefs, motivation, and achievement in writing: A review of the literature. *Reading & Writing Quarterly: Overcoming Learning Difficulties, 19,* 139–158.

Pajares, F., & Kranzler, J. (1995). Self-efficacy beliefs and general mental ability in mathematical problem-solving. *Contemporary Educational Psychology, 20*(4), 426–443.

Pajares, F., & Schunk, D. H. (2001). Self-beliefs and school success; Self-efficacy, self-concept, and school achievement. In R. J. Riding & S. G. Rayner (Eds.), *Self perception: International perpsectives in individual differences* (Vol. 2, pp. 239–265). Westport, CT: Ablex Publishing.

Pajares, F., & Schunk, D. H. (2002). Self and self-belief in psychology and education: A historical perspective. In J. Aronson (Ed.), *Improving academic achievement impact of psychological factors on education* (pp. 3–20). Amsterdam: Academic Press.

Palincsar, A. S., & Brown, A. L. (1984). Reciprocal teaching of comprehension fostering and comprehension-monitoring acivities. *Cognition and Instruction, 1,* 117–175.

Palincsar, A. S., and Herrenkohl, L. R. (2002). Designing collaboratiove learning contrexts. *Theory into Practice, 41*(1), 26–32.

Palincsar, A. S., Brown, A. L., & Campione, J. C. (1993). First-grade dialogues for knowledge acquisition and use. In E. A. Forman, N. Minick, & C. A. Stone (Eds.), *Contexts for learning sociocultural dynamics in children's development* (pp. 43–57). New York: Oxford University Press.

Panagos, R. J., & Dubois, D. L. (1999). Career self-efficacy development and students with learning disabilities. *Learning Disabilities Research & Practice, 14*(1), 25–34.

Papatheodorou, T. (2000). Management approaches employed by teachers to deal with children's behaviour problems in nursery classes. *School Psychology International, 21*(4), 415–440.

Papert, S. (1980). *Mindstorms.* New York: Basic Books.

Papert, S. (1990). *Constructionist learning.* Cambridge, MA: MIT Media Laboratory.

Paris, S. G., & Byrnes, J. P. (1989). The constructivist approach to self-regulation and learning in the classroom. In B. J. Zimmerman & D. H. Schunk (Eds.), *Self-regulated learning and academic achievement: Theory, research, and practice.* New York: Springer-Verlag.

Parke, R. D., & Buriel, R. (1998). Socialization in the family: Ethnic and ecological perspectives. In N. Eisenberg (Ed.), *Handbook of child psychology* (5th ed., Vol. 3, pp. 463–552). New York: Wiley.

Parkhurst, J., & Hopmeyer, A. (1998). Sociometric popularity and peer-perceived popularity: Two distinct dimensions of peer status. *Journal of Early Adolescence, 18,* 125–144.

Parry, L. J. (2000). Transcending national boundaries: Hilda Taba and the "new social studies" in Australia, 1969 to 1981. *Social Studies, 91*(2), 69–78.

Parsons, M. B., & Reid, D. H. (1999). Training basic teaching skills to paraeducators of students with severe disabilities. *Teaching Exceptional Children, 31*(4), 48–54.

Pascual-Leone, J. (2000). Is the French connection Neo-Piagetian? Not nearly enough! *Child Development, 71*(4), 43–45.

Patrick, H., Anderman, L. H., Ryan, A. M., Edelin, K., & Midgley C. (2001). Teachers' communications of goal orientatuiib in four fifth-grade classrooms. *The Elementary School Journal, 102*(1), 35–58.

Patton, J. R., & Baytops, J. L. (1995). Identifying and transforming the potential of young, gifted African Americans: A clarion call. In B. A. Ford, F. E. Obiakor, & J. M. Patton (Eds.), *Effective education of African American exceptional learners: New perspectives* (pp. 27–67). Austin, TX: Pro-Ed.

Patton, J. R., Jayanthi, M., & Polloway, E. A. (2001). Home-school collaboration about homework: What do we know and what should we do? *Reading and Writing Quarterly, 17,* 227–242.

Pavlov, I. P. (1902). *The work of the digestive glands* (H. W. Thompson, Trans.). London: Griffin.

Pavlov, I. P. (1927). *Conditioned reflexes* (G. V. Anrep, Trans.). London: Oxford University Press.

Pearson, D., Vyas, S., Sensale, L. M., & Kim, Y. (2001). Making our way through the assessment and accountability. Where do we go now? *The Clearing House, 74*(4), 175–182.

Pearson, P. D., Roehler, L. R., Dole, J. A., & Duffy, G. G. (1992). Developing expertise in reading. In S. J. Samuels & A. E. Farstrupt (Eds.), *What research has to say about reading instruction.* Newark DE International Reading Association.

Pearson, Q. M., & Nicholson, J. I. (2000). Comprehensive character education in the elementary school: Strategies for administrators, teachers, and counselors. *Journal of Humanistic Counseling, Education & Development, 38*(4), 243–251.

Pekrun, R., Gietz, T., Titz, W. & Perry, R. P. (2002). Academic emotions in students self-regulated learning and achievement: A program of qualitative and quantitative research. *Educational Psychologist, 37*(2), 91–105.

Pena, D. C. (2000). Parent involvement: Influencing factors and implications. *Journal of Educational Research, 94*(1), 42–54.

Perkins, D. N. (1993). Person-plus: A distributed view of thinking and learning. In G. Salomon (Ed.), *Distributed cognitions: Psychological and educational considerations* (pp. 88–110). New York: Cambridge University Press.

Perkins, D. N., & Salomon, G. (1989). Are cognitive skills context bound? *Educational Researcher, 17,* 16–25.

Perkins, D. N., Simmons, R., & Tishman, S. (1990). Teaching cognitive and metacognitive strategies. *Journal of Structured Learning, 10*(4), 285–303.

Perreault, G. (2000). The classroom impact of high-stress testing. *Education, 120*(4), 705–710.

Peskin, J. (1998). Constructing meaning when reading poetry: an expert-novice study. *Cognition and Instruction, 16*(3), 235–263.

Peterson, G. W., & Hann, D. (1999). Socializing children and parents in families. In M. B. Sussman, S. K. Steinmetz, & G. W. Peterson (Eds.), *Handbook of marriage and the family* (2nd ed., pp. 327–370). New York: Plenum Press.

Peterson, L. D., Young, K. R., West, R. P., & Peterson, M. H. (1999). Effects of student self-management on generalization of student performance to regular classrooms. *Education and Treatment of Children, 22*(3), 357–372.

Peterson, R. L., & Skiba, R. (2001). Creating school climates that prevent school violence. *The Clearing House, 74*(3), 155–163.

Pettigrew, T. F. (1958). The measurement of category width as a cognitive variable. *Journal of Personality, 26,* 532–544.

Peverly, S. T., & Wood, R. (2001). The effects of adjunct questions and feedback on improving the reading comprehension skills of learning-disabled adolescents. *Contemporary Educational Psychology, 26,* 25–43.

Phillips, D. C. (2000). *The expanded social scientist's beastiary*. Oxford: Rowman and Littlefield Publishers.

Phillips, S. (1977). The contributions of L. S. Vygotsky to cognitive psychology. *The Alberta Journal of Educational Research, 23*, 31–42.

Phillips, S. E. (1994). High stakes testing accommodations: Validity versus disabled rights. *Applied Measurement in Education, 7*(2), 93–120.

Phillips, S. U. (1983). *The invisible culture: Communication in classroom and community on the Warm Springs Indian Reservation*. Prospect Heights, IL: Waveland.

Phillips, S. U. (1985). Participant structures and communicative competence: Warm Springs children in community and classroom. In C. B. Cazden, V. P. John, & D. Hymes (Eds.), *Functions of language in the classroom* (pp. 370–394). Prospect Heights, IL: Waveland.

Piaget, J. (1924). *Judgment and reasoning in the child*. London: Routledge & Kegan Paul.

Piaget, J. (1927). The first year of life of the child. *British Journal of Psychology, 18*, 97–120.

Piaget, J. (1950). *The psychology of intelligence* (M. Piercy & D. Ellis, Trans.). London: Routledge & Kegan Paul.

Piaget, J. (1952). *The origins of intelligence in children*. New York: International Universities Press.

Piaget, J. (1954). *The construction of reality in the child* (M. Cook, Trans.). New York: Basic Books.

Piaget, J. (1962). *Play, dreams, and imitation*. New York: Norton.

Piaget, J. (1977). *The development of thought: Equilibration of cognitive structures*. New York: The Viking Press.

Piaget, J., & Inhelder, B. (1969). *The psychology of the child* (H. Weaver, Trans.). New York: Basic Books.

Piaget, J., & Szeminska, A. (1941). *The child's conception of number* (C. Gattegno & F. M. Hodgson, Trans.). Atlantic Highlands, NJ: Humanities Press.

Piechowski, M. M. (1997). *Emotional giftedness: An expanded view*. Paper presented at the World Conference of the World Council for Gifted and Talented Children, Seattle, WA.

Pierangelo, R., & Giuliani, G. A. (2002). *Assessment in special education: A practical approach*. Boston: Allyn & Bacon.

Piirto, J. (1999). *Talented children and adults: Their development and education* (2nd ed.). Upper Saddle River, NJ: Merrill.

Pintrich, P. R., & Schunk, D. H. (2002). *Motivation in education: Theory, research, and applications* (2nd ed.). Englewood Cliffs, NJ: Prentice Hall.

Pintrich, P. R., Marx, R. W., & Boyle, R. A. (1993). Beyond cold conceptual change: The role of motivational beliefs and classroom contextual factors in the process of conceptual change. *Review of Educational Research, 63*(2), 167–199.

Pisha, B., & Coyne, P. (2001). Smart from the start: The promise of universal design for learning. *Remedial and Special Education, 22*(4), 197–302.

Pittman, P., & Huefner, D. S. (2001). Will the courts go bi-bi? IDEA 1997, the courts, and deaf education. *Exceptional Children, 67*(2), 187–198.

Plato. (1987). *Theaetetus* (R. Waterfield, Trans.). Middlesex, England: Penguin Books

Plumert, J. M. (1994). Flexibility in children's use of spatial and categorical organizational strategies in recall. *Developmental Psychology, 30*, 738–747.

Pollock, E., Chandler, P., & Sweller, J. (2002). Assimilating complex information. *Learning and Instruction, 12*(1), 61–86.

Polloway, E. A., Bursuck, W. D., & Epstein, M. H. (2001). Homework for students with learning disabilities: The challenge of home-school communication. *Reading and Writing Quarterly, 17*, 181–187.

Polloway, E. A., Epstein, M. H., & Foley, R. (1992). A comparison of homework problems of students with learning disabilities and nonhandicapped students. *Learning Disabilities Research and Practice, 7*, 203–209.

Polson, M. C., & Richardson, J. J. (Eds.). (1988). *Foundations of intelligent tutoring systems*. Hillsdale, NJ: Erlbaum.

Polya, G. (1985). *How to solve it: A new aspect of mathematical method* (2nd ed.). Princeton, NJ: Princeton University Press,

Pomplun, M. (1997). When students with disabilities participate in cooperative groups. *Exceptional Children, 64*(1), 49–58.

Porter, L. (2000). *Behaviour in schools: Theory and practice for teachers*. Buckingham, England: Open University Press.

Posner, G. J., Strike, K. A., Hewson, P. W., & Gertzog, W. A. (1982). Accommodation of a scientific conception: Toward a theory of conceptual change. *Science Education, 66*, 211–277.

Postlethwaite, K., & Haggarty, L. (1998). Towards effective and transferable learning in secondary school: The development of an approach based on mastery learning. *British Educational Research Journal, 24*(3), 333–353.

Postlethwaite, T. N. (1994). Validity vs. utility: Personal experiences with the taxonomy. *Yearbook. National Society for the Study of Education, 93*, 174–180.

Potter, L., & Bulach, C. (2000). Do's and don'ts of parent-teacher conferences. *Education Digest, 66*(9), 37–40.

Prater, M. A. (1994). Improving academic and behavior skills through self-management procedures. *Preventing School Failure, 38*(4), 5–9.

Pratt, M. W., Golding, G., Hunter, W., & Sampson, R. (1988). Sex differences in adult moral orientation. *Journal of Personality, 36*, 373–391.

Premack, D. (1959). Toward empirical behavior laws: I. positive reinforcement. *Psychological review, 66*, 219–233.

Premack, D. (1965). Reinforcement theory. In D. Levine (Ed.), *Nebraska symposium on motivation* (pp. 123–179). Lincoln, NE: University of Nebraska.

Presno, C. (1997). Bruner's three forms of representation revisited: Action, pictures, and words for effective computer instruction. *Journal of Instructional Psychology, 24*(2), 112–118.

Pressley, M., & Wharton-McDonald, R. (1997). Skill comprehension and its development through instruction. *School Psychology Review, 26*(3), 448–466.

Pressley, M., & Woloshyn, V. (1995). *Cognitive strategy instruction that really improves children's academic performance* (2nd ed.). Cambridge, MA: Brookline Books.

Pressley, M., Goodchild, F., Fleet, J., Zajchowski, R., & Evans, E. D. (1989). The challenge of classroom strategy instruction. *The Elementary School Journal, 89*(3), 301–336.

Price, A. T., Martella, R. C., Marchand-Martella, N. E., & Cleanthous, C. C. (2002). A comparison of immediate feedback delivered via FM headset versus delayed feedback on the inappropriate verbalizations of a student with ADHD. *Education and Treatment of Children, 25*(2), 159–171.

Protheroe, N. (2002a). Teaching students to be efficient learners. *Principal, 82*(2), 48–51.

Protheroe, N. (2002b). More student learning strategies for deeper student learning. *The Education Digest, 68*(4), 25–28.

Pryor, D. B., & Tollerud, T. R. (1999). Applications of Adlerian principles in school settings. *Professional School Counseling, 2*(4), 299–304.

Putnam, M. L., Deshler, D. D., & Schumaker, J. B. (1993). The investigation of setting demands: A missing link in learning strategy instruction. In L. Meltzer (Ed.), *Strategy assessment and instruction for students with learning disabilities: From theory to practice* (pp. 325–354). Austin, TX: PRO-ED.

Pyryt, M. C. (1999). Putting the "g" back in gifted education. *Understanding Our Gifted, 12*(1), 16–18.

Quaiser-Pohl, C., & Lehmann, W. (2002). Girls' spatial abilities: Charting the contributions of experiences and attitudes in different academic groups. *British Journal of Educational Psychology, 72*, 245–260.

Quay, H. C. (1986). Classification. In H. C. Quay & J. S. Werry (Eds.), *Psychopathological disorders of childhood* (3rd ed.). New York: Wiley.

Radziszewska, B., & Rogoff, B. (1991). Children's guided participation in planning imaginary errands with skilled adult or peer partners. *Developmental Psychology, 27*(3), 381–389.

Rafoth., M. A., Leal, L. & Defabo, L. (1993). Strategies for learning and remembering. *Curriculum Review, 33*, 24.

Ramist, L., & Arbeiter, S. (1986). *Profiles, college bound seniors*. New York: College Entrance Examination Board.

Raschke, D., Alper, S., & Eggers, E. (1999). Recalling alphabet letter names: A mnemonic system to facilitate learning. *Preventing School Failure, 43*(2), 80–83.

Raskind, M. H., Goldberg, R., Higgins, E. L., & Herman, K. L. (2002). Teaching "life success' to students with LD: Lessons learned from a 20-year study." *Intervention in School & Clinic, 37*(4), 201–208.

Raths, L. E., Harmin, M., & Simon, S. B. (1978). *Values and teaching* (2nd ed.). Columbus, OH: Merrill.

Rathvon, N. (1999). *Effective school interventions: Strategies for enhancing academic achievement and social competence*. New York: Guilford.

Ratnesar, R. (1999, January 25). The homework ate my family. *Time*, 11.

Rattanapian, V., & Gibbs, W. J. (1995). Computerized drill and practice: Design options and learner characteristics. *International Journal of Instructional Media, 22*(1), 59–77.

Ravanis, K., & Bagakis, G. (1998). Science education in kindergarten: Sociocognitive perspective. *International Journal of Early Years Education, 6*(3), 315–327.

Raymond, E. B. (2000). *Learners with disabilities: A characteristics approach*. Boston: Allyn & Bacon.

Rayner, S., & Riding, R. (1997). Towards a categorization of cognitive styles and learning styles. *Educational Psychology, 17*(1/2), 5–28.

Reamer, R. B., Brady, M. P., & Hawkins, J. (1998). The effects of video self-modeling on parents' interactions with children with developmental disabilities. *Education and Training in Mental Retardation and Developmental Disabilities, 33*(2), 131–143.

Rebok, G. W., & Balcerak, L. J. (1989). Memory self-efficacy and performance differences in young and old adults: The effect of mnemonic training. *Developmental Psychology, 25*(5), 714–721.

Reeve, J. (1996). *Motivating others: Nurturing inner motivational resources*. Boston: Allyn & Bacon

Reeves, L., & Stein, J. V. (1999). Developmentally appropriate pedagogy and inclusion: "Don't put the cart before the horse!" *The Physical Educator, 56*(1), 2–7.

Reid, R. (1996). Research on self-monitoring with students with learning disabilities: The present, the prospects, the pitfalls. *Journal of Learning Disabilities, 29*, 317–331.

Reid, R. (1999). Attention deficit hyperactivity disorder: Effective methods for the classroom. *Focus on Exceptional Children, 32*(4), 1–20.

Reigeluth, C. M. (1997). Instructional theory, practitioner needs, and new directions: Some reflections. *Educational Technology, January-February*, 42–47.

Reigeluth, C. M., & Moore, J. (1999). Cognitive education and the cognitive domain. In C. M. Reigeluth (Ed.), *Instructional-design theories and models: Volume II. A new paradigm of instructional theory* (pp. 51–68). Mahwah, NJ: Erlbaum.

Reilly, L. (1999). IDEA'97 final regulations: Provisions of special interest to teachers. *Teaching Exceptional Children, 32*(1), 88–89.

Reis, S. M., & Renzulli, J. S. (1985). The secondary level enrichment triad model: Excellence without elitism. *NASSP Bulletin, 69*(482), 31–38.

Renninger, K. A. (1992). Individual interests and development: Implications for theory and practice. In K. A. Renninger, S. Hidi, & A. Krapp (Eds.), *The Role of interest in learning and development*. Hillsdale, NJ: Erlbaum.

Renninger, K. A. (1998). The roles of individual interest(s) and gender in learning: An overview of research on preschool and elementary school-aged children/students. In I. Hoffman, A. Krapp, K. Renninger, & J. Baumert (Eds.). *Interest and learning: Proceedings of the second conference on interest and gender* (pp. 165–175). Kiel, Germany: IPN.

Renzulli, J. S. (1977). *The enrichment triad model: A guide for developing defensible programs for the gifted and talented*. Wethersfield, CT: Creative Learning Press.

Renzulli, J. S. (2002). Expanding the conception of giftedness to include co-cognitive traits and to promote social capital. *Phi Delta Kappan, 84*(1), 33–40, 57–58.

Renzulli, J. S., & Dai, D. Y. (2001). Abilities, interests, and styles as aptitudes for learning: A person-situation interaction perspective. In R. J. Sternberg & L. Zhang (Eds.), *Perspectives on thinking, learning, and cognitive styles* (pp. 23–46). Mahwah, NJ: Erlbaum.

Reschly, D. J. (1997). Diagnostic and treatment utility of intelligence tests. In D. P. Flanagan, J. L. Genshaft, & P. L. Harrison (Eds.), *Contemporary intellectual assessment theories, tests, and issues* (pp. 437–466). New York: Guilford.

Rest, J., Narvaez, D., Bebeau, M., & Thoma, S. (1999). A neo-Kohlbergian approach to moral judgment: An overview of defining is-

sues test research. *Educational Psychology Review, 11*(4), 291–324.

Rich, J. M. (1984). Discipline, rules, and punishment. *Contemporary Education, 55*(2), 110–112.

Richardson, V. (1997). Constructivist teaching and teacher education: Theory and practice. In V. Richardson (Ed.), *Constructivist teacher education: Building new understandings* (pp. 3–14). London: Falmer Press.

Richey, R. C. (1996). *Robert M. Gagné's impact on instructional design theory and practice of the future*. Paper presented at the Association for Educational Communications and Technology, Indianapolis, IN.

Rickards, J. P., & Di Vesta, F. J. (1974). Type and frequency of questions in processing textual information. *Journal of Educational Psychology, 66*, 354–362.

Riding, R. (2001). The nature and effects of cognitive style. In R. J. Sternberg & L.-F. Zhang (Eds.), *Perspectives on thinking and cognitive styles* (pp. 47–72). Mahwah, NJ: Erlbaum.

Riding, R. J. (2000). Cognitive style: A review. In R. J. Riding & S. G. Rayner (Eds.), *International perspectives on individual differences* (Vol. I, pp. 315–346). Stamford, CT: Ablex Publishing.

Riding, R. J., & Cheema, I. (1991). Cognitive styles—an overview and integration. *Educational Psychology, 11*, 193–215.

Ridley, D. S., Schutz, P. A., Glanz, R. S., & Weinstein, C. E. (1992). Self-regulated learning: The interactive influence of metacognitive awareness and goal-setting. *Journal of Experimental Education, 60*(4), 293–306.

Rieber, L. P. (1992). Computer-based microworlds: A bridge between constructivism and direct instruction. *Educational Technology, 40*(1), 93–106.

Risemberg, R., and Zimmerman, B. J. (1992). Self-regulated learning in gifted students. *Roeper Review, 15*(2), 98–101.

Ritchie, D., & Karge, B. D. (1996). Making information memorable: Enhanced knowledge retention and recall through the elaboration process. *Preventing School Failure, 41*(1), 28–33.

Rittle-Johnson, B., & Siegler, R. S. (1998). The relation between conceptual and procedural knowledge in learning mathematics: A review. In C. Donlan (Ed.), *The development of mathematical skills. Studies in developmental psychology* (pp. 75–110). Hove, England: Psychology Press/Taylor & Francis.

Robbins, M. W. (1990, December 10). Sparing the child: How to intervene when you suspect abuse. *New York Magazine*, 42–53.

Robertson, H. M., Priest, B., & Fullwood, H. L. (2001). 20 ways to assist learners who are strategy-inefficient. *Intervention in School and Clinic, 36*(3), 182–184.

Robinson, F. P. (1961). *Effective study* (Revised ed.). New York: Harper & Row.

Roblyer, M. D., Edwards, J., & Havriluk, A. (1997). *Integrating educational technology into teaching*. Upper Saddle River, NJ: Prentice-Hall.

Roehler, L. R., & Duffy, G. G. (1984). Training teachers for instructional change in reading: A descriptive study. *Research Series, 143*, IRT-RS—143.

Rogers, P. J., & Aston, F. (1992). Teaching method, memory and learning: An enquiry with primary school children. *Educational Studies, 18*(2), 129–149.

Rogoff, B. (1981). Schooling and the development of cognitive skills. In H. C. Triandis &

A. Heron (Eds.), *Handbook of cross-cultural psychology* (Vol. 4). Boston: Allyn & Bacon.

Rogoff, B. (1982). Integrating context and cognitive development. In M. E. Lamb & A. L. Brown (Eds.), *Advances in developmental psychology* (Vol. 2, pp. 125–170). Hillsdale, NJ: Erlbaum.

Rogoff, B., & Chavajay, P. (1995). What's become of research on the cultural basis of cognitive development. *American Psychologist, 50*(10), 859–877.

Rogoff, B., & Morelli, G. (1989). Perspectives on children's development from cultural psychology. *American Psychologist, 44*:343–348.

Rogosa, D. (2001). Shoe shopping and the reliability coefficient. *Educational Assessment, 7*(4), 255–258.

Roid, G. H. (2003). *Stanford Binet Intelligence Scales* (Fifth ed.). Itasca, IL: Riverside Publishing

Romeo, F. F. (1998). The negative effects of using a group contingency system of classroom management. *Journal of Instructional Psychology, 25*(2), 130–133.

Rosch, E., Mervis, C. B., Gray, W. D., Johnson, D. M., & Boyes-Braem, P. (1976). Basic objects in natural categories. *Cognitive Psychology, 8*, 382–439.

Rose, D. H. (2000). Universal design for learning. *Journal of Special Education Technology, 15*(1), 67–70.

Rose, D. H. (2001). Universal design for learning: Deriving guiding principles from networks that learn. *Journal of Special Education Technology, 16*(2), 66–67.

Rose, D. H., Sethuraman, S., & Meo, G. J. (2000). Universal design for learning. *Journal of Special Education Technology, 15*(2), 56–60.

Rose, M. (1999). 6 surefire incentives for your students . . . *Instructor, 109*(4), 26.

Rosenshine, B. (1987). Explicit teaching and teacher training. *Journal of Teacher Education, 38*(3), 34–36.

Rosenshine, B., & Meister, C. (1992). The use of scaffolds for teaching higher-level cognitive strategies. *Educational Leadership, 47*(7), 26–33.

Rosenshine, B., & Meister, C. (1994). Reciprocal teaching: A review of the research. *Review of Educational Research, 64*(4), 479–530.

Rosenshine, B., & Stevens, R. (1986). Teaching functions. In M. C. Wittrock (Ed.), *Handbook of research on teaching* (3rd ed., pp. 376–391). New York: Macmillan.

Rosenthal, T. L., & Bandura, A. (1978). Psychological modeling: Theory and practice. In S. L. Garfield & A. E. Bergin (Eds.), *Handbook of psychotherapy and behavior change: An empirical analysis* (2nd ed., pp. 621–658). New York: Wiley.

Ross, B. H. (1989). Reminders in learning: objects and tools. In S. Vosniadou & A. Ortony (Eds.), *Similarity and Analogical Reasoning* (pp. 438–469). Cambridge: Cambridge University Press.

Rossi, P. H., Schuerman, J., & Budde, S. (1999). Understanding decisions about child maltreatment. *Evaluation Review, 23*(6), 579–598.

Roth, W.-M. (2001). Situating cognition. *Journal of the Learning Sciences, 10*(1/2), 27–61.

Rothbart, M., Hanley, D., & Albert, M. (1986). Gender differences in moral reasoning. *Sex Roles, 15*, 645–653.

Rothkopf, E. Z. (1966). Learning from written instruction materials: An exploration of the control of inspection behavior by test-like events. *American Educational Research Journal, 3,* 241–249.

Rothkopf, E. Z. (1970). The concept of math-emagenic activities. *Review of Educational Research, 40,* 325–336.

Rowan, J. (1999). Ascent and descent of Maslow's theory. *Journal of Humanistic Psychology, 39*(3), 125–133.

Rubin, K. H., Bukowski, W., & Parker, J. G. (1998). Peer interactions, relationships, and groups. In W. Damon (Editor-in-Chief) & N. Eisenberg (Vol. Ed.), *Handbook of child psychology: Vol. 3, Social, emotional, and personality development)* (5th ed., pp. 619–700). New York: John Wiley & Sons.

Ruble, D. N. (1983). The development of social-comparison processes and their role in achievement-related self-socialization. In E. T. Higgins, D. N. Ruble, & W. Hartup (Eds.). *Social cognition and social development* (pp. 134–157). New York: Cambridge University Press.

Ruble, D. N., & Martin, C. L. (1998). Gender development. In N. Eisenberg (Ed.), *Handbook of child psychology* (Vol. 3, pp. 933–1016). New York: John Wiley.

Ruff, H. A., & Lawson, K. R. (1990). Development of sustained, focused attention in young children during free play. *Child Development, 26,* 85–93.

Rugen, L., & Hartl, S. (1994). The lessons of learning expeditions. *Educational Leadership, 52*(3), 20–23.

Ruiz-Primo, M. A., & Shavelson, R. J. (1996). Problems and issues in the use of concept maps in science assessment. *Journal of Research in Science Teaching, 33*(6), 569–600.

Rumelhart, D. E., & Ortony, A. (1977). The representation of knowledge in memory. In R. C. Anderson, R. J. Spiro, & W. E. Montague (Eds.), *Schooling and the acquisition of knowedge.* (pp. 99–135). Hillsdale, NJ: Erlbaum.

Ryan, A. M. (2001). The peer group as a context for the development of young adolescent motivation and achievement. *Child Development, 72*(4), 1135–1150.

Ryan, G. (1997). Ensuring that students develop an adequate and well structured knowledge base. In D. Boud & G. I. Feletti (Eds.), *The challenge of problem-based learning* (2nd ed., pp. 28–35). London: Logan Page.

Ryle, G. (1949). *The concept of mind.* New York: Barnes & Noble.

Sadker, M., & Sadker, D. (1994). *Failing at fairness: How our schools cheat girls.* New York: Simon & Schuster.

Salend, S. J. (1998). *Effective mainstreaming: Creating inclusive classrooms* (3rd ed.). Upper Saddle River, NJ: Merrill.

Salend, S. J., & Duhaney, L. G. (1999). The impact of inclusion on students with and without disabilities and their educators. *Remedial and Special Education, 20,* 114–126.

Salend, S. J., & Gordon, B. D. (1987). A group-oriented timeout ribbon procedure. *Behavioral Disorders, 12*(2), 131–137.

Salend, S., & Meddaugh, D. (1985). Using a peer-mediated extinction procedure to decrease obscene language. *The Pointer, 30,* 8–11.

Salomon, G. (1993). Editor's introduction. In G. Salomon (Ed.), *Distributed cognitions psychological and educational considerations* (pp. xi–xxi). New York: Cambridge University Press.

Sampson, M. B. (2002). Confirming a K-W-L: Considering the source. *Reading Teacher, 55*(6), 528532.

Samuda, R. J. (1998). *Psychological testing of American minorities issues and consequences* (2nd ed.). Thousand Oaks, CA: Sage Publications.

Samway, K. D., & McKeon, D. (1999). *Myths and realities: Best practices for language minority students.* Portsmouth, NH: Heinemann.

Sasso, G. M., & Rude, H. A. (1987). Unprogrammed effects of training high-status peers to interact with severely handicapped children. *Journal of Applied Behavior Analysis, 20*(1), 35–44.

Savage, T. (2001). Shaping: A multiple contingencies analysis and its relevance to behaviour-based robotics. *Connection Science, 13*(3), 199–234.

Savage, T. V. (1999). *Teaching self-control through management and discipline* (2nd ed.). Boston: Allyn & Bacon.

Savin-Williams, R. C., & Berndt, T. J. (1990). Friendship and peer relations. In S. Feldman & G. Elliott (Eds.), *At the threshold: The developing adolescent.* Cambridge, MA: Harvard University Press.

Savoie, J. M., & Hughes, S. H. (1994). Problem-based learning as a classroom solution. *Educational Leadership, 52*(3), 54–57.

Schallert, D. L. (1982). The significance of knowledge: A synthesis of research related to schema theory. In W. Otto and S. White (Eds.), *Reading expository material.* New York: Academic Press.

Schamel, D. & Ayres, M. P. (1992). The minds-on approach: Student creativity and personal involvement in the undergraduate science laboratory. *Journal of College Science Teaching, 21*(4), 226–229.

Schank, R. C. (1975). *Conceptual information processing.* New York, Elsevier.

Schank, R. C., & Abelson, R. (1977). *Scripts, plans, goals and understanding.* Hillsdale, NJ: Lawrence Earlbaum.

Schank, R. C., Berman, T. R., & Macpherson, K. A. (1999). Learning by doing. In C. M. Reigeluth (Ed.). *Instructional-design theories and models: A new paradigm of instructional theory* (Vol. II). (pp. 161–182). Mahwah, NJ: Erlbaum.

Schank, R., Fano, A., Bell, B., & Jona, M. (1993). *The design of goal-based scenarios.* Evanston, IL: Northwestern University Press.

Schaps, E., & Williams, M. (1999). Character education: The foundation for teacher education. In M. Williams & E. Schaps (Eds.), *Character education: The foundation for teacher education* (pp. vii–xi). Washington, D.C.: Character Education Partnership.

Scheinman, A. J. (2000). 6 behavior tips that really work. *Instructor, 110*(1), 24.

Scher, S. J., & Osterman, N. M. (2002). Procrastination, conscientiousness, anxiety, and goals: Exploring the measurement and correlates of procrastination among school-aged children. *Psychology in the Schools, 39*(4), 385–398.

Scherer, M. (1999). The understanding pathway: A conversation with Howard Gardner. *Educational Leadership, 57*(3), 12–16.

Schiefele, U. (1991). Interest, learning, and motivation. *Educational Psychologist, 26,* 299–323.

Schiefele, U. (1992). Topic interest and levels of text comprehension. In K. A. Renninger, S. Hidi, & A. Krapp (Eds.), *The role of interest in learning and development* (pp. 151–182). Hillsdale, NJ: Erlbaum.

Schiever, S. W. & Maker, C. J. (1997). Enrichment and acceleration: An overview of new directions. In N. Coangelo & G. A. Davis (Eds.), *Handbook of gifted education* (2nd ed., pp. 113–125). Boston: Allyn & Bacon.

Schimmoeller, M. A. (1998, April). *Influence of private speech on the writing behaviors of young children: Four case studies.* Paper presented at the American Educational Research Association, San Diego.

Schloss, P. J., & Smith, M. A. (1994). *Applied behavior analysis in the classroom.* Boston: Allyn & Bacon.

Schmidt, P. (2000). Colleges prepare for the fall-out from state testing programs. *Chronicle of Higher Education, 46*(20), A26–A28.

Schneider, M. R. (1974). Turtle technique in the classroom. *Teaching Exceptional Children, 7,* 22–24.

Schneider, W. (1998). The development of procedural metamemory in childhood and adolescence. In G. Mazzoni & T. O. Nelson (Eds.), *Metacognition and cognitive neuropsychology: Monitoring and control processes.* Mahwah, NJ: Erlbaum.

Schorr, L. (1988). *Within our reach: Breaking the cycle of disadvantage.* New York: Anchor.

Schraw, G., Flowerday, T., & Lehman, S. (2001). Increasing situational interest in the classroom. *Educational Psychology Review, 13*(3), 211–224.

Schreiber, M. E. (1999). Time-outs for toddlers: Is our goal punishment or education? *Young Children, 54*(4), 22–25.

Schrumpf, F., Crawford, D., & Bodine, R. (1997). *Peer mediation: Conflict resolution in schools.* Champaign, IL: Research Press.

Schunk, D. (1989). Self-efficacy and cognitive achievement: Implications for students with learning problems. *Journal of Learning Disabilities, 22*(1), 14–22.

Schunk, D. (1996). Goal and self-evaluative influences during children's cognitive skill learning. *American Educational Research Journal 33,* 359–382.

Schunk, D. H. (1987). Peer models and children's behavioral change. *Review of Educational Research, 57*(2), 149–174.

Schunk, D. H. (1990). Goal setting and self-efficacy during self-regulated learning. *Educational Psychologist, 25:* 71–86.

Schunk, D. H. (1995). Social origins of self-regulatory competence: The role of observational learning through peer modeling. A paper presented at the biennial meeting of the Society for Research in Child Development, Indianapolis, IN.

Schunk, D. H. (1996). Self-evaluation and self-regulated learning (ERIC Document Reproduction Services No. ED403233).

Schunk, D. H. (2000). *Learning theories: An educational perspective* (3rd ed.). Upper Saddle River, NJ: Merrill.

Schunk, D. H. (2001). Social cognitive theory and self-regulated learning. In B. J. Zimmerman & D. H. Schunk (Eds.), *Self-regulated learning and academic achievement theoretical perspectives* (2nd ed., pp. 125–151). Mahwah, NJ: Erlbaum.

Schunk, D. H., & Pajares, F. (2002). The development of academic self-efficacy. In A. Wigfield & J. S. Eccles (Eds.), *Development of achievement motivation* (pp. 15–31). San Diego: Academic Press.

Schunk, D. H., & Rice, J. M. (1989). Learning goals and childrens reading comprehension. *Journal of Reading Behavior, XXI,*(3), 279–293.

Schunk, D. H., Hanson, A. R., & Cox, P. D. (1987). Peer-model attributes and children's achievement behaviors. *Journal of Educational Psychology, 79*(1), 54–61.

Schwartz, B. (1989). *Psychology of learning and behavior* (3rd ed.). New York: W. W. Norton.

Schwartz, N. H., Ellsworth, L. S., Graham, L., & Knight, B. (1998). Accessing prior knowledge to remember text: A comparison of advance organizers and maps. *Contemporary Educational Psychology, 23*, 65–89.

Schwartz, S. J., & Dunham, R., M. (2000). Identity status formulae: Generating continuous measures of the identity statuses from measures of exploration and commitment. *Adolescence, 35*(137), 147–165.

Schwebel, M., & Raph, J. (Eds.). (1973). *Piaget in the classroom.* New York: Basic Books.

Scruggs, T. E., & Mastropieri, M. A. (1991). Classroom applications of mnemonic instruction: Acquisition, maintenance, and generalization. *Exceptional Children, 58*, 219–229.

Scruggs, T. E., & Mastropieri, M. A. (1994). The construction of scientific knowledge by students with mild disabilities. *Journal of Special Education, 28*(3), 307–321.

Scruggs, T. E., & Mastropieri, M. A. (1996). Teacher perceptions of mainstreaming-inclusion, 1958–1995: A research synthesis. *Exceptional Children, 63*, 59–74.

Seels, B., & Glasgow, Z. (1998). *Making instructional design decisions* (2nd ed.). Upper Saddle, NJ: Merrill.

Seifert, K. L., & Hoffnung, R. J. (1994). *Child and adolescent development.* Boston: Houghton Mifflin.

Seligman, M. E. (1992). *Helplessness: On depression, development, and death.* San Francisco: W. H. Freeman.

Serna, L. A., & Forness, S. R. (1998). Intervention versus affirmation: Proposed solutions to the problem of disproportionate minority representation in special education. *Journal of Special Education, 32*(1), 48.

Settle, S. A., & Milich, R. (1999). Social persistence following failure in boys and girls with LD. *Journal of Learning Disabilities, 32*(3), 201–212.

Shapiro, E. S., & Cole, C. L. (1994). *Behavior change in the classroom: Self-management interventions.* New York: Guilford.

Shapiro, E. S., Browder, D. M., & D'Huyvetters, K. K. (1984). Increasing academic productivity of severely multihandicapped children with self-management: Idiosyncratic effects. *Analysis and Intervention in Developmental; Disabilities, 4*, 171–188.

Shapiro, E. S., Dupaul, G. J., & Bradley-Klug, K. L. (1998). Self-management as a strategy to improve the classroom behavior of adolescents with ADHD. *Journal of Learning Disabilities, 31*(6), 545–555.

Sharan, S., Kussell, P., Hertz-Lazarowitz, R., Bejarano, Y., Raviv, S., & Sharan, Y. (1984). *Cooperative learning in the classroom: Research in desegregated schools.* Hillsdale, NJ: Erlbaum.

Shaw, S. F., Scott, S. S., & McGuire, J. M. (2001). Teaching college students with learning disabilities. In *ERIC Digest.* Arlington, VA: ERIC Clearinghouse on Disabilities and Gifted Education (ED 459 548).

Sheets, R. H. (2002). "You're just a kid that's there"—Chicano perception of disciplinary events. *Journal of Latinos and Education, 1*(2), 105–122.

Shelton, T. L., & Barkely, R. A. (1994). Critical issues in the assessment of attention deficit disorders in children. *Journal of Learning Disabilities, 14*, 26–41.

Shepherd-Look, D. (1982). Sex differentiation and the development of sex roles. In B. Wolman (Ed.), *Handbook of developmental psychology.* Englewood Cliffs, NJ: Prentice Hall.

Sherman, J. (1983). Factors predicting girls' and boys' enrollment in college preparatory mathematics. *Psychology of Women Quarterly, 7*(3), 272–281.

Shiland, T. (2000). Questions on cue. *Science Teacher, 67*(8), 46–49.

Shimabukuro, S. M., Prater, M. A., Jenkins, A., & Edelen-Smith, P. (1999). The effects of self-monitoring of academic performance on students with learning disabilities and ADD/ADHD. *Education and Treatment of Children, 22*(4), 397–414.

Shimoff, E. (1998). Piagetian conservation in college students: A classroom demonstration. *Teaching of Psychology, 25*(1), 48–49.

Shrock, S. A. (1994). The media influence debate: Read the fine print, but don't lose sight of the big picture. *Educational Technology, Research and Development, 42*(2), 49–53.

Shrum, W., & Cheek, N. H. (1987). Social structure during the school years: Onset of the degrouping process. *American Sociological Review, 52*, 218–223.

Shute, V. J., & Glaser, R. (1990). A large-scale evaluation of an intelligent discovery world: Smithtown. *Interactive Learning Environments, 1*(1), 51–77.

Shweder, R. A., Mahapatra, M., & Miller, J. G. (1987). Culture and moral development. In J. Kagan & S. Lamb (Eds.), *The emergence of morality in young children* (pp. 1–82). Chicago: University of Chicago Press.

Siegel, L. S., Hodkin, L. S., & (1982). The garden path to the understanding of cognitive development: Has Piaget led us into the poison ivy? In In S. Modgil & C. Modgil (Eds.), *Jean Piaget: Consensus and controversy* (pp. 57–82). New York: Praeger.

Siegler, R. S. (1998). *Children's thinking* (3rd ed.). Upper Saddle River, NJ: Prentice Hall.

Silver, P., Bourke, A., & Strehorn, K. C. (1998). Universal instructional design in higher education: An approach for inclusion. *Equity & Excellence in Education, 31*, 47–51.

Simek, T. C., & O'Brien, R. M. (1981). *Total golf: A behavioral approach to lowering your score and getting more out of your game.* New York: Doubleday.

Simons, P. R. (1993). Constructive learning: The role of the learner. In T. M. Duffy, J. Lowyck, D. H. Jonassen, & T. M. Welch (Eds.), *Designing environments for constructive learning* (pp. 291–314). Berlin: Springer-Verlag.

Simpson, G. (2001). Learner characteristics, learning environments, and constructivist epistemologies. *Australian Science Teachers Journal, 47*(2), 17–20, 22–24.

Simpson, M. (2000). Why can't you tickle yourself? *Student BMJ, 9*, 451.

Simpson, R. L. (1998). Behavior modification for children with exceptionalities: Application of best practice methods. *Intervention in School and Clinic, 33*(4), 219–226.

Singley, M. K., & Anderson, J. R. (1989). *The transfer of cognitive skill.* Cambridge: Harvard University Press.

Skiba, R. J., & Peterson, R. L. (2000). School discipline at a crossroads: From zero tolerance to early response. *Exceptional Children, 66*(3), 335–347.

Skinner, B. F. (1938). *The behavior of organisms.* New York: Appleton-Century-Crofts.

Skinner, B. F. (1953). *Science and human behavior.* New York: McMillan.

Skinner, B. F. (1958a). Reinforcement today. *American Psychologist, 13*, 94–99.

Skinner, B. F. (1958b). Teaching machines. *Science, 128*(3330), 969–977.

Skinner, B. F. (1974). *About behaviorism.* New York: Knopf.

Skinner, B. F. (1984). The shame of American education. *American Psychologist, 39*(9), 947–958.

Skinner, B. F., & Epstein, R. (1982). *Skinner for the classroom.* Champaign, IL: Research Press.

Slade, P. D., & Owens, R. G. (1998). A dual process model of perfectionism based on reinforcement theory. *Behavior Modification, 22*(3), 372–390.

Slater, W. H., & Horstman, F. R. (2002). Teaching reading and writing to struggling middle school and high school students: The case for reciprocal teaching. *Preventing School Failure, 46*(4), 163–166.

Slavin, R. E. (1986). *Student team learning* (3rd ed.). Baltimore, MD: Center for Research on Elementary and Middle Schools, Johns Hopkins University.

Slavin, R. E. (1989a). Achievement effects of group-based mastery learning. In R. E. Slavin (Ed.), *School and classroom organization* (pp. 99–128). Hillsdale, NJ: Erlbaum.

Slavin, R. E. (1989b). On mastery learning and mastery teaching. *Educational Leadership, 46*(7), 77–79.

Slavin, R. E., Madden, N. A., Dolan, L. J., & Wasik, B. A. (1994). Roots and wings: Inspiring academic excellence. *Educational Leadership, 52*(3), 10–13.

Sliwiak, S. A., & Frissell, S. (2001). Some value orientations and their educational implications in American society. *Education, 108*(2), 155–163.

Small, R. V. (1997). *Motivation in instructional design.* Syracuse, NY: ERIC Clearinghouse on Information and Technology (ERIC Document Reproduction Services No. ED409895).

Small, R. V. (1999). An exploration of motivational strategies used by library media specialists during library and information skills instruction. (ERIC Document Reproduction Services No. ED409895).

Smith, D. D. (2001). *Introduction to special education: Teaching in an age of opportunity* (4th ed.). Boston: Allyn & Bacon.

Smith, J., Brooks-Gunn, J., & Klebanov, P. (1997). Consequences of living in poverty for young children's cognitive and verbal ability and early school achievement. In G. Duncan & J. Brooks-Gunn (Eds.), *Consequences of growing up poor* (pp. 132–189). New York: Russell Sage.

Smith, L., Dockrell, J., & Tomlinson, P. (Eds.). (1997). *Piaget, Vygotsky and beyond: Future issues for developmental psychology and education.* London: Routledge.

Smith, M. L. (1989). A qualitative study of teacher beliefs about retention. In L. A. Shepard & M. L. Smith (Eds.), *Flunking grades: Research and policies on grade retention.* New York: Falmer Press.

Smith, M., Duda, J., Allen, J., & Hall, H. (2002). Contemorary measures of approach and avoidance goal orientations: Similarities and differences. *British Journal of Educational Psychology, 72*, 155–190.

Smith, P. L., & Ragan, T. J. (1993). *Instructional design.* New York: Merrill.

Smith, S. W. (2000). Creating useful individualized education programs (IEPs). ERIC Clearinghouse on Disabilities and Gifted Education (ED449636).

Smith, T. C., Polloway, E. A., Patton, J. R., & Dowdy, C. A. (2001). *Teaching students with special needs in inclusive settings* (3rd ed.). Boston: Allyn & Bacon.

Smitherman, G. (1977). *Talkin' and testifyin': The language of Black America.* Boston: Houghton Mifflin.

Snarey, J. R. (1985). Cross-cultural universality of social-moral development: A critical review of Kohlbergian research. *Psychological Bulletin, 97*(2), 202–232.

Sneed, C. D. (2002). Correlates and implications for agreeableness in children. *Journal of Psychology, 136*(1), 59–68.

Snell, M., & Drake, G. P. (1994). Replacing cascades with supported education. *Journal of Special Education, 27*(4), 393–409.

Snow, R. E. & Jackson, D. N. (1994). Individual differences in conation: Selected constructs. In H. F. O'Neil & M. Drillings (Eds.), *Motivation: Theory and research* (pp. 71–100). Hillsdale, NJ: Erlbaum.

Snow, R. E., Corno, L., & Jackson, D. (1996). Individual differences in affective and conative functions. In D. C. Berliner & R. C. Calfee (Ed.), *Handbook of educational psychology* (pp. 243–310). New York: Macmillan.

Snyder, B., & Pressley, M. (1995). Introduction to cognitive learning strategies. In M. Pressley & V. Woloshyn (Eds.), *Cognitive strategy instruction that really improves children's academic performance* (2nd ed. pp. 1–18). Cambridge, MA: Brookline Book.

Snyderman, M., & Rothman, S. (1987). Survey of expert opinions on intelligence and aptitude-testing. *American Psychologist, 42,* 137–144.

Soar, R. S., & Soar, R. M. (1979). Emotional climate and management. In P. Peterson & H. Wahlberg (Eds.), *Research on teaching: Concepts, findings, and implications.* Berkley, CA: McCutchan.

Sobesky, W. E. (1983). The effects of situational factors on moral judgment. *Child Development, 54,* 575–584.

Solomon, J., & Hunter, J. (2002). A psychological view of spirituality and leadership. *School Administrator, 59*(8), 38–41.

Solter, A., & Mayer, R. E. (1978). Broader transfer produced by guided discovery of number concepts with preschool children. *Journal of Eductional Psychology, 70*(3), 363–371.

Somuncuoglu, Y., & Yildirim, A. (2001). Relationship between achievement goal orientations and use of learning strategies. *The Journal of Educational Research, 92*(5), 267–277.

Song, S. H., & Keller, J. M. (2001). Effectiveness of motivationally adaptive computer-assisted instruction on the dynamic aspects of motivation. *Educational Technology: Research and Development, 49*(2), 5–22.

Sorrell, A. L. (2000). Learning disabilities: From understanding to intervention. In F. E. Obiakor, S. A. Burkhardt, A. F. Rotatori, & T. Wahlberg (Eds.), *Intervention techniques for individuals with exceptionalities in inclusive settings* (pp. 53–78). Stamford, CT: JAI Press.

Southern, W. T., & Jones, E. D. (1991). Academic acceleration: Background issues. In W. T. Southern & E. D. Jones (Eds.), *The academic acceleration of gifted children* (pp. 1–28). New York: Teachers' College Press.

Spaulding, K., & Dwyer, F. M. (1999). Effect of job aids in facilitating learners' cognitive development. *International Journal of Instructional Media, 26*(1), 87–104.

Spearman, C. (1904). General intelligence, objectively determined and measured. *American Journal of Psychology, 15,* 201–293.

Spearman, C. (1927). *The abilities of man.* New York: Macmillan.

Spector, M. J. (2000, April). *Toward a philosophy of instructional design.* Paper presented at the American Educational Research Association, New Orleans, LA.

Spector, M. J. (2001). Philosophical implications for the design of instruction. *Instructional Science, 29*(4–5), 381–402.

Spence, I., & Hively, W. (1993). What makes Chris practice? *Educational Technology, 33*(10), 15–20.

Spence, J. T., & Helmreich, R. L. (1983). Achievement related motives and behaviors. In J. T. Spence (Ed.), *Achievement and achievement motives: Psychological and sociologicval approaches* (pp. 7–74). San Francisco: W. H. Freeman and Company.

Spielberger, C. D., & Starr, L. M. (1994). Curiosity and exploratory behavior. In H. F. O'Neil Jr. & M. Drillings (Eds.), *Motivation: Theory and research* (pp. 221–244). Hillsdale, NJ: Erlbaum.

Spiro, R. J., Coulson, R. L., Feltovich, P. J., & Anderson, D. K. (1988). *Cognitive flexibility theory: Advanced knowledge acquisition in ill-structured domains.* Paper presented at the Tenth Annual Conference of the Cognitive Science Society, Montreal.

Spiro, R. J., Feltovich, P. J., Coulson, R. L., & Anderson, D. K. (1989). Multiple analogies for complex concepts: Antidotes for analogy-induced misconceptions in advanced knowledge acquisition. In S. Vosniadou & A. Ortony (Eds.), *Similarity and analogical reasoning* (pp. 498–531). Cambridge: Cambridge University Press.

Spooner, F., & Spooner, D. (1984). A review of chaining techniques: Implications for future research and practice. *Education and Training of the Mentally Retarded, 19,* 114–124.

St. Charles, J., & Costantino, M. (2000). *Reading and the Native American learner.* Olympia: Washington Office of the State Superintendent of Public Instruction, Olympia, Office of Indian Education.

Stallings, D. T. (2002). A brief history of the United States Department of Education. *Phi Delta Kappan, 83*(9), 677–683.

Stallings, J., & Krasavage, E. M. (1986). Program implementation and student achievement in a four-year Madeline Hunter Follow-Through Project. *The Elementary School Journal, 87,* 117–138.

Stangor, C., & Ruble, D. N. (1987). Development of gender role knowledge and gender constancy. In L. S. Liben & M. L. Signorella (Eds.), *Children's gender schemata* (pp. 5–22). San Francisco: Jossey-Bass.

Stanley, J. C., & Benbow, C. P. (1983). SMYP's first decade: Ten years of posing problems and solving them. *Journal of Special Education, 17*(1), 11–25.

Stanley, J. C., & McGill, A. M. (1986). More about "young entrants to college: How did they fare?" *Gifted Child Quarterly, 30*(2), 70–73.

Stanley, J. C., Benbow, C. P., Brody, L. E., Dauber, S., & Lupkowski, A. E. (1991). Gender differences in eighty-six nationally standardized aptitude and achievement tests. In N. Colangelo, S. G. Assouline, & D. Ambrosen (Eds.), *National research symposium on talent development.* Iowa City: University of Iowa Press.

Stark, R., Mandl, H., Gruber, H., & Renkl, A. (1999). Instructional means to overcome transfer problems in the domain of economics: Empirical studies. *International Journal of Educational Research, 31*(7), 591–609.

Steel, S., & Funnell, E. (2001). Learning mathematics facts: A study of children taught by discovery methods in England. *Journal of Experimental Child Psychology, 79*(1), 37–55.

Steele, M. M., & Steele, J. W. (1999). DISCOVER: An intelligent tutoring system for teaching students with learning difficulties to solve word problems. *Journal of Computers in Mathematics and Science Teaching, 18*(4), 351–359.

Steenbarger, B. N. (1991). All the world is not a stage: emerging contextualist themes in counseling and development. *Journal of Counseling and Development, 70*(2), 288–296.

Stein, B. S., Littlefield, J., Bransford, J. D., & Persampieri, M. (1984). Elaboration and knowledge acquisition. *Memory and Cognition, 12*(5), 522–529.

Steinman, A. J. (1999). 6 behavior tips that really work. *Instructor, 110*(1), 24.

Stephens, K. R., & Karnes, F. A. (2000). State definitions for the gifted and talented revisited. *Exceptional Children, 66*(2), 219–238.

Stepien, W., & Gallagher, S. (1993). Problem-based learning: As authentic as it gets. *Educational Leadership, 50*(7), 25–28.

Sternberg, R. J. (1977). Component processes in analogical reasoning. *Psychological Review, 84,* 353–378.

Sternberg, R. J. (1980). Sketch of a componential subtheory of human intelligence. *The Behavioral and Brain Sciences, 3,* 573–614.

Sternberg, R. J. (1981). Intelligence as thinking and learning skills. *Educational Leadership, 39,* 18–20.

Sternberg, R. J. (1984). How can we teach intelligence? *Educational Leadership, 42,* 38–48.

Sternberg, R. J. (1985). *Beyond IQ: A triarchic theory of human intelligence.* New York: Cambridge University Press.

Sternberg, R. J. (1990). *Metaphors of mind: Conceptions of the nature of intelligence.* Cambridge: Cambridge University Press.

Sternberg, R. J. (1994). Diversifying instruction and assessment. *The Educational Forum, 59,* 47–52.

Sternberg, R. J. (1995). *A triarchic approach to giftedness.* Storrs, CT: National Research Center on the Gifted and Talented.

Sternberg, R. J. (1996). *Successful intelligence.* New York: Simon & Schuster.

Sternberg, R. J. (1997). The triarchic theory of intelligence. In D. P. Flanagan, J. L. Genshaft, & P. L. Harrison (Eds.), *Contemporary intellectual assessment theories, tests, and issues* (pp. 92–104). New York: Guilford.

Sternberg, R. J. (1998a). Ability testing, instruction, and assessment of achievement: Breaking out of the vicious circle. *NASSP Bulletin, 82,* 4–10.

Sternberg, R. J. (1998b). Applying the triarchic theory of intelligence in the classroom. In R. J. Sternberg & W. M. Williams (Eds.), *Intelligence, instruction, and assessment* (pp. 1–16). Mahwah, NJ: Erlbaum.

Sternberg, R. J. (1998c). Principles of teaching for successful intelligence. *Educational Psychologist, 33*(2/3), 65–72.

Sternberg, R. J. (1999a). A triarchic approach to understanding and assessment of intelligence in multicultural populations. *Journal of School Psychology, 37*(2), 145–159.

Sternberg, R. J. (2001a). How wise is it to teach for wisdom? A reply to five critiques. *Educational Psychologist, 36*(4), 269–272.

Sternberg, R. J. (2001b). Why schools should teach for wisdom: The balance theory of wisdom in educational settings. *Educational Psychologist, 36*(4), 227–245.

Sternberg, R. J. (2001c). Epilogue: Another mysterious affair at styles. In R. J. Sternberg & L. Zhang (Eds.), *Perspectives on thinking, learning, and cognitive styles* (pp. 249–252). Mahwah, NJ: Erlbaum.

Sternberg, R. J. (2002a). Teaching for wisdom after 911. *The Education Digest, 68*(1), 9–12.

Sternberg, R. J. (2002b). Teaching for wisdom in our schools. *Education Week, 22*(11), 56, 42.

Sternberg, R. J. (Ed.). (1999b). *Handbook of creativity*. Cambridge: Cambridge University Press.

Sternberg, R. J., & Gardner, M. K. (1982). A componential interpretation of the general factor in intelligence. In H. J. Eysenck (Ed.), *A model for intelligence* (pp. 231–254). Berlin: Springer.

Sternberg, R. J., & Grigorenko, E. L. (2000). *Teaching for successful intelligence to increase student learning and achievement*. Washington, D.C.: Office of Educational Research and Improvement.

Sternberg, R. J., & Grigorenko, E. L. (2001). A capsule history of theory and research on styles. In R. J. Sternberg & L. Zhang (Eds.), *Perspectives on thinking: learning and cognitive styles* (pp. 1–22). Mahwah, NJ: Erlbaum.

Sternberg, R. J., Ferrari, M., Clinkenbeard, P. R., & Grigorenko, E. L. (1996). Identification, instruction, and assessment of gifted children: A construct validation of a triarchic model. *Gifted Child Quarterly, 40*, 129–137.

Stevens, R. J., & Slavin, R. E. (1995). The cooperative elementary school: Effects on students' achievement, attitudes and social relations. *American Educational Research Journal, 32*, 321–351.

Stevens, S. (2000). A teacher looks at the elementary child with ADHD. In B. P. Guyer (Ed.), *ADHD: Achieving success in school and in life* (pp. 67–80). Boston: Allyn & Bacon.

Stiggins, R. J. (1985). Improving assessment where it means the most: In the classroom. *Educational Leadership, 43*(2), 69–74.

Stiggins, R. J. (1993). Two disciplines of educational assessment. *Evaluation in Counseling and Development, 26*(1), 94–104.

Stiggins, R. J. (2002). Assessment crisis: The absence of assessment for learning. *Phi Delta Kappan, 83*(10), 758–763.

Stiggins, R. J., & Bridgeford, N. J. (1985). The ecology of classroom assessment. *Journal of Educational Measurement, 22*(4), 271–286.

Stipek, D. J., & Hoffman, J M. (1980). Children's achievement-related expectancies as a function of academic performance histories and gender. *Journal of Educational Psychology, 72*, 861–865.

Stone, C. A., & May, A. L. (2002). The accuracy of academic self-evaluations in adolescents with learning disabilities. *Journal of Learning Disabilities, 35*(4), 370–383.

Stone, J. E. (1996). Developmentalism: An obscure but pervasive restriction on educational improvement. *Educational Policy Analysis Archives, 4*(8).

Storemont-Spurgin, M. (1997). I lost my homework: Strategies for improving organization. *Intervention in School & Clinic, 32*(5), 270–274.

Story, M. F., Mueller, J. L., & Mace, R. L. (1998). *The universal design file: Designing for people of all ages and abilities*. (Rev. ed.). Washington, D.C.: National Institute on Disability and Rehabilitation Research.

Stricker, L. J., Rock, D. A., & Burton, N. W. (1993). Sex differences in prediction of college grades from Scholastic Aptitude Test scores. *Journal of Educational Psychology, 85*(4), 710–718.

Strom, P. S., & Strom, R. D. (1999). Making students accountable for teamwork. *Community College Journal of Research & Practice, 23*(2), 171–182.

Strong, R. W., Silver, H. F., & Perini, M. J. (2001), Making students as important as standards. *Educational Leadership, 59*(3), 56–61.

Stuart-Hamilton, I., & McDonald, L. (2001). Do we need intelligence? Some reflections on the perceived importance of 'G'. *Educational Gerontology, 27*(5), 399–407.

Stumpf, H., & Jackson, D. N. (1994). Gender-related differences in cognitive abilities: Evidence from a medical school admissions testing program. *Personality and Individual Differences, 17*, 335–344.

Sturm, J. M., & Rankin-Erickson, J. L. (2002). Effects of hand-drawn and computer-generated concept mapping on the expository writing of middle school students with learning disabilities. *Learning Disabilities: Research & Practice, 17*(2), 124–139.

Suchman, J. R. (1962). The elementary school training program in scientific inquiry. Urbana, IL: Illinois University (ERIC Document Reproduction Services ED003530).

Sue, D. W. (1991). A diversity perspective on contextualism. *Journal of Counseling and Development, 70*(2), 300–301.

Sullivan, K. R., & Mahalik, J. R. (2000). Increasing career self-efficacy for women: Evaluating a group intervention. *Journal of Counseling & Development, 78*(1), 54–62.

Suls, J., & Wills, T. A. (Eds.). (1991). *Social comparison: Contemporary theory and research*. Hillsdale, NJ: Erlbaum.

Sulzer-Azaroff, B., & Mayer, G. R. (1991). *Behavior analysis for lasting change*. Forth Worth, TX: Holt, Rinehart, & Winston.

Surber, J. R., & Anderson, R. C. (1975). Delay-retention effect in natural classroom settings. *Journal of Educational Psychology, 67*, 170–173.

Susi, F. D. (2002). Behavior management: Principles and guidelines for art educators. *Art Education, 55*(1), 40–45.

Sutherland, K. S., Wehby, J. H., & Copeland, S. R. (2000). Effect of varying rates of behavior-specific praise on the on-task behavior of students with EBD. *Journal of Emotional & behavioral Disorders, 8*(1), 2–8.

Swaggert, B. L. (1998). Implementing a cognitive behavior management program. *Intervention in School and Clinic, 33*(4), 235–238.

Swanson, D. B., & Case, S. M. (1997). Assessment in basic science instruction: Directions for practice and research. *Advances in Health Sciences Assessment, 2*, 71–84.

Swanson, H. L. (1993). An information processing analysis of learning disabled children's problem solving. *American Educational Research Journal, 30*, 861–893.

Swanson, H. L. (1999). Instructional components that predict treatment outcomes for students with learning disabilities: Support for a combined strategy and Direct Instruction model. *Learning Disabilities Research & Practice, 14*(3), 129–140.

Swanson, H. L., & Siegel, L. (2001). Learning disabilities as a working memory deficit. *Issues in Education, 7*(1), 1–48.

Swanson, J. M., McBurnett, K., Wigal, T., Pfiffner, L. J., Lerner, M. A., Williams, L., et al. (1993). Effect of stimulant medication on children with attention deficit disorder. *Exceptional Children, 60*(2), 154–162.

Sweller, J. (1989). Cognitive technology: Some procedures for facilitating learning and problem solving in mathematics and science. *Journal of Educational Psychology, 81*(4), 457–466.

Sweller, J. (1999). *Instructional design in technical areas*. Melbourne: ACER.

Sweller, J., & Cooper, G. A. (1985). The use of worked examples as a substitute for problem solving in learning algebra. *Cognition and Instruction, 2*(1), 59–89.

Swiderek, B. (1997). Parent conferences. *Journal of Adolescence & Adult Literacy, 40*(7), 580–581.

Symons, F. J., McDonald, L. M., & Wehby, J. H. (1998). Functional assessment and teacher collected data. *Education and Treatment of Children, 21*(2), 135–159.

Tan, S. C., & Hung, D. W. L. (2002). Beyond information pumping: Creating a constructivist E-learning environment. *Educational Technology, 42*(5), 48–50, 52–54.

Tankersley, M. (1995). A group-oriented contingency management program: A review of research on the Good Behavior Game and implications for teachers. *Preventing School Failure, 40*, 19–24.

Tappan, M. B. (1998). Moral education in the zone of proximal development. *Journal of Moral Education, 27*(2), 141–160.

Tartre, L. A., & Fennema, E. (1995). Mathematics achievement and gender: A longitudinal study of selected cognitive and affective variables (grades 6–12). *Educational Studies in Mathematics, 28*, 199–217.

Tauber, R. T. (1990). Classical conditioning: Eliciting the right response. *NASSP Journal, 74*(526), 90–92.

Taylor, J. A., & Baker, R. A. (2001/2002). Discipline and special education students. *Educational Leadership, 59*(4), 28–30.

Tennyson, R. D., & Cocchiarella, M. J. (1986). An empirically based instructional design theory for teaching concepts. *Review of Educational Research, 56*, 40–71.

Terman, L. M. (1921). Intelligence and its measurement. *Journal of Educational Psychology, 12*, 127–133.

Terrace, H. S. (1966). Stimulus control. In W. K. Honig (Ed.), *Operant behavior: Areas of research and application*. New York: Appleton-Century-Crofts.

Tessmer, M. (1990). Environment analysis: A neglected state of instructional design. *Educational Technology: Research and Development, 38*(1), 55–64.

Tessmer, M., & Richey, R. (1997). The role of context in learning and instructional design. *Educational Technology Research and Development, 45*(20), 85–115.

"The first hour." *Instructor*. (2002). *112*(1), 44–46.

Thelen, M. H., Fry, R. A., Fehrenbach, P. A., & Frautsch, N. M. (1979).

Therapeutic videotape and film modeling: A review. *Psychological Bulletin, 86*(4), 701–720.

"The New ESEA." (2002). *American Teacher, 87*(2), 20.

Theodore, L. A., Bray, M. A., Kehle, T. J., & Jenson, W. R. (2001). Randomization of group contingencies and reinforcers to reduce classroom disruptive behavior. *Journal of School Psychology, 39*(3), 267–277.

Thomas, A., & Chess, S. (1980). *The dynamics of psychological development.* New York: Brunner/Mazel.

Thomas, R. M. (2000). *Comparing theories of child development,* (5th ed.). Belmont, CA: Wadsworth/Thomas Learning.

Thompson, S. K. (1975). Gender labels and early sex-role development. *Child Development, 46,* 339–347.

Thorndike, E. L. (1903). *Educational psychology.* New York: Lemke and Buechner.

Thorndike, E. L. (1905). *The elements of psychology.* New York: Seiler.

Thorndike, E. L. (1911). *Animal intelligence.* New York: Macmillan.

Thorndike, E. L. (1949). *Selected writings from a connectionist's psychology.* New York: Appleton-Century-Crofts.

Thorndike, E. L., & Woodworth, R. S. (1901). The influence of improvements in one mental function upon the efficiency of other functions. *Psychological Review, 8,* 247–261.

Thurstone, L. L. (1931). Multiple factor analysis. *Psychological Review, 38,* 406–427.

Thurstone, L. L. (1938). *Primary mental abilities.* Chicago: University of Chicago Press.

Tindal, G., Heath, B., Hollenbeck, K., Almond, P., & Harniss, M. (1998). Accommodating students with disabilities on large-scale tests: An experimental study. *Exceptional Children, 64*(4), 439–450.

Tobias, S. (1985). Test anxiety: Interference, defective skills, and cognitive capacity. *Educational Psychologist, 20,* 135–142.

Tolin, D. F. (2001). Case Study #58: Bibliotherapy and extinction treatment of obsessive-compulsive disorder in a 5-year-old boy. *Journal of the American Academy of Child & Adolescent Psychiatry, 40*(9), 1111–1114.

Torem, C. (2000). *Crisis intervention & nonviolent restraint: What's your action step?* Paper presented at the National Association of School Psychologists, New Orleans, LA (Ed 444 080).

Torff, B. (1999). Tacit knowledge in teaching: Folk pedagogy. In R. J. Sternberg & J. A. Horvath (Eds.), *Tacit knowledge in professional practice: Research and practitioner perspectives* (pp. 195–214). Mahwah, NJ: Erlbaum.

Torgesen, J. K. (1977). The role of nonspecific factors in the task performance of learning disabled children: A theoretical assessment. *Journal of Learning Disabilities, 10,* 27–34.

Torgesen, J. K. (2001). Learning disabilities as a working memory deficit: The important next questions. *Issues in Education, 7*(1), 93–92.

Torp, L., & Sage, S. (2002). *Problems as possibilities: Problem-based learning for K–16 education* (2nd Ed.), Alexandria, VA: ASCD.

Trammel, D. L., Schloss, P. J., & Alper, S. (1994). Using self-recording, evaluation, and grading to increase completion of homework assignments. *Journal of Learning Disabilities, 27*(2), 75–81.

Trautwein, U., & Köller, O. (2003). The relationship between homework and achievement—Still much of a mystery. *Educational Psychology Review, 15*(2), 115–145.

Trevarthen, C., Aitken, K., Papoudi, D., & Robarts, J. (1998). *Children with autism: Diagnosis and interventions to meet their need* (2nd ed.). London: Jessica Kingsley.

Tripp, M. K., Hermann, N. B., Parcel, G. S., Chamberlain, R. M., & Gritz, E. R. (2000). Sun protection is fun! A skin cancer prevention program for preschoolers. *Journal of School Health, 70*(10), 395–401.

Troia, G. A., & Graham, S. (2002). The effectiveness of a highly explicit, teacher-directed strategy instruction routine: changing writing performance of students with learning disabilities. *Journal of Learning Disabilities, 35*(4), 290–305.

Tsai, C.-C. (2003). Using a conflict map as an instructional tool to change student alternative conceptions in simple series electric-circuits. *International Journal of Science Education, 25*(3), 307–327.

Tucker, G., & Gunn, C. (Eds.). (1998). *Perspectives. Technology, integration, and learning environments. CEE monograph: The NAU centennial year of education.* Flagstaff, AZ: Northern Arizona University.

Tudge, J. (1990). Vygotsky, the zone of proximal development, and peer collaboration: Implications for classroom practice. In L. C. Moll (Ed.), *Vygotsky and education* (pp. 155–174). New York: Cambridge University Press.

Tulving, E. (1974). Recall and recognition of semantically encoded words. *Journal of Experimental Psychology, 102*(5), 778–787.

Tulving, E., & Osler, S. (1968). Effectiveness of retrieval cues in memory for words. *Journal of Experimental Psychology, 77*(4), 693–701

Turnbull, H. R., & Turnbull, A. P. (2000). *Free appropriate public education* (6th ed.). Denver: Love.

Turnbull, R., & Cilley, M. (1999). *Explanations and implications of the 1997 amendments to IDEA.* Upper Saddle River, NJ: Merrill/Prentice Hall.

Turner, H. S., & Watson, T. S. (1999). Consultant's guide for the use of time-out in the preschool and elementary classroom. *Psychology in the Schools, 36*(2), 135–147.

Turner, J. E., Husman, J., & Schallert, D. L. (2002). The importance of students' goals in the emotional exierence of academic failure: Investgating the precursors and consequences of shame. *Educational Psychologist, 37*(2), 79–89.

Twitmyer, E. B. (1974). A study of the knee jerk. *Journal of Experimental Psychology, 103*(6), 1047–1066.

Tyler, M. D. (2001). Resource consumption as a function of topic knowledge in nonnative and native comprehension. *Language Learning, 51*(2), 257–280.

United States Department of Education. (1997). *National Assessment of Educational Progress (indicator 32: Writing proficiency: Prepared by the Educational Testing Service).* Washington, D.C. (World Wide Web: http//www.ed/gov/nces).

United States Department of Education. (2000). Guide to the individualized education program. Washington, D.C.: (ERIC Document Reproduction Services 800-443).

Updegraff, K. A., Madden-Derdich, D. A., Estrada, A. U., Sales, L. J., & Leonard, S. A. (2002). Young adolescents' experiences with parents and friends: Exploring the connections. *Family Relations, 51*(1), 72–80.

Urberg, K. A., Degirmencioglu, S. M., Tolson, J. M., & Halliaday-Scher, K. (2000). Adoles-

cent social crowds: Measurement and relationship to friendships. *Journal of Adolescent Research, 15*(4), 427–445.

Utley, C., & Obiakor, F. E. (2000). Students with cognitive disabilities: Implementing effective instructional strategies in classroom settings. In F. E. Obiakor, S. A. Burkhardt, A. F. Rotatori, & T. Wahlberg (Eds.), *Intervention techniques for individuals with exceptionalities in inclusive settings* (pp. 21–52). Stamford, CT: JAI Press.

Vadeboncoeur, J. (1997). Child development and the purpose of education: A historical context for constructivism in teacher education. In V. Richardson (Ed.), *Constructivist teacher education: Building new understandings* (pp. 3–14). Washington, D.C.: Falmer Press.

Vaidya, S. (1999). Metacognitive learning strategies for students with learning disabilities. *Education, 120*(1), 186–188.

Valäs, H. (2001). Learned helplessness and psychological adjustment II: Effects of learning disabilities and low achievement. *Scandinavian Journal of Educational Research, 45*(2), 101–114.

Valli, L. (1986). *Becoming clerical workers.* Boston: Routledge and Kegan Paul.

van Boxtel, C., van der Linden, J., Roelofs, E., & Erkens, G. (2002). Collaborative concept mapping: Provoking and supporting meaningful discourse. *Theory into Practice, 41*(1), 40–46.

van den Hurk, M. M., Dolmans, D. J. M., Wolfhagen, I. H. A. P., & Van Der Vleuten, C. P. M. (2001). Quality of student-generated learning issues in a problem-based curriculum. *Medical Teacher 23*(6), 567–571.

van der Veer, R., & Valsiner, J. (1991). *Understanding Vygotsky: A quest of synthesis.* Cambridge, MA: Blackwell.

van Merrienboer, J. J. G., Clark, R. E., & De Croock, M. B. M. (2002). Blueprints for complex learning: The 4C/ID model. *Educational Technology: Research and Development, 50*(2), 39–64.

Van Riper, C., & Erickson, R. L. (1996). *Speech correction: An introduction to speech pathology and audiology* (9th ed.). Boston: Allyn & Bacon.

Vartanian, L. R. (2000). Revisiting the imaginary audience and personal fable constructs of adolescent egocentrism: A conceptual review. *Adolescence, 35*(140), 639–661.

Vartanian, L. R. (2001). Adolescents' reactions to hypothetical peer group conversations: Evidence for an imaginary audience? *Adolescence, 36*(142), 347–380.

Vaughn, S. (2001). The social functioning of students with learning disabilities: Implications for instruction. *Exceptionality, 9*(1), 47–65.

Vaughn, S. R., Elbaum, B. E., & Schumm, J. S. (1996). The effects of inclusion on the social functioning of students with learning disabilities. *Journal of Learning Disabilities, 29,* 598–608.

Vaughn, S., & Klinger, J. K. (1999). Teaching reading comprehension through collaborative strategic reading. *Intervention in School and Clinic, 35*(5), 284–292.

Vaughn, S., Bos, C. S., & Schumm, J. S. (2000). *Teaching exceptional, diverse, and at-risk students in the general education classroom* (2nd ed.). Boston: Allyn & Bacon.

Veenman, M. V. J., & Elshout, J. J. (1995). Differential effects of instructional support on learning in simulation environments. *Instructional Science, 22,* 363–383.

Veenman, S. (1984). Perceived problems of beginning teachers. *Review of Educational Research, 54*(2), 143–178.

Vellutino, F. R. (2001). Working memory deficits and learning disabilities: Reactions to Swanson and Siegel. *Issues in Education, 7*(1), 49–68.

Verschueren, K., & Marcoen, A. (2002). Perceptions of self and relationship with parents in aggressive and nonaggressive rejected children. *Journal of School Psychology, 40*(6), 501–522.

Vogt, L. A., Jordan, C., & Tharp, R. G. (1993). Explaining school failure, producing school success: Two cases. In E. Jacob & C. Jordan (Eds.), *Minority education: Anthropological perspectives* (pp. 53–66). Norwood, NJ: Ablex.

Volkmar, F. R., & Lord, C. (1998). Diagnosis and definition of autism and other pervasive disorders. In F. R. Volkmar (Ed.), *Autism and pervasive developmental disorders* (pp. 1–31). Cambridge: Cambridge University Press.

Vosniadou, S., & Brewer, W. F. (1987). Theories of knowledge restructuring in development. *Review of Educational Research, 57*, 51–67.

Vygotsky, L. S. (1962). *Thought and language* (E. H. G. Vakar, Trans.). Cambridge, MA: MIT Press.

Vygotsky, L. S. (1978). *Mind in society: The development of higher psychological processes.* Cambridge, MA: Harvard University Press.

Vygotsky, L. S. (1981). The genesis of higher mental functions. In J. V. Wertsch (Ed.), *The concept of activity in Soviet psychology* (pp. 144–188). Armonk, NY: Sharpe.

Vygotsky, L. S. (1987). *Thinking and speech* (N. Minick, Trans.). New York: Plenum.

Wadsworth, B. J. (1996). *Piaget's theory of cognitive and affective development: The origins of constructivism.* New York: Longman.

Wainer, H., & Steinberg, L. S. (1992). Sex differences on the mathematics section of the Scholastic Aptitude Test: A bidirectional validity study. *Harvard Educational Review, 62*(3), 323–336.

Walker, B. J. (2003). The cultivation of student self-efficacy in reading and writing. *Reading & Writing Quarterly: Overcoming Learning Difficulties, 19*, 173–187.

Walker, H. M. (1997). *The acting out child: Coping with classroom disruption* (2nd ed.). Longmont, CO: Sopris West.

Walker, H. M., Colvin, G., & Ramsey, E. (1995). *Antisocial behavior in school: Strategies for best practice.* Pacific Grove, CA: Brooks/Cole.

Walker, J. E., & Shea, T. M. (1995). *Behavior management a practical approach for educators* (6th ed.). Englewood Cliffs, NJ: Merrill.

Walker, L. J. (1984). Sex differences in the development of moral reasoning: A critical review. *Child Development, 55*, 677–691.

Walker, L. J. (1989). A longitudinal study of moral reasoning. *Child Development, 60*, 157–166.

Walker, L. J. (1991). Sex differences in moral reasoning. In W. M. Kurtines & J. L. Gewirtz (Eds.), *Handbook of moral behavior and development: Vol. 2. Research* (pp. 333–364). Hillsdale, NJ: Erlbaum.

Walker, L. J., DeVries, B., & Trevethan, S. (1987). Moral stages and moral orientation. *Child Development, 58*, 842–858.

Walker, M. H. (1998). 3 basics for better student output. *The Education Digest, 63*(9), 15–18.

Walker, S., Berthelsen, D., & Irving, K. (2001). Temperament and peer acceptance in early

childhood: Sex and social status differences. *Child Study Journal, 31*(3), 177–192.

Wallerstein, J. S., & Blakeslee, S. (1989). *Second chances.* New York: Ticknor & Fields.

Walters, J. M., & Gardner, H. (1986). The theory of multiple intelligences: Some issues and answers. In R. J. Sternberg & R. K. Wagner (Eds.), *Practical intelligence: Nature and origins of competence in the everyday world* (pp. 163–182). Cambridge: Cambridge University Press.

Walther-Thomas, C. S., & Brownell, M. T. (1998). An interview with Dr. Mitchell Yell: Changes in IDEA regarding suspension and expulsion. *Intervention in School and Clinic, 34*(1), 46–49.

Wang, M. C., Haertel, G. D., & Walberg, H. J. (1993). Toward a knowledge base for school learning. *Review of Educational Research, 63*(3), 249–294.

Ward, C. D. (2001). Under construction: On becoming a constructivist in view of the standards. *Mathematics Teacher, 94*, 94–96.

Ward, J., & Guyer, K. E. (2000). Medical management of ADHD. In B. P. Guyer (Ed.), *ADHD: Achieving success in school and in life* (pp. 38–54). Boston: Allyn & Bacon.

Warger, C. (2001). Five homework strategies for teaching students with disabilities. ERIC Document Reproduction Services No. ED452628.

Warger, C., & Burnette, J. (2000). Five strategies to reduce overrepresentation of culturally and linguistically diverse students in special education. ERIC Document Reproduction Services No. ED447627.

Warnemuende, C. (2000). The art of working with parents. *Montessori Life, 12*, 20–21.

Watson, J. B. (1913). Psychology as a behaviorist views it. *Psychological Review, 20*, 158–177.

Watson, J. B. (1919). *Psychology from the standpoint of a behaviorist.* Philadelphia: J. B. Lippincott.

Watts-Taffe, S., & Truscott, D. M. (2000). Using what we know about language and literacy development for ESL students in the mainstream classroom. *Language Arts, 77*(3), 258–265.

Waung, M., & Brice, T. S. (1998). The effects of conscientiousness and opportunity to caucus on group performance. *Small Group Research, 29*(5), 624–634.

Webb, N. M., & Farivar, S. (1994). Promoting helping behavior in cooperative small groups in middle school mathematics. *American Educational Research Journal, 31*(2), 369–395.

Wechsler, D. (2003). *Wechsler Intelligence Scale for Children—Fourth Edition (WISC-IV).* San Antonio, TX: The Psychological Corporation.

Wehmeyer, M. L., & Rousso, H. (2001). Addressing gender equity in special education services: An agenda for the twenty-first century. In H. Rousso & M. L. Wehmeyer (Eds.), *Double jeopardy: Addressing gender equity in special education* (pp. 375–386). New York: New York University Press.

Weimer, R. C. (1975). An analysis of discovery. *Educational Technology, 15*(9), 45–48.

Weiner, B. (1985). An attributional theory of achievement motivation and emotion. *Psychological Review, 92*(4), 548–573.

Weiner, B. (1992). *Human motivation: Metaphors, theories and research.* Newbury Park CA: Sage Publications.

Weiner, B. (1994). Integrating social and personal theories of achievement striving. *Review of Educational Research, 64*(4), 557–573.

Weiner, B., Graham, S., Taylor, S. & Meyer, W. (1982). Social cognition in the classroom. *Educational Psychologist, 18*, 109–124.

Weinert, F. E., & Helmke, A. (1995). Learning from wise mother nature or big brother instructor: The wrong choice as seen from an educational perspective. *Educational Psychologist, 30*(3), 135–142.

Weinstein, C. E., & Mayer, R. E. (1986). The teaching of learning strategies. In M. C. Wittrock (Ed.), *Handbook of research on teaching* (3rd ed, pp. 315–327.). New York: Macmillan.

Weinstein, C. S., Tomlinson-Clarke, S., & Curran, M. (2004). Toward a conception of culturally responsive classroom management. *Journal of Teacher Education, 55*(1), 25–38.

Wells, G. (1999). Using L1 to Master L2: A response to Antón and Di Camilla's "sociocognitive functions of L1 collaborative interactions in the L2 classroom." *The Modern Language Journal, 83*, 248–254.

Wentzel, K. R. (1992). Motivation and achievement in adolescence: A multiple goals perspective. In D. H. Schunk & J. L. Meece (Eds.), *Student perceptions in the classroom* (pp. 287–306). Hillsdale, NJ: Erlbaum.

Wentzel, K. R. (2002). Are effective teachers like good parents: Teaching styles and student adjustment in early adolescence. *Child Development, 73*(1), 287–301.

Werner, E. (1993). Risk, resilience, and recovery. Perspectives from the Kauai longitudinal study. *Development and Psychopathology, 5*, 503–515.

Werner, E. E. (1989). High-risk children in young adulthood: A longitudinal study from birth to 32 years. *American Journal of Orthopsychiatry, 59*(1), 72–81.

Wertsch, J. V. (1985). *Vygotsky and the social formation of mind.* Cambridge, MA: Harvard University Press.

Westberry, S. (1994). A review of learning strategies for adults with learning disabilities preparing for the GED exam. *Journal of Learning Disabilities, 27*(4), 202–210.

Weyandt, L. L. (2001). *An ADHD primer.* Boston: Allyn & Bacon.

White, A. G., & Bailey, J. S. (1990). Reducing disruptive behaviors of elementary physical education students with sit and watch. *Journal of Applied Behavior Analysis, 23*, 353–359.

White, D. A., & Breen, M. (1998). Edutainment: Gifted education and the multiple intelligence. *Gifted Child Today, 21*(2), 12–14, 16–17.

White, L. K. (1991). Detriments of divorce: A review of research in the eighties. In A. Booth (Ed.), *Contemporary families: Looking forward, looking back* (pp. 141–149). Minneapolis, MN: National Council on Family Relations.

Whitfield, G. W. (1999). Validating school social work: An evaluation of a cognitive-behavioral approach to reduce school violence. *Research on Social Work Practice, 9*(4), 399–426.

Wielkiewicz, R. M. (1995). *Behavior management in the schools: Principles and procedures.* Boston: Allyn & Bacon.

Wigfield, A., & Eccles, J. (1992). The development of achievement task values: A theoretical analysis. *Developmental Review, 12*, 265–310.

Williams, B. F. & Williams, R. L., & McLaughlin, T. F. (1989). The use of token economies with individuals who have developmental disabilities. In E. Cipani (Ed.), *The treatment of severe behavior disorders: Behavior analysis approaches* Washington, D.C.: AAMR.

Williams, J. A. (2001). Classroom conversations: Opportunities to learn for ESL students in mainstream classrooms. *Reading Teacher, 54*(8), 750–757.

Williams, K. (1998). Do Howard Gardner's multiple intelligences add up? (book review). *British Journal of Educational Studies, 48*(1), 107–108.

Williams, M. M. (2000). Models of character education: Perspectives and developmental issues. *Journal of Humanistic Counseling, Education & Development, 39*(1), 32–40.

Williams, S. M., Burgess, K. L., Bray, M. H., Bransford, J. D., and the Cognition and Technology Group at Vanderbilt. (1998). Technology and learning for thought classrooms. In C. Dede (Ed.), *ASCD yearbook: Learning with technology* (pp. 87–120). Alexandria, VA: Association for Supervision and Curriculum Development.

Willig, A. C. (1985). A meta-analysis of selected studies on the effectiveness of bilingual education. *Review of Educational Research, 55*(3), 269–317.

Willingham, W. W., & Cole, N. S. (1997), *Gender and fair assessment.* Mahwah, NJ: Erlbaum.

Willingham, W. W., Cole, N. S., Lewis, C., & Leung, S. W. (1997). Test performance. In W. W. Willingham & N. S. Cole (Eds.), *Gender and fair assessment* (pp. 55–126). Mahwah, NJ: Erlbaum.

Willis, J. (1998). Alternative instructional design paradigms: What's worth discussing and what isn't. *Educational Technology, 38*(3), 5–16.

Willis, J. (2000). Principles that can guide practice. *Educational Technology, 40*(1), 5–16.

Willis, P. (1977). *Learning to labour: How working class kids get working class jobs.* Farnborough, UK: Saxon House.

Wilson, B. G. (2002). Trends and futures of education: Implications for distance education. *The Quarterly Review of Distance Education, 3*(1), 91–103.

Wilson, K. M., & Swanson, H. L. (2001). Are mathematics disabilities due to a domain-general or a domain-specific working memory deficit. *Journal of Learning Disabilities, 34*(3), 237–248.

Windholz, G. L. (1993). Vagaries of science; priority, independent discovery, and the quest for recognition. *Psychological Record, 43*(3), 339–410.

Wine, J. D. (1980). Cognitive-attentional theory of test anxiety. In I. G. Sarason (Ed.), *Test anxiety: Theory, research, and applications.* Hillsdale, NJ: Erlbaum.

Winebrenner, S., & Devlin, B. (1991). *Cluster grouping fact sheet: How to provide full-time services for gifted students on existing budgets.* Lombard, IL: Phantom Press.

Wink, J., & Putney, L. (2002). *A vision of Vygotsky.* Boston: Allyn & Bacon.

Wise, J. B., & Trunnell, E. P. (2001). The influences of sources of self-efficacy upon efficacy strength. *Journal of Sport & Exercise Psychology, 23*(4), 268–280.

Witkin, H. A. (1950). Individual differences in the ease of perception of embedded figures. *Journal of Personality, 19,* 1–15.

Witkin, H. A., & Goodenough, D. R. (1978). Field dependence and interpersonal behavior. *Psychological Bulletin, 84,* 661–689.

Wolfe, E. W., & Miller, T. R. (1997). Barriers to the implementation of portfolio assessments in secondary education. *Applied Measurement in Education, 10*(3), 235–251.

Wolfe, P. (1998). Revisiting effective teaching. *Educational Leadership, 56*(3), 61–64.

Wolfe, V. V., Boyd, L. A., & Wolfe, D. A. (1983). Teaching cooperative play to behavior-problem preschool children. *Education and Treatment of Children, 6,* 1–9.

Wolfgang, C. H. (1999). *Solving discipline problems: Methods and models for today's teachers* (4th ed.). Boston: Allyn & Bacon.

Wolfgang, C. H., & Wolfgang, M. E. (1995). *The three faces of discipline for early childhood: Empowering teachers and students.* (pp. 223–225). Boston: Allyn & Bacon.

Wolford, P. L., Heward, W. L., & Alber, S. R. (2001). Teaching middle school students with learning disabilities to recruit peer assistance during cooperative learning group activities. *Learning Disabilities: Research & Practice, 16*(3), 161–173.

Woltzer, G. (2001). Learning disability and working memory: A commentary. *Issues in Education, 7*(1), 103–106.

Wood, D. (1989). Social interaction as tutoring. In M. H. Bornstein & J. S. Bruner (Eds.), *Interaction in human development* (pp. 59–82). Hillsdale, NJ: Erlbaum.

Wood, D., & Middleton, D. (1975). A study of assisted problem solving. *British Journal of Psychology, 66*(2), 181–191.

Wood, D., Bruner, J., & Ross, G. (1976). The role of tutoring in problem solving. *Journal of Child Psychology and Psychiatry, 17,* 89–100.

Wood, E., Woloshyn, V., & Willoughby, T. (1995). *Cognitive strategy instruction for middle and high schools.* Cambridge, MA: Brookline Books.

Woodward-Kron, R. (2004). 'Discourse communities' and 'writing apprenticeship': An investigation of these concepts in undergraduate education students' writing. *Journal of English for Academic Purposes, 3*(2), 139–161.

Yamnill, S., & McLean, G. N. (2001). Theories supporting transfer of training. *Human Development Resource Quarterly, 12*(2), 195–208.

Yates, G. C. R. (2000). Applying learning style research in the classroom: Some cautions and the way ahead. In R. J. Riding & S. G. Rayner (Eds.), *International perspectives on individual differences* (Vol. I, pp. 347–364). Stamford, CT: Ablex.

Yell, M. (1994). Timeout and students with behavior disorders: A legal analysis. *Education and Treatment of Children, 17*(3), 293–301.

Yell, M. L. (1995). The least restrictive environment mandate and the courts: Judicial activism or judicial restraint? *Exceptional Children, 61*(6), 578–581.

Yell, M. L., & Drasgow, E. (1999). A legal analysis of inclusion. *Preventing School Failure, 43*(3), 118–123.

Yelon, S. L. (1996). *Powerful principles of instruction.* White Plains, NY: Longman.

Young, J. W. (1991). Gender bias in predicting college academic performance: A new approach using item response theory. *Journal of Educational Measurement, 28,* 37–47.

Young, J. W. (1994). Differential prediction of college grades by gender and ethnicity: A replication study. *Educational and Psychological Measurement, 54,* 1022–1029.

Youniss, J., & Smollar, J. (1985). *Adolescent relations with mothers, fathers, and friends.* Chicago: University of Chicago Press.

Ysseldyke, J. (2001). Reflections on a research career: Generalizations from 25 years of research on assessment and instructional deci-

sion making. *Exceptional Children, 67*(3), 295–309.

Zabel, M. K. (1986). Time-out use with behaviorally disordered students. *Behavioral Disorders, 12,* 15–21.

Zarbatany, L., Hartmann, D. P., & Rankin, D. B. (1990). The psychological functions of preadolescent peer activities. *Child Development, 61,* 1067–1080.

Zeitz, C. M. (1994). Expert-novice differences in memory, abstraction, and reasoning in the domain of literature. *Cognition and Instruction, 12*(4), 277–312.

Zhang, D., & Katsiyannis, A. (2002). Minority representation in special education: A persistent challenge. *Remedial and Special Education, 23*(3), 180–187.

Ziegert, D. I., Kistner, J. A., Castro, R. & Robertson, B. (2001). Longitudinal study of young children's response to challenging achievement situations. *Child Development, 72*(2), 609–624.

Zimmerman, B. J. (1999). Attaining self-regulation: A social cognitive perspective. In M. Borkaerts, P. P. Pintrich, & M. Zeisner (Eds.), *Handbook of self-regulation* (pp. 13–39). San Diego: Academic Press.

Zimmerman, B. J. (2000). Self-efficacy: An essential motive to learn. *Contemporary Educational Psychology, 25*(1), 82–91.

Zimmerman, B. J., & Kitsantas, A. (1997). Developmental phases in self-regulation: Shifting from process goals to outcome goals. *Journal of Educational Psychology, 89*(1), 29–36.

Zimmerman, B. J., & Kitsantas, A. (1999). Acquiring writing revision skills: Shifting from process to outcome self-regulatory goals. *Journal of Educational Psychology, 91*(2), 241–250.

Zimmerman, B. J., & Martinez-Pons, M. (1990). Student differences in self-regulated learning: Relating grade, sex, and giftedness to self-efficacy and strategy use. *Journal of Educational Psychology, 82*(1), 51–59.

Zimmerman, B. J., Bandura, A., & Martinez-Pons, M. (1992). Self-motivation for academic attainment: The role of self-efficacy beliefs and personal goal setting. *American Educational Research Journal, 29,* 663–676.

Zimmerman, E. H., & Zimmerman, J. (1962). The alteration of behavior in a special education classroom situation. *Journal of the Experimental Analysis of Behavior, 5,* 59–60.

Zirpoli, T. J., & Melloy, K. J. (1997). *Behavior management applications for teachers and parents* (2nd ed.). Upper Saddle River, NJ: Merrill.

Zook, K. B. (1991). Effects of analogical processes on learning and misrepresentation. *Educational Psychology Review, 3,* 41–72.

Zook, K. B., & Di Vesta, F. J. (1991). Instructional analogies and conceptual misrepresentations. *Journal of Educational Psychology, 83*(2), 246–252.

Zook, K. B., & Maier, J. M. (1994). Systematic analysis of variables that contribute to the formation of analogical misconceptions. *Journal of Educational Psychology, 86*(4), 589–600.

Zumbach, J., & Reimann, P. (2002). Enhancing learning from hypertext by inducing a goal orientation: Comparing different approaches. *Instructional Science, 30,* 243–267.

Zurkowski, J. K., Kelly, P. S., & Griswold, D. E. (1998). Discipline and IDEA 1997: Instituting a new balance. *Intervention in School and Clinic, 34*(1), 3–9.

Index

Numbers followed by the letter f indicate figures; numbers followed by the letter t indicate tables.

Photo Credits

Page 1, © David Young-Wolff/Getty Images; 5, © David Young-Wolff/Photo Edit; 13, © Bob Daemmrich/The Image Works; 15, © Lindfors Photography; 17, © Richard Hutchings/Photo Edit; 25, © Jack Kurtz/The Image Works; 29, © Bettmann/CORBIS; 32, © Topham/The Image Works; 43, © Ellen Senisi/The Image Works; 44, © Dennis MacDonald/Photo Edit; 55, © Michael Newman/Photo Edit; 57, © Will Hart/Photo Edit; 65, © Michael Newman/Photo Edit; 69, Comstock Royalty Free Division/Comstock; 79, © James Marshall/The Image Works; 91, © Charles Gupton/CORBIS; 95, © Ellen Senisi/The Image Works; 101, © Kathy McLaughlin/The Image Works; 104, © Johnny Crawford/The Image Works; 111, © Mary Kate Denny/Photo Edit; 119, © Bob Daemmrich/The Image Works; 123, © Jeff Greenberg/The Image Works; 125, © Laura Dwight Photography; 133, © LWA-Dann Tardif/CORBIS; 146, © David Young-Wolff/Photo Edit; 155, © David Lassman/Syracuse Newspapers/The Image Works; 160, © Will & Deni McIntyre/Photo Researchers; 165, © Royalty-Free/CORBIS; 167, 174, © Gabe Palmer/CORBIS; 197, © Spencer Grant/Photo Edit; 201, © Lindfors Photographs; 209, © Bonnie Kamin/Photo Edit; 215, © Mark Richards/Photo Edit; 226, © Arthur Tilley/Getty Images; 241, © Michael Newman/Photo Edit; 251, © Bill Aron/Photo Edit; 260, © Charles Gupton/CORBIS; 267, © Bill Aron/ Photo Edit; 271, © Gabe Palmer/CORBIS; 281, © Tony Freeman/Photo Edit; 283, © Charles Gupton/ CORBIS; 289, © Bob Daemmrich/The Image Works; 308, © David Young-Wolff/Photo Edit; 313, © Mark Richards/Photo Edit; 321, © T. Lindfors Photography; 324, © Bill Freeman/Photo Edit; 326, © Richard Hutchings/Photo Edit; 337, © Tony Freeman/Photo Edit; 344, © John Henley/CORBIS; 355, © Jim Cummins/Getty Images; 359, © Laura Dwight/Photo Edit; 369, © Bob Daemmrich/The Image Works; 371, © Stephen Marks; 372, © Laura Dwight Photography; 393, © Elizabeth Crews/The Image Works; 397, © Chuck Savage/CORBIS; 415, © David Young-Wolff/Photo Edit; 417, © Tony Freeman/Photo Edit; 427, © Michael Newman/Photo Edit; 433, 436, © Bob Daemmrich/The Image Works; 447, © Will & Deni McIntyre/CORBIS; 452, © Jeff Greenberg/The Image Works; 462, © Mary Kate Denny/ Photo Edit; 466, © Dana White/Photo Edit.